Meet the Team Behind
REA's LSAT Logic Games

The best minds to help you get the best LSAT scores

In this book, you'll find our commitment to excellence, an enthusiasm for the subject matter, and an unrivaled ability to help you master the LSAT. REA's dedication to excellence and our passion for education make this book the very best source for preparing for the LSAT Analytical Reasoning section.

Robert Webking is Professor of Political Science at the University of Texas at El Paso, where he has taught since 1978. He is co-founder of UTEP's Law School Preparation Institute and in that role, has, since 1998, taught many students in a very intensive and thorough way how to work with the LSAT.

Jerry McLain is a graduate of the University of Texas at El Paso and of UTEP's Law School Preparation Institute. He is a graduate of Stanford Law School.

Clayton Holland is a graduate of the University of Texas at El Paso and of UTEP's Law School Preparation Institute. He is a student at the University of Virginia School of Law.

Daniel Avelar is a graduate of the University of Texas at El Paso and of UTEP's Law School Preparation Institute. He is a graduate of Texas Tech School of Law.

LSAT
LOGIC
Games

Research & Education Association
Visit our website at
www.rea.com

Research & Education Association
61 Ethel Road West
Piscataway, New Jersey 08854
E-mail: info@rea.com

LSAT Logic Games

Published 2009

Printed in the United States of America

Library of Congress Control Number 2005931422

ISBN 13: 978-0-7386-0111-3
ISBN 10: 0-7386-0111-X

Serious Games and the Logic of the LSAT

Passionate.

Disciplined.

Worldly-wise.

If you're getting ready to pursue a law degree, I'm reasonably sure I just described *you*.

But, of course, it doesn't end there. Law schools are seeking candidates with strong analytical and problem-solving skills, and with particular strength in logical reasoning. So it comes as no surprise that logical reasoning lies at the heart of the LSAT, the test required for admission to law schools across the United States and Canada.

Well-rounded you may be, but logical reasoning does not necessarily come naturally. In fact, there's no substitute for exposure to in-depth logic games to get you in shape for test day—and for law school generally.

The Association of American Law Schools, in describing the type of education appropriate for pre-law students, recommends preparation that helps candidates develop creative power in thinking.

The 100 challenging logic games in this book have been carefully honed by some of the best academic thinkers on this subject in North America to help you sharpen your creative power and thereby master the LSAT. The logic games contained herein are presented in a systematic progression to allow you to build your approach, and thus your confidence, from every facet.

Whatever other prep you're doing for the LSAT (or even tests like the GMAT!), you'll find REA's *LSAT Logic Games* to be an invaluable resource.

Larry B. Kling
Chief Editor

Table of Contents

ABOUT RESEARCH & EDUCATION ASSOCIATION

Founded in 1959, Research & Education Association is dedicated to publishing the finest and most effective educational materials—including software, study guides, and test preps—for students in middle school, high school, college, graduate school, and beyond.

REA's Test Preparation series includes books and software for all academic levels in almost all disciplines. REA publishes test preps for students who have not yet entered high school, as well as high school students preparing to enter college. Students from countries around the world seeking to attend college in the United States will find the assistance they need in REA's publications. For college students seeking advanced degrees, REA publishes test preps for many major graduate school admission examinations in a wide variety of disciplines, including engineering, law, and medicine. Students at every level, in every field, with every ambition can find what they are looking for among REA's publications.

REA's practice tests are always based upon the most recently administered exams, and include every type of question that can be expected on the actual exams.

REA's publications and educational materials are highly regarded and continually receive an unprecedented amount of praise from professionals, instructors, librarians, parents, and students. Our authors are as diverse as the fields represented in the books we publish. They are well-known in their respective disciplines and serve on the faculties of prestigious high schools, colleges, and universities throughout the United States and Canada.

We invite you to visit us at *www.rea.com* to find out how "REA is making the world smarter."

STAFF ACKNOWLEDGMENTS

In addition to our authors, we would like to thank Larry B. Kling, Vice President, Editorial, for his overall guidance; Pam Weston, Vice President, Publishing, for setting the quality standards for production integrity and managing the publication to completion; Christine Reilley, Senior Editor, for preflight editorial review; Diane Goldschmidt, Associate Editor, for post-production quality assurance; and Christine Saul, Senior Graphic Designer, for cover design.

Finally we gratefully acknowledge the team at Publication Services for editing, proofreading, page composition, and post-production file mapping.

Part I

An Approach to Analytical Reasoning Problems

Many different particular methodologies can be used to work with the problems presented in the analytical reasoning section of the LSAT. And they all have at least this much in common: You must interpret the rules correctly, represent the situation clearly on a diagram, and make as many accurate deductions as possible to move from what you know to what you don't know. There is no one right way to work through the LSAT analytical reasoning questions. And certainly it is not the case that you receive extra points for neatness or for consistency in methodology. The goal of any methodology is to help you analyze a problem accurately and thoroughly, so as to be able to answer several questions about what is going on.

As you work with the analytical reasoning games in this book, reread this introduction and methodology section from time to time. The explanations of the particular solutions to the games in this book will refer to this section, and it will become more clear to you the more games you do. Each game you practice on should help you understand the general approach and to learn how to apply principles that will make you more successful with the next one.

Five-Step Procedure

To work analytical reasoning problems efficiently and effectively, we suggest that you take the time to follow a five-step procedure before you tackle the questions. This procedure is more thoroughly explained through the analysis of the particular games, but its basic structure is as follows:

Step 1: Identify the Type

Each problem on an LSAT is unique, as are each of the problems included here, but it helps to think about them as being of three basic types that require you to do three different things:

1. Put items into groups
2. Put items in order
3. Put items into slots

These types are distinguished from one another by the kind of information you are given and by the approach you take to solve them. Most games are of one of these types, though many of them mix elements of two types or even three types. Since different types of games require different approaches, the first step in working any game is to examine the setup and scan the rules to determine what type of game you are working with. The different types of games will be discussed below.

Step 2: Draw the Diagram

Once you know the type of game you are working with, you should design the diagram that you will use to work out the game and answer the questions. Step 1 and this step are both critical, because here you are conceptualizing the problem. You are building the basic structure to understand what is going on in the situation with which you have been presented.

It is usually a good idea to make the diagram as large as you can so there will be enough room to apply information introduced in the individual questions to the basic scenario. It is also a good idea to save your work on the diagram from question to question since things you have learned about what must or might or cannot be the case are likely to be helpful with other questions.

Step 3: Simplify the Rules

The next step is to analyze the rules, making sure that you know exactly what each means. Rewrite each rule in short and clear symbols. Using symbols will enable you to access the rules easily by eliminating all those time-consuming words. Often the rules are stated in terms that make it a challenge to know precisely what they mean, but you must interpret them correctly in order to work the game correctly. Interpreting them and putting them in simple symbols makes what they mean clear and allows you to apply them with ease as you work through the questions.

Some rules will give clear information that can be applied directly to the diagram. In those cases (for example, "W always goes third"), use your diagram instead of writing a new symbol, always being certain to represent things that must be true on the diagram differently from other things that might be true only in some scenarios or for some questions.

Remember that sometimes there are key rules in the descriptive setup as well as in the list of rules that follows.

Step 4: Deductions

After the first three steps you should feel comfortable that you know what the game is about and should have a general idea of what is going on. If you don't, then you need to go back and look at the type, diagram, and rules again to figure out what is going on. Now you take the information you have and work with the clues in relation to one another: If *this* is true and *this* is true then what else must be true or false? The things that you deduce as true from the things explicitly stated in the rules are just as true for the game as if they had been written in the setup.

- Deductions are critical to any game — they are what a game is about.
- Relate the clues to one another.
- Where appropriate sketch out basic scenarios.
- Note on the diagram what must be true and what cannot be true.
- Be alert for the type of information that you need for the type of game you are working with.

This step is critical — it is what the analytical reasoning of the LSAT section is testing. Sometimes there will not be many deductions that you can make before moving on to the questions, and the game will seem uncomfortably uncertain. When that happens, try again. Look at each rule in relation to the others. If you still cannot make meaningful deductions, know that the questions will likely force you to make some. But don't rush to the questions. Try to make the deductions on your own first.

Step 5: Walk Around It

Wait! Do not go to the questions yet. Take a breath and look at what you have determined so far and what is going on in the game. Walk around the game for a while. Look at it from different perspectives. Use what you have learned from your experience (experience you can gain from working the problems in this book). Think about what are likely to be the keys on this type of game and identify key variables or issues for this game. Identify wild cards, groups, splits (these things are explained in the examples on the following pages), unusual rules and the like. What is the game going to make you do, and what do you need to be aware of with the questions? WAIT! Spend the time to figure out what is likely to be tested before you go on to the questions. There will be a lot that you do not know, but think about what that is, and what you will need to know to be more clear.

An analytical game describes a situation about which you can know some things, but not others. It is not a logic problem with a single solution, and it can be frustrating and discouraging to approach it that way. It presents a circumstance, but incompletely, so that you can be certain about some things but not others. The questions are testing how well you understand that circumstance.

Go through these steps before working the questions. It may seem slow, but in fact it will make dealing with the questions much easier and more efficient. Remember: What is being tested is your ability to understand the information presented and your ability to relate its parts to one another. You must be clear on the information, so take the time to analyze it. If you miss a deduction or a key rule, the questions will force you to discover it, but you are better off if you find it first. Focus consciously both on what you know and on what you do not know.

Basic Types

There are three common basic game types. The boundaries between them are sometimes fuzzy, and many games combine elements of more than one type, but it is useful to know the different pure types and to know how to approach them so that no matter what particular game you are faced with, you can decide what operations you will have to perform.

Type 1: Groups

One common type of game gives you a list of items and requires you to build from one to four groups made up of those items. The rules here are likely to involve "if" statements that are critical to interpret correctly. (If A is included in a group then C must be included.)

Interpreting the "if" statement takes these steps:

1. Simplify what it says. What is sufficient to produce what else? Make it clear. If A then C.
2. An "if" statement means exactly one other thing, called the "contrapositive." If the statement is "If A then C," then to get the contrapositive *reverse* and *negate* the two terms: "if not C then not A."
3. The statement TELLS YOU NOTHING ELSE. If you know that A is not included it tells you nothing about C. Likewise, if you know that C is included, it tells you nothing about A.

The ability to understand what "If" statements mean and do not mean is the single most tested reasoning skill on the LSAT.

Working with conditional statements

A conditional statement establishes a relationship between two things. It asserts that when one of those things is present (or perhaps absent) then another thing is present or absent.

Consider this statement:
If A is included, then C is included.

In the above statement A is a sufficient condition for C. That means that having A is enough to know that you must have C.

In that statement, C is a necessary condition for A, since you cannot have A without having C. It is necessary that C be there in the case that A is there.

Steps for working with conditional statements

1. Determine exactly what the statement means.

This step involves examining the statement to distinguish accurately between the sufficient condition and the necessary condition. It is crucial to know which is which.

The basic form is this: If the sufficient condition is there, then the necessary condition is there as well. That can be represented in this way: sufficient → necessary, which means, "If the sufficient condition then the necessary condition."

To determine which part of a statement is the sufficient condition, ask which item involved in the statement carries the other with it. In other words, ask which of the components of the statement is the one whose presence allows you to know for sure that the other one is there. The sufficient condition makes something else happen; it has consequences. You cannot have the sufficient condition present alone. It will always drag the necessary condition into the picture as well.

On the other hand, you can have the necessary condition alone (i.e., without the sufficient condition). The necessary condition can be present without the sufficient condition being present.

Once you have determined the relationship between the two items in a conditional statement, represent that relationship clearly with the sufficient condition, followed by an arrow, followed by the necessary condition to indicate that in the circumstance that the sufficient condition is there, the necessary condition is also there (S → N).

This act of interpretation can be difficult because there are very many different ways to say the same thing.

Each of the following statements means exactly the same thing as the others, and you can use this list as an aid in learning to interpret conditional statements:

> If you have measles, then you're sick.
> You are sick if you have measles.
> You can have measles only if you're sick.
> In the case that you have measles, you must be sick.
> Only if you're sick can you have measles.
> You cannot have measles unless you're sick.
> You cannot have measles without being sick.

Interpret the statement and put it in basic sufficient form: S → N. The first example in the above list fits this format exactly. You could symbolize this statement by writing, "measles → sick," or better yet, "M → S."

Here is a tip to help you on your way to interpreting conditional statements correctly. The part of the statement that follows the "if" is usually the sufficient condition. This changes, however, when the statement uses the language of "only if." "Only if" introduces the necessary condition. You can see this by comparing the first statement in the list above with the third. They mean exactly the same thing. "Unless" is a little more complicated. One way to approach "unless" is this: take the word "unless" to introduce the necessary condition, and then negate what comes before it to derive the sufficient condition. Thus "You cannot have measles unless you are sick" becomes "M → S."

Any conditional statement can be expressed in two different forms, and it is useful to state it in both forms when working through a game.

The basic form says if the sufficient condition is there, then the necessary condition is there: S → N.

The other form is called the "contrapositive." It follows the thought that if you do not have the necessary condition you cannot have the sufficient condition. So the statement "if A then C" also means "If not C then not A." The contrapositive is the second form.

Once you have the original conditional statement clear you can derive the contrapositive with this simple operation:

2.   Reverse the two items in the original conditional statement and negate them both.

> so S → N can also be expressed as -N → -S
> and A → C can also be expressed as -C → -A.

3.   Think about what the statement does not mean

A conditional statement does not create a group. The two items in a conditional statement *must* both be the case only in two of four possible situations involving those items (unless other rules apply).

In a conditional statement A → C , A and C must both be included when A is included. And since the statement also means -C → -A, it means that neither can be included in the case that C is not included. *But* the information that C is included alone tells us *nothing* about A. And the information that A is not included tells us *nothing* about C.

The analytical games will test to see that you understand both what the conditional statements mean, and what they do not mean.

4.   Summary

When dealing with conditional statements do these things:

1.   Interpret the statement to determine which is the sufficient condition and which is the necessary condition.
2.   Restate the statement in its contrapositive form.
3.   Take the two forms of the statement together and note that you cannot have the two sufficient conditions at the same time, but that you can (but not must) have the two necessary conditions at the same time.

Example:

Anyone with measles is a sick person.
1. Measles → Sick
2. Not sick → not measles
3. Cannot have measles and not sick, but could have sick and not measles.

With grouping games the questions often have to do with what you don't see — with ***side effects***. If a particular set of items is in group 1, what does that leave for group 2, and can that be possible?

When dealing with grouping games it is critical to be aware of items that must be together (**blocks**) and items that cannot be together (**splits**).

It is also important when dealing with grouping games to work out basic scenarios in order to know what is going on. When making deductions and walking around it, ask some basic questions to be clear about the situation.

•   Does each item have to be included?
•   Can an item be in more than one group?
•   Is there a set number in each group?
•   If not, what are the possibilities for the numbers of items in the groups?
•   What are the **wildcards**, or the items that no rules affect directly?
•   Are there two or three basic scenarios that will dominate the game?
•   Is there a item or two that controls several others?

These are the things that you identify when you are making deductions and walking around the game. They help you be alert for what the questions will do and they prepare you to deal with the questions efficiently.

Work through the following example:

GROUPING EXAMPLE

Eight items: A, B, C, D, E, F, G, and H must be placed in two groups of four each: group 1 and group 2. Each item must be placed in exactly one group, according to the following rules:

A and B must be in the same group.
C and D must be in different groups.
E is in group 2.
If F is in group 1 then G is in group 1.

Take this game though the five steps of working a game before going to the questions:

1. **Type:** This is the basic structure of any grouping game. A game may use names for the items or groups, and it might state the rules in more complex language, but if it is a game that requires you to put things in groups, it will boil down to something like this. If the test gives you names for items, reduce them to first letters (almost never will two use the same first letter). You don't care what the items are (people or things) or what the groups are doing. All you care about is that you are placing items in groups.

2. **Diagram:** The basic diagram for a grouping game will include a list of the items and a diagram distinguishing between the groups. Make it large and leave plenty of room to work. Ordinarily you do not want to waste time erasing. Also you want to keep your work from question to question so that you will know what scenarios work, should you encounter a question about what could or must be true.

ABCDEFGH

1 | 2

3. **Simplify the rules:** Now simplify the rules by stating them in symbols and place them beside the diagram so you can access them easily. The rule that places E into group 2 can be incorporated directly into the diagram.

ABCDEFGH

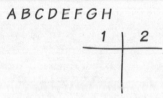

1 | 2
E

4. **Deductions:** Now look at the rules you have written down and ask what else they tell you about the groups. Begin with the "if" statement and write out its contrapositive. The statement, "If F is in 1 then G is in 1" also means that if G is not in 1 then F is not in 1. Now consider the FG rule in relation to the AB **block** and the CD **split**. The split means that either C or D must be in each group. You can incorporate this into the diagram. Since that is the case, it is not possible for the AB group and the FG group to be in 1 at the same time, because that would put five items into 1. You can state this as an if statement: If A/B is in 1, then F is not in 1, which places it in 2. And the contrapositive: if F is in 1 then AB are not in 1, which means they are in 2.

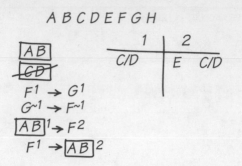

5. **"Walk Around It"**: Before you go to the questions, take the time to look at what you have and think about what is likely to be important in the game. The split you already have indicated on the diagram is sure to be a key in this type of game, as is the deduction you have made about AB and F. Remind yourself of what the "if" statement says and doesn't say: you could have G in 1 without F, or F in 2 with or without G. They are a group only when F is in 1 or when G is in 2. Remind yourself to be on the lookout for **side effects**: often the question will deal directly with the items in one group, but what you have to figure out are the effects of that for the other group. Note that H is a **wild card**: No rule affects it directly, but its placement could be very important.

QUESTIONS

1. Which of the following could be a complete and accurate list of the items in the two groups?

   (A)   1: C, A, F, B; 2: G, E, D, H
   (B)   1: B, F, G, C; 2: E, A, D, H
   (C)   1: D, F, G, C; 2: B, A, H, E
   (D)   1: C, A, H, B; 2: G, E, D, F
   (E)   1: G, D, E, F; 2: C, B, H, A

This is a typical first question. Very often, the first question is one that can be answered on the basis of the rules alone without any further deductions. Where the game involves some kind of list, the question will frequently do what this one does: give five lists and ask which of the five does not violate the rules. On these questions a good approach is to take the rules one by one and ask whether any of the answers violate that rule. An answer that violates a rule can be eliminated from further consideration. Not only does this enable you to answer the question quickly, it also gives you the opportunity to review the rules again and be certain that you understand them correctly. If you find no right answer or more than one right answer, then you have probably misunderstood a rule.

Take the AB block rule: answer (B) violates that, and so is eliminated.
Now take the CD split: answer (C) violates that, and so is eliminated (once an answer is eliminated, do not waste time checking it against the other rules).
The rule that E must be in 2 is violated by (E).
The FG rule is violated by (A).
Only answer (D) violates no rule.

2. Which is a pair of items that cannot both be in group 1?

   (A)   C, B
   (B)   H, F
   (C)   G, A
   (D)   B, F
   (E)   D, G

This question might be a rules question. The rules tell you that E cannot be in 1 and that C and D cannot be together in 1. Check first to see whether any of the answers violates one of those rules. When you see that the answers do not violate the rules, you know it is a question testing a deduction. In this case you have already made the deduction: **If A/B is in 1, then F is not in 1**, so you know the answer is (D). If you had not seen that key deduction before, then you would have to make it now. You could do so by testing the answers on your diagram until you find the one that could not work. Once you make that deduction, remember that it *always* applies in the game. It might be useful for future questions. Often a key deduction will provide the answer to several questions.

3. If H is in group 2, which is a pair of items that could also be in group 2?

    (A)   C, B
    (B)   D, F
    (C)   G, E
    (D)   A, C
    (E)   D, G

This is a **side effects** question. It calls your attention to group 2, but it is really about what is going on in group 1. You cannot have both FG and AB in group 1. If H is in 2, it is there with E and either C or D. Since there is only one place left in 2, AB cannot be in 2 and must be in 1. To prevent FG from being in 1 also, F must be placed in 2. This is testing your understanding of the relationship between F and G: they must both be in 1 when F is in 1, but G can be in 1 without F. So the answer is (B). Side effects questions like this are very common in grouping games.

Type 2: Ordering

Most LSATs will include a game that requires you to put items in order. A set of items will be presented and the task will be to put them in order from first to last (or low to high, inside to outside, left to right, east to west). The resulting order may place items in a specific spot in the order (e.g. "A ranks third"), but the critical point will not be filling discreet slots, but establishing a relative order among items.

The rules usually indicate most clearly that what is at hand is an ordering game. Typical rules for games which require you to put things in order establish the relative order of two or three of the items. In working the game, it is necessary to look at those rules in relation to one another to establish a basic order among the items and to identify items that are flexible. Questions will then ask about that overall order and sometimes add an additional piece of information to constrain the order further.

It is common to mix ordering problems with groups or slots. Sometimes it may be necessary to work a game as both a grouping game and, within the groups, as an ordering game. When it is not clear whether to approach a game as an ordering game or a slot game (see below) ask whether the key seems to be the relative order of the items, which determines the slot or slots each might occupy, or is it items relative to slots rather than to each other that dominates the game.

As a practical matter it will sometimes happen that you change approaches while working with a particular game because you discover you need to think about it differently in order to deal effectively with the questions. While a goal is to understand the type of game and to approach it most efficiently from the start, a more important goal is to answer questions correctly, and so such changes should be made as needed. The more practice you have, the more likely you will be to see how the game works from the start.

Things to be alert for in ordering games:

*   Be careful with the order: it may be first to last, highest to lowest, left to right, inside to outside, north to south, etc. Be certain to be clear on your diagram and in interpreting the rules which side is which.

- Be careful with the rules. Do they say that one item is **immediately** before another or **sometime** before another?
- If a rule mentions three items, be certain you have sorted out the relationships correctly. It is a good idea to separate out the relationships and represent them as separate rules.

ORDERING EXAMPLE

Six items: A, B, C, D, E, F must be ranked in order from low to high with place 1 being lowest and place 6 being highest. Each item occupies a unique place in the order. The order is governed by the following rules:

F is ranked lower than B.
C is ranked higher than B and lower than E.
A is ranked higher than F.
Take this game though the five steps for working a game before going to the questions:

1. **Type:** This is a pure ordering game. It does have places or slots from 1 to 6, but the rules are all about the items relative to one another. The order of the items will decide their places, so the order is what you will need to figure out in general, insofar as you can, and then with each question as new information is added.

2. **Diagram:** The basic diagram for an ordering game will include a list of the items and a notation to indicate the beginning and end of the order. Make it large and leave plenty of room to work. Ordinarily you do not want to waste time erasing. You also want to keep your work from question to question so that you will know what scenarios work, should you encounter a question about what could or must be true.

A B C D E F

1   6
LOW HIGH

3. **Simplify the rules:** Now simplify the rules by stating them in symbols and placing them beside the diagram so you can access them easily. Be certain that you have the relative relationships represented correctly. With ordering rules it is easy to reverse items in the order, so, in this example, be sure that you have represented B as lower than C and not as higher. Your symbols should clearly distinguish between what comes sometime before or after something else (as all the rules in this example do) and what comes immediately before or after something else. Now that the clues have been represented as symbols, you should be able to leave the words behind (except in the case that you use the first question to test your interpretation of the rules) and work only with your diagram and symbols.

A B C D E F F..B
       B..C
1   6 C..E
LOW HIGH F..A

4. **Deductions:** Now look at the rules you have written down and ask what else they tell you about the order of the items. With an ordering game it is a good idea to begin with an item that is mentioned more than once in the rules and just place it in the middle of the diagram. Then follow the other rules and establish the relative relationships. Take B here as the starter and write it down. Now add the information from the first rule: F..B. Next add the information from the second rule (actually these were stated initially as a single rule, but your splitting them apart makes it more likely that you will represent the order among the three accurately): F..B..C. You just deduced that C is higher than F. Now add the information about E: F..B..C..E. Although the rules didn't say so directly, they have enabled you to deduce the relative order of four of the six items. The final rule is not as constraining, but it does give some information about A and F directly, and about A and F, B, and C indirectly. While A must be higher than F, it can fall anywhere else in the order. There are rules that deal with five of the six items. Identify the sixth (D) and note that it can go anywhere in the order.

<pre>
                          A B C D E F   F..B
                                             B..C
         1   6   C..E
        LOW   HIGH   F..A
        ..A
      F..B..C..E
        ← D →
</pre>

5. **"Walk Around It":** Before you go to the questions, take the time to look at what you have and think about what is likely to be important in the game. One way to get comfortable with an ordering game is to think about what can come first and last. Here the only items that could be first are F and D, and that observation leads you to see that F can only be first or second. The last item might be D, E, or A, and having that thought reminds you of A's flexibility. There are only two real variables here: (1) Where is A? and (2) Where is F? Realize that you do not know those things, and that the questions might give you information to answer one or both of the questions.

QUESTIONS

1. Which of the following could be a complete and accurate list of the items listed from lowest to highest?

   (A)   D, A, F, B, C, E
   (B)   F, B, E, A, C, D
   (C)   D, F, B, C, A, E
   (D)   D, B, F, C, A, E
   (E)   F, D, C, A, B, E

This is a typical first question. Very often, the first question is one that can be answered on the basis of the rules alone without any further deductions. Where the game involves some kind of order, the question will frequently do what this one does: give five orders and ask which of the five does not violate the rules. On these questions a good approach is to take the rules one by one and ask whether any of the answers violate that rule. You will get to the correct answer quickly, and you will have an opportunity (though not a fool proof one) to check to see that you have not made mistakes in interpretation. An answer that violates a rule can be eliminated from further consideration. If you find no right answer or more than one right answer, then you have probably misunderstood a rule.

Start with the rule that F is lower than B. Answer (D) violates that rule, and so is eliminated. The rule that C must be higher than B is violated by answer (E), so it must not be correct. The rule that C is lower than E is violated by answer (B).

An Approach to Analytical Reasoning Problems

Answer (A) violates the rule that places A higher than F.
In this case the correct answer is (C), which obeys all the rules.

2. Which of the following is a complete and accurate list of items that could be in position 3?

    (A)   B, C
    (B)   F, B, C
    (C)   D, A, B
    (D)   C, D, B, A
    (E)   D, B, F, C, A

This question asks about an absolute slot, slot number 3. But, in fact, the question is about possible orders: how could these six items be put in order to leave different items in the third position? If you look at the six items, you know that both D and A are highly flexible and could easily be in the third position. F, on the other hand, is inflexible and can be only in the first or second positions. Similarly, E must be preceded by at least three other items and, thus, could not be in the third position. And so you deduce that the list of items that could be in position 3 includes D A B and C. The correct answer is located in the choice (D).

3. If D is adjacent to A, which of the following must be false?

    (A)   B is in position 2.
    (B)   C is in position 5.
    (C)   F is in position 1.
    (D)   A is in position 4.
    (E)   E is in position 5.

With the previous question you were able to figure out the answer and then locate the one answer choice that was correct. With questions that ask what "must be false" or what "could be true" it might take a little bit more work: it might be necessary to test each of the choices to determine whether it works. But try to do this efficiently, deducing what you can from what the question gives you and then asking, given your deductions, whether the positioning in the answer choice can take place. The question places D beside A. Since both of those items are highly flexible, their placement adjacent to each other would not seem to do much to constrain the other items. Since F must be some time before A, it does place F in position one, and so answer choice (C) must be true and cannot be false. A first glance may not reveal any problem with the remaining choices. But then look at answer (E). If D and A are together, either one of them is in the sixth position or E is in the sixth position. But if D or A is in the sixth position, then the other one of the pair is in the fifth position. So it would not be possible for E to be in the fifth position since only A, D, or E can be in the sixth position, and, therefore, if E is not in the sixth position, it must be in the fourth position. So the correct answer here, the one which indicates something that must be false, is (E).

Type 3: Slots

With grouping games your task is to collect items together, paying attention to which items must stay together and which items must be apart. Ordering games require you to focus on the positions of items relative to one another, and any absolute order that is produced will be created primarily by understanding that relative order. The third basic type of game creates discreet, well-defined slots that must be filled or not with individual items. Unlike grouping games, slot games do not collect items together, but place them in particular positions. And unlike ordering games, slot games do not deal with items relative to one another, but with items relative to slots.

In slot games, the slots are defined carefully by either one or two criteria. Often these are schedules, defining the slots as days of the week or hours of the day during which things take place. But they are not necessarily schedules, and can be defined in a variety of different ways. There might be several items which must be distributed among the slots, or it might be that each slot is filled with a yes or a no, an item included or an item excluded, or something of that sort.

With grouping games and ordering games it is most efficient to avoid making a matrix, since that suggests that each item has a permanent, distinct place, thereby obscuring the flexibility of the situation. With slot games, on the other hand, it is important to identify those distinct slots carefully. How can you tell when you first approach a game whether the most efficient way to work with it is to treat it as one that creates these distinct slots? If the rules have to do with the relative order of items, or if the rules lead to collecting things together without distinguishing places within the group, then it is probably not a game to work with slots. But if the rules have to do with absolute placement of items in something like days of the week, or cities, or places at a table, then it will be most effective to define the slots very carefully and to place or not place a single item in each as the rules and the questions require.

Distinguish between the criteria defining the slots and the items to be placed in them. The slots themselves are not variable, and it is important to define them well. If they are defined by two criteria, use a matrix and distinguish clearly between the criteria defining the slots. The items will be more variable and flexible in most cases, and they will be used to fill in and the places in the matrix or schedule. The danger with using a matrix, the reason why it is probably not a good idea to use one with grouping games or ordering games, is that it tends to suggest that there is only one possible solution. It is always important to remember that the games create situations about which you know some things and don't know others, and it is crucial to be as clear on what is flexible, on what you don't know, as it is to be clear on what to do know. And so in drawing a matrix for a slots game, it is important to identify clearly areas of uncertainty as well as definite placement of items in slots.

Keys to slots games:

- **Deductions** are especially important in these games. The rules may place an item or two, but often you can deduce the placement of several other items, and these deductions will be necessary to working the game well.
- Questions in these games often give one or two pieces of information that create a **chain reaction**. Knowing that an item is placed in a particular slot often constrains what can or must be placed in another slot, which, in turn, may determine what can or must be placed in a third slot.
- The situation in a slots game is often more constrained than it seems based only on the rules. Most of the time the placement of items into one or two slots will have critical effects for the rest of the situation. In walking around the game, consider those possibilities.

SLOTS EXAMPLE

Each of boxes W, X, Y, and Z is divided into two parts: 1 and 2. Each of eight items, two each of A, B, C and D, must be placed in exactly one part of one box, according to these conditions:

B's must be in part 2 of their boxes.
A's must be in part 1 of their boxes.
Any box containing a D must contain a C.
Part 1 of box X contains a C.
Box Y does not contain a D.

Take this game through the five steps before going to the questions.

An Approach to Analytical Reasoning Problems

1. **Type:** There's a lot going on in this setup. There are boxes with divisions and items to be placed into those divisions. The boxes and the divisions together create distinct slots. The items are more variable, and they are to be placed in the slots.

In identifying the game's type, remember the importance of maintaining flexibility, of identifying not only what you know, but also what you do not know. Avoid making the game more rigid than the rules make it. In this case, ask whether it makes sense to simplify it and to think of the game in terms of groups rather than the more rigid slots. The answer here is "no" because in this case the object is not to collect things together but to place individual items in individual slots.

Distinguishing Types

In identifying game types, the key is in the individual rules. Consider these examples, each of which involves distributing items over the days of a week:

Example 1:

Each of four people, P, Q, R, and S, arrives on exactly one of four sequential days, Monday, Tuesday, Wednesday, and Thursday. Each of the people arrives on a different day. P arrives sometime before R, and R arrives sometime after S and before Q.

Example 2:

Each of eight people, G, H, I, J, K, L, M, and N arrives on exactly one of four sequential days, Monday, Tuesday, Wednesday, and Thursday. No more than three of the people arrive on the same day. J and K arrive on different days, and M and N arrive on the same day.

Example 3:

Each of four people, W, X, Y, and Z, arrives on exactly one of four sequential days, Monday, Tuesday, Wednesday, and Thursday. There is exactly one day between the day on which W arrives and the day on which Y arrives. X arrives on either Monday or Thursday.

While each of three examples involves the days of the week, the three require very different operations. With Example 1 any question would require that you determine the order of the items relative to one another and then determine the possibilities for the days of the week. And so Example 1 is an ordering game. With Example 2 you are required to collect items together in groups of one, two, or three, using three or four of the days of the week. This does not create eight distinct slots for the items, but rather collections of uncertain size, and so it makes sense to think of this as a grouping game. But in Example 3 you are to place four items in the days of the week and the placement is relative to the day. So in Example 3 you make the slots distinctly and place the items relative to the slots. This one is a slot game, and to work it you will need to identify the slots carefully to place the items into them.

The game's type will not always be crystal clear. Indeed, sometimes you will set up a game as a particular type and end up working it as another type. Your experience and the questions will guide you to the appropriate way of dealing with the questions.

2. **Diagram:** Since this is a slot game you need to identify the criteria (in this case there are two) that define the slots. Then draw the diagram accordingly, making the boxes clear with the letters, W, X, Y, and Z on one side, and the numbers 1 and 2 on the other. Make the matrix as large as you can, remembering that you will have to deal with five to seven questions and with different possibilities and chain reactions in different questions. Include in the diagram a list of the items that need to be placed in the slots.

A A B B C C D D

	W	X	Y	Z
1				
2				

3. **Simplify the rules:** The next step is to interpret and simplify the rules. Make it clear that all B's must be in part 2's and all A's must be in part 1's. The third rule can be symbolized as $D \rightarrow C$. The final two rules can be added directly to the diagram.

A A B B C C D D

B,B = 2 only

A,A = 1 only

	W	X	Y	Z
1		C	~D	
2			~D	

4. **Deductions:** Now look at the rules you have written down and ask what else they tell you about the placement of the items into the slots. This step is critical in any game, but it is especially so in a slot game. Often an initial deduction will lead to a second and third, allowing you to fill in slots or at least to narrow the possibilities. Look for multiple rules that affect a particular item. Be sure to consider the number of items relative to the number of slots and the question of whether each item has to be used, and, if so, whether it has to be used exactly once.

In this case you have eight items, each of which must be used exactly once. Consider that fact in conjunction with the rule establishing a relationship between D and C. By itself the rule says that if a D is included a C must also be included permits a C to be in a box without a D. But in this case you can add that rule to the rules that tell you that you have exactly two D's and exactly two C's and that each C and D must be used exactly once. Since each D must be accompanied by a C in the same box, and each D must be used, each C must be reserved for a box containing a D. So despite the fact that $D \rightarrow C$ does not by itself create a block, that rule combined with the other rules in the game allows you to deduce that any box containing a D in one of its slots contains a C in the other, and any box containing a C contains a D. That key deduction enables you to fill in three more of the slots. Since every box containing a C must also contain a D, part 2 of box X contains a D. Furthermore, since no C can be in a box without a D, there can be no C in box Y. And since B's can be in part 2's only and A's can be in part 1's only, slot Y1 must contain an A and slot Y2 must contain a B. These deductions should be represented on the diagram by filling in the slots and making it clear that the placement of items in these slots is just as clear and as certain as if rules had stated directly that X2 contains a D, Y1 contains an A, and Y2 contains a B.

A A B B C C D D

B,B = 2 only

A,A = 1 only

	W	X	Y	Z
1		C	A ~D	
2		D	B ~D	

An Approach to Analytical Reasoning Problems

5. **"Walk Around It"**: Before you go to the questions, take the time to look at what you have and think about what is left to do. You know what is in half of the slots, and you don't know what is in the other half. But on reflection, you do know quite a bit about what will happen in the four remaining slots. Since each D must be accompanied by a C, and each C accompanied by a D, the remaining C and D will be together either in box X or in box Z, although you do not know which is in part 1 and which is in part 2. The other one of boxes X and Z must contain the remaining A and B, with A in part 1 and B in part 2. Any additional information that a question provides will cause a **chain reaction**, enabling you to know which items are in which boxes and, perhaps, which items are in which parts of the boxes. Basically there are two questions remaining: (1) Which of boxes X and Z contains the A and B, and which contains the C and D? (2) In the box containing the C and D, which is in part 1 and which is in part 2?

QUESTIONS

1. Which of the following could be a complete and accurate list of the items in the two parts of the boxes in order W, X, Y, Z?

    (A) 1: D, C, A, A 2: C, D, B, B
    (B) 1: A, C, A, D 2: B, C, B, D
    (C) 1: D, A, C, A 2: C, B, D, B
    (D) 1: C, C, B, A 2: D, D, A, B
    (E) 1: A, C, A, D 2: B, A, B, C

This is a typical first question. Very often, the first question is one that can be answered on the basis of the rules alone without any further deductions. Where the game involves some kind of list, the question will frequently do what this one does: give five lists and ask which of the five does not violate the rules. On these questions a good approach is to take the rules one by one and ask whether any of the answers violate that rule. An answer that violates a rule can be eliminated from further consideration. Not only does this enable you to answer the question quickly, it also gives you the opportunity to review the rules again and be certain that you understand them correctly. If you find no right answer or more than one right answer, then you have probably misunderstood a rule.

Begin with the rule that says that B's must be in part 2's of their boxes. This rule is violated by answer choice (D), and so that answer is eliminated.

The rule that says that A's must be in part one of their boxes is violated by answer choice (E), which is thereby eliminated.

Choice (B) violates the rule that says any box containing a D must contain a C, and so it is eliminated.

Finally the rule that states that X1 contains a C is violated by choice (C).

So the only answer choice that does not violate a rule is (A), which is the correct answer.

2. If the B's are not placed in boxes labeled with letters adjacent in the alphabet, which of the following must be true?

(A) Z1 has a C.
(B) Z2 has a C.
(C) Z1 has an A.
(D) W1 has a C.
(E) W1 has an A.

This question causes a chain reaction. If the B's are not to be in boxes with letters adjacent in the alphabet, then the box containing the A in part 1 and B in part 2 must be box W, leaving C and D to be in box Z. The only thing you do not know is which of C and D is in part 1 and which in part 2. That last bit of uncertainty figures heavily in the question, which asks for something that MUST be true. (A) and (B) *could* be true, but do not have to be. Only answer (E) *must* be true.

$$A\ A\ B\ B\ C\ C\ D\ D$$

		W	X	Y	Z
B,B = 2 only	1	A	C	A~D	C
A,A = 1 only	2	B	D	B~D	D

3. If part 1 of box Z has an item that is different from the item in any other part 1 slot, which of the following must be false?

(A) W1 has an A.
(B) Z2 has a C.
(C) Z2 has a D.
(D) W2 has a B.
(E) Y2 has a B.

This question creates another chain reaction, which is typical of slots games. This one gives you information that enables you to fill in all the slots. If Z1 is different from any other part 1 slot, it cannot have an A or a C, which are already in part 1's. It cannot have a B, which can never be in a part 1, so it must have a D. That enables you to put the remaining C in Z2, and then the A in W1 and the B in W2. The question asks for what must be false, and what must be false is answer (C). Everything else must be true.

$$A\ A\ B\ B\ C\ C\ D\ D$$

		W	X	Y	Z
B,B = 2 only	1	A	C	A~D	D
A,A = 1 only	2	B	D	B~D	C

How to Use This Book

This book is divided into three major parts: the games, their setups, and the analysis of the questions and answers. If you are just beginning to work with analytical reasoning problems, we suggest that for your first few games you begin by reading the game's basic setup and rules, and then set it up as best you can. Before you go to the questions, however, it might be helpful for you to consult the setup included here.

An Approach to Analytical Reasoning Problems

That will help you learn to go through the steps: to identify the type, prepare the diagram, and most especially to make deductions and to pause and think about what is going on before you move on to the questions. Then you should attempt to answer the questions, using the analysis of the questions as you need to in order to begin to see the things you need to see.

After you have practiced a while and are beginning to make good deductions and to answer questions without help, it is probably better to try to work each game on your own with as little assistance as possible. But then it is important after you have completed a game to read the setup in this book and to read the analysis of the questions so you can continue to learn how you might approach these exercises more efficiently. The explanations make every attempt to tie the particular problems in particular games to general rules and strategies that can be employed on other similar problems and games. If you look at the setup and analysis here while the game is still fresh in your experience, you can learn reasoning strategies that can make you more accurate and efficient in the future.

The games are intentionally presented in random order rather than by type or in order of difficulty. A key part of working a game is determining the type, so that task is left to the reader, although it is explained for each game in the setup. Similarly, it is probably better to approach each game without a predisposition as to whether it is difficult or not so difficult. Instead it is a good idea to approach each with the confidence that the information needed to find the one correct answer to each question about the situation is there, and working patiently and systematically will allow you to find it. The games here range from very difficult to relatively easy, but all are workable. If a game just seems too difficult, start by rereading the rules: Maybe there is something you have missed or something you are assuming is there that is not there. (Remember, the language in the game's rules will be exact.) Then if it still seems impenetrable, start reading the setup to see the deductions or perhaps the beginning of the deductions, which you can use as a hint to get going. Above all, learn from each game, and especially from the ones you find more challenging.

Finally, it is probably not a good idea to do a set of four of these as a timed imitation LSAT section. They are not designed with that in mind and they are not grouped as they would need to be for that purpose. The intent here is for you to be able to use each of these games to practice your technique and to develop your reasoning skills so that when you practice on actual timed LSAT sections, you will find yourself doing the problems in those sections more efficiently and effectively.

Part II

Games

Game 1

Each of five students, Christina, Bernie, Israel, Jamie, and Angela, will be assigned to give a report on one the following plays: *Merchant of Venice*, *Othello*, *King Lear*, *Hamlet*, and *Richard III*. Each student must report on exactly one play and no two students report on the same play. The reports are presented over a five-week period, one each week, with week one being the earliest week. The following conditions apply:

Jamie gives her report sometime after the report on *King Lear* is given and sometime before Christina gives her report.

The report on *Othllo* is given sometime after Angela gives her report.

Angela does not give the first report.

Neither *Othello* nor *Merchant of Venice* is the subject of the last report.

1. Which of the following could be a complete and accurate list from first to last of the order in which the students give reports?

    (A) Bernie, Jamie, Israel, Angela, Christina
    (B) Bernie, Israel, Angela, Christina, Jamie
    (C) Israel, Angela, Jamie, Christina, Bernie
    (D) Christina, Jamie, Israel, Bernie, Angela
    (E) Israel, Jamie, Christina, Angela, Bernie

2. Which is a complete and accurate list of the students who could give the first report?

    (A) Israel, Jamie, Angela, Christina
    (B) Bernie, Angela, Jamie, Israel
    (C) Bernie, Angela, Israel
    (D) Israel, Bernie
    (E) Bernie, Israel, Jamie

3. If Jamie reports on *Hamlet* and gives the second report, which of the following must be true?

    (A) Bernie is the first student to give a report.
    (B) The report on *Richard III* is given first.
    (C) The report on *Othello* is given third.
    (D) Christina is the fourth student to give a report.
    (E) The report on *Merchant of Venice* is given third.

4. If Angela reports on *King Lear* in the third week, which of the following must be true?

    (A) Christina reports on *Richard III*.
    (B) Israel reports on *Hamlet*.
    (C) Jamie reports on *Othello*.
    (D) Bernie reports on *Merchant of Venice*.
    (E) Jamie reports on *Hamlet*.

5. Which of the following must be false?

    (A) Israel reports on *Othello*.
    (B) Jamie reports on *Othello*.
    (C) Bernie reports immediately before Israel.
    (D) Angela reports sometime after Christina.
    (E) The report on *Merchant of Venice* is immediately before the report on *Othello*.

6. If Israel reports on *Hamlet* and Bernie reports on *Richard III*, which of the following could be true?

    (A) Jamie reports on *King Lear*.
    (B) Jamie reports on *Merchant of Venice*.
    (C) Angela reports on *Merchant of Venice*.
    (D) Bernie reports second.
    (E) Christina reports third.

7. If the condition requiring *Othello* to be reported on sometime after Angela reports is changed to require Angela to give a report on *Othello* and all other conditions remain the same, what is the maximum number of plays any one of which could be the subject of the first report?

    (A) 1
    (B) 2
    (C) 3
    (D) 4
    (E) 5

Game 2

Eight dinosaur species, Orodromeus, Pleurosaurus, Quetzocoatlus, Rhamphorhynchus, Synosauropteryx, Tenontosaurus, Utahraptor, and Velociraptor, each went extinct in one of three periods: the Early era, the Middle era, or the Late era, with the Middle era occurring after the Early era and before the Late era. Each species can go extinct in only one era, with no more than three dinosaurs going extinct in any one era. The following conditions apply:

The Orodromeus must go extinct sometime after the Pleurosaurus, but not necessarily in a later period.

The Pleurosaurus must go extinct sometime after the Tenontosaurus, but not necessarily in a later period.

The Synosauropteryx and the Orodromeus cannot go extinct in the same period.

The Tenontosaurus and the Utahraptor must go extinct in the same period.

The Utahraptor and the Velociraptor must go extinct in the same period.

1. Which of the following is an acceptable ordering of the extinctions of the dinosaurs?

    (A) Early era: Synosauropteryx, Quetzocoatlus, Velociraptor
    Middle era: Tenontosaurus, Pleurosaurus
    Late era: Orodromeus, Rhamphorhynchus, Utahraptor

    (B) Early era: Pleurosaurus, Rhamphorhynchus, Orodromeus
    Middle era: Synosauropteryx, Quetzocoatlus
    Late era: Velociraptor, Tenontosaurus, Utahraptor

    (C) Early era: Velociraptor, Tenontosaurus, Utahraptor
    Middle era: Pleurosaurus, Synosauropteryx, Rhamphorhynchus
    Late era: Orodromeus, Quetzocoatlus

    (D) Early era: Rhamphorhynchus, Quetzocoatlus
    Middle era: Tenontosaurus, Velociraptor, Utahraptor
    Late era: Pleurosaurus, Orodromeus, Synosauropteryx

    (E) Early era: Orodromeus, Rhamphorhynchus
    Middle era: Pleurosaurus, Synosauropteryx, Quetzocoatlus
    Late era: Tenontosaurus, Utahraptor, Velociraptor

2. If only two of the species go extinct in the Middle era, which of the following must be true?

    (A) The Utahraptor went extinct in the Early era.

    (B) The Orodromeus went extinct in the Middle era.

    (C) The Pleurosaurus went extinct in the Late era.

    (D) The Synosauropteryx went extinct sometime before the Velociraptor.

    (E) The Rhamphorhynchus went extinct in the Late era.

3. Which of the following CANNOT be true?

    (A) The Utahraptor went extinct in the Middle era.

    (B) The Synosauropteryx went extinct in the period immediately following the period in which the Velociraptor went extinct.

    (C) The Velociraptor went extinct in the Early era.

    (D) The Orodromeus and the Quetzocoatlus went extinct in the same era.

    (E) The Pleurosaurus went extinct in the Early era.

4. If the Utahraptor went extinct in the Middle era, which of the following must be true?

    (A) The Velociraptor went extinct in the Early era.

    (B) The Synosauropteryx went extinct in the Late era.

    (C) The Orodromeus and the Pleurosaurus went extinct in the same period.

    (D) The Quetzocoatlus went extinct in the Late era.

    (E) The Pleurosaurus and the Rhamphorhynchus went extinct in different periods.

5. Which of the following would allow us to know the period in which each dinosaur went extinct?

   (A) The Synosauropteryx and the Rhamphorhynchus were the only dinosaurs that went extinct in the Early era.

   (B) The Orodromeus and the Quetzocoatlus went extinct in the same period.

   (C) The Tenontosaurus and the Velociraptor both went extinct in the Middle era.

   (D) The Pleurosaurus went extinct in the period immediately following the period in which the Utahraptor went extinct.

   (E) The Synosauropteryx went extinct in the Middle era and the Orodromeus went extinct in the Late era.

6. Which of the following CANNOT be true?

   (A) Only two dinosaurs went extinct in the period in which the Pleurosaurus went extinct.

   (B) The Rhamphorhynchus went extinct before the Tenontosaurus.

   (C) The Synosauropteryx went extinct in the Late era.

   (D) The Rhamphorhynchus and the Velociraptor went extinct in the same period.

   (E) The Pleurosaurus and the Orodromeus went extinct in the same period.

Game 3

Seven students, Nathan, Travis, Rafael, Anne, Eddie, Jonathan, and Bernie, are beginning their first year of law school after having graduated from the same prestigious university. Each student will be assigned to one of four sections: section 1, section 2, section 3, or section 4. No section includes more than three of the seven students, and none of the seven is the only one of the seven in any section. Section assignments conform to the following constraints:

Nathan and Anne cannot be in the same section, and neither can be in a section with Travis.

Bernie and Rafael cannot be in the same section, and neither can be in a section with Travis.

Bernie and Nathan cannot be in the same section, and neither can be in a section with Eddie.

Whether or not they are in the same section, both Eddie and Anne are assigned either to section 2 or else to section 4.

1. Which of the following could be a complete and accurate list of assignments of the students to sections?

   (A) section 1: Bernie, Travis; section 2: Eddie, Rafael; section 3: none; section 4: Anne, Travis, Jonathan

   (B) section 1: none; section 2: Eddie, Travis; section 3: Nathan, Rafael; section 4: Anne, Bernie, Jonathan

   (C) section 1: Nathan, Travis; section 2: Anne, Eddie; section 3: none; section 4: Jonathan, Bernie, Rafael

   (D) section 1: none; section 2: Eddie, Jonathan; section 3: Anne, Bernie, Travis; section 4: Nathan, Rafael

   (E) section 1: Nathan, Rafael; section 2: Travis, Bernie, Jonathan; section 3: none; section 4: Anne, Eddie

2. Which of the following must be false?

   (A) Jonathan is one of three students assigned to section 3.

   (B) Eddie is one of three students assigned to section 4.

   (C) Section 2 includes Rafael, Nathan, and Travis.

   (D) Section 4 includes Jonathan, Anne, and Bernie.

   (E) Section 3 includes Nathan and Rafael only.

3. Which of the following is a pair of students who can be in a section with Travis?

   (A) Bernie, Eddie

   (B) Jonathan, Rafael

   (C) Eddie, Jonathan

   (D) Rafael, Nathan

   (E) Anne, Eddie

4. If Jonathan and Rafael are assigned to section 3, which of the following must be false?

   (A) Anne is assigned to section 2.

   (B) Eddie is assigned to section 4.

   (C) Travis is assigned to section 2.

   (D) Bernie is assigned to section 1.

   (E) Nathan is assigned to section 3.

5. If Bernie is one of three students assigned to section 2, which of the following must be true?

   (A) Eddie is assigned to section 2.

   (B) Travis is assigned to section 4.

   (C) Nathan is assigned to section 1.

   (D) Rafael is assigned to section 3.

   (E) Jonathan is assigned to section 4.

6. Which of the following pairs of students CANNOT be assigned to the same section?

   (A) Jonathan and Travis

   (B) Bernie and Anne

   (C) Rafael and Nathan

   (D) Eddie and Anne

   (E) Jonathan and Rafael

7. If Travis is assigned to a section with Jonathan, which of the following must be false?

   (A) Rafael is assigned to a section with two of the other seven students.

   (B) Eddie is assigned to a section with two of the other seven students.

   (C) Anne is assigned to a section with exactly one of the other seven students.

   (D) Bernie is assigned to a section with exactly one of the other seven students.

   (E) Nathan is assigned to a section with exactly one of the other seven students.

Game 4

Each of five customers, Brenda, Chris, Danny, Felix, and Glenda, buys a pizza from the Ruiz House of Pizza. Each customer buys a pizza with exactly two toppings selected from mushrooms, onions, pepperoni, and sausage in a manner consistent with these conditions:

Brenda and Felix order exactly the same toppings.
Felix and Chris do not order any of the same toppings.
Chris and Danny order exactly one topping in common.
Glenda and Brenda order exactly one topping in common.
Chris and Glenda order exactly one topping in common.
Chris orders pepperoni, Brenda orders onions, and Glenda orders sausage.
Danny and Glenda order toppings different from each other.

1. Which of the following could be a complete and accurate list of customers and toppings they order?

    (A) Brenda: onion, sausage; Chris: pepperoni, mushroom; Danny: onion, mushroom; Felix: mushroom, sausage; Glenda: sausage pepperoni

    (B) Brenda: mushroom, onion; Chris: onion, pepperoni; Danny: pepperoni, mushroom; Felix: mushroom, onion; Glenda: sausage, pepperoni

    (C) Brenda: onion, sausage; Chris: pepperoni, mushroom; Danny: onion, mushroom; Felix: onion, sausage; Glenda: sausage, pepperoni

    (D) Brenda: onion, mushroom; Chris: sausage, pepperoni; Danny: pepperoni, sausage; Felix: mushroom, onion; Glenda: sausage, mushroom

    (E) Brenda: sausage, onion; Chris: mushroom, pepperoni; Danny: pepperoni, sausage; Felix: sausage, onion; Glenda: onion, mushroom

2. If Chris orders sausage then which of the following must be true?

    (A) Danny orders onions.
    (B) Brenda orders sausage.
    (C) Glenda orders mushrooms.
    (D) Danny orders pepperoni.
    (E) Felix orders pepperoni.

3. If Glenda orders mushrooms and Chris does not, which of the following is a complete and accurate list of the toppings, each of which could be ordered by exactly three of the customers?

    (A) mushroom, onions
    (B) onions, pepperoni
    (C) sausage, mushroom
    (D) onion, mushroom, pepperoni
    (E) sausage, mushroom, onions

4. If Glenda does not order mushrooms and Felix orders sausage, then which of the following are toppings that Danny must order?

    (A) pepperoni and onions
    (B) onions and mushrooms
    (C) mushrooms and pepperoni
    (D) pepperoni and sausage
    (E) sausage and mushrooms

5. If exactly two customers order sausage, which of the following must be false?

    (A) Glenda orders mushrooms.
    (B) Danny orders mushrooms.
    (C) Danny orders onions.
    (D) Danny orders pepperoni.
    (E) Glenda orders pepperoni.

6. Which of the following must be false?

   (A) Exactly two customers order sausage.
   (B) Exactly three customers order sausage.
   (C) Exactly two customers order mushrooms.
   (D) Exactly two customers order pepperoni.
   (E) Exactly three customers order pepperoni.

7. If exactly two customers order mushrooms, which of the following could be true?

   (A) Danny and Glenda order mushrooms.
   (B) Chris and Danny order onions.
   (C) Chris and Glenda order sausage.
   (D) Chris and Glenda order pepperoni.
   (E) Glenda and Felix order onions.

Game 5

This semester Andres is taking courses in humanities, philosophy, math, government, sociology, anthropology, and literature. Each class takes place either on Monday, Wednesday, and Friday (MWF) or on Tuesday and Thursday (TTh), with at least two courses following each schedule. Andres carries exactly one notebook for each class; he carries the notebooks for the MWF classes in a red backpack and the notebooks for the TTh classes in a blue backpack.

The philosophy notebook and the humanities notebook are not in the same backpack.

If Andres takes government on TTh then he takes anthropology on MWF.

The sociology notebook is not in the blue backpack unless the anthropology notebook is in the blue backpack.

If Andres takes philosophy on MWF then the government notebook is not in the blue backpack.

If literature is on TTh then government is also on TTh.

1. Which of the following could be a complete and accurate list of the notebooks in each backpack?

   (A) Red: humanities, literature, government, philosophy; Blue: sociology, anthropology, math

   (B) Red: philosophy, literature, math; Blue: government, sociology, anthropology, humanities

   (C) Red: anthropology, math, humanities; Blue: literature, government, philosophy, sociology

   (D) Red: philosophy, literature, government, sociology; Blue: humanities, anthropology, math

   (E) Red: government, math, philosophy; Blue: literature, humanities, sociology, anthropology

2. If there are exactly two notebooks in the blue backpack, which of the following must be true?

   (A) Government is on TTh.
   (B) Literature in on MWF.
   (C) Government is on MWF.
   (D) Math is on TTh.
   (E) Humanities in on TTh.

3. If Andres carries his government notebook in the blue backpack, which of the following could be true?

   (A) Andres takes philosophy on MWF.
   (B) Andres takes sociology on TTh.
   (C) Andres takes literature on MWF.
   (D) Andres takes anthropology on TTh.
   (E) Andres takes humanities on TTh.

4. Which of the following could be true?

   (A) The notebooks for literature and humanities are both in the red backpack.

   (B) The notebooks for government and anthropology are both in the blue backpack.

   (C) The notebooks for government and sociology are both in the blue backpack.

   (D) The notebooks for literature and sociology are both in the blue backpack.

   (E) The notebooks for literature and humanities are both in the blue backpack.

5. If Andres takes literature on TTh, which of the following must be true?

   (A) He takes philosophy on MWF.
   (B) He takes anthropology on TTh.
   (C) He takes math on MWF.
   (D) He takes sociology on TTh.
   (E) He takes humanities on MWF.

6. If the notebooks for humanities, government, and anthropology are in the same backpack, which of the following must be true?

   (A) The notebook for literature is in the blue backpack.
   (B) The notebook for philosophy is in the red backpack.
   (C) The notebook for math is in the blue backpack.
   (D) The notebook for sociology is in the blue backpack.
   (E) The notebook for government is in the blue backpack.

7. If the condition requiring philosophy and humanities to be taken on different days is changed so that both philosophy and humanities are taken on MWF and all other conditions remain the same, which of the following must be a course taken on TTh?

   (A) Math
   (B) Anthropology
   (C) Government
   (D) Sociology
   (E) Literature

Game 6

An advertising company must assign teams to projects C, D, and F. Each team must include at least one of writers L and M and exactly two of graphic artists R, S, T, and V. Each writer and graphic designer is assigned to at least one team according to these restrictions:

No writer can be assigned to both C and D.
No graphic artist can be assigned to both D and F.
S is not on a team with T.
V is on a team with L.
V is assigned to project D.
S is assigned to C.

1. Which of the following could be a complete and accurate list of teams assigned to projects?

   (A) C: M, V, S   D: L, V, R   F: M, T, R
   (B) C: M, V, R   D: L, V, R   F: M, S, T
   (C) C: L, V, R   D: L, S, R   F: M, T, V
   (D) C: L, V, S   D: M, V, S   F: L, T, R
   (E) C: L, S, R   D: M, V, T   F: M, S, R

2. Which of the following can serve on only one team?

   (A) S
   (B) T
   (C) R
   (D) V
   (E) L

3. If T is on a team with R, which of the following must be true?

   (A) L is on project D.
   (B) M is on project F.
   (C) R is on project C.
   (D) R is on project F.
   (E) M is on project C.

4. If L is not on a team with S, which of the following must be true?

   (A) L is assigned to project F.
   (B) M is assigned to project D.
   (C) T is assigned to project D.
   (D) T is assigned to project F.
   (E) R is assigned to project D.

5. If M is on exactly two teams, which of the following CANNOT be a complete team assigned to one of the projects?

   (A) M, S, V
   (B) M, V, T
   (C) L, S, R
   (D) L, V, T
   (E) L, S, V

6. If R is assigned to exactly two projects, then which of the following must be true?

   (A) L is assigned to F.
   (B) T is assigned to F.
   (C) M is assigned to D.
   (D) S is assigned to D.
   (E) M is assigned to C.

7. What is the maximum number of different teams that could be assigned to project F?

   (A) 3
   (B) 4
   (C) 5
   (D) 6
   (E) 7

Game 7

Nine professionals are sitting in the first-class section of an airplane. Of the nine, three are accountants, G, H, and I; three are doctors, X, Y, and Z; and three are lawyers, M, N, and O. The seats are arranged into five rows of two, as follows:

	window	aisle
row 1	——	——
row 2	——	——
row 3	——	——
row 4	——	——
row 5	——	——

Each of the professionals must sit in one of these seats, and no professional can sit in more than one seat. The seating of the professionals must also conform to the following conditions:

G and N must sit in window seats.
If M sits in an aisle seat, then Z and I must sit in the same row as each other.
N must sit in a lower-numbered row than H and a higher-numbered row than Z.
If X sits in the same row as one of the lawyers, then two of the accountants must sit in the same row as each other.
None of the lawyers can sit in row 5.
I sits in the window seat in row 2.

1. Which of the following could be a complete and accurate list of the professionals in the aisle seats in rows 1 through 5 consecutively?

   (A) Z, X, N, Y, H
   (B) M, Z, X, H, Y
   (C) O, Z, Y, H, M
   (D) O, H, X, empty, Y
   (E) empty, I, X, M, H

2. If H is the only professional sitting in row 4 and M sits in the same row as N, which of the following is a row that X could be sitting in?

   (A) 1
   (B) 2
   (C) 3
   (D) 4
   (E) 5

3. If both H and O have window seats, which of the following must be false?

   (A) H sits in row 5.
   (B) Y sits in row 1.
   (C) O and X sit in row 4.
   (D) I and Z sit in the same row.
   (E) N sits in the row with the empty seat.

4. If Z sits in the window seat in row 3, then each of the following is a row in which X could be sitting EXCEPT:

   (A) 1
   (B) 2
   (C) 3
   (D) 4
   (E) 5

5. If G and Y both sit in row 4, then N could be seated

   (A) in row 1 with O.
   (B) in row 2 with I.
   (C) in row 3 with H.
   (D) in row 3 with M.
   (E) in row 3 with X.

6. If Z sits in the row with the empty seat, which of the following is a row in which G could be seated?

   (A) 1
   (B) 2
   (C) 3
   (D) 4
   (E) 5

7. Suppose that M, X, and Y sit in the aisle seats in rows 1, 3, and 5, respectively. If Y is the only professional sitting in row 5, then each of the following must be true EXCEPT:

   (A) H sits in an aisle seat.
   (B) G sits in row 3.
   (C) M sits next to another lawyer.
   (D) O sits in a window seat.
   (E) X sits in the same row as one of the lawyers.

Game 8

On a certain night a band called The Attack Marmots is playing at a local club. The band only knows ten songs, A, B, C, D, E, F, G, H, I, and J, and it will try to play as many of these as it can before it is kicked off the stage. After it is kicked off the stage it cannot play any more songs. The Attack Marmots can play each song no more than once, and the following conditions apply:

If the band plays either H or I, then it must be kicked off the stage immediately afterward.
The band cannot play D unless it also plays B and F, D being played sometime after B and sometime before F.
If the band plays either A or G, then it must play the other as well, and exactly one song must be played in between them.
If G is not played, then E must be the fourth song played.
If the band plays two or more songs, then C must be the second song played.

1. Which of the following could be a complete and accurate list of the songs played by the band that night?

    (A) B, C, A, I, G, D, F
    (B) B, C, E
    (C) E, C, F, G, D, A, B, I
    (D) F, C, G, A, H
    (E) J, C, F, E, B, H

2. If the band plays F immediately after it plays B and plays I sixth, then which of the following could be true?

    (A) A is the fifth song played.
    (B) B is the third song played.
    (C) E is the fourth song played.
    (D) F is the fifth song played.
    (E) J is the first song played.

3. Suppose that D is played fifth and I is played seventh. Which of the following is a complete and accurate list of the places in which J could be played?

    (A) first, third
    (B) first, third, fourth
    (C) first, third, sixth
    (D) fourth
    (E) fourth, eighth

4. If The Attack Marmots play H fifth, then which of the following is a song that the band CANNOT play?

    (A) A
    (B) D
    (C) E
    (D) F
    (E) J

5. If D is the fourth song played and the band plays as few songs as the rules permit before getting kicked off stage, then each of the following must be false EXCEPT:

    (A) A is played immediately before F.
    (B) B is played immediately before D.
    (C) E is the first song played.
    (D) G is the last song played.
    (E) G is played immediately before C.

6. If the band plays as few songs as the rules permit before getting kicked off stage then the number of songs that the band plays must be

    (A) 1.
    (B) 2.
    (C) 3.
    (D) 4.
    (E) 5.

7. If the band plays B third and F fifth, what is the fewest number of songs the band could play?

    (A) 5
    (B) 6
    (C) 7
    (D) 8
    (E) 9

Game 9

On Thursday, an automobile service center serviced each of six cars: a red car, a green car, a blue car, a silver car, a white car, and a tan car. The cars were serviced one at a time in the order in which they arrived at the service center. Each car arrived at the service center at a time different from the others.

The white car arrived sometime after the green car and sometime after the tan car.

The silver car arrived sometime after the white car.

The red car arrived sometime before the silver car.

1. Which of the following is a complete and accurate list of the order in which the cars arrived at the service center from first to last?

    (A) green, red, tan, silver, white, blue
    (B) green, tan, white, silver, red, blue
    (C) blue, green, tan, red, white, silver
    (D) green, blue, white, red, tan, silver
    (E) tan, white, red, green, silver, blue

2. Which of the following must be true?

    (A) The silver car arrived last.
    (B) The green car arrived first.
    (C) The silver car arrived after the blue car.
    (D) The silver car arrived after the green car.
    (E) The white car arrived after the red car.

3. What is the total number of cars any one of which could have arrived first?

    (A) 1
    (B) 2
    (C) 3
    (D) 4
    (E) 5

4. If the red car was the fifth car to arrive, then which of the following must be true?

    (A) The white car arrived fourth.
    (B) The silver car arrived sixth.
    (C) The blue car arrived second.
    (D) The tan car arrived third.
    (E) The green car arrived first.

5. Which of the following is the latest that the tan car could arrive?

    (A) second
    (B) third
    (C) fourth
    (D) fifth
    (E) sixth

6. If the blue car arrived third, which of the following provides sufficient information to know the exact order in which the cars arrived at the service center?

    (A) The red car arrived sometime after the blue car and immediately before the silver car.
    (B) The blue car arrived immediately after the tan car and sometime before the green car.
    (C) The tan car arrived sometime before the green car and sometime before the blue car.
    (D) The red car arrived sometime before the blue car and sometime before the white car.
    (E) The white car arrived immediately after the blue car and sometime before the red car.

7. If the blue car arrived second, which of the following must be false?

    (A) The silver car arrived sixth.
    (B) The green car arrived fourth.
    (C) The white car arrived third.
    (D) The red car arrived first.
    (E) The tan car arrived fourth.

Game 10

On a certain Monday eight students, A, B, C, D, E, F, G, and H, will use the same exercise bike. No other students will use the bike on that day and only one student can use the bike at a time. No student uses the bike more than once. The following rules govern the order in which the students can use the bike that Monday:

A, B, and C, no matter what their order relative to each other, must use the bike consecutively.
E and F must use the bike before C uses it.
G must be either the first or last student to use the bike.
Exactly one student must use the bike between A's use of the bike and F's, regardless of whether A uses the bike before F or not.
Exactly one student must use the bike between B's use of the bike and D's, regardless of whether B uses the bike before D or not.

1. If A is the seventh student to use the bike, which of the following must be true?

    (A)   B is the last student to use the bike.
    (B)   C is the sixth student to use the bike.
    (C)   D is the fourth student to use the bike.
    (D)   F is the last student to use the bike.
    (E)   H is the second student to use the bike.

2. If C uses the bike after as few students as the rules permit, which of the following is the position in which H must use the bike?

    (A)   fourth
    (B)   fifth
    (C)   sixth
    (D)   seventh
    (E)   eighth

3. If F is the fourth student to use the bike, which of the following CANNOT be true?

    (A)   B uses the bike immediately after F uses the bike.
    (B)   C uses the bike immediately before H uses it.
    (C)   D is the seventh student to use the bike.
    (D)   E is the first student to use the bike.
    (E)   H is the last student to use the bike.

4. If D is the second student to use the bike, then the fifth, sixth, and seventh students to use the bike, respectively, could be

    (A)   A, C, and H
    (B)   B, A, and H
    (C)   C, A, and B
    (D)   F, C, and A
    (E)   H, E, and G

5. If B uses the bike immediately after F, which of the following must be false?

    (A)   A is the fifth student to use the bike.
    (B)   B is the sixth student to use the bike.
    (C)   D is the first student to use the bike.
    (D)   E is the third student to use the bike.
    (E)   H is the first student to use the bike.

6. If A uses the bike sometime after C uses it, which of the following could be a position in which H uses the bike?

    (A)   1
    (B)   3
    (C)   5
    (D)   7
    (E)   8

7. If the conditions are changed so that D must be immediately after B and G must be the last student to use the bike, how many different possibilities are there for the order in which the students could use the bike?

    (A)   5
    (B)   6
    (C)   7
    (D)   8
    (E)   9

Game 11

Of nine students: H, I, J, K, L, M, N, O, and P, at least four will register for English and at least four will register for biology. The following conditions apply:

No more than two register for both courses.
M takes either biology or English, but not both.
K takes biology.
J does not take English unless H takes biology.
H will not take biology if I takes biology.
P and N take at least one course together.

1. Which one of the following could be a complete and accurate list of all the students who take the courses?

   (A) biology: P, N, M, K; English: J, M, I, O, K
   (B) biology: K, L, O, P, N; English: H, I, O, K, N
   (C) biology: P, N, K, H, M; English: I, H, J, P, K, N
   (D) biology: H, K, P, N, L; English: M, J, I, O
   (E) biology: P, N, H, K, I; English: J, M, I, O, L, N

2. What is the maximum number of students who could take biology at the same time?

   (A) five
   (B) six
   (C) seven
   (D) eight
   (E) nine

3. If the complete list of students taking English includes K, L, O, M, P, and N, which is a pair that could be taking biology together?

   (A) I, H
   (B) M, K
   (C) J, H
   (D) J, M
   (E) M, O

4. If the only students taking English are M, P, N, J, L, and O, which of the following is not a group that could be among the students taking biology?

   (A) K, I, L
   (B) P, K, J
   (C) N, P, K
   (D) K, J, O
   (E) H, K, N

5. If each student takes exactly one course, which of the following could be a complete and accurate list of the students registered for English?

   (A) P, N, O, M, L
   (B) J, I, K, P, N
   (C) M, I, O, L
   (D) P, I, J, M
   (E) J, M, O, L

6. Which of the following is a pair of students who CANNOT both be taking biology and English?

   (A) H, J
   (B) I, N
   (C) K, L
   (D) I, H
   (E) P, L

7. If P and N each take exactly one course, what is the minimum number of different students who could be registered for biology, English, or both?

   (A) five
   (B) six
   (C) seven
   (D) eight
   (E) nine

Game 12

Six bowlers, A, B, C, D, E, and F, are participating in the Scobey County Bowling Championship (SCBC). The SCBC consists of two rounds. The bowlers will be paired off into three two-person teams, with each bowler assigned to the same teammate for both rounds. No bowler can be on more than one team. Each team must be assigned to exactly one lane, either lane 1, lane 2, or lane 3, for each round. No team can occupy the same lane in both rounds. The following conditions also apply:

B and C cannot be on the same team.
D and F are on the same team.
If E is assigned to lane 3 in either round, then his partner must be B.
A is assigned to lane 1 in round two.

1. Which of the following could be the lane assignments for the first round?

    (A) lane 1: A, C;   lane 2: E, B;   lane 3: D, F
    (B) lane 1: B, E;   lane 2: D, C;   lane 3: A, F
    (C) lane 1: C, E;   lane 2: D, F;   lane 3: A, B
    (D) lane 1: D, F;   lane 2: A, E;   lane 3: B, C
    (E) lane 1: D, F;   lane 2: A, B;   lane 3: C, E

2. If B is assigned to lane 1 in the first round, then his teammate must be

    (A) A
    (B) C
    (C) D
    (D) E
    (E) F

3. Which of the following must be false?

    (A) A is not assigned to lane 3 in either round.
    (B) A and E are on the same team.
    (C) B and E are on the same team.
    (D) D is assigned to lane 2 in the first round.
    (E) F is assigned to lane 2 in the second round.

4. If A and B are assigned to the same team, then it must be true that

    (A) A and B are assigned to lane 3 in the first round.
    (B) C and E are assigned to lane 2 in the first round.
    (C) C and E are assigned to lane 3 in the second round.
    (D) D and F are assigned to lane 1 in the first round.
    (E) D and F are assigned to lane 2 in the second round.

5. If E is assigned to lane 2 in the first round, which of the following is a complete and accurate list of the bowlers who could be E's teammate?

    (A) A, B
    (B) A, B, C
    (C) A, C
    (D) B
    (E) B, C

6. If E is assigned to lane 3 in the first round, then which of the following is a pair of bowlers who must be assigned to lane 3 in the second round?

    (A) A and B
    (B) A and C
    (C) B and D
    (D) B and E
    (E) D and F

7. If E and C are teammates, which of the following must be true?

    (A) A is in lane 2 in round 1.
    (B) D is in lane 3 in round 2.
    (C) C is in lane 2 in round 1.
    (D) F is in lane 3 in round 1.
    (E) B is in lane 1 in round 1.

Game 13

A bridge tournament includes exactly four rounds and four players from each of group 1 and group 2. Group 1 consists of C, D, F, and G, and group 2 consists of P, Q, S and T. During each round a player from group 1 partners with a player from group 2. No two players are partners in more than one round, and each player participates in each round. The following conditions apply:

D's partner in round 1 is Q.
T's partner in round 3 is F.
G's partner in round 3 is D's partner in round 2.
F's partner in round 4 is C's partner in round 3.

1. Which of the following is a complete and accurate list of the players who could be D's partners in round 3?

    (A) Q, T, P
    (B) P, S, T, Q
    (C) P, S
    (D) P, S, T
    (E) P, T

2. Which of the following could be a complete and accurate list of C's partners in order from round 1 through round 4?

    (A) P, T, Q, S
    (B) S, Q, T, P
    (C) Q, S, P, T
    (D) T, P, S, Q
    (E) P, Q, S, T

3. Which of the following must be false?

    (A) S and F are partners in round 2.
    (B) T and D are partners in round 4.
    (C) Q and F are partners in round 2.
    (D) C and P are partners in round 4.
    (E) T and G are partners in round 1.

4. Which of the following could be true?

    (A) D is a partner with T in an earlier round than D is a partner with S.
    (B) F is a partner with P in an earlier round than F is a partner with S.
    (C) F is a partner with Q in an earlier round than F is a partner with T.
    (D) G is a partner with Q in an earlier round than G is a partner with T.
    (E) G is a partner with S in an earlier round than G is a partner with Q.

5. Which of the following is a complete and accurate list of the players any one of whom could be partners with P and S in consecutive rounds, although not necessarily in that order?

    (A) F, G
    (B) C, D, F
    (C) D, F, G
    (D) D, G
    (E) C, D, F, G

6. If S is G's partner in round 4, which of the following must be false?

    (A) G is partners with P in round 3.
    (B) D is partners with T in round 4.
    (C) F is partners with P in round 1.
    (D) C is partners with Q in round 3.
    (E) D is partners with S in round 2.

7. Which of the following is a list of partner combinations which must be made in consecutive rounds regardless of the order?

    (A) S and C, G and Q
    (B) F and T, C and P
    (C) S and D, F and T
    (D) D and T, C and Q
    (E) D and Q, F and P

Game 14

At a buffet lunch, Carol can select from the following dishes: beans, corn, rice, spaghetti, tomato, yogurt, meatballs, onions, and pork chops. Selection must conform to these regulations:

Corn and beans may not both be selected.
Anyone who chooses tomato must also choose corn.
Onions are selected by anyone who selects pork chops.
Rice is selected by anyone who selects onions.
Spaghetti is selected when rice is selected.
Beans are chosen when tomatoes are chosen.
No one who selects meatballs also selects rice.

1. Which of the following could be a complete and accurate list of dishes selected by Carol?

   (A) onions, rice, spaghetti, beans, yogurt
   (B) yogurt, pork chops, spaghetti, rice, corn
   (C) corn, meatballs, yogurt, spaghetti, beans
   (D) yogurt, spaghetti, meatballs, corn, rice
   (E) onions, rice, pork chops, tomato, corn

2. Which is a food that may not be selected?

   (A) yogurt
   (B) tomato
   (C) spaghetti
   (D) meatballs
   (E) corn

3. If exactly four foods are selected, which must be included?

   (A) pork chops
   (B) rice
   (C) spaghetti
   (D) meatballs
   (E) yogurt

4. What is the largest number of foods that could be selected?

   (A) 4
   (B) 5
   (C) 6
   (D) 7
   (E) 8

5. Which of the following is a pair of foods that could both be selected?

   (A) meatballs, rice
   (B) tomato, spaghetti
   (C) meatballs, spaghetti
   (D) tomato, corn
   (E) pork chops, meatballs

6. Which of the following is a pair of dishes that could NOT both be selected by Carol?

   (A) spaghetti, beans
   (B) pork chops, yogurt
   (C) onions, meatballs
   (D) onions, yogurt
   (E) pork chops, spaghetti

7. If meatballs are selected, what is the greatest number of foods that could be selected?

   (A) 2
   (B) 3
   (C) 4
   (D) 5
   (E) 6

Game 15

A company must send surveyors to visit four sites, numbered 1 through 4. Only six surveyors, Rey, Stark, Treehorn, Vargas, West, and Yeow, are available to visit sites. Each of these surveyors must be placed on only one of two three-member teams, team A and team B. Each of the four sites must be visited by exactly one team, and the visits must take place in accordance with one of the following plans:

Plan 1: All of the members of team A visit sites 1 and 2 and all of the members of team B visit sites 3 and 4.

Plan 2: All of the members of team A visit sites 1 and 3 and all of the members of team B visit sites 2 and 4. No other visits take place and the following conditions apply:

If Rey is on the team that visits site 3, then Rey must also visit site 4.

If Treehorn and Yeow are not on the same team, then Treehorn must be on the team that visits site 2.

Stark must be on team A.

West must be on team B.

Vargas cannot be on the team that visits site 3.

1. Which of the following could be a complete and accurate list of the surveyors and the sites they visit?

   (A) 1) Rey, Vargas, Treehorn; 2) Stark, Vargas, Yeow; 3) West, Treehorn, Rey; 4) Treehorn, Yeow, Rey

   (B) 1) Stark, Yeow, Treehorn; 2) West, Rey, Vargas; 3) Stark, Yeow, Treehorn; 4) West, Yeow, Rey

   (C) 1) Stark, Rey, Vargas; 2) Stark, Rey, Vargas; 3) Rey, West, Yeow; 4) Treehorn, West, Yeow

   (D) 1) Stark, Vargas, Yeow; 2) Stark, Vargas, Yeow; 3) Rey, West, Treehorn; 4) Rey, West, Yeow

   (E) 1) West, Vargas, Yeow; 2) Stark, Rey, Vargas; 3) Stark, Treehorn, Yeow; 4) Treehorn, Yeow, Rey

2. Which surveyor must visit site 2?

   (A) Rey
   (B) Stark
   (C) Treehorn
   (D) Vargas
   (E) Yeow

3. If Stark and Yeow are on the same team, then which of the following must be false?

   (A) Rey visits site 2.
   (B) Treehorn visits site 1.
   (C) Vargas is on team B.
   (D) Yeow visits site 2.
   (E) Yeow and Treehorn are on the same team.

4. If Vargas is on team B, then each of the following must be true EXCEPT:

   (A) Rey visits site 4.
   (B) Stark visits site 3.
   (C) Treehorn visits site 2.
   (D) West visits site 2.
   (E) Yeow is on team A.

5. If Treehorn visits site 3, then which of the following is a pair of surveyors that must be on different teams?

   (A) Rey and West
   (B) Rey and Yeow
   (C) Stark and Treehorn
   (D) Treehorn and Yeow
   (E) Vargas and West

6. Which of the following are two surveyors that could be on team A together?

   (A) Rey and Treehorn
   (B) Rey and Vargas
   (C) Stark and West
   (D) Treehorn and West
   (E) Vargas and Yeow

7. If Yeow is on the team that visits site 4, then which of the following is a surveyor that must visit site 2?

(A) Rey
(B) Stark
(C) Treehorn
(D) West
(E) Yeow

8. If Rey visits site 3, then which of the following are two surveyors that must visit site 1?

(A) Rey and Vargas
(B) Rey and Stark
(C) Stark and Treehorn
(D) Treehorn and Yeow
(E) Vargas and Yeow

Game 16

The feared Lilliputian army is planning a series of surprise invasions of seven countries: Andorra, Barbados, Chad, Denmark, Ethiopia, Fiji, and Guatemala. The Lilliputian army cannot invade two countries at the same time, and the following conditions govern the ordering of the invasions:

Chad must be invaded after Guatemala.
Denmark must be invaded before Guatemala.
Barbados must be invaded either immediately before or immediately after the invasion of Fiji.
Exactly two other invasions must occur between the invasions of Ethiopia and Chad.
Fiji cannot be invaded immediately before or after Chad.

1. Which of the following could be the order in which the invasions occur?

    (A) Denmark, Andorra, Guatemala, Chad, Barbados, Fiji, Ethiopia
    (B) Denmark, Ethiopia, Fiji, Barbados, Guatemala, Chad, Andorra
    (C) Andorra, Barbados, Denmark, Ethiopia, Fiji, Guatemala, Chad
    (D) Fiji, Barbados, Ethiopia, Andorra, Denmark, Chad, Guatemala
    (E) Ethiopia, Denmark, Guatemala, Chad, Fiji, Barbados, Andorra

2. Which of the following CANNOT be true about the order of the invasions?

    (A) Barbados is the last country invaded.
    (B) Barbados is invaded immediately after Ethiopia.
    (C) Chad is invaded sometime before Ethiopia.
    (D) Denmark is the fifth country invaded.
    (E) The invasion of Denmark falls immediately before the invasion of Fiji.

3. If Andorra is invaded immediately before Barbados, each of the following could be true about the invasions EXCEPT:

    (A) Andorra is the first country invaded.
    (B) Barbados is the second country invaded.
    (C) Denmark is invaded immediately before Guatemala and immediately after Ethiopia.
    (D) The invasion of Fiji is followed immediately by the invasion of Ethiopia.
    (E) Guatemala is the fifth country invaded.

4. If Ethiopia is invaded third, each of the following could be true about the other invasions EXCEPT:

    (A) Andorra is the last country invaded.
    (B) Barbados is the fourth country invaded.
    (C) Barbados is invaded immediately before the invasion of Chad.
    (D) Denmark is invaded immediately before Guatemala.
    (E) Fiji is the second country invaded.

5. If Andorra is invaded first and Denmark second, which of the following could be true?

    (A) Barbados is the last country invaded.
    (B) Chad is the third country invaded.
    (C) Ethiopia is the fourth country invaded.
    (D) Fiji is the third country invaded.
    (E) Guatemala is the sixth country invaded.

6. If Guatemala is the second country invaded, which of the following must be true about the invasion of Barbados?

    (A) It is the fourth country invaded.
    (B) It is the sixth country invaded.
    (C) It is invaded either immediately before or immediately after the invasion of Chad.
    (D) It occurs sometime before the invasion of Ethiopia.
    (E) It is invaded immediately after the invasion of Andorra and immediately before the invasion of Fiji.

7. How many countries could be the sixth country invaded?

    (A) 2
    (B) 3
    (C) 4
    (D) 5
    (E) 6

Game 17

In a certain week running Monday through Friday a presidential candidate will visit seven cities. Four of the cities to be visited are in Wyoming: Basin, Cheyenne, Douglas, and Evanston. The other three cities to be visited are in Montana: Roundup, Scobey, and Townsend. The candidate can only make one visit to each city, and each visit must last either an entire morning or an entire afternoon. No other visits are made during the week. During at least two consecutive mornings no visits will be made, and the following conditions also apply:

The Douglas and Townsend visits must take place on the same day.

The Evanston visit must take place sometime after the Scobey visit and sometime before the Cheyenne visit.

The first visit must be made in a Wyoming city, and the last must be made in a Montana city.

1. If the Townsend visit is made on Thursday morning, then which of the following must be true?

   (A) The Evanston visit takes place on Tuesday.
   (B) The Scobey visit takes place on Monday.
   (C) No visits are made on Tuesday morning.
   (D) No visits are made on Friday morning.
   (E) Two visits are made on Friday.

2. If no visits take place on Friday, then which of the following visits could take place on Thursday?

   (A) Evanston
   (B) Cheyenne
   (C) Roundup
   (D) Scobey
   (E) Townsend

3. If the Basin visit occurs on Friday, which of the following could be the third city visited that week?

   (A) Cheyenne
   (B) Douglas
   (C) Evanston
   (D) Scobey
   (E) Townsend

4. If no visits are made on Monday morning and Friday afternoon, the first and second cities visited, in that order, must be

   (A) Basin, Roundup
   (B) Basin, Scobey
   (C) Douglas, Townsend
   (D) Roundup, Douglas
   (E) Scobey, Evanston

5. Which of the following CANNOT be true?

   (A) Douglas is the first Wyoming city visited.
   (B) The Scobey visit takes place on Thursday morning.
   (C) The Roundup visit takes place on the day before the Basin visit.
   (D) The Townsend visit is the last of the week.
   (E) No visits take place on Monday.

6. If the Roundup visit occurs as early in the week as possible, then which of the following must be scheduled for a morning visit?

   (A) Cheyenne
   (B) Scobey
   (C) Evanston
   (D) Douglas
   (E) Townsend

7. Which of the following provides sufficient information to identify the day and time of each visit?

   (A) Douglas is visited sometime before Evanston, and there is only one city visited on Thursday.
   (B) Townsend is the second city visited, and there is only one city visited on Friday.
   (C) Cheyenne is the fourth city visited, and Scobey is visited on Tuesday.
   (D) Scobey and Cheyenne are visited on consecutive mornings, beginning on Wednesday, and there is no city visited on Thursday afternoon.
   (E) Basin and Scobey are visited on consecutive afternoons beginning on Monday, and there is only one city visited on Wednesday.

At an emergency veterinary clinic animals' injuries are initially classified as critical, serious, or mild. The veterinarian will treat critical injuries before serious ones and serious ones before mild ones. Within each group, the veterinarian will treat animals in the order they arrive in the clinic, treating earlier arrivals before later arrivals. Three cats, P, Q, and S, and three dogs, K, H, and J, and one goat, G, are waiting to be treated.

Exactly two cats and two dogs have serious injuries.

H is treated sometime before P and sometime after S.

J arrived in the clinic sometime before H and sometime after K.

K is treated either immediately before or immediately after P.

G does not have a serious injury.

1. Which of the following could be a complete and accurate list of the animals in the order in which they are treated?

   (A) S, H, G, Q, P, J, K
   (B) G, S, J, H, Q, P, K
   (C) Q, S, H, P, J, K, G
   (D) S, H, Q, G, K, P, J
   (E) Q, S, G, K, H, P, J

2. Which of the following must have a serious injury?

   (A) Q
   (B) J
   (C) K
   (D) H
   (E) S

3. Which of the following is a pair that cannot both have serious injuries?

   (A) S, H
   (B) K, P
   (C) Q, P
   (D) H, K
   (E) P, H

4. If the goat is the fifth animal treated, which of the following must be true?

   (A) S does not have a serious injury.
   (B) P has a serious injury.
   (C) J is injured more seriously than P.
   (D) H's injury is critical.
   (E) Q is injured more seriously than S.

5. If P is treated as early as possible, then which of the following must be true?

   (A) Q has a mild injury.
   (B) J is treated fifth.
   (C) G is treated seventh.
   (D) S has a serious injury.
   (E) H has a serious injury.

6. If there are no animals with mild injuries, which of the following could be the animal treated fourth?

   (A) G
   (B) H
   (C) S
   (D) Q
   (E) J

7. If there are no animals with critical injuries, which is an animal that CANNOT have a serious injury?

   (A) K
   (B) J
   (C) P
   (D) Q
   (E) H

Game 19

Denise is recording exactly seven songs on a CD in order from 1 through 7, with song 1 being farthest from the middle and song seven being closest to the middle of the CD. The 7 songs include H, K, L, M, N and two of P, Q, R, and S. The following conditions apply:

Song M is closer to the middle than L and farther from the middle than H.
Song K is closer to the middle than H and N.
If Q is included, it must be placed third from the middle.
P cannot be in positions 1 or 7.
If R is included it must be placed adjacent to N.

1. Which of the following is a complete and accurate list of songs in order from the outside to the middle?

    (A) S, L, M, N, R, P, K
    (B) L, M, Q, R, N, H, K
    (C) N, L, M, R, Q, H, K
    (D) L, P, M, N, R, II, K
    (E) L, M, P, H, K, N, S

2. How many different songs could occupy the position farthest from the middle?

    (A) 1
    (B) 2
    (C) 3
    (D) 4
    (E) 5

3. If Q and P are both included and P is closer to the middle than Q, then which of the following could be true?

    (A) M is adjacent to Q.
    (B) N is adjacent to P.
    (C) L is third from the outside.
    (D) M is third from the outside.
    (E) H is adjacent to P.

4. If K is as far from the middle as possible, then which of the following must be true?

    (A) K is sixth from the outside.
    (B) P is second from the middle.
    (C) L is farthest outside.
    (D) H is third from the outside.
    (E) H is fourth from the outside.

5. Which of the following is a pair of songs that could not both be adjacent to H on the same CD?

    (A) Q, N
    (B) M, S
    (C) R, Q
    (D) N, P
    (E) R, P

6. If neither S nor P is included on a CD, which of the following is a complete and accurate list of the songs that could be fourth from the middle?

    (A) R, N
    (B) II, M, R
    (C) M, R, N
    (D) H, M, R, N
    (E) M, N

7. If L is not closest to the outside and K is not closest to the middle, which of the following must be false of the songs on the CD?

    (A) R is closer to the middle than N.
    (B) P is farther outside than Q.
    (C) L is third from the outside.
    (D) K is third from the middle.
    (E) R is farther from the middle than Q.

Game 20

On a certain week, running Sunday through Saturday, Felix must clean six rooms of his house: the den, the garage, the kitchen, and three bedrooms, numbered 1 through 3. Felix must take one day off during which he will clean no rooms, and he must clean exactly one room every other day in the week. The following rules apply:

If Felix cleans a bedroom on Sunday or Saturday, then he cannot clean a bedroom on Thursday.

If Felix cleans the den and the garage on consecutive days, then he must clean bedroom 3 on the day immediately before his day off.

Felix must clean bedroom 1 exactly three days after he cleans the den.

Felix must clean the garage before Wednesday.

Felix must clean two of the bedrooms on consecutive days.

1. Each of the following must be false EXCEPT:

    (A) Felix cleans bedrooms on Sunday and Monday.
    (B) Felix cleans bedrooms on Sunday and Wednesday.
    (C) Felix cleans a bedroom on Sunday and the kitchen on Monday.
    (D) Felix cleans the garage on Monday and the den on Tuesday.
    (E) Felix cleans the garage on Tuesday and bedroom 3 on Wednesday.

2. If Felix takes Tuesday off, which of the following could be the day on which he cleans the kitchen?

    (A) Monday
    (B) Wednesday
    (C) Thursday
    (D) Friday
    (E) Saturday

3. If bedrooms are cleaned on Sunday and Saturday then Felix must clean the den on

    (A) Monday
    (B) Tuesday
    (C) Wednesday
    (D) Friday
    (E) Saturday

4. If Felix cleans the kitchen on Tuesday and does not clean any bedroom before Wednesday then each of the following must be false EXCEPT:

    (A) Felix cleans bedroom 1 on Thursday.
    (B) Felix cleans bedroom 1 on Friday.
    (C) Felix cleans bedroom 2 on Saturday.
    (D) Felix cleans bedroom 3 on Wednesday.
    (E) Felix takes Thursday off.

5. If Felix cleans the den on Sunday and the kitchen on Friday, which of the following could be the day on which he cleans bedroom 2?

    (A) Monday
    (B) Tuesday
    (C) Wednesday
    (D) Friday
    (E) Saturday

6. If Felix cleans bedroom 2 on Sunday, which of the following is a complete and accurate list of the days that Felix could take off?

    (A) Monday
    (B) Monday, Thursday, Friday, Saturday
    (C) Tuesday, Wednesday
    (D) Tuesday, Thursday
    (E) Thursday

7. If Felix cleans bedroom 3 on Sunday and bedroom 1 on Saturday, on how many different days would he be able to clean bedroom 2?

    (A) 1
    (B) 2
    (C) 3
    (D) 4
    (E) 5

Game 21

A government committee consists of five members, Q, R, S, T, and U. The committee is meeting to vote on one proposal. Each of the five committee members must vote either for or against the proposal during the meeting. If and only if the proposal is not adopted during the initial meeting but is voted for by at least one committee member, then the committee will hold a second meeting and vote again on the proposal, again with each of the five voting either for or against the proposal. The proposal will be adopted if and only if three or more of the members vote for it during either the initial meeting or the second meeting. Only one vote will be taken at each meeting, and the following conditions apply:

If Q votes for the proposal at a meeting, then a majority of the committee members votes for it at that meeting.

If Q votes against the proposal at a meeting, then a majority of the committee members votes against it at that meeting.

If there is a second meeting, then R votes the same way at both meetings.

If R and U vote the same way at a meeting, then T also votes that way at that same meeting.

S and U always vote the same way as each other.

S votes against the proposal in the initial meeting.

1. If R and U vote the same way at the initial meeting, it must be true that

    (A) Q votes for the proposal at the initial meeting.
    (B) Q and T do not vote the same way at the initial meeting.
    (C) T votes for the proposal at the second meeting.
    (D) At least two committee members vote for the proposal at the second meeting.
    (E) A second meeting is not held.

2. If exactly two committee members vote for the proposal during the first meeting and Q votes against it at a second meeting, what is the highest possible number of committee members who could vote for it at the second meeting?

    (A) 1
    (B) 2
    (C) 3
    (D) 4
    (E) 5

3. Which of the following must vote for the proposal at a second meeting if one is held?

    (A) Q
    (B) R
    (C) S
    (D) T
    (E) U

4. If the proposal is adopted at a second meeting, then which of the following is a pair of committee members who must vote for the proposal at the second meeting?

    (A) Q and S
    (B) Q and T
    (C) R and S
    (D) T and U
    (E) S and U

5. If at a second meeting U votes for the proposal, which of the following is a complete and accurate list of the committee members who must also vote for the proposal at the second meeting?

    (A) Q, R, S
    (B) Q, R, S, T
    (C) Q, S
    (D) Q, T
    (E) R, S, T

6. If S votes for the proposal at a second meeting, which of the following must be false?

(A) Q votes for the proposal at the second meeting.

(B) Q votes against the proposal during both meetings.

(C) R votes for the proposal during the second meeting.

(D) T votes against the proposal during the first meeting.

(E) T votes for the proposal at the second meeting.

Game 22

Bulgaria, Canada, Denmark, Estonia, Finland, Germany, Holland, and Iceland are the only participants in an international curling competition. The three teams with the highest scores receive medals. There can be no ties, and the following conditions apply:

Finland scores higher than Estonia but lower than Holland.

Iceland scores higher than Estonia but lower than Germany.

Both Bulgaria and Canada score higher than Holland.

If Denmark receives a medal, then Iceland does not receive a medal.

If Bulgaria receives a medal, then Holland also receives a medal.

1. Which of the following could be the three teams that receive medals?

    (A) Bulgaria, Holland, Germany
    (B) Canada, Denmark, Iceland
    (C) Germany, Iceland, Canada
    (D) Finland, Holland, Bulgaria
    (E) Denmark, Iceland, Germany

2. If Holland does not receive a medal, then which of the following are two teams that must receive medals?

    (A) Bulgaria and Germany
    (B) Canada and Germany
    (C) Canada and Finland
    (D) Denmark and Germany
    (E) Estonia and Iceland

3. If Germany scores lower than Bulgaria, then each of the following must be true EXCEPT?

    (A) Canada receives a medal.
    (B) Denmark scores higher than Bulgaria.
    (C) Germany scores lower than Holland.
    (D) Holland receives a medal.
    (E) Iceland does not receive a medal.

4. Which of the following is a team that CANNOT receive a medal?

    (A) Bulgaria
    (B) Iceland
    (C) Holland
    (D) Denmark
    (E) Finland

5. Which of the following teams must receive a medal if Iceland finishes in the top three?

    (A) Bulgaria
    (B) Canada
    (C) Denmark
    (D) Finland
    (E) Holland

6. If Finland scores lower than exactly four other teams, then which of the following must be true?

    (A) Denmark scores higher than Estonia.
    (B) Germany scores lower than Finland.
    (C) Iceland receives a medal.
    (D) Holland and Bulgaria receive medals.
    (E) Either Germany or Denmark receives a medal.

7. Which of the following is a team that must receive a medal?

    (A) Bulgaria
    (B) Canada
    (C) Denmark
    (D) Iceland
    (E) Germany

Game 23

A garage band that calls themselves The Screeching Eels is assembling a demo tape. The tape will consist of nine tracks, J, K, L, M, N, O, P, Q, and R. Each track will be placed on only one of two sides: side A or side B. Five songs will be placed on one of the sides and four will be placed on the other. The following restrictions apply:

If J is placed on side A then both M and N must be placed on side B.

If K is on one side then neither M nor R is on that side.

O must be the last track on the side with only four tracks.

P must be placed on the side with five tracks.

R must be either the second track on side A or the third track on side B.

K must be the fourth track on whichever side it is placed.

L is the third track on side A.

1. Which of the following could be a complete and accurate list of the songs included in order on the demo tape?

    (A) side A: Q, P, L, O, J;   side B: M, N, R, K
    (B) side A: M, R, L, O;   side B: J, N, K, P, Q
    (C) side A: M, J, L, K, P;   side B: Q, N, R, O
    (D) side A: P, J, L, K, Q;   side B: M, N, R, O
    (E) side A: M, Q, L, O;   side B: J, R, N, K, P

2. If K and N are on the same side, which of the following is a track that must also be on that side?

    (A) J
    (B) L
    (C) O
    (D) P
    (E) R

3. Which of the following must be true?

    (A) J and L are on the same side.
    (B) M is on side A.
    (C) M and R are on the same side.
    (D) N is on side B.
    (E) R is the second track on side B.

4. If Q is the third track on side B, which of the following is a list of tracks each of which must also be placed on side B?

    (A) J, M, N
    (B) J, N, P
    (C) K, M
    (D) K, P, R
    (E) O, R

5. If J and M are on the same side, each of the following must be false EXCEPT:

    (A) J is the third track on one of the sides.
    (B) M is the first track on side A.
    (C) N and O are on the same side.
    (D) P is placed immediately before Q on one of the sides.
    (E) R is placed immediately before L on one of the sides.

6. If O and J are on the same side, which of the following are three tracks that must be on side A?

    (A) J, M, R
    (B) J, K, Q
    (C) K, P, R
    (D) L, M, O
    (E) N, P, Q

7. Suppose that the rule stipulating that K must be fourth on whichever side it is placed is eliminated and all other rules remain in effect. If K and Q are placed on the same side, K falling immediately before Q, and J is fifth on side A, then P must be

    (A) first on side A.
    (B) fourth on side A.
    (C) second on side B.
    (D) third on side B.
    (E) fourth on side B.

Game 24

A pet store employee is placing seven dogs into cages, with exactly one dog in each cage. The cages are numbered 1 through 7, and consecutively numbered cages are considered adjacent. Three of the dogs are male: a beagle, a chow, and a dachshund. Four of the dogs are female: a maltese, a shar-pei, a terrier, and a yorkie. The beagle and the yorkie are adults and all of the other dogs are puppies. Each dog can only be placed in one of the seven cages, and the following conditions also apply:

Cages 1, 2, and 3 must all contain puppies, exactly two of which must be female.

Exactly two cages must lie between the cages in which the two adults are placed.

The maltese and the terrier cannot be placed in adjacent cages.

The beagle and the dachshund must be placed in adjacent cages.

The chow must be placed either in cage 2 or cage 6.

1. If a male dog is placed into cage 3, the dog in cage 5 could be the

   (A) beagle.
   (B) chow.
   (C) shar-pei.
   (D) terrier.
   (E) yorkie.

2. If the yorkie is placed into cage 4, which of the following could be true?

   (A) The chow is placed into cage 6.
   (B) The dachshund is placed into cage 5.
   (C) The maltese is placed into cage 2.
   (D) The shar-pei is placed into cage 2.
   (E) The terrier is placed into cage 5.

3. Which of the following is a complete and accurate list of the cages in which the dachshund could be placed?

   (A) 1, 2
   (B) 1, 2, 3
   (C) 1, 3, 4, 5
   (D) 3, 5, 6
   (E) 5, 6

4. If the shar-pei and the terrier are placed into adjacent cages, then which of the following could be true about the placement of the other dogs?

   (A) The beagle and the terrier are placed into adjacent cages.
   (B) The chow and the maltese are placed into adjacent cages.
   (C) The maltese is placed in a lower-numbered cage than the cage into which the dachshund is placed.
   (D) The dog placed in cage 3 is an adult.
   (E) The dog placed in cage 5 is a male.

5. Knowing which one of the following would make it possible to completely determine the placement of dogs into cages?

   (A) The dachshund is placed into cage 6.
   (B) The beagle is placed into cage 4.
   (C) The maltese is placed into cage 1.
   (D) The shar-pei is placed into cage 3.
   (E) The terrier is placed into cage 2.

6. If the shar-pei is placed into cage 6, the maltese could be placed in cage

   (A) 2.
   (B) 3.
   (C) 4.
   (D) 5.
   (E) 6.

7. If the maltese is placed in cage 1 and the chow is placed in cage 2, how many different combinations of dogs and cages are possible?

   (A) 2
   (B) 3
   (C) 4
   (D) 5
   (E) 6

Six *Star Trek* fans have just formed a club. Each of the six members, Alma, Bryce, Corey, Drexel, Ernst, Flor, must host one of the club's first six meetings. No meeting can be hosted by more than one member. No other meetings are held, and the following conditions apply:

Alma must host either the meeting immediately before or the meeting immediately after the meeting hosted by Ernst.

Exactly one meeting is held between the meetings hosted by Alma and Bryce, regardless of which comes first.

If Drexel hosts a meeting before Corey hosts a meeting, then Flor must host the sixth meeting.

Corey must host the fourth meeting.

1. Which of the following could be the order in which the members host the club's first six meetings, from first to sixth?

   (A) Alma, Flor, Bryce, Corey, Drexel, Ernst
   (B) Bryce, Ernst, Alma, Corey, Flor, Drexel
   (C) Drexel, Bryce, Corey, Alma, Ernst, Flor
   (D) Ernst, Alma, Drexel, Corey, Bryce, Flor
   (E) Flor, Drexel, Bryce, Corey, Alma, Ernst

2. If Bryce hosts the third meeting, then Flor could host either of which of the following pairs of meetings?

   (A) the first or the second
   (B) the first or the sixth
   (C) the second or the sixth
   (D) the second or the fifth
   (E) the fifth or the sixth

3. If the meeting hosted by Bryce is held either immediately before or immediately after the meeting hosted by Fern, then which of the following must be the meeting hosted by Drexel?

   (A) the first
   (B) the second
   (C) the third
   (D) the fifth
   (E) the sixth

4. The second meeting could be hosted by

   (A) Alma
   (B) Bryce
   (C) Drexel
   (D) Ernst
   (E) Flor

5. Which of the following is a complete and accurate list of the members that could host the third meeting?

   (A) Alma, Bryce
   (B) Alma, Drexel, Flor
   (C) Bryce, Ernst
   (D) Bryce, Drexel, Flor
   (E) Corey, Ernst, Flor

6. If the meeting hosted by Flor is held sometime before the meeting hosted by Alma, then which of the following must be true?

   (A) Alma hosts the fifth meeting.
   (B) Bryce hosts the first meeting.
   (C) Drexel hosts the fifth meeting.
   (D) Ernst hosts the sixth meeting.
   (E) Flor hosts the first meeting.

7. If the meeting hosted by Drexel is held sometime after the meeting hosted by Corey, then in how many different orders might the meetings be held?

   (A) 3
   (B) 4
   (C) 5
   (D) 6
   (E) 7

Game 26

A soft drink machine has six flavors of drinks indicated by buttons on the machine in order from top to bottom: root beer, orange, lemon-lime, cola, grape, and strawberry. The machine has been incorrectly stocked, so that it includes the six flavors on the buttons and each button produces exactly one flavor, but only one button when pushed will give the flavor it indicates. The other five will give a flavor other than the one on the button. The following is known about the machine.

The button that gives strawberry is higher than the one that gives root beer and lower than the one that gives lemon-lime.

The button that gives cola is either immediately above or immediately below the one that gives lemon-lime.

1. Which of the following could be a complete and accurate list of the flavors produced by the buttons from top to bottom?

   (A) strawberry, orange, cola, lemon-lime, root beer, grape

   (B) grape, orange, lemon-lime, cola, strawberry, root beer

   (C) orange, cola, lemon-lime, grape, strawberry, root beer

   (D) lemon-lime, strawberry, cola, root beer, orange, grape

   (E) orange, grape, lemon-lime, cola, strawberry, root beer

2. What is the maximum number of different flavors that could be produced from pressing the button labeled strawberry?

   (A) 1
   (B) 2
   (C) 3
   (D) 4
   (E) 5

3. If strawberry is produced by the button labeled lemon-lime, which of the following is the button that produces the flavor on its label?

   (A) orange
   (B) lemon-lime
   (C) cola
   (D) grape
   (E) root beer

4. If orange is produced by a button higher than the button that gives cola, which of the following must be false?

   (A) Orange comes from the button labeled orange.

   (B) Strawberry comes from the button labeled grape.

   (C) Grape comes from the button labeled orange.

   (D) Lemon-lime comes from the button labeled orange.

   (E) Root beer comes from the button labeled grape.

5. If grape is not the button accurately labeled, which of the following could be true?

   (A) Lemon-lime is produced by the button labeled root beer.

   (B) Strawberry is produced by the button labeled lemon-lime.

   (C) Orange is produced by the button labeled grape.

   (D) Orange is produced by the button labeled lemon-lime.

   (E) Strawberry is produced by the button labeled orange.

6. Which of the following is a pair of buttons both of which must be labeled incorrectly?

   (A) root beer, orange
   (B) cola, strawberry
   (C) lemon-lime, strawberry
   (D) grape, lemon-lime
   (E) orange, root beer

7. If grape is produced by the button immediately above or immediately below the button that gives cola, then which button produces the flavor on its label?

   (A) grape
   (B) cola
   (C) lemon-lime
   (D) root beer
   (E) orange

Game 27

The management at a company has decided to review its employees. Each of six employees, Ross, Saucedo, Turturro, Vaughan, Waters, and Ybarra, must be reviewed once by exactly one of the managers. Only three managers, I, J, and K, can review employees. The reviews will all take place in the same week over a three-day period running Monday through Wednesday, with at least one employee being reviewed each day. For each of the three days in the reviewing period only one manager will conduct reviews, and the following restrictions apply:

I cannot review Waters or Ybarra.
J cannot review Saucedo or Vaughan.
K cannot review Ross or Saucedo.
Ross must be reviewed on a day falling sometime before the day on which Ybarra is reviewed.
Saucedo must be reviewed on a day either immediately before or immediately after the day on which Waters is reviewed.
Vaughan must be reviewed on a day falling either immediately before or immediately after the day on which Ybarra is reviewed.
Turturro and Waters must be reviewed on the same day.

1. Which of the following could be a complete and accurate list of the employees reviewed by day?

   (A) Monday: Saucedo, Ross, Vaughan; Tuesday: Ybarra; Wednesday: Turturro, Waters

   (B) Monday: Ross, Vaughan; Tuesday: Ybarra, Waters; Wednesday: Saucedo, Turturro

   (C) Monday: Vaughan; Tuesday: Ybarra, Turturro, Waters; Wednesday: Ross, Saucedo

   (D) Monday: Ross; Tuesday: Ybarra, Turturro, Waters; Wednesday: Vaughan, Saucedo

   (E) Monday: Tururro, Waters, Ross; Tuesday: Saucedo, Ybarra; Wednesday: Vaughan

2. If K does not review any employees that week and Waters is reviewed on Tuesday, which of the following must be true?

   (A) Ross is reviewed by I.
   (B) Saucedo is reviewed on Monday.
   (C) Vaughan is reviewed on Wednesday.
   (D) I conducts the reviews on Wednesday.
   (E) J conducts the reviews on only one day.

3. If Ybarra is reviewed on Tuesday, which of the following must be true?

   (A) J conducts reviews on at least one day.
   (B) Vaughan is reviewed by I.
   (C) Saucedo is reviewed on Monday.
   (D) Turturro is reviewed by K.
   (E) J does not conduct reviews on Wednesday.

4. If K conducts reviews on Monday then the only employee whose reviewer CANNOT be determined is

   (A) Ross.
   (B) Saucedo.
   (C) Turturro.
   (D) Vaughan.
   (E) Ybarra.

5. Which of the following is a pair of workers whose reviews CANNOT both occur on Tuesday?

   (A) Ross and Saucedo
   (B) Ross and Turturro
   (C) Saucedo and Vaughan
   (D) Vaughan and Waters
   (E) Ybarra and Waters

6. If J conducts reviews on Tuesday and K conducts reviews on Wednesday, which of the following is an employee that must be reviewed by K?

   (A) Ross
   (B) Saucedo
   (C) Turturro
   (D) Vaughan
   (E) Ybarra

7. If I conducts reviews on Wednesday, which of the following must be false?

   (A) I reviews Vaughan on Wednesday.
   (B) J reviews Ross on Monday.
   (C) J reviews Ybarra on Tuesday.
   (D) K reviews Vaughan on Monday.
   (E) K reviews Waters on Tuesday.

Game 28

Johnson, the CEO for a major corporation must have exactly ten meetings during a certain week running Monday through Friday. Each meeting lasts either an entire morning or an entire afternoon, and Johnson cannot have a meeting with more than one person at a time. During the week he must meet with three accountants, two consultants, two executives, two lawyers, and one stockholder. The following conditions apply:

Johnson can meet with consultants only in the afternoon.

If Johnson meets with an accountant on a given day, then he must meet with at least one executive the following day.

Johnson's meetings with lawyers must be on days separated by exactly two days.

1. If Johnson meets with a consultant on Thursday and a lawyer on Friday, which of the following is a complete and accurate list of the days on which Johnson could meet with a stockholder?

   (A) Monday, Tuesday, Thursday
   (B) Monday, Wednesday, Friday
   (C) Tuesday
   (D) Tuesday, Thursday
   (E) Monday, Friday

2. If Johnson meets with executives on two consecutive days, which of the following could be his meetings on Tuesday?

   (A) morning: an accountant; afternoon: a consultant
   (B) morning: an executive; afternoon: an accountant
   (C) morning: a lawyer; afternoon: a consultant
   (D) morning: a stockholder; afternoon: an accountant
   (E) morning: a stockholder; afternoon: a lawyer

3. If Johnson does not meet with an accountant on Wednesday and he meets with a stockholder on Monday, which of the following are two days on which he must meet with executives?

   (A) Monday, Wednesday
   (B) Monday, Friday
   (C) Tuesday, Thursday
   (D) Tuesday, Friday
   (E) Wednesday, Friday

4. If Johnson meets with at least one accountant on Monday and one consultant on Tuesday, which of the following could be his meeting schedule for Friday?

   (A) morning: an executive; afternoon: a consultant
   (B) morning: an executive; afternoon: a lawyer
   (C) morning: a lawyer; afternoon: a consultant
   (D) morning: a lawyer; afternoon: a stockholder
   (E) morning: a stockholder; afternoon: a consultant

5. If Johnson meets with consultants on Tuesday and Friday, which of the following must be the day on which Johnson meets with a stockholder?

   (A) Monday
   (B) Tuesday
   (C) Wednesday
   (D) Thursday
   (E) Friday

6. If Johnson meets with exactly one accountant on Tuesday, which of the following is a complete and accurate list of the days on which Johnson could meet with a consultant?

   (A) Monday, Tuesday, Wednesday, Thursday, Friday
   (B) Monday, Tuesday, Thursday
   (C) Monday, Wednesday
   (D) Tuesday, Friday
   (E) Wednesday, Thursday

Game 29

A pair of film critics, Jones and Michaels, must each view each of three comedies, B, H, and W, and each of three dramas, F, Q, and L, during a particular week. Each views exactly one film per day, Monday through Saturday, and the two do not see the same film on the same day. The critics view the films according to the following conditions.

Jones cannot view a comedy unless Michaels has viewed it first.

Michaels cannot view comedies on successive days.

Neither critic sees either W or L on Monday or Saturday.

One critic sees Q on Thursday.

1. Which of the following could be a complete and accurate list of the movies seen by the critics in order from Monday through Saturday?

    (A) Jones: Q, L, H, F, W, B; Michaels: B, L, W, Q, H, F
    (B) Jones: F, H, W, L, Q, B; Michaels: H, B, W, F, L, Q
    (C) Jones: F, B, L, Q, W, H; Michaels: B, Q, W, L, H, F
    (D) Jones: Q, H, F, L, W, B; Michaels: W, F, H, Q, B, L
    (E) Jones: F, W, B, Q, L, H; Michaels: B, L, W, F, H, Q

2. Which of the following must be true?

    (A) Jones sees a comedy on Tuesday.
    (B) Michaels sees a drama on Wednesday.
    (C) Jones sees a comedy on Saturday.
    (D) Michaels sees a comedy on Thursday.
    (E) Jones sees a drama on Thursday.

3. Which of the following must be false?

    (A) Jones views H on Wednesday.
    (B) Michaels views Q on Saturday.
    (C) Jones views F on Monday.
    (D) Michaels views H on Wednesday.
    (E) Jones views B on Thursday.

4. If W is the first of the comedies that Jones views, which of the following could be false?

    (A) Jones views F sometime before Jones views L.
    (B) Michaels views L on Tuesday.
    (C) Jones views W on Thursday.
    (D) Michaels views L sometime before Michaels views Q.
    (E) Michaels views H on Friday.

5. If Michaels views L later in the week than Jones views L, then which of the following is a complete and accurate list of the days on which either of the critics might see F?

    (A) Monday, Tuesday
    (B) Monday, Saturday
    (C) Monday, Tuesday, Saturday
    (D) Monday, Wednesday, Saturday
    (E) Monday, Tuesday, Wednesday, Saturday

6. If Michaels sees F on a day sometime before seeing H, which of the following could be false?

    (A) Michaels sees Q after Jones sees Q.
    (B) Jones sees W on Friday.
    (C) Michaels sees H on Friday.
    (D) Jones sees L after Michaels sees L.
    (E) Michaels sees F after Jones sees F.

7. Which of the following provides sufficient information to know which critic sees which film on each of the six days?

    (A) Jones sees Q on the same day Michaels sees W.
    (B) Jones sees B and F on Wednesday and Thursday respectively.
    (C) Jones sees F and Q on Monday and Tuesday.
    (D) Jones sees H and F on Tuesday and Thursday respectively.
    (E) On Saturday Jones sees H and Michaels sees F.

Game 30

Three managers from the Buff Brewing Company, Arnold, Boris, and Chuck, must fire exactly five of the following eight employees: Doris, Elsa, Guillermo, Lionel, Henry, Otto, Siegfried, and Wayne. Only managers can fire employees. Each manager must fire at least one employee and no employee can be fired by more than one manager. The following conditions also apply:

Boris must fire exactly two employees.
If either Doris or Lionel is fired, then it must be by Chuck.
If either Elsa or Siegfried is fired, then the other is also fired by the same manager.
If Otto is fired, then Wayne and Henry are also fired.
Guillermo is fired.
If Wayne is fired, it must be by Boris.

1. Which of the following could be a complete and accurate list of the firings done by each manager?

    (A) Arnold: Doris, Guillermo
         Boris: Elsa, Siegfried
         Chuck: Wayne
    (B) Arnold: Elsa, Guillermo
         Boris: Henry, Wayne
         Chuck: Doris
    (C) Arnold: Henry
         Boris: Guillermo, Otto
         Chuck: Doris, Lionel
    (D) Arnold: Henry, Otto
         Boris: Wayne
         Chuck: Guillermo
    (E) Arnold: Guillermo, Otto
         Boris: Henry, Wayne
         Chuck: Doris

2. If both Henry and Lionel are not fired, then Guillermo could be fired

    (A) by Boris.
    (B) by Chuck.
    (C) by the same manager that fires Doris.
    (D) by the same manager that fires Otto.
    (E) by the same manager that fires Siegfried.

3. If Otto and Wayne are fired by the same manager, which of the following must be true?

    (A) Elsa is fired by Arnold.
    (B) Henry is fired by Arnold.
    (C) Lionel is fired by Chuck.
    (D) Guillermo and Doris are fired by the same manager.
    (E) Siegfried is not fired.

4. If Elsa is fired by Boris and Henry is fired by the same manager that fires Guillermo, which of the following must be true?

    (A) Chuck fires exactly one employee.
    (B) Henry is fired by Chuck.
    (C) Lionel is not fired.
    (D) Otto is fired by Arnold.
    (E) Wayne is fired by Boris.

5. Which of the following must be false?

    (A) Siegfried is fired by Boris.
    (B) Wayne is not fired.
    (C) Doris and Henry are fired by the same manager.
    (D) Elsa and Otto are both fired.
    (E) Guillermo and Otto are fired by the same manager.

6. If Guillermo and Otto are fired by the same manager, which of the following must be false?

    (A) Doris is not fired.
    (B) Guillermo is fired by Boris.
    (C) Lionel is fired by Chuck.
    (D) Otto is fired by Arnold.
    (E) Siegfried is not fired.

7. If Doris and Lionel are both fired, which of the following is a pair of employees that CANNOT also be fired?

    (A) Wayne and Henry
    (B) Elsa and Siegfried
    (C) Wayne and Siegfried
    (D) Guillermo and Wayne
    (E) Guillermo and Henry

Game 31

Eight flags will be placed on display. There is exactly one flag of each of the following colors: blue, green, orange, purple, red, silver, white, and yellow. Only flags that are in the same row and consecutively numbered are considered adjacent. Each flag must be placed into one of eight positions, numbered 1 through 8 and arranged as follows:

front row:	1	2	3	4
back row:	5	6	7	8

Each position faces exactly one position from the other row; positions 1 and 5 face each other, positions 2 and 6 face each other, positions 3 and 7 face each other, and positions 4 and 8 face each other. Each flag can be placed in only one position, and the following restrictions also apply:

The orange and silver flags cannot be placed in adjacent positions.

The white and yellow flags must be placed in adjacent positions.

The silver flag must be placed into position 6.

If the red and yellow flags face each other, then the blue flag must be placed into position 3.

If the green flag is placed in the front row, then the orange flag must be placed in the back row.

1. In no particular order, which of the following could be the four flags placed in the front row?

    (A) blue, green, purple, red
    (B) blue, orange, white, yellow
    (C) green, orange, white, yellow
    (D) green, purple, red, yellow
    (E) purple, silver, white, yellow

2. If the purple flag is placed in position 8, then which of the following are three flags that must be placed in the front row?

    (A) blue, white, yellow
    (B) blue, red, orange
    (C) green, red, yellow
    (D) orange, white, yellow
    (E) red, white, yellow

3. If the green flag is placed in position 2 and the orange and white flags are placed into positions facing each other, which of the following is a flag that could be placed into position 7?

    (A) blue
    (B) orange
    (C) red
    (D) silver
    (E) yellow

4. If the purple and the blue flags are placed in positions 4 and 5, respectively, then which of the following CANNOT be true?

    (A) The green flag is placed in position 3.
    (B) The orange flag is placed in a position facing the red flag.
    (C) The purple and red flags are placed in adjacent positions.
    (D) The white flag is placed in position 7.
    (E) The yellow flag is placed in position 1.

5. If the purple and red flags are placed in positions 2 and 3, respectively, then the green flag could be placed in

    (A) position 1.
    (B) position 4.
    (C) position 5.
    (D) position 7.
    (E) position 8.

6. If the green flag is placed in position 1, then which of the following must be false?

    (A) The red flag is placed in position 4.
    (B) The white flag is placed in position 3.
    (C) The green and yellow flags are placed in adjacent positions.
    (D) The purple flag is placed in a position facing the silver flag.
    (E) The red and yellow flags are placed into positions facing each other.

Game 32

Six of eight folk singers, Gill, Hyatt, Imus, Jesse, Kyle, Leanne, Maggie, and Naomi, must give solo performances at a hoe-down. Only one performance will be given at a time, and each singer can give only one performance. The following conditions apply:

Gill must give a performance, and it must be either the first or the fifth performance.

If Hyatt gives a performance, then Maggie must also give a performance, Maggie's performance coming immediately before Hyatt's.

If Imus gives a performance, then it can be only the second, fourth, or sixth.

If Leanne gives a performance, then Kyle must also give a performance, Leanne's performance falling sometime before Kyle's.

If Naomi gives a performance, then it cannot fall either immediately before or immediately after Gill's.

1. If Hyatt, and Naomi give performances and Hyatt's performance falls second, then which of the following could be the position in which Naomi gives her performance?

    (A)   first
    (B)   third
    (C)   fourth
    (D)   fifth
    (E)   sixth

2. If Maggie gives the sixth performance, then which of the following is a singer who must give a performance?

    (A)   Hyatt
    (B)   Imus
    (C)   Jesse
    (D)   Kyle
    (E)   Leanne

3. If Leanne gives the fourth performance and Hyatt and Imus also give performances, which of the following must be false?

    (A)   Gill gives the first performance.
    (B)   Jesse does not give a performance.
    (C)   Kyle gives the sixth performance.
    (D)   Leanne's performance falls sometime after Hyatt's.
    (E)   Maggie's performance falls immediately after Gill's.

4. If Leanne gives the third performance and Hyatt gives a performance sometime after Leanne's, which of the following is a singer who CANNOT give a performance?

    (A)   Gill
    (B)   Imus
    (C)   Kyle
    (D)   Maggie
    (E)   Naomi

5. Suppose Kyle does not give a performance. If Jesse gives the fourth performance, then which of the following could be true?

    (A)   Leanne gives the second performance.
    (B)   Maggie gives the third performance.
    (C)   Maggie gives the fifth performance.
    (D)   Naomi gives the second performance.
    (E)   Naomi gives the sixth performance.

6. If Naomi gives the second performance and Imus gives the fourth performance, which of the following must be true?

    (A)   Hyatt does not give a performance.
    (B)   Imus gives the sixth performance.
    (C)   If Jesse gives a performance, it must be the third performance.
    (D)   If Kyle gives a performance, it must be the sixth performance.
    (E)   Kyle does not give a performance.

7. If Leanne performs fourth and Imus performs second, which of the following must be false?

    (A)   Gill gives the first performance.
    (B)   Gill gives the fifth performance.
    (C)   Jesse gives the first performance.
    (D)   Maggie gives the third performance.
    (E)   Hyatt gives the sixth performance.

Game 33

Eight children, Barry, Jimbo, Kearney, Lisa, Marty, Nelson, Rob, and Toby, are members of the Springfield Elementary School football team. Each child will be assigned to one and only one of three squads: Offense, Defense, or Special Teams. At least two children must be assigned to each squad. The following conditions govern the assignments.

Barry cannot be assigned to Defense.
If Kearney is assigned to Defense, then Jimbo and Nelson are also assigned to Defense.
Lisa and Marty must be assigned to different squads.
If Marty is assigned to Special Teams, then Jimbo is also assigned to Special Teams.
Rob and Toby must be assigned to the same squad.

1. Which of the following is a possible assignment of children to the three squads?

    (A) Offense: Barry, Rob, Toby; Defense: Jimbo, Lisa, Marty; Special Teams: Kearney, Nelson

    (B) Offense: Barry, Lisa; Defense: Jimbo, Kearney, Nelson; Special Teams: Marty, Rob, Toby

    (C) Offense: Kearney, Marty; Defense: Nelson, Rob, Toby; Special Teams: Barry, Jimbo, Lisa

    (D) Offense: Marty, Toby; Defense: Jimbo, Kearney, Nelson; Special Teams: Barry, Lisa, Rob

    (E) Offense: Rob, Toby, Lisa; Defense: Marty; Special Teams: Barry, Jimbo, Kearney, Nelson

2. If Rob and Toby are the only children assigned to Offense and Nelson is assigned to Special Teams, which of the following is a complete and accurate list of the children any one of whom could be assigned to Defense?

    (A) Barry, Lisa, Marty
    (B) Jimbo, Marty, Lisa
    (C) Kearney, Lisa, Marty
    (D) Kearney, Marty
    (E) Kearney, Jimbo, Lisa, Marty,

3. Knowing which one of the following makes it possible to determine all of the assignments?

    (A) Barry is assigned to the same squad as Jimbo and Marty.
    (B) Kearney is assigned to Defense and Lisa is assigned to Offense.
    (C) Both Marty and Kearney are assigned to Defense.
    (D) Marty and Nelson are the only children assigned to Offense.
    (E) Both Rob and Lisa are assigned to Defense.

4. If Marty and Toby are assigned to Special Teams, then which of the following CANNOT be true?

    (A) Barry is assigned to Offense.
    (B) Jimbo is assigned to Special Teams.
    (C) Kearney is assigned to Offense.
    (D) Lisa is assigned to Defense.
    (E) Nelson is assigned to Offense.

5. If Jimbo and Lisa are two of four children assigned to Offense, then which of the following must be false?

    (A) Barry is one of the four children assigned to Offense.
    (B) Nelson is assigned to Special Teams.
    (C) Both Rob and Toby are assigned to Special Teams.
    (D) Jimbo and Barry are assigned to the same squad.
    (E) Lisa and Kearney are assigned to the same squad.

6. Suppose that a new condition is added stipulating that Marty and Kearney must be assigned to the same squad, and all other conditions remain in effect. If Rob and Jimbo are assigned to Defense, which of the following could be true?

    (A) Kearney is assigned to Special Teams.
    (B) Lisa is assigned to Offense.
    (C) Marty is assigned to Defense.
    (D) Barry, Lisa, and Nelson are assigned to the same squad.
    (E) Four children are assigned to Offense.

Game 34

A research company is assigning workers to projects. Three workers, Lemuel, Martin, and Nat, are available for assignment to five projects: C, D, E, F, and G. Each project must have at least one worker assigned to it. Additionally, each of the workers must be assigned to at least two but no more than three of the five projects. The following conditions also apply:

All three workers must be assigned to exactly one project in common.
G must be assigned to only one worker.
Lemuel cannot be assigned to either C or D.
If a worker is assigned to C that worker must also be assigned to F.

1. Which of the following could be a complete and accurate record of the assignments?

	C	D	E	F	G
(A)	Nat	Martin	Lemuel, Martin, Nat	Lemuel, Nat	Lemuel, Martin
(B)	Martin	Lemuel, Nat	Nat	Lemuel, Martin, Nat	Martin
(C)	Martin, Nat	Nat	Lemuel, Martin, Nat	Martin	Lemuel
(D)	Martin, Nat	Nat	Lemuel	Nat, Martin	Martin
(E)	Nat	Martin, Nat	Lemuel, Martin, Nat	Martin	Lemuel

2. If Martin is assigned to D and E and no other projects, then which of the following must be true?

   (A) Lemuel is assigned to F.
   (B) Lemuel is assigned to G.
   (C) Nat is assigned to D.
   (D) Nat is assigned to G.
   (E) Nat is not assigned to F.

3. If Lemuel is assigned to only two projects, and one of the other two workers is assigned to both E and F and no other projects, then which of the following must be true about the assignments?

   (A) Lemuel is assigned to F.
   (B) Martin is assigned to C.
   (C) Nat is assigned to G.
   (D) Exactly two workers are assigned to E.
   (E) Exactly two workers are assigned to F.

4. If Lemuel and Martin are the only workers assigned to F, each of the following must be true about the assignments EXCEPT:

   (A) Lemuel is assigned to G.
   (B) Lemuel is assigned to E.
   (C) Martin is assigned to C.
   (D) Nat is assigned to D.
   (E) Only one worker is assigned to D.

5. If Martin is assigned to G and only one other project, then Nat must be assigned to

   (A) C, D, F.
   (B) C, F.
   (C) C, F, G.
   (D) D, E, F.
   (E) D, E.

6. If two workers are assigned to D, which of the following must be true?

   (A) Martin is assigned to F.
   (B) Lemuel is assigned to three projects.
   (C) Martin is assigned to G.
   (D) Nat is assigned to C.
   (E) All three workers are assigned to E.

7. If Nat is assigned to projects E and D only, which of the following could be false?

   (A) Martin is assigned to E.
   (B) Martin is assigned to F.
   (C) Lemuel is assigned to G.
   (D) Lemuel is assigned to F.
   (E) Martin is assigned to C.

Game 35

During a five-day period from Monday through Friday, Freddie follows a special diet which allows him only three meals per day, breakfast, lunch, and dinner, and each meal must be made up of exactly one serving of only one of four foods: cake, ice cream, pie, or sardines. The following dietary restrictions apply:

During the week Freddie may have no more than four servings of any food.

Freddie does not eat the same food twice in the same day or for lunch on two consecutive days.

For exactly two days in a row Freddie eats the same food for dinner.

For exactly two days in a row Freddie eats the same food for breakfast.

Freddie has ice cream on Monday and Wednesday for breakfast and on Tuesday for lunch.

Lunch and dinner on Thursday are pie and sardines respectively.

Freddie eats no sardines on Friday.

1. Which of the following could be true of what Freddie eats during the week?

   (A) Freddie eats sardines for dinner four times.
   (B) Freddie eats pie at exactly two meals.
   (C) Freddie eats cake for breakfast three times.
   (D) Freddie eats pie for lunch three times.
   (E) Freddie eats ice cream for dinner once.

2. Which could be an accurate list of the things Freddie eats for breakfast, lunch, and dinner respectively on Friday?

   (A) ice cream, cake, pie
   (B) pie, sardines, cake
   (C) cake, ice cream, cake
   (D) cake, ice cream, pie
   (E) pie, ice cream, cake

3. Which of the following must be false?

   (A) Freddie eats ice cream for Friday lunch and sardines for Wednesday dinner.
   (B) Freddie eats sardines for Wednesday lunch, ice cream for Monday dinner, and pie on Tuesday.
   (C) Freddie eats sardines for Tuesday breakfast, Monday lunch, and Wednesday dinner.
   (D) Freddie eats cake for Tuesday dinner, sardines for Monday dinner, and pie for Friday dinner.
   (E) Freddie eats pie for Monday dinner, cake for Wednesday dinner, and sardines on Tuesday.

4. If Freddie eats sardines for dinner only once during the week, which of the following must be true?

   (A) Freddie eats sardines twice for lunch.
   (B) If Freddie eats sardines for lunch on Monday, he eats cake on Wednesday.
   (C) If Freddie eats cake on Monday, it is for dinner.
   (D) If Freddie eats pie for Monday lunch, he eats cake for Tuesday dinner.
   (E) If Freddie eats pie for Wednesday dinner, he eats cake for Wednesday lunch.

5. If Freddie eats sardines no more than three times and for Tuesday dinner, which of the following must be false?

   (A) Freddie eats cake for Wednesday dinner.
   (B) Freddie eats pie for Tuesday breakfast.
   (C) Freddie eats pie four days in a row.
   (D) Freddie eats pie for Monday lunch.
   (E) Freddie eats cake for Tuesday breakfast.

6. If Freddie eats each of the foods for lunch at least once, then which of the following must be true?

   (A) If Freddie has cake for Monday lunch, he has cake for Tuesday dinner.
   (B) If Freddie has pie for Tuesday dinner, he has sardines for Wednesday lunch.
   (C) Freddie has sardines exactly four times during the week.
   (D) Freddie has pie exactly four times during the week.
   (E) If Freddie has cake on Tuesday dinner, he has sardines for Monday lunch.

Game 36

Freeze Gopher, a punk band, is having auditions for a lead singer. The auditions will take place over a two-week period. Exactly one person will audition each day, Monday through Saturday, and no auditions will take place on Sundays. Exactly six singers will audition for the job, Razor, Slick, Trash, Ulcer, Vicious, and William. Each singer will have exactly one audition the first week and exactly one the second week. No other auditions are held. The following conditions govern the order of the auditions:

In both weeks Razor's audition occurs earlier in the week than Slick's.

Slick's audition during the first week is on the same day of the week as his audition during the second week.

In both weeks Ulcer's audition cannot fall on a day either immediately before or immediately after the day on which William auditions.

Trash and Vicious must audition on consecutive days during both weeks.

William has his auditions on Thursday of the first week and Tuesday of the second week.

1. If Slick has an audition on Saturday of the second week, which of the following could be the days on which Razor has his auditions?

   (A) first week: Monday; second week: Monday
   (B) first week: Monday; second week: Wednesday
   (C) first week: Wednesday; second week: Friday
   (D) first week: Friday; second week: Monday
   (E) first week: Friday; second week: Thursday

2. If Razor has an audition on Tuesday of the first week, which of the following could be true?

   (A) Razor has an audition on Wednesday of the second week.
   (B) Slick has an audition on Saturday of the first week.
   (C) Trash has an audition on Wednesday of the second week.
   (D) Ulcer has an audition on Friday of the second week.
   (E) Vicious has an audition on Saturday of the second week.

3. If both of Ulcer's auditions are held as early in the week as possible, which of the following is a complete and accurate list of the days of the week on which Trash could have an audition?

   (A) Monday, Tuesday
   (B) Monday, Tuesday, Wednesday
   (C) Tuesday, Wednesday, Friday, Saturday
   (D) Wednesday, Thursday, Friday, Saturday
   (E) Friday, Saturday

4. If Razor has one of his auditions on a Friday, which of the following must be another day on which he has an audition?

   (A) Monday
   (B) Tuesday
   (C) Wednesday
   (D) Thursday
   (E) Saturday

5. If both of Razor's auditions come as late in the week as possible, then which of the following is a day in both the first and second weeks on which either Trash or Vicious must audition?

   (A) Monday
   (B) Tuesday
   (C) Wednesday
   (D) Friday
   (E) Saturday

6. If Trash has one of his auditions on a Monday, then which of the following could be the days on which Ulcer has his auditions?

   (A) first week: Monday, second week: Saturday
   (B) first week: Tuesday; second week: Thursday
   (C) first week: Tuesday; second week: Friday
   (D) first week: Saturday; second week: Thursday
   (E) first week: Saturday; second week: Saturday

7. Which of the following could not be a complete and accurate list of auditions in order Monday through Saturday for one of the weeks?

(A) Vicious, Trash, Razor, William, Slick, Ulcer

(B) Ulcer, Trash, Vicious, William, Razor, Slick

(C) Razor, William, Trash, Slick, Vicious, Ulcer

(D) Razor, Trash, Vicious, William, Slick, Ulcer

(E) Razor, William, Trash, Vicious, Ulcer, Slick

Game 37

The manager of a convenience store must hire employees to work three shifts: morning, afternoon, and night. Only seven applicants, R, S, T, V, W, X, and Y, are being considered to fill the positions. For each shift the manager must hire either one applicant to work full-time or two applicants to work part-time. None of the applicants can be hired to work more than one shift and no other hirings are made.

The following restrictions apply:

R cannot be hired unless both T and V are hired.

If one of the applicants is hired full-time for the afternoon shift, then two applicants must be hired part-time to work the night shift.

Neither X nor V can be hired for any shift except the afternoon shift, and X cannot be hired if V is hired.

If more than two applicants are hired part-time then both S and W must be hired for the night shift.

W must be hired part-time.

1. Which of the following could be a complete and accurate list of the applicants hired to work the morning and afternoon shifts?

   (A)   morning: R, V; afternoon: S, T
   (B)   morning: S; afternoon: X, Y
   (C)   morning: S, T; afternoon: W
   (D)   morning: S; afternoon: T, W
   (E)   morning: Y; afternoon: R, S

2. If Y is not hired and T is hired to work the afternoon shift, then which of the following is an applicant that CANNOT work part time?

   (A)   R
   (B)   S
   (C)   T
   (D)   V
   (E)   W

3. If T is the only applicant hired full-time, then which of the following must be false?

   (A)   R is hired.
   (B)   T is hired to work the morning shift.
   (C)   V is not hired.
   (D)   W is hired to work the night shift.
   (E)   Y is hired to work the morning shift.

4. If Y is hired to work the night shift, then which of the following must be false?

   (A)   S is hired to work the afternoon shift.
   (B)   T is hired to work the night shift.
   (C)   V is not hired.
   (D)   W is hired to work the night shift.
   (E)   X is hired to work the afternoon shift.

5. If R is hired part-time to work the morning shift, then each of the following must be true EXCEPT:

   (A)   S is hired.
   (B)   T is hired part-time.
   (C)   X is not hired.
   (D)   Y is not hired full-time.
   (E)   Exactly five applicants are hired.

6. If S is hired full-time and T is hired part-time, then which of the following must be false?

   (A)   T is hired to work the morning shift.
   (B)   Neither V nor Y is hired.
   (C)   Both W and T are hired to work the night shift.
   (D)   X is hired to work the afternoon shift.
   (E)   Y is hired full time.

7. Which one of the following CANNOT be hired to work a morning shift?

   (A)   S
   (B)   R
   (C)   Y
   (D)   W
   (E)   T

Game 38

Out of eight students, A, B, C, D, E, F, G, and H, at least four must be selected to attend a spelling bee. The following conditions govern the selection of students:

If A is selected, then B is not selected.
If C and F are selected, then A is also selected.
D is not selected unless E is not selected.
If F and G are selected, then B is also selected.
If H is selected, then C is selected.

1. Which of the following could be a complete and accurate list of the students selected to attend the spelling bee?

   (A) A, C, D, E
   (B) A, D, F, G, H
   (C) B, C, D, G, H
   (D) B, C, E, F, G
   (E) B, F, G, H

2. What is the highest possible number of students that could be selected to attend the spelling bee?

   (A) 4
   (B) 5
   (C) 6
   (D) 7
   (E) 8

3. If five students are selected to attend the spelling bee, which of the following is a pair of students who must be selected?

   (A) A and H
   (B) B and C
   (C) C and H
   (D) D and E
   (E) E and G

4. If H and G are among the students selected to attend the spelling bee, which of the following is a student who CANNOT be selected?

   (A) A
   (B) B
   (C) D
   (D) E
   (E) F

5. Suppose that A is selected to attend the spelling bee. Which of the following could be a list of the students who are also selected?

   (A) B, C, D, and G
   (B) C, D, E, H
   (C) C, E, F
   (D) C, F, G
   (E) D, F, H

6. If C is not selected to attend the spelling bee, which of the following is a student who also must not be selected?

   (A) A
   (B) B
   (C) E
   (D) F
   (E) G

7. Which of the following is a pair of students at least one of whom must be selected to attend the spelling bee?

   (A) C, D
   (B) H, C
   (C) F, C
   (D) D, E
   (E) A, B

Game 39

The Sanchez family bought a home badly in need of remodeling. They will remodel it themselves doing exactly one room at a time. The rooms to be remodeled are the kitchen, living room, den, master bedroom, bathroom, guest room, and study. The rooms are remodeled according to the following conditions:

The bathroom and kitchen must be remodeled consecutively, though in either order.
The den is remodeled sometime after the master bedroom and sometime before the guest room.
The living room is remodeled sometime after the guest room and sometime after the study

1. Which of the following is a complete and accurate list of the order in which the rooms could be remodeled?

   (A) master bedroom, den, study, bathroom, kitchen, guest room, living room
   (B) study, guest room, den, master bedroom, living room, kitchen, bathroom
   (C) master bedroom, den, bathroom, guest room, study, kitchen, living room
   (D) master bedroom, den, guest room, kitchen, bathroom, living room, study
   (E) study, master bedroom, bathroom, kitchen, den, living room, guest room

2. Which of the following is a pair of rooms that could not be remodeled consecutively?

   (A) the study and the guest room
   (B) the den and the living room
   (C) the master bedroom and the study
   (D) the bathroom and the guest room
   (E) the living room and the kitchen

3. How many different rooms could be the last room remodeled?

   (A) 2
   (B) 3
   (C) 4
   (D) 5
   (E) 6

4. If the study is the fourth room remodeled, which of the following must be false?

   (A) The den is the fifth room remodeled.
   (B) The bathroom is the sixth room remodeled.
   (C) The master bedroom is remodeled third.
   (D) The living room is the fifth room remodeled.
   (E) The living room is remodeled sixth.

5. If the guest room is the fourth room remodeled, which of the following must be true?

   (A) The study is remodeled sometime before the master bedroom.
   (B) The living room is the last room remodeled.
   (C) The kitchen is remodeled sometime after the living room.
   (D) The bathroom is remodeled sometime after the guest room.
   (E) The study is remodeled sometime after the den.

6. If the master bedroom is the third room remodeled, which of the following is a complete and accurate list of the rooms that could be remodeled sixth?

   (A) den, guest room, study
   (B) living room, study, guest room
   (C) bathroom, kitchen
   (D) study, living room
   (E) study, guest room

7. If the kitchen is the third room remodeled and the master bedroom is the first room remodeled, how many different rooms could be the second room remodeled?

   (A) 1
   (B) 2
   (C) 3
   (D) 4
   (E) 5

Game 40

Three children, Fern, Guillermo, and Heinrich, are each participating in exactly two events during the Camp Quinnipiac summer games. They will each participate in one of three individual events: archery, badminton, and croquet; and one of three team events: rugby, soccer, and tug-of-war. The following conditions apply:

If Fern and Guillermo participate in the same team event, then they must also participate in the same individual event.

Fern and Heinrich do not participate in the same individual event.

Guillermo and Heinrich do not participate in the same team event.

Heinrich must participate in either croquet or soccer, or both.

Guillermo participates in archery.

1. Which of the following could be a complete and accurate list of the three individual sports and the three team sports played by the children, each category listed in the order of Fern, Guillermo, and Heinrich, respectively?

    (A)   Individual: croquet, archery, croquet; Team: rugby, tug-of-war, rugby
    (B)   Individual: badminton, badminton, archery; Team: tug-of-war, tug-of-war, soccer
    (C)   Individual: archery, archery, croquet; Team: rugby, tug-of-war, soccer
    (D)   Individual: badminton, archery, croquet; Team: rugby, rugby, tug-of-war
    (E)   Individual: croquet, archery, badminton; Team: rugby, soccer, soccer

2. If Heinrich participates in the badminton competition and Fern and Heinrich participate in the same team event, then which of the following must be true?

    (A)   Fern participates in archery.
    (B)   Fern participates in soccer.
    (C)   Guillermo participates in rugby.
    (D)   Guillermo participates in soccer.
    (E)   Heinrich participates in tug-of-war.

3. If both Fern and Guillermo participate in the tug-of-war competition, then how many possible combinations of individual and team events can Heinrich participate in?

    (A)   2
    (B)   3
    (C)   4
    (D)   5
    (E)   6

4. If none of the three children participate in croquet or tug-of-war and Fern takes part in the badminton competition, then which of the following must be true?

    (A)   Fern and Heinrich participate in the same team event.
    (B)   Guillermo and Fern participate in the same individual event.
    (C)   Guillermo is the only of the three children participating in archery.
    (D)   Guillermo participates in soccer.
    (E)   Heinrich participates in badminton.

5. If none of the three children participate in badminton and Guillermo participates in soccer, then Fern must participate in which of the following events?

    (A)   soccer
    (B)   croquet
    (C)   rugby
    (D)   archery
    (E)   tug-of-war

6. If Heinrich participates in archery, then each of the following can be true EXCEPT:

    (A)   Fern does not participate in archery.
    (B)   Fern and Guillermo participate in the same team sport.
    (C)   Fern participates in soccer.
    (D)   Guillermo participates in either rugby or tug-of-war.
    (E)   Heinrich participates in soccer.

The rectangular fifth floor of an insurance company's office building has ten cubicles of equal size and dimensions around a central reception area: one cubicle in each corner, two non-corner cubicles on both the east and west sides, and one non-corner cubicle on both the north and south sides. Nine employees, each of four adjustors: B, C, D, and E, and each of five salespersons: T, U, V, W, and X, must be assigned to exactly one cubicle, according to the following restrictions:

W's cubicle and T's cubicle are adjacent non-corner cubicles.

V is in a corner cubicle.

No adjustor has a cubicle immediately next to the cubicle of another adjustor.

D is the only adjustor who does not have a corner cubicle.

X's cubicle is directly across from U's cubicle.

1. If W is on the west side, which is a list of all cubicles which could be directly across from W?

(A) B, V, C
(B) empty, D
(C) X, D, empty
(D) B, C
(E) X, empty

2. Which of the following is a pair of employees whose cubicles must be adjacent to one another?

(A) B, U
(B) C, T
(C) D, V
(D) X, E
(E) V, X

3. If the empty cubicle is as far north as possible on the west side, who occupies the cubicle on the southwest corner?

(A) E
(B) B
(C) C
(D) U
(E) V

4. If D's cubicle is as far south as possible, which of the following could be a list from west to east of the cubicles on the north wall?

(A) V, X, B
(B) B, empty, E
(C) B, U, C
(D) U, C, X
(E) C, empty, V

5. If V and B are diagonally across from each other, which of the following is a complete and accurate list of the cubicles which could be beside B's cubicle?

(A) T, X, W, U
(B) empty, D, U, X
(C) T, X, W
(D) T, X, U, W, empty
(E) empty, D, X

6. If B is beside an empty cubicle, on the south wall, which is not a pair that could also be on the south wall?

(A) E, U
(B) B, X
(C) V, X
(D) U, B
(E) C, X

Game 42

Spaceman Spiff, interplanetary explorer extraordinaire, is planning his vacation. During his vacation Spiff must explore at least two of three nebulas: nebula 1, nebula 2, and nebula 3. Spiff must also explore at least one of six planets, Urgak, Vlog, Warg, Xerx, Yorglak, and Zorg.

If Urgak is explored, then Vlog must also be explored.
Either Urgak or Xerx must be explored, but not both.
If Zorg is explored, then Vlog cannot be explored.
If nebula 1 is explored, then Vlog and Warg must also be explored.
If nebula 3 is explored, then Zorg must also be explored.

1. Which of the following could be a complete and accurate list of the nebulas and planets explored during Spiff's vacation?

    (A) 1, 2, Vlog, Warg, Yorglak
    (B) 1, 2, Vlog, Xerx, Yorglak
    (C) 1, 3, Urgak, Vlog, Warg, Zorg
    (D) 2, 3, Urgak, Warg, Yorglak
    (E) 2, 3, Warg, Xerx, Zorg,

2. Which of the following could be true?

    (A) Spiff explores both Urgak and Warg.
    (B) Spiff explores both Urgak and Zorg.
    (C) Spiff does not explore either Vlog or Zorg.
    (D) Spiff explores exactly five planets.
    (E) Spiff does not explore nebula 2.

3. If exactly four planets are explored, which of the following is a planet that must be explored?

    (A) Urgak
    (B) Vlog
    (C) Warg
    (D) Xerx
    (E) Zorg

4. If Spiff does not explore Warg, then which of the following CANNOT be true?

    (A) Spiff explores Xerx.
    (B) Spiff explores Urgak.
    (C) Spiff explores Yorglak.
    (D) Spiff explores nebula 3.
    (E) Spiff explores exactly three planets.

5. If Spiff explores as few planets as possible, which of the following is a complete and accurate list of the planets he must explore?

    (A) Urgak
    (B) Xerx
    (C) Xerx, Zorg
    (D) Warg, Vlog
    (E) Vlog, Warg, Xerx

6. If Spiff explores Urgak and exactly two other planets, then which of the following must be explored by Spiff?

    (A) nebula 3
    (B) Warg
    (C) Xerx
    (D) Yorglak
    (E) Zorg

7. If Spiff explores nebula 1 and nebula 2, then which of the following planets must be explored by Spiff?

    (A) Urgak
    (B) Zorg
    (C) Xerx
    (D) Yorglak
    (E) Vlog

Exactly nine guests will attend a banquet held to attract overseas investors. Each of the guests must be seated at one of three tables, exactly three guests per table. Each of the guests speaks only one of four languages: French, Japanese, German, or Spanish. Exactly one company representative will be assigned to each of the three tables and no representative can be assigned to more than one table. Each representative must speak all of the languages spoken by the guests at the table to which he or she is assigned. The three representatives that will be assigned to tables are Bateman, Cuevas, and Diaz. Bateman speaks only French, German, and Japanese. Cuevas speaks only German and Spanish. Diaz speaks only French and Spanish. The following conditions govern the seating arrangements:

If a French-speaking guest is seated at the first table, then at least one French-speaking guest must be seated at the third table.

At least two German-speaking guests must be seated at the same table.

At least three of the guests are Spanish speakers.

If a Spanish speaker is seated at the first table, then Bateman must be assigned to the second table.

If Cuevas is not assigned to the third table, then Diaz cannot be assigned to the first table.

1. If a French-speaking guest and a Spanish-speaking guest are seated at the second table then the guests seated at the first table could be

    (A) one French speaker and two German speakers.
    (B) one French speaker and two Japanese speakers.
    (C) one German speaker and two Japanese speakers.
    (D) two German speakers and one Spanish speaker.
    (E) three Spanish speakers.

2. If three French-speaking guests are seated at the first table, then which of the following must be true?

    (A) No German-speaking guests are seated at the second table.
    (B) A Japanese-speaking guest is seated at the third table.
    (C) At least two Spanish-speaking guests are seated at the third table.
    (D) Bateman is assigned to the second table.
    (E) Cuevas is assigned to the first table.

3. If one French-speaking guest and two Japanese-speaking guests are seated at the same table then the guests seated at the second table could be

    (A) one French speaker and two German speakers.
    (B) one French speaker and two Spanish speakers.
    (C) two French speakers and one Spanish speaker.
    (D) one German speaker and two Spanish speakers.
    (E) two German speakers and one Spanish speaker.

4. If a French-speaking guest and a Japanese-speaking guest are seated at the third table, then which of the following must be true?

    (A) No French-speaking guests are seated at the second table.
    (B) At least two German-speaking guests are seated at the second table.
    (C) At least two Spanish-speaking guests are seated at the table to which Cuevas is assigned.
    (D) Bateman is assigned to the second table.
    (E) Cuevas is assigned to the third table.

5. If two of the guests are French speakers and five are Spanish speakers, then the guests seated at the third table could be

   (A) a French speaker and two German speakers.
   (B) a French speaker and two Spanish speakers.
   (C) two French speakers and a Spanish speaker.
   (D) one German speaker and two Spanish speakers.
   (E) two German speakers and a Spanish speaker.

6. If at least one German-speaking guest is seated at the second table and at least one German-speaking guest is seated at the third table, then each of the following must be false EXCEPT:

   (A) One French speaker is seated at the first table.
   (B) Two Japanese speakers are seated at the first table.
   (C) One French speaker is seated at the second table.
   (D) Two Spanish speakers are seated at the second table.
   (E) One Japanese speaker is seated at the third table.

Seven students must enroll in a foreign language course. Four of the students are boys, J, K, L, and M. Three of the students are girls, X, Y, and Z. Each student must enroll in one and only one of four courses: beginner's French, advanced French, beginner's Spanish, or advanced Spanish. No other students enroll in courses. At least one of the students must enroll in each class, and the following restrictions apply:

If K enrolls in a French course, then L and X also enroll in French courses, but not necessarily the same course.

If M enrolls in a Spanish course, then Y enrolls in advanced Spanish.

Y and Z must enroll in the same course.

At least two boys must enroll in beginner's Spanish.

No girl enrolls in beginner's French.

1. Which of the following could be a complete and accurate list of the students enrolled in advanced courses?

   (A)   French: J, X; Spanish: K
   (B)   French: K, Y, Z; Spanish: X
   (C)   French: K, X; Spanish: Y, Z
   (D)   French: L, Z; Spanish: X
   (E)   French: Y, Z; Spanish: M, X

2. Which of the following must be false?

   (A)   Exactly one student takes advanced French.
   (B)   Exactly one student takes advanced Spanish.
   (C)   Exactly four students take advanced courses.
   (D)   Exactly three students take beginner's French.
   (E)   Exactly three students take advanced Spanish.

3. If Y enrolls in a French course, which of the following is a student who must enroll in a Spanish course?

   (A)   J
   (B)   K
   (C)   L
   (D)   M
   (E)   X

4. If L and Y both enroll in French courses then each of the following must be false EXCEPT:

   (A)   J enrolls in a French course.
   (B)   K enrolls in advanced Spanish.
   (C)   M enrolls in an advanced course.
   (D)   X enrolls in the same course as Y.
   (E)   X enrolls in beginner's Spanish.

5. If K enrolls in advanced French, which of the following is a student who must take a course in which he or she is the only student enrolled?

   (A)   J
   (B)   L
   (C)   M
   (D)   X
   (E)   Z

6. If M and J both take beginner's Spanish, which of the following must be false?

   (A)   K takes a Spanish course.
   (B)   L takes advanced French.
   (C)   X takes a beginner's course.
   (D)   X takes advanced French.
   (E)   Z takes an advanced course.

7. If M enrolls in advanced Spanish, then each of the following must be true EXCEPT:

   (A)   J enrolls in a Spanish course.
   (B)   K enrolls in a Spanish course.
   (C)   L enrolls in a beginner's course.
   (D)   Only one student is enrolled in advanced French.
   (E)   Only one boy enrolls in a French course.

For each of five consecutive days, Monday through Friday, the editor of a local newspaper decides what stories to run on the paper's front page. Each front page story deals with exactly one of four topics: politics, war, economics, or crime. On each day the editor includes as many different stories on the front page as she judges appropriate, and the outcome of the front pages conform to these characteristics:

Any topic which is not covered on Tuesday is covered on Thursday, and no topic that is covered on Thursday is covered on Tuesday.

Any topic that is not covered on Monday is covered on Friday, and no topic that is covered on Friday is covered on Monday.

Tuesday's front page and Friday's front page include stories on politics.

Fridays front page and Thursday's front page include stories on crime.

On Friday, fewer topics are covered than on Wednesday, but more topics are covered than on Tuesday, and the number of topics covered on Friday is not the same as the number of topics covered on any other day.

1. On which of the following days are the fewest topics included in front page stories?

    (A) Monday
    (B) Tuesday
    (C) Wednesday
    (D) Thursday
    (E) Friday

2. Which of the following must be true of the topics covered on the front page?

    (A) War is covered on Monday.
    (B) War is covered on Tuesday.
    (C) War is covered on Wednesday.
    (D) War is covered on Thursday.
    (E) War is covered on Friday.

3. If war is covered on Friday and economics is covered on three consecutive days, which of the following must be true?

    (A) Crime is covered on Monday.
    (B) War is covered on Thursday.
    (C) Economics is covered on Friday.
    (D) War is covered on Tuesday.
    (E) Economics is covered on Thursday.

4. For how many of the topics is it possible to be covered on exactly four of the five days?

    (A) 0
    (B) 1
    (C) 2
    (D) 3
    (E) 4

5. If economics is covered on Friday and the days on which war is covered are not all consecutive, which of the following must be false?

    (A) Crime is covered on Wednesday.
    (B) War is covered on Monday.
    (C) Economics is covered on Tuesday.
    (D) Economics is covered on Thursday.
    (E) War is covered on Thursday.

6. If economics is covered on Monday, how many different combinations of days and topics are possible for the week?

    (A) 1
    (B) 2
    (C) 3
    (D) 4
    (E) 5

7. If war is covered on Tuesday and as few of the topics as possible are covered on consecutive days, which of the following must be false?

    (A) War is covered on Wednesday and Friday.
    (B) Economics is covered on Monday and Wednesday.
    (C) Politics is covered on three non-consecutive days.
    (D) War is covered on three non-consecutive days.
    (E) Economics is covered on Friday and Tuesday.

Game 46

In a certain week, Monday through Friday, four students, Raul, Marizza, Eddie, and Jessica, must eat lunch at one of four restaurants, Apple's, Burger's, Chick's, and the Deli. No two students can eat at the same place on the same day, and the following conditions apply:

No student can eat at the same place more than two times during the week.

Marizza is the only student who eats at Apple's on two of the weekdays, and one of the days that she eats at Apple's is Thursday.

Raul eats at Burger's on Monday and Tuesday.

Jessica eats at the Deli on Tuesday and Wednesday.

Eddie eats at Apple's on Friday.

1. Which one of the following could be a complete list of the restaurants at which Jessica eats?

    (A) Monday: Chick's; Tuesday: the Deli; Wednesday: the Deli; Thursday: Apple's; Friday: Burger's

    (B) Monday: Apple's; Tuesday: the Deli; Wednesday: the Deli; Thursday: Chick's; Friday: Chick's

    (C) Monday: Chick's; Tuesday: the Deli; Wednesday: the Deli; Thursday: Burger's; Friday: Chick's

    (D) Monday: Apple's; Tuesday: the Deli; Wednesday: the Deli; Thursday: Apple's; Friday: Chick's

    (E) Monday: Chick's; Tuesday: the Deli; Wednesday: the Deli; Thursday: Burger's; Friday: Burger's

2. Which one of the following must be true?

    (A) Raul does not eat at Chick's.
    (B) Marizza eats only at Apple's, Chick's, and the Deli.
    (C) All of the students eat at the Deli.
    (D) All of the students eat at Chick's.
    (E) All of the students eat at Apple's.

3. If Marizza eats at the Deli on Monday, which of the following must be true?

    (A) Raul eats at the Deli on Thursday.
    (B) Marizza eats Burger's on Wednesday.
    (C) Jessica eats at Burger's on Friday.
    (D) Marizza eats at Chick's on Wednesday.
    (E) Eddie eats at Chick's on Wednesday.

4. Which of the following is a complete and accurate list of the restaurants any of which Raul could eat at on Friday?

    (A) Chick's
    (B) Apple's
    (C) Chick's, the Deli
    (D) Chick's, Apple's
    (E) Chick's, Apple's, the Deli

5. If Eddie eats at Burger's two times during the week, which of the following CANNOT be true?

    (A) Eddie eats at the Deli on Monday.
    (B) Marizza eats at Burger's on Wednesday.
    (C) Jessica eats at Chick's on Thursday.
    (D) Raul eats at the Deli on Thursday.
    (E) Raul eats at the Deli on Friday.

6. Which of the following is the day on which Jessica eats at Apple's?

    (A) Monday
    (B) Tuesday
    (C) Wednesday
    (D) Thursday
    (E) Friday

7. If Raul eats at Chick's on Thursday and Eddie eats at Chick's on Monday, which of the following must be true?

    (A) Eddie eats at Burger's on Thursday.
    (B) Jessica eats at Chick's on Friday.
    (C) Marizza eats at Chick's on Wednesday.
    (D) Raul eats at Chick's on Friday.
    (E) Raul eats at the Deli on Friday.

Game 47

Each of eight students, L, M, N, O, P, R, S, and T must take a make-up test that lasts one hour during a particular week. Testing times are Monday through Friday at 8:00 and 9:00, and only one student can be tested at a time, although no student is tested on Wednesday at 8:00. The schedule for a make-up test must be consistent with the following conditions:

P must be tested sometime before N is tested.
O is tested on the same day that M is tested.
If L is tested at 8:00 on any day, then R is tested at 8:00 on another day.
S is tested at 9:00 on Tuesday.

1. Which could be a complete and accurate list of the students tested at 8:00 from Monday through Friday respectively?

    (A) O, N, none, P, T
    (B) L, T, none, P, R
    (C) O, P, none, L, N
    (D) R, T, none, P, M
    (E) O, L, none, M, R

2. If N is tested at 8:00 on Friday, what is the latest day and time that M could be tested?

    (A) Thursday at 8:00
    (B) Wednesday at 9:00
    (C) Thursday at 9:00
    (D) Friday at 9:00
    (E) Monday at 9:00

3. If T and N are both tested sometime before S, then which of the following CANNOT be true?

    (A) M is tested sometime on Thursday.
    (B) R is tested on Thursday at 8:00.
    (C) L is tested on Thursday at 8:00.
    (D) L is tested on Wednesday at 9:00.
    (E) T and P are tested on the same day.

4. If N and O are both tested sometime before T, which is the earliest exam that T could take?

    (A) Thursday, 8:00
    (B) Tuesday, 8:00
    (C) Wednesday, 9:00
    (D) Thursday, 9:00
    (E) Friday, 9:00

5. If no one is tested on Thursday at 8:00, then which of the following could be true?

    (A) L is tested at 8:00 on Tuesday and N is tested at 8:00 on Friday.
    (B) N is tested sometime before S and P is tested sometime after M.
    (C) P is tested Monday at 9:00 and N is tested Friday at 9:00.
    (D) L is tested Tuesday at 8:00 and O is tested sometime before R.
    (E) P is tested at 8:00 and L is tested at 8:00.

6. If R and T are tested in succession on Thursday and Friday at 8:00, which of the following could be true?

    (A) O is tested sometime after S.
    (B) L is tested on Wednesday at 9:00.
    (C) N is tested on Tuesday at 8:00.
    (D) L is tested on Monday at 9:00.
    (E) O and N are tested on consecutive days.

Game 48

Mayor Caballo must visit seven schools: E, F, G, H, I, J, and S. The following conditions govern the ordering of the visits:

Caballo visits for E before F.
Caballo visits F before I.
Caballo visits I after G.
Caballo visits H after G.
Caballo visits J after I.
Caballo cannot visit S either immediately before or after he visits either F or I.

1. Which of the following could be a complete and accurate ordering of Caballo's visits?

    (A) E, F, G, S, I, J, H
    (B) E, H, F, G, I, J, S
    (C) E, S, G, F, J, H, I
    (D) G, E, F, I, H, S, J
    (E) G, E, H, S, F, I, J

2. Which of the following CANNOT be true about the ordering of the visits?

    (A) F is fifth.
    (B) G is preceded by exactly three other visits.
    (C) H is second.
    (D) S is fifth.
    (E) S falls immediately before J.

3. If H is visited second, then S could be visited

    (A) third.
    (B) fourth.
    (C) fifth.
    (D) sixth.
    (E) seventh.

4. If E and G are visited first and second, respectively, in how many different places in the order could S be visited?

    (A) 2
    (B) 3
    (C) 4
    (D) 5
    (E) 6

5. If S is visited sometime after E and J is visited sixth, the fourth and fifth schools visited could be which of the following?

    (A) fourth: F   fifth: I
    (B) fourth: G   fifth: F
    (C) fourth: G   fifth: S
    (D) fourth: H   fifth: S
    (E) fourth: S   fifth: G

6. Which of the following gives sufficient information to determine the exact order of the visits?

    (A) H is visited second.
    (B) S is visited fourth.
    (C) G is visited sixth.
    (D) S is visited fifth.
    (E) J is visited sixth.

Game 49

A certain professor must assign each of sixteen students; Willie, Sandra, Tom, Carlos, Eddie, Oscar, Liz, Molly, Mike, Maria, Melissa, Jessica, Natalie, Denise, Brian, and Paul to one of four moot court teams: Marshall, Story, Taft, or Holmes. The following rules apply:

Sandra is not on a team unless Willie is on the same team.

Each team must have exactly four students.

Tom and Carlos are not on the same team.

If Liz is not on team Story then Oscar is not on team Story.

Jessica is not on a team unless Sandra is on the same team.

Oscar will serve only on a team named after a 19th century Supreme Court Justice.

Brian will serve only on a team named after a Supreme Court Chief Justice.

The professor wants Paul and Brian to learn to work together, and so assigns them together.

Jessica must be assigned to team Holmes.

Paul cannot serve on team Taft.

Eddie is on the same team as Oscar.

To avoid confusion, no team may include two members with the same first initial.

Marshall was a 19th century Supreme Court Chief Justice.

Story was a 19th century Supreme Court Justice, although he was not a Chief Justice.

Taft was a 20th century Supreme Court Chief Justice.

Holmes was a 20th century Supreme Court Justice but not a Chief Justice.

1. Which of the following could be an accurate list of the people on team Taft?

   (A) Liz, Natalie, Sandra, Maria
   (B) Jessica, Molly, Paul, Denise
   (C) Sandra, Melissa, Natalie, Tom
   (D) Carlos, Mike, Denise, Natalie
   (E) Denise, Natalie, Carlos, Jessica

2. On which team or teams could Brian serve?

   (A) Holmes or Taft
   (B) Taft only
   (C) Marshall only
   (D) Marshall, Taft, or Holmes
   (E) Marshall, Taft, Story, or Holmes

3. Which is a pair of students who can work together on team Holmes?

   (A) Sandra and Carlos
   (B) Oscar and Maria
   (C) Willie and Molly
   (D) Jessica and Tom
   (E) Melissa and Carlos

4. If Maria is on team Taft and Molly is on team Marshall, then which of the following is a pair of students who could work with Maria?

   (A) Natalie and Oscar
   (B) Denise and Eddie
   (C) Denise and Melissa
   (D) Natalie and Brian
   (E) Carlos and Denise

5. If Tom is on the same team as Natalie, then which is a pair that could be on the same team with Brian?

   (A) Oscar and Maria
   (B) Melissa and Carlos
   (C) Denise and Carlos
   (D) Mike and Denise
   (E) Eddie and Sandra

6. Which is a group of three who could not be on the same team?

   (A) Paul, Brian, and Molly
   (B) Natalie, Denise, and Tom
   (C) Mike, Tom, and Willie
   (D) Maria, Oscar, and Liz
   (E) Brian, Paul, and Tom

Game 50

A movie theater must show ten movies: H, I, J, K, L, M, N, O, P, and Q on a certain week on either Friday or Saturday. No movie can be shown on both days. Exactly five movies must be shown on each day and the following rules apply:

If H is shown on Saturday, then P must be shown on Friday.

If L is shown on Friday, then both J and K must be shown on Saturday.

If N is shown on Friday, then K must be shown on Saturday.

If O is shown on Friday, then M must be shown on Friday.

I must be shown on Friday.

Q must be shown on Saturday.

1. Which of the following could be the schedule for the showings?

   (A) Friday: H, I, J, K, N; Saturday: L, N, O, P, Q
   (B) Friday: H, I L, N, O; Saturday: J, K, M, P, Q
   (C) Friday: H, I, L, M, P; Saturday: J, K, N, O, Q
   (D) Friday: I, J, L, N, P; Saturday: K, H, M, O, Q
   (E) Friday: I, J, M, N, O; Saturday: H, K, L, P, Q

2. If P is shown on Saturday, which of the following is a movie that must be shown on Friday?

   (A) H
   (B) J
   (C) L
   (D) M
   (E) N

3. If M is shown on Saturday, which of the following is a movie that must be shown on Friday?

   (A) H
   (B) J
   (C) K
   (D) L
   (E) N

4. If both J and M are shown on Saturday, which of the following is a movie that must also be shown on Saturday?

   (A) H
   (B) K
   (C) L
   (D) N
   (E) P

5. If L, M, and P are all shown on the same day, which of the following is a pair of movies that must be shown on the same day, though not necessarily the day on which L, M, and P are shown?

   (A) H and I
   (B) J and Q
   (C) K and N
   (D) M and N
   (E) M and O

6. If L is shown on Friday and H is shown on Saturday, which of the following is a pair of movies that CANNOT be shown on the same day?

   (A) H and K
   (B) K and Q
   (C) L and P
   (D) M and N
   (E) N and O

7. If P is shown on Saturday and K is shown on Friday, which of the following is a list of movies any one of which could be shown on Saturday?

   (A) H, L, J
   (B) M, J, L
   (C) O, N, J
   (D) M, O, P
   (E) O, M, J

Game 51

Lisa is loading songs on an MP3 player. The player will hold exactly three long songs from songs C, D, and F or exactly six short songs from songs H, J, K L, P, Q. Each short song takes exactly half the space of any long song. Julie uses all available space in the MP3 player. The following conditions apply:

If J is included, then L is included.
If C is included, then K is not included.
If L is in included, then C is included.
If either P or D is included, then both are included.
If C is included, then Q is included.
If F is included, then D is not included.

1. Which of the following could be a complete and accurate list of the songs loaded?

   (A)   C, H, Q, J, P
   (B)   D, P, Q, F
   (C)   P, Q, D, K, H
   (D)   C, P, F, H
   (E)   Q, C, D, L

2. If L is included among the songs loaded, which of the following CANNOT be included?

   (A)   J
   (B)   F
   (C)   C
   (D)   P
   (E)   H

3. If exactly 2 long songs are loaded, which of the following must also be loaded?

   (A)   Q
   (B)   P
   (C)   L
   (D)   H
   (E)   K

4. If J is loaded, all of the following must also be loaded EXCEPT:

   (A)   L
   (B)   C
   (C)   Q
   (D)   H
   (E)   P

5. If H is not among the group of songs loaded, then which of the following is a pair that could be loaded?

   (A)   J, Q
   (B)   F, P
   (C)   D, L
   (D)   C, P
   (E)   K, P

6. Which of the following is a pair that CANNOT be loaded together?

   (A)   C, D
   (B)   Q, F
   (C)   F, L
   (D)   H, F
   (E)   L, P

7. If exactly 4 songs are loaded and one of them is L, which of the following could be among the four songs?

   (A)   H
   (B)   F
   (C)   P
   (D)   D
   (E)   J

Over a period of three days, Monday through Wednesday, three piano players must each learn exactly three of six pieces. The pieces are numbered one through six, consecutively, according to their difficulty, with piece 1 being the easiest and piece six being the most difficult. The students, Ali, Ben, and Claire, must learn one piece per day. Each piece is learned by at least one, but not more than two of the students, and no student can learn a piece that is easier than a piece they have previously learned. The following conditions also apply:

On Tuesday Ali must learn the piece that Ben learns on Monday.
Ben learns piece 4 on Tuesday.
Claire does not learn piece 4.
The piece Claire learns on Wednesday is not more difficult than the piece Ben learns on Wednesday.

1. Which of the following could be a complete and accurate list of the pieces learned by the three students?

   (A) Ali: 2, 3, 5; Ben: 3, 4, 6; Claire: 2, 5, 6
   (B) Ali: 2, 3, 4; Ben: 3, 4, 5; Claire: 1, 5, 6
   (C) Ali: 1, 2, 5; Ben: 1, 2, 6; Claire: 2, 3, 6
   (D) Ali: 2, 3, 5; Ben: 3, 5, 6; Claire: 1, 2, 6
   (E) Ali: 2, 3, 4; Ben: 2, 4, 5; Claire: 1, 3, 6

2. Which of the following is a piece that CANNOT be learned by Ben?

   (A) 1
   (B) 2
   (C) 3
   (D) 5
   (E) 6

3. If Ben learns piece 5, which of the following must be a piece learned by Ali?

   (A) 2
   (B) 3
   (C) 4
   (D) 5
   (E) 6

4. Which of the following must be false?

   (A) Exactly two students learn piece 1 on Monday.
   (B) Exactly two students learn piece 6 on Wednesday.
   (C) Exactly two students learn piece 4 on Tuesday.
   (D) Exactly two students learn piece 2 on Monday.
   (E) Exactly two students learn piece 5 on Wednesday.

5. If Ali learns the most difficult pieces allowed for her, then which of the following must be true?

   (A) Ali learns piece 5 on Wednesday.
   (B) Claire learns piece 6 on Wednesday.
   (C) Ali learns piece 4 on Tuesday.
   (D) Ben learns piece 2 on Tuesday.
   (E) Claire learns piece 2 on Tuesday.

6. If both Ali and Claire learn piece 3, which is a piece that must be learned by only one student?

   (A) 1
   (B) 2
   (C) 3
   (D) 5
   (E) 6

7. If piece six is removed from the list and all other conditions remain the same, which of the following is a piece that must be learned by two students?

   (A) 1
   (B) 2
   (C) 3
   (D) 4
   (E) 5

Game 53

On a particular morning, Dr. Johnson sees seven patients: Kathy, Luther, Mark, Nestor, Peter, Quincy, and Tina. Each patient is seen exactly once at the beginning of an hour. Dr. Johnson is available to see patients between 8:00 a.m. and just before noon. There are two examining rooms: A and B. In any hour, Dr. Johnson sees no more than two patients and no more than one patient in any examining room. The order in which Dr. Johnson sees the patients is governed by the following conditions:

Kathy and Mark are seen in the same hour.
Exactly one other hour begins between the hour when Peter sees the doctor and the hour when Quincy sees the doctor.
Nestor and Peter must be in room B.

1. Which could be an accurate list of patients in the two rooms from earliest to latest?

    (A) A: Luther, B: Peter; A: Tina, B: Nestor; A: Kathy, B: Mark; A: Quincy, B: none
    (B) A: Luther, B: Peter; A: Kathy, B: Tina; A: Quincy, B: Mark; A: Nestor, B: none
    (C) A: Nestor, B: Tina; A: Quincy, B: none; A: Mark, B: Kathy; A: Luther, B: Peter
    (D) A: Luther, B: Nestor; A: Kathy, Quincy, B: Mark; A: Tina, B: none; A: none, B: Peter
    (E) A: Quincy, B: Nestor; A: Kathy, B: Mark; A: Luther, B: Peter; A: Tina, B: none

2. If Mark sees Dr. Johnson at 11:00 and there is no patient in room B at 10:00, then which one of the following must be true?

    (A) Peter is in room B at 9:00.
    (B) Peter is in room A at 8:00.
    (C) Luther is in room B at 9:00.
    (D) Quincy is in room A at 10:00.
    (E) Nestor is in room B at 8:00.

3. If Nestor immediately follows Kathy, and Tina is at 10:00, which is a room and time in which Dr. Johnson could see Luther?

    (A) in room B at 11:00
    (B) in room B at 10:00
    (C) in room A at 8:00
    (D) in room B at 9:00
    (E) in room A at 9:00

4. Which one of the following is an accurate list of patients who could not both be seen in room B?

    (A) Tina, Luther
    (B) Kathy, Luther
    (C) Nestor, Tina
    (D) Mark, Luther
    (E) Quincy, Peter

5. If there is no patient in room B at 8:00 then which one of the following could be true?

    (A) Quincy is seen at 9:00 in room A and Kathy is seen at 11:00.
    (B) Quincy is seen at 8:00 and Peter is seen at 11:00.
    (C) Nestor is seen at 10:00 and Peter is seen at 11:00.
    (D) Luther is seen at 9:00 in room A and Quincy is seen at 8:00.
    (E) Nestor is seen at 10:00 and Luther is seen at 11:00.

6. If Kathy is in room A at 10:00 and room A is empty at 11:00, then which of the following is an accurate list of patients who could be in room B at 9:00?

    (A) Luther, Quincy
    (B) Nestor, Luther
    (C) Nestor, Luther, Peter,
    (D) Nestor, Luther, Peter, Tina
    (E) Quincy, Tina, Luther, Peter, Nestor

7. Which of the following CANNOT be true?

    (A) Kathy is in room A at 9:00 and Peter is in room B at 10:00.
    (B) Kathy is in room B at 10:00 and Tina is in room A at 11:00.
    (C) Luther is in room A at 10:00 and Nestor is in room B at 9:00.
    (D) Kathy is in room A at 8:00 and Quincy is in room A at 10:00.
    (E) Tina is in room A at 9:00 and Mark is in room B at 11:00.

Seven paddlers will ride canoes down a river. Three of the paddlers, A, B, and C, are experienced. Four of the paddlers, Q, R, S, and T, are inexperienced. Each of the paddlers must ride in exactly one of six canoes, numbered 1 through 6. If any of the paddlers rides in a canoe, then at least one experienced paddler or two inexperienced paddlers must ride in that canoe. No more than two paddlers can ride in any one canoe, and the following restrictions apply:

Q must ride in either canoe 1 or canoe 2.

If T rides in the same canoe as an experienced paddler, then no paddler can ride in either canoe 5 or canoe 6.

If S rides in the same canoe as an experienced paddler, then S must ride in the same canoe as B.

A and Q cannot ride in the same canoe.

C must ride in canoe 3.

R must ride in canoe 4.

1. If S rides in canoe 2 and B rides in canoe 6, which of the following is a canoe in which T could ride?

    (A) 1
    (B) 2
    (C) 4
    (D) 5
    (E) 6

2. If no paddler rides in canoe 2 and B rides in canoe 3, then A must ride in

    (A) canoe 1.
    (B) canoe 1 or else canoe 4.
    (C) canoe 2 or else canoe 4.
    (D) canoe 5 or else canoe 6.
    (E) canoe 4 , canoe 5 or canoe 6.

3. If S rides in canoe 6, which of the following must be true?

    (A) A rides in the same canoe as R.
    (B) B rides in canoe 5.
    (C) B rides in the same canoe as S.
    (D) Q rides in the same canoe as an expert.
    (E) T rides in the same canoe as Q.

4. If at least one inexperienced paddler rides in canoe 3, then each of the following must be false EXCEPT:

    (A) A rides in canoe 1 and S rides in canoe 4.
    (B) A rides in canoe 2 and T rides in canoe 1.
    (C) B and S ride in canoe 1.
    (D) B rides in canoe 5 and S rides in canoe 2.
    (E) S rides in canoe 2 and Q rides in canoe 1.

5. If B rides in canoe 4, which of the following CANNOT be true?

    (A) No paddlers ride in canoe 2.
    (B) The three experienced paddlers ride in consecutively numbered canoes.
    (C) A rides in canoe 1.
    (D) S rides in canoe 1.
    (E) Q rides in the same canoe as another inexperienced paddler.

6. If A rides in canoe 6, which of the following is a canoe in which B CANNOT ride?

    (A) 1
    (B) 3
    (C) 4
    (D) 5
    (E) 6

Game 55

Six prisoners, Chainsaw, Fingers, Ice-pick, Jewels, Lefty, and Snake, will all have parole hearings on a certain week between Monday and Saturday. No two inmates can have their hearings on the same day, and the following conditions apply:

Chainsaw's hearing must occur earlier in the week than the day on which Fingers is scheduled.

Ice-pick can only be scheduled for the day immediately before or after the day of Chainsaw's hearing.

Jewels must be scheduled for Tuesday.

Snake's hearing can only be scheduled on Wednesday or Saturday.

1. If Fingers is scheduled for Saturday, which of the following could be true?

   (A) Lefty's hearing falls after Snake's.
   (B) Chainsaw is scheduled for Monday.
   (C) Chainsaw is scheduled for Wednesday
   (D) Chainsaw is scheduled for the day immediately before the day of Snake's hearing.
   (E) Ice-pick is scheduled for Friday.

2. Which one of the following CANNOT be true?

   (A) Chainsaw is scheduled for Friday.
   (B) Fingers is scheduled for Friday.
   (C) Ice-pick is scheduled for Wednesday.
   (D) Ice-pick is scheduled later in the week than Snake.
   (E) Lefty is scheduled for Wednesday.

3. Which one of the following is a complete and accurate list of the days on which Fingers could have his hearing?

   (A) Monday, Tuesday
   (B) Tuesday, Wednesday
   (C) Wednesday, Thursday
   (D) Thursday, Friday
   (E) Friday, Saturday

4. Which one of the following must be true?

   (A) Lefty is scheduled for Monday.
   (B) Snake is scheduled for Wednesday.
   (C) Ice-pick is scheduled for Thursday.
   (D) Fingers is scheduled for Saturday.
   (E) Chainsaw's hearing day is later in the week than Snake's.

5. Which one of the following inmates could be scheduled for Thursday?

   (A) Chainsaw
   (B) Fingers
   (C) Jewels
   (D) Lefty
   (E) Snake

6. Which of the following is a complete and accurate list of the inmates any one of whom could be scheduled for Friday?

   (A) Fingers
   (B) Ice-pick, Chainsaw
   (C) Ice-pick, Chainsaw, Fingers
   (D) Chainsaw, Fingers
   (E) Ice-pick, Chainsaw, Fingers, Lefty

7. If the condition requiring Jewels's hearing to be on Tuesday is changed such that Jewels's hearing must be on Thursday and all other conditions remain the same, then if Snake's hearing is scheduled for Wednesday, how many different schedules for the parole hearings are possible?

   (A) 2
   (B) 3
   (C) 4
   (D) 5
   (E) 6

Game 56

A group of political party activists is being organized to campaign door to door in a small town for their party's presidential candidate. Activists are selected from among A, B, C, D, and F, the party's liberal wing members, and from among a group of the party's moderate activists: Q, R, S, and Z. At least one liberal and at least one moderate must be in the group of campaigners, which may not contain fewer than three or more than six members in total. The selection is made according to the following conditions:

If B campaigns, then R must also campaign.
S is not included if R is included.
If Z is not included, then B must campaign.
Either A or Z campaigns, but they do not campaign together.
R does not campaign unless F campaigns.

1. Which of the following could be a complete and accurate list of the campaigners?

    (A) S, Z, C, D
    (B) F, D, R, B, Q
    (C) R, D, A, F
    (D) C, A, Q, R, Z
    (E) Z, C, R, S, Q

2. If A campaigns, what is the minimum number of people who could make up the list of campaigners?

    (A) two
    (B) three
    (C) four
    (D) five
    (E) six

3. If S is in the group, which liberals could be included in the group that campaigns?

    (A) A, C, D
    (B) Z, C, D, Q
    (C) C, D
    (D) B, C, D
    (E) C, D, F

4. If Z is included and S is not included, which of the following is an accurate list of all those who could campaign, though not necessarily together?

    (A) Z, Q, C, D
    (B) Z, Q, R, C, D
    (C) Z, R, Q, B, C, D, F
    (D) Z, R, Q, C, D, F
    (E) Z, Q, B, C, D, F

5. If S and Z are the only moderates selected, which of the following could be included in the group of campaigners?

    (A) F
    (B) R
    (C) A
    (D) Q
    (E) B

6. If A is included and exactly two moderates are chosen to campaign, which of the following is a pair of activists that could not be included among the campaigners?

    (A) Q, F
    (B) C, D
    (C) R, C
    (D) Q, D
    (E) B, F

7. If Z is the only moderate included in the group of campaigners, what is the largest number of activists that could be included in the group?

    (A) 3
    (B) 4
    (C) 5
    (D) 6
    (E) 7

Game 57

During a five-hour shift, a personal trainer will work with exactly seven clients: H, J, K, L, M, N, and P. Each client works with the trainer for exactly one of the five hours, and the trainer works with no more than two clients in any hour.

K trains in an hour sometime after P and sometime before H.

P trains in an hour sometime before N and sometime after L.

Both M and P are the only clients trained in the hours in which they are trained.

J trains sometime earlier than N.

1. Which of the following could be a complete and accurate list of people trained in order from the earliest hour to the latest?

	1	2	3	4	5
(A)	J	M	P	K, L	H, N
(B)	M	L, J	K	P	H, N
(C)	L	J	P	M, K	H, N
(D)	L	P	M	H, J	K, N
(E)	M	L, J	P	K, N	H

2. If L is the only person trained in a particular hour, which of the following must be true?

   (A) M is trained in the fourth hour.
   (B) J is trained together with H.
   (C) P is trained in the second hour.
   (D) H is trained together with N.
   (E) L is trained in the second hour.

3. If H trains alone, how many different people could be trained in the first hour?

   (A) 1
   (B) 2
   (C) 3
   (D) 4
   (E) 5

4. Which of the following must be false?

   (A) N trains in the same hour as H.
   (B) J trains in the same hour as K.
   (C) K trains alone.
   (D) H trains in the same hour as J.
   (E) M trains in the fourth hour.

5. If the first and last hours are the only hours in which two people train, which of the following must be true?

   (A) P trains in the second hour.
   (B) K trains alone.
   (C) M trains in the second hour.
   (D) J trains in the fifth hour.
   (E) K trains in the third hour.

6. If only one client trains in the third hour, how many different clients could be that one person?

   (A) 2
   (B) 3
   (C) 4
   (D) 5
   (E) 6

7. If P is the fourth client trained, which of the following could be true?

   (A) J trains with K.
   (B) N trains with K.
   (C) M trains in the fourth hour.
   (D) K trains in the third hour.
   (E) L trains alone.

The Oakview Nuclear Power Plant has three nuclear safety technicians, Carl, Harry, and Lewis. The work week runs from Monday to Saturday, and there must be at least one of the three technicians working at the plant during each of these days. In addition, there must be meltdowns on exactly two days each week. The following conditions also apply:

No technician can work three days in a row.

The three technicians must each have at least two consecutive days off during the same week.

No two technicians can work together on the same day more than two times during the week.

The meltdowns can only occur on days when Harry is the only technician on duty.

Harry works at least three days each week.

1. Which of the following could be a complete and accurate work schedule for the three technicians on a given week?

    (A) Monday: Lewis; Tuesday: Harry, Lewis; Wednesday: Harry, Carl; Thursday: Lewis; Friday: Carl; Saturday: Harry

    (B) Monday: Carl, Lewis; Tuesday: Harry, Carl, Lewis; Wednesday: Harry; Thursday: Lewis; Friday: Carl; Saturday: Harry

    (C) Monday: Harry; Tuesday: Carl, Lewis; Wednesday: Lewis; Thursday: Harry, Lewis; Friday: Harry; Saturday: Carl

    (D) Monday: Carl, Lewis; Tuesday: Harry; Wednesday: Carl; Thursday: Harry; Fri: Carl, Lewis; Saturday: Harry

    (E) Monday: Harry; Tuesday: Carl, Lewis; Wednesday: Carl, Lewis; Thursday: Lewis; Friday: Harry; Saturday: Carl, Harry, Lewis

2. If on a certain week Carl works on every day that Lewis works and Lewis does not work on any day on which Carl does not work, each of following statements about that week must be false EXCEPT:

    (A) Carl works on Tuesday.
    (B) Harry works on Wednesday.
    (C) Harry works on exactly three days that week.
    (D) A meltdown occurs on Thursday.
    (E) Meltdowns occur on Monday and Tuesday.

3. If on a certain week Carl does not work any days and meltdowns occur on Tuesday and Thursday, each of the following must true about that week EXCEPT:

    (A) Harry works on Monday.
    (B) Lewis works on Wednesday.
    (C) Lewis does not work on Monday.
    (D) Harry works more days than Lewis.
    (E) A meltdown does not occur on Saturday.

4. If Harry and Lewis work together on Tuesday and Friday, a meltdown must occur on

    (A) Monday.
    (B) Tuesday.
    (C) Wednesday.
    (D) Thursday.
    (E) Friday.

5. If Carl works on Tuesday and Thursday, Lewis works on Saturday, and Harry works on Thursday, then Harry must also work on which of the following days?

    (A) Monday
    (B) Tuesday
    (C) Wednesday
    (D) Friday
    (E) Saturday

Game 59

The radio in Carlos's car has eight buttons numbered consecutively from 1 to 8, each of which will be programmed to play exactly one of the three types of radio stations: rock, oldies, and alternative, and each type is assigned to no more than three buttons. The following conditions apply:

Each of buttons 3, 4, and 5 is assigned to a type of music different from the other two.
Buttons 6 and 5 are not assigned to the same type of music.
Neither 1 nor 7 is alternative, but both are the same type of music.
If 6 is not rock, then 2 is alternative.

1. Which of the following could be a complete and accurate list of the way stations are programmed?

(A) rock: 1, 7, 3; alternative: 6, 4, 8; oldies: 5, 2
(B) rock: 7, 3, 6; alternative: 5, 8; oldies: 1, 4, 2
(C) rock: 3, 6, 8; alternative: 5, 2; oldies: 4, 7, 1
(D) rock: 8, 1, 7; alternative: 4, 6, 2; oldies: 3, 5
(E) rock: 5, 2, 6; alternative: 4, 8; oldies: 1, 7, 3

2. Which is a pair of buttons that CANNOT play the same type of music?

(A) 2, 5
(B) 1, 6
(C) 3, 7
(D) 4, 8
(E) 2, 8

3. If button 2 plays a rock station, which of the following must be true?

(A) Button 5 plays alternative.
(B) Button 4 plays rock.
(C) Button 3 plays oldies.
(D) Button 8 plays rock.
(E) Button 7 plays oldies.

4. If buttons 5 and 8 play rock, which of the following must be false?

(A) Buttons 1 and 4 play oldies.
(B) Buttons 6 and 3 play alternative.
(C) Buttons 2 and 4 play alternative.
(D) Exactly three buttons play rock.
(E) Exactly three buttons play oldies.

5. If buttons 6 and 8 are programmed to play the same type of music, which of the following must be true?

(A) Button 2 is programmed to play alternative.
(B) Button 7 is programmed to play rock.
(C) Button 5 is programmed to play alternative.
(D) Button 3 is programmed to play rock.
(E) Button 8 is programmed to play rock.

6. Which of the following is a pair of buttons that CANNOT both play oldies?

(A) 8, 4
(B) 1, 5
(C) 5, 2
(D) 1, 4
(E) 4, 6

7. If button 6 plays alternative and button 5 plays the same kind of music as button 8, how many different combinations of buttons and stations are possible?

(A) 2
(B) 3
(C) 4
(D) 5
(E) 6

Nine campers will participate in the Camp Quotient relay races. Three of the campers are girls: Olsa, Percy, and Quinn. The other six campers are boys: Rupert, Silas, Tariq, Ulysses, Vernon, and Walt. The campers will be divided into three teams: the Koalas, the Lemurs, and the Marmots. Three campers must be assigned to each team, and each of the campers must be assigned to only one team. One girl must be assigned to each team, and the following conditions also apply:

If Olsa is assigned to the Lemurs, then Quinn is assigned to the Marmots.

Olsa and Silas must be assigned to the same team.

Rupert and Tariq must be assigned to the same team.

Vernon and Quinn cannot be assigned to the same team.

Vernon and Walt cannot be assigned to the same team.

Ulysses is assigned to the Marmots.

1. Which of the following could be the three campers assigned to the Lemurs?

   (A) Olsa, Percy, Silas
   (B) Olsa, Quinn, Silas
   (C) Percy, Vernon, Walt
   (D) Quinn, Rupert, Tariq
   (E) Rupert, Tariq, Vernon

2. If Quinn and Walt are assigned to the same team, which of the following is a camper who must also be assigned to that team?

   (A) Percy
   (B) Silas
   (C) Tariq
   (D) Ulysses
   (E) Vernon

3. If Vernon is assigned to the Koalas, then each of the following must be true EXCEPT:

   (A) Olsa is assigned to the Koalas.
   (B) Percy is assigned to the Lemurs.
   (C) Silas is assigned to the Koalas.
   (D) Tariq is assigned to the Lemurs.
   (E) Walt is assigned to the Marmots.

4. If Vernon is assigned to the Marmots, which of the following must be the three campers assigned to the Koalas?

   (A) Olsa, Silas, Walt
   (B) Percy, Olsa, Silas
   (C) Percy, Rupert, Tariq
   (D) Quinn, Rupert, Tariq
   (E) Quinn, Tariq, Walt

5. If Walt is assigned to the Koalas, which of the following must be true?

   (A) Olsa is assigned to the Marmots.
   (B) Percy is assigned to the Koalas.
   (C) Quinn is assigned to the Lemurs.
   (D) Percy is assigned to the Lemurs.
   (E) Vernon is assigned to the Koalas.

6. Which of the following is a camper who CANNOT be assigned to the Lemurs?

   (A) Percy
   (B) Walt
   (C) Quinn
   (D) Olsa
   (E) Rupert

A chemical research company is currently assigning researchers to three new research projects: project Ralph, project Spam, and project Toad. The researchers, A, B, C, D, and E, are assigned to the projects either as assistants or as managers. No researcher can be assigned to a project as both a manager and an assistant. Exactly one manager and at least one assistant must be assigned to each project. No researcher can be assigned to all three projects and no researcher can be assigned as a manager to more than one project. The following conditions also apply:

The most experienced researcher assigned to a project will be that project's manager.
A is the most experienced researcher.
B is the second most experienced researcher.
C is the third most experienced researcher.
D is the fourth most experienced researcher.
E is the least experienced researcher.
At least two assistants must be assigned to project Ralph.
If B is assigned to a project, then E is also assigned to that project.
C is assigned as a manager to one of the projects.
D is assigned to project Toad.

1. Which of the following could be a complete and accurate list of the researchers assigned to projects Ralph, Spam, and Toad?

   (A) Ralph: A, B, E; Spam: C, B, E; Toad: D, E
   (B) Ralph: B, D, E; Spam: A, C, D; Toad: B, D, E
   (C) Ralph: C, D, E; Spam: A, B, E; Toad: A, D
   (D) Ralph: A, C, D; Spam: B, E; Toad: C, D, E
   (E) Ralph: A, B, E; Spam: C, B, D; Toad: D, E

2. If B is assigned as manager to project Ralph and D is assigned as manager to project Toad, which of the following must be assigned to project Spam as an assistant?

   (A) A
   (B) B
   (C) C
   (D) D
   (E) E

3. If B is not assigned to any of the projects and D is assigned as an assistant to project Spam, which of the following must be false?

   (A) A is assigned to only one project.
   (B) C is assigned to project R and project S.
   (C) C and E are assigned to project T.
   (D) E is not assigned to project S.
   (E) E is assigned to project R.

4. If B is one of exactly two researchers who are assigned to two of the projects, which of the following must be true?

   (A) A is not assigned to project Ralph.
   (B) B is assigned manager to project Toad.
   (C) C is not assigned to project Ralph.
   (D) E is not assigned to project Toad.
   (E) C is assigned to project Spam.

5. If E is assigned to project Spam and no other projects, each of the following must be false EXCEPT:

   (A) A is assigned to project Spam.
   (B) B is not assigned to a project.
   (C) C is assigned to project Toad.
   (D) D is assigned to project Spam.
   (E) D is assigned as manager to project Toad.

6. Suppose that C is assigned to project Spam and no other projects. If B is the manager for project Ralph, which of the following must be true?

   (A) A is assigned to project Toad.
   (B) B is assigned to two projects.
   (C) D is assigned to project Spam.
   (D) E is assigned to project Toad.
   (E) E is assigned to all three projects.

7. If C and D are the two assistants assigned to project Ralph, which of the following must be false?

   (A) A and D are assigned to project Ralph.
   (B) B and C are assigned to project Spam.
   (C) B and E are assigned to project Toad.
   (D) C and D are assigned to project Toad.
   (E) C and E are assigned to project Spam.

Game 62

Seven people, J, K, L, N, O, P, and Q, are going on a river-rafting trip. Each of the people must ride in exactly one of four boats: the blue boat, the green boat, the red boat, or the yellow boat. Only two people can ride in the blue boat, only three people can ride in the green boat, only four people can ride in the red boat, and only one person can ride in the yellow boat. A boat is used if one or more people ride in it and not used otherwise. The following restrictions apply:

If N and O ride in the same boat, no one else rides in that boat.
If N rides in the red boat, then K must ride in the red boat.
If P rides in the blue boat, then K must ride in the green boat.
O cannot ride in the same boat with L or with P.
L cannot ride in the same boat as P.
Q rides in the blue boat.

1. Which of the following could be a complete and accurate list of the people that ride in the red and yellow boats?

    (A) red: J, K; yellow: N
    (B) red: J, L, N; yellow: K
    (C) red: K, N, O; yellow: P
    (D) red: L, P; yellow: empty
    (E) red: N, P, K; yellow: empty

2. If the yellow boat is not used, which of the following must be false?

    (A) K rides in the blue boat.
    (B) N rides in the red boat.
    (C) P rides in the blue boat.
    (D) J and L ride in the same boat.
    (E) N and O ride in the green boat.

3. If K rides in the blue boat, which of the following must be false?

    (A) L is the only person who rides in the red boat.
    (B) N rides in the yellow boat.
    (C) J rides in the red boat with L.
    (D) J and N ride in the same boat.
    (E) N and O ride in the same boat.

4. If O rides in the green boat and K rides in the yellow boat, J could ride

    (A) in the blue boat with Q.
    (B) in the green boat with N.
    (C) in the green boat with L.
    (D) in the red boat with L.
    (E) in the red boat with P.

5. If L rides in the green boat and N rides in the red boat, which of the following CANNOT be true?

    (A) J does not ride in the green boat.
    (B) Both J and P ride in the red boat.
    (C) O and Q ride in the same boat and J rides in the red boat.
    (D) Q is the only person that rides in the blue boat and P rides in the red boat.
    (E) The yellow boat is not used and J rides in the blue boat.

6. If N and O ride in the same boat and J rides in the yellow boat, then which of the following must be true?

    (A) K rides in the green boat.
    (B) L rides in the blue boat.
    (C) L rides in the red boat.
    (D) N rides in the red boat.
    (E) P rides in the green boat.

7. If four people ride in the red boat, which of the following must ride on the red boat?

    (A) P
    (B) L
    (C) O
    (D) N
    (E) Q

Game 63

Four salespersons, D, E, F, and G, and five technicians, M, N, O, P, and Q, form three teams of three people each to make presentations to potential clients. Each team includes a salesperson. Four pieces of equipment—two multimedia computers and two VCR's—are used by the teams, with each piece of equipment being used by exactly one team, each team using at least one piece of equipment, and no team using two of the same type of equipment. The following conditions govern the teams:

P and N must be on different teams.
If D is on a team with a VCR, then F is not on a team with a VCR.
If G can use a VCR, then P cannot use a multimedia computer.
M and Q work together on a team with only one type of equipment.

1. Which of the following could be a complete and accurate list of the three teams?

   (A) MQE, NGP, DFO
   (B) EMQ, DFPO, GN
   (C) DFP, MQO, NGE
   (D) GPO, NMO, FEQ
   (E) GDP, ENO, MQF

2. If M is on a team that can use a VCR, which of the following must be on a team without a VCR?

   (A) F
   (B) G
   (C) D
   (D) P
   (E) N

3. If F and G are together on a team that has a VCR, which of the following must be true?

   (A) D is on a team with O.
   (B) Q is on a team with E.
   (C) G is on a team with P.
   (D) O is on a team with E.
   (E) F is on a team with N.

4. If G does not have access to a VCR, which of the following could be a team with access to both kinds of equipment?

   (A) P, F, O
   (B) D, N, F
   (C) E, N, D
   (D) E, O, D
   (E) F, O, E

5. If P is on a team with a multimedia computer only, which of the following must be false?

   (A) M is on a team with a VCR only.
   (B) F is on a team with a VCR only.
   (C) D is on a team with both kinds of equipment.
   (D) N is on a team with a VCR only.
   (E) O is on a team with both kinds of equipment.

6. If O is on a team with D, which of the following is a pair that could be together on a team?

   (A) F, O
   (B) G, M
   (C) F, P
   (D) G, Q
   (E) O, E

7. If N, F, and O are on the same team, which of the following must be true?

   (A) M is on a team with E.
   (B) G is on a team with E.
   (C) G is on a team with P.
   (D) Q is on a team with D.
   (E) G is on a team with D.

Game 64

Six customers are at a delicatessen at lunchtime ordering sandwiches. The deli serves the following types of sandwiches: roast beef, pastrami, chicken salad, ham, tuna, and veggie. No two customers place their orders at exactly the same time. The following is known about the orders:

Each customer orders a different type of sandwich.

The customer who orders ham orders sometime before the customer who orders chicken salad and sometime after the customer who orders tuna.

The customer who orders pastrami orders sometime before the customer who orders chicken salad and does not order first.

The customer who orders veggie orders sometime after the customer who orders ham, but does not order last.

Exactly one of the customers, but not the one who orders first or the one who orders last, orders exactly two sandwiches of the same type.

1. Which one of the following could be a complete and accurate list in order from first to last of the sandwiches ordered?

   (A) pastrami, roast beef, tuna, ham, veggie, chicken salad
   (B) roast beef, pastrami, tuna, ham, chicken salad, veggie
   (C) tuna, pastrami, ham, roast beef, veggie, chicken salad
   (D) roast beef, tuna, pastrami, ham, chicken salad, veggie
   (E) ham, pastrami, tuna, roast beef, veggie, chicken salad

2. Which order could be the latest position in which pastrami is ordered?

   (A) second
   (B) third
   (C) fourth
   (D) fifth
   (E) sixth

3. If chicken salad is ordered sometime before veggie, which could be an accurate list, in order, of the first three orders?

   (A) tuna, ham, chicken salad
   (B) tuna, pastrami, ham
   (C) roast beef, tuna, pastrami
   (D) roast beef, tuna, ham
   (E) tuna, roast beef, ham

4. If ham is ordered as late as possible and tuna is not ordered first, which of the following is a pair neither of which could be the one with two sandwiches ordered?

   (A) pastrami, chicken salad
   (B) tuna, roast beef
   (C) roast beef, ham
   (D) chicken salad, roast beef
   (E) pastrami, ham

5. Which of the following gives sufficient information to determine the exact order in which the sandwiches are ordered?

   (A) Tuna is ordered second and pastrami is ordered sometime before veggie.
   (B) Roast beef is ordered first and two ham sandwiches are ordered.
   (C) Tuna is ordered first and two pastrami sandwiches are ordered.
   (D) Pastrami is ordered sometime after veggie and two tuna sandwiches are ordered.
   (E) Ham is ordered immediately after tuna and two chicken salad sandwiches are ordered.

6. If two chicken salad sandwiches are ordered, which of the following must be false?

   (A) Tuna is ordered first.
   (B) Ham is ordered third.
   (C) Pastrami is ordered second.
   (D) Ham is ordered fourth.
   (E) Chicken salad is ordered fourth.

Game 65

Each of the satellite television channels that Luis watches on Saturday is one of four sports channels, five movie channels, three music video channels, or one game show channel. He watches shows on Saturday on at least six and at most eight channels according to these stipulations:

The total number of the sports and music video channels Luis watches is either three or four.

If and only if Luis watches the game show channel, does he watch more sports channels than movie channels.

If Luis watches three or more movie channels, he does not watch two or more music video channels.

1. Which of the following must be true about the channels Luis watches?

   (A) They include the game show channel.
   (B) They do not include the game show channel.
   (C) They include at least one movie channel.
   (D) They include at least one sports channel.
   (E) They include at least one music video channel.

2. If Luis watches at least two music video channels, which of the following must be false?

   (A) He watches exactly one movie channel.
   (B) He watches exactly six different channels.
   (C) He watches exactly seven different channels.
   (D) He watches the game show channel.
   (E) He watches exactly two movie channels.

3. If Luis watches the game show channel, then he can also watch at most

   (A) three sports channels.
   (B) two movie channels.
   (C) two sports channels.
   (D) one music video channel.
   (E) two music video channels.

4. If Luis watches exactly three sports channels, which of the following could be a complete and accurate list of the remaining channels that he watches?

   (A) two music video channels and three movie channels
   (B) one music video channel and one movie channel
   (C) one music video channel, one game show channel, and two movie channels
   (D) one music video channel, four movie channels, and one game show channel
   (E) three movie channels and one game show channel

5. If Luis watches exactly eight channels, which of the following CANNOT be true?

   (A) He watches exactly two movie channels.
   (B) He watches exactly three sports channels
   (C) He watches exactly two sports channels.
   (D) He watches the game show channel.
   (E) He does not watch the game show channel.

6. If Luis watches exactly two music video channels, which of the following must be true?

   (A) He watches the game show channel.
   (B) He watches exactly two sports channels.
   (C) He watches exactly one movie channel.
   (D) He watches exactly four movie channels.
   (E) He does not watch the game show channel.

7. If Luis watches exactly seven channels, exactly three of which are movie channels, then he must also watch

   (A) exactly one sports channel.
   (B) exactly one music video channel.
   (C) the game show channel.
   (D) exactly two sports channels.
   (E) exactly four sports channels.

Game 66

A student is choosing one of five schools, T, S, A, O, W, to continue his education. He will give each school a ranking of 1 to 5 with 1 being the highest and 5 being the lowest on each of three criteria: cost, location, and quality. No schools are given the same rank on any of the criteria and no school receives the same rank on any two criteria. The following conditions apply:

A is ranked 3 in location and 4 in cost.
S receives exactly two higher ranks than T.
T receives exactly 2 higher rankings than A.
W is ranked 1 in Quality.
O is ranked below W in all three criteria.

1. Which of the following is a pair that can have no number 1 rankings?

    (A)   T, O
    (B)   S, O
    (C)   S, A
    (D)   O, A
    (E)   S, T

2. If T is ranked 1 in location, which of the following CANNOT be ranked 5 in any category?

    (A)   T
    (B)   S
    (C)   A
    (D)   O
    (E)   W

3. Which of the following must be false?

    (A)   W ranks 2 in cost.
    (B)   W ranks 2 in location.
    (C)   O ranks 5 in quality.
    (D)   A ranks 5 in quality.
    (E)   A ranks 2 in quality.

4. If W is ranked 4 in location, which of the following must be true?

    (A)   O is ranked 5 in quality.
    (B)   S is ranked 3 in cost.
    (C)   O is ranked 3 in cost.
    (D)   T is ranked 2 in quality.
    (E)   T is ranked 3 in cost.

5. If S is ranked 2 in location, which of the following must be ranked 2 in quality?

    (A)   T
    (B)   S
    (C)   A
    (D)   O
    (E)   W

6. If W is ranked 3 in cost, which of the following could be true?

    (A)   S is ranked 5 in location.
    (B)   O is ranked 4 in quality.
    (C)   W is ranked 4 in location.
    (D)   T is ranked 3 in cost.
    (E)   A is ranked 4 in quality.

7. If O is ranked 2 in quality and W is ranked 2 in cost, the sum of the three rankings is lowest for which of the following?

    (A)   T
    (B)   S
    (C)   A
    (D)   O
    (E)   W

Game 67

Seven friends, Cat, Diana, Eddie, Frank, Giselle, Horatio, and Jaime, go to the movies. Each sees exactly one of *Righteous*, *Terrified*, *Ambitious*, or *Baffling*, and each sees the movie at a matinee showing, an evening showing, or a late night showing. The following conditions apply:

Each of movies is seen by at least one of the friends.
Terrified has no matinee showing.
Baffling is available as a matinee or as a late night showing.
Ambitious is available at all three times.
Righteous is available only in the evening.
Cat and Jaime go to the same movie.
If Cat goes in the evening, then Frank goes to *Ambitious*.
Giselle and Horatio go to the same movie.
Diana sees *Ambitious*
Eddie and Frank go to different movies.

1. Which of the following could be a complete and accurate list of the friends who see *Baffling*?

    (A) Giselle, Horatio, Diana
    (B) Cat, Jaime, Horatio
    (C) Eddie, Cat, Jaime, Frank
    (D) Giselle, Jaime, Horatio, Cat
    (E) Horatio, Jaime, Giselle

2. If Cat goes to see *Righteous*, what is the largest number of friends who could attend matinee showings?

    (A) three
    (B) four
    (C) five
    (D) six
    (E) seven

3. If Horatio and Jaime attend evening showings, which is a friend who could see *Baffling*?

    (A) Frank
    (B) Cat
    (C) Giselle
    (D) Diana
    (E) Jaime

4. If exactly three friends see *Baffling*, which of the following could be a group of friends for each of whom going to a matinee would be impossible?

    (A) Eddie, Giselle, Frank
    (B) Giselle, Cat, Eddie
    (C) Jaime, Frank, Cat
    (D) Diana, Eddie, Horatio
    (E) Jaime, Horatio, Frank

5. Which of the following must be false?

    (A) Diana is the only friend to see *Ambitious*.
    (B) Exactly three friends see *Baffling*.
    (C) None of the friends attends a matinee.
    (D) Eddie is one of three friends to see *Terrified*.
    (E) Jaime is one of three friends to see *Righteous*.

6. If exactly six friends attend late night showings, which of the following is sufficient to be able to determine which movie each sees?

    (A) Eddie sees *Righteous* and Frank sees *Ambitious*.
    (B) Cat sees *Terrified* and Horatio goes to a movie that has a matinee available.
    (C) Frank accompanies Diana, and Horatio goes to a movie that has a matinee available.
    (D) Eddie sees *Ambitious* and Frank goes to an evening show.
    (E) Cat goes to *Baffling* and Giselle does not see *Righteous*.

Seven runners, L, M, N, O, P, Q, and R, will run in a marathon. No other runners participate. The following restrictions govern the order in which they finish:

O must finish sometime after L and sometime before R.

P must finish sometime after L and sometime after M.

N must finish sometime after R.

O cannot finish either immediately before or immediately after P.

Q must finish after exactly two other runners.

1. Which of the following is a complete and accurate list of the runners finishing from first to seventh?

    (A)   L, O, Q, N, M, R, P
    (B)   M, L, Q, O, R, P, N
    (C)   L, M, Q, O, P, R, N
    (D)   M, O, Q, R, P, N, L
    (E)   O, L, Q, R, N, M, P

2. Which of the following CANNOT be the fifth runner to finish the race?

    (A)   M
    (B)   N
    (C)   O
    (D)   R
    (E)   P

3. If R finishes sixth, then the runner that finishes fourth could be

    (A)   L.
    (B)   M.
    (C)   O.
    (D)   P.
    (E)   Q.

4. The earliest that P could finish the race is

    (A)   first.
    (B)   second.
    (C)   fourth.
    (D)   fifth.
    (E)   sixth.

5. If O finishes the race after Q, then which of the following must be true?

    (A)   M is the first runner to finish the race.
    (B)   N is the last runner to finish the race.
    (C)   N and R finish the race consecutively.
    (D)   O is the fourth runner to finish the race.
    (E)   P finishes the race immediately after R.

6. Which of the following must be false?

    (A)   M is the first runner to finish the race.
    (B)   N is the sixth runner to finish the race.
    (C)   O is the second runner to finish the race.
    (D)   P is the fourth runner to finish the race.
    (E)   R is the fourth runner to finish the race.

7. How many different positions could M finish the race?

    (A)   2
    (B)   3
    (C)   4
    (D)   5
    (E)   6

8. Suppose the rule that Q must finish after exactly two other runners is altered so that Q must finish after exactly four other runners. If O finishes third, which of the following must be true?

    (A)   L finishes sometime before M.
    (B)   M finishes immediately after O.
    (C)   N finishes last.
    (D)   P finishes sometime before N.
    (E)   R finishes immediately before Q.

Game 69

Each of five shirts—blue, red, green, plaid, white—and each of four pairs of pants—jeans, dress, casual, and shorts—must be packed in one of two overnight bags, with bag 1 having more articles than bag 2. Each article must be packed in exactly one bag and there are no other items in the bags. Each bag must have at least one shirt and at least two pairs of pants.

The dress pants and shorts cannot be in the same bag.

If the blue shirt is in a bag, then the white shirt is in the same bag.

Shorts cannot be included in the same bag if the white shirt is included.

The green shirt cannot go with jeans.

1. Which of the following could be a complete and accurate list of the contents of bag 1?

    (A) dress pants, blue shirt, white shirt, shorts, plaid shirt, casual pants
    (B) casual pants, shorts, red shirt, green shirt
    (C) green shirt, red shirt, plaid shirt, jeans, casual pants
    (D) green shirt, shorts, casual pants, red shirt, plaid shirt
    (E) dress pants, casual pants, blue shirt, plaid shirt, jeans, white shirt

2. If the blue shirt is in bag 2, which of the following must be true?

    (A) There are exactly five items in bag 1.
    (B) There are exactly six items in bag 1.
    (C) The plaid shirt is in bag 2.
    (D) There are three shirts in bag 2.
    (E) The shorts are in bag 2.

3. If the green shirt is in bag 2, which of the following must be false?

    (A) The blue shirt is in bag 2.
    (B) The plaid shirt is in bag 2.
    (C) The shorts are in bag 1.
    (D) The casual pants are in bag 1.
    (E) The jeans are in bag 1.

4. If the shorts are in bag 1, which of the following must be true?

    (A) The jeans are in bag 1.
    (B) There are exactly six items in bag 1.
    (C) The plaid shirt is in bag 1.
    (D) The green shirt is in bag 2.
    (E) The red shirt is in bag 2.

5. Which of the following could be a complete and accurate list of the contents of bag 2?

    (A) dress pants, casual pants, plaid shirt
    (B) white shirt, jeans, shorts, plaid shirt
    (C) shorts, jeans, plaid shirt, red shirt
    (D) shorts, jeans, casual pants
    (E) shorts, casual pants, plaid shirt, jeans

6. Which of the following could be false?

    (A) If the blue shirt is in bag 1, the shorts are in bag 2.
    (B) If the jeans are in bag 1, the casual pants are in bag 2.
    (C) If the shorts are in bag 1, the white shirt is in bag 2.
    (D) If the plaid shirt is in bag 2, the dress pants are in bag 1.
    (E) If the plaid shirt is in bag 2, the shorts are in bag 1.

7. If there are exactly six items in bag 1, how many possible combinations of items could there be in bag 2?

    (A) 2
    (B) 3
    (C) 4
    (D) 5
    (E) 6

8. Which of the following is a pair of items that could not be included together in bag 2?

    (A) the plaid and white shirts
    (B) the shorts and plaid shirt
    (C) the green shirt and casual pants
    (D) the red shirt and shorts
    (E) the jeans and dress pants

A casting director is holding auditions over a two-day period, Thursday and Friday. Exactly six actors, Larimore, Macdonald, Perry, Rappaport, Stephens, and Walker, will audition on Thursday. Of these six exactly three will have a second audition on Friday. No other auditions are held and the following restrictions apply:

Larimore's Thursday audition must fall immediately before Macdonald's.

If Perry and Stephens have non-consecutive auditions on Thursday then both actors audition on Friday.

The actor that auditions last on Thursday must be the first to audition on Friday.

The actor that auditions second on Thursday must be the third to audition on Friday.

Larimore must audition on Friday.

Walker must be the fourth actor to audition on Thursday.

1. Which of the following could be a list of the three actors to audition on Friday in the order in which they audition?

   (A) first: Macdonald; second: Larimore; third: Perry

   (B) first: Macdonald; second: Stephens; third: Rappaport

   (C) first: Rappaport; second: Larimore; third: Macdonald

   (D) first: Stephens; second: Larimore, third: Perry

   (E) first: Larimore; second: Walker; third: Stephens

2. If Rappaport's audition occurs sometime after Walker's, then each of the following could be true EXCEPT:

   (A) Larimore is the third actor to audition on Friday.

   (B) Macdonald does not audition on Friday.

   (C) Perry is the second actor to audition on Friday.

   (D) Rappaport is the first actor to audition on Friday.

   (E) Stephens auditions on Friday.

3. If Perry is the third actor to audition on Thursday, then the first and third actors to audition on Friday could be, respectively,

   (A) Larimore and Macdonald.

   (B) Larimore and Rappaport.

   (C) Macdonald and Stephens.

   (D) Rappaport and Macdonald.

   (E) Stephens and Walker.

4. If Walker auditions on Friday, then which of the following could be true?

   (A) Larimore's audition on Thursday falls sometime after Walker's.

   (B) Perry's audition on Thursday falls sometime after Macdonald's.

   (C) Rappaport's audition on Thursday falls sometime after Larimore's.

   (D) Rappaport's audition on Thursday falls sometime after Stephens's.

   (E) Walker's audition on Friday falls sometime after Larimore's.

5. If Stephens is the second actor to audition on Friday, then the fifth actor to audition on Thursday could be

   (A) Larimore.

   (B) Macdonald.

   (C) Perry.

   (D) Stephens.

   (E) Walker.

6. If Perry's and Stephens's auditions on Thursday are not consecutive, then Rappaport's Thursday audition must be the

   (A) first.

   (B) second.

   (C) third.

   (D) fifth.

   (E) sixth.

Game 71

On each of seven consecutive days, Sunday through Saturday, Bianca will eat exactly one kind of soup for lunch. The only soups available are chicken, tomato, vegetable, lentil, bean, and mushroom. Bianca eats each soup at least once and does not eat the same soup on consecutive days.

Bean soup must be eaten on the day immediately before or immediately after any day on which chicken soup is eaten.

Lentil soup and mushroom soup cannot be eaten on consecutive days.

Mushroom soup cannot be eaten on Monday.
Vegetable soup is eaten on Thursday.

1. Which could be a complete and accurate list of the soups eaten in order from Sunday through Saturday?

    (A) tomato, chicken, lentil, bean, vegetable, mushroom, vegetable
    (B) vegetable, lentil, tomato, mushroom, vegetable, bean, chicken
    (C) mushroom, tomato, lentil, vegetable, chicken, bean, tomato
    (D) chicken, bean, tomato, mushroom, vegetable, tomato, bean
    (E) tomato, mushroom, lentil, tomato, vegetable, chicken, bean

2. Which of the following is not a pair of days on both of which mushroom soup could be eaten?

    (A) Sunday, Friday
    (B) Wednesday, Sunday
    (C) Friday, Wednesday
    (D) Sunday, Saturday
    (E) Tuesday, Friday

3. If Bianca has tomato soup on Monday and lentil soup on Wednesday, it CANNOT be true that she has

    (A) bean soup on Tuesday.
    (B) chicken soup on Friday.
    (C) bean soup on Friday.
    (D) vegetable soup on Sunday.
    (E) vegetable soup on Tuesday.

4. If Bianca eats chicken soup twice during the week, which of the following is a complete and accurate list of the days on which she could eat tomato soup?

    (A) Friday, Saturday
    (B) Sunday, Saturday
    (C) Sunday, Friday, Saturday
    (D) Wednesday, Friday, Saturday
    (E) Sunday, Wednesday, Friday, Saturday

5. If Bianca eats chicken soup on Saturday, which of the following could be a complete and accurate list of the soups any one of which she could eat twice during the week?

    (A) tomato, vegetable
    (B) tomato, vegetable, bean
    (C) bean, lentil, vegetable
    (D) tomato, mushroom, lentil
    (E) tomato, vegetable, mushroom, lentil

6. If Bianca eats chicken soup on Sunday, which of the following could be a complete and accurate list of the soups she eats on Friday and Saturday respectively?

    (A) chicken, bean
    (B) bean, lentil
    (C) tomato, vegetable
    (D) vegetable, mushroom
    (E) mushroom, lentil

7. If mushroom soup is eaten twice during the week, how many different soups could be eaten on Tuesday?

    (A) 1
    (B) 2
    (C) 3
    (D) 4
    (E) 5

A cook is making two dishes, dish X and dish Y. Each of the dishes must include exactly four dashes of seasoning. Only five seasonings can be used in the dishes: basil, ginger, oregano, paprika, and tarragon. Only two dashes of basil, two dashes of ginger, three dashes of oregano, three dashes of paprika, and one dash of tarragon are available for use in the two dishes. No other seasonings can be used and each dash can be used in only one dish. The following rules govern the use of the seasonings:

If the cook uses a dash of basil in a given dish, then both dashes of basil must be used in that dish.

If the cook uses any ginger in a dish, then the cook cannot use any oregano in that dish.

At least three different seasonings are used in dish X.

If the cook uses any paprika in dish X, then he must use one dash of tarragon in dish Y.

1. Which of the following could be used in dish X?

   (A) two dashes basil, one dash ginger, one dash tarragon
   (B) two dashes basil, one dash ginger, one dash oregano
   (C) one dash basil, one dash oregano, two dashes paprika
   (D) two dashes oregano, two dashes paprika
   (E) one dash oregano, two dashes paprika, one dash tarragon

2. If the cook uses at least one dash of oregano and one dash of tarragon in dish X, which of the following must he use in dish Y?

   (A) exactly two dashes of basil
   (B) at least two dashes of ginger
   (C) exactly two dashes of oregano
   (D) at least two dashes of paprika
   (E) exactly one dash of tarragon

3. The cook could use two dashes of which of the following seasonings in dish X?

   (A) basil
   (B) ginger
   (C) oregano
   (D) paprika
   (E) tarragon

4. If the cook uses two dashes of paprika and two dashes of oregano in dish Y, which of the following must be used in dish X?

   (A) exactly one dash of basil
   (B) exactly two dashes of ginger
   (C) exactly one dash of oregano
   (D) exactly one dash of paprika
   (E) exactly one dash of tarragon

5. Which of the following must be false?

   (A) No ginger is used in the dishes.
   (B) All three dashes of oregano are used in the dishes.
   (C) No tarragon is used in the dishes.
   (D) Three dashes of oregano are used in dish Y.
   (E) No paprika is used in dish Y.

6. If no dashes of oregano are used in the dishes, which of the following could be used in dish Y?

   (A) two dashes of basil, one dash of ginger, and one dash of tarragon
   (B) two dashes of basil and two dashes of paprika
   (C) one dash of ginger, two dashes of paprika, and one dash of tarragon
   (D) two dashes of ginger and two dashes of paprika
   (E) three dashes of paprika and one dash of tarragon

Game 73

A therapist has a split personality patient named Mr. Norton. Mr. Norton has three and only three personalities, Ed, Cornelius, and Tyler. On any given day at least one of his three personalities must surface. However, all three personalities never surface on the same day. The therapist is trying to determine which personalities will surface during a five-day period running from Monday to Friday. Mr. Norton cannot adopt the same personality for three consecutive days, and the following conditions also apply:

Of two days, Tuesday and Friday, Tyler must surface at least once.

Of three days, Monday, Wednesday, and Friday, Cornelius must surface exactly twice.

Tyler and Cornelius cannot surface on the same day.

If Ed surfaces on a given day, then Cornelius must also surface on that same day.

Tyler does not surface on Thursday.

1. Which of the following is a pair of days on which Cornelius must surface?

   (A) Monday, Wednesday
   (B) Tuesday, Friday
   (C) Wednesday, Friday
   (D) Thursday, Monday
   (E) Friday, Monday

2. Which of the following CANNOT be true?

   (A) Ed surfaces on Monday, Wednesday, and Thursday.
   (B) Ed does not surface.
   (C) Ed and Cornelius both surface on Monday.
   (D) Tyler and one other personality surface on Tuesday.
   (E) Tyler surfaces on Tuesday and Wednesday.

3. If Tyler surfaces on Friday, then which of the following must be true?

   (A) Cornelius surfaces on Tuesday.
   (B) Ed surfaces on Monday.
   (C) Ed surfaces on Thursday.
   (D) Tyler surfaces on Tuesday.
   (E) Tyler surfaces on Wednesday.

4. If Ed surfaces on Friday, then which of the following must be true?

   (A) Cornelius surfaces on Wednesday.
   (B) Ed surfaces on Monday.
   (C) Ed surfaces on Thursday.
   (D) Tyler surfaces on Monday.
   (E) Tyler surfaces on Wednesday.

5. Which of the following CANNOT be true?

   (A) Cornelius does not surface on Tuesday.
   (B) Ed does not surface on Monday.
   (C) Ed surfaces on Monday, Thursday, and Friday.
   (D) Tyler surfaces on Friday and only one other day.
   (E) Tyler surfaces on three days.

6. Which of the following is a day on which Ed CANNOT surface?

   (A) Monday
   (B) Tuesday
   (C) Wednesday
   (D) Thursday
   (E) Friday

Game 74

Four friends, Felix, Gail, Helmut, and Ignacio, are ordering meals at a steak house. Each must order exactly one of three types of steaks: ribeye, sirloin, or T-bone. Each of the four may or may not order a pie for dessert. Any pie ordered must be either apple or cherry. Each person can at most order one steak and one pie. The meals ordered by the friends must also meet the following conditions:

If one of the friends orders a ribeye, then he or she must also order an apple pie.

If one of the friends orders a T-bone, then he or she must also order a cherry pie.

At least as many ribeyes are ordered as sirloins.

If Helmut does not order a sirloin, then Ignacio does not order a sirloin.

Gail cannot order any steak or pie ordered by Helmut.

Gail orders an apple pie.

1. Which of the following could be a complete and accurate list of the orders?

   (A) Felix: ribeye, apple pie; Gail: ribeye, apple pie; Helmut: sirloin; Ignacio: T-bone, cherry pie
   (B) Felix: ribeye, apple pie; Gail: T-bone, apple pie; Helmut: sirloin; Ignacio: ribeye, apple pie
   (C) Felix: sirloin; Gail: ribeye, apple pie; Helmut: sirloin; Ignacio: T-bone, cherry pie
   (D) Felix: sirloin; Gail: ribeye, apple pie Helmut: ribeye, apple pie; Ignacio: T-bone, cherry pie
   (E) Felix: T-bone, cherry pie; Gail: ribeye, apple pie; Helmut: T-bone, cherry pie; Ignacio: sirloin, apple pie

2. If exactly one apple pie is ordered, which of the following must be true?

   (A) Felix orders a cherry pie.
   (B) Felix orders a ribeye.
   (C) Helmut orders a T-bone.
   (D) Ignacio orders a sirloin.
   (E) Ignacio orders a cherry pie.

3. If Gail does not order a ribeye, then each of the following must be false EXCEPT:

   (A) Helmut does not order a pie.
   (B) Ignacio orders a sirloin.
   (C) Felix and Gail order the same steak.
   (D) Helmut and Ignacio order the same steak.
   (E) Only one person orders an apple pie.

4. If as few pies are ordered as the conditions will allow, which of the following must be true?

   (A) Felix orders a ribeye.
   (B) Helmut orders a pie.
   (C) Ignacio does not order a pie.
   (D) Two apple pies are ordered.
   (E) Exactly three pies are ordered.

5. If Felix orders the same steak as Ignacio, which of the following must be false?

   (A) Exactly two ribeyes are ordered.
   (B) Exactly three T-bones are ordered.
   (C) Exactly two pies are ordered.
   (D) Exactly three cherry pies are ordered.
   (E) All four friends order a pie.

6. If Felix is the only person who orders a T-bone, which of the following could be true?

   (A) Gail orders a cherry pie.
   (B) Helmut orders a cherry pie.
   (C) Ignacio orders a cherry pie.
   (D) Ignacio orders a sirloin.
   (E) Only two pies are ordered.

7. If Gail orders a sirloin and Felix orders a cherry pie, which of the following must be true?

   (A) Exactly three T-bones are ordered.
   (B) Exactly two ribeyes are ordered.
   (C) Helmut orders a sirloin.
   (D) Felix and Ignacio order the same kind of pie.
   (E) Exactly four pies are ordered.

A strip mall has storefronts for six shops. The storefronts are immediately beside one another and form a row from west to east. They are numbered consecutively one through six from west to east. Exactly one storefront is occupied by each of the following shops: Florist, Hair Stylist, Computer Repair, Delicatessen, Vacuum Cleaner, and Optician. The following rules govern the placement of the shops:

Exactly three shops are between the Vacuum Cleaner and the Delicatessen.

There is at least one shop between the Optician and the Florist.

Exactly one shop is adjacent to the Computer Repair shop.

1. Which could be a complete and accurate list of the shops from west to east?

   (A) Vacuum Cleaner, Optician, Computer Repair, Florist, Delicatessen, Hair Stylist
   (B) Computer Repair, Delicatessen, Hair Stylist, Optician, Vacuum Cleaner, Florist
   (C) Computer Repair, Vacuum Cleaner, Optician, Florist, Hair Stylist, Delicatessen
   (D) Delicatessen, Optician, Hair Stylist, Florist, Vacuum Cleaner, Computer Repair
   (E) Computer Repair, Florist, Vacuum Cleaner, Optician, Hair Stylist, Delicatessen

2. Which of the following could be true?

   (A) Delicatessen is the third store from the west.
   (B) Computer Repair is immediately beside Optician.
   (C) Optician is the third store from the west.
   (D) Vacuum Cleaner is the fourth store from the west.
   (E) Delicatessen is immediately beside Hair Stylist.

3. Which of the following is a storefront that the Hair Stylist could occupy?

   (A) 1
   (B) 2
   (C) 3
   (D) 5
   (E) 6

4. Which of the following must be false?

   (A) Computer Repair is adjacent to Delicatessen.
   (B) Vacuum Cleaner is adjacent to Florist.
   (C) Delicatessen is adjacent to Optician.
   (D) Hair Stylist is adjacent to Vacuum Cleaner.
   (E) Optician is adjacent to Hair Stylist.

5. Which of the following is a pair of stores either one of which might occupy either the third or fourth storefront?

   (A) Hair Stylist and Optician
   (B) Delicatessen and Florist
   (C) Florist and Vacuum Cleaner
   (D) Hair Stylist and Delicatessen
   (E) Optician and Delicatessen

6. Which of the following is a complete and accurate list of shops what might occupy storefront 2?

   (A) Delicatessen, Vacuum Cleaner
   (B) Optician, Florist
   (C) Optician, Florist, Hair Stylist
   (D) Delicatessen, Vacuum Cleaner, Optician, Florist
   (E) Delicatessen, Vacuum Cleaner, Optician, Florist, Hair Stylist

7. If the Optician is located in a storefront that is farther east than the storefront occupied by the Computer Repair shop, which of the following must be true?

   (A) Delicatessen is in storefront 2.
   (B) Optician is in storefront 5.
   (C) Vacuum Cleaner is in storefront 6.
   (D) Florist is in storefront 3.
   (E) Hair Stylist is in storefront 4.

Game 76

Six students, Chunze, Doris, Ephraim, Fern, Gwen, and Horace, will each take one and only one of four courses: Philosophy, Sociology, Theatre, or Zoology. Three professors, K, L, and M, will teach the courses. Each course must be taught by only one professor and each professor must teach at least one course. Each of the four courses must be taken by at least one student. The assignment of students and professors to courses must be in accordance with the following conditions:

Any course taught by L cannot be taken by more than one student.

Chunze must take a course taught by K.

If Fern takes Sociology, then Horace must also take Sociology.

Neither Gwen nor Horace takes a course taught by M.

Doris takes Philosophy.

Ephraim takes Theatre.

Theatre is taught by K.

1. Which of the following could be the assignment of students and professors to courses?

	Philosophy	Sociology	Theatre	Zoology
(A)	K; Chunze, Doris, Horace	L; Gwen	K; Ephraim	M; Fern
(B)	L; Doris	K; Gwen	K; Chunze, Ephraim, Fern	L; Horace
(C)	L; Doris	K; Gwen	K; Ephraim, Horace	M; Chunze, Fern
(D)	M; Doris	L; Fern	K; Ephraim, Horace	K; Chunze, Gwen
(E)	M; Doris, Gwen	M; Horace	K; Chunze, Ephraim	L; Fern

2. If Fern and Gwen each take a course in which there is only one student and M teaches exactly two courses, which of the following must be true?

(A) K teaches a course taken by three students.
(B) L teaches a course taken by Horace.
(C) Doris and Horace take the same course.
(D) Chunze takes Philosophy.
(E) Fern takes Sociology.

3. If Chunze and Horace take Zoology, which of the following could be true?

(A) Fern takes Zoology.
(B) Gwen takes Philosophy.
(C) K teaches a course taken by Gwen.
(D) L teaches a course taken by Fern.
(E) M teaches Sociology.

4. If Fern takes Sociology, which of the following must be true?

(A) Ephraim and Chunze take the same course.
(B) Gwen takes Theatre.
(C) K teaches Zoology.
(D) L teaches two courses.
(E) M teaches Philosophy.

5. If M teaches only one course and as many students as possible take that course, then which of the following could be true?

(A) Fern takes Sociology.
(B) Gwen takes Philosophy.
(C) Chunze and Gwen take Sociology.
(D) Chunze and Horace take Theatre.
(E) Gwen and Horace take Zoology.

6. If Gwen takes a course taught by K and Horace also takes a course taught by K, but not necessarily the same course as Gwen, then which of the following CANNOT be true?

(A) Chunze takes Theatre.
(B) Fern takes a course taught by M.
(C) Gwen takes Sociology.
(D) Horace takes Zoology.
(E) L teaches Philosophy.

7. If the rules are changed such that Horace and Gwen must take a course together that is taught by M, and if K teaches exactly one course, which of the following must be true?

(A) L teaches once.
(B) Horace takes Sociology.
(C) Gwen takes Zoology.
(D) M teaches Zoology.
(E) M teaches twice.

During her ten-week summer vacation Ellen will read each of eight books: *Ivanhoe, Billy Budd, Huckleberry Finn, Moby Dick, Walden, The Great Gatsby, The Ambassadors*, and *The Pioneers*. Ellen reads each book in one and only one of the ten weeks and reads no other books during the period. The following conditions apply:

The Ambassadors, Moby Dick, and *The Great Gatsby* are read in consecutive weeks, though not necessarily in that order.

Billy Budd is read sometime before *Moby Dick* and sometime before *The Pioneers*.

Walden is read in a week immediately before or immediately after a vacation week in which none of the books is read.

Ivanhoe is not read in a week immediately before or after a vacation week in which none of the books is read.

The Pioneers is read sometime before *Walden*, which is read sometime after *Ivanhoe*.

1. Which of the following could be a complete and accurate list of the order in which the books are read, from first to last?

   (A) *Huckleberry Finn, The Pioneers, Billy Budd, Ivanhoe, Moby Dick, The Ambassadors, The Great Gatsby, Walden*

   (B) *Billy Budd, The Great Gatsby, The Ambassadors, Moby Dick, The Pioneers, Walden, Ivanhoe, Huckleberry Finn*

   (C) *Billy Budd, Ivanhoe, Walden, The Ambassadors, Moby Dick, The Great Gatsby, The Pioneers, Huckleberry Finn*

   (D) *Billy Budd, Ivanhoe, Moby Dick, The Ambassadors, The Great Gatsby, The Pioneers, Huckleberry Finn, Walden*

   (E) *Huckleberry Finn, Billy Budd, The Great Gatsby, Moby Dick, The Pioneers, The Ambassadors, Huckleberry Finn, Walden*

2. How many different books could be the first book Ellen reads during her vacation?

   (A) 1
   (B) 2
   (C) 3
   (D) 4
   (E) 5

3. Which of the following must be false?

   (A) *The Great Gatsby* is read immediately before *The Pioneers*.
   (B) *Walden* is read immediately after *Billy Budd*.
   (C) *Ivanhoe* is read immediately before *The Pioneers*.
   (D) *Moby Dick* is read immediately after *Walden*.
   (E) *The Pioneers* is read immediately before *Moby Dick*.

4. If *Great Gatsby* is the third book read and is in the week following the week in which *Billy Budd* is read, which of the following is a complete and accurate list of books that could be the sixth book read?

   (A) *Walden, The Pioneers*
   (B) *Huckleberry Finn, Ivanhoe*
   (C) *Ivanhoe, Walden, The Pioneers, Huckleberry Finn*
   (D) *Huckleberry Finn, Ivanhoe, The Pioneers*
   (E) *The Ambassadors, The Pioneers, Huckleberry Finn*

5. If Ellen reads no book in the ninth or tenth week of her vacation, which of the following must be false?

   (A) *Billy Budd* is read sometime after *Ivanhoe*.
   (B) *Ivanhoe* is read sometime after *Huckleberry Finn*.
   (C) *The Pioneers* is read sometime after *The Great Gatsby*.
   (D) *Ivanhoe* is read sometime after *The Ambassadors*.
   (E) *Huckleberry Finn* is read sometime after *Walden*.

6. If Ellen reads *Walden* in the sixth week of her vacation and reads *Ivanhoe* in the fourth week, which of the following must be false?

   (A) Ellen reads no book in the seventh week.
   (B) Ellen reads no book in the ninth week.
   (C) Ellen reads no book in the second week.
   (D) Ellen reads The Pioneers in the fifth week.
   (E) Ellen reads Billy Budd in the second week.

7. Which week is the earliest of the ten vacation weeks that could be the second week in which Ellen reads no book?

   (A) 4
   (B) 5
   (C) 6
   (D) 7
   (E) 8

Three children, Eugene, Fern, and Giles, are ordering ice cream sundaes. Each child orders exactly one sundae, and each sundae has exactly three parts. Each part must be one of five flavors, butterscotch, chocolate, pineapple, strawberry, or vanilla. The following conditions govern the composition of the sundaes:

If any chocolate parts are used in making the sundaes, then the total number of strawberry parts used in making the three sundaes must be greater than the total number of chocolate parts used.

If a sundae has one or more parts butterscotch, it cannot contain any parts strawberry.

If a sundae has one or more parts vanilla, it cannot contain any parts pineapple.

Fern's sundae must use a greater number of flavors than Giles'.

Fern's sundae must have at least one part vanilla.

1. Which of the following could be a complete and accurate list of the flavors ordered by Fern and Giles?

   (A) Fern: butterscotch, vanilla, strawberry; Giles: strawberry, strawberry, vanilla
   (B) Fern: vanilla, pineapple, chocolate; Giles: strawberry, chocolate, chocolate
   (C) Fern: vanilla, vanilla, butterscotch; Giles: strawberry, strawberry, chocolate
   (D) Fern: vanilla, chocolate, chocolate; Giles: strawberry, strawberry, strawberry
   (E) Fern: vanilla, vanilla, pineapple; Giles: strawberry, strawberry, butterscotch

2. If Giles' sundae has one part chocolate and one part pineapple, which of the following must be true about Eugene's sundae?

   (A) It must contain exactly one part butterscotch.
   (B) It must contain at least one part pineapple.
   (C) It must contain exactly one part strawberry.
   (D) It must contain at least two parts strawberry.
   (E) It must contain at least two different flavors.

3. If Giles' sundae contains one part pineapple and one part butterscotch, what is the greatest number of parts vanilla that can be used in the sundaes?

   (A) 3
   (B) 4
   (C) 5
   (D) 6
   (E) 7

4. If Fern's sundae contains two parts butterscotch, which of the following must be false?

   (A) Eugene's sundae contains two parts chocolate.
   (B) Eugene's sundae contains three different flavors.
   (C) Giles' sundae contains at least one part chocolate.
   (D) No strawberry parts are used in making the sundaes.
   (E) Four parts vanilla are used in making the sundaes.

5. Which of the following CANNOT be true?

   (A) Eugene's and Giles' sundaes each contain one part chocolate and one part pineapple.
   (B) Fern's sundae has two parts vanilla.
   (C) Fern's and Giles' sundaes have no flavors in common.
   (D) Eight parts strawberry are used in making the sundaes.
   (E) Two children order sundaes containing no flavor other than pineapple.

6. If exactly four parts pineapple and two parts vanilla are used in making the sundaes, which of the following must be false?

(A) Eugene's sundae contains at least one part butterscotch.

(B) Eugene's sundae contains three different flavors.

(C) Fern's sundae contains at least one part chocolate.

(D) Giles' sundae contains at least two parts strawberry.

(E) Giles' sundae contains only one flavor.

7. If exactly two parts chocolate are used in making the sundaes and Fern's sundae contains neither chocolate nor strawberry, which of the following must be true?

(A) Eugene's sundae contains one part strawberry.

(B) Eugene's sundae contains exactly three parts strawberry.

(C) Fern's sundae contains no parts butterscotch.

(D) Giles' sundae contains three parts strawberry.

(E) Giles' sundae contains exactly two parts chocolate.

Part Two

Game 79

Teachers C, D, F, G, H, J, K, and L are available for assignment to classes 1, 2, and 3. Each class has either 15 or 20 students. A class with 20 students is assigned exactly three teachers and a class with 15 students is assigned exactly two teachers. No teacher teaches more than one class. The assignment of teachers is governed by the following conditions:

F and K are assigned to classes, but not to the same class.

J and D are assigned to classes, but not the same class.

If C and L are assigned to the same class, then it must be to a class with 20 students.

If G and K are assigned to the same class, then it is to a class of 15 students.

1. Which of the following could be a complete and accurate list of assignments to classes?

   (A) 1: L, J;   2: C, K, H; 3: F, D
   (B) 1: J, C;   2: K, D, G; 3: F, H, L
   (C) 1: F, H;   2: K, L, J; 3: C, G
   (D) 1: D, G, C; 2: J, L;   3: H, F, K
   (E) 1: F, H, D; 2: G, L;   3: K, J, H

2. If each class has 15 students and L and K are assigned to class 2, which of the following CANNOT be the teachers assigned to class 3?

   (A) D, G
   (B) F, H
   (C) H, J
   (D) F, D
   (E) J, F

3. If all eight teachers are assigned to classes and C, F, and H are assigned to class 3, which of the following CANNOT be two teachers assigned to class 2?

   (A) J, L
   (B) K, D
   (C) G, K
   (D) G, L
   (E) D, G

4. If C and L are assigned to class 1 and H is not assigned to a class, which of the following could be the teachers assigned to class 3?

   (A) J, K, G
   (B) F, D, K
   (C) J, F, G
   (D) D, G
   (E) K, F

5. If G and K are assigned to class 2 and H and F are assigned to class 1, which of the following must be true?

   (A) Three teachers are assigned to class 3.
   (B) Three teachers are assigned to class 2.
   (C) Three teachers are assigned to class 1.
   (D) Two teachers are assigned to class 3.
   (E) Two teachers are assigned to class 1.

6. Which of the following must be false?

   (A) Six teachers are assigned to classes, with G and F in class 1 and D and L in class 3.
   (B) Seven teachers are assigned to classes, with C and L in class 2 and F and G in class 3.
   (C) Eight teachers are assigned to classes, with G and K in class 1 and F, H, and L in class 3.
   (D) Eight teachers are assigned to classes, with G and K in class 2 and L, D, and C in class 1.
   (E) Seven teachers are assigned to classes, with C and F in class 3 and G and D in class 2.

7. If classes 1 and 3 have 20 students each and H and G are assigned to class 2, which of the following is a pair that CANNOT be assigned to class 3?

   (A) L and D
   (B) F and J
   (C) C and F
   (D) C and L
   (E) K and D

Game 80

Ten golfers: C, D, E, F, G, H, J, K, M, N will form two groups of four, foursome A and foursome B, to play a round of golf. No golfer can be in both foursomes and the foursomes are made according to these criteria:

If D is in a foursome, neither G nor J is included in a foursome.

If F is in a foursome, K is in the other foursome.

If either M or C is in a foursome, the other is also in that foursome.

K is not in foursome B.

N is in neither foursome unless E is in foursome A.

Foursome A includes either D or J.

1. Which of the following could be a complete and accurate list of the two foursomes?

   (A)   A: K, H, E, J;   B: N, F, M, C
   (B)   A: D, E, H, K;   B: F, M, C, G
   (C)   A: J, N, E, H;   B: M, F, C, G
   (D)   A: D, H, K, N;   B: G, C, M, F
   (E)   A: J, M, H, K;   B: F, E, N, C

2. Which of the following must be included in one of the foursomes?

   (A)   D
   (B)   E
   (C)   J
   (D)   F
   (E)   N

3. Which of the following could be the two golfers not included in either foursome?

   (A)   K, G
   (B)   F, D
   (C)   M, N
   (D)   E, D
   (E)   H, N

4. If E is in the same foursome as F, which of the following must be true?

   (A)   K is not in a foursome.
   (B)   D is not in a foursome.
   (C)   G is not in a foursome.
   (D)   M is not in a foursome.
   (E)   F is not in a foursome.

5. If M and K play on the same foursome, which of the following could be true?

   (A)   J and F are in the same foursome.
   (B)   M and D are in the same foursome.
   (C)   E and M are in the same foursome.
   (D)   F and H are in the same foursome.
   (E)   C and H are in the same foursome.

6. If D is included in a foursome, which of the following could be false?

   (A)   G is not included in a foursome.
   (B)   E is in foursome A.
   (C)   F is in foursome B.
   (D)   N is in foursome A.
   (E)   C is in foursome B.

7. If H is not included in a foursome, which of the following is a pair of golfers who could be on the same foursome?

   (A)   E, F
   (B)   N, G
   (C)   G, J
   (D)   J, M
   (E)   D, E

A tennis tournament will consist of exactly seven matches, numbered 1 through 7. Eight players will compete in the tournament: E, F, M, N, S, T, Y, and Z. Each match consists of exactly two players and exactly one of the two must win; there are no ties. No other matches occur. The matches will be played as follows:

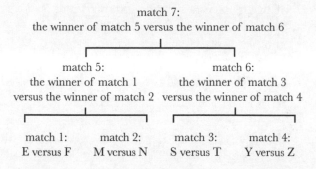

match 7:
the winner of match 5 versus the winner of match 6

match 5:
the winner of match 1
versus the winner of match 2

match 6:
the winner of match 3
versus the winner of match 4

match 1:
E versus F

match 2:
M versus N

match 3:
S versus T

match 4:
Y versus Z

The winner of match 7 will be the tournament champion. The following conditions apply:

E and N cannot meet in a match.
If M wins match 2, then he must meet F in match 5 and S must win match 3.
The champion cannot be N, S, or T.
If Z wins match 6, then M must win match 2.
If T and Y meet each other in a match, then T must win that match.

1. Which of the following could be a pair of players that meet in match 7?

   (A)   E and S
   (B)   M and T
   (C)   M and Y
   (D)   N and S
   (E)   N and Z

2. If N wins match 5, which of the following is a pair of players who must meet in a match?

   (A)   E and N
   (B)   N and Z
   (C)   S and Y
   (D)   T and Y
   (E)   T and Z

3. If N wins match 2 and T wins match 3, which of the following must be true?

   (A)   F wins match 5.
   (B)   N is the tournament champion.
   (C)   S wins match 3.
   (D)   Z is the tournament champion.
   (E)   Y wins match 6.

4. If Y wins match 4 and the winner of match 1 does not win match 5, which of the following must be false?

   (A)   M wins the championship.
   (B)   N wins match 2.
   (C)   S wins match 6.
   (D)   T wins match 3.
   (E)   Y does not win match 6.

5. If N wins match 5, which of the following is a player who must win at least two matches?

   (A)   F
   (B)   S
   (C)   T
   (D)   Y
   (E)   Z

6. If T wins at least one match, which of the following is a player who could be the champion?

   (A)   E
   (B)   F
   (C)   M
   (D)   N
   (E)   Z

7. If N wins match 2, what is the maximum number of players, any one of whom could be the champion?

   (A)   1
   (B)   2
   (C)   3
   (D)   4
   (E)   5

Game 82

Seven campers, O, P, Q, R, S, T, and U, are erecting tents beside a river. Each tent must be one of three colors: brown, green, or navy, and each tent must be either a large or a small. Exactly two campers will sleep in each of the large tents that are erected and exactly one camper will sleep in each of the small tents erected. Each camper must sleep in one and only one of the tents. The first tent erected will be designated tent 1, the second tent erected will be designated tent 2, the third tent 3, and so on. The following rules govern the sleeping arrangements:

There are at least four and no more than five tents.
No two consecutively numbered tents can be the same color.
If a tent is navy colored, then only one person sleeps in that tent.
O and U must each sleep in a green tent, which may or may not be the same tent.
P must sleep in a brown tent.
Q and R sleep in tent 2.

1. If only four tents are erected, which of the following must be false?

   (A) O is the only camper assigned to tent 4.
   (B) P is assigned to tent 1.
   (C) S and T each sleeps in a navy tent.
   (D) Tent 3 is brown.
   (E) No navy tents are erected.

2. If O and T sleep in tent 4, then S must sleep in which of the following tents?

   (A) tent 1, a green tent
   (B) tent 3, a brown tent
   (C) tent 3, a navy tent
   (D) tent 5, a brown tent
   (E) tent 5, a navy tent

3. If S sleeps in tent 3 and that tent is brown, then which of the following is a pair of campers who must sleep in the same tent?

   (A) O and S
   (B) O and U
   (C) P and Q
   (D) P and T
   (E) S and T

4. If five tents are erected and tents 1 and 5 are navy, then which of the following is a complete and accurate list of the tents in which T could sleep?

   (A) 1, 3, 4, 5
   (B) 1, 3, 5
   (C) 1, 5
   (D) 2, 3, 4
   (E) 3, 4

5. If only four tents are erected and O and U sleep in separate tents, which one of the following must be false?

   (A) O is the only camper that sleeps in tent 3.
   (B) P sleeps in tent 3.
   (C) S and U sleep in tent 1.
   (D) T sleeps in a brown tent.
   (E) U sleeps in tent 3.

6. Assume the conditions are altered so that exactly six tents must be erected, but all other conditions remain in effect. If P sleeps in tent 1, which of the following must be true?

   (A) S sleeps in tent 3.
   (B) Tent 5 is navy.
   (C) Tents 4 and 6 are green.
   (D) Exactly two brown tents are erected.
   (E) No navy tents are erected.

Game 83

Three children, Eddie, Jessica, and Angelica, are taken to the toy store on each of three consecutive days, Monday through Wednesday, by their grandparents. Each day, each child buys exactly one toy: either a puzzle, a yo-yo, a scooter, or a video game. No two children buy the same kind of toy any day and no child buys the same kind of toy on more than one day. Each kind of toy is bought at least once. The following conditions apply:

Angelica does not buy a puzzle.
Jessica buys a yo-yo on Tuesday and Eddie buys a yo-yo on Monday.
Eddie buys on Wednesday what Angelica buys on Monday.

1. Which of the following could be a complete and accurate list of the toys each child is bought in order, Monday through Wednesday?

   (A) Eddie: yo-yo, scooter, puzzle; Jessica: puzzle, yo-yo, scooter; Angelica: video game, scooter, yo-yo
   (B) Eddie: yo-yo, puzzle, scooter; Jessica: puzzle, yo-yo, video game; Angelica: scooter, video game, yo-yo
   (C) Eddie: yo-yo, video game, scooter; Jessica: puzzle, yo-yo, puzzle; Angelica: scooter, video game, yo-yo
   (D) Eddie: yo-yo, puzzle, scooter; Jessica: puzzle, scooter, video game; Angelica: scooter, video game, yo-yo
   (E) Eddie: yo-yo, puzzle, scooter; Jessica: puzzle, yo-yo, video game; Angelica: scooter, video game, puzzle

2. If Jessica buys a scooter on Monday, which of the following must be true?

   (A) Eddie gets a scooter on Tuesday.
   (B) Jessica buys a puzzle on Wednesday.
   (C) Eddie buys a scooter on Wednesday.
   (D) Angelica buys a video game on Tuesday.
   (E) Jessica buys a video game on Wednesday.

3. If Jessica buys a video game on Wednesday, which of the following must be true?

   (A) Eddie buys a video game on Wednesday.
   (B) Angelica buys a video game on Monday.
   (C) Jessica buys a puzzle on Monday.
   (D) Angelica buys a scooter on Tuesday.
   (E) Eddie buys a scooter on Tuesday.

4. Which of the following must be true?

   (A) Eddie buys a puzzle on Tuesday.
   (B) Jessica does not buy a scooter on Wednesday.
   (C) Angelica buys a scooter on Monday.
   (D) Eddie buys a puzzle on Wednesday.
   (E) Jessica buys a scooter on Monday.

5. Which of the following must be false?

   (A) Jessica buys a scooter on Wednesday.
   (B) Jessica buys a puzzle on Wednesday.
   (C) Eddie buys a scooter on Tuesday.
   (D) Eddie buys a scooter on Wednesday.
   (E) Angelica buys a scooter on Tuesday.

6. Which of the following is sufficient to determine what each child buys on each day?

   (A) Angelica buys a video game Tuesday.
   (B) Eddie buys a scooter on Wednesday.
   (C) Angelica buys a video game on Monday.
   (D) Jessica buys a scooter on Wednesday.
   (E) Jessica buys a puzzle on Wednesday.

7. Each of the following must be false EXCEPT:

   (A) Exactly two yo-yo's are bought.
   (B) Exactly three scooters are bought.
   (C) Exactly two puzzles are bought.
   (D) Exactly three puzzles are bought.
   (E) Exactly three video games are bought.

Game 84

In a track meet eight events, labeled O, P, Q, R, S, T, U, and V, will be held over an eight-day period. Exactly one event will be held each day. The following restrictions govern the scheduling of the events:

V can be held only on day 1 or else day 2.
The days on which P and T are held must be separated by exactly one day.
The days on which Q and R are held must be separated by exactly one day.
The days on which T and U are held must be separated by exactly one day.
Q and U cannot be held on consecutive days.
S must be held sometime before U, but not on the day immediately before U.
R must be held sometime before P.
There must be at least one event after Q.

1. Which of the following could be a complete and accurate list of the track events held in order from day one to day eight?

   (A) V S Q R P O T U
   (B) V R S Q T U O P
   (C) R V Q U P O T S
   (D) R V Q P S T O U
   (E) S Q V R U P O T

2. If S is held on day 5, which of the following is a day on which O could be held?

   (A) 1
   (B) 2
   (C) 4
   (D) 6
   (E) 7

3. If T and P are held respectively on days 5 and 7, which of the following is a day on which O could be held?

   (A) 1
   (B) 2
   (C) 3
   (D) 6
   (E) 8

4. If P is held on a day sometime before U, which of the following must be false?

   (A) S is sometime before P.
   (B) O is sometime after T.
   (C) S goes third.
   (D) R goes third
   (E) O is sometime after P.

5. If Q is held on day 7, which of the following is a day on which O could be held?

   (A) 2
   (B) 3
   (C) 4
   (D) 6
   (E) 8

6. If Q is held immediately after T, which of the following could be true?

   (A) P is the sixth event held.
   (B) R is the third event held.
   (C) S is the third event held.
   (D) U is the last event held.
   (E) V is the first event held.

7. If R is held after as many events as the restrictions permit, then which of the following must be false?

   (A) O is held sometime before U.
   (B) Q is the third event held.
   (C) S is held on day 2.
   (D) T is held on day 6.
   (E) U is held sometime before T.

Game 85

A landscaping company has been hired to plant three trees at each of four adjacent townhouses, house 1, house 2, house 3, and house 4. The townhouses are lined up in a row from west to east. The company has four different types of trees, elm, oak, apple, and pine, and has four trees of each type. The trees must be planted in a manner consistent with the following rules:

No townhouse can have more than one oak tree or more than one elm tree.

Each townhouse must have at least two different types of trees, but no two townhouses can have the same three types of trees

There must be at least one apple tree planted at the third house from the west.

There cannot be pine trees at adjacent townhouses.

There cannot be apple trees at adjacent townhouses.

1. Which of the following could be a complete and accurate list of the trees that are planted at each house?

    (A)   house 1: apple, apple, elm; house 2: pine, oak, elm; house 3: apple, apple, elm; house 4: pine, pine, elm

    (B)   house 1: apple, elm, elm; house 2: pine, oak, elm; house 3: apple, apple, oak; house 4: pine, pine, oak

    (C)   house 1: pine, pine, elm; house 2: apple, apple, elm; house 3: apple, apple, oak; house 4: pine, elm, oak

    (D)   house 1: apple, apple, oak; house 2: pine, pine, elm; house 3: apple, elm, oak; house 4: pine, pine, oak

    (E)   house 1: apple, elm, pine; house 2: elm, oak, pine; house 3: apple, apple, oak; house 4: pine, pine, elm

2. If all four oak trees are planted, which of the following must be true?

    (A)   Three elm trees are planted.
    (B)   Two apple trees are planted.
    (C)   Two pine trees are planted.
    (D)   Four elm trees are planted.
    (E)   Two elm trees are planted.

3. If house 2 has exactly three kinds of trees, which of the following could be true?

    (A)   House 4 has three kinds of trees.
    (B)   House 1 and house 3 have three different kinds of trees.
    (C)   House 4 has an oak tree, an elm tree, and an apple tree.
    (D)   Exactly two pine trees are planted.
    (E)   House 3 has exactly three kinds of trees.

4. If more elm trees are planted than oak trees, which of the following must be true?

    (A)   Exactly three oak trees are planted.
    (B)   Exactly one oak tree could be planted.
    (C)   Exactly two pine trees are planted.
    (D)   Exactly two oak trees are planted.
    (E)   Exactly four apple trees are planted.

5. If all four pine trees and all four apple trees are planted, which of the following could be false?

    (A)   Exactly two oak trees are planted.
    (B)   No oak tree is planted at a house where an elm tree is planted.
    (C)   No house where an elm tree is planted is adjacent to another house where an elm tree is planted.
    (D)   Exactly two elm trees are planted.
    (E)   The number of oak trees planted is exactly equal to the number of elm trees planted.

6. If more apple trees are planted than pine trees and more oak trees are planted than elm trees, then which of the following could be true?

(A) Exactly three apple trees are planted.

(B) Exactly four oak trees are planted.

(C) No house has both an apple tree and an elm tree.

(D) No house has both a pine tree and an oak tree.

(E) More pine trees are planted than elm trees.

7. If house number three has exactly one apple tree, then which of the following must be true?

(A) House 4 has exactly three kinds of trees.

(B) No more than one house can have three kinds of trees.

(C) Exactly two houses must have exactly two kinds of trees.

(D) Exactly three apple trees are planted among the four houses.

(E) Exactly three elm trees are planted among the four houses.

There are two bookcases—white and black—with 4 shelves each. The shelves are numbered 1 through 4 from bottom to top. There are seven kinds of books that are to be placed in the shelves: geography, mystery, philosophy, sci-fi, nonfiction, cooking, and British literature. Each type goes on exactly one shelf except for philosophy, which occupies two shelves, one directly on top of the other, on the same bookcase. The following conditions apply:

Mystery and sci-fi are on the top shelves.
British literature is on the second shelf.
Cooking and nonfiction are on different bookcases.

1. Which of the following could be a complete and accurate list of the books on shelves 1 to 4, respectively, in the two cases?

    (A) white bookcase: philosophy, philosophy, geography, sci-fi; black bookcase: cooking, British literature, nonfiction, mystery
    (B) white bookcase: philosophy, nonfiction, philosophy, sci-fi; black bookcase: geography, British literature, cooking, mystery
    (C) white bookcase: nonfiction, geography, British literature, mystery; black bookcase: cooking, philosophy, philosophy, sci-fi
    (D) white bookcase: cooking, philosophy, philosophy, mystery; black bookcase: geography, British literature, nonfiction, sci-fi
    (E) white bookcase: nonfiction, philosophy, philosophy, geography; black bookcase: nonfiction, British literature, mystery, sci-fi.

2. If British literature is on the white bookcase, which of the following must be true?

    (A) Cooking is on shelf 1 of the white case.
    (B) Philosophy is on shelf 2 of the black case.
    (C) Mystery is on shelf 4 of the white case.
    (D) Philosophy is on shelf 3 of the black case.
    (E) Geography is on shelf 3 of the white case.

3. Which of the following must be false?

    (A) British literature and cooking are on the same bookcase.
    (B) Nonfiction and geography are on the same bookcase.
    (C) Sci-fi and philosophy are on the same bookcase.
    (D) Philosophy and geography are on the same bookcase.
    (E) British literature and nonfiction are on the same bookcase.

4. If philosophy is in the white case on shelf 1, how many different kinds of books could be in the black case on shelf 1?

    (A) 1
    (B) 2
    (C) 3
    (D) 4
    (E) 5

5. If nonfiction is on a lower-numbered shelf than cooking, which of the following must be true?

    (A) Nonfiction is on a first shelf.
    (B) Cooking is on a second shelf.
    (C) Philosophy is on a first shelf.
    (D) Philosophy and geography are on the same shelf.
    (E) Nonfiction and geography are on the same shelf.

6. If British literature is on the white bookcase on a shelf below cooking, how many possible combinations of books are possible on the black shelf?

    (A) 2
    (B) 3
    (C) 4
    (D) 5
    (E) 6

Game 87

During a five-hour period two hair stylists, Deb and Frank, each give five haircuts, numbered one through five, to five different clients. Both Deb and Frank see only one client per hour. For each of the stylists, exactly four of the clients, an adult woman, an adult man, and two children, have appointments, while the other client, who could be an adult woman, an adult man, or a child, does not. The following restrictions apply:

During any of the five hours, Deb and Frank do not both give haircuts to adults or children.

The clients without appointments receive haircuts in neither the first nor the last hour.

1. Which of the following could be a complete an accurate list of the clients served by each stylist in order from earliest to latest?

    (A) Deb: man, child, man, child, woman; Frank: child, man, man, woman, child

    (B) Deb: child, child, man, woman, child; Frank: woman, man, child, child, man

    (C) Deb: child, woman, child, child, man; Frank: child, man, woman, child, child

    (D) Deb: man, woman, child, child, woman; Frank: woman, child, child, child, man

    (E) Deb: child, man, child, child, man; Frank: woman, child, man, man, child

2. If Deb's five clients, in order from earliest to latest, are child, man, child, woman, and child, which of the following could be true of Frank's clients?

    (A) His third client is a child.
    (B) His fifth client is a child.
    (C) His second client is not a child.
    (D) His fourth client is a woman.
    (E) His third client is not a man.

3. Which of the following must be false?

    (A) Frank's first client is a man and Frank's third client is a man.

    (B) Deb's second client is a child and Deb's third client is a child.

    (C) Frank's fourth client is a child and Deb's first client is a child.

    (D) Deb's first client is a woman and Deb's fifth client is a woman.

    (E) Deb's third client is a man and Frank's fourth client is a man.

4. Which of the following must be true of the ten clients served by Deb and Frank?

    (A) They must include exactly two men.
    (B) They must include exactly five children.
    (C) They must include exactly three women.
    (D) They must include exactly four children.
    (E) They must include exactly four men.

5. Which of the following could be included among the ten clients served by Deb and Frank?

    (A) exactly three women and exactly three men

    (B) exactly three women and exactly five children

    (C) exactly four children and exactly two women

    (D) exactly two men and exactly four women

    (E) exactly two men and exactly two women

6. If Deb's client without an appointment is a woman and if Frank does not serve any two children in consecutive hours, which of the following could be true?

    (A) Frank's second client is a child.
    (B) Deb's third client is a man.
    (C) Franks fifth client is a woman.
    (D) Deb's fifth client is a woman.
    (E) Frank's third client is a woman.

Game 88

Each of three parents (C, D, and F) and five children (Q, R, S, T, and V) is traveling in exactly one of two vehicles (an SUV and a Minivan) on a school field trip to the museum. There are exactly four occupants in each vehicle with exactly one parent driving each vehicle. These regulations apply:

S is in the vehicle with more children.
T is not in any vehicle that F is in.
If R is in the SUV, then V is in the SUV.
S is in the SUV if D is in the Minivan.
F does not drive the vehicle that Q rides in.

1. Which of the following could be a complete and accurate list of assignments to vehicles?

   (A)   SUV: T, Q, F, S; Minivan: R, C, V, D
   (B)   SUV: R, V, F, D; Minivan: T, C, S, Q
   (C)   SUV: D, C, Q, F; Minivan: S, T, V, R
   (D)   SUV: F, C, R, V; Minivan: S, Q, T, D
   (E)   SUV: T, Q, F, S; Minivan: R, C, V, D

2. If C and T are not in the same vehicle, which is a pair that must be in the same vehicle?

   (A)   D, V
   (B)   R, T
   (C)   S, T
   (D)   C, Q
   (E)   F, Q

3. If C and D are in the same vehicle, which is a pair that must be in the same vehicle?

   (A)   V, T
   (B)   Q, F
   (C)   T, R
   (D)   F, R
   (E)   S, Q

4. If D is in the SUV and Q is in the Minivan, which of the following must be true?

   (A)   R is in the Minivan.
   (B)   F is in the Minivan.
   (C)   C is in the Minivan.
   (D)   S is in the SUV.
   (E)   S is in the Minivan.

5. Which of the following could be true?

   (A)   V and T are in the Minivan.
   (B)   R and T are the only children in the Minivan.
   (C)   Q and T are in the SUV.
   (D)   D is the only parent in the Minivan.
   (E)   R is in the SUV with C and Q.

6. Which of the following must be false?

   (A)   S and T are in the Minivan.
   (B)   R and T are in the SUV.
   (C)   D and C are in the Minivan.
   (D)   R and S are in the SUV.
   (E)   Q and S are in the SUV.

7. If the rule forbidding F from driving Q is removed and all other conditions remain the same, which of the following could be true?

   (A)   Q, F, and R are in the SUV.
   (B)   D, R, and Q are in the Minivan.
   (C)   C, R, and D are in the SUV.
   (D)   S, F, and D are in the Minivan.
   (E)   F, T, and Q are in the Minivan.

Game 89

Sarah and Anita are planning a short vacation that will last three days, Thursday through Saturday. On each day they must see no fewer than two sights. Over the three days they must see exactly eight sights, which must consist of one beach, three landmarks, two museums, and two parks. If they see exactly three sights on Thursday, then they must see exactly three sites on Friday. If they see exactly two sights on Friday, then they must see exactly two sites on Saturday. The following restrictions also apply:

If on a given day Sarah and Anita see two or more landmarks, then they must also visit a beach on that day.

If on a given day Sarah and Anita see a museum, then they must also see a park on that day.

If Sarah and Anita see two museums on the same day, then it must be on Saturday.

Sarah and Anita must see a landmark on Thursday.

1. Which of the following could be a complete and accurate list of the sights that Sarah and Anita see over the three day period?

   (A) Thursday: landmark, park; Friday: beach, museum, park, landmark; Saturday: landmark, museum

   (B) Thursday: landmark, landmark, beach; Friday: landmark, park; Saturday: museum, museum, park

   (C) Thursday: landmark, landmark, museum, park; Friday: museum, park; Saturday: landmark, beach

   (D) Thursday: landmark, park; Friday: landmark, landmark, beach; Saturday: museum, park, museum

   (E) Thursday: landmark, landmark, beach; Friday: museum, museum, park; Saturday: landmark, park

2. Which of the following could be a complete and accurate list of the sights that Sarah and Anita see on Saturday?

   (A) one beach and one landmark
   (B) one landmark and one museum
   (C) one landmark and one park
   (D) one beach, one museum and one park
   (E) one beach and two landmarks

3. If Sarah and Anita see a museum on Thursday, then each of the following must be false EXCEPT?

   (A) They see a beach on Thursday.
   (B) They see a landmark and a park on Friday.
   (C) They see two parks on Friday.
   (D) They see a landmark and a park on Saturday.
   (E) They see two landmarks on Saturday.

4. If Sarah and Anita see a beach and a landmark on Friday, then which of the following could be true?

   (A) They see two landmarks on Thursday.
   (B) They see a museum on Thursday.
   (C) They see a park on Friday.
   (D) They see a landmark on Saturday.
   (E) They see two parks on Saturday.

5. If Sarah and Anita see two museums on the same day, then each of the following must be false EXCEPT?

   (A) They see two landmarks on Thursday.
   (B) They see a beach on Thursday.
   (C) They see two landmarks on Friday.
   (D) They see a park on Friday.
   (E) They see a landmark on Saturday.

6. If Sarah and Anita do not see a park on Friday, then which of the following must be true?

   (A) They see a beach on Thursday.
   (B) They see a museum on Friday.
   (C) They see two landmarks on Friday.
   (D) They see two museums on Saturday.
   (E) They see a landmark on Saturday.

7. If Sarah and Anita see a landmark and a park on Saturday, then which of the following could be true?

   (A) They see a park on Thursday.
   (B) They see a park on Friday.
   (C) They see a beach on Friday.
   (D) They see a beach on Saturday.
   (E) They see two museums on Saturday.

A volleyball squad with members B, C, D, E, F, G, H, I, J, K, L, and M is being divided into two teams, X and Y, for a scrimmage. Each team has six members numbered one to six, and the members serve in order from one to six. The following regulations govern the makeup of the teams:

K is on a team with C, but not with M and serves neither first nor last.

C serves third.

J and L are on different teams.

G is not on the same team as H

D serves fourth from last on team Y

E, G, and B serve fourth, fifth, and sixth, though not necessarily respectively and not necessarily on the same team.

1. Which of the following could be a complete and accurate list from first to serve to last to serve of the members of team Y?

   (A) L, B, D, H, E, M
   (B) J, I, D, G, F, E
   (C) M, K, D, L, E, B
   (D) L, I, D, B, M, G
   (E) H, M, D, E, G, B

2. If F is on the same team as and serves immediately before K, then which of the following could be true?

   (A) F serves second on team X.
   (B) F serves fourth on team Y.
   (C) F serves sometime after G.
   (D) F serves later than H.
   (E) K serves immediately after C.

3. If B and F are on team Y, which of the following must be on team X?

   (A) G
   (B) L
   (C) I
   (D) J
   (E) H

4. If J, H, and M serve consecutively on the same team, which of the following must be true?

   (A) G serves sixth on one of the teams.
   (B) L serves first on team X.
   (C) F serves sometime after C.
   (D) I serves first or second on team X.
   (E) F and L are on the same team.

5. Which of the following CANNOT be true?

   (A) B and G are on Team X, and L is on team Y.
   (B) F and I are on Team X, and B and E are on Team Y.
   (C) G, B, and I are all on Team Y.
   (D) F and K are the two who serve second and M serves fourth.
   (E) B, E, and F are all on Team X.

6. If J and L are the two who serve second and if I, G, and B, respectively, serve consecutively on the same team, which of the following could be false?

   (A) K serves fifth on team X
   (B) M serves first on team Y.
   (C) E serves fourth on team X.
   (D) F serves first on team X
   (E) I serves fourth on team Y.

Game 91

During a wedding ceremony, each of four bridesmaids, Eve, Fran, Gwen, and Harriet will walk down the aisle in a pair with one of four groomsmen, Abe, Bill, Chad, and Dan. The four pairs walk down the aisle in succession, from first to fourth according to the following rules:

Chad walks down the aisle sometime before Fran.
Gwen walks down the aisle sometime before Bill.
Dan walks down the aisle sometime after Bill and sometime after Chad.
Bill and Fran do not form a pair together.

1. Which of the following could be a complete and accurate list of the pairs in the order they walk down the aisle from first to fourth?

    (A) 1: Gwen, Chad; 2: Eve, Bill; 3: Harriet, Dan; 4: Fran, Abe
    (B) 1: Eve, Abe; 2: Gwen, Dan; 3: Fran, Chad; 4: Harriet, Bill
    (C) 1: Gwen, Chad; 2: Fran, Dan; 3: Harriet, Bill; 4: Eve, Abe
    (D) 1: Harriet, Abe; 2: Gwen, Chad; 3: Fran, Bill; 4: Eve, Dan
    (E) 1: Eve, Chad; 2: Harriet, Bill; 3: Fran, Abe; 4: Gwen, Dan

2. Which of the following could form a pair with any of four others?

    (A) Chad
    (B) Fran
    (C) Bill
    (D) Harriet
    (E) Dan

3. Which of the following CANNOT form a pair together?

    (A) Dan and Fran
    (B) Abe and Fran
    (C) Dan and Gwen
    (D) Eve and Bill
    (E) Gwen and Chad

4. If Harriet and Abe walk second, how many different pairs could walk fourth?

    (A) 1
    (B) 2
    (C) 3
    (D) 4
    (E) 5

5. If Abe walks down the aisle sometime before Gwen, which of the following could be false?

    (A) Abe walks in the first pair.
    (B) Bill walks in the third pair.
    (C) Gwen is paired with Chad.
    (D) Fran is paired with Dan.
    (E) Bill is paired with Eve.

6. If Harriet walks in the third pair with Dan, which of the following must be true?

    (A) Abe walks sometime before Bill.
    (B) Eve walks sometime after Chad.
    (C) Harriet and Bill walk together.
    (D) Eve and Chad walk together.
    (E) Gwen walks sometime after Chad.

7. Which of the following gives sufficient information to determine the makeup of the pairs and the order in which they walk?

    (A) Dan and Eve are the fourth pair.
    (B) Gwen and Chad are the first pair.
    (C) Bill and Harriet are the second pair.
    (D) Harriet and Abe are the fourth pair.
    (E) Dan and Fran are the third pair.

Game 92

Ralph must monitor wind direction for four consecutive days. On each of the four days, Ralph must take two recordings, once in the morning and once in the afternoon. For each recording he must record the wind direction as exactly one of the following: north, south, east, or west. He does not record the same wind direction for both the morning and afternoon of any day. Also, he does not record the same wind direction for consecutive mornings or consecutive afternoons. The following conditions apply:

He does not record the wind direction as both north and south on the same day, and he cannot record the wind direction as both east and west on the same day.

If he records the wind direction as east on the morning of a given day, then he must record the wind direction as north on that afternoon.

If he records the wind direction as either north or west on any day except day 4 then he must record the wind direction as south on the following day.

1. What is the fewest number of times during the four days that Ralph could make recordings of south?

    (A) 0
    (B) 1
    (C) 2
    (D) 3
    (E) 4

2. Which of the following CANNOT be Ralph's recordings for the morning of day 3 and the afternoon of day 4, respectively?

    (A) north and east
    (B) north and south
    (C) south and west
    (D) east and west
    (E) west and south

3. If Ralph records the wind direction as west on the afternoon of day 3 and east on the afternoon of day 4, then which of the following must be true?

    (A) Ralph records the wind direction as east on the morning of day 1.
    (B) Ralph records the wind direction as south on the morning of day 2.
    (C) Ralph records the wind direction as south on the afternoon of day 2.
    (D) Ralph records the wind direction as east on the morning of day 3.
    (E) Ralph records the wind direction as north on the morning of day 4.

4. If Ralph records the wind direction as south on the afternoons of days 1 and 4, then which of the following could be his recordings for the wind directions on day 3?

    (A) morning: north; afternoon: east
    (B) morning: north; afternoon: west
    (C) morning: east; afternoon: west
    (D) morning: east; afternoon: south
    (E) morning: west; afternoon: north

5. If Ralph records the wind direction as north on the afternoon of day 2 and south on the morning of day 4, then which of the following could be his recordings for the wind directions on the mornings of days 1, 2, and 3, respectively?

    (A) north, south, west
    (B) south, east, west
    (C) south, west, east
    (D) east, west, east
    (E) west, east, north

6. If Ralph records the wind direction as west on the afternoon of day 1 and north on the morning of day 3, then which of the following could be true?

(A) Ralph records the wind direction as south on the morning of day 1.

(B) Ralph records the wind direction as west on the morning of day 2.

(C) Ralph records the wind direction as south on the afternoon of day 2.

(D) Ralph records the wind direction as west on the afternoon of day 3.

(E) Ralph records the wind direction as east on the morning of day 4.

7. If Ralph records the wind direction as south on the morning of day 1 and west on the morning of day 3, then which of the following must be false?

(A) Ralph records the wind direction as east on the afternoon of day 1.

(B) Ralph records the wind direction as north on the morning of day 2.

(C) Ralph records the wind direction as east on the afternoon of day 2.

(D) Ralph records the wind direction as south on the afternoon of day 3.

(E) Ralph records the wind direction as west on the afternoon of day 4.

Game 93

The city zoo has just finished construction of five new cages, numbered 1 through 5. Seven types of animals, dingoes, elephants, giraffes, hyenas, jackals, kangaroos, and leopards, are being considered for relocation into the cages. Of these exactly four types will be selected for relocation into the new cages. Each cage can house only one type of animal and one cage will remain empty. If dingoes selected then they must be placed in cage 1. If leopards are selected then they must be placed in cage 2. If kangaroos are selected then they must be placed in cage 4. The following conditions also govern the assignment of animals to cages:

Only consecutively numbered cages are considered adjacent.

If either elephants or giraffes are selected, then both must be selected and placed in adjacent cages.

If elephants are selected, then leopards must also be selected.

Either hyenas or kangaroos must be selected, but not both.

1. Which of the following could be an acceptable assignment of animals to cages?

   (A) cage 1: hyenas, cage 2: leopards, cage 3: elephants, cage 4: giraffes, cage 5: jackals
   (B) cage 1: empty, cage 2: elephants, cage 3: giraffes, cage 4: jackals, cage 5: hyena
   (C) cage 1: dingoes, cage 2: leopards, cage 3: jackals, cage 4: kangaroos, cage 5: empty
   (D) cage 1: hyenas, cage 2: leopards, cage 3: empty, cage 4: elephants, cage 5: kangaroos
   (E) cage 1: dingoes, cage 2: hyenas, cage 3: leopards, cage 4: elephants, cage 5: empty

2. If elephants are placed in cage 3, then which of the following must be true?

   (A) The dingoes are selected to move into a new cage.
   (B) The jackals are selected to move into a new cage.
   (C) The hyenas are selected to move into a new cage.
   (D) Cage 4 is empty.
   (E) Cage 5 is empty.

3. Which of the following must be true?

   (A) The jackals are selected to move into a new cage.
   (B) The leopards are selected to move into a new cage.
   (C) Cage 3 is empty.
   (D) Cage 5 is empty.
   (E) Either elephants or giraffes are placed in cage 4.

4. Which of the following could be placed in cage 1?

   (A) elephants
   (B) giraffes
   (C) hyenas
   (D) kangaroos
   (E) leopards

5. If the jackals are placed in a cage adjacent to the empty cage, then which of the following are three types of animals that CANNOT be selected for placement into one of the new cages?

   (A) dingoes, elephants, kangaroos
   (B) elephants, hyenas, leopards
   (C) elephants, giraffes, kangaroos
   (D) giraffes, hyenas, kangaroos
   (E) giraffes, hyenas, leopards

6. Suppose the condition that one cage remain empty is altered so that two of the new cages must remain empty and three will be filled with animals. All other conditions remain in effect. If jackals are placed in cage 2, then each of the following could be true about the hyenas EXCEPT:

   (A) They are placed in cage 1.
   (B) They are placed in cage 3.
   (C) They are placed in cage 5.
   (D) They are not selected.
   (E) They are placed between the two empty cages.

Three types of flowers, roses, carnations, and irises, are available to a florist to make a flower arrangement that includes exactly nine flowers. The roses are available in red, yellow, and pink, with exactly two of each color. The carnations are available in pink, red, and white, with exactly two of each color. Irises are available in white and yellow, with exactly three of each color. The following restrictions govern the arrangement:

The arrangement must include at least one of each of the three types of flowers.

There must be more roses than carnations in the arrangement.

There must not be fewer carnations than irises in the arrangement.

There must be more white than pink flowers in the arrangement.

There must not be fewer red than pink flowers in the arrangement.

There must not be fewer yellow than red flowers in the arrangement.

1. Which of the following could be a complete and accurate list of the flowers in the arrangement?

   (A) Roses: two yellow, two pink; Carnations: two red, one white; Irises: one white, one yellow

   (B) Roses: one yellow, one pink, two red; Carnations: two red, one white; Irises: one yellow, one white

   (C) Roses: two red, one yellow; Carnations: two white, one red; Irises: one white, one yellow

   (D) Roses: two yellow, two red; Carnations: two pink, one white; Irises: two white

   (E) Roses: two red, one pink, two yellow; Carnations: one red, one white; Irises: one white, two yellow

2. If the only irises used in the arrangement are white, which of the following must be true?

   (A) There are exactly three red flowers.
   (B) There are exactly two white flowers.
   (C) There are exactly three pink flowers.
   (D) There are exactly three yellow flowers.
   (E) There are exactly two yellow flowers.

3. If the arrangement includes four red flowers, which of the following must be true of the arrangement?

   (A) It includes exactly three white flowers.
   (B) It includes exactly one white flower.
   (C) It includes exactly one pink flower.
   (D) It includes exactly two white flowers.
   (E) It includes exactly two yellow flowers.

4. If there are no pink flowers in the arrangement, which of the following could be false?

   (A) There are exactly two yellow roses.
   (B) There are exactly two red roses.
   (C) There is one white carnation.
   (D) There are exactly four roses.
   (E) There are three carnations.

5. Which of the following must be false?

   (A) The arrangement includes two pink roses.
   (B) The arrangement includes three yellow flowers.
   (C) The arrangement includes exactly one white flower.
   (D) The only irises in the arrangement are yellow.
   (E) The only carnations in the arrangement are red.

6. If the arrangement includes the maximum possible number of pink flowers, it must include which of the following?

   (A) exactly two red carnations
   (B) at least one white carnation
   (C) at least one pink carnation
   (D) at least one red carnation
   (E) exactly two pink carnations

7. If the arrangement includes exactly two pink carnations, which of the following could be a complete and accurate list of the roses included?

   (A) one pink, one yellow, two red
   (B) two red, two yellow, one pink
   (C) two red, two pink, one yellow
   (D) two red, two yellow
   (E) one red, two yellow, one pink

Game 95

A basketball coach is selecting her starting line-up. There are eight players on the team that could be placed into the starting line-up: G, H, I, J, K, L, M, and O. No other players can be placed into the starting line-up. The starting line-up consists of exactly five positions, numbered 1 through 5. The coach must select exactly one player to fill each of the five positions and no player can play more than one position. The following conditions apply:

The only players that can be placed into position 1 are G, H, and I.
The only players that can be placed into position 2 are G, H, and J.
The only players that can be placed into position 3 are G, K, M, and O.
The only players that can be placed into position 4 are L, M, and K.
The only players that can be placed into position 5 are L and M.
If J is placed into the starting line-up, then M must be placed into position 5.
If I is placed into the starting line-up, then K cannot be placed into the starting line-up.
If both G and M are placed into the starting line-up, then K must also be placed into the starting line-up.
If L is placed into position 4, then G must be placed into position 1.

1. Which of the following could be a complete and accurate list of the players chosen for the starting line-up in positions 1 through 5, respectively?

   (A) I, H, K, L, M
   (B) G, J, K, M, L
   (C) H, J, K, L, M
   (D) G, H, O, M, L
   (E) H, G, K, M, L

2. If M is not placed into the starting line-up, which of the following must be true?

   (A) H is placed into position 1.
   (B) I is placed into position 1.
   (C) K is not placed into the starting line-up.
   (D) L is placed into position 4.
   (E) O is placed into position 3.

3. If both I and M are placed into the starting line-up, which of the following are two players that could be placed in positions 2 and 4, respectively?

   (A) G and L
   (B) H and M
   (C) H and L
   (D) J and K
   (E) J and L

4. Which of the following gives sufficient information to know the exact starting line-up?

   (A) H is in position 1.
   (B) J is in position 2.
   (C) G is in position 3.
   (D) L is in position 4.
   (E) M is in position 5.

5. If K is not placed into the starting line-up, which of the following is a player that CANNOT be placed into the starting line-up?

   (A) G
   (B) H
   (C) I
   (D) M
   (E) O

6. If I is placed into position 1, which of the following are two players that must be placed into consecutively numbered positions?

   (A) G and H
   (B) G and M
   (C) H and O
   (D) I and J
   (E) K and L

7. If K is placed in position 3, which of the following CANNOT be true?

   (A) G is not placed into the starting line-up.
   (B) H is placed into position 1.
   (C) H is not placed into the starting line-up.
   (D) L is placed into position 5.
   (E) J is placed into the starting line-up.

Game 96

Six kites are being flown in a park on Saturday. Each kite is either red, green, blue, or yellow. There is at least one kite of each color and there cannot be more than two of any particular color. Each kite is flying at a different altitude from the others.

The same red kite that is higher than a blue kite is also lower than a green kite.
A blue kite is higher than a green kite.
No blue kite is highest or lowest among the kites.
No blue kite is immediately higher or lower than a green kite.

1. Which of the following could be a complete and accurate list of the kites from highest to lowest?

    (A) yellow, green, red, blue, red, green
    (B) red, green, yellow, blue, yellow, green
    (C) yellow, green, red, blue, red, yellow
    (D) blue, yellow, green, red, blue, yellow
    (E) red, green, red, blue, green, yellow

2. Which of the following must be true?

    (A) There is exactly one red kite.
    (B) There is exactly one yellow kite.
    (C) There are exactly two red kites.
    (D) There are exactly two green kites.
    (E) There are exactly two blue kites.

3. Which of the following must be true?

    (A) A yellow kite is highest or lowest.
    (B) A green kite is either highest or lowest.
    (C) A blue kite is immediately above the lowest kite.
    (D) A red kite is immediately below the highest kite.
    (E) Exactly two kites separate the highest kite and a red kite.

4. If yellow kites are immediately below the highest kite and above the lowest kite, which of the following must be false?

    (A) A green kite is highest
    (B) There is exactly one blue kite
    (C) There are exactly two red kites
    (D) A yellow kite is immediately above a red kite.
    (E) A blue kite is immediately above a yellow kite.

5. If a red kite is the highest, which of the following must be false?

    (A) A blue kite is immediately above a yellow kite.
    (B) A green kite is immediately above a red kite.
    (C) A red kite is immediately above a blue kite.
    (D) The lowest kite is yellow.
    (E) The lowest kite is green.

6. If two kites of the same color are adjacent in height, one immediately above the other, which of the following must be false?

    (A) There are two yellow kites.
    (B) There are two red kites.
    (C) There are two blue kites.
    (D) A yellow kite is adjacent to a red kite in height.
    (E) A yellow kite is adjacent to a green kite in height.

7. If there is exactly one red kite, in how many different positions from lowest to highest could that kite be flying?

    (A) 1
    (B) 2
    (C) 3
    (D) 4
    (E) 5

Game 97

Each of five awards, for service, GPA, leadership, citizenship, and research, is presented to exactly one of five graduates, Brenda, Daniel, Felix, Kellie, and Natalie, at a graduation awards ceremony. The awards are given according to the following criteria:

If the award for leadership does not go to Kellie, then the award for GPA goes to Kellie and the award for leadership goes to Brenda.

In the circumstance that Natalie receives the service award, the award for GPA goes to Daniel, unless it goes to Felix.

Felix cannot receive the awards for service or research unless Daniel does not receive an award for either service or research.

Brenda does not receive the leadership award only if Natalie receives the service award.

1. Which of the following could be a complete and accurate list of the awards received by Brenda, Daniel, Felix, Kellie, and Natalie, respectively?

   (A) citizenship, leadership, research, GPA, service
   (B) leadership, service, citizenship, GPA, research
   (C) leadership, research, citizenship, GPA, service
   (D) leadership, service, research, GPA, citizenship
   (E) GPA, research, citizenship, leadership, service

2. What is the total number of graduates any one of whom could win the award for GPA?

   (A) 1
   (B) 2
   (C) 3
   (D) 4
   (E) 5

3. If Brenda receives the award for citizenship, which of the following could be true?

   (A) Daniel receives the award for leadership.
   (B) Felix receives the award for leadership.
   (C) Kellie receives the award for service.
   (D) Daniel receives the award for research.
   (E) Kellie receives the award for research.

4. Which of the following is a complete and accurate list of the awards which might be presented to Natalie?

   (A) service
   (B) service, research
   (C) service, research, GPA
   (D) service, research, citizenship
   (E) service, research, citizenship, GPA

5. If Kellie does not receive the award for leadership and Daniel does not receive the award for citizenship, which of the following must be false?

   (A) Brenda receives the award for leadership.
   (B) Felix receives the award for citizenship.
   (C) Daniel receives the award for research.
   (D) Natalie receives the award for research.
   (E) Kellie receives the award for GPA.

6. If Natalie receives the award for service, which of the following is a complete and accurate list of the graduates who might receive the award for citizenship?

   (A) Brenda
   (B) Brenda, Daniel
   (C) Brenda, Felix
   (D) Brenda, Daniel, Felix
   (E) Brenda, Daniel, Felix, Kellie

7. Which of the following must be false?

(A) Felix receives the award for citizenship and Natalie receives the award for service.

(B) Daniel receives the award for citizenship and Kellie receives the award for GPA.

(C) Brenda receives the award for research and Felix receives the award for service.

(D) Daniel receives the award for citizenship and Natalie receives the award for research.

(E) Felix receives the award for citizenship and Daniel receives the award for service.

Game 98

Nine students, Zachary, Jessica, Scratch, Lily, Ripper, Katie, Geek 1, Geek 2, and Geek 3, are all participants on the Bayview High School High-Q team. Mr. Balding is assigning each of the nine students to either the junior varsity squad or the varsity squad. The junior varsity squad must have exactly four students and the varsity team must have exactly five students. The students can be assigned to only one squad. The assignments must be made in accordance with the following rules:

Either Zachary or Geek 3 must be on the junior varsity squad, but not both.

Ripper is not on the varsity squad unless Katie is on the varsity squad.

If Zachary is on the junior varsity squad, then Scratch must be on the varsity squad.

If Jessica is not on the junior varsity squad, then Scratch is not on the varsity squad.

Geek 1 and Geek 2 are not assigned to the same squad.

Geek 2 is assigned to the junior varsity squad only if Geek 3 is assigned to the junior varsity squad.

1. Which of the following could be a complete and accurate list of the students assigned to the varsity squad?

   (A) Ripper, Geek 1, Katie, Jessica, Lily
   (B) Geek 2, Ripper, Scratch, Zachary, Katie
   (C) Scratch, Geek 3, Jessica, Geek 1, Lily
   (D) Zachary, Lily, Katie, Jessica, Ripper
   (E) Zachary, Ripper, Geek 2, Jessica, Lily

2. If Geek 3 is assigned to the varsity squad, which of the following is a student who must also be assigned to the varsity squad?

   (A) Lily
   (B) Katie
   (C) Jessica
   (D) Ripper
   (E) Geek 1

3. Which of the following could be true?

   (A) Katie is on the junior varsity squad and Ripper is on the varsity squad.
   (B) Geek 3 is on the varsity squad and Geek 2 is on the junior varsity squad.
   (C) Scratch is on the junior varsity squad and Zachary is on the junior varsity squad.
   (D) Geek 3 is on the junior varsity squad and Geek 2 is on the varsity squad.
   (E) Scratch is on the varsity squad and Jessica is on the varsity squad.

4. Which of the following provides sufficient information to determine which squad each of the nine students is assigned to?

   (A) Ripper and Geek 3 are together on the varsity squad.
   (B) Jessica and Geek 3 are together on the junior varsity squad.
   (C) Zachary and Geek 1 are together on the varsity squad.
   (D) Scratch and Geek 1 are together on the junior varsity squad.
   (E) Geek 2 and Zachary are together on the varsity squad.

5. If Geek 2 is on the varsity squad, which of the following must be false?

   (A) Ripper is on the junior varsity squad.
   (B) Zachary is on the varsity squad.
   (C) Katie is on the junior varsity squad.
   (D) Lily is on the junior varsity squad.
   (E) Scratch is on the varsity squad.

6. If Zachary is on the junior varsity squad, which of the following could be a pair of students who are both assigned to the varsity squad?

   (A) Geek 1, Geek 3
   (B) Lily, Ripper
   (C) Jessica, Katie
   (D) Ripper, Geek 2
   (E) Katie, Geek 1

Aaron is on a shopping spree at an electronics superstore. He buys at least four and at most six of a TV, VCR, DVD, laptop, PDA, camera, blender, refrigerator, and washing machine. Aaron makes his purchases in accordance with the following:

He does not buy a laptop if he buys both a DVD and a VCR.

He does not buy a PDA or a camera unless he buys neither a blender nor a refrigerator.

He buys a TV if he buys neither a DVD nor a VCR.

He does not buy a TV unless he also buys a PDA and a laptop.

One of the things he buys is a blender, a refrigerator, or a washing machine.

1. Which of the following could be a complete and accurate list of the items that Aaron purchases?

   (A) PDA, refrigerator, TV, DVD
   (B) laptop, VCR, blender, refrigerator, camera
   (C) camera, TV, laptop, PDA, DVD
   (D) laptop, PDA, washing machine, camera
   (E) refrigerator, VCR, DVD, camera, laptop

2. If Aaron buys a camera, which of the following must he also buy?

   (A) DVD
   (B) TV
   (C) refrigerator
   (D) washing machine
   (E) VCR

3. Which of the following is a pair of items both of which CANNOT be among the items Aaron buys?

   (A) VCR and DVD
   (B) TV and camera
   (C) refrigerator and TV
   (D) laptop and washing machine
   (E) DVD and PDA

4. If Aaron buys exactly four items, including a PDA, a washing machine, and a camera, he could also buy a

   (A) refrigerator.
   (B) laptop.
   (C) TV.
   (D) DVD.
   (E) blender.

5. If Aaron buys a refrigerator and a blender but not a DVD, he must also buy

   (A) a washing machine.
   (B) a camera.
   (C) a VCR.
   (D) a laptop.
   (E) a PDA.

6. If Aaron buys a VCR, a camera, and a DVD, which of the following must be true?

   (A) He buys a PDA.
   (B) He buys a TV.
   (C) He buys at most four items.
   (D) He buys at most five items.
   (E) He buys at most six items.

7. If Aaron buys exactly four items, including a laptop and a refrigerator, the other two items that he buys could be

   (A) a camera and a VCR.
   (B) a washing machine and a PDA.
   (C) a washing machine and a DVD.
   (D) a VCR and a TV.
   (E) a DVD and a VCR.

Game 100

Six students, Brenda, Chris, Danny, Margaret, Weston, and Jessica sit in six desks numbered 1 to 6 in a row in a classroom. Desk 1 is in the front, and desk 6 is in the rear. Each is wearing exactly one of the following shirts: New York, orange, plaid, red, silver, and Texas. The following conditions apply:

The student in the Texas shirt sits two seats away from the student in the New York shirt.

The student in the Texas shirt sits directly behind the student in the plaid shirt.

The student in the red shirt sits in desk 6.

Brenda never sits in desk 1.

Chris would never wear either a plaid shirt or a Texas shirt.

Jessica sits closer to the front than Danny.

Margaret sits closer to the front than Chris.

Danny sits closer to the front than Weston and Margaret and wears the New York shirt.

Brenda sits directly in front of Chris.

Chris is in desk 5 or desk 6.

1. If Brenda sits in the fourth seat from the front, which shirt must Weston wear?

    (A) orange
    (B) silver
    (C) red
    (D) plaid
    (E) Texas

2. Which of the following is a complete list of people who could wear red?

    (A) Danny, Weston, Chris
    (B) Margaret, Jessica, Weston
    (C) Weston, Chris
    (D) Brenda, Danny, Jessica
    (E) Chris, Margaret, Weston

3. If Chris sits in the fifth seat from the front, which is a list of shirts that Jessica could wear?

    (A) Texas, orange
    (B) plaid
    (C) silver, plaid
    (D) plaid, orange
    (E) orange

4. If Brenda wears the Texas shirt, which of the following could be true?

    (A) Chris wears plaid.
    (B) Jessica wears plaid.
    (C) Margaret wears orange.
    (D) Weston wears plaid.
    (E) Weston wears red.

5. Which of the following is a complete and accurate list of the shirts Margaret could wear?

    (A) silver, orange, Texas
    (B) silver, orange
    (C) plaid, Texas
    (D) Texas, New York
    (E) plaid, orange, silver

Part III

Setups

1. **Type:** In this game there are elements of both slots and ordering games. There are slots because there are three different variables: students, plays, and weeks. However, a quick reading of the rules tells you that you will have to deal with the order of both the students and the plays over the five-week period. In other words, the order will establish the places the items take in the slots.

2. **Diagram:** The order is going to be the key to this game, so the five weeks are going to play a central role. The five weeks should be written as columns across the top of your diagram. The two remaining categories, students and plays, should be the two rows. This creates a distinct slot for each book and for each student over the five-week period. You will have to place a student or a book in each slot based on the conditions given in the rules.

3. **Simplify the rules:** Simplify the rules by converting them into symbols wherever you can. If you can't, try to write the rule as briefly as possible near your diagram so you don't have to look at the rules again. Don't forget the information contained in the setup paragraph. Every student will be used exactly once and every play will be used exactly once. Thus, every slot will be filled with a unique piece of information. The first rule in the rules list gives you two pieces of information, one of which mixes information about students and plays: J must be after K (K..J) and J must be before C (J..C). The second rule says O is after A (A..O), again mixing information about students and plays. The third and fourth rules give you hard facts that can be placed directly on the diagram: A cannot be first and neither M nor V can be last.

4. **Deductions:** At this point it doesn't seem like you know very much, or even that you *can* know very much. However, consider the sequences that the rules gave you. J must be after K, so J cannot be the first student and K cannot be the last play. Mark these things down on your diagram. J must also be before C, so J cannot be the last student and C cannot be the first student. Now you know that none of A, J, and C can be the first student to give a report, leaving either B or I as the first student. You also know that O, M, and K cannot be the last plays, leaving either H or R as the last play. Now the information about the order of the students and plays becomes even more important because it is more restrictive. The rules tell you that A must be before O. Since O cannot be the last play and A cannot be the first student, you are only left with weeks 2, 3, and 4 to work with. Since A must be before O, A can only fit in week 2 or 3 and O can only fit in week 3 or 4. Furthermore, J must be before C and J cannot be in week 1 so it would appear that the earliest C can be is in third (which would occur if J were second). However, since A must be in either week 2 or 3, if J is in week 2 then A must be in week 3, and vice versa. So in reality C must come after both J and A, and neither J nor A can be first. Thus, there is no room for C until week 4 or 5. These deductions have limited the possible placement of students and plays and will help you complete this game successfully.

5. **"Walk Around It":** The key here is to keep track of not only which students must be before which students and which plays must be before which plays, but also which plays must be before which students and which students must be before which plays. The relationship between the order of the students and the plays restricts the available slots for many of the students and plays. Anything that places C, J, or A in a specific slot will constrain things a great deal. Thus, the deductions will be very helpful in solving the questions.

Setups

1. **Type:** In this game there are eight dinosaur species that must be assigned to one of three periods, the Early, Middle, and Late periods. Based solely on this information it would be easy to classify this as a grouping game. However, if you look at the rules it becomes clear that the groups are going to depend on the order specified in the rules. You have to deal with the order of dinosaurs and this order will determine the composition of the groups. This is a hybrid between a grouping game and an ordering game. The first thing to do is determine the relative order that the rules establish and then determine the effects of this order on the groups.

2. **Diagram:** Since this is a hybrid between a grouping and an ordering game, it will be helpful to draw two diagrams. The groups can be represented by drawing three columns labeled E, M, and L, respectively, to represent the three periods in which the dinosaurs go extinct. Each group can have no more than three dinosaurs in it. The other diagram will be a list of relative order. Drawing out the groups will help you visualize the effects that the order has on the groups.

3. **Simplify the rules:** This game is a great example of why it is important to simplify and symbolize the rules. The game talks about eight types of dinosaurs with names like Rhamphorhynchus. Writing these names out or even thinking them is a waste of time. Abbreviate them by using the first letter so that Rhamphorhynchus becomes simply R, etc. The rules tell you that S and O cannot be in the same period, creating a split. P must go extinct after T (T...P) although T and P do not have to be in different groups. Furthermore, O must go extinct after P (P..O), although P and O do not have to be in different groups. The last two rules create two blocks: TU and UV.

4. **Deductions:** Now is the time to make deductions. Relate the rules to each other and determine what additional information you can discover. The easiest way to make deductions is to find two or more rules that deal with the same item. For instance, look at the two groups: TU and UV. If T must be with U and U must be with V then it must be the case that there is a larger group of T, U, and V (TUV). This group of three dinosaurs that must go extinct in the same era will fill up one era, because no more than three dinosaurs can go extinct in any one era. Another rule says that T must be before P. Thus, you know that the TUV block must come sometime before P. Lastly, you know that P must come sometime before O. You end up with a list of relative order that looks like this: TUV..P..O. Although the rules said T and P do not necessarily have to be in different groups, you just deduced that they must. On the other hand, you still do not know whether P and O are in different groups. From this list of relative order you can further deduce that the TUV block can only be in the Early or Middle era and that the earliest P can be is in the Middle era because it must come after the TUV block. If the TUV block is in the Early era, you do not know very much additional information. If it is in the Middle era, you know that both P and O must be in the Late era. Since O and S cannot be in the same group, if the TUV block goes extinct in the Middle era you also know that S must go extinct in the Early era.

5. **"Walk Around It":** There are only two main scenarios. Which scenario you are dealing with depends on the position of the TUV block in either the Early era or the Middle era. Placing the TUV block in the Middle Period is more restrictive. Both Q and R are wildcards in this game, while S is restricted because it cannot be in the same group as O. You are now ready for the questions.

1. **Type:** The first step in solving any game is to figure out what it is that you are actually dealing with. Here, you must distribute seven students among four different sections, or groups. This, then, is a grouping game.

2. **Diagram:** The diagram for this game, as with any grouping game, is simply a drawing that reflects the number of groups that are involved in the game. Here there are four groups, so you can draw four columns, each labeled, in this case, one through four.

3. **Simplify the rules:** Simplify the rules by converting them into symbols. The process of converting each rule into a symbol benefits you by forcing you to consider what each rule means, as well as by providing you with symbols to work with rather than words. This will help you move through the game faster. Many times there are very important rules in the setup paragraph, so do not gloss over the information contained there. The setup paragraph, in addition to providing the key to knowing what type of game this is, also includes the vital restrictions that no more than three of the seven students can be in one section together and that none of the seven students can be alone in a section. These two rules simply mean that each section that students are assigned to must have at least two and no more than three of the seven students assigned to it. Notice that nowhere is it stated that all four of the sections must be used. The rest of the rules are contained in the rules list. The rules list provides a long list of splits, or groups of students who cannot be together. None of the following pairs can be together: NA, NT, AT, BR, BT, RT, BN, BE, or NE. You can show this by writing these pairs and then crossing them out so that you know these pairs are prohibited rather than required. The final rule says that E is in either section 2 or section 4 and that A is in either section 2 or section 4, but E and A do not have to be together.

4. **Deductions:** Once you have the diagram and the rules in front of you, think about how the rules relate to each other. In other words, make deductions. As in most grouping games, it is very helpful to consider the possible numerical distribution of the items. In this game there are seven students and four groups. There is also a requirement that each group that has somebody assigned to it must have two or three people assigned to it. The only way to divide up seven people in groups of two's or three's is if there are two groups of two and one group of three. Thus, the numerical distribution for this game is 2-2-3, though not necessarily in that order. This reveals that none of the seven students will be assigned to one of the four sections, or, in other words, one section will not be used. Now consider the rules about the pairs of students who cannot be together. The three students who are most constrained are N, B, and T. N cannot be with B or T, and B and T cannot be together either. In other words, N, B, and T must be all be separated from each other. Thus, each one of the three groups used must include exactly one of N, B, or T. Now you can use the rules about who cannot be together to determine who can be with each of N, B, and T, respectively. N cannot be with B, T, A, or E, so N must be with R or J (or both). B cannot be with N, T, R, or E, so B must be with A or J (or both). T cannot be with A, B, N, or R, so T must be with E or J (or both). Looking carefully at these lists reveals that N is the only one of the three who can be with R, so N and R must be together. B is the only one of the three who can be with A, so B and A must be together. Similarly, T is the only one of the three who can be paired with E, so T must be with E. J was included in each of these lists, so J can be grouped with anybody. Thus, before even going to the questions you know that N and R are together, B and A are together, and T and E are together. J can be the third member of any of these groups.

5. **"Walk Around It":** Before moving on to the questions, review what you know so far. The seven students must be assigned to exactly three of the four sections. One section will have three students and the remaining two will have exactly two students. You already know the three basic groups: NR, BA, and TE. J can be the third student in any of these groups. Also, bear in mind that both A and E are restricted to section 2 or 4, and it is now clear that A and E cannot go together, and so the unused section is either section 1 or section 3.

1. **Type:** In this game there are five customers who must each buy exactly two of four toppings for their pizza. As you work this game, you will want to see what each customer does and does not buy. Thus, there are in effect three categories: customers, toppings, and whether or not they buy a topping. It is most useful to consider this as a slots game. It is tempting to approach this as a grouping game, but the rules indicate that chain reactions will be key, and these are easier to see in a slots setup.

2. **Diagram:** The diagram should indicate clearly the slots that are created by the two categories. For this game it is easiest to use a matrix with the five customers, B, C, D, F, and G, on the horizontal axis, and the four types of toppings, M, O, P, and S, on the vertical axis. Since you will want to see what each customer does and does not buy, you can fill in your diagram with checks and X's.

3. **Simplify the rules:** Go through the rules one by one and convert them into symbols. This keeps the rules close to your work and also forces you to think about what the rules actually say. Don't leave out any rules that are contained within the setup paragraph. Here, the setup paragraph tells you that each customer buys exactly two toppings. Next, tackle the list of rules. One rule says that B and F must order the same foods (B=F). Two other rules tell you that two pairs of customers cannot order the same foods: F cannot order the same toppings as C (F≠C) and D cannot order the same toppings as G (D≠G). There are three rules that, rather than saying that two customers order exactly the same thing, tell you that pairs of customers must have only one topping in common: C and D must order exactly one topping that is the same, G and B must order exactly one topping that is the same, and C and G must order exactly one topping that is the same. Symbolize these in any way that makes sense to you. For example, you could write: C & D=1 same, etc. The remaining rule makes

specific assignments to the diagram: C orders P, B orders O, and G orders S. Place a check on the matrix in the appropriate slots to indicate that a certain customer orders a specific topping.

4. **Deductions:** After simplifying the rules, you know what the rules say, but what do they really mean? How do they relate to each other? This is the key to every game. Take the time to make deductions. Relate the rules to each other and see what else you can determine. The first two rules in the rules list tell you 1) that B and F order the same thing and 2) that C and F must order different things. Since B and F order the same thing while C and F must order different things, you can determine that B and C cannot order the same thing. Thus, you have deduced an additional relationship: B≠C. Now look at the specific assignments made to the various slots. Since B must order O, and B and F must order the same toppings, F must order an O. Since C cannot order the same toppings as either B or F, C cannot order O. Likewise, since C orders P, neither B nor F can order P. Both B and C are left with one topping to order and they cannot order the same thing as each other so one must order M and one must order S. You cannot determine which one orders which. You will have to rely on the questions to give you additional information that will allow you to determine which topping they order. The one remaining assignment is that G orders S. G and D cannot order the same toppings, so D cannot order S. This is everything that you can deduce from the specific assignments. The only rules left are the rules that specify pairs of customers who buy one topping in common. Notice that each of B and C must have one topping in common with G, but since B and C cannot order the same topping, each of B and C must have a different topping in common with G. As you've already determined, G must have an S and exactly one of B or C must have an S. G's second topping could be any of the other three toppings, but the other of B or C that does not have an S must have the same topping as G's second topping. Notice also that C must share a topping with each of D and G, but D and G cannot have the same toppings. You cannot deduce anything firm from this relationship, but it is important to notice the relationship nonetheless.

5. **"Walk Around It":** Before jumping into the questions, take a brief moment to review what you do know and what you don't know. You know exactly one of the two toppings for B, C, F, and G. B and F must order the same two toppings. C must order different toppings than do both B and F. For both B and C, the only toppings left are M and S. Since B and C cannot order the same toppings, one must order M and the other must order S. It is vital that you recognize that there are effectively only two possibilities, one where B and F order S and C orders M and another where B and F order M and C orders S. If you feel compelled you can work out both these scenarios, or you can just remember that the setup is very limited. In any case, both B and C must have exactly one topping in common with G. Whoever orders the S will have met this requirement since G must order an S. C must also have one topping in common with D, but D and G cannot have the same toppings. The only thing that you know about D is that he cannot order S. The questions will place something on the diagram and require you to determine the side effects. Watch closely for the interplay among B, C, and F. The placement of one will determine the placement of all the others. All you will be left with is the relationship between D and G, and their orders will be restricted by the requirement that both B and C have exactly one topping in common with G and that C also has one topping in common with D. This game will be about chain reactions. Almost any given information will result in a lot of additional information, as is evident once you have made the deductions.

1. **Type:** In this game you have to assign various notebooks to one of two different colored backpacks. These two different colored backpacks also represent different days of the week. If you realize that the color of the backpacks and the days of the week that the classes are taken are interchangeable, then it is apparent that this is a grouping game with two groups.

2. **Diagram:** The diagram should clearly show the two groups by having two columns labeled R and B for the red and blue backpacks. You should also make note on the diagram that R means the same thing as a class taken on Monday, Wednesday, and Friday (MWF) and B means the same thing as a class taken on Tuesday and Thursday (TTh).

3. **Simplify the rules:** Simplify the rules by converting them into symbols. This is easy to do for conditional statements like those found in this game. Be sure to write them down correctly! Don't forget the simple rules in the setup paragraph, such as the rule that says Andres takes at least two courses on each day, which means that there must be at least two notebooks in each backpack. One very helpful thing to do in this game, once you realize that the color of the backpack and the days of the week of the classes describe the same thing, is to pick either the color of the backpacks or the days of the week as the standard method of notation for each of the rules. For this explanation, color will be used. In other words, the rule that says if Andres takes government on Tuesday and Thursday then he takes anthropology on Monday, Wednesday, and Friday becomes if G is in B (B is the same as TTh) then A is in R (R is the same as MWF). This rule can be symbolized as: $G_B \rightarrow A_R$. Follow the same approach for the other conditional statements, inserting R or B wherever MWF or TTh is used. The one rule that may cause trouble is the rule that says S is not in the blue backpack unless A is in the blue backpack. To work the game correctly you must interpret this rule correctly. In order to interpret this rule correctly, you must determine what is sufficient to produce what. Is A's being in the blue backpack sufficient to force S into the blue backpack? Or is it the other way

around? The statement says that there is no way for S to be in the blue backpack unless A is in the blue backpack. In other words, S can be in the blue backpack only if A is in the blue backpack. A's being in the blue backpack is a necessary condition for S to be in the blue backpack. Translated into an "if...then" statement, this becomes: if S is in B then A must also be in B. Remember, one way to approach "unless" is to consider that "unless" always introduces a necessary condition, not a sufficient condition. Knowing this allows you to determine that the correct way to interpret this rule is, as already mentioned, "if S is in B then A must also be in B." Consider an example: You cannot do well on the Law School Admissions Test unless you have a pencil. Does having a pencil ensure a good performance? No! Having a pencil is a necessary condition for doing well while doing well is sufficient to show that you had a pencil. Thus, as an "if..then" statement, the example becomes: If you do well on the Law School Admissions Test then you had a pencil. Another way to think about any statement with "unless" is to convert "unless" to "if not." Thus, the statement "S is not in the blue backpack unless A is in the blue backpack" can be changed to read "S is not in B if A is not in B." Rearranged, this statement reads "if A is not in B then S is not in B," which is the contrapositive of "if S is in B then A is in B." Consider the same example as above: You cannot do well on the LSAT unless you have a pencil. You can convert the "unless" into "if not" such that the statement becomes "You cannot do well on the LSAT if you do not have a pencil." Rearranged, this becomes "If you do not have a pencil then you cannot do well on the LSAT," which is the contrapositive of "If you do well on the LSAT then you had a pencil." The ability to sort out the precise meaning of conditional statements is vital. If you ever have trouble, think of this example.

4. **Deductions:** The deductions step is vital to working the game correctly and quickly. Remember, when you have to choose between speed and accuracy, accuracy counts more. More wrong answers do not help you, while getting everything right that you spend your precious time on counts a great deal. This can become a reality if you take the time to make deductions and think about the game before jumping directly into the questions. In fact, you do not have to choose speed or accuracy,

one over the other. By making deductions and thinking about the game, you not only increase your accuracy, but your speed as well. Think of the deductions step as an investment. The return on this investment will be a better understanding of the game, which leads to increased confidence and better performance. Thus, accuracy yields speed. After the pep talk, are you ready for the deductions? A good place to start making deductions in a game that contains conditional statements is with the contrapositive of each conditional statement. Go through each "if...then" statement and reverse and negate it in order to find the contrapositive. For example, the rule that says if G is in B then A is in R becomes if A is not in R then G is not in B. Since there are only two groups and since each notebook must be used, if A is not in R then it is in B and if G is not in B then it is in R. Thus, the contrapositive becomes if A is in B then G is in R. Follow this same procedure for the rest of the conditional statements. Now that you have written down what each rule means, try to relate the rules to each other. Look for rules that contain the same notebooks, or for rules that affect each other. It turns out here that you can determine a few rather lengthy chains of causation. One rule says if S is in B then A is in B, a contrapositive says if A is in B then G is in R, and another contrapositive says that if G is in R then L is in R. Thus, one chain looks like this: If S is in B then A is in B then G is in R then L is in R ($S_B \rightarrow A_B \rightarrow G_R \rightarrow L_R$). Remember, you can jump in anywhere on the chain but if you do not start with S then only the things that follow on the right must be true. For instance if you know A is in B then it must be true that G is in R and L is in R, but you cannot determine whether S is in B. The contrapositive of this chain is also true: If L is in B then G is in B, if G is in B then A is in R, and if A is in R then S is in R ($L_B \rightarrow G_B \rightarrow A_R \rightarrow S_R$). This chain also allows you to determine a shoot off chain concerning the placement of P and H since if G is in B then P is in B and if P is in B then H is in R. Written out this chain says: $L_B \rightarrow G_B \rightarrow P_B \rightarrow H_R$. Don't forget the contrapositive of this little chain as well: HB and $P_R \rightarrow G_R \rightarrow L_R$. The same thing holds true for these chains: If you know one item, then only the things that follow on the right in the chain must be true; you do not know anything about what comes before that item.

5. **"Walk Around It"**: Now you have quite a bit of information. All but one of the notebooks, M, are included in the rules. Since there are no rules about M, M is the wildcard. The rest of the notebooks are restricted. Any information about any of the notebooks will most likely let you know the placement of still other notebooks. All you need to do is follow the chains of causation. If you affirm any of the information, then you know that its consequences must be true but you do not know anything about its antecedents. If you understand this concept, this game will be much easier. Just to be sure that you understand this concept, try an example. Suppose this chain is true: If Charlie has the measles then he is sick, if he is sick then he does not go to school, if he does not go to school then he will miss a test, and if he misses a test then he will fail the course. If you know that Charlie does not go to school then it must be true that he misses a test and that he fails the course. However, you cannot say for certain that Charlie had measles or even that he was sick. There could be any number of causes for Charlie's absence from school. Perhaps he was out drinking too late with his friends and slept in, or perhaps he was camping out for tickets to the latest episode of Star Wars. Once you understand this concept, you are ready for the questions.

1. **Type:** First think about what type of game you are dealing with. This game tells you that you must assign teams to projects C, D, and F. This should indicate to you that this is a grouping game. Within each group you will have to deal with the categories of writers and graphic artists, but it is easy to keep track of them within the groups instead of making this a slots game. However, be sure to pay attention to who is a writer and who is a graphic artist.

2. **Diagram:** The diagram should clearly show the three groups: C, D, and F. In each of these groups there will be at least one writer and exactly two graphic artists. In order to show the three groups, you can make three columns labeled C, D, and F. If you insist on showing the distinction between writers and graphic artists, you could also create two rows labeled W for writer and G for graphic artist. If you set the game up like this, it will be unlike normal slots games because more than one item can, and in some cases must, go in the slot. It might be easiest just to have the three columns and within each column draw four spaces, since that is the largest number of people that can be in each group. You will have exactly two G's and at least one W.

3. **Simplify the rules:** It is important to go through the rules carefully and simplify them by converting them into symbols. This will help you save time in the long run by allowing you to avoid reading bothersome and time-consuming words all the time. It also forces you to ponder the meaning of each rule. Do not forget the rules contained in the setup paragraph. The setup paragraph here provides some information about the numerical distribution of writers and graphic artists: There must be exactly two graphic artists in each group and at least one of the two writers in each group. The first two rules in the rules list will help you deduce more precisely the distribution of writers and graphic artists: 1) No writer can be in both C and D, and 2) No graphic artist can be

in both D and F. You next have a split and a block: S cannot be with T and V must be with L. Be careful with this block of V and L. It merely says that V is assigned to a team with L, it does not say that wherever V is, L is, or wherever L is, V is. It simply says that on at least one of the teams, V and L must be together. There might still be instances where they are apart. Finally, there are two direct assignments that you can place on the diagram: V is in D and S is in C.

4. **Deductions:** Once you have pondered the meaning of each rule individually, you need to ponder the significance of each rule, especially as it relates to the other rules. This allows you to determine side effects and make deductions. For instance, the first rule says that no writer can be in both C and D. The setup paragraph tells you that there are only two writers, L and M, and that at least one must be assigned to every group. Since one of L or M must be assigned to C, it is impossible for whichever one is in C to be in D also. Since there must be a writer in D, the one that is not in C must be in D. In other words, exactly one of L or M must be in C and the other must be in D. The fact that only one of the writers is in each of C and D means that there must be exactly three people in groups C and D (two graphic artists plus one writer). The rules told you that S is in C and that V is in D, so at this point you know that S and L/M are in C while V and L/M are in D. In both C and D there must be exactly one other graphic artist. Since T cannot be with S, the remaining graphic artist in C must be either R or V. Now look at group D. Since V is a graphic artist who is definitely in D and no graphic artist can be in both D and F, V cannot be in F. Therefore, in order for there to be exactly two graphic artists in F, there must be exactly two of R, S, and T. Since S and T cannot be together, R must be in F with exactly one of S and T. Because R must be in F, you can deduce that R cannot also be used in D. Since V is already used in D and R cannot be used in D, the remaining graphic artist in D must either be S or T. You now know that either S or T must be in D and that either S or T must be in F. Since S and T are both graphic artists and no graphic

artists can be in both D and F, if you know where the S or T is between D and F, you also know where the other is. Lastly, keep in mind that V must be with L somewhere, so if V is not used somewhere else (C is the only place that another V could be used besides the V in D), then L must be with V in group D. These rules gave you a lot to chew on, but it is worth it. If you try to swallow too soon, you'll choke.

5. **"Walk Around It":** The deductions step was critical in determining the possible distribution of writers and graphic artists. If you took the time to make the deductions, you now know that in C you must have S, R/V, and L/M, in D you must have V, S/T, and L/M, and in F you must have R, S/T, and one or both of L and M. There must be exactly three people in both C and D while there could either be three or four people in F. If you know where the L or M is in C or D, then you know where the other one is. This will also affect whether R or V is in C, since V must be with L in one of the groups. If V is not used in C, or rather, if R is used in C, then you know L must be in D because L must be with V somewhere. The contrapositive of this statement is also true: If M is in D then L is in C and therefore V must be in C in order to be with L. Finally, if you know where the S or T is in D or F, then you know where the other is. You might also notice that T can be used only once and S must be used exactly twice. The others are more flexible. Before even looking at the questions you know quite a bit! This quick review reveals that the key aspects to this game will be the relationship between L, M, and V, as well as the relationship between S and T.

1. **Type:** In this game there are nine people who must be placed into ten well-defined slots. There are five rows of two. Since the slots are well-defined and the people must be placed in those slots, this is a slots game.

2. **Diagram:** The setup of this game gives you a model diagram. Set up a similar one that you can work with. You can replicate the given diagram exactly, with two columns, one labeled W for window, and one labeled A for aisle, and five rows labeled one through five. Or you could rotate the diagram and convert the five rows into columns and designate two rows for the window and aisle seats.

3. **Simplify the rules:** Once you have a diagram, go through the rules one by one and interpret what each means. Convert the rules into symbols that will help you picture the rules in your mind. The rules are fairly straightforward. One thing to watch for when any ordering is involved is the specific language. There is one rule that says N must sit in a lower-numbered row than H and a higher-numbered row than Z. Be careful when you convert this rule into symbols. Lower-numbered means just that, a lower number. Row 1 is lower numbered than row 2. This is easy to interpret incorrectly. Take the time to get it right. In this case the rule says Z is lower than N (Z.. N) and N is lower than H (N..H). Place as much information as you can directly on the diagram. For instance, you can place I in the window seat of row 2, you can write down next to the window row or column (depending on your diagram) that G and N must sit in window seats, and, since no L's can sit in row 5, you can list that row 5 cannot contain M, N, or O. There are also two conditional statements to deal with: 1) If M is in an aisle seat then Z and I must sit in the same row and 2) If X sits in the same row as an L (M, N, or O) then two A's must sit in the same row.

4. **Deductions:** Stop! Don't go to the questions yet. This is a vital step. In order to avoid reinventing the wheel on every question, take a moment to make deductions. These deductions will help you solve every question more easily. Making deductions is not difficult, but it does take patience and practice. Relate the rules to each other and see if you notice any new relationships. Before you do so, it is helpful to note the contrapositive of each conditional statement. You can determine the contrapositive by reversing and negating the statement. For example, the rule that says if M is in an aisle seat, then Z and I must sit in the same row; this also means that if Z and I are not in the same row, then M is not in an aisle seat. Finding the contrapositives will help you see the exact meaning of the rules. Now for the deductions! In this case there is a rule that says I sits in the window seat in row 2. There is another rule that says if M sits in an aisle seat, then Z and I must sit in the same row as each other. By coupling these two rules together you can deduce that if M sits in an aisle seat, Z sits in the aisle seat in row 2. The contrapositive of this deduction is also true: If Z does not sit in the aisle seat of row 2 then M does not sit in an aisle seat. Another rule to look at is the rule that says if X sits with a lawyer (M, N, or O) then two accountants sit in the same row. The only accountants are G, H, and I. You already know that I is sitting in the window seat in row 2. If either G or H were to sit with I, it would be in the aisle seat in row 2. However, another rule says that G must sit in a window seat, so G cannot sit with I, leaving H as the only accountant who can sit with I. But there is still another rule that says both Z and N must sit in lower numbered seats than H. Thus, the lowest numbered row that H can sit in is row 3; H, therefore, cannot sit with I in row 2 either. It is impossible for I to sit with either of the other accountants, so if two accountants are to sit in the same row as each other, they must be G and H, with G in the window seat and H in the aisle seat. The deduction, then, is that if X sits with a lawyer, then G and H must sit together, with G in the window seat and H in the aisle seat. Now go back to the ordering rule. Z must be in a lower numbered row than N, who must be in a lower numbered row than H. Thus, the lowest numbered row H can be in is row 3, and the highest numbered row that Z can be in is row 3. Notice what this does to N. N must sit in a window seat and must be have at least Z above him and at least H below him. Thus, N could be in the range of row 2 to row 4. However, I is sitting in the window seat in row 2, so N can

only be in the window seat of row 3 or row 4, which means also that H can only sit in row 4 or row 5.

5. **"Walk Around It":** There are a number of variables to keep track of in this game. First, there are ten slots, but only nine professionals, so there will be one empty space. Second, there is a basic order of Z..N..H that you must deal with. N must always sit in a window seat and must sit in row 3 or 4, which limits the placement of both Z and H. Second, the job of each professional must always be in the back of your mind. Keep track of whether or not X is sitting with a lawyer and keep in mind that no lawyers can sit in row 5. Lastly, watch for the placement of M, especially if M is in an aisle seat. If M is in an aisle seat then Z must be in row 2 in the aisle seat, which forces the entire Z..N..H order to begin in row 2.

1. **Type:** First ask yourself what type of game you are dealing with. In this game the rules tell you what type of game it is. There is a band that must play some number of songs and it will be your task to determine the order in which the songs are played. This is an ordering game, albeit it is a little different from standard ordering games in that you do not know how many songs must be used at all times.

2. **Diagram:** Your diagram, as any diagram for an ordering game, should reflect the relative position of the players in the game. If you know a fixed position, place it where it needs to go. Other than that, all you will know is the relative order.

3. **Simplify the rules:** Simplify the rules by transposing them onto your workplace as symbols. This will save you time and help you to understand the rules a little better. Make sure that you are clear on all the rules. The rule that says *if* the band plays either H or I, then it must be kicked off the stage immediately afterwards means only that if H or I is used, then that song is the last one. It does not mean that either H or I must be the last song. Also, the rule that says the band cannot play D unless it also plays B and F, D being played sometime after B and sometime before F means that if D is played, then B and F must be played. The condition that D must be sometime after B and sometime before F can be represented like this: B..D..F.

4. Deductions: When there are "if…then" statements involved in a game, it is easy to start making the deductions. The most basic deductions, and often the most helpful, are the contrapositives. The contrapositives in this game tell you that if B, D and F are not in the order of B..D..F, then D is not a song that is played; if A and G are not separated by one, then neither A nor G are songs that are played; if E is not fourth, then G (and thus A as well) is a song that is played; and finally, if C is not second, then there are fewer than two songs, or, in other words, there is one song that is played. The next step is to look at the rules and contrapositives and see how they relate to each other. One thing to notice is that if there are more than two songs, then C is played second. If either A or G is played, then both must be played, meaning that there are at least two songs, which forces C to be the second song. No other rules directly apply, so it is possible to have just three songs with A, C, and G, as long as C is second. More songs could be included but you cannot be certain without additional information. On the other hand, if G is not used (meaning that A cannot be used either), then according to the rules E must be the fourth song. In this situation there are at least four songs, so C must be the second song once again. In other words, C is always second.

5. "Walk Around It": There is a lot going on in this game. The first thing to be aware of is that you do not know how many songs are actually played. However, you do know that C must always be the second song played and that the band must always play at least three songs. Thus, the fewest number of songs that the band can play is three. Because once the band has played one of H or I the band is kicked off the stage, the band can never play both H and I, so the maximum number of songs that the band can play is nine. Many of the other rules deal with or are affected by the number of songs that are played. If you know the position of either H or I, then you know the total number of songs played. If you know the number of songs played, this will affect your ability to use the B..D..F sequence, as well as your ability to meet the requirement that A and G be separated by exactly one space.

1. Type: In this game an automobile service center works on six cars in the order in which they arrive. This is clearly an ordering game.

2. Diagram: The diagram for an ordering game is simple. There are six cars, so the basic diagram should have six spaces numbered one through six. For instance, the diagram could simply be this: _ _ _ _ _ _. Indicate clearly the poles for the order from first to sixth. Most of the work will be done in the space beneath this diagram where you will sketch out the basic possibilities for the order as they will be developed by the rules and deductions.

3. Simplify the rules: In this game every rule deals with the relative order of different cars. Simplify these rules by changing them into simple statements showing that relative order. The rule that says the white car arrived sometime after the green car and sometime after the tan car should be split up into two different statements: G..W and T..W. Next, the silver car arrived after the white car becomes W..S and the last rule, that the red car arrived sometime before the silver car, becomes R..S.

4. Deductions: This is the most critical step. Before going to the questions, look at the rules and see how they relate to one another. Ordering games are usually easier than the other types of games because it is relatively easy to make all the deductions. Take all the ordering rules that contain information about the same car and write one longer list of relative order. G and T must both be before W, which must be before S. R must be sometime before S. B is the wild card. Now you've just deduced that both G and T must be before S.

Setups

5. **"Walk Around It":** Take a moment to look at the game more closely. It is often very helpful to look at which pieces could be first and last on the list. In this case, any one of G, T, B, or R could be first. The sixth position is more constrained. Only S or B could be sixth. Other things to look for are how early or late certain items could be. For instance, what is the earliest and latest W could be? W must have both G and T before it, so the earliest W can be is third. W could also have B and R before it so the latest it could be is fifth. Now you are ready for the questions.

1. **Type:** This game deals solely with the order in which eight students use an exercise bike. It is an ordering game.

2. **Diagram:** The basic diagram is simply eight empty spaces: _ _ _ _ _ _ _ _. The poles, one and eight, should be clearly indicated. Between those poles you will work with the relative order of the items.

3. **Simplify the rules:** Take the rules one by one and determine what order each rule establishes, writing the relative order like this: E..C, F..C, etc. In your diagram, don't forget to show that A, B, and C must be consecutive, but that they can vary in their relative order to each other. Clearly show that there is one space between A and F (A_F) and B and D (B_D), but that you do not know the relative order of A to F or B to D. For instance, you could draw a double arrow between A and F, showing that they are interchangeable.

4. **Deductions:** In ordering games your diagram reflects the deductions. Here the only thing your diagram will show is that both E and F must come before the ABC block. Since F must be before A and there must be one space between A and F, A must either be the first student in the ABC block or the second student in the ABC block. Since both E and F must be before the ABC block, you can also determine that the earliest that the ABC block can begin is in the third position.

5. **"Walk Around It":** The placement of A or F and B or D will tell you a lot about the order of the students, so watch closely for the placement of one of these pairs. Consider the possibilities: where can F be? Can D be both before and after the ABC block? It is also helpful to note that H is the wildcard.

1. **Type:** In this game there are nine students, H, I, J, K, L, M, N, O, and P, who must be assigned to either an English class or a biology class. The two classes make up two groups to which the students must be assigned. This is a standard grouping game.

2. **Diagram:** The diagram should clearly show the two groups, which is easily accomplished by drawing two columns labeled English and biology.

3. **Simplify the rules:** Once you have the diagram, go through the rules one by one and simplify them by converting them into symbols. Don't forget the rules that are contained in the setup paragraph. In this case, the setup paragraph says that at least four students in each group. Now go through the rules list. In typical grouping game fashion, most of the rules are conditional statements and one creates a block. The first rule says that no more than two students can register for both courses, which tells you that some people can register for both courses. The next rule says that M takes either biology or English, but not both, so M is not one of those people that can register for both courses. K takes biology, which is not to say that K does not take English as well. All you know is that K must, at the least, take biology. The rule that says J does not take English unless H takes biology is an easy one to misinterpret, so be careful. Maybe a more realistic example will help to understand this statement a little better. What if someone said, "I cannot eat out unless I have money." Does this mean if he has money, he is going to eat out? No! If he has money he can eat out, but it does not say that he will. However, you can say for certain that if he eats out then he has money. Applying this same reasoning to the rule at hand, you can say for certain that if J takes English then H takes biology. If H takes biology, you do not know whether J takes English or not, only that he can. The next rule says H will not take biology if I takes biology. This is a normal conditional

statement presented in a reversed order. It simply says if I takes biology then H will not take biology. Lastly, P and N must take at least one course together, creating a PN block. Be careful though, they must be together only once, but either one or both could possibly take both classes.

4. **Deductions:** After you have simplified the rules, you are ready to make deductions. The first step where there are conditional statements is to write down the contrapositives. In order to get the contrapositives, go through the conditional statements and reverse and negate them (e.g., if I takes biology then H does not take biology means also that if H does take biology then I does not take biology). After you have the contrapositives, think about the rules, what they mean, and how they relate to each other. Take the two rules about general placement: There are at least four students in each group and no more than two can register for both courses. There are nine students but the fact that up to two can double up and register for two courses means that you can really use up to eleven items (even though there are still only nine students): nine students plus the two who register for both classes. With a minimum of four in each group, the maximum number of students that can register for one class is seven, while the minimum is, of course, four. Moving on to the other rules, look for rules that share variables. For instance, one rule says that if J is in English then H is in biology while the contrapositive of another rule says that if H is in biology then I is not in biology. Adding these two together tells you that if J is in English then I is not in biology. The contrapositive of this deduction is also true.

5. **"Walk Around It":** Before rushing on to the questions, take a moment to think about what you do and do not know about the game, for this will provide a clue as to what the questions are likely to test. The rules do not say that every student must be used, so you can work with anywhere from eight to eleven items, but there must be at least four students in each group. Just because there must be four students in each class does not

mean that eight different students must be used. Since up to two students can register for both classes, there could be as few as six different students: two students registered for both classes and then two more students in each class to meet the minimum of four. The maximum number of different students that can be used is, of course, nine since there are only nine students. You also know that M must be in one of the classes, that K must be in biology, and that P and N must be together for at least one course. You do not know much else. The numerical composition is likely to be as important as the specific students in each group. Go to the questions with the rules in mind.

1. **Type:** In this game six bowlers must participate in a bowling tournament, playing in three pairs of two. Each pair must be assigned to one of three lanes over two rounds. The lanes and rounds are distinct and fixed categories. The only variables are the players themselves. This game is a slots game. However, unlike most slots games, this game requires you to place groups of two into each slot, so this game also has some elements of a grouping game. You must determine which groups go in which slots.

2. **Diagram:** The diagram should clearly show the three lanes and two rounds. You can accomplish this by making three columns and two rows labeled appropriately: something like L1, L2, and L3 across the top and 1 and 2 down the side.

3. **Simplify the rules:** Simplify the rules by converting them into symbols. Where possible, place the information directly on the diagram. The rules here are pretty self-explanatory. Each provides restrictions as far as who can and cannot go with whom. Don't overlook the key rules contained within the body of the setup: Each bowler is assigned to the same teammate for both rounds and no bowler can be in the same lane both rounds.

4. **Deductions:** After simplifying the rules individually, relate the rules to each other to see if there are any deductions to make. The game consists of three two-person teams. According to the rules, D and F are teammates, so one of the teams must consist of D and F. You must determine how the remaining four bowlers, A, B, C, and E are divided into two two-person teams. These remaining two teams are constrained by the rule that says B and C cannot be on the same team. Any combination that leaves B and C together cannot be correct. If A and E are together then B and C must be together, so A and E cannot be teammates. Since A and E cannot be on the same team, A must

be teammates with either B or C. The rules assigned A to lane 1 in round 2, so A and either B or C must be in lane 1 in round 2. Another rule says if E is in lane 3 then his partner must be B. From what you have determined about A's teammate, you know that if E's partner is B then A's partner is C. Thus, if E is in lane 3 then E's partner is B and A's partner is C. The contrapositive of this deduction says if A's partner is not C, which is the same as saying that if A's partner is B, then E's partners is C and this EC team cannot be in lane 3. Finally, since A is in lane 1 for round 2 and since no team can occupy the same lane in both rounds, A and his partner (either B or C) must occupy lane 2 or lane 3 in round 1.

5. **"Walk Around It":** Once you have made as many deductions as you can, take a moment to look at the game overall. There are three pairs of partners: D and F, A and either B or C, and E and either B or C. Watch for any information about B or C, because then you can determine every partnership. For example, the placement of E in lane 3 forces E's teammate to be B, and A's to be C. Also, since A must be in lane 1 for round 2 and no bowler can be in the same land for both rounds, any information about B or C being in lane 1 for round 1 will tell you who A's partner is in round 2.

1. **Type:** This game creates four distinct groups by creating four rounds. However, these groups are not groups like teams or people that work together. Each round has all eight players split up into four partnerships so within each of the four rounds there are four pairs of partners.

2. **Diagram:** The diagram for this game should clearly show the four categories, which are the four rounds in the bridge tournament. These categories can be represented by four columns. Be sure to draw the diagram large enough to be able to work with the four pairs of partners within each of the rounds.

3. **Simplify the rules:** It is vital to understand the rules. You cannot logically reach the correct answer to any of the questions if you do not understand the rules. Often there is critical information in the setup paragraph that is important for working the game. In this case the setup paragraph establishes that the people in group 1 must partner with people from group 2, that every person must participate in each round, and that no pair of players can be partners in more than one round. Following the setup paragraph there is only a short list of rules, all of which you can place directly on the diagram. The rules establish a few of the pairs of partners that will participate in the game.

4. **Deductions:** The rules say that during each round a player from group 1 (C, D, F, and G) pairs up with a player from group 2 (P, Q, S, and T). This allows you to place one of each player from either group 1 or group 2 on your diagram in each round. For example, you could place C, D, F, and G in each round as one part of each partnership. The rules further say that no pair of players can be partners in more than one round, and each player participates in each round. This means that every person from each group will partner with every person from the other group over the course of the four

rounds. D and Q are partners in round 1, so D cannot be with Q in any subsequent round. Go through and mark this down: Wherever D is in rounds 2 through 4, Q cannot be his partner. According to the rules, in round 3 F is with T, and G is with D's partner from round two. D's partner in round two cannot be Q, so G cannot be with Q in round 3. In round 3 D cannot be partners with Q either since D is partners with Q in round 1. Thus, in order for Q to participate in round 3, he must partner with C. Since C and Q are partners in round 3, go through and mark down that Q cannot be partners with C in round 1, 2, or 4. In round 4, F is partners with C's partner from round 3, which is what you just determined, so now you know that F is with Q in round 4. Go through the diagram and mark down that F cannot be partners with Q or vice versa in any of the remaining rounds. In round 2 this leaves you with a situation where D, C, and F cannot be partners with Q, leaving only G to be partners with Q. Now you know Q's partner in every round. In round 1 D and Q are partners, in round 2 G and Q are partners, in round 3 C and Q are partners, and in round 4 F and Q are partners. The fact that T is F's partner in round 3 means that T cannot be partners with anyone else in round 3. Because G cannot be with T in round 3, and in round 3 G is partners with D's partner in round 2, you know D's partner in round 2 cannot be T either. Thus, in round 1 D is partners with Q, in round 2 D cannot be with T, and in round 3 D cannot be with T. Therefore, D is partners with T in round 4. Look at what this does in round 2. G is already with Q, so none of the other players can partner with Q. F and D are both with T in other rounds, so they cannot be with T in round 2. This leaves C as T's partner in round 2. Now C cannot be partners with T in any other round, so mark that down on the diagram. In round 1, D is with Q and both C and F cannot be with T; thus, G is partners with T in round 1. Now you know T's partner in every round as well. In round 1 G is with T, in round 2 C is with T, in round 3 F is with T, and in round 4 D is with T. While you know Q's partners and T's partners in every round, you do not know the partners of P or S in any round. This is all that there is left to determine.

5. **"Walk Around It":** After working through the deductions you know quite a bit of information. Any additional information concerning P or S in any round will carry you through the same process that you went through in the deductions stage and will allow you to determine the remaining partnerships. In every round there are two people whose partners you do not know. In each case, their partner is either P or S so if you know something about one partnership, you know the other partner, and then you can go through and mark this down for the other groups, which will further restrict the partnerships until you know the entire setup. For instance, look at round 1: D is with Q, G is with T, and C and F must be with one of either P or S. If you know that P is with C, then you know that S is with F. Then you would go to later rounds and mark down that C cannot be with P and that S cannot be with F. Once you have this information, you would know that C must be with S in round 4 and that F must be with P in round 2. This chain reaction would continue and would allow you to fill in the rest of the diagram.

1. **Type:** In this game you have to create a group of foods that Carol orders, but there are not distinct groups or categories to put the foods in. Likewise, there is no ordering. This game requires you to actually build a single group.

2. **Diagram:** There is no firm diagram for this game because there is no set number of how many pieces you are working with.

3. **Simplify the rules:** Go through the rules one by one and simplify them by converting them into symbols. This is also a good opportunity to ensure that you understand what the rules mean. The challenge in this game is in interpreting the rules correctly. You must take the statements that they give you and change them into "if…then" statements that you can work with. For example, one rule says that anyone who chooses tomato (T) must also choose corn (C). This becomes the "if…then" statement: if T then C (T → C). The next rule says onions (O) are selected by anyone who selects pork chops (P). This means that if someone selects P, then they must select O (P → O). The next rule says rice (R) is selected by anyone who selects onions (O). This would become: If O then R (O → R). Next, spaghetti (S) is selected when R is selected. This means that that if R is selected then S is selected (R → S). The last "if…then" rule is the rule that says that beans (B) are chosen when T is chosen. When this becomes an "if…then" statement, it becomes if T is chosen then B is chosen (T → B). The first and last rules both create pairs of food that cannot both be ordered. C and B cannot be together and M and R cannot be together.

4. **Deductions:** As in any game with "if…then" statements, the first place to start when making deductions is to write down the contrapositives of the "if…then" statements. To determine the contrapositive, simply negate both sides of the statement and reverse the order. For example, if T then C becomes if not C then not T (~C → ~T). The next step is to determine how the rules relate to each other. Are there any common terms in different rules? In this game there is a short chain of "if…then" statements that are all connected. One rule says if P then O, the next rule says if O then R, and the rule after that says if R then S. If you put these three rules together then you know that if P is chosen then O is also, which means that R is also, which means that S is chosen as well (P→O→R→S). Similarly, if O is chosen then R and S are chosen. In other words, you can jump into this chain anywhere, but only that which is to the right of what you know must follow. If O is included then you do not know anything about P. This chain of deductions is also related to the rule that says M and R cannot be together. From the deduction you just made, you know that if P or O is chosen, then R must be chosen. If R is chosen, then M cannot be chosen. Thus, if P or O is chosen, then M cannot be chosen. Don't forget the contrapositives of the deductions either. For instance, the contrapositive of the deduction you just made says that if M is chosen, then neither P nor O can be chosen. Lastly, there are two rules that contain T. If T is chosen, then both C and B must be chosen. However, another rule says that C and B cannot be chosen together. Thus, in order to satisfy the condition that C and B are not together, T can never be one of the foods chosen.

5. **"Walk Around It":** After making deductions, take a moment to walk around the game to see what the variables are and what information is likely to be key in working the game. There are nine total foods but T cannot be chosen, so really you can only work with eight foods. Of these eight foods there are two pairs that are either/or. C and B cannot be together and M and R cannot be together. Thus, there are eight possible choices, but the greatest number of items that Carol can order is six. If P is chosen, then there must automatically be three additional foods chosen (O, R, and S) and M cannot be chosen. If, on the other hand, M is chosen, then neither P nor O can be chosen, so look out for M. The only dish that does not have a rule to govern its participation is yogurt (Y). Y is the wildcard.

1. **Type:** First ask yourself what type of game this is. At first it might seem a little confusing with all the talk about different plans, teams, building sites, and surveyors. However, as even the first question clearly shows, the main task here is assigning the surveyors to the different building sites. This is a grouping game. While the main groups are the four building sites, it is very helpful to keep track of the teams as well, if only in your head.

2. **Diagram:** The diagram for this, as any grouping game, needs to clearly show the different groups. You can accomplish this by creating four columns labeled one through four to represent the four building sites. You will have to assign the six surveyors to different sites according to the two possible plans.

3. **Simplify the rules:** At this point, you have a basic understanding of what the game is going to require you to do. The next step is to determine the constraints on the placement of the surveyors. Go through the rules and take the time to interpret each one and convert them into symbols. Do not forget to include the rules that are contained within the setup paragraph itself. For instance, the setup paragraph tells you that there are two teams, A and B, that each team has three people, and that each team will visit exactly two sites. The sites they visit will be determined by which plan they are following. In plan 1 all the members of team A visit 1 and 2 while all of team B visits 3 and 4. In plan 2 all the members of team A visit 1 and 3 while all of team B visits 2 and 4. The rules list contains more specific restrictions: If R visits 3 then R visits 4, if T and Y are not on the same team then T visits 2, S is on team A, W is on team B, and V cannot visit 3.

4. **Deductions:** Here you have two different plans that assign the two teams of surveyors to different sites. If you look at and think carefully about the two plans, you can determine that in both plans only team A can visit site 1 and only team B can visit site 4. This means that if you find out which team someone is on, then you will know at least one of the sites that he visits. For instance, if you know someone is on team B, you know he must at least visit site 4 and he cannot visit site 1. This works in the opposite direction as well. If you know that someone visits site 1 or site 4 then you know what team he is on. This is an important concept to grasp. This deduction coupled with the information that S is on team A and that W is on team B allows you to place S at site 1 and W at site 4. The second site that A and B visit will depend on which plan you are following. Continue analyzing the rules for any additional information that you can ascertain by relating them to each other. The first rule says that if R is in 3 then R is in 4. If R visits both site 3 and site 4 then you must be dealing with plan 1 because only in plan 1 can someone visit both 3 and 4. Thus, to say that if R is in 3, then R is in 4 is the same as saying that if R is in 3 then the surveyors are following plan 1. The contrapositive of this deduction says that if you are not dealing with plan 1, which would mean that you are dealing with plan 2, then R cannot visit site 3. In plan 2, team B is the team that does not visit site 3, so if you are following plan 2 then R must be on team B and must visit sites 2 and 4. The next rule says that if T and Y are not together then T visits site 2. The contrapositive of this rule says that if T does not visit 2 then T and Y are together. If it is the case that T is not in 2 then T must either be on team B in plan 1 and visit sites 3 and 4 or be on team A in plan 2 and visit sites 1 and 3. Either way, if T is not in 2, then T must be in 3. Since T and Y must be together when T is not in 2, both T and Y must be in 3. In other words, if T is not in 2 then T and Y must be together in 3. Whether T and Y also visit site 1 or 4 will depend upon which plan you are following. You already deduced one assignment for both S and W, so move on to the last rule: V does not visit site 3. Since V does not visit site 3, V must either be on team A in plan 1 and visit sites 1 and 2 or be on team B in plan 2 and visit sites 2 and 4. Either way, V must visit 2, so V must always visit site 2. Once again, the other site that V visits will depend upon which plan you are following. At this point you know that S must always visit site 1, V must always visit

site 2, and that W must always visit site 4. The other site that each of these surveyors visits depends upon which plan you are following. Any information that allows you to determine what plan to follow will tell you the other placement of each of these people. Since there are only two plans, you can use each plan as a basic scenario. Work them out now so that you do not have to repeat the work over and over for the questions. If you know you are dealing with plan 1, then S must visit sites 1 and 2, V must visit sites 1 and 2, and W must visit sites 3 and 4. You are left with R, T, and Y to assign to the sites. If T and Y are not together, then T must be assigned to 2 and since this is plan 1, T would also have to be assigned to 1, leaving R and Y for sites 3 and 4. On the other hand, T and Y could be together with W at sites 3 and 4, leaving R at sites 1 and 2. Thus, there are two possible scenarios using plan 1: 1) S, V, T; 2) S, V, T; 3) W, Y, R; and 4) W, Y, R or 1) S, V, R; 2) S, V, R; 3) W, T, Y; and 4) W, T, Y. If you know you are dealing with plan 2, then you immediately know that S visits sites 1 and 3, that V visits sites 2 and 4, and that W visits sites 2 and 4. Thus, by knowing that you are following plan 2, you can immediately determine that V and W are two of the three people that visit sites 2 and 4. Furthermore, according to the deductions, if you are in plan 2 then R must visit 2 and 4. Therefore, in plan 2, you actually know all three of the surveyors that must visit sites 2 and 4: V, W, and R. The remaining three surveyors, S, T, and Y, must visits sites 1 and 3. Thus, if you know you are using plan 2 then the setup looks like this: 1) S, T, Y; 2) V, W, R; 3) S, T, Y; and 4) V, W, R. Congratulations, you just determined that there are only three possibilities for the setup. This knowledge will make the questions a breeze.

5. **"Walk Around It":** With only three possible scenarios, all you need to do is determine which scenario each question places you in and then work from there.

1. **Type:** First ask what type of game it is. This one is plain: When you read the setup it becomes clear that you are dealing with a classic ordering game.

2. **Diagram:** Because of the nature of the game, at this point your diagram will consist of a list of the items (reduced to their first letters) that have to be placed in order along with a 1 and a 7 to indicate the direction from first to last.

3. **Simplify the rules:** Now go over the rules and see what they mean. Linear order rules are easily misinterpreted. Be careful not to reverse any of the rules. If you do not understand what a rule is trying to say, go back and check it again. These are fairly straightforward, but be certain to get the E and C rule correctly: They must be separated by exactly two spaces (E _ _ C), but you cannot say for sure whether E is before C or C is before E, which you can indicate with a double arrow showing that E and C are interchangeable.

4. **Deductions:** Start by looking for items mentioned in more than one rule. G is mentioned twice; using those two rules you can develop the basic order: D...G...C. Furthermore, C and E must have exactly two spaces in between them, but it is important to realize that you do not know the relative order of C and E. E could be either before or after C. Because E and C are interchangeable, the game is not quite very restricted.

5. **"Walk Around It":** Now take a second to walk around the game. Look at your diagram and consider the possibilities. The key to this game is the two-space gap between C and E. Which countries can fill this gap? Since B and F must be adjacent they could fill the gap, but neither can be used to fill the gap without the other (and, of course, if they fill the gap, F cannot be beside C). If B and F do not fill the gap, the gap will have to be filled by a combination of two of D, G, and A, but be aware that D must be before G and both must be before C.

1. Type: This game is a slots game. You have five days, Monday through Friday, with two parts to each day, morning and afternoon. You have to fill those slots with various towns. However, you can see from the rules that the order of the slots is going to be very important.

2. Diagram: Your diagram should consist of five columns for the five days and two rows for each column representing the morning and afternoon.

3. Simplify the rules: You cannot understand the situation that the game creates without understanding the restrictions that create that situation. In other words, you cannot understand the game without understanding the rules. Not only must you understand the rules, you must internalize them and be able to work with them. In order to do that better, it is helpful to simplify the rules into symbols. You will be able to understand the symbols quickly, plus the process of converting the rules into symbols makes you think about what they mean; it gives you a chance to interpret the rules. Do not leave out rules that are stated in the setup paragraph. In this game there are seven cities that are either in Wyoming or Montana. These seven cities must be visited over the course of five days, either in the morning or afternoon. There are at least two consecutive mornings that are empty. This creates a block of at least two empty mornings. These rules are all contained within the setup paragraph. Now consider the rules in the rules list. D and T are visited on the same day, creating a DT block that will fill up an entire day. E is after S but before C, creating a list of relative order that look like S..E..C. Be careful with this ordering rule, for it does not tell you during what time of day these cities are visited or even that they are visited on three different days. S is still before E if S is in the morning of one day and E is in the afternoon. The last rule provides some information about the cities that can be visited first and last. The first city visited must be in Wyoming and the last city visited must be in Montana. Notice that this does not mean that on Monday morning, a Wyoming city must be visited. You do not yet know on what days the first and last visit will take place.

4. Deductions: Look at the rules and how they relate to each other. What does combining different rules tell you? Here you know that the first visit must be a Wyoming city, which means that the first city visited must be one of B, C, D, or E. However, the rules also tell you that S must be visited before E and C, so neither E nor C can be first. Thus, the first visit must be B or D. The same analysis applies to the last visit. The last visit must be a Montana city, which means that the last city must be one of R, S, or T. But since S must be before both E and C, S cannot be last, which means that the only two possibilities for the last stop are R and T. Watch out for how these deductions about the first and last cities relate to the rule placing D and T on the same day. If D is the first city, then T must be visited on that same day, which means that T cannot be the last city visited. Since T cannot be last in this scenario, R must be last. Thus, if D is the first city then R must be the last city. Likewise, if T is the last city then D must be on that same day, which means that D can no longer be the first city. Since D can no longer be first, B must be first. In other words, if T is last then B is first. Be careful with this deduction. It does not mean that the DT block is either on the first day or the last day, for B could be first and R could be last, placing the DT block somewhere in between.

5. "Walk Around It": Walk around the game and get a feel for what it is doing and what it will likely test you on. You have seven towns and ten slots to fill, so there are going to be three empty slots, at least two of which, according to the rules, are on consecutive mornings. Also, pay close attention to the first/last rule and your deduction. Either B or D must be the first city and either R or T must be the last city. Watch out for how this relates to the rule placing D and T on the same day. Also, since D and T will fill up an entire day, the location of the two consecutive empty morning slots will be powerful. The placement of the DT block and the empty slots are likely to be key components of this game.

1. **Type:** First ask yourself what kind of game you are dealing with. This one may appear confusing because it contains elements of different types of games. The setup paragraph says that there are three classifications of injuries. These classifications create three different groups. However, the rules make it apparent that you will also have to deal with the order in which the animals are treated. This game contains elements of both grouping and ordering. The key here will be the ordering because the order will help determine the composition of the groups. A glance at the first question is a hint that working out this game will require you to put the animals in order.

2. **Diagram:** Because this is a hybrid game, you will not be able to create a firm diagram. When you are working on the order, deal with the game as an ordering game. You will need to make a list of the relative order of the different animals. Keep in mind that there are also three groups: C, S, and M.

3. **Simplify the rules:** Now go to the rules. Invest sometime in understanding the rules and converting them into easily understandable symbols that you can look at in your workspace. There are three cats, P, Q, and S, three dogs, K, H, and J, and one goat, G. They are treated in a particular order. This order is governed by two things: 1) Critical injuries are treated before serious injuries and serious injuries are treated before mild injuries; 2) Within each injury category the animals are treated in the order in which they arrive. The first rule in the rules list says that exactly two cats and two dogs have serious injuries. You now know the injury classification of four of the seven animals. The next few rules deal with the order, both of arrival and treatment. H is treated sometime before P and sometime after S, which can be written like this: S..H..P. Next, J arrived in the clinic sometime before H and sometime after K, which can be symbolized like this: K..J..H. The remaining rule dealing

with ordering says that K is immediately before or after P, which can be written like this: KP, along with a double-ended arrow, to indicate that they are interchangeable. Be very careful with the language in these rules. The rules gave you information on both arrivals and treatments, so be careful that you stay within each category as you relate them to each other and try to make deductions. The last rule tells you that G does not have a serious injury.

4. **Deductions:** This is the most critical part of the game and is the difference between understanding and exasperation. Once you have the deductions, you will know the basic scenarios and the key to the game. Remember, the rules gave you information about both treatment and arrivals. Take a look at the treatments first. You have a list or relative order that looks like this: S..H.. P. Since K and P must be next to each other, this turns into: S..H..KP, although the K and P are interchangeable. Now look at the information on arrivals. This is the key part of the game. Compare the list of treatments with the list of arrivals. H arrived before K but gets treated after K. What does this tell you? First, it tells you that H and K cannot be in the same injury category; otherwise K would have to be treated before H. Second, because H is treated before K it must be the case that H has a more serious injury than K. These are very important deductions. What else can you determine? Remember, two cats and two dogs have serious injuries. There are only three dogs: K, H, and J. You just determined that K and H must be in different categories. Therefore, in order for there to be two dogs with a serious injury, one of K or H must have a serious injury and J must have a serious injury. In other words, J must always be in the serious injury category. If J is in the serious group with K, then because J arrived after K, J must be treated after K. If, on the other hand, J is in the serious group with H, then because J arrived before H, J must be treated before H. Thus, there are two basic scenarios for the order of treatment built from the previously deduced list. The earlier list looked like this: S..H..KP. If J is with K in the serious group, then the treatment schedule

looks like this: S..H..KP.J, where at least J and K are in the serious group and since H must have a more serious injury than K, at least S and H are in the critical group. If, on the other hand, J is with H in the serious group, then the treatment schedule looks like this: S.J..H..KP, where at least J and H are in the serious group and since H must have a more serious injury than K, at least K is in the mild group. In both of these scenarios K and P are interchangeable and G and Q are the wildcards. However, G is not as free as it first appears. Remember, G cannot have a serious injury. In a list of all seven animals where four consecutive spaces must represent animals with serious injuries, it must be the case that G is not in the fourth position. Placing G fourth would not leave room for four serious injuries. With these two basic treatment schedules worked out and the deduction about G, you are ready for the questions. A confusing game has become manageable.

5. **"Walk Around It":** Take a moment to think about the game as a whole and from different directions. This is a hybrid between an ordering game and a grouping game, but the real work will be in determining the order. The order will determine the groups and in some instances the requirements of the groups will restrict the ordering. The two treatment scenarios are governed by the question of whether it is K or H that has a serious injury along with J. Determining which four animals have serious injuries while keeping K and H separate will probably be the key to this game.

1. **Type:** In this game you must determine the order of seven songs on a CD, so this is a standard ordering game. The only variation from a classic ordering game is that not every piece must be used. There are five songs that must be used, H, K, L, M, N, and then two out of P, Q, R, and S that must be used. However, the key here is still the order.

2. **Diagram:** For the diagram, simply write down seven spaces labeled one through seven. Be clear that song 1 is farthest from the middle and song 7 is closest to the middle. This diagram will help you conceptualize the game, but most of the work will be done with the list of relative order that you obtain from the rules.

3. **Simplify the rules:** The next step is to simplify the rules. Convert them into symbols that you can interpret at a glance. There are not any particularly difficult rules here. As you simplify the rules, be clear about the relative order. Remember, song 1 is farthest from the middle and song 7 is closest to the middle. It is helpful to break up rules that contain two pieces of information into separate rules. Thus, the rule that says that M is closer to the middle than L and farther from the middle than H can be split into two separate rules where one says M is closer to the middle than L (L..M) and another that says M is farther from the middle than H (M..H). Also, the rule says K is closer to the middle than H and N should be split up into two rules that say K is closer to the middle than H (H..K) and K is closer to the middle than N (N..K).

4. **Deductions:** Once you understand the rules individually, relate them to each other. In ordering games, this process is fairly easy. Combine the individual statements about relative order into one large statement. Since L is before M and M is before H and H is before K, you know the order must look something like this: L..M..H..K. Furthermore, N must be sometime before K, although you do not know N's position relative to L, M, or H. This basic list of relative order will be the key to the entire game. The CD must also include two of P, Q, R, and S. P, Q, and R are all restricted by the rules: If P is included then P cannot be first or seventh, if Q is included then Q must be fifth, and if R is included then R must be next to N. If R is next to N then, just like N, R must always be before K. As with any ordering game, it is helpful to consider right away which songs could be first and which songs could be last. Out of the main five songs only L or N could be first while only K could be last. Out of songs P, Q, R, and S, either R or S could be first while only S could be last. Thus, L, N, R, or S could be first, while only K or S could be last.

5. **"Walk Around It":** Before moving on to the questions, take a moment to think about what you know. The order of L, M, H, K, and N, the five songs that must be included, is fairly clear although N is freer than the others to move around. The CD must also include two of P, Q, R, and S. If P is used then P cannot be 1 or 7, if R is used then it must be adjacent to N and closer to the outside than K, and if Q is used then it must be third from the middle, or song 5. Thus, P, Q, and R are restricted in some way by the rules, while S is a wildcard.

1. **Type:** As always, the first question to ask yourself is "What type of game is this?" In this game Felix must clean six rooms, one per day, during a seven-day week. It is evident from the information paragraph and the rules that the game requires you to determine when Felix cleans each room during the week. Because the game deals more with absolute order than relative order, this is a slots/scheduling game.

2. **Diagram:** The diagram should show what you know. In this case, you only know there are seven days, Sunday through Saturday. The diagram should have seven columns labeled Sunday through Saturday. Use abbreviations. Sunday can be abbreviated as Su and Saturday as Sa. However you do it, be sure you can distinguish between Saturday and Sunday and Tuesday and Thursday.

3. **Simplify the rules:** This step involves changing the rules into symbols and placing information directly on the diagram. The symbols are meant to save you time in the long run, not to confuse you every time you glance at them, so regardless of how exactly you symbolize the rules, make them easy for you to understand. The first two rules in the rules list are standard "if…then" statements and the rest are general rules. The two conditional statements are straightforward: 1) If Felix cleans a bedroom (B1, B2, or B3) on Saturday or Sunday then he cannot clean a bedroom (B1, B2, or B3) on Thursday, and 2) If Felix cleans the den and garage on consecutive days then he must clean bedroom 3 immediately before the day off. The next three rules may require a little clarification. Felix must clean bedroom 1 exactly three days after he cleans the den. This means that there are exactly two days in between the den and bedroom 1. For instance, if he cleans the den on Sunday, then he must clean bedroom 1 on Wednesday. Next, Felix must clean the garage before Wednesday, which means the garage must be cleaned on Su, M, or T. Finally, Felix must clean two of the bedrooms on consecutive days. You do not know which two bedrooms must be consecutive, but two of three must be.

Setups

4. **Deductions:** After each rule is written down on your workspace, examine the relationships between the different rules. The first thing to do when there are "if…then" rules is to write down the contrapositives. Remember, an "if…then" statement means only one other thing and you can determine what that is by reversing and negating it. The first rule says that if Felix cleans a bedroom on Sunday or Saturday then he cannot clean a bedroom on Thursday. The contrapositive says if Felix cleans a bedroom on Thursday then he cannot clean a bedroom on Saturday or Sunday. The next rule says if Felix cleans the den and the garage on consecutive days then he must clean bedroom 3 on the day immediately before his day off. The contrapositive says if Felix does not clean bedroom 3 immediately before his day off, then Felix does not clean the den and the garage on consecutive days. Now look at the other rules. The garage (G) must be cleaned before Wednesday, which means the garage must be cleaned on Su, M, or T. Felix must clean B1 exactly three days after he cleans the den (D), which is to say that there must be exactly two spaces in between them. There are only seven days, so this rule means that the latest D can be is Wednesday and the earliest B1 can be cleaned is Wednesday. Since neither D nor G is cleaned later than Wednesday, only some combination of the bedrooms (B1, B2, and B3), the kitchen (K) and the day off can be cleaned on Thursday, Friday, and Saturday. One rule says if Felix cleans a bedroom on Saturday or Sunday then he cannot clean a bedroom on Thursday. This restricts the possibilities for Thursday even more, leaving only K or the day off. Thus, this rule has the potential to cause a chain reaction. There is not much else to deduce. While these deductions are important, most of your information will come from the questions themselves.

5. **"Walk Around It":** The final step in the prequestions routine is to walk around the game. The garage must be cleaned on Su, M, or T. The latest the den (D) can be cleaned is Wednesday, which means the D can be cleaned Su, M, T, or W. There is a rule that says if D and G are consecutive then Felix must clean B3 on the day immediately before his day off. Furthermore, the placement of D fixes the placement of B1. Knowing that D and G are consecutive will give you information about five of the seven items you need to place: D, G, B1, B3, and the day off. Therefore, watch out for the placement of D and G. Always consider whether they can or cannot be adjacent. Lastly, don't forget that there need to be two consecutive days on which a bedroom is cleaned and that if a bedroom is cleaned on Saturday or Sunday then no bedroom can be cleaned on Thursday, leaving only K or the day off for Thursday.

1. **Type:** In this game there are five people, Q, R, S, T, and U, who must vote either for or against a proposal in either a first or second meeting. Thus, in this game there are two fixed categories: votes for and against, and meetings one and two. The variables here are the people themselves. Because there are two fixed categories, you can approach this game as a slots game. However, unlike most slots games, here you can have more than one item in each slot.

2. **Diagram:** Your diagram should be a matrix that represents the fixed categories. You could have two columns labeled 1 and 2 to represent the meetings and two rows labeled F and A to represent votes for and against.

3. **Simplify the rules:** Go through the rules and simplify them into easily understandable symbols. If they are not easy to symbolize, shorten them as much as you can. This is also your opportunity to make sure that you understand what the rules are saying. Don't forget the rules that are contained in the setup paragraph. There are a number of generalities about the meetings and the voting: If the proposal is not adopted during the first meeting, then there is a second meting, but only if one or two people vote for the proposal. If the proposal is adopted, then a majority voted for it, and if the proposal is adopted in the first meeting, then there is no second meeting. Finally you reach a list of specifics: If Q votes for the proposal, then a majority votes for the proposal. If Q votes against the proposal, then a majority votes against. If there is a second meeting, then R votes the same way in both meetings. If R and U vote the same way, then T votes the same way as R and U, S and U always vote the same way, and S votes against the proposal in the first meeting. Again, symbolize or shorten these rules as best as you can. For instance the rule that says if Q votes for the proposal then a majority votes for the proposal might become "Q for → majority for." Place the information about S voting against the proposal in the first meeting directly on the diagram.

4. **Deductions:** This is the most vital step in the game. Take the time to see how the rules relate to one another before you go to the questions. The most obvious deduction in this game is based on the two rules that S and U must always vote together and that S must vote against in the first meeting. This means that U must vote against in the first meeting. The other rule concerning U involves his relationship to R. If R and U are together then T votes the same way. If R and U vote together in the first meeting (they would both have to vote against the proposal), then S, U, R, and T would all vote against the proposal, leaving you with only Q. From the rules you can deduce that Q must always vote with the majority, so since S, U, R, and T make up a majority, Q would have to vote against the proposal as well. This scenario has all five of the committee members voting against the proposal, which means that they would not hold a second meeting. Thus, if R votes against the proposal in the first meeting, then there is no second meeting. Don't forget the contrapositive of the deductions: If there is a second meeting, then R votes for the proposal in the first meeting. There is also another rule concerning R that tells you that if there is a second meeting, then R votes the same way at both. Thus, if there is a second meeting then R votes for the proposal at both meetings. Another rule concerning the second meeting is that if a majority votes for the proposal at the first meeting, then there is not a second meeting. Since Q votes with the majority you know that if Q votes for the proposal in the first meeting then there is no second meeting. The contrapositive is also true. If there is a second meeting, then Q does not vote for the proposal in the first meeting, which is the same as saying that Q votes against the proposal in the first meeting.

5. **"Walk Around It":** Based on your deductions, you know that the placement of R and Q will tell you a lot of information. Watch for these two key players.

1. **Type:** First ask yourself what kind of game this is. This is a linear order game that also contains a few conditional statements. You can tell this is a linear order game by looking at the rules: F scores higher than…I scores higher than… These rules tell you that the game is about the relative position of the competitors. The position of the top three scoring teams is especially important since the three teams with the highest scores receive medals.

2. **Diagram:** The initial diagram is just a list of eight spaces numbered one through eight. Other diagrams that will help you solve the questions will only emerge after going through the rules and making deductions.

3. **Simplify the rules:** Go through the rules and convert them into symbols. This is easy to do in ordering games. When a rule contains two pieces of information, it is usually helpful to break it up into two separate rules. Be especially careful with ordering games in interpreting what "higher" and "lower" mean. Put things that are higher on the left and things that are lower on the right. For example, the rule that says I scores higher than E but lower than G should be split up into two rules that read: I..E and G..I.

4. **Deductions:** The deductions in an ordering game usually come from the relative order of the pieces. Go through the rules that you have written and combine those that share a common term to obtain a more complete list of the order. Thus, the first rule can be put back into a sequence that looks like this: H..F.. E. Both B and C must be before H, although you do not know the relative order of B and C. Furthermore, I must be before E and G must be before I (G..I..E). Because you do not know the order of G and I relative to the list you already have, write them above the main sequence. Keep in mind that G could go all the way to the beginning of the list. Lastly, the only country about which there is no rule is D, so D is the wildcard. Now that you have

an idea of the order, look at what additional deductions you can make. First, the earliest that H can be is third because both B and C must be in front of it. Also, since only the highest three finishers win a medal, no one that scores lower than H can win a medal. In other words, neither F nor E can win a medal. Furthermore, only E or D could finish last. In this game it is also necessary to see how the conditional statements relate to the order. The rules say that B and C must be before H and that if B wins a medal then H must win a medal. If H wins a medal, then H must be in the top three, and because B and C must be before H, H must be third, with B and C finishing first and second, not necessarily in that order. Thus, if B wins a medal, then both C and H win a medal as well, with H in third. What must happen when B does not win a medal? In order for B not to receive a medal, B must come in fourth or lower, which means that there must be at least three other countries in front of B so that B can be knocked out of the top three. The only countries that could possibly score higher than B are C, G, I, and D. Because of the rule that says if D wins a medal then I does not win a medal, it is impossible for both I and D to win medals. One of I or D can win a medal, but not both. Therefore, if B does not win a medal, C, G, and either I or D must all win medals. To recap what you have determined so far, if B wins a medal then B, C, and H win medals. If B does not win a medal then G, C, and I or D win medals. In both cases, C wins a medal. Thus, C must always win a medal. With these deductions, the game is rather simple.

5. **"Walk Around It":** Take a moment to walk around the game in order to see what the questions will likely test. You have the relative order and know that if B wins a medal then both C and H do as well. The contrapositive of this is also true: If B, C, and H are not the three that win medals, then B does not win a medal. If B does not win a medal then G, C, and I/D win medals. C must always win a medal. Based on these deductions, it is likely that the most important aspect of this game is determining whether B wins a medal. Now you are ready to move on to the questions.

1. **Type:** This game consists of two groups, A and B, and nine songs that must be placed in order within each of those groups. Thus, it is a hybrid between a grouping and an ordering game.

2. **Diagram:** Your diagram should show the two groups clearly, which is easily accomplished with two columns labeled A and B. Make sure you have room to work with the ordering within those groups.

3. **Simplify the rules:** Simplify the rules by converting them into easily understandable symbols. This is your chance to clarify the meaning of any rule that you do not understand. These rules are fairly straightforward. They consist of two conditional statements in standard "if…then" form and a number of more firm rules about the placement of particular songs.

4. **Deductions:** Take a moment and see how the rules relate to one another. Here the first thing to notice is that the rules establish two basic scenarios. Since one side will have four tracks and the other side five, the only two scenarios are: side A has five while B has four, or side A has four while side B has five. Draw these two scenarios on your diagram and then see what the rules tell you about each scenario. If side A has five tracks, then you know the following about side A: 1) L is 3, 2) K is 4 (K must always be on the side with 5 because O must be 4 on the side with four tracks, which in this case is side B), and 3) P is somewhere on side A because side A has five tracks. You also know the following about side B: 1) O is 4, 2) R is 3 because it cannot be on the same side as K and R can only be 2 on A or 3 on B, and 3) M is somewhere on side B because M cannot be on the same side as K. Scenario 1 leaves you with J, N, and Q to work with. They can be in either group. Now work out the remaining scenario. If side A has four tracks then you know the following about side A: 1) O is 4, 2) L is 3, and 3) because K

is on side B, both M and R must be on side A with M as 1 and R as 2 since if R is on side A, R must be the second track on side A. You also know the following about side B: 1) K is 4, and 2) since side A is full, P, J, N, and Q must also be on side B in some order. Scenario 2 determines what group each song is in and the entire order on side A, but leaves the order uncertain for side B. Now that you know the two possible scenarios, see if there are any patterns or similarities between the two. You will notice that O, M, and R are always together and that P and K must always be together.

5. **"Walk Around It":** As you work the game, look for the clues that will tell you which scenario you are dealing with. This will limit the possible choices and make the game much easier than it appears.

1. **Type:** In this game you have seven numbered cages in which you must place different species of dogs. You have two different groups of dogs to work with: male and female, and adult and puppy. While there are definitely elements of ordering in this game, the focus is not on relative order, but on absolute order, as in slots games. Each dog must go into a discreet place. Thus, this is a slots game with elements of an ordering game.

2. **Diagram:** Your diagram need only consist of seven spaces numbered 1 through 7.

3. **Simplify the rules:** Go to the rules and see what they mean and how you can simplify them. Here the rules are fairly straightforward. The first rule tells you that the first three cages all contain puppies and that two of the first three are female. Next, the two adults must be separated by exactly two cages. The remaining rules tell you that M is not adjacent to T, B must be adjacent to D, and C must be either 2 or 6.

4. **Deductions:** Here you know that B and Y are adults, and that the adults are separated from each other by exactly two spaces, so the diagram will have B and Y separated by exactly two spaces (B _ _ Y). Notice however, that you do not know whether B is before or after Y, so draw a double arrow showing that they are interchangeable. The other relationships among the rules are a little more difficult to see. But take a moment to think them through. The rules tell you that cages 1 through 3 contain puppies, two of which must be female. This means that there is one male in cages 1 through 3. You know it cannot be B because B is an adult. Because B cannot be in cages 1 through 3, the one male that is in one of the first three cages must be either C or D. C is constrained by the rule that says that C must be in either 2 or 6. This is an invitation to work out the two scenarios. If C is 2, it is the male that is in one of the first three cages, but if C is 6, D must be the male

that is in one of the first three cages. Continue to work out what happens if C is in cage 6. D must be adjacent to B but B cannot be in any of the first three cages, so if C is in 6 and D is one of the first three cages, D must be in 3 in order to be next to B in 4, which forces Y into 7. Here's what you have: _ _ D B _ C Y. Since M cannot be next to T, one of M and T must be in 5, leaving the other of M and T, as well as S for 1 or 2. This is the first scenario. You actually know quite a bit if C is in cage 6. But what if C is in cage 2? If C is in cage 2 you cannot determine as much. You have C in 2 and you can also determine that the B _ _ Y separation must be in 4 and 7, but you don't know in which order (Y could be in 4). The dogs in cages 1 and 3 would have to be female but you can choose from M, S, and T. D will have to be adjacent to B, depending on whether B is in cage 4 or 7. This means that in this scenario D is limited to either cage 5 or 6, taking up one of the spaces in between B and Y. The second cage in between B and Y must be filled with the one female that was not used in cages 1 through 3. This is the second scenario.

5. **"Walk Around It":** You now have two scenarios. Scenario 1, where C is in cage 6, tells you almost everything. Scenario 2, where C is in cage 2, while not giving you as much information as scenario 1, does limit the possibilities a great deal. How do you distinguish between the two scenarios? You can determine which scenario you are in by the placement of C or D, or likewise, by information about cage 2 or cage 3. Watch out for any information about these two dogs and these two cages.

1. **Type:** This game deals with the order in which six *Star Trek* fans host a club meeting. However, what matters here is the absolute placement of each person as a host at a specific meeting, or their location in the sequence and not the relative order of each club member. You have to deal with absolute places, blocks, and conditional statements as well as relative order. Thus, this is a slots-based scheduling game rather than simply a linear ordering game.

2. **Diagram:** Your diagram for this scheduling game should show the six meetings. You can do this by drawing six columns or by showing that you have six spaces.

3. **Simplify the rules:** When the rules tell you specific places, write them directly on the diagram; for example, C must be fourth. You have two rules concerning A. A must be immediately before or after E and must be separated from B by exactly one space. Lastly, if D is before C then F is sixth (D..C → F=6).

4. **Deductions:** The key to successfully working any game is usually the deductions that you can draw from the rules. Relate the rules to each other and determine what else you know. There are two rules concerning the placement of A: A must be immediately beside E and A must be separated from B by exactly one space. Notice the effects of this

last rule in relation to the placement of C. C must be fourth, so there is no way for A or B to be second, fourth, or sixth. Thus, you already know that this A_B split must be first and third or third and fifth. If A and B are first and third, though not necessarily in that order, then E must be second in order for E to be adjacent to A, leaving D and F to take up slots five and six, though not necessarily in that order. In other words, if A and B are first and third, the setup looks like this: AEBCDF, with A and B interchangeable and D and F interchangeable. This is the first scenario. Now determine the effects of placing A and B third and fifth. First of all, you should realize that if A is fifth, E would have to be sixth, forcing D to be before C. But if D is before C then F must be sixth, so this cannot work. In other words, A cannot be fifth, so the only way for this second scenario to work is if A is third. If A is third then E is second and B is fifth. Thus, the second scenario is: _EACB_, with D and F interchangeable in positions 1 and 6. These two basic scenarios tell you quite a bit of information: A can only be in position 1 or 3, B can be in position 1, 3, or 5, E must always be second, and either D or F must be sixth.

5. **"Walk Around It":** With these two basic scenarios in front of you, there is not much left to determine. Rely on the questions to give you a piece of information that will allow you to determine which scenario you are working with or, if you still cannot determine which scenario you are in based on the information provided, simply compare the answer choices to both scenarios.

1. Type: The first step in approaching a game is to determine what type of game it is. In this game there are six buttons on a soda machine, five of which are mislabeled and give a different type of drink than the type specified by the button. The labels create six different slots into which you must place the types of drinks. Thus, this is partially a slots game. This game also contains elements of linear order because it deals with the relative position of the drinks themselves. The rules give you information about certain drinks being assigned to a higher or lower position relative to the other types of drinks. The relative position of the drinks will determine the placement of the drinks in the different slots.

2. Diagram: The diagram should show the six slots (the six buttons): R, O, L, C, G, and S. The setup says that this is the order of the buttons from top to bottom. You can either work with this list vertically or turn it horizontally. If you do make it a horizontal list, make sure that you pay attention to what higher and lower mean. R is the highest button and S is the lowest. This list will be a reference point once you work out the relative order as much as you can. Once you have the relative order for each question, you can compare that order to the list of buttons and determine what type of soda each button gives.

3. Simplify the rules: There are only two rules in the rules list but be sure to include any rules contained within the setup paragraph itself or else you will not make it very far in this game. The setup paragraph provides a key piece of information. It says that exactly one button will give the flavor that it indicates while the other five are mislabeled and will give flavors other than the one indicated. Keep this in mind while working out the questions! The two rules in the rules list are simple to interpret and convert into symbols. They deal strictly with the relative order of the flavors. L is higher than S, which is higher than R, and C is immediately above or below L. As you convert these rules into symbols, be sure to keep track of the meaning of higher and lower and above and below, especially

if you are working horizontally rather than vertically. These two rules can be symbolized like this: L..S, S..R, and CL, with a double arrow above or below C and L indicating that C and L are interchangeable.

4. Deductions: The first step in making deductions in any game that contains elements of linear order is to create one large list of relative order. The rules said that L is higher than S and that S is higher than R. This gives you a list that looks like this: L... S...R. Furthermore, C is immediately above or below L. Thus, the list now looks like this: LC…S...R. Keep in mind that C could be immediately above L as well. You should note this by drawing a double arrow between L and C showing that they are interchangeable. Now that you have this list of relative order, you know quite a bit of information. Remember, the order of the buttons from top to bottom is R, O, L, C, G, S. Compare the order of the buttons to the list of the relative order of the flavors that you just deduced. R must come below at least three other drinks: C, L, and S. This means that R cannot be produced by any of the first three buttons, which means that R cannot be produced by the R button, the O button, or the L button. Now you know that R cannot be the button labeled correctly. Don't forget to mark all these deductions on the diagram. S must also come after at least two other drinks: C and L. Thus, S cannot be one of the first two drinks. In other words, S cannot be produced by the R button or the O button. You have just determined the earliest (highest) that S and R can be. This same process works for finding out the latest (lowest) that C, L, and S can be. S must be above R so S cannot be last. In other words, S cannot be produced by the S button; S cannot be the button labeled correctly. Both C and L must be above S and R so there must be at least two buttons below the buttons that produce C and L. This means that neither C nor L can be produced by the S button and that neither C nor L can be produced by the G button. Furthermore, notice that the buttons that produce C and L must be consecutive and also that the buttons labeled C and L are consecutive. Since only one button can produce the type of drink that it indicates, it is impossible for C to be in the C slot and for L to be in the L slot at the same time. If C is in the C slot then S and R are forced into the two slots below C, while L is forced into the slot immediately above C. This arrangement puts both C and L with their corresponding buttons in direct violation of the rules. Thus, C cannot be in the slot labeled C. In other words, C cannot be the button labeled correctly. L is not as limited as C. If L is in the slot labeled L, C would not have to be in the slot labeled C. C could be produced by the button labeled O. Before even going to the questions you know that R, S, and C cannot be labeled correctly. Since none of these three buttons can be labeled correctly, one of the remaining buttons, O, G, or L, must be labeled correctly.

5. **"Walk Around It":** There are six flavors and the rules only deal with four of them (S, R, L, and C), so G and O are wildcards. Of the six buttons, only one of the buttons can be labeled correctly. In other words, exactly one button will have its corresponding flavor. One of O, G, or L must be the button that is labeled correctly. Pay careful attention to the order that each question gives you and how that order relates to the requirement that one button is labeled correctly. Be careful with the placement of C and L because they both cannot correspond to their buttons at the same time.

Setup Game 27

1. **Type:** In this game there is a three-day period, Monday through Wednesday, over which the managers must review the employees. Since it is not clear how many employees are reviewed each day and since there are no specific slots created by the rules, the only category required is the days of the week. This can be approached as a grouping game, albeit there is an element of ordering or scheduling since the days of the week are sequential.

2. **Diagram:** Your diagram should show the groups by having three columns labeled Monday, Tuesday, and Wednesday. You can fill in the extra information about which employees are reviewed and which manager is doing the reviewing once you find out more information. If you feel compelled, you can also create two rows as well, one for the employees and one for the managers, but it is easy enough to keep track of these categories within the groups themselves.

3. **Simplify the rules:** It is vital that you understand the rules and can work with them effectively. To do so, it is helpful to simplify the rules into symbols that you can work with on your workspace. Go through the rules one at a time and simplify them. Be extra careful with ordering statements so that you write down the correct order. In this case, for instance, the rules say that Ross must be reviewed on a day falling sometime before the day on which Ybarra is reviewed. This should be simplified to R..Y. The rest of the rules are pretty straightforward. It might be helpful to convert the rules telling you which employees each manager cannot review into a list of the employees that each manager can review. For example, the rules say that I *cannot* review W or Y. This means that I *can* review R, S, T and V. Likewise, J can review R, T, W, and Y and K can review T, V, W, and Y.

4. **Deductions:** The most important step in the whole process of successfully completing a game is analyzing what the rules really signify

as they relate to other rules, or, in other words, the most important step is the deduction-making step. Not making deductions can only lead to extra work and probably a few gray hairs as you try to complete the games in a timely manner, so take a deep breath and concentrate on the rules, not the questions. If you look at the restrictions on each manager as to whom they can review, you will notice that both J and K cannot review employee S. In other words, only I can review S. Since each of the six employees must be reviewed, I must review S on one of the days. Stated simply, I must be used as a reviewer. On whichever day S is reviewed, I is the reviewer for that day. But don't be fooled. This does not mean that there is an SI block. I could conceivably review employees on two days, and S would only be on one of those two days. In other words, the condition that says if S is reviewed on a given day then I is the reviewer on that day does not necessarily mean if I is the reviewer on a given day then S is reviewed on that day. In what other ways is the placement of S constrained? S must be reviewed on a day either immediately before or immediately after the day on which W is reviewed. Another rule says that T and W must be reviewed on the same day. Thus, S is immediately before or after both W and T. Out of the three reviewers, only J and K can review both W and T. So either J or K must be the reviewer on the day that T and W are reviewed. Now look at the game more generally. There are only three days: Monday, Tuesday, and Wednesday. If S is immediately before or after the day on which T and W are reviewed, either S or the TW block must be reviewed on Tuesday. Likewise, V must be reviewed on a day falling either immediately before or after the day on which Y is reviewed. Once again, since there are only three days available and V and Y must be on two consecutive days out of those three, then on Tuesday either V or Y is going to be reviewed. Thus, on Tuesday, exactly one of either S or the TW group must be reviewed and exactly one of either V or Y must be reviewed. If S is reviewed on Tuesday then I must be the reviewer and between V and Y, I can only review V. So if S is reviewed on Tuesday then V must be reviewed on Tuesday as well. The contrapositive of this deduction says that if V is not reviewed on Tuesday (meaning that Y is) then S cannot be reviewed on Tuesday (which means that T and W are). It is probably better to write this contrapositive in the positive form, which says that if Y is reviewed on Tuesday then the TW block is also reviewed on Tuesday.

5. **"Walk Around It":** There is one last step before heading to the questions. Walk around the game to see what the key elements are likely to be. Here there are three sequential groups. There must be one manager at each group, so each group must have exactly one of I, J, or K. Whoever the manager is on any day will limit the employees that can be reviewed that day. Likewise, if you are given information about the employees reviewed on a certain day then the manager who can do the reviewing on that day will probably be limited. Thus, perhaps the most important task in this game will be to keep track of which employees each manager can review. The deductions are also likely to be key. Keep your eyes open for the placement of S and TW, as well as V and Y. One of each of these pairs must be on Tuesday. Once you know something about one of them, then you also know something about the other. Y is even more restricted because R must be reviewed on a day before Y.

1. **Type:** This game consists of five days, Monday through Friday, with two parts to each day, a.m. and p.m. These are fixed categories. Johnson must meet with various clients. It will be your task to place the accountants, consultants, executives, lawyers, and the stockholder within this schedule. Thus, this is a standard slots game.

2. **Diagram:** Your diagram should have five columns, labeled Monday through Friday, and two rows labeled a.m. and p.m. You can abbreviate Monday through Friday using letters such as M, T, W, R, and F. Just be sure that you are clear on the difference between Tuesday and Thursday.

3. **Simplify the rules:** Go to the rules and write them down in your workspace as understandable symbols. As you write them down, think about what they mean. The rules here are fairly straightforward. The C's can only be in the afternoon (C's = p.m.), there must be an E on the day after any A (A → E the next day), and the L's are separated by exactly two days (L _ _ L). Be careful; this does not tell you whether the L's are in the morning or afternoon.

4. **Deductions:** While there are not many rules in this game, there are a few deductions that you can make by relating the rules to each other and considering their side effects. Think of the effects of the rule that says if Johnson meets with an A on a given day then he must meet with at least one E the following day. Keep in mind that there are 3 A's and only 2 E's. If all three A's were on separate days, then there wouldn't be enough E's to satisfy the rule. Therefore, in order to satisfy this rule there must be one day with 2 A's. Also, this rule means that an A cannot be on the last day. Thus, there will be one day with 2 A's and one with 1 A and the latest that either of these days can be is Thursday (R). Next, the rule that the L's must be separated by exactly two days means they must be on M and R or on T and F.

5. **"Walk Around It":** The only variable about which there are no rules is S. Every other player in this game is constrained by some rule or by the location of another player. The three rules in this game are interconnected. The placement of the L's restricts the location of the block of two A's. The location of the A's, in turn, will determine the location of the E's and vice versa. Also, you already know quite a bit of information about the people who have meetings in the afternoon. Both C's must have their meetings in the afternoon and one day must have two A's, so at least one A is also in the afternoon. Thus, you already know three of the five people that have meetings in the afternoon.

Setup Game 29

1. **Type:** First ask yourself what type of game you are dealing with. In this game there are a number of variables: critics, films, types of films, and days of the week. You need to determine exactly what the game is going to force you to work with. The two critics and the five days of the week are fixed and will never vary. What can vary, however, is which movies they see on any given day. Thus, this is a slots game, where you must build a schedule for each critic over the six days. Knowing the type of each film will help you determine the schedule.

2. **Diagram:** The setup tells you that each critic views exactly one film per day Monday through Saturday and the two do not see the same film. This tells you what the diagram should look like: six columns representing the days of the week and two rows representing the two film critics. Make sure that you label the rows and columns correctly.

3. **Simplify the rules:** The rules are the driving force in any game. The rules are why a game is a game. If there were no rules there would be nothing to figure out. Because the rules are so important, go through them one by one and be sure that you understand them. As you do so, convert them into symbols that you can comprehend at a glance. This will prevent you from reading and rereading all those bothersome and time-consuming words. The first rule says that J cannot view a comedy unless M has viewed it first. This means that if J sees a comedy, M must have already seen that comedy. In other words, for all the comedies, M is before J. The second rule tells you that M cannot view comedies on successive days. This one might be hard to symbolize, but try your best to come up with something that tells you M cannot have two consecutive comedies. The two remaining rules can be placed directly on the diagram: Neither critic sees W or L on Monday or Saturday and one of the critics sees Q on Thursday. Be careful when placing Q on the diagram because you don't know which critic sees it. You may want to place it above or below the Thursday column so that you don't confuse yourself.

4. **Deductions:** The next step is to make deductions. Think about how the rules relate to each other and the side effects of each. If M must see the comedies before J, it is impossible for J to see a comedy on Monday. Thus, J views a drama on Monday. Out of the three dramas, J cannot view L on Monday, so J must view either F or Q on Monday. Furthermore, since M must see the comedies before J, it is also impossible for M to see a comedy on Saturday. Thus, M must see a drama on Saturday. M cannot view L on Saturday, so the drama that M sees on Saturday must be either F or Q. You now know that J must see either F or Q on Monday and M must see either F or Q on Saturday. Write these down on your diagram! With M viewing a drama on Saturday, there are three comedies left for M to view sometime during Monday through Friday. Since M cannot view two comedies on successive days, M must view a comedy on Monday, Wednesday, and Friday, leaving Tuesday, Thursday, and Saturday for the dramas. Now look at the next rule: Neither critic sees W or L on Monday or Saturday. W is a comedy and M must see comedies before J. Since J cannot see W on Saturday, he must see W before Saturday. This means that M must see W before Friday. Since M sees comedies only on Monday, Wednesday, and Friday, but cannot see W on Monday or Friday, M sees W on Wednesday. Since M sees W on Wednesday, M must see one of B or H on Monday and the other on Friday. Whichever of B or H that M sees on Friday, J must see on Saturday, since J views each comedy sometime after M has seen it. Thus, J must see either B or H on Saturday. Furthermore, since J can only view comedies after M and M views W on Wednesday, J can only view W on Thursday or Friday.

5. **"Walk Around It"**: The rules allowed you to make a number of important deductions that will save you time in the long run. Take what you know with you to the questions; that is why you do the work ahead of time. At this point you know that J must see a drama, either F or Q, on Monday, W on either Thursday or Friday, and a comedy, either B or H, on Saturday. M must see a comedy, either B or H, on Monday and Friday and must see the remaining comedy, W, on Wednesday. Lastly, M must see either F or Q on Saturday. The relationship between F and Q is going to be important because either J or M must see Q on Thursday. Knowing where one critic views Q can have effects on where the other critic views Q. For instance, if J sees Q on Monday then M must be the one that sees Q on Thursday. If M sees Q on Thursday then M must see F on Saturday. Keep your eyes open for any questions testing this relationship.

1. **Type:** First ask what type of game this is. There are three managers who must fire five of eight employees. Each manager fires at least one person. In effect, the three managers make up three groups into which five of the eight employees must be placed. Thus, this is a grouping game. The other pieces will be placed into these groups according to the rules.

2. **Diagram:** The diagram for this grouping game, as with all grouping games, is easy to make. It should clearly show the three groups into which the other pieces will go. You can easily accomplish this by drawing three columns labeled A, B, and C.

3. **Simplify the rules:** The next step is to simplify the rules. Go through the setup paragraph and the rules list and write down each rule in your workspace. Convert the rules into symbols so that you can work with them. In the list of rules for this game there are two rules that can be broken up into two rules each. For example, the rule that says if either D or L is fired then it must be by C should be changed into two rules: If D is fired then it is by C, and if L is fired it must be by C. The other rule that can be split up into two is the rule that says if O is fired then W and H are also fired. This becomes two separate rules: If O is fired, then W is fired, and if O is fired then H is fired. Breaking down the rules like this will help you see each rule better, although you just might combine them again when working the game. Two of the other rules create constants: B must fire exactly two employees and G must be fired. The fact that B must fire exactly two employees can be placed directly on the diagram by placing a "2" above the B column. The rule that says if either E or S is fired, then the other is also fired by the same manager, creates a block of E and S if either one of them is fired. Finally, if W is fired, it must be by B. Thus, if W is ever used, it must go in B.

4. **Deductions:** After all the rules have been simplified, take the time to make deductions. The first thing to notice is the distribution of the five employees among the three managers. Five of eight employees must be fired by the three managers, A, B, and C. Each manager fires at least one employee while B must fire exactly two. Since B fires exactly two of the five that are fired, A and C must fire a total of three combined, which means either A will have two and C will have one or A will have one and C will have two. Next, relate the rules to each other and see if there are common variables among different rules. The first two rules that have common variables are the rules that say if O is fired then W is fired and if W is fired then he is fired by B. Combining these two rules tells you if O is fired then W is fired by B. Since B must fire exactly two people, there would be no room for the ES block in group B, so if O is fired, then E and S are not fired by B. There is something larger going on here as well. Watch what happens if O is fired. If O is fired, then both W and H are fired. In addition, G must always be fired, so if O is fired then you know four of the five people who are fired. This leaves no room for the ES block at all. The fifth person must be either D or L. So not only do you know that if O is fired, then E and S are not fired by B, but you also know if O is fired, then both E and S are not fired by anyone. Thus, if O is fired then O, H, W, G, and D/L are the employees who are fired. Regardless of whether D or L is the one fired, D or L must be fired by C. The contrapositive of this deduction concerning E, S, and O is also true. If E or S is fired then O is not fired at all. Furthermore, if E and S are fired by B, then you also know that W is not fired. In fact, the placement of E and S anywhere is very constraining because they will fill whichever group they are in. As mentioned, the placement of E or S in B will tell you something about W because B is the only person that can fire W. Notice how this affects the placement of D and L as well. If E and S are fired by C, then there is no room for C to fire D or L, who, if they are fired, must be fired by C. Therefore, if E and S are fired by C, then neither D nor L is fired. Likewise, if D or L is fired then neither E nor S can be fired by C.

5. **"Walk Around It":** Take a deep breath before moving on to the questions. Look at the game as a whole. Think about what you know, what you don't know, and what information will be the most helpful. You know that the ES block is important. If E and S are fired then O is not, and if O is fired E and S are not. Furthermore, the numerical distribution of the employees fired will also be important. B must fire exactly two and the most any manager can fire is two. You know certain employees must be fired by certain managers, so the ES block will be limited by the placement of any other employees and vice versa. For instance, if W is used and fired by B, there is no room for E and S in B. Likewise, if D or L is fired by C, there is no room for C to fire E and S.

1. **Type:** First determine what kind of game you are dealing with. By what you see in the rules and how the positions are arranged, you can tell that this is a slots game. You have eight variables that must be placed into eight well-defined slots.

2. **Diagram:** There are very few games that give you an example for a diagram, but when they do, use it to create your own. You can simply draw and label two rows of four. Be sure to number the slots correctly.

3. **Simplify the rules:** The next step is to simplify the rules. There are one or two rules that are straightforward and there are others that need a little more analysis. The first condition says that O and S cannot be adjacent. These variables will always be separated by at least one space. On the other hand, the second rule says that W and Y are always adjacent. This will be important in the deductions. The third rule is one of those rules that does not need much interpretation: S must be placed in 6. This can be directly applied to the diagram. The fourth rule is a little more difficult. It says if R and Y face each other, then B is in 3. Make sure that you understand your symbols for this rule. The fifth and final rule says that if G is in the front row, then O is in the back row. Again, be sure that you can understand your symbols for these rules.

4. **Deductions:** Are there any deductions you can make? This is a crucial step. Try and see how the rules relate to one another. If O and S are not adjacent and S is in position 6, then O cannot be in position 5 or in position 7. There is one more rule that deals with the placement of O. If G is in the front row then O is in the back row. O cannot be in 5, 6, or 7, so if O is in the back row then O must be in position 8. Thus, if G is in the front row then O is in the back row in position 8. The contrapositive is also true: If O is not in 8, then G is not in the front row (which is the same as saying that G is in the back row). Next, you know that W and Y must be adjacent. The only room for this WY sequence on the back row is in 7 and 8. If you couple this with the deduction you just made, the placement of either O or the WY sequence will tell you quite a bit of information. If you know G is in the front row (which forces O into the back row), or only that O is in the back row, then the WY sequence must be in the front row. The contrapositive of this deduction is also true: If W and Y are in the back row, then O must be in the front row, which in turn means that G must be in the back row. Finally, look at the conditional statement that says if R and Y face each other, then B is in 3. Think about how that condition relates to the rule that places S in the sixth slot. If R and Y face each other, placing B in 3, then R and Y could only be placed in 1 and 5 or in 4 and 8 because position 3 and position 6 are already filled.

5. **"Walk Around It":** Now you can take a second to look at the game and see what the game is most likely to test. The key in this game is likely to be the relationship between the WY sequence and O, which is also related to the placement of G.

1. Type: This game deals with the order of performances given at a hoe-down. However, what matters here is the absolute location of each performer, their location in the sequence, not the relative order of each performer. Thus, this is a slots-based scheduling game rather than a linear ordering game.

2. Diagram: Your diagram should be a simple list of positions 1 through 6.

3. Simplify the rules: Break down the rules into easily understandable symbols. At the same time, make sure that you understand what the rules are saying. Here you have eight singers but only six will be used. G must give a performance and must be either first or fifth. The rest of the rules are fairly straightforward. Be sure to write down the ordering correctly. For instance, one rule says that if H performs, then M is *immediately before* H. This can be symbolized as: H → MH.

4. Deductions: Look at how the rules relate to each other and determine what additional information you can deduce. One rule says that if H is included, then M is immediately before H (MH). This means that H cannot be first, and that if M is sixth, you cannot use H. The rule that says if L is included then L is before K (L..K) means that L cannot be sixth and also that if there is no K, then there is no L.

5. "Walk Around It": The placement of G looks like it is going to be important. He must perform first or fifth, but he cannot be next to N. Furthermore, if H is used there will be a sequence of MH, which might be difficult to place in the setup if you already know the location of other performers.

1. Type: To begin, ask what type of game this is. Since you must assign variables in three different areas, this is a grouping game. The groups are the three squads. Each child must be assigned to one squad.

2. Diagram: The diagram for this grouping should show the three groups: Offense, Defense, and Special Teams. This is easily done by creating three columns labeled appropriately with abbreviations like O, D, and S.

3. Simplify the rules: Go through the rules and convert them into symbols that you can easily understand. This is also the time to interpret the rules and clarify any of them that might seem confusing. In this game the rules are straightforward. The first rule can be marked directly on the diagram: B cannot be assigned to defense. The rules create a block, RT, and a split of L and M. The rest of the rules are standard conditional statements. The first conditional statement, which says that if K is on Defense then both J and N are on Defense, should be broken up into two separate statements: If K is on Defense then J is on Defense, and if K is on Defense N is on Defense.

4. Deductions: When you run into grouping games and there are two or three groups in which to place variables, always make sure to see how many have to be in each group and how many can be in each group. In this game each person must be assigned to a group so you can determine the possible distributions. Everyone must be used and there must be at least two in every group. There are only two ways to divide up eight items into three groups with each group having at least two items: 3,3,2 and 4,2,2, although you cannot determine which group has which number. The questions will give you that information. Also, as usual with "if…then" statements, look at the contrapositives and then relate as many rules as possible to each other. In this case, one rule says if M is assigned to Special Teams, then J is assigned to Special Teams. The contrapositive of a previous rule says that if J is not assigned to Defense, then K is not assigned to Defense either. Thus if M is assigned to Special Teams then K is not assigned to Defense. The contrapositive of this deduction is also true: If K is assigned to Defense, then M is assigned to Special Teams.

5. **"Walk Around It":** The key to this game will be keeping L and M separate and also keeping R and T together, which is expected since splits and blocks are usually keys in grouping games. You will certainly find questions forcing you to try to violate these rules. Keep in mind also the effects of placing K in D. According to the rules, if K is in D then both J and N must be in D as well, which means that if K is in D then you know the placement of three of the eight children. You would just have to place the five others according to the rules. Any information about J will be very helpful. There are two rules concerning J: If K is in D, then J is in D, and if M is in S, then J is in S. If you know the placement of J, then you know which team he will not be on, which will cause the appropriate contrapositive to come into effect. Do not worry too much if you do not have that many deductions or no deductions at all so long as you have taken the time to try to find them. Trust the questions because they will give you everything you need.

1. **Type:** First ask yourself what type of game you are working with. This will help you set up the game. In this game there are three workers that must be assigned to at least two but no more than three of five different projects. The projects and the workers are fixed categories. The only variable in this game is the assignment of the workers to their projects. Because there are two fixed categories and only one variable, this game is a slots game and can be set up as a matrix.

2. **Diagram:** The diagram for this game is a simple matrix, with the five projects, C, D, E, F, and G, each comprising a separate column and the three workers, L, M, and N, each comprising a separate row. To mark an assignment of a certain person to a certain project, simply place a check mark in the appropriate box. Similarly, if there are restrictions about a certain worker being assigned to a project, simply cross out the appropriate slot.

3. **Simplify the rules:** After drawing the diagram, go to the rules and convert them into simple symbols. Where possible, place the information directly on the diagram. For instance, the rule that says L cannot be assigned to either C or D means that you can cross out the boxes in the L row under columns C and D. The remaining rules are fairly straightforward.

4. Deductions: After converting the rules into symbols it is very important to look at the rules and the diagram and see how the rules relate to each other. In this case, one rule says that L cannot be assigned to C or D, another says that only one worker can be assigned to project G, and another says that all three workers must be assigned to exactly one project in common. These three rules combined indicate that all three workers cannot be assigned to projects C, D, or G. Thus, all three workers must be assigned to either E or F. Also, do not forget the contrapositives of the "if…then" statements. One rule says that if a worker is assigned to C then that worker must also be assigned to F. The contrapositive of this rule says that if a worker is not assigned to F, then that worker is not assigned to project C.

5. "Walk Around It": Using the rules and the deductions you know that all three workers must be assigned to either project E or F, only one worker can be assigned to project G, and only M and N can possibly be assigned to projects C and D. Also, each worker can only be used two or three times, so the fact that if a worker is assigned to project C he must also be assigned to project F means that if a worker is assigned to project C, then that worker has already used two of his assignments. On the other hand, if a worker has been assigned to two projects other than C and F, this means that the worker cannot be assigned to C for his third assignment. It is important to grasp this limitation on the assignment of workers based on the number of projects that they can be assigned to.

1. Type: In this game, there are five days, M through F, where Freddie follows a special diet that includes three meals per day. The days and the meals do not change. The only variables in the game are the types of food Freddie eats: cake (C), ice cream (I), pie (P), or sardines (S). This game sets up fifteen distinct slots that must be filled with one of the types of food. This is a typical slots game.

2. Diagram: The diagram for this slots game is easy to draw. Since there are five days on which Freddie must follow his diet, you can make these five days, Monday through Friday, the columns. Each day is further divided into three meals: breakfast, lunch, and dinner. Make these three divisions into three rows. You now have fifteen slots.

3. Simplify the rules: Simplify the rules by going through them one by one and converting them into symbols. This is also the time to interpret the rules so that you are sure you understand what each rule says. The rules in this game are easy to interpret but harder to symbolize; just do the best you can: There cannot be more than four servings of any one food. There cannot be two consecutive lunches that have the same food. There cannot be two servings of the same food on one day. There are exactly two dinners in a row where Freddie eats the same type of food. There are exactly two breakfasts in a row where Freddie eats the same food. The remaining rules are rules that can be placed directly on the diagram: Freddie eats I on Monday and Wednesday for breakfast and on Tuesday for lunch, Freddie eats P and S on Thursday for lunch and for dinner respectively, and he does not eat S on Friday.

4. **Deductions:** The deductions step is the critical step. This is what the game is all about: the ability to carry out related statements to their logical, although often hidden, conclusions. Take the time to see how the rules relate to each other. First, there are already three I's used, so there can only be one more. Second, there are no S's on Friday and Freddie cannot eat the same food twice in one day, so on Friday Freddie must eat some combination of C, I, and P. Now you know that there is a fourth I on Friday, so no more I's can be used in the game. Third, since the fourth I is on Friday and there must be two days in a row where Freddie eats the same food for breakfast, the food that Freddie eats for those two consecutive days cannot be I. Since the food that Freddie has for two consecutive breakfasts is not I, the two consecutive days where Freddie eats the same food for breakfast must be Thursday and Friday because those are the only two consecutive days available. This means that there cannot be an I for breakfast on Friday. Since Freddie cannot eat I for breakfast on Friday, he must eat either C or P. Whichever of these two foods Freddie eats on Friday for breakfast he will also eat for breakfast on Thursday. Fourth, Freddie does not eat two of the same foods on any day and he is already eating P for lunch on Thursday. Thus, it turns out that Freddie cannot eat P for breakfast on Thursday. Since Freddie cannot have P for breakfast on Thursday, he must have C for breakfast on Thursday. Since Freddie eats the same food for breakfast on Thursday and Friday, Freddie eats C for breakfast on Friday as well. Fifth, since Freddie has C for breakfast on Thursday and P for lunch on Thursday and he cannot have two of the same foods in the same day and cannot have any more I's, Freddie must eat S for dinner on Thursday. Sixth, Freddie does not eat the same food for lunch on two consecutive days. Since Freddie eats P for lunch on Thursday, he cannot eat P for lunch on Friday. Remember, Freddie must eat some combination of C, I, and P on Friday. He eats C for breakfast and cannot have P for lunch, so he must eat P for dinner and have I for lunch. For the remaining slots keep in mind that there cannot be any additional I's. Also, since Freddie cannot have the same food for two consecutive lunches and he eats P for lunch on Thursday, he cannot have P for lunch on Wednesday. This eliminates P and I for lunch on Wednesday, leaving either C or S. This is everything that you can deduce from the rules. At this point, you have nine of the fifteen slots completely filled in and one narrowed down to two possibilities before you even start working the questions.

5. **"Walk Around It":** After making deductions, do not rush on to the questions. Take a moment to look at what you have determined and the rules that govern the game in order to see if you can determine what will be the key in answering the questions. You know the entire setup for Thursday and Friday. Since there are four I's, there cannot be any additional I's. The rules that say Freddie cannot eat the same food for two consecutive lunches and that Freddie cannot eat the same food twice in one day will be important, especially coupled with the rule that there must be two consecutive dinners for which Freddie eats the same food. The consecutive days on which Freddie must eat the same food for dinner must be Monday-Tuesday, Tuesday-Wednesday, or Wednesday-Thursday. Since there cannot be any more I's, I cannot be the food that is eaten for two consecutive dinners. The only possibilities are C, P, and S. There are already two C's and two P's used on Thursday and Friday, so if either C or P is used as the food that is eaten consecutively for dinner, then there could not be any additional C's or P's. With all this in mind, go to the questions.

1. **Type:** In this game there are six days, Monday through Saturday, over two weeks. This is a hint that you will need to draw a grid or matrix. This, then, is a slots game. However, the basic concept is the order of the auditions within each week.

2. **Diagram:** The diagram should have the days of the week as columns and two rows representing week 1 and week 2.

3. **Simplify the rules:** Next, go through the rules and make sure that you understand them as you convert them into easily understandable symbols. In this game the rules are straightforward. R must be before S in both weeks and the audition for S is held on the same day in both weeks. The next rule creates a TV sequence for both weeks though the order of the two can vary. U and W, on the other hand, must be separated by at least one slot. The last rule can be placed directly on the diagram: W auditions on Thursday in week 1 and on Tuesday in week 2.

4. **Deductions:** This is a critical step. Take the time to make deductions; it will save time in the long run. To make deductions, look at how the rules relate to each other. First, R must be before S and S must be on the same day both weeks. W auditions on Tuesday and Thursday, so it is impossible for S to audition on either of those days, and since R must be before S, S cannot audition on Monday either. Thus, S must audition on Wednesday, Friday, or Saturday. Remember to mark what cannot be true on the diagram as well. In other words, put it directly on the diagram that S cannot audition on Monday in either week, etc. The next variables that are covered by the rules are T and V. In both weeks T and V must be consecutive. In week 2, W auditions on Tuesday, so neither T nor V can audition on Monday in week 2. The next rule says that U cannot audition on a day immediately before or immediately after a day on which W auditions. Since the rules assigned W to Thursday in week 1, U cannot audition on Wednesday or Friday in week 1. In week 2, W auditions on Tuesday, so U cannot audition on Monday or Wednesday. Look at what you know about Monday in week 2: U, T, V, S, and W cannot audition on Monday. The only person that can, and therefore must, audition on Monday in week 2 is R.

5. **"Walk Around It":** After you have made deductions, take a moment to look at the game and determine what the questions will likely test. The deduction that R must be on Monday in week 2 is sure to be critical. Because S must be on the same day in both weeks, the placement of S will restrict the placement of everyone else, especially the TV sequence. The placement of T or V will likewise restrict the placement of everyone else. In fact, keep an eye on T and V, because this is likely to be the key to this game.

1. **Type:** In this game you have seven applicants who are being hired for either full-time or part-time work in one of three groups: morning, afternoon, or night. The category of full-time and part-time workers seems to complicate things, but the setup reveals that whether someone is hired as full-time or part-time is actually related to the number of people in each group. Thus, while the setup might appear confusing, it is really a basic grouping game.

2. **Diagram:** Your diagram should reflect your three groups by having three columns labeled morning, afternoon, and night, preferably with abbreviations like M, A, and N.

3. **Simplify the rules:** Simplify the rules as best you can. Make sure you understand what they mean. First of all, there are either part-time or full-time workers. When there is a full-time worker, he is alone during a shift, and conversely if there is only one person working a shift then he is a full-time worker. When there is a part-time worker, he must work with one other person during a shift, and the converse is true too; if there are two people working, then they are part-time workers. If a person is hired full-time, he will be alone during his shift. If a person is hired part-time, there will be two people during that shift. The rule that says R cannot be hired unless both T and V are hired might also confuse you. This simply means that if R is hired, then both T and V are also. Notice that this rule tells you absolutely nothing about which shift T and V are hired for when R is hired. The other rules tell you that if a full-time worker works in A then two part-time workers work in N, that if V works then X cannot, if V works then V is in A, if X works then X is in A, W works part-time, and that if there are three or more hired part-time, then S and W must be in N.

4. **Deductions:** This is the critical part of the game, the part that the test makers are actually testing, so take sometime to analyze the rules and determine how they relate to

one another. The rules tell you that W works part-time. This means that there must be another person who will be working part-time with W. Already you know that there must be at least two people working part-time. Since there are already two part-time workers, only one more is required to satisfy the condition that there are more than two and if there are more than two then S and W must work the night shift. Another rule dealing with the assignment of part-time and full-time workers is the rule that says if one of the applicants is hired full-time for the afternoon shift then two applicants must be hired part-time to work the night shift. Consider the significance of this rule as it relates to the requirements that W works part time and that if there are more than two part-time workers then S and W work on the night shift. If an applicant is hired full-time for the afternoon shift, then the two part-time workers for the night shift could include W and one other worker, or theoretically, it could include two other part-time workers besides W. However, if it is the case that two other people besides W work part-time during the night shift then there would be more than two people working part-time, because W would be working part-time somewhere else. According to the rules, if there are more than two part-time workers then W (and S) must be hired for the night shift. Thus, no matter what, *if there is a full-time worker in the afternoon then W must work the night shift with one other person.* The contrapositive of this deduction is also true: If W does not work the night shift, then there is not a full-time worker in the afternoon, which is the same as saying that there must be two part-time workers in the afternoon. If there are two part-time workers in the afternoon and one of them is not W, then once again there will be more than two part-time workers again, which would force S and W into the night shift, which cannot be since the condition was that W is not working the night shift. So if W is not hired for the night shift then W must be one of the workers hired part-time for the afternoon. Thus, *if W is not working the night shift, then there must be two part-time workers in the afternoon, one of whom must be W.* What does this mean? Either W works the night shift or W works the afternoon shift, which is the same as saying that W cannot work the morning shift. The rest of the deductions are not that difficult to reach. According to the rules, if R works, then V must work in the afternoon. Another rule states that if V works, then X cannot work. Thus, if R works, then X cannot work. The contrapositive is also true: If X works, then R does not work.

5. **"Walk Around It":** After you've had your fill of the deductions, look at the game as a whole and see what information you have as well as what information is likely to be important in determining any possible scenarios. First of all, there are seven workers and three groups. However, V and X cannot work at the same time, which effectively limits the game to six people at the most. If six people are hired, then they must all be hired part-time, or, in other words, there would be two people in each group. But be careful, not everybody has to be used. All you know for certain is that there must at least be two part-time workers. If the other two shifts are filled by full-time workers then there would be four people. Therefore, there are between four and six people hired. The deductions also show that the relationship of W with the other rules about part-time workers is going to be important and cause various side effects. W must either work in the afternoon or the night and must work part-time, or, in other words, must work with somebody else. If there is a third person working part-time, then S and W work together in the night shift. Because W is so important, watch out for any information about W or about any other employees besides W who are hired part-time.

1. **Type:** First ask yourself what type of game this is. You do not have to place anything in order, nor do you have distinct slots for items. This is a grouping game, but one that differs from most other grouping games in that there is only one group to build.

2. **Diagram:** There is no general diagram for this game. The game requires you to build a group of anywhere from four to eight students while adhering to the rules, which are all conditional statements. The key is to build the possible scenarios from the conditional statements. These scenarios will be the diagrams for this game.

3. **Simplify the rules:** Simplify the rules by converting them into symbols. This is also the time to clarify the meaning of each rule. In this case every rule is a conditional statement. The only rule that requires special attention is the rule that says D is not selected unless E is not selected. The word "unless" introduces the necessary condition, or, in other words, the consequent. Thus, the consequent to this conditional statement is that E is not selected. What is sufficient to bring about this consequent? In other words, what is it that allows you to know for certain that E is not selected? What allows you to determine this is if you know that D is selected. If D is selected, then it must be the case that E is not selected, for D cannot be selected without E not being selected. Consider an example: Tom is not successful unless Frank is not successful. This says that the only way for Tom to be successful is if Frank is not, but it does not say that Frank's success will determine Tom's success. Rather, Tom's success will allow you to determine Frank's. As an "if…then" statement, this becomes: If Tom is successful then Frank is not successful. Similarly, the rule that says D is not selected unless E is not selected becomes: If D is selected then E is not selected ($D \rightarrow \sim E$). The remaining rules are straightforward and easy to symbolize: If A is selected then B is not ($A \rightarrow \sim B$), if both C and F are selected then A is also ($C + F \rightarrow A$), if F and G are selected then B is selected ($F + G \rightarrow B$), and if H is selected then C is selected ($H \rightarrow C$).

4. **Deductions:** The first step in making deductions in games that contain "if...then" statements is to determine the contrapositives. Be careful with the contrapositives of the two rules that say if C and F are selected then A is selected, and if F and G are selected then B is selected. The contrapositive of the former says if A is not selected then C and F are not selected. However, this does not meant that neither C nor F is selected, but that C and F cannot *both* be selected at the same time. You can have one without the other. The same holds true for the second of these two rules. Often it is very helpful to think first about the numerical distribution that the game requires. Does everyone have to be used? How many times can everybody be used? In this game not everybody must be used, but nobody can be used twice. There must be at least four students selected and there are eight students, so it first might seem that you are dealing with anywhere between four and eight items; however, two rules create "either/or" restrictions. If A is included, then B is not, and if D is included, then E is not. Thus, you can never use both A and B at the same time, and you can never use both D and E at the same time. Right away you know that instead of eight possible attendees at the spelling bee, there are actually only six. You must choose one of A or B, one of D or E, C, F, G, and H. At this point, begin looking for any relationships among the different rules; in other words, look for rules that contain information about the same variable. Also look at how those rules relate to the numerical distribution that you have discovered. The restrictions will allow you to build a few scenarios. To begin, the first two rules contain information about A. The second rule says if C and F are selected, then A is also selected. The first rule says if A is selected, then B is not. Putting these two rules together you know that if C and F are selected, then A is selected and B is not selected. The contrapositive of the other rule affecting F and B, the rule that says if F and G are selected then B is also selected, says that if B is not selected then F and G cannot both be selected at the same time. Thus, if C and F are selected, then B is not selected, and if B is not selected, then F and G cannot both be selected. However, F is already included in

the C and F pair, so this is the same as saying that if C and F are selected, then G cannot be selected. Work this deduction out as a possible scenario. If F and C are selected, then A is also selected. That gives you three people. Since there must be at least four selected, you need to look for the other students who could be included. Since F and C are selected, from the deductions you know that B and G cannot be selected, leaving only D/E and H. Thus, the first scenario is if F and C are included and the setup looks like this: F, C, A, D/E, H, where one or both of D/E and H must be included. You can follow this same reasoning and create another scenario where F and G are selected. If F and G are selected, then B is selected. If B is selected, then A is not selected, so if F and G are selected, then B is selected and A is not. If A is not selected, then C and F cannot both be selected at the same time. F is already included in the F and G pair, so if F and G are selected, then C cannot be selected. Furthermore, if C is not selected, then H is not selected. Now you can work this set of deductions out as another possible scenario. If F and G are selected, then B must be selected. Once again, this only gives you three people. If F and G are selected, then from the deductions you know that A, C, and H cannot be selected, leaving only D/E as the fourth student. Thus, the second scenario looks like this: F, G, B, D/E. Notice how these two scenarios revolved around the relationship between F and either C or G. It is important to note that these two scenarios do not exhaust the possibilities. There are two more conceivable scenarios, one where F is included but neither C nor G is included and one where F is not included at all. If neither C nor G is included, then, in order to have four students, one of A or B would have to be selected, one of D or E would have to be selected, F would have to be selected, and H would have to be selected. However, H drags C along with it, so this scenario does not work. What happens if F is not included at all? If F is not included then the rules do not reveal anything more about who is or is not included. Everyone else could be selected; however, both the A and B pair and the D and E pair are "either/or," so only one of each of them could be included. Thus the setup for the third scenario where

F is not included looks like this: A/B, D/E, H, C, G, while only four must be selected. In this scenario the relationship between H and C is very important. With these three scenarios in front of you before even going to the questions, this game is easy to work out. Notice that in each of these three scenarios the maximum number of students who can be selected for the spelling bee is five.

5. **"Walk Around It":** While the deductions step might have taken a little longer than usual, it will be well worth the effort. There are only three possible basic scenarios: 1) F and C are included, which gives you F, C, A, and one or both of D/E and H as the students selected; 2) F and G are included, which gives you F, G, B, and D/E as the four students selected, and 3) one scenario without F, which gives you at least four of A/B, D/E, H, C, and G as the students selected. The key will be to know which scenario each question refers to. Also, remember that four students must be included, but five may be included depending on the scenario.

1. **Type:** In this game there are seven rooms that are remodeled according to various conditions. A glance at these conditions clearly shows that the focus of this game will be on ordering the rooms based on when they are remodeled. This is an ordering game.

2. **Diagram:** In ordering games such as this, the real diagram will be the complete list of relative order that you obtain in the deductions step. However, writing down some basic information will help you out. For the diagram, write down that you have seven spaces to work with and all seven of the rooms: K, L, D, M, B, G, and S.

3. **Simplify the rules:** Simplify the rules by converting them into symbols. Instead of rereading each rule countless times throughout the game, you can simply glance at the symbols and, ideally, understand what each means without additional thought. As in all ordering games, be careful to interpret what each rule says accurately. In other words, make sure that you symbolize "after" as after and "before" as before. There are only three rules in the rules list, but two of them can be broken down into more than one rule. First, B and K must be remodeled consecutively. In other words, B and K must be next to each other, although you do not know which one comes first. The second rule says that D is after M and before G. Write this initially as two separate rules: M..D and D..G. The third rule says L is after G and after S. This should also be written as two separate rules: G..L and S..L. That takes care of the rules.

4. Deductions: Now comes the vital step of making deductions. In ordering games, this step is simple. Combine the rules where possible so that you create one large list of relative order. For instance, in this case, you know that M is before D, that D is before G, and that G is before L. Thus, you get a list that looks something like this: M..D..G..L. Furthermore, S must be before L. Be careful, for you do not know the order of S in relation to M, D, or G. You only know that S must be sometime before L. You can represent this in the list of relative order by writing in S above or below the M..D..G..L sequence. The rules do not allow you to determine the position of B or K relative to the other rooms, so B and K can be anywhere as long as they are consecutive. Pay attention to what the deduced list of relative order tells you. It tells you what could be first (M, S, B, or K), what could be last (L, B, or K), as well as the earliest and latest that certain rooms can be remodeled.

5. "Walk Around It": At this point, before you have even gone to the questions, you know something about every room. The basic order must be M..D..G..L, with S sometime before L, and B and K as wildcards as long as they are consecutive. There really isn't too much left to determine. Take the information that the questions give you and work them out based on this list of order.

1. Type: In this game there are two fixed categories: the three children and the types of events, individual and team. The only variable is which event each child plays for the individual event and for the team event. Thus, the children and game type create slots into which you must place the actual event that each child plays. This is a slots game.

2. Diagram: The diagram should clearly show the slots. You can accomplish this easily by drawing three columns labeled with the first letter of each child's name to represent the three children and two rows labeled I and T to represent the categories of individual and team events. You will have to assign one of the three individual and team events to each child.

3. Simplify the rules: Take the time to convert the rules into symbols. Write these symbols directly in your workspace so you do not have to reread the rules over and over again. The symbols will save you precious time. This also gives you a chance to ensure that you really understand what the rules mean, for you cannot symbolize them correctly without understanding what they mean. The rules here are fairly straightforward; there is nothing difficult to interpret. First, if F and G have the same team event then they have the same individual event. Second, F and H do not have the same individual event. Similarly, G and H do not have the same team event. H must have a C or an S, where C is an individual event and S is a team event. H must have at least one of C or S, but could have both. Finally, the rule that assigns A to G can be placed directly on the diagram. A is an individual event so be sure to place it in the appropriate slot.

4. Deductions: The next step is to make deductions. How do the rules relate to each other? Does more than one rule govern the same variable? In this case, there is not much to go on, but there is something. According to the rules, if F and G have the same

Setups

team event, then they must have the same individual event as well. Since G must always have A as his individual event, if F and G have the same team event, then they must both have A as their individual event. Since G will always have an A, you can restate this by saying if F and G have the same team event, then F must participate in A for the individual event. The contraposition of this statement also holds: If F does not participate in A for the individual event, then F and G cannot participate in the same team event. There is not much else to deduce.

5. **"Walk Around It":** Before moving on to the questions, think about the game as a whole. Think about what you do and do not know. There are six slots and you know the contents of one: G must participate in A for his individual event. The rules make it explicit that the children can participate in the same events as each other, except where specifically forbidden by the rules. There are two such exceptions: H cannot have the same individual event as F, and H cannot have the same team event as G, so knowledge of any of the sports that H plays or the sports that F and G play will give you information about the other of H or F of G. Furthermore, H must participate in at least one of C or S so information that H does not participate in C for his individual event tells you that he participates in S for his team event. Likewise, any information that tells you that H does not participate in S for his team event tells you that H participates in C for his individual event. Watch out for this relationship between C and S for H, as well as H's relationship to the other two children. Lastly, don't forget to use your deductions as you reason out the questions.

1. **Type:** In this game there are ten cubicles surrounding an empty space. There are nine workers, four adjustors, and five salespersons. You must place each person in a cubicle. This is an unusual game in that it does not fit neatly into any of the standard categories (ordering, grouping, slots). Often such games are fairly easy once you make peace with their difference.

2. **Diagram:** The diagram for this game should follow the description given in the setup paragraph. There are ten cubicles arranged with one cubicle in each corner, two non-corner cubicles on both the east and west sides, and one non-corner cubicle on both the north and south sides. The diagram should look something like this:

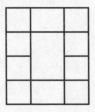

3. **Simplify the rules:** Go through the rules one at a time and interpret them. Convert them into symbols and place them directly on the diagram wherever possible. The first rule says that W and T are in adjacent non-corner cubicles. W and T must be next to each other, but neither can be in a corner office. On the other hand, V must be in a corner cubicle. No adjustor has a cubicle immediately next to the cubicle of another adjustor. D is the only adjustor who does not have a corner cubicle. This means that the rest of the adjustors do have corner cubicles. Finally, X's cubicle is directly across from U's cubicle.

4. **Deductions:** Once you understand the rules, take the time to relate them to one another and make deductions. First of all, it is helpful to think about the game in general, about the number of pieces in the game and the number of slots available. Here, since there are ten cubicles and only nine people, every person must be used

exactly once and there will be one empty cubicle. Next, go to the rules list. The first rule says that W and T are in adjacent non-corner cubicles. Since only the east and west sides have adjacent non-corner cubicles, W and T must be next to each other on either the east or west side in the two available non-corner cubicles. Since one side of either east or west has W and T next to each other, in order for X to be directly across from U, U and X must be in the non-corner cubicles on the north and south sides. Furthermore, the rules provide you with the employees in all four corner cubicles: All the adjustors except for D must have corner cubicles and so does V. Thus, V, B, C, and E are in the four corner cubicles. This means that the one remaining adjustor, D, must have a non-corner cubicle. Every non-corner cubicle is next to at least one corner cubicle, so D must be adjacent to one of B, C, E, or V. However, because no adjustor has a cubicle immediately next to another adjustor, D cannot be next to B, C, or E. Therefore, D must be in a non-corner cubicle next to V, the only person who has a corner cubicle that is not an adjustor. Think about what this means. V must be in a corner cubicle and D must be in a non-corner cubicle next to V. X and U are already in the non-corner cubicles on the north and south sides, so D must be in a non-corner cubicle on the east or west side. W and T fill up one side entirely, so D must be on the opposite side from W and T and must be adjacent to the empty cubicle.

5. **"Walk Around It":** Walk around the game to get a feel for what is going on. At this point, you know almost everything. B, C, E, and V are in the corner positions. X and U are in the non-corner cubicles on the north and south sides. D is in a non-corner cubicle on the east or west side and is immediately next to V. The empty cubicle is the non-corner cubicle adjacent to D. W and T are in the non-corner cubicles on the opposite side of D and the empty cubicle. The only thing you do not know is which side of the building each piece is on.

1. **Type:** Ask yourself what type of game this is. The rules and conditions of this game are easy to classify. It is a grouping game where your task is to create a single group of planets and nebulae that Spiff visits. This is slightly different from other grouping games where you must assign people or things to different groups. Here you will select different planets and nebulae to make a single group.

2. **Diagram:** Since there is really only one group, you may not use the diagram much.

3. **Simplify the rules:** Go to the rules and see what they mean. Break them down so you can understand them. This game has a list of conditional statements that are easy to interpret. Don't forget to write down the rules contained in the opening paragraph as well: You need at least two of the three nebulae and at least one of the six planets.

4. **Deductions:** In a game like this that has a list of conditional statements, it is helpful to start by writing down the contrapositives. It is almost guaranteed that there will be at least one question that tests your understanding of a contrapositive. Next, examine how the rules relate to one another. Notice that there are three rules that deal with V: *If U then V (if not V then not U). If Z then not V (if V then not Z). If nebula 1 then V (if not V then not nebula 1).* If you put those rules together, what happens? Combine the first and second and you get: *If U then not Z.* Combine the second and third and you get: *If Z then not nebula 1* (Note: Don't forget to take the contrapositive of your deductions, such as, *If nebula 1, then not Z.* That deduction leads to a connection with another rule: *If nebula 3 then Z.* Putting those two rules together gives you: *If nebula 3 then not nebula 1,* as well as the contrapositive: *If nebula 1 then not nebula 3.* Bells should be going off in your head. You're on your way to a huge deduction. If Spiff must visit at least two nebulae, and if he visits nebula 1 but not nebula 3, then one scenario is nebula 1 and

nebula 2, and the second possible scenario is nebula 3 and nebula 2. Now you must see what happens within your two possible scenarios. Begin with the first scenario: Spiff visits nebula 1 and nebula 2. Go to the rules and see which planets Spiff must visit. Knowing which nebulae Spiff visits creates a long chain reaction. If Spiff visits nebula 1, then you know that Spiff visits V and W for certain, one of U or X for certain, and that he cannot visit Z. You don't know anything about Y, so he could or could not visit Y. Thus, in the first scenario Spiff visits nebula 1, nebula 2, V, W, U/X, and possibly Y. Now go to scenario 2, where Spiff visits nebula 2 and nebula 3. If he visits nebula 3, then he must visit Z. Your rules say *If Z, then not V*, and one of your contrapositives tells you *If not V, then not U*, so Spiff cannot visit V or U. Since there must be one of U or X, and there cannot be a U, there must be an X. Thus, in scenario 2 Spiff must visit nebula 2, nebula 3, Z, and X. You don't know anything about W or Y, so you could have them, or you could not.

5. **"Walk Around It":** Now that the game is limited to only two scenarios, the questions will be much easier to answer. In each question look for any information that will allow you to determine which scenario you are dealing with. Also, make sure that you understand the distinction between what you have to have in each scenario and the items that you could have.

1. **Type:** In this game there are three tables at a banquet. It will be your task to place nine guests at these tables. At each table there is also one company representative, so you must place the representative as well. Thus, the only definite information that you have is that there are three tables with three guests and one company representative each. Since there are tables and two different types of people you might be inclined to set up this game as a slots game. However, the slots are not well defined; there will be three guests at each table and one company representative. You can set this up as a grouping game, but keep track of the company representatives and the languages they speak.

2. **Diagram:** Your diagram should simply show the three tables as three columns. There must be three guests at each table, so you can place that information on your diagram as well. Along with the three guests there must be a representative. The representative's placement will be determined by the languages spoken at each table.

3. **Simplify the rules:** Now is the time to interpret the rules and write them down in your workspace. Convert the rules into symbols that will help you understand what is going on. In this game there is not much information to place directly on the diagram, but when it is possible be sure to do it. Don't forget to write down the rules that are contained in the setup paragraph as well. In this case, the critical information of what languages each representative can speak is found in the setup. Then go to the rules list and focus on those rules. The rules here are straightforward. There are a few "if…then" statements that are easy to simplify and a couple of more general rules which say there must be at least two German-speaking guests seated at the same table and that there must be at least three Spanish-speaking guests.

4. **Deductions:** The easiest place to begin making deductions when there are "if…then" statements is with the "if…then" statements. It is easy to determine the contrapositives, simply negate both sides and then reverse the statement. For example, the rule that says if a Spanish speaker is seated at the first table then Bateman must be assigned to the second table can be changed into the contrapositive by saying if Bateman is not assigned to the second table then there is not a Spanish speaker seated at the first table. Next, look at how the individual rules relate to each other. The first rule says if there is an F at table 1 then there must be an F at table 3. Only B and D can speak F, so if there is an F at table 1, then B and D must be at the first and third tables, though not necessarily in that order. C is left over and must be assigned to table 2. Thus, if there is an F at table 1, then C is the representative at table 2. Now look at the rule that says if C is not assigned to table 3, then D is not assigned to table 1. If there is an F at table 1, then C is assigned to table 2, which means that C is not assigned to table 3, so D cannot be assigned to table 1. Thus, D must be assigned to table 3 and B must be assigned to table 1. So if you know that there is an F at the first table, you can determine the assignment for every representative: C is at table 2, D is at table 3, and B is at table 1. The contrapositive of this deduction is also true. If the assignment of representatives to tables does not conform to this setup then there is no F at table 1. There is another rule, the consequence of which does not conform to this setup. If there is an S at table 1, then B must be assigned to table 2. This means that B is not at table 1 so there cannot be an F at table 1. There are not any additional deductions that stand out immediately so quickly take a moment to walk around the game.

5. **"Walk Around It":** The main key to this game is merely keeping track of which representative speaks which language. If you know that a certain language is spoken at a table, then you can narrow down who the representative will be at that table. Similarly, if you know which representative is at a table, then you can determine what languages can be spoken at that table. Any information at all will probably cause a rule to come into play. For instance, if you know that there is an F at table 1, then you know that B is at table 1, C is at table 2, and D is at table 3. Likewise, if a situation does not have B at table 1, C at table 2, or D at table 3, then there cannot be an F at table 1. At one table you need to have at least two G's, and there must be at least three S's used in the game. Have the conscious thought that you do not have to have any F's or J's, though it is likely you will. It is a lot to keep track of, but you can do it.

1. Type: First, ask yourself what type of game this is. The rules establish four different groups: beginner's French, advanced French, beginner's Spanish, and advanced Spanish. It is your job to place different combinations of boys and girls within those groups. It is a grouping game.

2. Diagram: The diagram is easy to make for grouping games. There are four groups. Simply make each group a separate column. Place whatever information you can directly on the diagram.

3. Simplify the rules: The first two rules in the rules list contain "if…then" statements that are easy to convert into symbols. The first rule, however, actually provides two pieces of information, so it can and should be broken up into two rules: One rule that says if K is in a French course, then L is in a French course. The other rule says if K is in a French course, then X is in a French course. The third rule establishes a block: Y and Z must enroll in the same course. The last two rules tell you that there are at least two boys in beginner's Spanish, and that there are no girls in beginner's French. These last two rules you can put directly on the diagram.

4. Deductions: Look at the rules in relation to one another in order to make deductions. This is a critical step. It will allow you to use your time more efficiently. Rather than trying to reinvent the wheel on every question, you will be able to know beforehand what the rules mean and how they relate to each other. A good way to begin the deductions process is to write down the contrapositives for each conditional statement. You can obtain the contrapositive by reversing the conditional statement and negating both sides. The three contrapositives for the three conditional statements are thus: 1) If L is not in French, then K is not in French. 2) If X is not in French, then K is not in French. 3) If Y is not in advanced Spanish, then M

is not in Spanish. Now you can relate the rules and contrapositives to each other. In grouping games, it is often helpful to think first about the possible numerical distribution of the items over the groups. In this game there are seven students to place in four groups. There must be at least one student in each of the four groups and, according to the rules, there must be at least two boys in beginner's Spanish and at least one boy in beginner's French. This entails that there can never be four students in any one group. Since there must be two boys in beginner's Spanish, there can never be four students in any one group. The numerical distribution must either be 3-2-1-1 (not necessarily in that order) or 2-2-2-1 (not necessarily in that order), with beginner's Spanish as one of the courses with two or more students. Since no girls enroll in beginner's French, if any of X, Y, or Z is in a French course, she must be in advanced French. With none of the three girls in beginner's French and at least two boys in beginner's Spanish, there can only be at most two students in beginner's French, and both of those two students would have to be boys. Next, consider the conditional statements as they relate to each other and the rules about the distribution of boys and girls. The first rule says that if K is in French, then X is in French. X is one of the three girls and no girl can enroll in beginner's French, so if K is in French, then X must be in advanced French. The first rule also says that if K (a boy) is in French, then L (a boy) is in French. There must still be two boys in beginner's Spanish and the only two boys remaining are J and M. Therefore, if K is in French, then J and M are in beginner's Spanish. The one remaining conditional statement tells you that if M is in Spanish, then Y is in advanced Spanish. Y and Z must enroll in the same course, so if M is in Spanish, then Y and Z are in advanced Spanish. As mentioned, if K is in French, then J and M must be in beginner's Spanish; so when K is in French, M is in Spanish, which forces Y and Z into advanced Spanish. Notice how much information you are able to deduce if the only thing you know is that K is in a French course. If K is in a French course then L and X must both be in French courses with at least X in advanced French. J and M would have to be in beginner's Spanish, which forces Y and Z into advanced Spanish. Thus, if K is in a French course, then you know something about the placement of every student. The only remaining question is whether K and L are in beginner's French or advanced French. The contrapositive of this string of deductions is also valid. The contrapositive reveals that there is only one other basic scenario. As mentioned, no distribution of students allows four students to take the same language course. There must always be at least two boys in beginner's Spanish, so if the YZ block is not in advanced Spanish, then it cannot be in beginner's Spanish. Furthermore, no girls enroll in beginner's French, so if the YZ block is not in advanced Spanish, then Y and Z must be in advanced French. Thus, the YZ block is either in advanced French or advanced Spanish.

5. **"Walk Around It":** Before moving on to the questions, take the time to get a feel for what the game is doing and what it is going to test you on. There are four groups and seven students. Each student must be assigned to exactly one course. Each group must have at least one person in it. Pay close attention to who the boys are and who the girls are, for there must be two boys in beginner's Spanish and if a girl is in French then she must be in advanced French. The YZ block is restricted to either advanced French or advanced Spanish, and its placement will either be determined by or a determinant of the placement of K, so pay close attention to the placement of K. If K is in a French class, then you can almost place every student in a group. If any student is not in the class in which he or she would be if K were in French, then you know that K cannot be in French and will most likely be able to deduce other facts as well using other rules.

1. **Type:** In this game an editor must decide which stories to include on the front page for five days. She can choose from four different topics. The topics and the days of the week create fixed categories. It might be tempting to set this up as a grouping game with the days of the week as the groups, or as a scheduling game since you have the days of the week. In fact, a grouping setup *will* work as long as you thoroughly understand what is going on. However, since you want to see the relationship between the topics and the days of the week, you are better off to set this up as a slots game. With a matrix, you will be able to see more clearly what can and cannot be used on each day of the week.

2. **Diagram:** The diagram for this game should be a matrix with the days of the week on one axis and the four topics on the other. Draw five columns labeled as the days of the week and then draw four rows labeled P, W, E, and C to represent the four topics. When you know that a certain topic must be used on a certain day, place a check mark in the appropriate slot. Likewise, if you know that a certain topic cannot be used on a certain day, mark this, perhaps with an X, in the appropriate slot. If you insist on working this as a grouping game, you can simply draw five columns to represent the five days of the week.

3. **Simplify the rules:** Simplify the rules by converting them into symbols that you can quickly glance at when you need to check the rules. Going through each rule and converting it into symbols will also force you to interpret each rule and decipher exactly what it says. A few of the rules for this game can be broken up into two or more conditional statements. When this is the case, go ahead and write them down as separate rules. The first and second rules in the rules list are rules than can be broken up into two rules each. The first rule says two things: If a topic is not covered on Tuesday, then it is covered on Thursday. And if a topic is covered on Thursday, then

it is not covered on Tuesday. The second rule says the same about Monday and Friday: If a topic is not covered on Monday, then it is covered on Friday. And if a topic is covered on Friday, then it is not covered on Monday. These rules create strong relationships between Tuesday and Thursday and Monday and Friday. All four topics will be covered between Tuesday and Thursday and all four topics will be covered between Monday and Friday. What is covered on one day in each pair cannot be covered on the other and what is not covered on one day in each pair must be covered on the other. The next two rules give you assignments that you can place directly on the diagram: P is covered on Tuesday and Friday, and C is covered on Thursday and Friday. The last rule is long and convoluted and actually gives you three distinct pieces of information: Wednesday's front page covers more topics than Friday's, Friday's covers more than Tuesday's, and no other day's front page can cover the same number of topics as Friday's. It is vital that you understand each of these rules. Do try your best to convert them into symbols. Getting rid of the words will prevent you from reading and rereading. Instead you can simply glance at your symbols and understand what is meant right away. Don't waste your time with words.

4. **Deductions:** Once you have simplified the rules and converted them into symbols, analyze them. How do the rules relate to each other? What more can you determine? Two of the rules make specific assignments, so it is easy to start there. On both Tuesday and Friday, P must be one of the topics covered on the front page. From the other rules, you know that if a topic is covered on Tuesday, then that topic cannot be covered on Thursday. Thus, P cannot be covered on Thursday. Furthermore, if a topic is covered on Friday then it cannot be covered on Monday. Thus, P cannot be covered on Monday either. The other specific assignment is that C must be covered on both Thursday and Friday. Since what is covered on Thursday cannot be covered on Tuesday, C cannot be covered on Tuesday, and since what is covered on Friday cannot be covered on Monday, C cannot be covered on Monday. Now comes the tricky, but vital step. You

must still deal with the rule that tells you first of all that no other day can cover the same number of topics as are covered on Friday and second that Friday's front page must have fewer topics than does Wednesday's but more topics than Tuesday's. From the placements that the rules gave you, you know that F must already cover at least two topics, and since F covers those two topics, M cannot cover those two topics. This leaves two topics remaining on both days. If on Friday the front page were to only cover those two topics that have already been assigned to Friday, then Monday would be forced to cover the two topics that Friday's front page does not, which means that if F only covered two topics then M would cover two topics as well, which breaks the rule that no other day covers the same number of topics as Friday does. Thus, the front page on Friday must cover more than two topics. However, Friday's front page must also have a fewer number of topics than does Wednesday's, so in fact Friday's front page must cover exactly three topics, the P and the C that are already covered on Friday and exactly one of W or E. The one topic that is not covered on Friday must be covered on Monday. In other words, the front page on Monday must cover exactly one topic, one of W or E, and the front page on Friday must cover exactly three topics, P, C, and one of W or E. Since you now know that Friday's front page covers three topics, you also know that no other day's paper can cover exactly three topics. Furthermore, since Friday's front page covers exactly three topics and Wednesday's front page must cover more topics than Friday's, all four topics must be covered on Wednesday. Friday's front page must also cover more topics than does Tuesday's so Tuesday's front page must cover one or two topics. Now focus on the relationship between Tuesday's front page and Thursday's front page. Tuesday and Thursday have the same relationship as Monday and Friday, what is covered on one day cannot be covered on the other, and what is not covered on one day must be covered on the other. For both pairs, either one day must cover one topic and the other three, or both days must cover exactly two topics. Since no day other than Friday can cover exactly three topics, neither Tuesday nor Thursday can cover three topics, which means that neither of them can cover only one topic as well. In other words, both Tuesday's and Thursday's front page must cover exactly two topics. You now know the number of topics covered by each day's front page: Monday's must cover exactly one topic, either W or E; Tuesday's must cover exactly two topics, P and either W or E; Wednesday's must cover all four topics; Thursday's must cover exactly two topics, C, and either W or E; and Friday's must cover exactly three topics, P, C, and one of W or E.

5. **"Walk Around It":** After making the necessary deductions, it is apparent that the game is much more restricted than it first appeared. Wednesday is completely filled and must cover all four topics. Monday and Friday both need one additional topic so that Monday has one and Friday has three. Whichever one Monday covers, Friday does not and, likewise, whichever one Friday covers, Monday does not. Tuesday and Thursday also both need one additional topic so that they will both be covering exactly two. The only two topics to choose from for both Tuesday and Thursday are W and E, so one day will cover one and the other will cover the one remaining topic. The questions will make you work out the relationship between Monday and Friday as well as the relationship between Tuesday and Thursday. Once you are comfortable with the game and what you have to do, move on to the questions.

1. **Type:** In this game four students must go to one of four restaurants over a period of five days. The four students, R, M, E, and J, make up one set category, while the days of the week make up another. The only variables are the restaurants that each student eats at each day. The students and the days of the weeks create well-defined slots in which you must place the variables. This is a slots game.

2. **Diagram:** This game is best set up as a matrix with the days of the week as five columns and the students as four rows. This setup creates twenty slots that you must fill. The rules will help you fill some, while you must depend on the questions to fill others.

3. **Simplify the rules:** Once you know the type of game you are dealing with and have a good idea what the diagram looks like, go through the rules. As you go through them, convert them into symbols or place them directly on the diagram where possible. Don't forget the rules contained in the setup paragraph. In this case, the setup paragraph tells you that no students can eat at the same place on the same day. Thus, for each day, each of the four restaurants must be visited by one student. The first rule in the rules list says that no student can eat at the same place more than two times during the week. While this is hard to symbolize, it is easy to understand. A student can eat at the same restaurant twice during the week, but no more than twice. Notice that this rule does not say that a student can only eat at one restaurant twice; therefore, you do not know for sure from the rules whether each student eats at every restaurant. The second rule in the rules list plays off the previous rule. M is the only student who eats at A two times; furthermore, one of those days is Thursday. This second part you can place directly on the diagram. M eats at A on Thursday and also one other time during the week. The last three rules all contain information that you can and should place directly on the diagram. R eats at B on Monday and Tuesday, J eats at D on Tuesday and Wednesday, and E eats at A on Friday.

4. **Deductions:** The rules may seem not to give you very much information, but take the time to see how they relate to each other and you might be surprised what happens. First, on the larger scale, there are five days of the week, only four restaurants, and no student can eat at the same place more than two times during the week, so at least one of the restaurants must be visited twice. Also, each restaurant must be used each day. Since M eats at A twice and is the only student to do so, there are three other days on which A must be visited. There are only three other students, so each student must visit A. Fortunately, you have enough information to determine when each student eats at A. But first, for both R and J you know the restaurant that they must visit twice. Since they cannot visit that restaurant again, you can go across the row and mark down that R cannot visit B on Wednesday, Thursday, or Friday, and that J cannot visit D on Monday, Thursday, or Friday. Furthermore, since M is the only student who eats at A on two days and the rules say that E eats at A on F, you can mark that E cannot eat at A on Monday, Tuesday, Wednesday, or Thursday. Now that you've taken care of the rows, go to the columns. No two students can eat at the same place on the same day. Every day, each of the four restaurants must be used. Start with E on Friday. E eats at A on Friday, so no one else can eat at A on Friday. Go down the column and mark that R, M, and J cannot eat at A on Friday. M eats at A on Thursday, so you can mark that R, M, and J cannot eat at A on Thursday. Since J eats at D on Tuesday and Wednesday, nobody else can eat at D on Tuesday or Wednesday, and since R eats at B on Monday and Tuesday, nobody else can eat at B on Monday or Tuesday. Now that you've finished marking down what cannot be where, look at the implications of what you have done. E cannot eat at A, B, or D on Tuesday; thus, E must eat at C on Tuesday. With E eating at C, M cannot eat at C. Since M cannot eat at C, B, or D on Tuesday, M must eat at A. Now you know both days that M eats at A. Thus, you can say for certain that M does not eat at A on Monday or Wednesday. Next, take a look at what has happened on Monday. R eats at B and neither M nor E can eat at A. Thus, J must be the person who eats

at A on Monday. The only person for whom you have determined the day on which they eat at A is R. He must eat at A sometime, and now it is clear that R cannot eat at A on Monday, Tuesday, Thursday, or Friday. Thus, R eats at A on Wednesday. This is everything that you can determine for certain. At this point you know ten of the twenty slots, while many of the others are narrowed down to two choices. On Monday, M and E must visit C or D. On Tuesday, you know the restaurant that each student visits. On Wednesday, M and E must both eat at B or C. For Thursday and Friday you do not know very much information, although you do know some.

5. **"Walk Around It":** The questions will test both what you do know and what you don't. Once you know any additional information, it will likely set off a chain of events that will allow you to fill in even more slots. For example, on Monday, M and E must eat at C or D. If you know that M eats at D, then E must eat at C, which makes two C's for E, which forces E to eat at B on Wednesday, and so on. Make yourself comfortable with how this process works. Lastly, realize that while each person must visit at least one of the restaurants twice, since there is no requirement that each person visits each restaurant, it is possible that one or more people actually visits two restaurants twice. Now you are ready for the questions.

1. **Type:** In this game you have to schedule a series of make-up tests for Monday through Friday for either 8:00 a.m. or 9:00 p.m. These are fixed slots. The only variables in this game are the placement of the people themselves. This is a slots game.

2. **Diagram:** The diagram for this slots game should show the fixed slots. There should be five columns labeled as M through F, for Monday through Friday. There should also be two rows labeled 8 and 9. The setup paragraph says that no student can be tested on Wednesday at 8:00, so cross out or shade in this slot so that you know no one can be placed there.

3. **Simplify the rules:** The rules list here is not very lengthy. Go through the rules one by one, interpret them, and convert them into symbols. P must be tested sometime before N. This is a little trickier than a normal ordering rule because each day is divided into two parts. This rule does not mean that P must be on a day earlier than N, only that P must be tested in an earlier time slot than N. P only has to be before N. P could be on one day at 8:00 while N is on the same day at 9:00. O and M must be tested on the same day, which means that O and M will take up an entire day, although you do not know whether O or M is at 8:00. The rule that says S is tested at 9:00 on Tuesday should be placed directly on the diagram. The one remaining rule is a conditional statement: If L is at 8 then R is also at 8.

4. **Deductions:** The deductions step is a critical step. In this game, however, there are not many deductions to make. You cannot create a list of relative order and there are not that many "if…then" statements to work with, although there is one. Don't forget the contrapositive of the one "if…then" rule. Now look at the diagram and go through the rules with the diagram in mind. The fact that O and M are on the same day means that they take up an entire day, but S is already on Tuesday and on Wednesday no one is tested at 8:00, so O and M cannot be on Tuesday or Wednesday. Thus, the O and M block must be on Monday, Thursday, or Friday. There is not anything left to deduce, so move to the next step.

5. **"Walk Around It":** There are eight people and nine slots, so there will be one empty slot. O and M constitute a block that takes up an entire day, which forces O and M to be on Monday, Thursday, or Friday. The placement of any other person will probably restrict the placement of O and M. Finally, make sure P is always before N and watch out for the placement of L, because if L is at 8:00, then R must be at 8:00 on another day.

Setup Game 48

1. **Type:** In this game Mayor Caballo must visit seven schools. The rules only deal with the order in which he visits those schools, so it is apparent that this is an ordering game.

2. **Diagram:** The diagram for an ordering is very easy. For this game, simply put down seven spaces labeled 1 through 7.

3. **Simplify the rules:** Convert the rules into symbols that you can easily understand. Each of these rules deals with the order in which the mayor visits the schools. Take the rules one at a time and write down the order of the two schools that are mentioned. For example, the first rule says that Caballo visits E before F. This should be written as: E..F. Follow this procedure for the rest of the rules.

4. **Deductions:** After simplifying the rules, the next step is to make deductions. The deductions for ordering games are easy to make. Pick a school that is described more than once in the rules and create a list of the relative order of all the schools that you can based on that one letter. For example, F is mentioned in the first two rules, so start with F. E must be before F and F must be before I. This should be written as: E..F..I. Another rule says that I..J, so add that to your list and you get: E..F..I..J. You also know that G must be sometime before I on this list, and that H must be after G. It is important to note that you do not know the order of G relative to either E or F, nor do you know the order of H relative to any of the other schools. Since you do not know how G relates to E or F, you should write G above or below this basic list of order, but do it in such a way that you are clear G must be before I. Wherever you write the G, also write the H, such that you understand G is before H, but that you do not know how the order of H relates to any other school. Keep in mind that S cannot be next to F or I. Now that you have a completed diagram, you know quite a bit more information than you did when you started.

5. **"Walk Around It":** Now take a moment to see how this game will be played. You are going to have to determine the order of the schools. What information can you see from the list of the relative order? It is helpful to look at what can be first and what can be last. In this game E, G, or S could be first and J, H, or S could be last. That doesn't narrow it down too much, but it should help you get a feel for the game. Notice how the requirement that S cannot be next to F or I severely restricts the placement of S. F and I must be somewhere in the middle and S must be separated from both by at least one. G, H, J, and E are the possible buffers that will allow you to keep S and both F and I separated. This rule will definitely be an important one.

1. **Type:** Here there are sixteen students that must be assigned to one of four moot court competition teams. This is clearly a grouping game where each of the four teams is a group. It is also pretty clear that there are an unusually large number of items to place and rules to deal with. You will not see a game on the LSAT that looks exactly like this. However, you will see games that force you to do the same thing. The same skills are being tested. Your task is to sift through and interpret a mass of information and then answer questions that test your ability to understand that information. If you take the time to understand the game before going to the questions, especially by making deductions and walking around it, this game is no more difficult than any other, and is, in fact, easier than many.

2. **Diagram:** The diagram for this grouping game should consist of four columns labeled M, S, T, and H to represent the four teams.

3. **Simplify the rules:** Simplify the rules by converting them into symbols, thereby eliminating those pesky words that serve only to take up your precious time. Wherever possible, place the information directly on the diagram. For instance, the fact that there are exactly four students on each team, that Jessica must be assigned to team Holmes, that Paul cannot serve on team Taft, and even all four rules that specify who Marshall, Story, Taft, and Holmes were can be placed directly on the diagram. There is nothing surprising about the remaining rules. As in any grouping game, the rules largely consist of blocks, splits, and conditional statements. The rules create three blocks. First, one rule says that S is not on a team unless W is on the same team. According to the setup paragraph, all sixteen students must be assigned to a team, so S is indeed on a team. Since S is on a team, W must be on the same team. Thus, there is an SW block. Another rule creates a block in exactly the same fashion: J is not on a team unless S is on the same team. According to

the setup paragraph, all sixteen students must be assigned to a team, so J is on a team. Since J is on a team, J and S must always be on the same team. Thus, there is a JS block. The rules also clearly establish a PB block and an EO block. The rules create only one split: T and C cannot work together. T and C must therefore be on different teams. There is only one real conditional statement left (the other conditional statements actually created blocks): If L is not on S then O is not on S. This is a straightforward "if…then" statement that can be symbolized easily: $L \neq S \rightarrow O \neq S$. The remaining few rules give you some helpful tidbits of information: O must be on a team named after a 19th century Justice, B must be on a team named after a Chief Justice, and no team may include two members with the same first initial.

4. **Deductions:** As with any logic game, the key is to make deductions, to relate the rules to each other to see if they lead you to any additional conclusions. This is especially true in this game, as making deductions will practically allow you to determine the entire setup. First of all, there are four students in every group. No team may include two members with the same first initial. There are four students with the same first initial: Mo, Mi, Ma, and Me. Since none of these four can be with any of the others, there must be exactly one person with the first initial "M" in each of the four groups. Next, the rules assigned J to team H. S must be assigned to the same group as J and W must be assigned to the same group as S, so both S and W must be assigned to team H with J and one of the "M" students. Team H is effectively filled, although you don't know which one of Mo, Mi, Ma, or Me is the fourth student. There are also two rules dealing with the placement of P: P must be with B, and P cannot be assigned to team T. This means that the PB block must be assigned to either team M or team S. However, B must be assigned to a team named after a Chief Justice. The teams not named after a Chief Justice are S and H, so B cannot be assigned there. So the PB block must be assigned to team M. The only block left to place is the EO block. O must be assigned to a team named after a 19th century

justice, which means that O must be assigned to either team M or team S. Since P, B, and one of the M's must be assigned to team M, there is not room for the OE block in team M. Thus, the OE block must be assigned to team S. The one conditional statement said that if L is not in S, then O is not in S. It turns out that O must be in S, which means that L must also be in S. Thus, team S must contain O, E, L, and one of the four M's. At this point you know the four students assigned to team S (O, E, L, and one of the M's) and the four students assigned to team H (J, S, W, and one of the M's). Since team S and team H are, for all intents and purposes, filled, you are only left with teams M and T. At this point all the blocks have been accounted for, but the TC split has not been. T and C must be on different teams, and the only two teams left are team M and team T. Thus, one of T or C must be on team M and the other must be on team T. With one of T or C on team M, team M has reached the maximum of four students (P, B, T/C, and one of the four M's). Since team M, team S, and team H are effectively filled, the remaining students must be assigned to team T, which means that team T must include one of T or C, one of the four M's, and the two students whose placement was not directly restricted by the rules, N and D.

5. **"Walk Around It":** It turns out that this game is extremely limited: Team M must contain P, B, T/C, and one of the four M's; team S must contain O, E, L, and one of the four M's; team T must contain T/C, N, D, and one of the four M's; and team H must contain J, S, W, and one of the four M's. The only variables in the entire game are the exact placement of T and C and the exact placement of the four M's (Mo, Mi, Ma, and Me). What looked overly complex and confusing has revealed itself to be an easy game. The situation has very few variables.

1. **Type:** To begin, ask yourself what type of game this is. This is clearly a game that requires you to put items into groups.

2. **Diagram:** Now design your diagram. The diagram for this game is very simple. Since you will have to place items into two distinct groups, make two groups labeled F and S for Friday and Saturday. You should also write out the ten items you have to deal with; abbreviate to save time.

3. **Simplify the rules:** The rules begin in the setup paragraph. Every item must be used exactly once and each movie must go in either the Friday or Saturday group. The majority of the rules contained in the rules list are simple conditional statements that are easily converted into symbols. The rules involving I and Q can be applied directly to the diagram: I is on Friday and Q is on Saturday.

4. **Deductions:** A good starting point for making deductions whenever there are conditional statements is to work out the contrapositives. Since each item must be used exactly once, and since there are only two groups, the contrapositives are very specific. If a movie is not on Friday then it must be on Saturday. Thus, the first rule, which says if H is in S then P is in F, means also that if P is in S then H must be in F. But be careful, these rules do not create simple splits: P and H could be together in F (but not in S) without violating any rules. The same applies to all the other conditionals. For example, one rule says if O is on F, then M must be on F, which also means if M is in S then O is in S. However, M could be in F and O in S at the same time and not violate this rule. After you have the contrapositives, look at the rules and see if any rules contain common variables. In this case, the contrapositives help you see a relationship that wasn't so easy to see before: If K is on F, then both L and N must be on S. This relationship might turn out to be important, especially as it relates to the number of movies on each day.

5. **"Walk Around It":** Take a moment to consider what you do and do not know about the setup. With I and Q fixed in F and S respectively, you really only have to place four items in each group. There are blocks to be aware of: If O is in F or if M is in S, then O and M form a block. Remember, this is not a fixed block because O could be in S with M in F. Also, putting L in F creates a JK block in S. Lastly, if K is in F, then L and N must both be in S. Keeping track of these pairs will be important, especially with regard to the number of movies on each day. The questions are likely to be about these blocks.

1. **Type:** This game requires you to build a group of songs from some combination of short and long songs. This is not a typical grouping game where you have to place items in different groups; rather, you have to build one group from a number of different pieces.

2. **Diagram:** Because your task is to build the group, there is not really a general diagram. It is likely that you will need to make a new diagram for each question.

3. **Simplify the rules:** Go through the rules one by one and convert them into symbols. This is also the time to make sure that you understand each rule. The rules are the foundation of the game so make sure that you write them down correctly. The conditional statements in this game are straightforward and easy to symbolize.

4. **Deductions:** After you have a general idea of what the game involves, try to analyze the game. Find out how the rules relate to each other. What restrictions are there? Does one rule affect another? Your task is to build a group of songs. There is room on the MP3 player for exactly three long songs or six short songs. The rules further clarify that each short song takes up exactly half the space of a long song. Thus, the MP3 player could include three long songs, six short songs, or some combination of the two. The only two combinations are: two longs songs and two short songs or one long song and four short songs. Now go to the rules and see how they relate to each other. Don't forget to include the contrapositives when you are trying to make deductions. The rules for this game create a chain reaction. If J is included, then L is included. If L is included, then C is included. If C is included, then Q is included and K cannot be included. Knowing that J is included tells you that three other songs are included as well. Only one of the songs, C, is a long song, while the other three, J, L, and Q, are short songs. According to the possible

scenarios, this means that there must be one more short song to fill up the MP3 player. The remaining short songs are H, P, and K; however, since C is included, K cannot be included. Thus, the only two short songs available are H or P. But, since there is only space for one more short song, there is no space for any more long songs. Therefore, neither D nor F can be included. If D is not included then P cannot be included. With P eliminated, it must be true that H is included. Thus, if J is included, you know the entire group: J, L, C, Q, and H (one long song and four short songs). There are other, smaller deductions as well, some of which you might have determined as you worked out the chain beginning with J. Nevertheless, it is important to mention them. If J is included, then C must be included, and if C is included, then K cannot be included. Therefore, if J is included, then K cannot be included. Also, the last rule says if F is included, then D is not included. Since if either P or D is included then both are, if F is included, then P cannot be included either.

5. **"Walk Around It":** Before leaping into the game take a moment to think about what sort of deductions you made and what the questions are likely to test. The deductions you made involved following the chains of logic that were created by the conditional statements. In fact, these are the only rules that there are. Since you know the entire setup if J is included, look for J or maybe even an indication that J cannot be included. Furthermore, the deductions were only possible because you knew the number of long and short songs based on the information given. Be on the watch for any information that will let you know how many long and short songs you are dealing with and work from there.

1. **Type:** First ask what type of game you are dealing with. In this game there are three piano players, A, B, and C, and three days, Monday, Tuesday, and Wednesday, over which the three players must learn three of six pieces of music. There two fixed categories: days and people. These categories create well-defined slots into which you will place the only variable: the music pieces.

2. **Diagram:** Once you understand what type of game you are dealing with, design your diagram. The diagram should have the three days of the week on the top as columns and the three students on the side as rows. Make the diagram large enough so that you have enough space to include deductions and various situations.

3. **Simplify the rules:** The next step is to interpret the rules and state them with symbols. Each of items 1–6 must be used at least once but not more than twice. Write a list of the items next to the diagram, noting that each item must be used one or two times. Each music piece that each piano player learns must be more difficult (numerically higher) than the one to the left of it. Most of the rules can be put directly into the diagram. This saves space and it reminds you of what you know for sure. Be careful to represent things that you know for sure differently from things that can change. For example, the rule that says B learns song 4 on Tuesday can simply be applied to the diagram. The rule that says that the piece Claire learns on Wednesday is not more difficult than the piece Ben learns on Wednesday should be clarified and written beside the diagram: $Cw \leq Bw$.

4. **Deductions:** Now it is time to make deductions. Relate the rules to one another and see what additional information you can glean from the rules. Start with B. Since B learns 4 on Tuesday and since no student can learn a song that is easier than a song he or she learned earlier in the week, B must learn either 5 or 6 on Wednesday. Furthermore, since B learns 4 on Tuesday, B must learn 1, 2, or 3 on Monday. However, since B must learn the same piece on Monday as A learns on Tuesday and it is impossible for A to learn 1 on Tuesday, B must learn either 2 or 3 on Monday and A must learn either 2 or 3 on Tuesday. Also, since A learns either 2 or 3 on Tuesday, A must learn either 1 or 2 on Monday. The next deduction you can get from applying the conditions in the main paragraph to the deduction just made concerning A and B. Since each piece is learned by at least one, but not more than two of the students, whatever piece B learns Monday and A learns on Tuesday, C cannot learn on any day. Thus, C can only learn one of 2 and 3, but not both. C cannot learn 4 either, which restricts C to only four possible pieces. C must learn three of 1, 2/3, 5, and 6. This deduction also reveals that C must learn either 5 or 6 on Wednesday.

5. **"Walk Around It":** Now that you have made deductions you can take a second to take a breath and look at what is going on. The deductions have greatly restricted the game by limiting the songs that each player can learn. The songs that C learns are especially restricted and are heavily dependent upon the songs that the others learn and vice versa. You will know which of 2 and 3 C can learn by knowing which one A and B learn. Furthermore, the piece that C learns on Wednesday cannot be more difficult than that piece B learns on Wednesday. Thus, if C learns 6 on Wednesday then B must learn 6 on Wednesday and if B learns 5 on Wednesday then C must learn 5 on Wednesday. Lastly, keep in mind that every piece must be used at least once.

1. **Type:** In this game there is a series of times, 8 through 11, and two rooms, A and B, in which a doctor must see seven patients. The times and the rooms create a number of distinct slots in which each person must go. This is a slots game.

2. **Diagram:** The diagram should show the distinct slots. You can do this by creating columns and rows. In this game the columns are the hours. The setup says that Dr. Johnson is available for patients between 8 and noon. Be careful with this statement. The doctor does not see patients at noon, only until noon. Thus, there should be four columns labeled 8, 9, 10, and 11. The two examining rooms, A and B, should be the rows. This diagram creates eight slots while there are only seven people. There will be one empty slot.

3. **Simplify the rules:** Before trying to work the game, go through the rules and convert them into symbols that you can work with directly in your workspace. This is also a good time to see if you are interpreting the rules correctly. Oftentimes there are rules stated in the setup paragraph as well and not only in the list of rules. Be sure to include those "hidden" rules. The setup paragraph says that in any hour Dr. J sees no more than two patients and no more than one in any examining room. This simply means that there is only one person per slot. The first rule in the rules list says that K and M are seen in the same hour, which is pretty self-explanatory. This rule creates a block of K and M, but keep in mind that this rule does not tell you which patient is in which room. The second rule in the rules list says that P and Q are separated by one hour. This question does not tell you the relative order of P and Q, nor does it tell you which room they are in, although the next rule does say that P must be in room B. Q could be in room A or B. Lastly, N and P must be in room B.

4. Deductions: The next step is to make deductions. Look at what the rules mean and how they relate to each other. First, with the KM block, one of K or M must be in room B, so in addition to N and P either K or M must be in room B, leaving only one slot remaining for a patient to be seen in room B. Next, the rule that separates P and Q by one slot means that P and Q must be in either 8 and 10 or 9 and 11. There are not that many deductions to make in this game, but that is okay. Determine what you can figure out and move on.

5. "Walk Around It": You do not have very much firm information or fixed positions before heading into the questions. N, P, and K/M must be in room B, leaving only one slot. You do not know which room Q is in, although Q must be separated from P by one hour, which means P and Q are in 8 and 10 or 9 and 11. Watch for the placement of the KM block because it will tell you which hours P and Q will be in. For example, if K and M are in 8, then P and Q must be in 9 and 11. Lastly, L and T are wildcards and there will be one empty slot.

1. Type: In this game there are seven paddlers to place in six canoes numbered one through six. This is a grouping game.

2. Diagram: Draw six columns to represent the six canoes and label them one through six.

3. Simplify the rules: Make sure you understand what the rules are telling you. Here you have experienced and inexperienced paddlers. There are one or two people in every canoe used. Only experienced canoers can be alone, which means inexperienced canoers must share with one other paddler. However, this does not mean that experienced canoers must be alone. There are a few conditional statements: If T is with an experienced paddler, then there is nobody in 5 or 6, and if S is with an experienced paddler, then S must be with B. The rules create a split: A and Q cannot ride in the same canoe. There are also a few more firm rules that you should indicate directly on the diagram: Q must be in either 1 or 2, C is in 3, and R is in 4.

4. Deductions: Take the time to make deductions. Whenever there are conditional statements you can always start making deductions by determining the contrapositives. The rule that says if T is with an experienced paddler, then there is nobody in 5 or 6, also means that if there are paddlers in either 5 or 6, then T is not with an experienced paddler. Likewise, the rule that says if S is with an experienced paddler, then S must be with B also means that if S is not with B, then S is not with an experienced paddler. Notice that this rule means that S cannot be with either A or C. Since C must be in canoe 4, S cannot be in canoe 4. While this exhausts the contrapositives, it does not exhaust the possible deductions. In grouping games it is often useful to consider the possible numerical distribution of the items among the groups. In this game there are seven paddlers. One or two of them must be in every canoe that is used, although you cannot determine right away how many canoes are used. If as few canoes as possible are used, then there will be three canoes with two paddlers in them and one canoe with exactly one paddler. This reveals that there must always be at least one paddler alone. Only experienced paddlers can be alone so there must be at least one experienced paddler alone in one of the canoes. Furthermore, this also reveals that at least four canoes must be used. On the other hand, if all three of the experienced paddlers are alone and the four inexperienced paddlers are divided among two canoes then there will be five canoes. Thus, there must either be four or five canoes used and there must be at least one experienced paddler alone in one of those canoes. The rules already made clear that canoes 3 and 4 must be used since C, an experienced paddler, must be in 3 and R, an inexperienced paddler, must be in canoe 4. Since C is experienced, he could be alone, but does not have to be. On the other hand, since R is inexperienced there must be somebody else in canoe 4 with R.

5. **"Walk Around It":** Get a feel for what is going on. There must be four or five canoes used and there must be at least one experienced paddler alone in one of the canoes. If you find out the placement of any of the inexperienced paddlers then you will know that there are two people in that canoe. It will be important to keep track of which canoes must have two people in them, especially as this information relates to the total number of canoers. Keep in mind the AQ split, as well as what happens to T if there is somebody in canoe 5 or 6.

1. **Type:** You can tell from the rules that this is an ordering game where you must place six prisoners in the order of their parole hearings. Though the game has elements of absolute placement, the relative order will usually establish the final placements.

2. **Diagram:** Your diagram should have six spaces that represent Monday through Saturday (M T W R F S). Then go through the rules and put down any fixed positions, as well as any relative order.

3. **Simplify the rules:** Break down the rules into simple understandable symbols. C must be before F (C..F), I is immediately before or after C (IC, though not necessarily in that order), S is on either Wednesday or Saturday (S=W/S), and J is scheduled for Tuesday, which you can place directly on the diagram.

4. **Deductions:** The rules give you two definite scenarios by telling you that S is either on Wednesday or Saturday. Try both of these scenarios out and see what happens. If S is on Wednesday, then, since J is on Tuesday and I and C must be consecutive, I and C must be after W. I and C must also be before F, which means that F must be on Saturday, and I and C must be on Thursday and Friday, although not necessarily in that order. The only day left is Monday and the only person left to have a hearing is L, so L is on Monday. Thus, placing S on Wednesday creates one scenario: L, J, S, C, I, F, with I and C interchangeable. Now test the other scenario, where S has his hearing on Saturday. J is still on Tuesday, so the rules placing I and C and placing F after C mean that the I and C must be on Wednesday and Thursday and F must be on Friday, leaving L again for Monday. Thus, scenario two looks like this: L, J, C, I, F, S, with C and I interchangeable. Those are your two scenarios. Notice that one of your deductions is that L is on Monday. Congratulations! You've done all the work that you need to answer all but one of the questions in this game.

5. **"Walk Around It"**: With your two scenarios, it is easy to see what will be going on in this game. For each question you need to know which scenario you are dealing with. Once you do, you will know the entire schedule except for the relative position of I and C because both I and C are interchangeable.

1. **Type:** In this game there are two categories of party activists, liberals and moderates, who must be grouped together into one group of between three and six people. This is a grouping game, but different from most because there is only one group. You have to build the group according to the rules.

2. **Diagram:** There really is no diagram for this game. There will be one group that consists of anywhere from three to six people. You will have to build a new group for each question.

3. **Simplify the rules:** While simplifying the rules, don't forget the rules that are contained in the setup paragraph, such as the rule that at least one liberal and at least one moderate must be included. The rules for this game are fairly straightforward. The only rule that might be difficult to interpret is the rule that says R does not campaign unless F campaigns. Think carefully about what this means. The statement says that there is no way for R to campaign unless F campaigns. In other words, R can campaign only if F does. F's campaigning is a necessary condition for R to campaign. Translated into an "if..then" statement, this becomes: If R campaigns then F campaigns ($R \rightarrow F$). Note carefully that if F campaigns you do not know anything about R; R may or may not campaign. Another way to think about any statement with "unless" is to convert "unless" to "if not." In other words, the statement "R does not campaign unless F campaigns" can be changed to read "not R if not F." Rearranged, this statement reads "if not F then not R," which is the contrapositive of "if R then F." Convert the rest of the rules to symbols as well: $B \rightarrow R$, $R \rightarrow \sim S$, $\sim Z \rightarrow B$, and A/Z but not both ($A \rightarrow \sim Z$ and $Z \rightarrow \sim A$).

4. **Deductions:** After you understand the rules individually, take the time to relate them to each other. Before you look for rules that share a common person, don't forget to write down the contrapositives. Once you have the contrapositives look for rules that contain information about the same person. For example, the first rule says if B campaigns, then R must campaign, and the second rule says if R campaigns, then S cannot campaign. By combining these two rules you can deduce that if B campaigns, then S does not. There is also a rule that says if R campaigns, then F must campaign. If it is the case that B campaigns, then it must be the case that R campaigns, and if R campaigns, then F must also campaign. This allows you to deduce that if B campaigns, then both R and F must campaign while S does not. There are also two rules dealing with Z. Either A or Z must be included but not both. Thus, if A is included, then Z is not included. Another rule says if Z is not included, then B must be included. Therefore, if A is included in the group, then Z cannot be included, which means that B must be included and if B is included, then S cannot be included while R must be included, and if R is included, then F must be included. Thus, knowing that A campaigns allows you to determine that B, R, and F campaign as well. Don't forget the contrapositives of each of these deductions. Now that you've exhausted the obvious relationships among the rules, take a moment to Walk Around the Game.

5. **"Walk Around It":** You must create a group of between three and six people that must include either A or Z, but not both. From the rules and the deductions you actually have quite a bit of information. First of all, either A or Z must be included. If A is included, then you know B, R, and F must be included and that Z and S cannot be included. On the other hand, if Z is included, you do not know any additional information. It is vital that you understand exactly what the rules mean. The rule that says if B campaigns then R must campaign does not create a block of B and R. If B is included then R must be, but R can still be included without B. Likewise, the rule that says if R campaigns then F campaigns does not create a block of R and F. F can be included without R. Lastly, keep in mind that there are no rules about C, D, and Q; C, D, and Q are the wildcards.

1. **Type:** In this game a personal trainer must train seven clients over a five-hour period. There can be at the most two people during each hour. The rules make it clear that the focus here is on placing the clients in the order in which they are trained. The only variation from the basic ordering game style is that in this case there will be exactly two hours that have two people.

2. **Diagram:** The most basic diagram for ordering games is a list of the spaces that you will be dealing with. In this case there are five hours, so there will be five spaces. Keep in mind that two of these spaces must be filled with two people. Your working diagram will show the relative order of as many of the clients as you are given information about, but you cannot create this diagram until after you have gone through the rules.

3. **Simplify the rules:** The first two rules in the rules list should be broken down into four rules: P is before K, K is before H, P is before N, and L is before P. These rules can be symbolized like this: P..K, K..H, P..N, and L..P. The third rule in the rules list says that M and P are both alone in the hours in which they are trained. Neither M nor P can be in one of the hours where two people are trained. In other words, M is alone and P is alone. Finally, the last rule gives you another tidbit of information about the relative order in which the personal trainer sees the clients: J..N.

4. **Deductions:** In order to make the deductions that will help you work through this game relatively painlessly, you need to build a longer list of relative order out of the information provided in the rules. It doesn't really matter which person you start with, but it is best to build the longest list that you can. For instance, from the rules you can build a list that looks like this: L..P..K..H. Since these four people must be separated, no two of them can be in the same hour. Thus, now you know one person in four of the five

hours, although you do not know exactly which hours they are in. And although you do not know the order of M relative to any other people, you do know that M is alone in an hour. Thus, now you have one person in all five hours: L, P, K, H, and M must all be in separate hours. The two remaining clients are J and N. Since they are the only two clients left, you know for sure that J and N must share their hours with somebody else. According to the rules, P and M are the only clients trained in the hours in which they are trained, so P and M cannot share their hours with anybody. Because P and M are alone, J and N must be in the same hour with some combination of L, K, and H, but the requirements that J is before N and that N is after P restricts this even more. Since N must come after P and L must be before P, N cannot share with L. Thus, N must share with either K or H. Furthermore, since J must be before N and the latest that N can be is in the hour with H, J cannot share with H. J must therefore share with either L or K.

5. **"Walk Around It":** Before moving on to the questions, it is helpful to be clear on what you do know and what you don't. Look at the game as a whole. This will often help you find the key to the game, or what is going to be tested. If nothing else, this allows you to recap quickly what you have discovered. Before even going to the questions you know that L, P, K, H, and M will be in separate hours and that L, P, K, and H must be in that order. M is free to move around. Both J and N must share their hours with other people and the only people that they could possibly share with are L, K, or H. J and N are also restricted by the two rules about their order: P..N and J..N. These two rules restrict the placement of J and N such that J must share with either L or K while N must share with either K or H. Thus, only J can share with L and only N can share with H. The placement of J and N is likely to be the key to this game.

1. **Type:** The first step in every game is to determine what type of game you are dealing with. This will help you get in the appropriate frame of mind and let you know what sort of information will be helpful to get the answers right. In this game there are three people, C, H, and L, who must be work during a week that runs Monday through Saturday. You can tell by the information given to you that you will have to schedule which days each employee works. What will be important is the absolute order of the workers, not their relative order. This, then is a slots game, or, if you like, a scheduling game.

2. **Diagram:** The diagram for a scheduling game is rather simple. You are going to place the workers on the days that they work, so the only thing you need in your diagram is the schedule of Monday through Saturday. You can represent this as six columns labeled M, T, W, R, F, and S.

3. **Simplify the rules:** Now go to the rules and convert them into symbols that you can place directly on your workspace. Sometimes the rules are not easy to convert into symbols, but do the best you can. Pay close attention to the language of the rules so that you interpret them correctly. For example, consider the rule that says the meltdowns can only occur on days when H is the only technician on duty. This rule really means that whenever there is a meltdown, H is the only technician on duty. The rest of the rules are very general: Every worker must have at least two consecutive days off. No two workers can be scheduled for the same day more than twice. No technician can work for three days in a row. And H must work for at least three days.

4. Deductions: After you have all the rules written down, analyze the rules and see how they relate to one another. Is there any information that you can deduce? Are there two rules dealing with the same item? In this game, the setup paragraph tells you that there must be exactly two meltdowns during the week. Another rule tells you if there is a meltdown, then H must be the only technician on duty that day. In other words, there must be two meltdowns and on the days when there is a meltdown, H is alone. Put these two rules together and you know that there are at least two days on which H is the only technician on duty. But the rules also require that H is scheduled for at least three days. The number of times H, or for that matter, C or L, is scheduled is further limited by the additional requirement that the three technicians must each have at least two consecutive days off during the week. Since there are six days and each worker must have at least two of those days off, the greatest number of days that any technician work is four. Furthermore, no technician can work three days in a row. What this means for H is that H must work at least three days, but cannot work three consecutive days, and must have at least two consecutive days off. H's schedule is much more restricted than the other technicians, so watch closely for the placement of H. There really is not much more you can deduce immediately, so move to the next step and walk around the game.

5. "Walk Around It": Take a moment to see how much information you have and what sort of information you will need in order to be able to solve the problems. It looks like the placement of H is going to be the most important variable in this game. H is really the only technician that you know anything about. Be sure, however, to keep track of the number of times C and L are scheduled and that they have the required two days off.

1. Type: The first step is to determine what type of game this is. Is it a slots game? Is it an ordering game? Or is it a grouping game? For this particular game, it might at first be a little difficult to say which type of game it is. At first glance, it looks like this is an ordering game because the setup paragraph says that there are eight buttons numbered consecutively. However, notice what you will have to do with these eight buttons. Each button must be assigned to one of three types of music: rock (R), oldies (O), or alternative (A). As the rules make clear, this game is about assigning the numbered buttons to one of the three groups. Thus, this is a grouping game.

2. Diagram: The diagram for grouping games is simple enough. Create three columns labeled R, O, and A to represent rock, oldies, and alternative. You will have to place no more than three buttons in each group.

3. Simplify the rules: In order to gain a better understanding of the game, go through the rules one by one and convert them into easily understandable symbols. This will not only help you by placing the rules directly onto your workspace, but it will also force you to think about what each rule means. The first rule in the rules list says that buttons 3, 4, and 5 must be assigned to types of music that are different from each other. The next rule creates a split between 5 and 6. They must be in different groups. The rules also create a block of 1 and 7. This block cannot be in A. Lastly, there is a conditional statement: If 6 is not in R, then 2 must be in A.

Setups

4. **Deductions:** Before moving on to the questions, it is critical to take a moment to make deductions. Analyze the rules and how they relate to each other. This is the reason this is called the analytical reasoning section, and it will be what is tested in the questions. Knowing the mechanics of the game beforehand will allow you to answer the questions more quickly. First of all, there are eight buttons to assign to one of three different types of music (the three groups). No more than three buttons can be assigned to each type of music. In other words, no group can contain more than three buttons. In order to distribute the eight buttons over the three groups with no group containing more than three buttons, the distribution must be 3:3:2, though not necessarily in that order. Next, consider the rules about specific buttons. The first rule in the rules list says that 3, 4, and 5 must be in different groups. Since there are only three groups, one of 3, 4, or 5 will be in each group. Taken together with the rule that creates a block of 1 and 7, you know that 1, 7, and one of 3, 4, or 5 must be in one of the three groups. Since there can be no more than three buttons assigned to any one type of music, this group of 1, 7, and 3/4/5 will fill one of the groups completely. Since 1 and 7 cannot be in A, this block must be in either R or O. When the game provides you with an either/or situation like this one, it is generally a good idea to try to quickly work out both possibilities. First, determine what happens if 1, 7, and 3/4/5 are in R. If 1, 7, and 3/4/5 are in R, then there is no room for 6 in R, so, since 6 is not in R, 2 would have to be in A. This, then, is one possible basic scenario: 1, 7, and 3/4/5 in R, at least 2 and 3/4/5 in A, and at least 3/4/5 in O. You are left with 6 and 8 to place in either O or A. The only rule that applies to 6 is that you cannot place 6 with 5, while there are no rules about 8; 8 is the wildcard piece. There can be at most three buttons assigned to each type of music, so at least one of 6 and 8 must be assigned to O. Notice that there is still a little uncertainty in this basic scenario. That is all right. Get used to uncertainty. It would take far too much time to work out every specific scenario; you are just looking for the skeletal structure of each setup. Then you will know what must be true and what could be true. The other

possibility here is that 1, 7, and 3/4/5 are in O rather than R. If 1, 7, and 3/4/5 are in O, then you cannot immediately determine the placement of any other pieces. However, you are left mainly with 2, 6, and 8 to distribute among the groups. In this scenario, the rule concerning 6 and 2 becomes the key. The rule says if 6 is not in R, then 2 must be in A, while the contrapositive says that if 2 is not in A, then 6 must be in R (note that this does not mean that if 6 is in R, then 2 cannot be in A). Since the only two groups are R and A, if 6 is not in R, 6 must be in A, which would force both 6 and 2 into A along with 3/4 (not 5 since 5 and 6 cannot be together), thereby forcing 8 into R. Thus, this looks like: R: 8, 3/4/5; O: 1, 7, 3/4/5; A: 2, 6, 3/4. At this point you have worked out two scenarios: 1) When the block of 1, 7, 3/4/5 is in R. 2) When the block of 1, 7, and 3/4/5 is placed in O and 6 is not in R. The one remaining possibility is if the block of 1, 7, and 3/4/5 is placed in O and 6 is in R. This setup does not allow you to determine anything else, but the only two buttons that you do not know anything about are 2 and 8. This setup looks like this: at least 6 and 3/4/5 in R, the block of 1, 7, 3/4/5 in O, and at least 3/4/5 in A. Again, there can be no more than three buttons assigned to each type of music, so at least one of 2 and 8 must be assigned to A. Remember, just because 6 is in R does not mean that 2 cannot be in A.

5. **"Walk Around It":** The rules actually restricted this game quite a bit. There are only three basic scenarios. The most important information to look for is information that lets you know which scenario you are working with. The key here is to know whether 1, 7, and 3/4/5 are in R or O. The next step is fixing the positions of 2 and 6. The wildcard is 8. Lastly, don't forget the rule that separates 5 and 6.

1. **Type:** The key to determining the type of game is the sentence: *The campers will be divided into three teams.* The rules go on to tell you that you must have three people on each team and other conditions concerning the number of boys and girls. This is a grouping game.

2. **Diagram:** Draw a diagram that clearly shows your three groups, K, L, and M, by making three columns labeled appropriately.

3. **Simplify the rules:** Before simplifying the rules in the rules list, don't forget to note the rules contained within the setup paragraph. Here, the setup paragraph tells you that there must be one girl on each team. There are only three girls, so you know that you will use one and only one in each of the three groups. The rules in the rules list establish a number of blocks and splits: an OS block, an RT block, a VQ split, and a VW split. The one conditional statement included in the rules says that if O is assigned to L, then Q is assigned to M, which is fairly easy to interpret and symbolize. Be aware that Q can be assigned to M without O being assigned to L. The last rule, which says U must be assigned to M, can be placed directly on the diagram.

4. **Deductions:** Since there must be one girl in each group, and U must be in M, you can determine that one of the other two campers assigned to M must be a girl, either O, P, or Q, which leaves no room for the RT block in M. Thus, the RT block cannot be in M. Likewise, the third person in the group with R and T must be a girl. The three girls to choose from are O, P, and Q, but O must always be in a group with S. The RT block and the OS block can never be together. Thus, the girl assigned to the same group as R and T must either be P or Q. Consider what happens if P is assigned to the group that contains R and T. If one group contains P, R, and T then there are only two groups left to deal with, one of which must contain the OS block and the other of which must contain the one

remaining girl, Q. According to the rules, V and Q cannot be together, so V would have to be in the group with O and S. The remaining boys must be assigned to the group with Q. Thus, if P, R, and T are together in one group, then the other two groups must consist of 1) O, S, and V, and 2) Q, W, and U. The group composed of Q, W, and U must be in M. Next, consider what happens if, on the other hand, Q is assigned to the group that contains R and T. If one group contains Q, R, and T, then there are only two groups left to deal with, one of which must contain the OS block and the other of which must contain the one remaining girl, P. According to the rules, V and W cannot be together, so one of V or W must be in each of the two remaining groups. Thus, if one group contains Q, R and T, then the two other groups must consist of 1) O, S, and V/W, and 2) P, V/W, and U. These deductions reveal that there are only two basic scenarios, one where P, R, and T are together and one where Q, R, and T are together. When P, R, and T are together there is only one possibility, while when Q, R, and T are together there are still two possibilities, depending on the placement of V and W.

5. **"Walk Around It":** The deductions revealed that this game is very restricted. In fact there are only three possible variations in the composition of the groups: 1) PRT, OSV, and QWU; 2) QRT, OSV, and PWU; and 3) QRT, OSW, and PVU. Remember, whichever group contains U must be in M. For each question, you will have to determine which scenario you are dealing with and then which team each group of three students is actually on.

1. **Type:** This game is a hybrid of two types of games. Five researchers are assigned to one of three projects. In this sense, this is a grouping game. However, within those groups, there are also assignments of managers and assistants, with the manager as the most experienced researcher within that group. The rules tell you the relative experience of all the researchers. Thus, it is easy to set up this aspect of the game like an ordering game. Stated simply, there are three groups, within which you will have to order the researchers based upon their experience.

2. **Diagram:** This hybrid game first deals with the groups, so the diagram should have three columns representing the three groups: R, S and T. Leave sufficient space to be able to work with the ordering aspect of the game within each of those groups.

3. **Simplify the rules:** Now focus on the rules themselves. Convert the rules into easily understandable symbols. This is a good opportunity to make sure that you understand what each rule says. Here the rules are fairly straightforward. Notice how the rules give you a list of the relative experience of all the researchers. Each of these rules is best simplified by putting the list together into a long list of the relative experience of all the researchers. The list should look like this: A..B..C..D..E, moving from the most experienced to the least experienced. Other than this, you also know that no researcher can be assigned to all three projects, that no researcher can be a manager for more than one project, that there must be at least one assistant and exactly one manager at every project, that there are at least two assistants assigned to R (add the manager and this means that there are at least three people assigned to R), that if B is assigned to a project then E must be assigned to that project (B→E), and that C is the manager for one of the projects. The rule that says D is assigned to project T can be placed directly onto the diagram. Also, do not forget that the researcher with the most experience at each project will be the manager for that project. Lastly, it is important to note that the rules do not say that every researcher must be assigned to a project.

4. **Deductions:** Now that you understand the rules individually, take a moment to relate the rules to each other and get a larger picture of what is happening in the game. This is a vital step that will save you time in the long run. Since E is the least experienced and there must be at least two researchers for every project, you can deduce that E can never be a manager. The fact that D is the fourth most experienced (or second to last) means that if he is ever a manager, the only assistant he can have is E. Since if D is a manager, there can only be two people assigned to that project. If D is the manager, he cannot be the manager of project R. These deductions should point out that you must be careful with the rule that says if B is assigned to a project, then E is also assigned to that project. Know that you can have E without B; otherwise, D could never be a manager. Now look at the other side of the spectrum. Of what significance is it that A is the most experienced researcher? If the most experienced researcher is always the manager, then wherever A is, he will be the manager. Another rule says that no researcher can be manager for more than one project. Thus, A cannot be in more than one project, because this would make him the manager in more than one project.

5. **"Walk Around It":** Take a moment to look at the game as a whole now that you have determined what the rules mean and how they relate to each other. You need to place one manager and at least one assistant in each of the three groups. Project R will have at least two assistants. A, B, C, and D can be managers, but wherever A is he will be the manager, so A can only be assigned to one project if, in fact, he is assigned to one at all. The fact that B takes E with him will limit the placement of both E and B, especially coupled with the fact that if D is a manager E must be the assistant and that the only possible choices for assistants where C is the manager are D and/or E. These rules together show that the rule that says no researcher can be used at all three projects is going to be important in the game, so keep track of the number of times you use any researcher. Don't forget also that not every researcher must be assigned to a project.

1. **Type:** In this game there are seven people who must be assigned to one of four boats. The four boats comprise four different groups. This is a basic grouping game.

2. **Diagram:** The diagram should reflect the four different groups. You can do this by making four columns labeled B for blue, G for green, R for red, and Y for yellow. The setup paragraph establishes how many people may ride in each boat, so place those numbers on your diagram as well.

3. **Simplify the rules:** Simplify the rules by converting them into symbols in your work area. In this game there are the standard "if...then" statements, as well as a number of rules establishing "splits," or pairs of people who cannot be together in the same boat. The rules are fairly straightforward. When dealing with rules that actually contain two separate rules, it is best to break the statement up into the two separate rules. For example, the rule that says O cannot ride in the same boat with L or with P should be written as two rules: O cannot ride with L and O cannot ride with P.

4. **Deductions:** You've simplified the rules, now try to understand how they work in relation to each other and see if you can make any deductions. You have seven people to place in the groups. The rules tell you the maximum number for each group. In order to use all seven people without going over the maximum number in any group, you must use R (add up B, G, and Y, and you only have six people). Thus, R must be used. Next, there are two rules that deal with K. When this is the case, it is often helpful to combine the two rules and see if you can make a new statement. The rules tell you if N=R, then

K=R, and if P=B, then K=G. Put the two rules together and you know that if N=R, then P is not in B, as well as if P=B, then N is not R. There are also two rules dealing with N. If N and O are together, then no one else can be with them. Furthermore, if N=R, then K=R. So if N and K are both in R, O cannot be there with them. This can be stated as: If N=R, then not NO (or O is not in R). As always, don't forget your contrapositives. They are very helpful! Finally, notice the rules concerning O, L, and P. P must be separated from both O and L, while O and L must be separated from each other. What does this mean? It means that P, O, and L all have to be in different groups and three boats must be used.

5. **"Walk Around It":** This is a critical step. Get a feel for what is happening in the game, as well as what might be the key for understanding the game. P, O, and L must be in separate boats, indicating that at least three of the boats must be used. R must be one of the boats that are used in order to use all seven people and follow the restrictions on the number of people in each boat. An understanding of this relationship between P, O, and L, coupled with the number of people in each group is likely to be the key to this game.

1. **Type:** The first step is to determine which type of game you are dealing with. While the setup may sound confusing, look specifically at what the game requires you to do. In this game a number of salespersons and technicians must be assigned to one of three teams. Thus, this is a grouping game.

2. **Diagram:** Since this is a grouping game, the basic structure is simple enough: There are three groups, so the diagram should contain three columns. The tricky part in this game is figuring out just what the groups are. Should you label the groups as one, two, and three, and then try to assign both people and equipment to the groups? You could, and if you approach it in this way, you could add two rows to the diagram: people and equipment. The easiest way to approach the game, and perhaps the hardest to see, is to define the groups by the equipment. There are four pieces of equipment, two computers and two VCR's, with each piece of equipment used by exactly one team and no team using two of the same type of equipment. Dividing the four pieces of equipment among the three groups in a manner consistent with the rules, there must be one group with only a VCR, one group with only a computer, and one group with both a computer and a VCR. Thus, the three groups can be labeled: VCR, computer, and mix. If you began with the three groups labeled as one, two, and three, and then created two rows labeled equipment and people, the effect would be the same. One group must have only a VCR, one must have only a computer, and one must have one of both. Each group will have three people assigned to it. The questions will make you assign people to the groups, but will define the groups by what type of equipment they have. Thus, it is helpful to think of the groups in that manner.

3. **Simplify the rules:** By determining how to label the diagram, you have already completed the major simplification task. However, go through the remaining rules and simplify them into symbols where possible. Above all, be sure that you understand what each rule means. Before looking over the rules in the rules list, do not forget to find other rules contained within the setup paragraph. The remaining rule in the setup paragraph says that each team must include a salesperson. The rules contained in the rules list are fairly straightforward. The first rule creates a split between P and N. They must be on different teams. The last rule creates a block of M and Q. They must work on the same team, but on a team with only one type of equipment. Thus, M and Q must either be in the VCR group or the computer group. The second and third rules are standard conditional statements. First, if D is on a team with a VCR, then F is not on a team with a VCR. There are two teams with VCR's: VCR and mixed. Thus, this rule says that if D is on the VCR only or mixed team, then F must be on the computer only team. Lastly, if G can use a VCR, then P cannot use a computer. Again, there are two teams that can use a VCR (VCR and mixed), and only one team that cannot use a computer (VCR only). So this rule says if G is on either the VCR team or the mixed team, then P must be on the VCR only team. These conditional statements will be important when making deductions.

4. **Deductions:** The deductions step is probably the easiest to skip and the most important one not to skip. If you are having trouble knowing where to begin, start with the contrapositives of the conditional statements. Next, look at the rules and how they relate to each other. For instance, the rules say that M and Q must be on the same team and on a team with only one type of equipment. Since M and Q must be on a team with only one type of equipment, they must be on the VCR team or on the computer team (not the mixed team). Since both M and Q are technicians, the third person on whichever team they are on must be a salesperson. P and N are not salespersons, so neither one of them can be on the team with M and Q. Furthermore, P and N must be on different teams, so one of P or N must be on both the other two teams. Since there are only two possibilities for the MQ block, work out the possible scenarios. First, work out what happens if M and Q are on the VCR team. If M and Q are on the VCR team, then one of P or N must be on both the computer team and the mixed team. In either case, P must be on a team that can use a computer. Since P has to be on a team that can use a computer,

G cannot be on a team that can use a VCR. The only team that cannot use a VCR is the computer only team, so G is on the computer team. With G and one of P or N on the computer team, there is only one space left. This is where the conditional statement concerning D and F becomes critical. The rule (and contrapositive) says if either one is with a VCR, then the other one cannot be with a VCR. Since there is only one spot left in the computer-only group, one of D or F must be with a VCR, forcing the other one into the computer group. Thus, the computer group looks like this: G, P/N, D/F. With the computer group filled and one space left on the VCR group that must be filled by a salesperson, O must be in the mixed group. To recap, if M and Q are in the VCR group, the groups look like this: VCR: M, Q, salesperson (D, E or F); Mixed: O, P/N, salesperson (D, E, or F); Computer: G, P/N, D/F. Now check what happens when M and Q are on the computer team. If M and Q are on the computer team, then one of P or N must be on both the VCR and the mixed team. Since there is only one spot left in the computer group, once again one of D or F must be in a group with a VCR, forcing the other one into the computer group. Thus, the three people in the computer group are M, Q, and D/F. With the computer group filled you know that G must be in group with a VCR. Since G can use a VCR, P cannot use a computer. The only group that cannot use a computer is the VCR group, so P is in the VCR group, which forces N into the mixed group. Therefore, if M and Q are on the computer team, then M, Q, and D/F must be on the computer team, P must be on the VCR team, and N must be on the mixed team. In this scenario you are left with E, D/F, O, and G to place in the VCR and mixed groups. With the two main scenarios worked out ahead of time, you are armed with enough information to answer the questions easily.

5. **"Walk Around It":** In this game there are two basic scenarios: when the MQ block is in the VCR group, and when the MQ block is in the computer group. If M and Q are in the VCR group, the groups look like this: VCR: M, Q, salesperson (D, E or F); Mixed: O, P/N, salesperson (D, E, or F); Computer: G, P/N, D/F. On the other hand, if M and Q are on the computer team, then M, Q, and D/F must be on the computer team, P must be on the VCR team, and N must be on the mixed team. In this scenario you are left with E, D/F, O, and G to place in the VCR and mixed groups. For each question, determine which scenario you are working with and from there you will know what information you do know and what information you do not know.

1. **Type:** In this game there are six customers at a delicatessen who order sandwiches of various types: roast beef (R), pastrami (P), chicken salad (C), ham (H), tuna (T), and veggie (V). From the rules it is apparent that you will be dealing with the order in which these sandwiches are ordered. Thus, this is an ordering game.

2. **Diagram:** The diagram for an ordering game is simple. When you are reading through the setup paragraph you can make a skeleton diagram showing you what you will be working with. In this case there are six sandwiches, so you can draw six spaces (_ _ _ _ _ _) labeled one through six. The most important diagram, however, will be the one that you create after making deductions. This diagram should show the relative order of all the pieces of the game.

3. **Simplify the rules:** Simplify the rules by converting them into easily understandable symbols. In ordering games the rules are straightforward but are easy to mix up. Make sure that you keep your "before's" and "after's" straight. The rules list for this game has a number of rules that establish the relative order of many of the sandwiches. When a rule contains two pieces of information, split the rule into two parts and write down each part separately. For example, the first ordering rule says that the customer who orders H orders sometime before the customer who orders C and sometime after the customer who orders T. Interpret this as two separate rules, one that says H is before C (H..C) and one that says H is after T (T..H). Follow this same pattern for the rest of the ordering rules. In addition to the ordering rules there are also two instances where the rules specify that a certain sandwich cannot be in a certain position, like the rule that says the customer who orders P does not order first (P/1). These rules are very helpful when coupled with the rules about the relative order, so keep this in mind. The last rule is a little trickier to interpret. It says that exactly one of the customers, but not the one who orders first or the one who orders last, orders exactly two sandwiches of the same type. This does not mean that there will be another space. There are still only six customers who order sandwiches and only six spaces. But one of the people orders two sandwiches. The person who does so cannot be the first or last to order. This information will help you if you know which sandwich is ordered twice because then you know that that particular sandwich cannot be ordered first or last and likewise, if you know which sandwiches are ordered first and last, then you know that that particular sandwich cannot be the sandwich that is ordered twice.

4. **Deductions:** The easiest and most important deductions in an ordering game are the deductions about the relative order of all the pieces of the game. Pick two that share a common item. In this case, you can start with the first rule that says H..C and T..H. You can expand this into the list: T..H..C. The two other ordering rules do not establish such firm positions. One rule says P..C and the other H..V. Add these rules to the list of relative order, but be careful. You know that P must be before C, but you do not know the relative order of P and H or P and T. Thus, these last two rules you should add to the diagram in such a way that you understand this ambiguous relationship. You can accomplish this by adding P above the T..H..C row with a line showing that P must be before C. Do the same for the H..V rule. In order to limit the possibility for confusion, you may want to add V below the T..H..C row since P is already above it. Now you have a pretty good idea of the relative order. The only sandwich that you do not know anything about is R. R is the wildcard and can be placed anywhere in the order. After you have a diagram showing the relative order of the sandwiches, it is helpful to look at what could be first and what could be last. T is at the beginning of the ordering list, so T could be first while H, C, and V cannot. R is the wildcard, so R could be first as well. From the diagram it also looks like P could be first, but there is a rule that specifically says that P cannot be first. Thus, either R or T is in position 1. Do the same

thing for position 6. C is at the end of the diagram, so C could be last while T, H, and P must all be before C, so they cannot be last. R is the wildcard so R could be last. From the diagram it also looks like V could be last, but there is a rule that specifically says that V cannot be last. Thus, either R or C is in position 6, or is ordered by the sixth customer.

5. **"Walk Around It":** With the relative order determined you are well on your way to complete this game quickly and correctly. T is before H, which is before C. V must be sometime after H, and P must be sometime before C. R is the wildcard. The sandwich that is ordered first must either be R or T, while the sandwich that is ordered by the last customer must either be R or C. These two deductions about the first and last positions both contain R, so once you know something about the placement of R, you will know something about the first and/or last position. Now you are ready to face the questions with confidence.

1. **Type:** In this game there are a number of different types of channels that must be grouped together to form a group of between six and eight channels. Because it is your task to create a group or at least to determine the makeup of a group, this is a grouping game, albeit somewhat different than most grouping games because in this case there is only one group and it does not involve a fixed number of items.

2. **Diagram:** Because there is only one group, there is no diagram. You will have to build a different group for each question.

3. **Simplify the rules:** Simplify the rules by converting them all into symbols. This also has the benefit of forcing you to decide what the rules say. The basic conditions of this game are that there are four sports channels (4 S's), five movie channels (5 M's), three music video channels (3 V's), and one game show channel (1 G) that must be put together in some combination to create a group of between six and eight channels. The setup is restricted by the three rules in the rules list. The first of these says that the number of S's and V's combined is either three or four. In other words, the number of S's plus the number of V's is either three or four (S + V = 3/4). The second rule says that Luis watches more S's than M's if and only if he watches the G. This is different than a normal "if...then" statement because it says "if and only if;" there are actually two conditions included here: "if" and "only if." Luis watching the G becomes both a sufficient and a necessary condition for Luis watching more S's than M's. Thus, there are two conditions to draw from this rule. First is the more obvious condition that if Luis watches the G, then he watches more S's than M's. Second is the condition that if Luis watches more S's than M's, then he must also watch the G. The third rule contained in the rules list is a standard conditional statement that says if Luis watches three or more M's, then he does not watch two or more V's. In other words, if Luis watches three or more M's, he watches no more than one V (but he does not have to watch a V).

Setups

4. **Deductions:** After considering the rules individually, consider how they relate to each other and the general game restrictions. Luis must watch six to eight different channels. The first rule says that three or four of these channels must be some combination of S's and V's. Since S's and V's can account for at most four channels, Luis must watch at least two other channels. These two or more channels must be some combination of M's and G. There is only one G available, so, no matter what, Luis must watch at least one M.

5. **"Walk Around It":** Besides the basic deduction that Luis must watch at least one M, there is not much else to discover before moving on to the questions. This game is therefore likely to be less about deductions and more about the rules. Simply take the information that each question gives you and work from there using the rules.

1. **Type:** The first step in tackling any game is to determine what type of game you will be working with. You can glean this information from the setup and the rules. In this game there are five schools that must be ranked from one to five on three criteria: cost, location, and quality. The schools and the three criteria are fixed while the rankings are variable. Thus, the schools and the criteria create fixed slots into which you will place the rankings. This is a slots game that can be setup as a matrix.

2. **Diagram:** The matrix for this slots game should include the five schools as five columns and the three criteria as three rows. Label the columns and rows appropriately and abbreviate to save time. You will have to place a numerical ranking into each of these slots according to the rules. Be sure to give yourself enough room for deductions and for working out the questions.

3. **Simplify the rules:** The next step is to go through the rules, simplify them, and check that you understand them appropriately. Simplify them by converting them into easily understandable symbols and abbreviations. Where possible, apply the rules directly to the diagram. For instance, you can place the rules that say A is ranked 3 in location and 4 in cost and that W is ranked 1 in quality directly in the appropriate slots. The remaining rules you should write near the diagram for easy reference. Don't forget any pertinent information in the setup paragraph itself. The remaining rules tell you that no schools receive the same rank on any of the criteria, that no school receives the same rank for two criteria, that S receives exactly two higher ranks than T, that T receives exactly two higher rankings than A, and that O is ranked below W in all three criteria. Although it should go without saying, be clear that a higher ranking is a lower number.

4. **Deductions:** This, the deductions step, is perhaps the most crucial step. Of course, every step is helpful, but this is where you

can determine the key to the game. Begin by analyzing the effects of the rankings that the rules gave you. W is 1 in quality so it cannot receive a 1 in cost or location and no other school can receive a 1 in quality. Since A receives a 3 on location and a 4 on cost, no other schools can receive a 3 or 4 in location or cost, respectively. Furthermore, A cannot receive a 3 or 4 in quality. All these restrictions you should note on the diagram. Since A cannot receive a 3, 4, or 1 in quality, it must receive either a 2 or a 5. Another rule says that O is ranked below W in all three criteria. This means that it is impossible for W to receive a 5 in any category as well as that O cannot receive a 1 in any category. If W cannot receive a 1 or a 5 in cost or location and cannot receive a 4 in cost or a 3 in location, then you know W must receive either a 2 or a 3 in cost and either a 2 or a 4 in location. Now look at O. Remember, O must be ranked lower than W, which means that O must have a higher number than W. In the location category, since O must have a higher number than W and the lowest W can receive is a 2, then the lowest O can receive in location is a 3. However, O cannot receive a 3 in location because A already receives a 3 in location. Thus, O must receive either a 4 or a 5 in location. The same reasoning leads you to deduce that O can only receive a 3 or a 5 in the cost category because the lowest W can receive in cost is 2, which means that the lowest O could receive is 3, and since A receives a 4 in cost, O cannot receive a 4, leaving only 3 and 5. Look at the relationship that you have determined among O and W in the areas of cost and location. If O receives a 3 in cost, then W must receive a 2, forcing W to receive a 4 in location, which causes O to receive a 5 in location. If O receives a 5 in cost, then O receives a 4 in location, forcing W to receive a 2 in location, which forces W to receive a 3 in cost. Thus, you know that O must receive a 5 in either cost or location. This, in turn, means that O cannot receive a 5 in quality. These two different scenarios also let you know what two ranks are left over for T and S in the categories of cost and location. This relationship between O and W is difficult to see at this point. The questions will test you on it, so the earlier you discover it, the better. If you didn't or still don't see it, do not worry too much. You still know a lot and can work the game with confidence. You will be forced to make this deduction in question three.

5. **"Walk Around It":** The interplay between O and W is likely to be very important. Any information about O or W in cost or location will allow you to fill in both O and W for cost and location. Also, keep in mind that T has two rankings that are higher than A and that S has two rankings higher than T. Be aware that almost any information will cause a chain reaction, so look for new information and see what it leads to. Try to keep it all straight, take a deep breath, and move on to the questions.

1. **Type:** In this game there are seven friends who go to the movies to watch one of four movies, *Righteous*, *Terrified*, *Ambitious*, or *Baffling*. Each movie has three showings, so it might make sense to approach this as a slots game, where you must place each of the seven friends in one of the time slots for each movie. However, since not all the slots must be used and there are also multiple friends who see the same movie in the same time slot, it probably makes more sense to approach this as a grouping game, where the show times merely modify the groups rather than create distinct slots.

2. **Diagram:** The diagram should clearly show the four movies, or four groups. You can accomplish this by drawing four columns labeled appropriately. A few of the rules will force you to modify the groups because certain movies do not have certain showings.

3. **Simplify the rules:** Go through the rules and interpret exactly what they mean as you convert them into easily understandable symbols. The first rule says simply that each movie must be seen. The next rule says that *Terrified* has no matinee showing. This rule, and the others like it, allows you to modify the groups shown in the diagram. For this rule you can note that *Terrified* does not have a matinee showing. Thus, whoever sees *Terrified* must see either an evening or late showing. Another rule allows you to eliminate the evening showing for *Baffling*, which means that whoever sees *Baffling* must see either a matinee or a late night showing. Still another allows you to eliminate the matinee and late night showings for *Righteous*, which means that whoever sees *Righteous* must see an evening showing. There are also a few rules that establish blocks and splits. C and J constitute a block, as do G and H. On the other hand, E and F must be split. There are two rules left to review. One assigns D to *Ambitious*, but does not tell you which showing of *Ambitious* she attends. You can and should place this information on the diagram. The remaining rule is the only "if…then"

statement: If C goes in the evening then Frank goes to *Ambitious*. This is a straightforward "if…then" statement.

4. **Deductions:** Every once in awhile, you get a game like this where there are not many evident deductions. However, just because they are not evident does not mean that there are not any. In grouping games, it is often helpful to first consider the big picture, the numerical distribution of items in the groups. In this game there are four groups, which are the four movies. There must be at least one friend at each movie and there are only seven friends. The distribution is further constrained by the blocks and splits: there are two blocks, CJ and GH, and one split, E and F. Lastly, D must watch *Ambitious*. These rules and requirements allow you to determine the possible numerical distributions of friends at movies. If the CJ and GH blocks are in separate groups, then the four groups must be split like this: CJ, GH, D, E/F, though not necessarily in that order. Since E and F cannot be together, the other of E or F would have to be with either one of the blocks or with D. Thus, the distribution could either be 3:2:2:1 or 2:2:2:1, though not necessarily in that order. The remaining possibility is if the two blocks are together, which would create a distribution of 4:1:1:1, again, not necessarily in that order. Regardless of the setup, these distributions reveal that one of E or F will always be alone in a group. Next, consider how the specific rules relate to each other. The only two rules that directly relate to each other are the two rules dealing with C: C must be with J and if C goes to an evening showing then Frank goes to *Ambitious*. From these two statements you can deduce that the rule that says if C goes to an evening showing really says that if C and J go to an evening showing then Frank goes to *Ambitious*.

5. **"Walk Around It":** The possible distribution of friends to movies is quite limited by the blocks and splits. The deductions revealed that those blocks and splits will play a big role in this game. Thus, keep track of CJ and GH, as well as E and F. Due to the blocks and splits and the requirement that there be at least one person at each movie, one of E or F must always be alone.

1. **Type:** First ask what type of game it is. After reading the set-up in the main paragraph and the rules it becomes clear that this is an ordering game.

2. **Diagram:** Now that you have the type of game in mind, you should design your diagram so that you can place the items in order. Your diagram will consist of a list of the items you are working with and the extremes of the order (first on the left and seventh on the right) so you are clear about the direction in which you are working.

3. **Simplify the rules:** Now go to the rules and simplify what they tell you. Be especially careful with the first two, each of which contains three items. For clarity, you might want to separate them into two rules each. For example, the first rule means these two things: L..O and O..R. Be careful with the last rule since it is not one that places an item relative to others, but in an absolute spot.

4. **Deductions:** The next step is to make deductions. Check the rules to see how each relates to the others. In this case, start with what you know for sure. For example, you know that L comes before O, O comes before R, and R comes before N. Put this line of items from left to right in the diagram. Now add that P comes after L and that M comes before P. These rules are all relative, so they should be placed near, not on, the diagram. On the other hand, incorporate the Q rule directly on the diagram by placing it third. With this order, you have quite a bit of information. Consider what you have: Two people will have to finish before Q. L will have to be one of them, and the other must be either O or M. The only ones that can be first are M and L. Look at who might come last: only N or P. M and P appear quite flexible, but don't lose track of P. Both L and M must be before P, and Q must be third, so it seems that the earliest P could finish is fourth. However, if P were fourth, O, R, and N would have to be fifth, sixth, and seventh, respectively, which puts O and P next to each other in violation of the rules. Thus, P cannot be fourth either. Notice that this same reasoning holds true if O is fifth, because it again forces P into fourth place. Therefore, O cannot finish fifth. Because O must finish before R and N, O cannot finish sixth or seventh either. Thus, the latest that O can finish is fourth. With Q third, you also know that O cannot be third. Furthermore, you already know that O cannot finish first since L must be before O. Thus, O must finish either second or fourth. The earliest that P can finish is fifth, and then only if O finishes second.

5. **"Walk Around It":** The last deduction concerning P and his relationship with O reveals what is likely to be the key in this game. Watch out for the placement of O and P, especially in relation to the L..O..R..N sequence and the fact that P must come after both L and M. When you are comfortable with what is going on in, go to the questions.

Setups

Setup Game 69

1. **Type:** In this game there are two bags, 1 and 2, into which must be placed five shirts and four pairs of jeans. Although there are two types of items to place into the bags (shirts and pants), this game is easiest if approached as a simple grouping game, where the two bags create two groups.

2. **Diagram:** Since this is a grouping game, the diagram is easy to draw. Draw two columns labeled 1 and 2 to represent the two bags. Keep in mind that there are rules about the shirts and pants but that these two types of clothing are not represented in the diagram. You will have to keep them straight in your head.

3. **Simplify the rules:** Go through the rules and simplify them by converting them into symbols. Don't forget to include rules that are in the setup paragraph, such as the information that bag 1 must have more articles of clothing than bag 2 and that each bag must have at least one shirt and at least two pairs of pants. Next go to the rules list. For this game, the rules are of the type typical of a grouping game: blocks, splits, and conditional statements. Most of the rules are in standard format and should be easy to understand and symbolize. One rule that might be tricky is the rule that says if blue is in a bag then white is in the same bag. The setup paragraph says that each of the types of shirt must be used, so blue must always be used. Thus, blue and white must always be in the same group. Blue (B) and white (W) make up a block. The same holds true for the remaining conditional statement, which says that if W is included in a bag, then S cannot be in that bag. W must always be in one of the bags, so this rule actually creates a WS split. When all is said and done, the rules create a BW block, a WS split, a DS split, and a GJ split.

4. **Deductions:** This is a very important step. Making deductions is the key to working out the game quickly and correctly. First, as in most grouping games, it is helpful to consider the possible numerical distribution of the items between the groups. In this case there are nine items, all of which must be used, and there must be at least one shirt and two pairs of pants in each bag. This means that the minimum number of items that can be in a bag is three. But since bag 1 must have more items of clothing than bag 2, only bag 2 could contain three items. Hence, one possible distribution is if there are six items in bag 1 and three items in bag 2. The greatest number of items that bag 2 can have while still having less than bag 1 is four, so the only other possible distribution is if there are five items in bag 1 and four items in bag 2. Now go through the other rules and see how they relate to each other. First of all, B and W are a block. Another rule creates a WS split. Thus, whichever bag B and W are in is not the bag that S is in. Since there are only two bags and one rule says that D and S cannot be together, in whichever bag S is, D must be in the other of the two bags. Therefore, D must also be in whichever bag B and W are in. The block has just grown by one: BWD. This block must include another pair of pants to go with D. It cannot be S, so it must either be C or J. There is one thing to note about C. Since D and S cannot be together, it must be the case that C and J cannot be together, because that would force D and S to be together. The rules also say that G and J cannot be together. Thus, J must be in a different bag than both C and G. Therefore C and G must always be together, making up another block. If the BWD block is with this CG block, then that bag will have five items. Since the maximum number of items that can be in bag 2 is four, if the BWD block is with CG, they must be in bag 1. Bag 2 would have to contain J, S, and at least one of R and P. On the other hand, if the BWD block is with J, then C, G, and S must be in the other bag. This setup does not allow you to determine which bag the BWDJ block is in. It could be in either bag 1 or 2, but if it is in bag 2 then bag 2 is completely filled. Another way to say this is if BWD is in bag 1 then it could be with either J or CG. If the BWD block is in bag 2 then it is with J.

5. **"Walk Around It":** The key to this game is the placement of the BWD block. The block must be with one other pair of pants, either J or C. It turns out that C and G form another block, so really the BWD block must be with either J or both C and G. These requirements limit the game to only three possibilities. If the BWD block is in bag 1 with J, then C, G, and S must be in bag 2, and at least one of R and P must be in bag 1 (since there can be at most four articles of clothing in bag 2). On the other hand, if the BWD block is in bag 2 with J, then bag 2 is full and the remaining items must be in bag 1. The only other possibility is if the BWD block is with both C and G. If the BWD block is with the CG block, these articles of clothing must be in bag 1, since the greatest number of items that can be in bag 2 is four. Bag 2 would then have to include S and J, and one or both of R and P. You will have to determine which scenario you are dealing with. The scenarios are driven by the placement of the BWD block. In determining the placement of the BWD block, the numerical distribution will play an important role. Remember, the distribution can either be 6:3 or 5:4.

1. **Type:** The first step to every game is to determine what type of game it is. The information paragraph and the rules will give you hints. In this game there are two days of auditions for a movie. On Thursday there are six auditions and on Thursday there are three. It is your job to determine which actors audition on each day. In this respect, this is a grouping game. From the rules it is also easy to see that you will have to determine the order of the auditions on each day. In this respect, this is an ordering game. Thus, this is a hybrid between a grouping and an ordering game.

2. **Diagram:** Once you've identified the components of the game, it is easy to draw a diagram including all the necessary parts. You need two columns representing Thursday and Friday, and within each column you need to leave room for the ordering task. On Thursday you need six spaces while on Friday you only need three. Now move on to the rules.

3. **Simplify the rules:** Simplify the rules into symbols that you can understand. This step helps you by reminding you of the rules as well as keeping everything in a small workspace so that you do not have to keep returning to the top of the page to look at the rules. The rules that tell you that the sixth actor on Thursday is the first actor on Friday and that the second actor on Thursday is the third actor on Friday can be simplified like this: $R_6 = F_1$ and $R_2 = F_3$. You can place W directly on your diagram in position 4 on Thursday. The remaining rules are easy to interpret and simplify: L must be immediately before M, L must audition on Friday, and if P and S are not consecutive on Thursday then both P and S audition on Friday.

4. **Deductions:** This is perhaps the most vital step (besides getting the answers right, but this will help you accomplish that goal). Take a moment to analyze the rules and how they relate to each other. The first rule says that L's

audition on Thursday must be immediately before M's audition. This means that the latest L can be is fifth and the earliest that M can audition is second. Another rule says that the actor that auditions last (sixth) on Thursday must be the first to audition on Friday. If the latest L can be is fifth, you can deduce that, because L cannot ever be sixth on Thursday, L cannot ever be first on Friday. Another way to state it is that L must be second or third on Friday. This is a vital deduction. There is also the contrapositive of the rule that says if P and S have non-consecutive auditions on Thursday, then both actors audition on Friday. The contrapositive says that if both P and S do not audition on Friday, then P and S have consecutive auditions on Thursday. This PS block and the LM block really restrict the number of possibilities. You cannot immediately determine much else so take a few seconds to walk around the game.

5. **"Walk Around It":** Although you do not have much specific information, the rules are quite restrictive. Any information at all will allow you to determine some specifics about P and S. Your ability to understand the interplay between P and S and the other actors, especially the LM sequence, is going to be important. Furthermore, pay close attention to the rules that tell you the second actor on Thursday must be third on Friday and that the sixth actor on Thursday must be the first actor on Friday. Once you know any of these positions you can fill out the corresponding position on the other day and then take it from there.

1. **Type:** The first thing that you should determine about each game is the general type. Do you have to place items in groups? Do you have to order a number of items? Do you have to place items in distinct slots? The rules will determine what type of game you are dealing with. Grouping games involve blocks, splits, and conditional statements. Ordering games involve the relative position of various items. Slots games often contain various types of rules, depending on what type of slots game it is. One general type of slots game is a scheduling game, often dealing with the days of the week. In this game there are seven consecutive days on which Bianca eats soup. While it might seem like an ordering game, there are not really any rules about relative order. Instead, this is a slots/scheduling game where the slots are identified by the days of the week. You will have to place certain items on different days and determine the effects of those placements.

2. **Diagram:** The diagram is merely the seven days of the week, Sunday through Saturday. You can draw this as you would an ordering game with seven spaces labeled with an abbreviation so you know which space corresponds to each day. Thus, your diagram could look like this:

$$\underline{\quad} \quad \underline{\quad} \quad \underline{\quad} \quad \underline{\quad} \quad \underline{\quad} \quad \underline{\quad} \quad \underline{\quad}$$
$$\text{Su} \quad \text{M} \quad \text{T} \quad \text{W} \quad \text{R} \quad \text{F} \quad \text{S}$$

3. **Simplify the rules:** Simplify the rules by converting them into symbols that you can understand at a glance. This also gives you an opportunity to go through the rules and understand exactly what each says. The only rule that might confuse you here is the rule that says bean soup must be eaten on a day immediately before or immediately after any day on which chicken soup is eaten. Your initial reaction might be to simply say that B and C must always be on consecutive days. However, this is not what the rule says. It says that wherever there is a chicken soup (C), there must be a bean (B) soup on a

consecutive day. In other words, if there is a C then there must be a B next to it. You can still have a B without a C. The remaining rules are simple: Bianca does not eat the same soup on consecutive days, L and M cannot be next to each other, M cannot be on Monday, and V is on Thursday (which you should place directly on the diagram).

4. **Deductions:** Take the time to made deductions. Analyze the rules and how they relate to each other. First of all, the rules placed V on Thursday. The setup paragraph says that Bianca does not eat the same soup on consecutive days, so Bianca cannot eat V on either Wednesday or Friday. Furthermore, in this game there are seven days while there are only six soup choices. Because Bianca must eat each soup at least once, you know that there will be one soup that Bianca eats exactly twice, while the others must be eaten exactly once. Since C must be eaten at least once, there will be a CB sequence. If the soup that is ordered twice is C, there must be a B next to each C. In order to accomplish this without using two B's as well, the order would have to be CBC. Therefore, if C is used twice, there will be a CBC sequence. If it seems as though you have not learned very much from these deductions, don't worry. The questions will give you the information you need to solve the problems. Just make sure that you understand what the game requires of you.

5. **"Walk Around It":** You have seven days and six soups. Every soup must be used and one will be used exactly twice. M cannot be eaten on Monday. With V on Thursday and at least a CB sequence (remember, it could be CBC), the key will be to keep L and M separated. The schedule becomes even more restricted if there are two L's or two M's.

1. **Type:** The first sentence of this game establishes what type of game you are dealing with. You have two dishes X and Y, with four items in each dish. This is clearly a grouping game.

2. **Diagram:** This is a grouping game, so your diagram should reflect clearly the two groups you will be dealing with: X and Y. Make two columns, one for each and label them appropriately.

3. **Simplify the rules:** It is vital to understand what the rules say. You know you have two groups, X and Y, with four items in each group. The items you have to work with are 2B's, 2G's, 3O's, 3P's, and 1T. The rules constrain you in how you can arrange these items within the groups: If a B is used in a dish, then both B's must be used in that dish. If G is used in a dish, then there cannot be any O in that dish. There must be at least three types of spice in X. And if P is used in X, then T is used in Y. Understand what these rules mean. For instance, you can have T in Y without P in X, but if there is a P in X, then there must be a T in Y.

4. **Deductions:** Always make note of the contrapositives. In this case you know that if there is an O in a dish, then there cannot be a G in that dish and also that if T is not in dish Y, then P is not in dish X. Next, relate the rules to each other to see what additional information you can glean from them. First of all, look at the numerical distribution of the spices. There must be four dashes of spice in each dish, but not necessarily four different spices. However, you know for certain that there must be at least three different spices in dish X. The spices to choose from are B, G, O, P, and T. At least three out of these five spices must be included in dish X. However, both G and O can never be included in the same dish, due to the rule that says if G is in a dish then O is not included in that dish and the contrapositive of this rule, which says if O is in dish then G is not included in that dish. For

the purpose of placing at least three different spices in dish X, this means that you really can only choose from among four spices: B, P, T, and G/O. However, there is yet another rule that says P and T cannot both be together in dish X (if P is in dish X, then T is in dish Y). Now dish X is restricted even more. There must be at least three different spices, but there cannot be both a G and an O; neither can there be both a P and a T. Thus, in order to have at least three different spices, dish X must include either G or O, either P or T, and B. In other words, dish X must include exactly three spices, one of which must be B. Since B must be included in dish X, both B's must be in dish X. Therefore, dish X must have 2B, exactly one dash of either G or O, and exactly one dash of either P or T. Since both B's must be included in dish X, there cannot be any B's in dish Y.

5. **"Walk Around It":** Before moving on to the questions, quickly review what you do know and what you do not know. Look for what the game is likely to test you on. You know that in dish X you must have 2B, 1G/O, and 1P/T. You know a lot less about dish Y, but the important point to remember is that dish Y must have exactly four dashes as well, though there are no rules about the number of different spices in dish Y. In other words, keep track of how many dashes you have used of each spice because this will be important as you try to get four dashes in dish Y.

1. **Type:** In this game you have five days, Monday through Friday, and three personalities that must surface over those five days. Because you want to know which personalities do and do not appear on every day, you could approach this as a slots game. On the other hand, it has elements of a grouping game since you do not know exactly how many personalities appear on each day.

2. **Diagram:** You could set this up as a simple grouping game, with five columns labeled M through F or you could create a matrix with five columns labeled M through F, and three rows labeled E, C, and T. Either way will serve your purposes.

3. **Simplify the rules:** Go through the rules and make sure you understand them. As you go through them, simplify them and write them next to your diagram. Here, the rules are fairly straightforward. Make sure that you understand that T must be on at least one of Tuesday or Friday. That means that he could be on both. C, on the other hand, must be on exactly two of Monday, Wednesday, or Friday. Lastly, realize that the rule that says if E surfaces on a given day, then C must also surface on that same day means that whenever there is an E, there is also a C, but you could have a C without an E.

4. **Deductions:** Now that you understand what the rules mean, try to see how they relate to each other. For instance, there is a rule that says if E surfaces on a given day, then C must also surface on that same day. There is also a rule that says T and C cannot surface on the same day. Thus, if E surfaces on any day, then C surfaces on that day, while T cannot surface on that day. The contrapositive of this is that if T surfaces, then C cannot surface and since C cannot surface, neither can E. This means that on whatever day that T surfaces, T must be alone on that day (not C and not E). On the other hand, whenever T does not surface, there must be at least one of

E or C. But whenever E surfaces, C surfaces as well. Thus, C must always surface on any day that T does not surface. On any given day, then, either T or C must surface. Now look at how this relationship between T and C relates to the other rules about T and C. First of all, the rules tell you that T cannot surface on Thursday. Immediately, then, you know that C must surface on Thursday. Next, T must surface on at least one of Tuesday and Friday, while C must surface on exactly two of Monday, Wednesday, and Friday. Both T and C have a rule concerning their appearance on Friday. Since every day must have one of T or C, Friday must also have either T or C. This gives you two basic scenarios that you can quickly work out, one with T on Friday and one with C on Friday. In both cases you already know that C must surface on Thursday. If T surfaces on Friday, then C must surface on Monday and Wednesday. Since no personality can surface on three consecutive days, C cannot surface on Tuesday. If C cannot surface on Tuesday, then E cannot surface on Tuesday either. With C and E eliminated, T must surface on Tuesday. This, then, is one scenario: C on Monday, T on Tuesday, C on Wednesday, C on Thursday, and T on Friday. The only uncertainty remaining is whether E surfaces on the days on which C surfaces, Monday, Wednesday, and Thursday. The second scenario is if C surfaces Friday. Remember, C must surface on Thursday as well. If C surfaces on Friday, then C cannot surface on Wednesday, because placing C on Wednesday would place three C's in a row. Since C cannot be on Wednesday, neither can E, which means that T must be on Wednesday. According to the rules, T must be on at least one of Tuesday and Friday, and in this case C is on Friday so T must also surface on Tuesday. With T on Tuesday and Wednesday, it is impossible for T to also surface on Monday. Since T cannot surface on Monday, C must and E could possibly surface on Monday. This then is the second scenario: C on Monday, T on Tuesday, T on Wednesday, C on Thursday, and C on Friday. Again, the only uncertainty here is whether E surfaces on the days on which C surfaces. Notice that in both scenarios T must surface on Tuesday and C must surface on Thursday and Monday. Generally, when a game gives you two basic scenarios (T or C but not both on Friday) it is worth your while to work them out. In this case it makes the game much easier by making it clear that there are only two basic possible outcomes for C and T and, given those, the only other variable is whether E is with C. You could have also deduced these two scenarios by realizing that C must surface on Thursday and then realizing that this means that C cannot be on both Wednesday and Friday, leaving C to surface on either Monday and Wednesday or Monday and Friday.

5. **"Walk Around It":** There are five days over which at least one of three personalities must surface. From the deductions it is clear that there are only two basic scenarios. The key in answering the questions will be to determine which scenario you are dealing with. The only real variable is E. E may or may not surface on any day on which C surfaces. In fact, you do not even know whether E surfaces during the week at all.

1. **Type:** In this game there are four friends, F, G, H, and I. Each friend must order one of the three types of steaks and possibly one of the two types of pies. In effect, you are placing a type of steak and, perhaps, a type of pie in each of the four main groups. This is a hybrid between a slots game and a grouping game, but since the items and number of items included within each group are variable, you can treat it as a grouping game.

2. **Diagram:** Your diagram should have four columns, F, G, H, and I. You will have to assign a type of steak and possibly a type of pie to each person. If you insist on setting this up as a slots game, the four friends should still be four columns, but you would also need to include two rows labeled S and P, for steak and pie. These categories would create slots in which to place the specific type of steak or pie.

3. **Simplify the rules:** Go through the rules and convert them into symbols. This will force you to interpret exactly what the rules mean. Be clear on what the rule means that says that at least as many R's are ordered as S's. The number of R's must be equal to or greater than the number of S's. Also, everyone must order a steak, but each person is not required to order a pie. The remaining rules are straightforward: If someone orders an R, then he must order an A (R → A). If someone orders a T then he orders a C (T → C). If H does not order an S, then I does not order an S (H ≠ S → I ≠ S). And G does not order anything that H orders and vice versa (G ≠ H). The last rule you can place directly on the diagram, G orders an A.

4. **Deductions:** First, always remember to determine consciously the contrapositives to the "if...then" statements. One that will help you here is the contrapositive to the rule if H does not order an S then I does not order an S. The contrapositive is: If I orders an S, then H orders an S. Next, look at the rules and see if there are any relationships between the rules that you can discern. One rule says that G cannot order the same steak or pie as H and the next rule then tells you that G orders an apple pie. This means that H does not order an apple pie. If H orders a pie, then it must be cherry. Because H cannot order an apple pie, he cannot order an R either, for if one of the friends orders an R then he must also order an apple pie. H must order either an S or a T. Furthermore, since G must order an apple pie, you know that G cannot order a T. G must order either an R or an S. Then there is the rule that tells you that the total number of R's must be equal to or greater than the total number of S's. There are only four total steaks, which means that the greatest number of S's that can be used is two. If I orders an S, then H orders an S. This would use up the two possible S's and require that both F and G order an R. Thus, if I orders an S, then H orders an S and both F and G order an R. The contrapositive of this deduction tells you that if F and G do not both order an R, then I cannot order an S.

5. **"Walk Around It":** Look at the game as a whole and see what variables are left to deal with. You do not know how many of the friends order a pie, only that G must order an apple pie. If someone orders an R, then he must order an apple pie, and if someone orders a T, then he must order a cherry pie. If someone orders an S, you do not know whether or not he orders a pie. Keep careful tally of the number of S's and R's distributed among the four friends. Remember, if I orders an S, then H must order an S, which forces both F and G to order R's.

1. Type: In this game there are six shops numbered consecutively one through six from west to east. It will be your task to place the different stores in the proper order according to the rules. This is an ordering game, with some characteristics of a slots game as well.

2. Diagram: The basic diagram for an ordering game is a series of numbered blanks, in this case one through six. However, the working diagram you can obtain only after going through the rules and determining the relative order of the different shops. Be careful to get your directions right: west is on the left and east is on the right.

3. Simplify the rules: This game has only three rules in the rules list, which does not at first seem like very much information. With a little thought, it soon becomes clear that these three rules give you all the information you need to determine everything you need to know in order to answer the questions. The three rules are fairly straightforward. First, there must be exactly three shops between the Vacuum Cleaners (V) and the Delicatessen (D). To convert this into symbols, write V, add three blanks, and then write D (V _ _ _ D). Be careful; this rule does not say that V is before D, so draw a double arrow connecting V and D, letting you know that D could be before V. The second rule says that there is at least one shop between the Optician (O) and the Florist (F). Again, this rule does not tell you the relative order of O and F, just that there is at least one space in between them. The third rule requires only slightly more interpretation. It says that exactly one shop is adjacent to the Computer Repair Shop (C). For it to be true that C is next to only one shop, C must be either the first or the sixth shop.

4. Deductions: Once you have simplified the rules and converted them into symbols, relate the rules to each other and build a working diagram. The rule concerning V and D is going to be very important because it involves five of the six spaces. V and D must either be first and fifth or second and sixth. It is also the case that C must either be first or sixth, so C, V, and D will fill up either 1, 2, and 6 or 1, 5, and 6. Either way, three of the six spaces are filled, leaving only the three spaces in between V and D to fill with O, F, and H. The second rule says that O and F must be separated by at least one space. O and F must be inside V and D, and since there are only three spaces inside V and D, they must be separated by exactly one space. H must be in the remaining space. You need to make this an understandable diagram. If C is first the order looks like this: C V _ _ _ D, keeping in mind that V and D are interchangeable. O and F must be separated by at least one space, so O and F must be inside V and D: C V O _ F D, keeping in mind that O and F are interchangeable. H must be in the one remaining space. Thus, your diagram should look like this: C V O H F D, with double arrows indicating that V and D are interchangeable and that O and F are interchangeable. C could also be sixth, and if this is the case, then V or D must be first and fifth, not necessarily in that order, O and F must be second and fourth, not necessarily in that order, and H must be third. Thus, if C is sixth the diagram should be: V O H F D C, with double arrows indicating that V and D are interchangeable and that O and F are interchangeable. To recap, if C is first then V or D must be second and sixth, though not necessarily in that order, O and F must be third and fifth, not necessarily in that order, and H must be fourth. If C is sixth then V or D must be first and fifth, not necessarily in that order, O and F must be second and fourth, not necessarily in that order, and H must be third. Just remember that V and D are interchangeable, as are O and F. Only H is fixed, but its position depends on whether C is first or sixth.

5. "Walk Around It": The rules actually allowed you to determine a complete diagram. The key is to understand what effect placing C first or sixth has on the order. Once you have a diagram and a good understanding of it, go on to the questions with confidence.

Setup Game 76

1. **Type:** Begin working the game by asking yourself what type of game you are dealing with. In this game the constants are the courses, P, S, T, and Z, and the categories of people within those courses: professors and students. It will be your task to place the professors and students in the appropriate course, so the courses are groups and this is a grouping game.

2. **Diagram:** The diagram should reflect the four courses that make up the four groups. This is easily accomplished by making four columns labeled appropriately. Be sure to keep track of the difference between students and professors. If you have trouble remembering who is what, it might be helpful to create two rows that separate these classes of people.

3. **Simplify the rules:** Next, interpret the rules one by one and simplify them into symbols where possible. In this game each of six students takes one of the four courses. Each of the four courses is taught by exactly one of the three professors and all three professors must teach at least one course, which means that exactly one professor will teach two classes. The rules contained in the rules list are fairly straightforward and easy to interpret and symbolize. There are four groups, there must be one teacher in each group, and at least one student in each of the four groups. The rules list says that if L teaches a course then there is only one student in that class (L→ 1 student). Be careful with the next rule. The rule that says C must take a course taught by K does not mean that C takes every course taught by K, but only that C must take one of the courses taught by K (K could possibly teach more than one course). C being in a course is sufficient to know that K teaches that course. Thus, this rule can be approached as a conditional: If C is in a course, then K teaches that course (C→K). The third rule is a standard conditional: If F takes S, then H takes S (F=S→H=S). The rule that says neither G nor H takes a course taught by M can be simplified into two rules: If M then not G (M→~G). And if M then not H (M→~H). The remaining rules can all be placed directly on the diagram: D takes P, E takes T, and K teaches T.

4. **Deductions:** This step is very important. Not only will you find new relationships that were not obvious at first, but you will also gain a better sense of what the rules mean and how they relate to each other. A good first place to start is with the contrapositives. Go through each conditional statement and find the contrapositive, which you can obtain by reversing the conditional and negating both sides. For example, C→K becomes ~K→ ~C. Do this for the remaining conditional statements. Next, notice the general rule that each student takes only one of the four courses and that each of the three professors must teach one of the four courses. As has been mentioned, this means that one of the professors will teach two courses. This has ramifications for the rule that says C must be in a course taught by K. According to the rules, K must teach T, but it could also be true that K teaches another course. If K teaches two courses, then you do not know which of the two courses C is in; however, if K teaches only one course, then you know that K only teaches T and that both E and C take that course. Thus, the deduction is that if K is used only once then C is in T. The contrapositive of this deduction is also true: If C is not in T, then K is used twice. Furthermore, the conditions that each student takes only one of the four courses and that there is at least one student in each class restricts the distribution of the six students as well. There can only be two numerical arrangements of students: 3:1:1:1 or 2:2:1:1. Next, there are two rules governing the placement of H: If F is in S, then H is in S, and if H is in a class, then M is not the teacher (the contrapositive of the M→~H rule). Combining these two rules tells you that if F is in S, M cannot teach S.

5. **"Walk Around It":** The fact that there are only two scenarios for the distribution of the students is very important. There can be either three students in one class and one student in the remaining three classes or there can be two students in two classes and one student in the remaining two classes. Knowing practically any information at all will allow you to determine which scenario you are working with. Look out for questions that force exactly two or three students into a class. Likewise if more than three students (four is the maximum) are assigned to a teacher then you know that that teacher must teach two classes. The distribution will also let you know which classes L can teach since L can only teach classes taken by one student. The relationship among M, G, and H is also likely to be a key to successfully working this game.

1. **Type:** A quick reading of the setup and the rules makes it clear that your task in this game is to place the eight books in the order in which they were read over the ten-week period. This, then, is an ordering game.

2. **Diagram:** As with all ordering games, the working diagram can only be created after you go through the rules. However, it is a good idea to quickly write down the basics. You will have ten spaces numbered one through ten and have eight books: I, B, H, M, W, G, A, and P.

3. **Simplify the rules:** Now go through the rules. You need to interpret them and then convert them into easily understandable symbols. The first rule creates a sequence of three of the books: A, M, and G. These three books will always be next to each other, though not necessarily in that order. Perhaps the most important thing about this sequence is that it takes up three consecutive weeks. Next, B is read sometime before M and sometime before P. This creates two conditions: B..M and B..P. The third rule says that W is next to a week in which nothing is read. W must be next to an empty space. On the other hand, I cannot be next to an empty space. Be careful with the final rule, which actually contains two rules: P..W and I..W.

4. **Deductions:** Here is where the real work of most games should take place. Once you understand the rules and have simplified them, relate the rules to each other. This will allow you to build a diagram of the relative order of many of the books. In order to do this, simply pick one of the books that is mentioned in more than one rule and expand from there. For instance, one rule says B is before P, another says that P is before W, and yet another says that W must be adjacent to an empty space. This gives you a basic list that looks like this: B..P..W_, where W and the empty space are interchangeable. Furthermore, one rule says that B must be before M. Since M, A, and G must

be consecutive, this means that B must be before M, A, and G. You can draw this sequence above or below the line you already have so that you do not get confused and think that you know anything about the relative order of M, A, and G to P or W. Lastly, I must be before W. Thus, you have a basic list that looks like this: B..P.W_, while the MAG sequence comes sometime after B and I comes sometime before W. Don't forget also that M, A, and G are not necessarily in that order and that W and the empty space are interchangeable. With this list in front of you, you know many things, including which books can be read first (B, H, or I) and which books can be read last (W, M, A, or G). With this list, you have enough information to answer anything that the questions can throw at you.

5. **"Walk Around It":** Before you move on to the questions, take a moment to think about the big picture. You have B..P.W_, with W and the empty space interchangeable, the MAG sequence sometime after B, and I sometime before W. Remember, you do not know anything about the relative order of the MAG sequence with any book except B and you do not know anything about the relative order of I with any book except W. H is the only book about which there is no rule, so H is the wildcard. There is also one more empty space to place in the list of ten. Remember, I cannot be next to an empty space. The MAG sequence is likely to be important since it takes up three consecutive spaces. Now that you have a good idea of what the game involves and how it works, move on to the questions.

1. **Type:** In this game you have three children, E, F, and G, each of whom is going to have a sundae that is composed of three parts. You could conceptualize this game in two ways: as a grouping game, where you will have to determine which flavors go to each child, or, since there are three fixed parts for each child's sundae, as a slots game, where you will have to determine which flavor goes in each slot. In the end it does not matter which way you set it up as long as you can clearly visualize what you are dealing with and what the game requires you to do.

2. **Diagram:** Your diagram at the least should show clearly the three groups, E, F, and G. You can accomplish this by drawing three columns labeled E, F, and G, respectively. If you work this game as a slots game, then you should also include three rows labeled one through three to represent the three parts of the sundae that each child must have. If you do work this game as a grouping game, be very careful about the rules. There must be three parts in each child's sundae but this does not mean that there are three different flavors in each sundae.

3. **Simplify the rules:** Simplify the rules into understandable symbols that will allow you to work with them more easily. Also, this is the time to make sure you understand all the rules. The first rule in the list tells you that if there are any chocolates (C) used in any sundae, then there must be more total strawberries (S) than there are total chocolates. The next two rules tell you that if any butterscotch (B) is used in a sundae, then that sundae cannot contain any S, and that if any vanilla (V) is used in a sundae, then that sundae cannot also contain any pineapple (P). Lastly, the rules give you a few specifics. F must have more flavors than G, and F must have at least one vanilla.

4. **Deductions:** Examine how the rules relate to one another. Before you do so, it is usually helpful to write down the contrapositives for all the conditional statements in the rules. Remember,

any conditional statement means exactly one other thing, the contrapositive. You obtain the contrapositive by reversing the conditional statement and negating both sides; or, in fancy logic language, by denying the consequent. Thus, the rule that says if V is included in a sundae, then P cannot be included in that sundae means exactly one other thing: If P is included, then V is not. Follow this same process for the other rules. Once you have the rules and all their meanings in front of you, you can more easily relate the rules to each other. A key rule here is that F's sundae must have more flavors than G's. This means that F cannot have only one flavor, but rather must have either two or three flavors. Likewise, since G's sundae has fewer flavors than F's, G cannot have three flavors, but rather must have either one or two flavors. Thus, since E could have at most three flavors, F could have at most three flavors, and G could have at most two flavors, the setup could include at most eight flavors. On the other hand, since E must have at least one flavor, F must have at least two flavors, and G must have at least one flavor, there must be at least four flavors. The rules already assigned a V to F's sundae. Since F's sundae contains a V, F's sundae cannot contain a P. Thus, the only flavors left to include in the remaining two parts of F's sundae are some combination of another V, some C's, and some of either B or S. (Nobody can have both B and S.) If F's sundae has three flavors then, in addition to the one V that is already part of F's sundae, F must have exactly one C, and exactly one of B or S. On the other hand, if F only has two flavors, then the flavors for F's sundae are not as restricted. F could have two V's, two C's, or two of B or S.

5. **"Walk Around It":** The F is greater than G rule will restrict what you can use in each group. Be mindful of those restrictions. F needs at least two flavors, while G can have at most two flavors. If F has three flavors, then F's sundae must include V, C, and one of B or S (because if B then no S and vice versa). However, if F only has two flavors, you cannot determine which flavors must be included. F could have two Vs, two Cs, or two of either B or S. Finally, always pay attention to the number of C's that are used. Anytime that a C is mentioned, take note of how many spaces you need in order to have more S's than C's overall.

1. **Type:** Although this game throws some different categories and variables at you, it is not that difficult to classify. There are eight teachers, some combination of whom must be assigned to one of three classes. Thus, you are dealing with three groups and you must build those groups according to the rules. The number of students within the three classes will tell you how many teachers are in each class.

2. **Diagram:** The diagram for this grouping game is rather simple. All you need are three columns labeled 1, 2, and 3 to represent the three classes.

3. **Simplify the rules:** The rules are fairly straightforward. In the rules list you are told that there are eight teachers and no teacher can be assigned to two classes. The classes either have 15 or 20 students, and the size of the class determines the number of teachers assigned to it, either 2 or 3 teachers. The first two rules in the rules list create two splits, an FK split and a JD split, while at the same time telling you that F, K, J, and D must all be used. The last two rules in the rules list are simple conditional statements: If C and L are together, then they are in a class with 20 students. If G and K are together, then they are in a class with 15 students.

4. **Deductions:** The rules establish some situational constraints. Your job in the deductions step is to make explicit what those constraints are. Relate the rules to each other and find out what additional information you can determine. First of all, you need to realize that knowing the number of students in any class is the same as knowing how many teachers are assigned to a class. Each class must have either 15 or 20 students. If a class has 15 students, then there are only two teachers, and if there are 20 students, then there are exactly three teachers. This tells you that the group sizes are limited to only two or three teachers. While you do not

know how many of the teachers you have to use in every instance, you must use at least six (three groups of two), and four of these must be F, K, J, and D. You can relate what you know about the possible group sizes to the two conditional statements. If C and L are together, then there are 20 children in that class. This means that there are three teachers, so there must be one teacher in addition to C and L assigned to that same class. It also means that the minimum number of teachers assigned to classes is seven. On the other hand, if G and K are together, then there are only 15 students in the class. Where there are only 15 students there are only two teachers, so if G and K are together, then that group is full.

5. **"Walk Around It":** There were not many deductions to make, but be comfortable with the game. The questions will give you everything you need in order to get them right. But before moving on to the questions, think about what you will have to deal with. The items that you will have to deal with to answer the questions are, first of all, the size of the three groups and, secondly, the two splits. No matter how many teachers are assigned, you must use F, K, J, and D while keeping F and K separated and J and D separated. As you go through the questions, pay close attention to how the group size relates to these splits and vice versa.

1. **Type:** In this game there are ten golfers who must be placed into two groups of four, foursome A and B. There are no other variables, so this is a grouping game.

2. **Diagram:** The diagram for this game should show the two groups, A and B, by making two columns labeled A and B. Be sure to note that there are exactly four people within each group.

3. **Simplify the rules:** Now focus on the rules. Go through the rules one by one and determine what they mean. Once you know what the rules mean, convert them into symbols directly on your workspace. There is only one rule that is not straightforward, the rule that says N is in neither foursome unless E is in foursome A. This does not say that if E is in a foursome then N must be also. It says that N cannot be in a foursome unless E is in A. E playing in foursome A is a necessary condition for N playing. To translate, this means that if N is in a foursome, then E must be in foursome A. The rest of the rules are more or less standard "if…then" statements that are easy to symbolize. Don't lose track of what exactly the condition in each statement is. For instance, the first rule says that if D is in a foursome, then neither G nor J is included in a foursome. This rule is dealing with generalities: If D is included in one of the two foursomes (regardless of which one), then neither G nor J can be included in either foursome (regardless of which one). Note that this rule actually contains two pieces of information, so it is best to break it into two rules: If D, then not G (D → ~G). If D then not J (D → ~J).

4. **Deductions:** The next step is to link rules that share common information together so that you can see how the rules relate to one another. This will allow you to make deductions that will be critical in finding solutions to the questions that follow. First, start with the simplest deductions, the contrapositives. Every "if…then" statement can be changed into one other statement that means exactly the same thing. You can obtain this statement by negating both sides of the "if…then" statement and then reversing the statement. Thus, the rule that says if D is in a foursome, then G is not in a foursome becomes a rule that says if G is in a foursome, then D is not in a foursome. Writing down the contrapositives will often help you to see relationships between the rules that are hard to see otherwise. After writing down the contrapositives, look for rules that contain information about the same pieces of the game. In this case, there are two rules dealing with the placement of K: First, if F is in a foursome, then K is in the other foursome. Second, K is not in foursome B. This second rule tells you that if K is in a foursome, then K can only be in foursome A. The first rule tells you that K's location is determined by the placement of F such that if F is in foursome A then K is in foursome B and if F is in foursome B then K is in foursome A. But K's location is restricted to only foursome A. If F and K are in different groups and K can only be in foursome A, then the only foursome that F can be in is foursome B. Thus, if F is in a foursome, then F is in foursome B and K is in foursome A. The remaining deductions are a little more difficult to see, but they are there for you to determine if you take the time. The setup paragraph tells you that there are ten golfers while there are only two foursomes that play golf. Thus, there are two people who do not play. With this idea in mind, look at the rule that says if D is included then neither G nor J can be included. If D is included, then G and J are the two players who do not play, which means that all the other golfers must be included. Since in this case D plays and J does not, and since one of D or J must be in foursome A, then D must be in foursome A. Since F plays, F must be in foursome B and K must be in foursome A. This setup also forces N to play, which means that E must

be in foursome A. This setup gives you D, E, and K in foursome A, which leaves no room for M and C to be together in foursome A, so M and C must be together in foursome B. Now you have three players in foursome A: D, K, and E, and three players in foursome B: F, M, and C. You need one more player on each foursome and there are only two people left, N and H. There are no rules that tell you which side they must be on, so they could both be in either foursome. Thus, the first scenario, where D is included, results in D, E, K, and one of N or H being assigned to foursome A, and F, M, C, and one of N or H being assigned to foursome B. The only other possibility is that D does not play. First of all, if D does not play and one of D or J must be assigned to foursome A, then J would have to be assigned to foursome A. Furthermore, if D does not play, then there can only be one other person in addition to D who does not play. Notice the rule that says if M or C plays in a foursome, then the other must play in that foursome as well. If there is only room for one more person to sit out, then one of M or C must play in a foursome, thus forcing both of them to play in a foursome. Now you know that M and C must always be used. Another rule says if N plays, then E must play in foursome A. Since there can only be one other person sitting out in addition to D, either N plays or he does not. If he plays, then E is used in foursome A. If he does not play, then D and N must be the two golfers not included in a foursome, which means that E is used again, although not necessarily in foursome A. Therefore, E must also always be used. Finally, within this second scenario where D and one other person are sitting out, there is one other rule that allows you to make a deduction. This is the rule that says if F is in a foursome, then K is used in the other foursome. In terms of this scenario, this rule means that either F plays or he doesn't. If F plays, then K must be used. If F does not play, then that makes two people sitting out, so K must still be used. These, then, are the deductions concerning the scenario where D is not included in a foursome: J, M, C, E, and K, with both J and K in foursome A, must always be used, and if F plays then F is in foursome B.

5. **"Walk Around It":** After making deductions, you are armed with quite a bit of information. There are ten golfers but only eight can be used. Thus, there will be two people who sit out. The only possible scenarios are one in which D plays and G and J sit out, or one in which D and one other person sit out. M, C, E, and K can never sit out, and so must always be used. Since K is always used and cannot be in foursome B, K must be in foursome A, which is a piece of information that you can place directly on the diagram. Notice that the scenario in which D is included is very constrained—there is only one variable. On the other hand, the scenario in which D is not included is much more flexible. The key in this game then will be to know which scenario you are working with. There are two ways to figure this out. Since in the first scenario G and J must sit out, if you know that somebody other than those two are sitting out then you know you are dealing with the second scenario. Also, there is a rule that says either D or J must be used in foursome A. The rules say if D is used, then J is not, and if J is used, then D is not. In other words, if you know which one of D or J is used in foursome A, then you know which scenario you are dealing with.

1. **Type:** Right away you can tell that this game does not resemble any of the three main types of games. This game involves a tournament of tennis players and you must determine who can advance through each round. Whatever you do, do not let the fact that it is an unusual game cause you to panic. Like all games, it will give you the information you need to answer the questions. Come to grips with it and move on.

2. **Diagram:** This game actually contains a diagram as part of the setup. Use it.

3. **Simplify the rules:** Simplify the rules by changing them into symbols that you can easily understand. The rules here are fairly straightforward. The rule that says if M wins match 2, then he must meet F in match 5, and that S must win match 3, should be broken down into two separate rules. Thus, one rule says if M wins match 2, then he must meet F in match 5, and the other rule says if M wins match 2, then S wins match 3. Keep in mind also that the statement "if M wins match 2" is the same as saying "if M plays in match 5" because if he wins the lower match, he will advance to the higher match.

4. **Deductions:** Now is your chance to do a little detective work. You have the rules in front of you, but what do they really mean? See how they relate to each other and what extra information you can glean from them. As usual, it is a good idea to start with the contrapositives. Start with the "if...then" statement that you broke down into two different rules. The first part says if M wins match 2, then he must meet F in match 5. The contrapositive says if F is not in match 5, then M does not win match 2. The second part says if M wins match 2, then S must win match 3. The contrapositive, on the other hand, says if S does not win match 3, then M does not win match 2. Follow the same procedure and write down the contrapositives of the other "if...then"

statements. Next, look at the first two rules: E and N cannot meet in a match and if M wins match 2 then he must meet F in match 5. Just as the rule stated, if M wins match 2 then F wins match 1. What about when N wins match 2? Because N cannot meet E in a match, F must win match 1. Thus, either way, *F must win match 1*. Now you have at least one solid piece of information. Now go to the rule that says the champion cannot be N, S, or T. The champion is the winner of match 7, so N, S, and T cannot win match 7. That is easily avoided if they play somebody else, but if they play each other, one would have to be the winner. Thus, no combination of N, S, and T can play in the championship match. Since N is on one side of the tournament and S and T are on the other, what this really means is *if N is in match 7, he cannot play either S or T, and if either S or T plays in match 7, he cannot play N*. The last rule says if T and Y meet each other in a match, then T must win that match. Add this to the deduction you just made and you also know that *if T and Y meet in a match* (which would have to be match 6) *then N cannot win match 5*. Finally, there is more than one rule that contains information about M winning match 2, so put those rules together and see what you get. If Z wins match 6, then M must win match 2. If M wins match 2, then two things happen: M must meet F in match 5 (which you already knew anyway because F must always win match 1) and S must win match 3. Write this down as a new rule: If Z wins match 6 (which is the same as saying if Z plays in match 7), then S wins match 3. That means Z and S played together in match 6, if Z is in the championship game. Since you know that F and M play each other in game 5, Z's opponent in game 7 will have to be either F or M (which is the same as saying it cannot be N). To restate that last little bit, *if Z makes it to match 7, Z played S in match 6 and plays either F or M in match 7*. This is really two deductions. The contrapositives are true as well. That was a lot to work through, but it was important and believe it or not, will save you time. Now you have a good idea of how the game will work.

5. **"Walk Around It":** The deduction step led you through a lot of the game. Hopefully you gained a sense of how the game will work and what some of the key variables will be. F will always advance to match 5, which saves you some work. Keep your eye on M, because the fact that M advanced or didn't advance tells you quite a bit of information. Also, remember that N, S, and T cannot be the champion. Since the possibilities are limited for the players in match 5 and 6, go ahead and write down the list of possibilities directly on the diagram. F must play either M or N in match 5. Match 6 is more open, but there are still only four possibilities. If S wins match 3, he plays either Y or Z (S v. Y, S v. Z) and if T wins match 3, he plays either Y or Z (T v. Y, T v. Z).

1. **Type:** This game seems a little complex because there are a few different variables: the number of tents, the color of the tents, and the person or people sleeping in the tent. Since there is a possibility of including more than one person in each tent, this is not exactly a slots game. This is closer to a grouping game in which there are four to five groups (the tents). However, these groups will be modified by their colors as well.

2. **Diagram:** Your diagram should represent the different tents. There are at least four tents and at most five, so you can draw five columns labeled one through five to represent the tents. There are two pieces of information that you must determine about each tent: its color and the people in it. If it helps, these two categories can be drawn as two rows, one labeled P for people and the other labeled C for color. Otherwise, you can just keep track of the color within the groups.

3. **Simplify the rules:** Simplify the rules by converting them into symbols or by shortening them as much as possible when symbols do not seem to work. The rules for this game are: There cannot be two consecutive tents of the same color. O is in a green tent. U is in a green tent. P is in a brown tent. Q and R are in tent 2. And if a tent is navy, then it has exactly one camper in it.

4. **Deductions:** Take the time to look at the rules and see if there are any connections between them. Don't forget to write down or at least think about the contrapositives of any conditional statement. Here there is really only one conditional statement. It states that if a tent is navy, then it can only have one person in it. The contrapositive of this rule says that if a tent has two people in it then it is not navy. Since Q and R are together in tent 2, then you know that tent 2 cannot be navy. Hence, tent 2 is either brown or green. There are also some general considerations to think about. There must either be four or five tents. If there are only four tents, then in order to use all seven people there must be three tents with two people in them and exactly one tent with one person in it. On the other hand, if there are five tents, then there must be exactly two tents with two people in them and exactly three tents with only one person in them

5. **"Walk Around It":** Although you are undoubtedly anxious to move on to and enjoy the questions, it is important to quickly review what you do and do not know. Tent 2 is brown or green and P must be in a brown tent. But there cannot be two consecutive tents of the same color, so always watch for the placement of P. If P is in tent 1 or 3, then tent 2 must be green, and then you must be aware of the placement of O and U, who must both be in a green tent. The reverse also holds true for the placement of O and U. O and U must both be in a green tent, so if O and U are in a tent adjacent to tent 2, then tent 2 must be brown, but then be aware of the placement of P. Also, keep track of how many campers are in each tent. There must either be two tents with two people and three tents with one person or three tents with two people and one tent with only one person in it.

1. **Type:** In this game there are three children who go to the store on three days and on each of those three days must buy exactly one of four types of toys. Thus, there are three different categories: children, days, and toys. The children and the days are fixed and will never vary. The type of toy that each child buys on each day is the only variable. Because this is so, the children and days create fixed, well-defined slots. It will be your task to place the type of toy within these slots.

2. **Diagram:** You can easily set this slots game up as a matrix, with three columns representing the days of the week labeled M, T, and W and three rows representing the three children labeled E, J, and A. You will have to place one of P, Y, S, or V in each slot.

3. **Simplify the rules:** In order to work out any game quickly and, more importantly, correctly, you must understand what the rules say. Before diving into the questions, spend sometime thinking about the rules. As you do so, convert them into symbols that you can easily comprehend at a glance. While the rules list contains only three rules, do not forget the rules contained within the setup paragraph. In this game each type of toy must be used at least once, but no child can buy two of the same toy. Likewise, no two children can buy the same toy on the same day. The first three rules in the rules list you can place directly on the diagram: A does not buy a P on any day. J buys a Y on Tuesday. And E buys a Y on Monday. The final rule links two slots: What E buys on Wednesday, A must buy on Monday ($E_W = A_M$).

4. **Deductions:** Once you understand what each rule means individually, take the time to relate them to each other. How do the rules constrain each other and what additional information can you learn if they do? Begin with the first rule: A does not buy a P. Since there are four toys, three days, and no repeats and since A does not buy a P, A must buy a Y, an S, and a V over her three days, although not necessarily in that order. The rules also tell you that no two children can buy the same toy on the same day. E buys a Y on Monday and J buys a Y on Tuesday, so in order for A to buy a Y, A must buy a Y on Wednesday. Since A buys a Y on Wednesday, A must buy exactly one of either S or V on both Monday and Tuesday. Now look closely at the relationship between A and E. What A buys on Monday, E buys on Wednesday, so E must buy either an S or a V on Wednesday. Also, since A must buy the one of S or V on Tuesday that she did not buy on Monday, E cannot buy the other of S or V on Tuesday. Thus, E must buy a Y on Monday, an S or a V on Wednesday, but cannot buy the other of S or V on Tuesday because A must buy it on that day. E must, therefore, buy a P on Tuesday. For example, if A buys an S on Monday, then A buys a V on Tuesday and E buys an S on Wednesday. E cannot buy a Y on Tuesday since he got one on Monday. He cannot buy an S because he buys one on Wednesday. And he cannot buy a V because A buys a V on Tuesday. Thus, the only toy that E can buy on Tuesday is P. You now have some sort of information about seven of the nine slots. You know the least about J. However, since E buys on Wednesday what A buys on Monday, either S or V, J will only be able to use one of S or V. Therefore, the three toys that J must buy are a Y, a P, and one of S or V. Whichever toy that A and E both buy on those two days, J will not be able to buy. Thus, the two remaining slots must be filled with a P or an S/V.

5. **"Walk Around It":** Although you might feel ready to move on to the questions, there is one last step. Review quickly what you do and do not know. Look for things that the game will likely test you on. E must buy a Y, a P, and either S or V, in that order. J must buy a P, a Y, and either S or V, but not necessarily in that order. J could buy the S/V on Monday and the P on Wednesday. A must buy one of S or V on Monday, the other on Tuesday, and a Y on Wednesday. Obviously, a vital part of this game is determining the location of the S or V for each child. Once you know which one of S or V a child receives and on what day he or she receives it, a chain reaction starts that allows you to determine other information. You will also need to fix the placement of the P that J buys on either Monday or Wednesday. Thus, in order to determine the entire setup, you will need some information that tells you which one of S or V that J buys, on what day J buys the P, and which toy A and E buy on Monday and Wednesday, respectively. Almost any information will cause chain reactions.

1. **Type:** As always, the first step is to determine what type of game you are dealing with. This will prepare you mentally for what the game is going to require you to do, as well as attune you to the likely keys to the game. In this game you have eight track events that must be scheduled over a period of eight days with one event per day. This setup should make it clear that this is a game where you have to place the eight events in the order in which they are held. The relative order of items will be important, but, judging from a quick glance at the questions, that placement into numerical slots will also be a factor.

2. **Diagram:** The diagram for any ordering game is rather loose because the key is really the relative order of the different events and you can only determine that relative order after going through the rules. However, for this step you can draw the eight track events and the eight spaces that you will be working with. Label the spaces one through eight so you can keep everything straight.

3. **Simplify the rules:** Do not be overwhelmed by the number of rules. The large number of rules may even turn into a blessing because the order of the events is heavily restricted by the rules. In order to determine exactly what the rules tell you, go through each and take the time to interpret it and convert it into symbols. The rules here are fairly straightforward. First, V must be first or second. The second, third, and fourth rules all tell you two events that must be separated by one: P_T, Q_R, and T_U. Be careful with these rules because you only know that each pair is separated by one, not the order in which they are held. T could be before P, R could be before Q, and U could be before T. This is easy to symbolize with double arrows connecting each pair. Fifth, Q and U cannot be adjacent. The last two rules tell you a little about the relative order of the events: S is sometime before U, but not on the day immediately before U (S..U), and R is before P (R..P).

4. Deductions: Take the time to understand what is really going on in the game. This is a critical step. Relate the rules to each other to see what else you can determine, what the rules mean as a group rather than just individually. You can accomplish this by finding rules that contain information about the same events. For instance, you can start with the P_T rule and relate it to the rule that says T_U. Putting these two rules together you can create a list of order that looks like this: P_T_U. Remember, since you do not know the order of P as it relates to T, or U as it relates to T, this list could also be: U_T_P. This little block, whatever the order, will account for five of the eight events. Furthermore, since there are only two basic possibilities, P_T_U or U_P_T, you can try to build scenarios with the remaining rules. Determine how the remaining rules relate to these two sequences. First, consider the sequence of P_T_U. You must still account for the Q_R separation and the rule that says R must be before P. Keeping both Q and R in front of P gives you a list that looks like this: Q_R..P_T_U, where Q and R are interchangeable. If you count the spaces used in this scenario, you will find that there are eight, so in this setup either Q or R is first and U is eighth. According to the rules, V must be first or second so with Q or R first, V must be second. Thus, at this point you have: QVRP_T_U, with Q and R interchangeable. The two remaining spaces, the fifth and seventh events, must be filled with O and S. S must be before U but not immediately before U, so S must be fifth and O must be seventh. Thus, one possible scenario looks like this: QVRPSTOU, where Q and R are interchangeable. This scenario occurs when P is before U (P_T_U) and when both Q and R are before P. The rule, however, says only that R must be before P, so it is possible for the Q to come after P. If this is the case, then the setup must look like this: RPQT_U. You are left with S, V, and O. S must be before U, but not immediately before U, so S cannot fill the gap between T and U, and V must be either first or second, so V cannot fill the gap between T and U either. Therefore, O must fill the gap, forcing the setup to look like this: RPQTOU, leaving S and V interchangeable as the first and second events. These are

the only two possibilities using the P_T_U sequence: 1) QVRPSTOU, with Q and R interchangeable, and 2) SVRPQTOU, with S and V interchangeable. Now check the possibilities if you use the U_T_P sequence. Since S must be before U the sequence must actually be: S..U_T_P, and there must be at least one space between S and U. If there is only one space between S and U, then the setup must be S_U_T_P, using seven of the eight spaces. In this setup S must always be in front of at least six other events. Since there are only eight events, the latest S could be is second. V must either be first or second, so V could either be before S, making S second, or V could be immediately after S, making S first and separating S from U by two spaces. Thus, whenever the U_T_P sequence is used, one of S or V must be first and the other must be second. With the first and second events taken care of, you are left with days three through eight, or six more events, five of which must be contained within the U_T_P sequence. This U_T_P sequence could immediately follow V and S in the third position, leaving the eighth event open (SVU_T_P_; notice that if U is third, S must be first since S cannot be immediately before U) or the U_T_P sequence could begin in the fourth position, leaving the third position open (SV_U_T_P, where S and V are interchangeable). Q cannot be next to U, so in either case Q cannot come immediately before or after U, which means that the earliest that Q can be is sometime after T. But the placement of Q is further restricted because Q cannot be the last event. Q must, therefore, be in between T and P in both cases. The placement of Q also determines the placement of R, for R must be separated from Q by exactly one space and R must also be before P. Thus, in both instances, Q must be immediately after T, placing Q in between T and P, and R must be immediately before T, placing R in the space in between U and T. Thus, whenever the sequence of U_T_P is used, the empty spaces must be filled with R and Q, respectively, such that the order looks like this: URTQP. Knowing that either S or V is first and that there is a sequence of URTQP leaves only O to place in the order. If the URTQP sequence is third through seventh then O must be eighth (SVURTQPO; again, S and V are not interchangeable here because S cannot be immediately before U) and if the URTQP sequence is fourth through eighth then O must be third (SVOURTQP, where S and V are interchangeable). These, then, are the only two scenarios if you use the U_T_P sequence: 1) SVURTQPO and 2) SVOURTQP, with S and V interchangeable. In sum, there are four possible scenarios: 1) QVRPSTOU, with Q and R interchangeable, 2) SVRPQTOU, with S and V interchangeable, 3) SVURTQPO, and 4) SVOURTQP, with S and V interchangeable. You have taken a mass of information and, by following through what each rule says individually and how all the rules, as a group, relate to each other, you have narrowed the possibilities significantly. It is important to note that this deductions section is unusual in that it is so extensive. This is not a case where you know right away that there are only four scenarios and that you are going to work them out, but once you start making deductions and working through the logic of the rules, you are led to them. If you do not do them here, you will end up doing them later in order to answer the questions.

5. **"Walk Around It":** With four basic scenarios, all you need to determine is which scenario, or, if more than one, which scenarios you are dealing with for each question. Compare the answer choices to the work you have already done; that is why you take the time to do it in the first place. Take a deep breath and head to the questions.

1. **Type:** In this game there are four adjacent townhouses. Three trees are planted at each house. There are four types of trees, E, O, A, P, and there are four of each type of tree available. It is your job to place the trees with the appropriate townhouse. Thus, this is a grouping game. The four townhouses are four groups and the trees are the items that you must place in the groups. There will be three trees in each group.

2. **Diagram:** Because this is a grouping game, the diagram is easy to draw. It should consist of four columns labeled 1 through 4 in order to represent the four townhouses.

3. **Simplify the rules:** This game is not as complex as it seems. Go through the rules and simplify them into symbols where possible. Write these rules directly on your workspace for easy and quick reference. Don't forget the rules contained in the setup paragraph. The setup paragraph tells you that there are 4 E's, 4 O's, 4 A's, and 4 P's. Once you have the rules from the setup paragraph, go through the rules list. First, no townhouse has more than one O or more than one E. The next rule says two things: No two townhouses can have the same three types of trees (or no two houses can have the exact same set of three trees). Each townhouse must have at least two types of trees. The rule that says that there is at least one A in the third townhouse from the west can be placed directly on the diagram. Be sure to leave room for the other two trees at the third house. The last two rules tell you that there are no P's in adjacent townhouses and no A's in adjacent townhouses. Some of these rules are not easy to convert into symbols; do the best that you can. Just be sure that you can understand what you write down. The game will be easier to understand and easier to work quickly if you think and work as much as you can in symbols. It cuts down on the time that you spend reading and interpreting.

4. **Deductions:** Once you understand each rule by itself, relate the rules to each other and see if you can glean any extra information that will assist you in working out the questions. The first rule in the rules list says that no townhouse can have more than one O or more than one E. Since the only types of trees available are O's, E's, A's, and P's, in order for any house to have three trees (as they must), at least one of those trees must be an A or a P. In other words, there must be either an A or a P at each of the four houses, but, according to the rules, none of the P's can be at adjacent townhouses and none of the A's can be at adjacent townhouses. These requirements, coupled with the rule that assigns an A to the third house, allow you to determine a great deal about the setup for this game. Since there must be an A at house 3, there cannot be an A at house 2 or house 4. As already discovered, every house must have at least one A or P. Since neither house 2 nor house 4 can have an A, both must have at least one P. Next, since house 2 has a P, house 1 cannot have a P. Because house 1 cannot have a P, house 1 must have at least one A. Thus, houses 1 and 3 must have at least one A, while houses 2 and 4 must have at least one P. According to the rules, each house must have two types of trees, so the greatest number of A's that can be included at each of house 1 and house 3 is two (which means both house 1 and house 3 must have at least one E or O) and the greatest number of P's that can be included at each of houses 2 and 4 is two (which means that houses 2 and 4 must also have at least one E or O). Therefore, houses 1 and 3 must each have either one or two A's and houses 2 and 4 must each have either one or two P's. If there is only one A or P at any house the other two trees at that house must be one each of O and E. One of the remaining rules says that no two townhouses can have the exact same set of three trees, so it is impossible for both house 1 and house 3 to have only one A (this would force both houses to have a setup of AEO) and it is impossible for both house 2 and house 4 to have only one P (this would force both houses to have a setup of PEO). This reveals that one or both of houses 1 and 3 must have two A's and that one or both of houses 2 and 4 must have two P's. Thus, the possible numerical distribution of A's and P's is limited. There could be two A's at house 1 or house 3 and two A's in the other, or there could be two A's at either house 1 or house 3 and one A in the other. Likewise, there could be two P's at both house 2 and house 4 or there could be two P's at one of house 2 or house 4 and only one P at the other.

5. **"Walk Around It":** From the deductions you now know that there are only four basic scenarios: first, where both 1 and 3 have two A's and both 2 and 4 have two P's; second, where only one of 1 and 3 has two A's and the other has only one while both 2 and 4 have two P's; third, where both 1 and 3 have two A's while only one of 2 or 4 has two P's and the other only has one; fourth, where there are two A's in one of 1 or 3 and one in the other while there are two P's in one of 2 or 4 and one in the other. The questions will place you in one of these scenarios. You need to figure out which one and then determine what else must be true in that specific scenario. It is important to keep track of the O's and E's.

1. **Type:** The first thing to determine is the type of game. In this game there are two bookcases, both of which have four shelves labeled one through four from bottom to top. There are seven different books to place on the shelves. The two bookcases, one white and one black, and the four shelves create well-defined slots into which the books must be placed. This, then, is a slots game.

2. **Diagram:** You can diagram this game horizontally with the two bookcases creating two rows and the four shelves creating four columns or vertically with the two bookcases creating two columns and the four shelves creating four rows. Either way, the diagram will show eight slots. Be sure to label the columns and rows appropriately and be clear which shelves are the top shelves and which shelves are the bottom shelves.

3. **Simplify the rules:** Once you have a grasp of the type of game it is and the type of diagram that is required, go to the rules. Go through the rules, making sure you understand what they mean, and converting them into symbols. Make sure to include the rules contained within the setup paragraph itself, such as the rule that says that each type of book occupies exactly one shelf, except for P, which occupies two shelves, one on top of the other, on the same bookshelf. Thus, P is used twice and the two must be in consecutive bookshelves in the same bookcase. The rules list contains the remaining rules. The first rule says that M and S are on the top shelves. You can place this directly on the diagram as long as you are clear that you do not know whether M or S is on the white or black bookcase. You can represent this by drawing a two-way arrow between M and S or by placing M/S on the top shelf of both bookcases. The second rule says B is on the second shelf, although it does not say which bookcase it is on. Finally, C and N are on different bookcases. One must be on the white bookcase and the other must be on the black bookcase.

4. **Deductions:** With a firm grasp of the rules and the diagram in front of you, relate the rules

to each other and make deductions. You know that M and S are on a top shelf, shelf 4, and that B must be on shelf 2 in whichever bookcase it is. With the top shelf filled, the bookcase that has B will only have shelf 1 and shelf 3 left empty. The two P's must be on consecutive shelves in the same bookcase. In whichever bookcase B is, there is not room for the two consecutive P's. This means that the B and the two P's must be on different bookcases. Furthermore, since the two P's must be on consecutive shelves and the only shelves available on that bookcase are 1, 2, and 3, a P must always be on shelf 2. Shelf 2 of the two bookcases will therefore be filled with one P and one B. You cannot determine which shelf the P's are on and which shelf the B is on without additional information. Now consider what other books could be in the bookcase with the P's. The two P's will take up two shelves and one of M or S also fills a shelf. This leaves only one shelf. The only remaining types of books are C, N, and G. C and N must be in different bookcases. This means that each bookcase must have one of C or N. Thus, the bookcase that has the two P's must have the two P's, with one on shelf 2 and the other on either shelf 1 or 3, one of M or S on shelf 4, and one of C or N on either shelf 1 or shelf 3. The bookcase that has B, on the other hand, must have B on shelf 2, one of M or S on shelf 4, one of C or N on either shelf 1 or shelf 3, and G on either shelf 1 or shelf 3. You now have quite a bit of information.

5. **"Walk Around It":** The deductions make it clear that the key to this game is the relationship between B and the two P's. One side of the bookcase will have M or S on shelf 4 and B on shelf 2, leaving G and one of C and N for shelves 1 and 3, though not necessarily in that order. The other bookshelf will have one of M or S on shelf 4 and P on shelf 2, leaving P and one of C and N for shelves 1 and 3, though not necessarily in that order. Knowing which side B or P is on allows you to almost determine completely the books that are in each bookcase. The placement of M and S as well as C and N always remains somewhat flexible because without additional information you cannot know which case they must be in. You also do not know exactly which books must be on shelves 1 or 3 in either bookcase, though the selection is very limited for each. You are now ready for the questions.

1. **Type:** In this game there are two hairstylists, D and F, who must each give five haircuts over a five-hour period, with one haircut per hour. Because the five hours and the two hair stylists create ten well-defined slots into which exactly one person must be placed, this is a slots game.

2. **Diagram:** The diagram for this game should show five columns labeled one through five to represent the five hours and two columns labeled D and F to represent the two hair stylists. You will have to place a client within each of the ten slots.

3. **Simplify the rules:** Simplify the rules by converting them into symbols. Do not ignore the rules contained within the setup paragraph. Here there are two stylists who must each see a W, an M, a C, and a C. Each stylist must also see one additional client who does not have an appointment. The rules list says that these clients without appointments cannot be first or last. The one remaining rule requires some interpretation. It says that during the five fours, D and F do not both give haircuts to adults or children. In other words, in no hour can both D and F give haircuts to adults and in no hour can both D and F give haircuts to C's. Since this is the case, during any hour in which one of the hairstylists gives a haircut to a C, the other hairstylist must give a haircut to an adult (either M or W). Likewise, during any hour in which one of the hairstylists gives a haircut to an adult (either M or W), the other stylist must give a haircut to a C.

4. **Deductions:** Once you have deciphered what the rules mean and converted them into symbols, try to make deductions by relating the rules to each other. First of all, each stylist is required to see a W, an M, and two C's. They both must see exactly one more client. This last client must be either an adult (M or W) or a C. According to the rules, in whichever hour one of the hairstylists has a C the other hairstylist must have an M or a W and vice versa. If one of the stylists has an adult (either M or W) as their one remaining client then that stylist will see three adults and two C's over the five hour period. In each of the three hours that this stylist sees an adult, the other stylist will have to see a C and in each of the two hours that this stylist sees a C, the other stylist will have to see an adult (either an M or a W). Thus, it must always be the case that one stylist sees three adults and two C's and the other sees exactly three C's and two adults.

5. **"Walk Around It":** Each of the two hairstylists must have a W, an M, two C's, and a fifth client. One of the stylists sees a C as their fifth client and the other sees an adult, meaning that one stylist will see three adults and two C's and the other will see three C's and two adults. The questions are likely to test your understanding of the required number of adults and children. Don't forget that the first and last hours must be by appointment, so if you know that someone is in the first or fifth hour then you also know that that person had an appointment. Likewise, if you know that someone did not have an appointment, then you also know that that person does not get a haircut in the first or fifth hour.

1. **Type:** In this game you must assign eight people to one of two different vehicles, an SUV or a Minivan. This is clearly a grouping game, which means that blocks and splits will probably be very important. You do need to keep track of who the parents are, but you can accomplish this using the basic grouping setup.

2. **Diagram:** The diagram needs to show the two groups, which in this case are the two vehicles. Draw two columns labeled S and M to represent the two vehicles. You should note on the diagram that both groups must contain exactly four occupants.

3. **Simplify the rules:** The key to any game is to thoroughly understand the rules and how they relate to each other. The first step in this process is to understand what the rules say individually. Go through the rules one by one and take however much time is necessary for you to grasp what they say. As you do so, convert the rules into symbols. Do not leave out the rules contained within the setup paragraph. In this game there are eight people and exactly four occupants in each vehicle. There are three parents and five children. The first rule in the rules list says that S is in the vehicle with more children. This works two ways: If you know S is in one of the vehicles, then that vehicle must contain more children than the other, and if you know that one vehicle contains more children than the other, then you know that S is in that vehicle. The second rule creates a split between T and F. The next two rules give you conditional statements: If R is in the SUV, then V is in the SUV, and if D is in the Minivan, then S in the SUV. These conditional statements are straightforward and are easy to symbolize. The final rule is a little tricky: F does not drive the vehicle that Q rides in. This does not say that F and Q cannot be in the same vehicle. What it does say is that F cannot be the driver of the vehicle that Q is in. In other words, if F and Q are together then there is another parent in addition to F who is the driver.

4. **Deductions:** The next step is to make deductions. Relate the rules to each other and see if you can determine any additional information. Whenever there are conditional statements, it is helpful to first write down their contrapositives. You find the contrapositive by reversing the order of the statement and then negating both sides. Thus, the contrapositive of the rule that says "If R is in the SUV then V is in the SUV" is "If V is not in the SUV (which means that V is in the Minivan), then R is not in the SUV (which means that R is in the Minivan). Follow this same process for the remaining conditional statements. Once you have all the contrapositives, you can more easily relate the rules to each other. In grouping games, it is often helpful to make general deductions about the numerical distribution, especially when there are different categories of people to assign to the groups. For instance, there are three parents and two groups. There must be at least one parent in each group. Thus, one vehicle is going to have one parent and three children and the other vehicle is going to have two parents and two children. The first rule in the rules list says that S is in the vehicle with more children, so S must be in the group that has one parent and three children. Next, look at the rules governing the placement of the parents and children. There are two rules dealing with F, who is a parent: F cannot be with T and F cannot be the driver of Q. Since all of the people must be used, T must be in the vehicle that F is not in. In other words, F will be in one vehicle and T will be in the other. Since F cannot be with T, the only children that F can be with are R, S, V, and Q, although F cannot be the driver of Q. Each parent must be with at least two children, so F must be with at least two of V, R, S, and Q. If F is the only parent, then F must be with V, R, and S, since Q cannot be in the vehicle if F is the driver. With F, V, R, and S in one vehicle, the other vehicle would have to contain C, D, Q, and T. On the other hand, if F is one of two parents in a vehicle, then S can no longer be with F because S must be in the car with only one parent. S would have to be in the vehicle with T. In other words, F, C/D, and two of V, R, and Q would have to be in one vehicle, while the other vehicle would have to include C/D,

T, S, and one of V, R, or Q. Thus, there are only two basic scenarios: when F is the only parent and when F is with another parent. Notice that these scenarios do not allow you to determine which vehicle each set of four travels in. You will have to rely on the questions to provide extra information that will allow you to do so.

5. **"Walk Around It":** Before moving on to the questions, take a moment to walk around the game and get a feel for it. What do you know? What don't you know? From the deductions you know that there are only two basic scenarios. When F is the only parent, one vehicle contains F, V, R, and S, and the other contains C, D, Q, and T. When F is with another parent, one vehicle contains F, C/D, and two of V, R, and Q, and the other contains C/D, S, T, and one of V, R, and Q. Pay attention to the remaining rules, especially the relationships between D and S and the relationship between V and R, which will often allow you to determine which vehicle each group of four is actually in once you are given some additional information.

1. **Type:** In this game there are three days, Thursday through Saturday, in which the two travelers must visit eight sights. You can tell that this game is a grouping game because the key is the placement of each of the eight sights within the groups of Thursday, Friday, and Saturday.

2. **Diagram:** Since this is a grouping game, your diagram should clearly show the three groups with three columns labeled T, F, and S for Thursday, Friday, and Saturday.

3. **Simplify the rules:** Go through the rules one by one and turn them into symbols that you can more easily use and understand. This is also your opportunity to decipher exactly what each rule means. The rules here are fairly straightforward.

4. **Deductions:** It is very important to take a moment to examine exactly how the rules relate to each other, as well as to look for the side effects of those rules. A good first step in doing so is determining the contrapositive for each of the conditional statements. This will help you see what each rule actually means. After you have all the contrapositives, think carefully about the interplay among the rules. What else can you determine? The setup paragraph tells you that the travelers must see exactly eight sights over the three days and that they must visit at least two sights every day. Notice the effect that these two rules have on the possible numerical distribution of the eight sights. If as many days as possible have only two sights, then two days will have exactly two sights and the third day will have four. Thus, one possible distribution is 4–2–2. The only other distribution is if only one day has two sights. This would force the remaining two days to divide up six sights among them and the only way to do so without either of them having two sights is if both have three. Thus, the second basic distribution is 2–3–3. If at any time you know that there are four sights seen on a given day, then you

immediately know that the two remaining days must have two sights. Likewise, if you know that there are exactly three sights seen on any given day, then one other day must also have three sights while one day must have exactly two sights. Notice that neither of these distributions tells you exactly which day has which amount of sights. However, there are a limited number of possibilities due to the two rules dealing specifically with the numerical distribution. Look at the 2–3–3 distribution. The rules tell you that if three sights are seen on Thursday then three sights must be seen on Friday, which, according to the numerical distribution, means that they must see two sights on Saturday. Keeping the 2–3–3 distribution, if there are not three sights on Thursday, then there are only two, which means that there would be three sights on both Friday and Saturday. Thus, there are really only two possible distributions if the basic numerical distribution follows the 2–3–3 setup. In order from Thursday to Saturday these two possibilities are: 3–3–2 and 2–3–3. Now look at the 4–2–2 distribution. A rule says that if two sights are seen on Friday, then two sights must be seen on Saturday, which means that four sights must be seen on Thursday. Keeping the 4–2–2 distribution, if there are not two sights seen on Friday, then there must be four sights seen on Friday, which means that exactly two sights must be seen on both Thursday and Saturday. Just as with the 2–3–3 distribution, using the basic 4–2–2 distribution there are only two different possibilities, which from Thursday to Saturday are: 4–2–2 and 2–4–2. Notice that there can never be four sights seen on Saturday, since that would leave two sights on Friday, which, by rule, requires two sights

on Saturday. Although these deductions do not deal with the specific placement of sights to days, the knowledge about the numerical distribution will be vital, especially as it relates to the conditional statements that create links between different sights. Lastly, there are two rules dealing with M. If an M is seen on any day, then a P must be seen on that day as well. However, if there are two M's on the same day, then that day must be Saturday. There are only two M's and two P's. If the two M's are seen on different days, then the two P's must be seen on different days as well, one P seen on each day that an M is seen. However, if a P is seen on a day that an M is not seen, then both M's would have to be seen on the same day, which means that the two M's would have to be seen on Saturday along with the one remaining P.

5. **"Walk Around It"**: After you've worked on the deductions, pause for a quick overview of the game. This will help you to get a feel for what variables will affect the game. Pay close attention to the numerical distribution for each question. The only possibilities are, in order of Thursday to Saturday, 3–3–2, 2–3–3, 4–2–2, and 2–4–2. Once you know how many sights have to be or can be visited on a certain day, then the rules dealing with specific placements become important. For instance, the rule that says if M then P will be important. If there is an M somewhere, you know there must also be a P, which gives you at least two sights on that day. Remember, if there are two M's, then they must be seen on Saturday. Finally, although it goes without saying, keep track of the number of B's, L's, M's, and P's you have used.

1. **Type:** In this game there is a volleyball squad that must be divided into two teams of six people, team X and team Y. Within each of these teams the six players serve in order from one to six. Thus, there are two groups and within each of those groups there is an element of ordering. The grouping is more general while the ordering is more specific.

2. **Diagram:** The diagram should clearly show team X and team Y, which is easily done by drawing two columns labeled X and Y. Within each team, draw six spaces.

3. **Simplify the rules:** Like any grouping game, blocks, and splits are very important. The rules establish these blocks and splits. The first rule says that K is on a team with C but not with M, and serves neither first nor last. Actually, this rule contains three rules. It establishes a KC block, a KM split, and has an element of ordering by saying that K cannot be first or last. The rules establish two additional splits: J and L cannot be together, and G and H cannot be together. In addition to the blocks and splits, the rules fix C in the third spot on one of the teams, although it does not say on which team, and D in the fourth position from last on team Y. Since you know which team D must be on, put D directly on the diagram. If you count four positions forward from the sixth space on team Y, then you will see that D must be third on team Y. The remaining rule might be hard to understand at first. E, G, and B must serve fourth, fifth, and sixth, though not necessarily respectively, and not necessarily on the same team. This rule means that whichever team E, G, and B are on, they must be either fourth, fifth, or sixth. After you have simplified the rules and taken a moment to understand the rules individually, you are ready to make deductions.

4. **Deductions:** It initially appeared that you could not determine which team C was on, but after placing D on team Y as the third person, it is clear that C must be third on team X. The rules created a KC block which means that K must be on team X as well. Since K is on team X, and K and M cannot be on the same team, M must be on team Y. There are two other splits: J and L cannot be together, and G and H cannot be together. There are only two teams, so one person from each of those splits must play on each team. In other words, on team X you must have C, K, one of J or L, and one of G and H. Similarly, on team Y you must have D, M, one of J or L, and one of G or H. Thus, on both teams you know something about four of the six people. Each team therefore only has space for two additional players. The additional players include B, E, F, and I. The remaining rules do not allow you to make any firm deductions so you can move on to the "Walk Around It" step.

5. **"Walk Around It":** Team X includes C, K, one of J or L, and one of G or H. The order of the players on team X is restricted because K cannot serve first or last and C is third. Team Y includes D, M, one of J or L, and one of G or H. The only restriction on the order of the players on team Y is that D is third. On both teams, you know something about four out of the six players, leaving room for only two additional players per team. The players to choose from are B, E, F, and I. E and B are constrained by the rule that says E, G, and B serve fourth, fifth, and sixth, though not necessarily in that order and not necessarily on the same team. This rule means that if you know E, G, or B's position on one of the teams, then you know that the other two cannot be in the same position on the other team. Furthermore, if you know that some other person serves fourth, for example, on one team, then you know that since E, G, and B must serve fourth, fifth, and sixth in some combination, that one of them will be fourth on the other team. Also, the fact that E, G, and B must be fourth, fifth, and sixth means that all three of them are excluded from serving first or second on either team. Therefore, the players who can be first or second are limited. This interplay among E, G, and B is likely to be the key to working this game.

Setup Game 91

1. **Type:** In this game there are four couples that consist of one bridesmaid and one groomsman. These couples walk down the aisle in succession from first to fourth. Thus, there are three categories: order from first through fourth, bridesmaids, and groomsmen. These three categories create well-defined slots that you must place each bridesmaid and groomsman into. However, it is readily apparent that the game deals mainly with the order that the individuals and couples walk down the aisle. This is a hybrid game that creates slots but focuses on the order.

2. **Diagram:** As a slots game the diagram should have four columns labeled 1 through 4 and two rows labeled in some manner to represent bridesmaids and groomsmen. You will place a bridesmaid into each bridesmaid slot and one groomsman into each groomsman slot. Because this is largely an ordering game, you may not need to use this complete diagram for every question; rather, you may need to create a separate list of order for each question.

3. **Simplify the rules:** In order to have at least a glimmer of hope of answering the questions correctly, you must understand the rules. Take the time to convert them into symbols, not only so that you have to interpret them in order to do so, but also that you get rid of all the pesky, time-wasting words. Instead, create a list of symbols that you can glance at and comprehend instantly. This is relatively easy with ordering games. For instance, the first two rules can be symbolized as: C..F and G..B. The third rule can be split into two rules: B..D and C..D. The final rule focuses on the slots aspect of the game: B and F do not form a pair. They must occupy two different positions in the order.

4. **Deductions:** The next step is to make deductions. Relate the rules to each other to see what additional information you can determine. Once again, in ordering situations this is relatively easy. Combine the rules that contain the same item. For instance, from the two rules that tell you G..B and B..D, you can determine that the order must look like this: G..B..D. You are left with two pieces of information about C: C..F and C..D. Since you know something about the placement of D you also know that C must be before D. Be careful, because you do not know the placement of C relative to G or B and neither do you know the placement of F relative to G, B, or D, although you do know that B cannot be paired with F. Now that you have this list of relative order, it is important to remember that you have two categories of people: bridesmaids and groomsmen. Label each of these people as either a bridesmaid or groomsman so that you can keep track of everybody. B, C, and D are all groomsmen. A is the wildcard groomsman. G and F are bridesmaids. E and H are the wildcard bridesmaids. Using this setup, ask yourself what you know at this point. What must be true? Out of the four groomsmen, you know that both B and C must be before D, so the earliest that D can be is third. There are only four spaces so D must be third or fourth. Out of the bridesmaids you know something about the placement of G and F. First, consider what you know about G. G must be before both B and D, so G cannot be third or fourth. The latest in the order that G can be is second. Furthermore, since G must be before both B and D, G cannot be paired with either B or D. Thus, G must walk down the aisle with either A or C. Next, consider what you know about F. The placement of F is restricted by two requirements: F must be after C, and F cannot be paired with B. Because F must come after C, F cannot be part of the first pair to walk down the aisle. The two rules governing the placement of F also reveal that F cannot be paired with B or C, which means that F must walk down the aisle with either A or D. This is everything that stands out, so quickly review what you know as you walk around the game and then move on to the questions.

5. **"Walk Around It":** Here you have a strange ordering game where you also have to keep track of who is a bridesmaid and who is a groomsman. The main sequence that you have is: G..B..D. Since these three people must be in separate couples, you know at least one person in three of the four couples. This tells you right away that the latest G could be is second and that the earliest that D could be is third. You also know that C is before D and that F must come sometime after C. E, H, and A are the wildcards, meaning that their placement is not restricted by any rule directly. Watch out for any information that allows you to determine at least one person in each of the four couples. For instance, placing someone before G or after D allows you to know at least one person in each of the four couples. From there you can apply the other rules and determine other things. Keep track of B and F because they cannot be a couple.

1. **Type:** In this game there are four days, 1 through 4, on which Ralph must record the direction of the wind in the morning and in the afternoon. He must record the wind direction as north (N), south (S), east (E), or west (W). This setup shows that the only variable in this game is the direction of the wind, while the other categories remain fixed. This makes it a slots game.

2. **Diagram:** The diagram for this game should show the fixed categories of days 1 through 4 as well as the morning and afternoon of each day. This is easily accomplished by making four columns labeled 1 through 4 and two rows labeled a.m. and p.m.

3. **Simplify the rules:** Now go to the rules and read them carefully so that you understand what each says. If possible, turn the rules into easily understandable symbols and write them down in your workspace. This will not only help you save time in the long run by keeping your work in a single area, but it will also force you to understand what the rules are saying. Don't forget the rules that are contained in the setup paragraph itself, which, in this case, are the rules that say that Ralph cannot record the same wind direction for the morning and afternoon of any day, and that he cannot record the same wind direction for consecutive mornings or afternoons. The rules in the rules list are fairly straightforward. First, the wind direction cannot be both N and S in the same day, nor can it be both E and W in the same day. Second, if Ralph records the wind direction as E in the morning, then the direction is N in that afternoon. The third statement means that if the wind is recorded as N or W on days 1 through 3, then there must be an S on the following day.

Setups

4. **Deductions:** Now that you know what the rules mean as they are stated, it is time to go back to the rules and determine the ramifications of each rule, especially as each rule relates to the other rules. As usual, a good place to start is with the contrapositives. Find the "if…then" statements and then reverse and negate them. For example, the rule that says that if Ralph records the wind direction as E in the morning, then the direction is N in that afternoon, also means that if the direction is not N in the afternoon, then the wind direction is not E in the morning. The next conditional statement says that if the wind is recorded as N or W on days 1 through 3, then there must be an S on the following day. The contrapositive of this rule is that if there is no S on any given day, then there is neither an N nor a W on the previous day. What does this mean? If there is no N or W on a day, then that day must have an S and an E. The previous contrapositive revealed that if there is no N in the afternoon, then there is no E in the morning, so in the case where the two recordings for a day are S and E (with no N in the afternoon), the S must be in the morning and the E must be in the afternoon. Thus, putting the pieces together, this contrapositive demonstrates that if there is no S on any given day, then the previous day must have an S and an E, with the S in the morning, and the E in the afternoon. After looking at the contrapositives, think about how the remaining rules relate to each other. It is important to realize that Ralph cannot record the same wind direction for both readings on any day and that he cannot record both N and S or both E and W on any day. What these two rules mean, when taken together, is that if Ralph records the wind direction as either N or S on any day, then the other reading for that day can neither be an N nor an S. In other words, if Ralph records the wind direction as either N or S for one reading during a day, then the second reading

for that day must be E or W. Likewise, if an E or W is used on any given day, then the second direction for that day must be either N or S. Thus, one of N or S and one of E or W must be used on every day. This helps clarify the deduction made about any day that does not include an S. You already know that any day that does not have an S must be preceded by a day that includes an S in the morning and an E in the afternoon. But it is also the case that any day that does not include an S must include an N. According to one of the conditional statements, if there is an N on any day 1, day 2, or day 3, then the following day must include an S. Thus, if one of day 1 through 3 does not include an S, then the following day must include an S. Therefore, the rules require that any day that does not have an S be preceded by a day that has an S and followed by a day that has an S. Lastly, the two conditional rules allow you to make a final deduction. The first conditional statement says that if there is an E in the morning, then there is an N in that afternoon, and the second conditional statement says that if there is an N on days 1 through 3, then there must be an S on the following day. These two rules together reveal that if there is an E in the morning of one of days 1 through 3, then there is an S on the following day.

5. **"Walk Around It":** Based on your deductions, you can see that the rules are very interrelated. Any information about S will tell you quite a bit of information, so watch for S, especially if there is no S on any day. If there is no S then there must be an S in the previous morning, an E in the previous afternoon, and an S on the following day. Also, keep in mind the rule that there can be no consecutive mornings or afternoons that are the same, and that there cannot be both N and S or both E and W on the same day.

1. **Type:** While reading the setup and the rules for the game, try to decide what basic type of game it is. In this game there are five cages, four of which must be filled with exactly one of seven types of animal. You might think of this game as a mix between a grouping game and a slots game. It has elements of grouping in that you must determine the group of four animals that are relocated to the new cages. It has elements of a slots game because you then have to place each of those four animals in a distinct slot, or cage.

2. **Diagram:** Your diagram should include five columns labeled 1 through 5 to represent the five cages.

3. **Simplify the rules:** Look at the rules one by one and simplify them. Don't forget the rules contained within the setup paragraph. Here the rules are fairly straightforward: There are five cages but one will remain empty. Each type of animal can only be in one cage. If D then D is in cage 1. If L then L is in cage 2. If K then K is in cage 4. If either E or G, then both must be used and must be in adjacent cages. If E then L, and exactly one of H or K must be used. Convert all these rules into symbols that you can understand and work with easily.

4. **Deductions:** Look at the rules and see how they relate to one another. A good place to start is by writing down the contrapositives to all the conditional statements. After you have the contrapositives written down, think about the setup and how the rules relate to that setup and to each other. There are five cages but only four cages need to be filled; there are seven animals with which to fill these four cages. One cage must have one of H or K, but not both. Since H and K cannot both be used, there are effectively only six items to choose from: D, E, G, J, L, and H/K. Four of these items will have to be used. Since H/K must be used, the remaining three cages must be filled with three of D, E, H, J, and L. The remaining rules largely deal with the placement of E. If you have E, then you must also have G and L, which gives you all four animals: E, G, L, and H/K. L would have to be in cage 2, and since E and G must be consecutive, they would have to be in either cages 3 and 4 or cages 4 and 5. Either way, cage 4 would be filled. Since if K is used then K is in cage 4, you know that if E is used then there is no K, or, in other words, since either H or K must be used, if E is used then H is used. The contrapositive of this deduction is that if K is used, then E is not. Thus, using an E produces a scenario where L, E, G, and H are the four types of animals that fill the four used cages, although not in that order. Now consider what happens if you do not use an E. If there is no E, then there is no G, leaving you with only D, J, and L to fill the three remaining cages. Thus, if E is not used, which must be the case if K is used, then the scenario that results is one in which D, J, L, and H/K fill the four used cages. In either scenario L must be included, and if L, then L=2. Therefore, L will always be in cage 2.

5. **"Walk Around It":** The key for this game will be to know which scenario you are working with. The first scenario, where E is included, includes E, G, L, and H as the four animals that must be in the four cages that are filled with animals. L must be in cage 2 and E and G must be in adjacent cages. The second scenario, where E is not included, includes D, J, L, and H/K as the animals that fill the four cages. D must be in cage 1 and L must be in cage 2. You will know which scenario you are dealing with if you know whether are not E is included (E must be and can only be in the first scenario), whether or not D is included (D must be and can only be in the second scenario), whether or not J is included (J must be and can only be included in the second scenario), and if you know that K is included, since K can only be included in the second scenario. Be sure to note the placement of the empty cage, for any information about which cage is empty might allow you to determine which animals can and cannot be included. For example, if cage 1 is empty, then D cannot be included because D can only be in cage 1. If D is not included, then you must be dealing with scenario 1. Now you are ready for the questions.

1. **Type:** In this game there are eighteen flowers from which a florist can choose to create a flower arrangement that includes exactly nine flowers. These nine flowers are one of three types, R, C, or I. Each type of flower has six flowers of various colors available. This is a grouping game, because you must build one group of nine flowers. However, you might also think of the three types of flowers as three different groups, into which you must place the various colors. Regardless, it will be your task to determine the number and color of the flowers included from each type of flower in the arrangement.

2. **Diagram:** In this grouping game, you will have to build a group of nine flowers with three types of flowers. Each type of flower can only be certain colors. If you consider this as only one group, there will be no clear diagram. You will have to create a new diagram for each question. On the other hand, if you think of this game as having three groups, you can draw three columns labeled R, C, and I to represent the three types of flowers, and then you can place into those three columns the number and colors of that type of flower that are used.

3. **Simplify the rules:** Simplify the rules by converting them into symbols. These symbols will help save time and the process of converting the rules into symbols has the added benefit of requiring you to think about and interpret the rules. First, there are the basic rules in the setup: There are R's, C's, and I's, with various colors of each available. You should write down all the colors available for each type of flower in your workspace. The rules list contains the bulk of the game. First, all three types of flowers must be used. Second, there must be more R's than C's (R > C). Third, there must not be fewer C's than I's. This requires some thought. If there must not be fewer C's then I's, then there must be at least as many C's as I's. In other words, the number of C's included must be greater than or equal to the number of I's (C ≥ I).

Fourth, there must be more white flowers than pink flowers (w > p). Finally, the fifth and sixth rules require the same interpretation as the rule above concerning the number of C's and I's: The number of red flowers must be greater than or equal to the number of pink flowers (r ≥ p) and the number of yellow flowers must be greater than or equal to the number of red flowers (y ≥ r).

4. **Deductions:** The next step is to make deductions. You make deductions by relating the rules to each other. Often, two or more different rules, when combined, will reveal additional restraints on the setup or other additional information. This additional information will be extremely useful throughout the game. First, consider the three groups and the numerical distribution of flowers among those groups. There must be nine flowers in the arrangement and there must be at least one of each type of flower. There must be more R's than C's, and the number of C's must be greater than or equal to the number of I's. These requirements restrict the number of flowers that can be in the three groups. For instance, it is possible that there is only one I. If there is only one I, then there must be eight flowers distributed among R and C, but since there must be more R's than C's, the way in which those flowers can be distributed is restricted to either six R's and two C's or five R's and three C's. On the other hand, if there are two I's, then there must be seven flowers distributed among R and C, but since there must be more R's than C's and at least as many C's as I's, the way in which those seven flowers can be distributed is restricted to either five R's and two C's or four R's and three C's. If there were three I's, then there would also have to be at least three C's, which in turn would require that there be at least four R's. This is too many flowers. Thus, there must either be one or two I's, restricting the game to the four numerical distributions determined above, where there can be one or two I's, two or three C's, and anywhere between four and six R's. Next, consider the rules about the number of colors included in the arrangement. The rules say that the number of yellow flowers is greater than or equal to the number of red flowers and that the number of red flowers must be greater than or equal to the number of pink flowers. In other

words, the rules allow you to build a list of the relative number of colors that looks like this: $y \geq r \geq p$. Additionally, there must be more white flowers than pink flowers ($w > p$). Be careful, this does not tell you anything directly about the number of white flowers relative to the number of yellow flowers or the number of red flowers; however, it does tell you something vital about white flowers. If there must be more white flowers than pink flowers, it is impossible for there to ever be no white flowers included in the arrangement. In other words, there must always be at least one white flower. Because there must be at least one white flower, there must be at the most eight total yellow, red, and pink flowers. Since there can be at most eight total yellow, red, and pink flowers, and because the number of both red and yellow flowers must be greater than the number of pink flowers, it is impossible for there to be more than two pink flowers. To check this, see what would happen if there were three pink flowers. If there were three pink flowers then there would have to be at least three red flowers, at least three yellow flowers, and at least one white flower, giving you at least ten flowers. Thus, there can be at the most two pink flowers.

5. **"Walk Around It":** Walk around the game for a moment and get a feel for what the game will require you to do. There are two basic factors here: First, there is the numerical distribution of the nine flowers among the three groups and second, there is the numerical distribution of the colors of the nine flowers. These two categories (type of flower and color) are closely related, for each type of flower can only include certain colors. The questions will likely test your understanding of each of these categories separately, as well as force you to notice the relationships across categories. For instance, you might have to determine the effect of having three red flowers on the number of white flowers or you might have to determine the effect of having three red flowers on the number of R's. As in this brief example, each question will probably introduce some condition and require you to work out the consequences. As you do so, use the deductions and always be on the lookout for side effects.

1. **Type:** First ask what type of game you are dealing with here. There are items that must be placed into fixed, well-defined positions. Even though there is more than one option for each position, the coach must select exactly one player to fill each of the five positions. You have a slots game.

2. **Diagram:** The spots in the game are identified by a single variable, a number 1 through 5. The simplest and clearest diagram is just to write the numbers 1 through 5 as columns, leaving plenty of room to chart out different solutions. Drawing lines may result in extra work, messiness and perhaps confusion.

3. **Simplify the rules:** Now go to the rules and interpret them. Do not be overwhelmed by the number of rules. Half of them are actually part of the basic setup and can be incorporated directly on the diagram to save time and space, and, more importantly, to gain clarity. So for the first rule, under column 1, you would write G, H, and I to indicate that those are the only items that might be placed in that spot. Do the same for the rest of the rules that give you items for positions 2 though 5. The last four rules are conditional statements. Convert these into symbols. These conditional statements are what the questions will test.

4. **Deductions:** The critical step is to make deductions. First, write down the contrapositives for every conditional statement: If M is not in position 5, then J is not in the starting line-up. If K is placed in the line-up, then I is not, if K is not used then G and M cannot both be used. And if G is not in position 1, then L is not in position 4. Once you have written out the rules and their contrapositives, you have in front of you everything that the game will be testing. However, the true task is not only to understand and interpret the rules individually, but also to understand how

the rules relate to each other. This ability to comprehend how various rules interrelate and bring about different consequences under different conditions is the essence of analytical thinking. This is what these games are all about, so take the time to do the work and thinking that is required of you. First of all, it is helpful to notice that there are a few players that are unique to some positions. For instance, I can only be placed in position 1, J can only be assigned to position 2, and O can only be assigned to position 3. Additionally, position 5 is very limited; it must contain either L or M. Next, think about how these restricted placements relate to the conditional statements. One rule says if I is included in the starting line-up, then K cannot be included. Remember, if I is included, I must be in position 1, so if I is in position 1, then K cannot be included. If K is not included then, according to one of the contrapositives, G and M cannot both be used. It is important to note that this does not mean that neither G nor M can be used, but that they cannot both be used at the same time. In other words, at least one of G or M will not be used. Furthermore, since K cannot be included, K is no longer an option for position 3 or 4. This limits position 4 to only L or M, similar to position 5. However, if I is included in position 1, then it must also be the case that G is not in position 1, which, according to another contrapositive, means that L cannot be in position 4. Since position 4 was limited to L or M and now cannot be L, M must be assigned to position 4, which in turn means that L must be assigned to position 5. Remember, since K is not included, G and M cannot be included in the starting line-up and now that you know M must be included when I is, you also know that G cannot be included. Since G and K cannot be included and M is already assigned to position 4, position 3 must be assigned to O. Only position 2 remains to be filled and it must be filled with either H or J. However, since M is not in position 5, J cannot be in position 2. Thus, if I is included, you can determine the entire setup. To recap, if I is included, then I is in position 1, H must

be assigned to position 2, O must be assigned to position 3, M must be assigned to position 4, and L must be assigned to position 5. This also reveals that if I is included, G cannot be included, K cannot be included, and J cannot be included. If any of these consequences are not true for any of the questions, then you know immediately that I is not included. Whew! That was what happened when I was included. The two other players who are absolutely restricted are J and O. However, knowing that J or O is included does not allow you to deduce a long chain as did including I. If J is included, then J must be assigned to position 2 and, because J is included, M must be assigned to position 5. This leaves you with positions 1, 3, and 4, and the relationship between G, M, and K becomes very important. If O is included, then O must be assigned to position 3. This does not allow you to determine anything else. This was a lot of work and a lot to deduce, but if you did not do it now, you would be forced to do it later on and under more constraints such that you probably would not notice that it is a deduction that must be true at all times, the same as if it were written in the rules.

5. **"Walk Around It":** Because you may have spent a lot of time making deductions, you might feel compelled to rush on to the questions. However, it is still smart to think one more time about what you do and do not know, as well as what the keys to this game are likely to be. Working out the deduction concerning I really helps you get a feel for how this game will work. Obviously the deduction about I will be vital, but it also showed you that any information will likely cause a chain reaction. Position 5 is the most restricted of all the positions. Knowing that either L or M is used anywhere else or, on the other hand, not used at all will tell you who must be assigned to position 5. Information about position 5 will in turn tell you something about J, etc. There goes that chain reaction again! You are now ready for the questions.

1. **Type:** In this game there are six kites that fly at six different altitudes. Your task is to determine as much as you can about the relative altitude of the different kites. The rules give you information about the altitudes. Don't let the terminology confuse this; this is a standard ordering game that talks about "altitude," "higher," and "lower" instead of "order," "before," and "after."

2. **Diagram:** The basic diagram for this, as for other ordering games, is a list of the spaces that you will be dealing with. Here, since there are six kites, each of which is at a different altitude, there will be six spaces. Right now, that is all you know. You can either work with the spaces vertically so that you can visualize the altitudes or you can work horizontally. If you work horizontally, be clear on which end is higher and which end is lower. The working diagram will actually be a list of the relative order of the different kites that you will compile from the rules.

3. **Simplify the rules:** Simplify the rules by converting them into symbols. In ordering games, this is easy to do. The first rule says there is an R that is higher than a B and lower than a G. Since the rules specifies that it is the same R that is lower than G and higher than B, this gives you a small list of the relative order of the kites: G..R..B. The second rule says a B is higher than a G, which becomes: B..G. The last two rules tell you that a B cannot be first or last and that no B can be immediately next to a G. This step is a great opportunity to make sure that you understand what the rules mean. As always, don't forget the rules contained within the setup paragraph. In this case, the setup paragraph tells you that every color must be used and that the setup includes no more than two of any particular color.

4. **Deductions:** Making deductions allows you to see the big picture. To make deductions, think about how the various rules relate to each other and what side effects each rule has. First, start with the condition that no more than two of the six kites are the same color. If there are six kites, at least one of each of the four different colors, and no more than two kites that have the same color, then there must be exactly two doubles. In other words, there will be one of each different color and then one more of two different colors. This is important to know. Now move on to what you were given about the relative order of the kites. The information about relative order included in this game is somewhat different than most games because there could be (and must be) more than one of a few of the colors. Because there can be more than one of each color of kite, the relative order given to you in the rules is somewhat flexible. The two rules about relative order are: G..R..B and B..G. Because of the flexibility in the number of the same colored kites, these two rules create two different scenarios. A B must be above a G, but you cannot yet determine whether that B is the same B that is in the G..R..B sequence. If it is, then the order would be G..R..B..G. Since there could be more than one B, the B that is above a G could be above the entire G..R..B sequence. Thus, the other possible order of kites is B..G..R..B. Take a look at the first scenario: G..R..B..G. According to the rules, no B can be adjacent to a G, so there must be at least one kite in between the B and the G such that the scenario is now G..R..B.._..G. The kite between the B and the G cannot be another B or another G, so it must either be an R or a Y (G..R..B..R/Y..G). Filling the gap gives you five of the six kites. The sixth kite's color and placement in the order can vary depending on what color kite fills the gap between B and G. No matter what, the sixth kite cannot be a G, since two G's have already been used. Since the sixth kite cannot be a G, it could be one of B, R, or Y. If it is B, you must still keep the B's and G's separated. Also, note that according to the rules, there must be at least one kite of each color. In this scenario, there is not yet a Y. Now look at the second possible order: B..G..R..B, placing the B that must be above a G above the entire G..R..B sequence. Again,

there would have to be a kite in between the B and the G such that the order is B.._..G.. R..B. However, according to the rules, no B is highest or lowest. In this setup a B would have to be either highest or lowest no matter where you place the sixth kite, so in actuality, this is not a possible scenario. Thus, there is only one scenario: G..R..B..R/Y..G, with the sixth kite relatively unrestrained.

5. **"Walk Around It":** Before even going to the questions, you know that there is only one basic scenario that works for this game: G..R.. B..R/Y..G. The sixth kite's color and order largely depends on which kite is in between the B and the G and vice versa. Again, do not forget that no matter what, there must be a Y, and you do not yet have one in the order of kites.

1. **Type:** In this game there are five awards that must be assigned to each of five students. Each student will receive exactly one award. Since each student will have a unique award, you might consider this a slots game. However, a glance at the rules reveals that they are not standard slots rules. They are all conditional statements in some form or another. You have no hard and fast information to work with. Essentially what you will have to do is match students to awards by applying the appropriate rules.

2. **Diagram:** There is no diagram for this game. What you end up with after simplifying the rules and making deductions is simply a long chain of conditional statements that will aid you in matching students to awards.

3. **Simplify the rules:** A large part of this game (as in any game) is interpreting the rules correctly. Without determining what it is that the rules actually say, you cannot work through the game correctly. Here, that task is complicated by complex rules with wording that requires careful interpretation. As you decipher each rule, convert it into easily understandable symbols. If any rule needs to be split into two separate rules, do so. The first rule here says that if K does not receive L, then K receives G and B receives L. This rule actually provides you with two pieces of information. First, K must receive either L or G (because if K doesn't receive L, K receives G). Second, if K does not receive L, which means that K does receive G, then B must receive L. Thus, there are two pieces of information here: 1) $K = L/G$ and 2) $K_G \rightarrow B_L$. The second rule is oddly worded and requires careful interpretation. It begins by saying "In the circumstance that N receives S," so you know that this is really a conditional statement that can be interpreted as "if N receives S, then…" What must result when N receives S is that D receives G, unless F receives G. Simply stated, this means that when N receives S, either D is going to receive G or F is going to receive G. Thus, this rule

can be simplified to say that if N receives S then either D or F receives G ($N_S \rightarrow D_G/F_G$). The third rule is another rule that contains "unless," which is a bit tricky to interpret at times. The rule states that F cannot receive the award for S or R unless D does not receive an award for S or R. Stated differently, there is no way for F to receive S or R unless D does not receive S or R. F can receive S or R only if D does not receive either S or R. D not receiving an S or R is a necessary condition for F receiving S or R, or is the consequence of F receiving S or R. Translated into an "if… then" statement, this becomes "If F receives S or R, then D does not receive S or R." This reveals one of the general approaches to an "unless" statement. "Unless" can be seen as introducing the necessary condition, or the consequent. The other part of the statement can then be negated, and becomes the antecedent. Consider the above rule again: F cannot receive the award for S or R unless D does not receive an award for S or R. Leaving what follows "unless" as is and negating the first part of the statement gives you the conditional: If F receives S or R, then D does not receive S or R. The final rule is another conditional statement, this time with an "only if": B does not receive L only if N receives S. "Only if" always introduces the necessary condition, or the consequent. Rewritten as a standard "if…then" statement, this rule becomes "If B does not receive L, then N receives S" ($\sim B_L \rightarrow N_S$).

4. **Deductions:** The next step is to make deductions, to see if the relationships among the rules lead to any new information. In order to better see what each rule says, it is usually helpful to write down the contrapositive of each of the conditional statements. You can obtain the contrapositive by reversing the statement and negating both sides. For example, the rule that says if B does not receive L then N receives S also means that if N does not receive S then B receives L. Once you have determined the contrapositives, look for any rules that deal with the same person or award. There are two rules that deal with N receiving or not receiving S, so start there. One rule tells you the effects of N receiving S, while the

contrapositive just mentioned tells you the effects of N not receiving S. No matter what, N must either receive S or not receive S, so these two rules provide you with the key to this game. There are only two possible scenarios, one where N receives S and one where N does not, so take the time to work through both of these scenarios. First, consider what happens when N does not receive S. According to the rules, if N does not receive S then B receives L. In this case, N does not receive S, so B must receive L. Since B receives L, K cannot receive L, which means that K must receive G. With B receiving L and K receiving G, you are left with awards S, C, and R for graduates D, F, and N. One of the rules states that if F receives S or R, then D does not receive S or R. In this scenario, S, C, and R are the only awards left, so one of F or D will have to receive either S or R. Thus, the other of D or F cannot receive S or R, which, in this case, means that that person must receive C. Thus, either D or F must receive C. This leaves N and the other of D or F to receive S and R, though not necessarily in that order. However, the condition that introduced this scenario, that N does not receive S, allows you to determine that N must, in this case, receive R, leaving the one of D or F that does not receive the C to receive the S. Working out this chain reveals that knowing that N does not receive S allows you to determine a great deal about the awards. When N does not receive S, B must receive L, K must receive G, one of D or F must receive C, the other one of D or F must receive S, and N must receive R. Now that you have determined what results when N does not receives S, take a moment to determine what results when N does receive S. According to the rules, if N receives S then either D or F must receive G. Although, you cannot determine which one of D or F receives G, you know for certain that it is impossible for K to receive G. According to one of the rules, K must either receive L or G. Since G is no longer an option here, K must receive L. With N receiving S, F or D receiving G, and K receiving L, you are left with awards C and R for graduates B and the other of D or F, though not necessarily in that order. The rules by themselves do not provide enough information to allow you to determine exactly who receives C and R. Working out this second scenario, where N receives S, allows you to determine that one of D or F must receive G, that K must receive L, that B must receive one of C or R, and that the other of D or F must also receive one of C or R. Interpreting the rules correctly reveal only two scenarios for this game, which will simplify the game a great deal.

5. **"Walk Around It":** The rules lead to only two scenarios, one where N does not receive S and one where N does receive S. When N does not receive S, B must receive L, K must receive G, one of D or F must receive C, the other one of D or F must receive S, and N must receive R. The only uncertainty in this scenario is that you do not know which one of D or F receives C and which one of D or F receives S. When N does receives S, one of D or F must receive G, K must receive L, B must receive one of C or R, and the other of D or F must also receive one of C or R. The remaining uncertainties in this scenario are that you do not know which one of D or F receives G, which one of D or F receives C or R, and whether B receives C or R. These two scenarios will make the questions much easier to approach. Simply determine which scenario you are dealing with in each question and work from there.

1. **Type:** In this game, nine students must each be assigned to one of two teams. Thus, this is a standard grouping game.

2. **Diagram:** The diagram for this grouping game is simply two columns. These columns should be labeled "J" or "JV" for the junior varsity squad and "V" for the varsity squad.

3. **Simplify the rules:** In order to work through the game correctly, you must understand the rules of the game, so take the time to understand them. Go through the rules and determine exactly what each means. As you do so, convert the rules into easily understandable symbols. Write these symbols down in your work area so that you can access them quickly. Do not forget the rules that are contained within the setup paragraph, such as the rule that says the JV squad has four people on it and the varsity squad has five. The bulk of the rules in this game are conditional statements. In order to symbolize them correctly, you must determine which part of the statement is the antecedent and which part of the statement is the consequent. In other words, you must determine what part of the statement is sufficient to produce the other. The first conditional rule says that R is not on the varsity squad unless K is on the varsity squad. Conditional statements that include "unless" require careful interpretation. This statement does not mean that if K is on the varsity squad then R must be on the varsity squad. It says that there is no way for R to be on the varsity squad unless K is there. In other words, R can be on the varsity squad only if K is there. K's presence on the varsity squad is a necessary condition for R being on the varsity squad, not a sufficient one. Since K's presence on the varsity squad is a necessary condition for R being on the varsity squad, R's presence on the varsity squad is enough to tell you that K is on the varsity squad. R's presence on the varsity squad is sufficient for K being on the varsity squad. As a standard "if...then" statement, this becomes "If R is on varsity, then K is on varsity" $(R_V \rightarrow K_V)$. Remember, "unless" introduces the necessary condition,

or the consequent. Negate the remainder of the statement and that becomes the sufficient condition, or the antecedent. Another approach is to translate "unless" as "if not." You might have approached this rule by translating "unless" to "if not" such that it read, "R is not on the varsity squad if K is not on the varsity squad." The contrapositive of this statement then says, "If R is on the varsity squad, then K is not on the varsity squad" ($R_V \rightarrow K_V$). When it comes to "unless" it is often helpful to keep an example in mind: You cannot do well on the LSAT unless you have a pencil. Having a pencil is a necessary, not a sufficient, condition for doing well. Rather, doing well is sufficient to know that you had a pencil. The next two conditional statements are in standard form and are easy to symbolize: $Z_{JV} \rightarrow S_V$ and $J_V \rightarrow S_{JV}$ (Note that for this second conditional the rule said, "If J is not on the junior varsity squad then S is not on the varsity squad..." but since there are only two squads and everybody must be included on a squad, if J is not on the junior varsity squad then J must be on the varsity squad. Likewise, if S is not on the varsity squad, then S must be on the junior varsity squad. This reasoning only applies when there are only two groups and everybody must be used). The final conditional statement says that Geek 2 is assigned to the varsity squad only if Geek 3 is assigned to the varsity squad. Like "unless," "only if" requires careful interpretation. "Only if" introduces a necessary condition, or the consequent. Thus, this rule means that if Geek 2 is assigned to the varsity squad, then Geek 3 is assigned to the varsity squad. It is important to note that these conditional statements do not create blocks and splits. For instance, the rule that says (in its revised form) if R is on varsity then K is on varsity does not create a block of R and K. R and K must be together whenever R is on varsity, but it is possible for R to be on junior varsity without K. Likewise, the rule that says if Z is on the junior varsity squad then S is on the varsity squad does not create a split between Z and S. Z and S must be on different squads when Z is on the junior varsity squad, but Z and S could still be together on the varsity squad. The two remaining rules tell you that exactly one of Z or Geek 3 must be on the junior varsity squad and that there is a split between Geek 1 and Geek 2.

4. **Deductions:** The next step is to make deductions. What can you deduce from the interplay among the rules? In order to make deductions more effectively, write down the contrapositives to all the conditional statements. You find the contrapositive by reversing and negating the statement. Look, for instance, at the first conditional statement, which says that if R is on V, then K is on V. Reversing and negating, the contrapositive becomes if K is on JV (not on V), then R is on JV (not on V). Again, this rule does not create a block of R and K. It is possible for R to be on JV and K to be on V. Do the same for the remaining conditional statements. Once you have the contrapositives, try to relate the rules to each other. In this game you are pointed in the right direction by the rules themselves. The very first rule says that either Z or Geek 3 is on the JV squad, but not both. This rule just restricted the game to two basic scenarios. When a game limits the possibilities like this, go ahead and work out the scenarios. First, consider what occurs when Z is assigned to the JV squad. There are two immediate results of Z being on the JV squad. First, Geek 3 must be assigned to the varsity squad, and, second, S must be assigned to the varsity squad. Look at the effects of both of these placements. One of the contrapositives says that if Geek 3 is on the varsity squad, then Geek 2 must also be on the varsity squad. With Geek 2 now on varsity, you can place Geek 1 on JV since Geek 1 and Geek 2 can never be on the same squad. Now look at the result of placing S on the varsity squad. According to a contrapositive, if S is on varsity, then J must be on JV. Recapping what you've learned so far, placing Z on JV allows you to determine immediately that Z, Geek 1, and J are on the JV squad and that Geek 3, Geek 2, and S are on the varsity squad. Now the numerical distribution becomes important. At this point you know three of the four people on the JV squad. The fourth person must be one of R, K, or L. However, according to a contrapositive, if K is on JV, then R is on JV. In other words, placing K on JV carries R along as well. But there is not room for both K and R on JV, so it cannot be the case that K is on the JV squad. Since K cannot be on JV, K must be on varsity. Now both squads are missing one person, and the

only students left are R and L (Note that K's being on varsity does not tell you anything about the placement of R). Exactly one of R or L must be on each squad. You now know practically everything about the groups, except for the exact placement of R and L. This is the first scenario. When Z is on JV then the Z, Geek 1, J, and one or R or L must be on the JV squad and Geek 3, Geek 2, S, K, and the other of R or L must be on the varsity squad. Now consider the second scenario, when Geek 3 is assigned to the JV squad. This scenario lacks many of the constraints of the first. All that you can immediately determine is that Z is on the varsity squad. Since Geek 1 and Geek 2 can never be on the same squad, one of Geek 1 or Geek 2 must be on each squad. Thus, the JV squad would have to include Geek 3 and one of Geek 1 or 2, leaving exactly two positions on the JV squad. These two positions seem completely flexible, but look closer. One of the rules says that if J is on varsity then S is on JV. The contrapositive says that if S is on varsity, then J is on JV. This rule tells you that it is impossible for J and S to be together on the varsity squad (though they could be together on the JV squad). Since J and S cannot be together on the varsity squad, at least one of J or S must be on the JV squad, which means that you know something about three of the four positions of the JV squad. Just as in the first scenario, there is now no longer room for both K and R, and if K were on JV, then R would have to be there as well. Thus, K cannot be on the JV squad and must instead be on the varsity squad (but this doesn't tell you anything about R!). The second scenario now has Geek 3, exactly one of Geek 1 or 2, and at least one of S or J on the JV squad and Z, the other of Geek 1 or 2, and K on the varsity squad. Again, R and L are left over, but in this case they can be on either squad. You should also note that in both scenarios, K must be on the varsity squad. This is as certain as if it were stated as a rule.

5. **"Walk Around It":** The rules allowed you to deduce that there are only two basic scenarios, one in which Z is on the JV squad and one in which Geek 3 is on the JV squad. When Z is on the JV squad, then the JV squad must include Z, Geek 1, J, and one of R or L, while the varsity squad must include Geek 3, Geek 2, S, K, and the other of R or L. The only uncertainty is the exact placement of R and L. The second scenario is more flexible. When Geek 3 is on the JV squad, then the JV squad must consist of Geek 3, one of Geek 1 and 2, and at least one of S or J, while the varsity squad must consist of Z, the other of Geek 1 or 2, K, and two other students. R and L are again free, restrained only by the numerical requirements. As you go through the questions, watch for which scenario you are asked to deal with.

1. Type: In this game Aaron must purchase anywhere from four to six out of nine possible items. It will be your task to build this group of four to six items. This is, therefore, a grouping game, but is unlike many grouping games because there is essentially only one group. You will have to determine the effects of including or not including certain items in the group.

2. Diagram: There is no diagram for this game. There is only one group and you do not even know with certainty the size of that group. You will probably have to build a new group of items for each question. What you end up with after simplifying the rules and making deductions is simply a long chain of conditional statements that will help you determine the effects of including or excluding certain items.

3. Simplify the rules: Games are all about the rules, so it is vital to comprehend what they say and then to apply them as you work through the questions. In order to apply the rules quickly and efficiently, convert them into symbols. This has the added benefit of forcing you to determine what each rule actually means. The bulk of the rules for this game are conditional statements, two in standard "if…then" form and two others in the more difficult "unless" form. Look first at the rules that are in standard "if…then" form. The very first rule in the rules list says that Aaron does not buy a laptop if he buys both a D and a V. This, in symbols, becomes: $D + V \rightarrow \sim L$. Be careful with this rule. Knowing only that Aaron purchased a D or only that he purchased a V does not tell you anything about L. Knowing that Aaron purchased *both* a D and a V is sufficient to know that he did not buy an L. The third rule in the rules list says that Aaron buys a TV if he buys neither a D nor a V. Thus, if he does not buy a D *and* he does not buy a V, then he does buy a T. This, in symbols, becomes: $\sim D + \sim V \rightarrow T$. Again, in order for this conditional statement to tell you with certainty that Aaron buys a T based on this rule, you would have to know that he did not purchase a D and that he did not purchase a V. If only one of those conditions is satisfied

then you cannot determine anything about T. The remaining two conditional statements are in the "unless" form. Interpreting statements with "unless" require extra care, for they are prone to misinterpretation. The first "unless" rule says that Aaron does not buy a P or a C unless he buys neither a B nor an R, or that he does not buy a P or a C unless he does not buy a B and he does not buy an R. What this rule says is that there is no way for Aaron to buy a P or C unless he does not buy a B and he does not buy an R. In other words, he can buy a P or a C only if he does not buy a B and he does not buy an R. Knowing that Aaron bought a P or a C is sufficient to know that he did not buy a B and he did not buy an R. In standard "if…then" form, this rule becomes: If he buys a P or a C, then he did not buy a B and he did not buy an R. In this case, knowing that Aaron purchased either one of P or C is enough to know that he did not buy a B and that he did not buy an R. Thus, this rule can actually be broken up into four different statements: 1) $P \rightarrow \sim B$, 2) $P \rightarrow \sim R$, 3) $C \rightarrow \sim B$, and 4) $C \rightarrow \sim R$. This process reveals the basic approach to "unless" statements: What follows "unless" is the necessary condition and should be left as the consequent, while the rest of the statement should be negated and then becomes the antecedent. Try it out with the next "unless" rule: He does not buy a T unless he also buys a P and an L. What follows the "unless" stays as it is and becomes the consequent. Thus, the consequent is "he also buys a P and an L." The rest of the statement ("He does not buy a T") is negated and then becomes the antecedent. Therefore, the antecedent here is that he does buy a T and the consequent is that he also buys a P and an L. In symbols this becomes: $T \rightarrow P + L$. This might further be broken up into two statements: $T \rightarrow P$ and $T \rightarrow L$. The one remaining rule simply states that Aaron must buy at least one of a B, an R, or a W.

4. Deductions: Each rule in isolation does not provide you with much information, but you have not been given a list of rules in isolation. Each rule must be true at the same time that all the others are true. You need to determine how the rules relate to each other. This process is called making deductions. If one rule says this and another says that, then what must be the case? In order to facilitate the deduction-making process, it is helpful to write down the contrapositive to each of the conditional statements. You obtain the contrapositive by reversing the statement and negating both sides. For example, the simplified rule that says that if Aaron buys a P then he does not buy a B (P → ~B) also means that if Aaron buys a B then he does not buy a P (B → ~P). Follow the same process for the remaining rules. Be careful with the two rules that have two components in the antecedent: the D + V → ~L rule and the ~D + ~V → T rule. To find the contrapositive you follow the same process: reverse and negate. However, be sure to negate the antecedent as a whole. Thus, the contrapositive of the D + V → ~L rule says that if Aaron buys an L, then he does not buy both a D and a V (L → ~ (D + V). This does not mean that if he buys an L, then he does not buy a D and that he does not buy a V, but only that he can't buy *both* a D and a V. In other words, if he buys an L, then it must be the case that he does not buy at least one of D or V, or maybe both. Likewise, the contrapositive of the ~D + ~V → T rule would be: ~T → ~ (~D + ~V), which would mean that if he does not buy a T, then it is not the case that both he doesn't buy a D and he doesn't buy a V. In other words, if he does not buy a T, then he must buy at least one of D or V, or maybe both. Once you have the contrapositives, you are ready to make deductions. Look for conditional statements that link to other statements such that they form a chain. In other words, look for a conditional statement whose consequent is the antecedent for another statement and so on. Notice that one rule says that if Aaron does not buy a D and does not buy a V, then he must buy a T (~D + ~V → T). Another rule says that if Aaron buys a T, then he must buy a P and an L (T → P + L). The purchase of both P and L have additional effects, each creating a new branch of the chain. If he buys a P, then he does not buy a B and he does not buy an R. Since he must buy at least one of a B, an R, and a W, if he buys a P, then he must buy also buy a W (Notice that this same reasoning about P holds true for C. If he buys a C, then he cannot buy a B or an R, and so he must buy a W). Similarly, purchasing an L has additional effects. If Aaron buys

an L, then he cannot buy both of D and L, though he still might buy one of them. The contrapositive of this entire chain is also the case, such that if the necessary consequences of Aaron purchasing a P (that he purchase a W) or the necessary consequences of Aaron purchasing an L (that he does not buy both D and V) are not present, then the antecedent that would have brought about that necessary consequent is also not present. For example, if Aaron does not buy a W, then he cannot buy a P, and if he cannot buy a P, then he cannot buy a T, which in turn means that he cannot *not* buy a D and a V, or, in other words, that he must buy at least one of a D or a V.

5. **"Walk Around It":** The rules allowed you to deduce a long chain of conditional statements. Knowing that Aaron buys or doesn't buy a particular item will most likely trigger chain reactions that result in other items that Aaron must or cannot buy. As you work with this long chain of conditional statements, it is important to remember that if you affirm any of the information in the chain, then you know that its consequences must be true but you do not know anything about its antecedents. If you understand this concept, this game will be much easier. Just to be sure that you understand this concept, try an example. Suppose this chain is true: If Charlie has the measles, then he is sick. If he is sick, then he does not go to school. If he does not go to school, then he will miss a test. And if he misses a test, then he will fail the course. If you know that Charlie does not go to school, then it must be true that he misses a test and that he fails the course. However, you cannot say for certain that Charlie had measles or even that he was sick. There could be any number of causes for Charlie's absence from school. Perhaps he was out drinking too late with his friends and slept in or perhaps he was camping out for tickets to the latest episode of The Matrix. As you work, do not forget the numerical requirement: He must purchase from four to six items. The number of items will be important. Watch out for conditional statements that drag extra items along with it, for these could very well violate the numerical requirement depending on the circumstances.

1. **Type:** In this game there are six students who must be assigned to seats 1 through 6. In addition to determining who is sitting where, you must also determine who is wearing which shirt. The rules deal with both the order of the students and the order of the shirts. Since you have to determine the order of two variables, students and shirts, this can be thought of as a slots game.

2. **Diagram:** The diagram for this game should create distinct slots for the student and the shirt that each student wears for each of the six desks. You can accomplish this by creating six columns labeled 1 through 6 to represent the six desks and creating two rows, one for the students and one for the shirts.

3. **Simplify the rules:** Because the rules create the situation that the questions will test, it is important to understand what the rules say. However, it is a waste of time to read and reread the rules over and over again, question after question. To use your time wisely, go through each rule and convert it into symbols. The symbols will save you time by being closer to your workspace and by eliminating time-wasting words. The process of converting the rules into symbols will also force you to clarify what each rule says. The first items to symbolize are the items in the game. Here there are six students who can simply be labeled B, C, D, M, W, and J. There are also six shirts, and these can be labeled N, O, P, R, S, T. Next, move to the rules list. The first rule says the student wearing T is two seats away from the student wearing N. You must be careful how you interpret this. The fact that they are two seats away from each other does not mean that there are two seats in between them, but rather that there is exactly one seat between them. For instance, if the student wearing T is in desk 1, then two seats away would be desk 3. Thus, there must be one seat between the student wearing T and the student wearing N (T_N) although you do not know the order in which they appear. The remaining rules

are fairly straightforward: There are not two seats between the student wearing S and the student wearing O. The student wearing T is immediately after the student wearing P (PT). The student wearing R sits at desk 6 (you can place this directly on the diagram). B never sits at desk 1 (you can also note this directly on the diagram). C does not wear P. C does not wear T. J is closer to the front than D (J..D). M is closer to the front than C (M..C). D is closer to the front than W (D..W). D is closer to the front than M (D..M). D wears N. B is directly in front of C (BC). And C sits in desk 5 or 6.

4. **Deductions:** The next and most important step is to make deductions. In games that involve ordering, making deductions is largely a function of building a longer list of the relative order of the items included in the game. Here there are two categories that must be placed in order: students and shirts. Begin with the students. According to the rules, J is before D, D is before M, M is before C, and B is immediately before C. Taken together, these rules create a list of relative order that looks like this: J..D..M..BC. W, the only student remaining, must come after D, although you do not know the order of W relative to M or the BC sequence. It is clear from this list of relative order that the only variation in order can come after D. In other words, J must always be first and D must always be second. The person sitting in desks 3 through 6 can vary only slightly, depending upon the placement of W. Now that you know the relative order of the students, you can easily determine the relative order of the shirts. The rules gave you the placement of one of the shirts: The student wearing R must sit at desk 6. The order of the students allows you to determine even more. For instance, D must sit at desk 2 and D must wear N. Furthermore, because there must be exactly one seat between the student wearing T and the student wearing N, the student wearing T must sit at desk 4. Since the student wearing T sits immediately behind the student wearing P, the student wearing P must sit at desk 3. There are now only two shirts remaining, the O and the S, and only two desks left, desks 1 and 5. The placement of shirts is, therefore, very restricted. The only uncertainty remaining is which of O or S is at desk 1 and which is at desk 5.

5. **"Walk Around It":** The rules restricted the game to a limited number of possible scenarios for both students and shirts. The basic order of the students must look like this: J..D..M..BC, with W coming sometime after D. The shirts must be ordered like this: O/S, N, P, T, O/S, and R. Determining the placement of W will be important in the order of students and determining the exact placement of O and S will be important in the order of shirts.

Part IV

Question Analysis and Answers

1) The first question is somewhat more complicated than a typical rules question because it asks for a possible order of the students while there is only one rule that deals specifically with the order of a student to other students: J..C. This rule allows you to eliminate (B) and (D). In order to eliminate the remaining answer choices, you must use the deduction that A must be in week 2 or 3. This allows you to eliminate (A) and (E). The correct answer here is (C).

2) Question two asks for a complete list of the students who could give the first report. From the deductions, you know that either B or I must give the first report. (D) contains both B and I, so (D) is the correct answer. If you did not make this deduction earlier, you would be forced to make it now. Here is a brief review of how you can determine that B or I must be first: The rules tell you that A cannot be first and because K must be before J, and J must be before C, neither J nor C can be first. Because neither A nor J nor C can be first, only B or I can.

3) This question gives you two conditions: J reports on H and does so in week 2. Start with what you know about the students. From the deductions, you know that A must be second or third, but because J is now second, A must be third. You cannot determine anything else about the order of the students, so go to the plays. Because A is third and O must come after A, O must be the fourth play. Furthermore, K must be before J and J is in week 2, so K must be the first play. The question also says that H is in week 2. Because the fifth play can only be H or R and in this case H is second, the fifth play must be R. The only play remaining is M and the only week left is week 3, so the report on M must be given third. This setup allowed you to determine the order of the plays entirely but leaves the order of the students rather flexible. Go through the answer choices and find the one that must be true based on what you have determined. The correct answer is (E); it must be true that the report on M is given third.

4) Question four assigns A to give a report on K in week 3. Think about the side effects of placing A and K in the third week. J must come after K and C must come after J, so J must be the student who gives a report in week 4 and C must be the student who gives a report in week 5. Because O must come after A and cannot be fifth, O must be the subject of the report that J reports on in week 4. This is everything that you can determine based on the information provided in the question. You do not know whether B or I is the first student, whether H or R is the last play, or the week in which M is reported on. Once you have a good grasp on what you do know and what you don't, go through the answer choices and look for the one that must be true. The correct answer is (C). J must report on O.

5) Question five asks for something that must be false. Because the question does not introduce any conditions or provide any information, you are going to have to go through each answer and determine whether or not it could be true. The good news is that the answer most likely depends on something you already know. Go through each choice and compare it to your diagram, which should be labeled well enough to tell you that either B or I must be the first student, that either H or R must be the last play, that A must be the student who gives a report during week 2 or week 3, that O must be the third or fourth play reported on, and that C must give the fourth or fifth report. (A) does not have to be false because you do not know the placement of I. This one tries to trick you by making you think that I must be in the first week. Only if that were the case would it be impossible for I to report on O. But I does not have to be in the first week. (B) was the solution to the previous question, so it is clear that it does not have to be false. (C) could have also happened in the previous question. If B were first, then I could be second, A could be third, J could be fourth, and C could be fifth. (D) must be false and is the correct answer, which is immediately apparent if you made the deductions concerning the placement of A and the placement of C. A must be in either week 2 or 3 while C must be in either week 4 or 5, so A can never give a report after C. (E) could be true because M is the wildcard of the plays and can be almost anywhere.

6) According to the deductions, either B or I must be the first student to give a report, and either H or R must be the last play reported on. If I reports on H and B reports on R, then one of these pairs must report during week 1 and the other must report during week 5. Because the first and fifth weeks will be filled, you are only left with weeks 2, 3, and 4. The rules about relative order are now much more restrictive. The rules tell you that K must be before J and J must be before C, and because there are only three weeks available, K must be the play in the second week, J must be the student in the third week, and C must be the student in the fourth week. The only student left is A and the only week in which A could give a report is week 2. Thus, A is the student in week 2. O must come after A, so O must be the play in either week 3 or 4. M must also be in week 3 or 4. You now have a tentative setup for every student and every book. You do not know whether I and H are first or fifth and the same goes for B and R. You also do not know whether M is in week three or four and the same goes for O. Based on this setup, the only answer choice that could be true is (B). J, who gives the third report, could report on M.

7) This question changes the rule that says A must be before O to a condition where A must report on O. The question tries to fool you by then asking how many reports could be first. At first it might seem like O could now be the first play because it no longer has to come after A, but since all other conditions remain the same, A still cannot be first. Thus, O still cannot be first. There are no other conditions about the first report, so the remaining four plays could all be first. The correct answer is (D).

1) The first question is a typical rules question. Go down rule by rule to see whether each answer violates the particular rule you are looking at. Once you have eliminated an answer, do not test it for the other rules. This is also your chance to review the rules to catch any you may have missed or misunderstood. You will know this is the case if you have more than one right answer or no right answer at all. The correct answer here is (C).

2) If you took the time to make the deductions concerning the TUV block and its placement, this question is very easy. If only two species go extinct in the Middle era, then the TUV block cannot go extinct in the Middle era, and, therefore, it must go extinct in the Early era, which is really the only firm fact that you can determine. Since this is a "must be true" question, stop once you have determined something that must be true and look for it in an answer choice. In this case, look for an answer choice that says T, U, or V must go extinct in the Early era. The correct answer is (A).

3) Question three asks for what cannot be true. A good way to approach this type of question is to go through the answer choices and ask yourself whether each answer choice could be true. If it could be true then it is not the correct answer; if it could not be true then it is the correct answer. Since this question does not introduce any new conditions, the answer is likely to depend only on the rules and the deductions. The basic order of the extinctions must be TUV..P..O, which reveals that there are only two scenarios, one with the TUV block in the Early era and one with the TUV block in the Middle era. The earliest P can go extinct is the Middle era. Placing the TUV block in the Middle era is more restrictive because it forces S to the Early era, while placing the TUV block in the Early period tells you very little because P and O do not have to be together. With these possibilities in mind, go through the answer choices and find the one that cannot be true. The correct answer is (E). It cannot be true that P went extinct in the Early era because it must go extinct after the TUV block.

4) If U went extinct in the Middle period, then the TUV block is in the Middle era. In this scenario P and O are forced into the Late era and S is forced into the Early era. This is everything that must be true, so go through the answer choices and find the one that must be true. The correct answer here is (C). O and P must have gone extinct in the same period.

5) Every once in awhile you will see a question like this one where you are asked what information will allow you to determine the entire setup. These questions may sometimes require slightly more work, but they are not a reason to panic. Think about what you do and do not know. You will need something that tells you whether the TUV block is in the Early or Middle era. Also, in order to determine the entire order, you will need some sort of information that allows you to place the two wildcards, Q and R, in groups. As mentioned, the scenario where T, U, and V are in the Middle era is much more restrictive, so the answer is likely going to place the TUV block in the Middle era. Knowing what is required to fix every position, go to the answer choices. Ask yourself if it tells you where the TUV block is and if it allows you to determine the positions of Q and R. Luckily, in this question you do not have to go very far. The correct answer is (A). If S and R are the only dinosaurs that went extinct in the Early period, then the TUV block must be in the Middle era, and you know that Q must be with P and O in the Late period.

6) Once again, this question asks for something that cannot be true without offering any additional conditions. With the two possible scenarios in mind, look at the answer choices and ask yourself if each choice could be true. If not, then you have found the right answer. Hopefully, after merely glancing at the answer choices, the answer will stand out. The correct answer is (D). Since T, U, and V must always go extinct in the same period, it is impossible for R and V to go extinct in the same period.

1) The first question is a typical rules question. Go down rule by rule to see whether each answer violates the particular rule you are looking at. Once you have eliminated an answer, do not test it for the other rules. This is also your chance to review the rules to catch any you may have missed or misunderstood. You will know this is the case if you have more than one right answer or no right answer at all. The correct answer here is (B).

2) Question two asks for something that must be false without providing any additional conditions that would restrict the game any more than the rules already do. This is usually a good clue that you can find the correct answer by focusing on the rules and the deductions. Go through each answer choice and consider whether or not it violates any of the rules about prohibited pairs. Remember, one section must include N and R, one section must include B and A, and the other section must include T and E. J is the wildcard. (A) does not have to be false because J is the wildcard student. (B) does not have to be false, because E could be assigned to section four with T and J. (C) assigns a specific group of students to section 2: R, N, and T. The rules specifically state that N cannot be with T. (C) is therefore the correct answer. The section assignments in both (D) and (E) can be true because they are consistent with the possible section assignments. If you did not make the deductions previously, this question would be more difficult to solve, as it would require you to work through each answer choice. If this were the case, however, you should notice how restricted the game really is.

3) To determine a pair of students who can be in a section with T, all you need to do is determine who the students are who cannot be in a section with Travis. You may have already done this work, which makes the answer quite simple. Travis must be with E and can also be with J. The correct answer is therefore (C). If you did not do the work previously, this question reveals that it is helpful to go through all the students and determine who they can be assigned to sections with.

4) Question four assigns J and R to section 3. J and R are the only two students who can be assigned to a section with N, or, rather, N must be assigned to the same section as R and can also be with J. Since R and J are both assigned to section 3, N must be assigned to section 3 as well. Since N, R, and J are assigned to a section together, the two remaining groups must be BA and TE. Both of these groups include one of A and E, and both A and E must be assigned to either section 2 or section 4, though they cannot be together. Thus, either the BA group or the TE group must be in section 2 and the other must be in section 4. No matter what, students will be assigned to section 2, section 3, and section 4. Any answer choice that assigns someone to section 1 must therefore be false. (D) assigns B to section 1 and is thus the correct answer.

5) If B is one of three students assigned section 2, then B must be with both A and J, since A and J are the only two students who can be assigned to a section with B. With three students in section 2, section 2 is full. The remaining two groups must include N and R in one group and T and E in the other. E must be assigned to section 4 since section 2 is full, which means that T and E must be assigned to section 4, while N and R must be assigned to either section 1 or section 3. Go to the answer choices and find what must be true. The correct answer is (B). T must be assigned to section 4 because T must be paired with E and E must be assigned to section 4.

6) Question six asks for a pair of students who cannot be assigned to the same section. You already know the three basic groups: NR, BA, and TE. J could be the third student in any of these groups. With this information in mind, go through the answer choices and find a pair of students who cannot be together. (A) could be true because J is the wildcard. (B) must be true; B and A always have to be together. (C) must also be true; R and N must always be together. (D) assigns E and A to the same group. E must always be with T in one section while A must always be with B in a different section. Thus, it is impossible for E and A to be assigned to the same section. The correct answer is (D). If you must know, (E) could be true because J is the wildcard.

7) If T is assigned to a section with J, then not only do you know that T, E, and J are assigned to the same section, but you also know that the remaining two groups must be NR and BA. Thus, the three groups must be TEJ, BA, and NR, though not necessarily in that order. The groups containing E and A must be assigned to sections 2 and 4, though not necessarily in that order, while the third group must be assigned to either section 1 or section 3. At this point you can go through the answer choices and easily find what must be false, or cannot be true. The correct answer is (A). R cannot be assigned to a section with two other students because R is with N and only N.

1) The first question is a typical rules question. Go down rule by rule to see whether each answer violates the particular rule you are looking at. Once you have eliminated an answer, do not test it for the other rules. This is also your chance to review the rules to catch any you may have missed or misunderstood. You will know this is the case if you have more than one right answer or no right answer at all. The correct answer here is (C).

2) Question two makes a specific assignment: C orders S. Since C orders S, C's two toppings are P and S. Neither B nor F can order the same toppings as C, so B and F cannot order S and must therefore order O and M for their two toppings. Unfortunately, this is not one of the answer choices so you must delve a little deeper. Since C orders S and P, and D cannot order S, in order for C to have one topping in common with D, D must order P. This is one of the answer choices so you don't need to go any further. The correct answer is (D).

3) If G orders M, then G's two toppings are M and S. Since D and G cannot order any of the same toppings, D must now order O and P. Since the question also says that C does not order M, C must order S, making C's two toppings P and S. Since C orders S and since C and B cannot order the same thing, B cannot order S and must therefore order M. Furthermore, because B and F order the same toppings, F must also order M. At this point you know the two toppings that each customer orders: B orders M and O, C orders P and S, D orders O and P, F orders M and O, and G orders M and S. The question asks for a complete list of the toppings ordered by three people. In this setup both M and O are ordered by three people. Thus, the correct answer is (A). This question might be answered more efficiently if you consider the information from question two. Question two made you work out the basic scenario where C orders S and B orders M. This question just adds additional information to that scenario. Nevertheless, the correct answer is still (A).

4) Question four gives you two conditions that will have some effect on the toppings that D orders. These conditions are 1) that G does not order M and 2) that F orders S. No matter which condition you start with, you will find the correct answer if you follow the chain reaction, but it might be easier to look at what people do order rather than what they do not. If F orders S then B must also order S. Since B orders S, C must order M. Both B and C must have one topping in common with G. B must order S, so B and G already have their one topping in common. Since B and G can only have one topping in common, G cannot order O. Since G cannot order M or O, G must order S and P. Since G and D do not order any of the same toppings, D cannot order S or P. Instead, D must order M and O. The correct answer is therefore (B).

5) For this question, the number of customers who buy S is limited to two. G must already order an S, so you need to find the one remaining S. Either B or C must order an S, but since B and F must order the same thing, if B were to order an S there would be three S's. Thus, B cannot order an S, which means that C must order the second S. C's two toppings must therefore be S and P. Since C orders S, B and F must both order M, making their two toppings O and M. You can check the answer choices at this point, but unfortunately the correct answer is not there. You must keep looking. You still need to ensure that both B and C have one topping in common with G and that C has one topping in common with D. C orders an S, so C and G already have one topping in common. In order for C and D to have one topping in common, D must order P (remember, C orders S and P, but D cannot order S). D and G cannot order the same topping, so G cannot order P. Check the answer choices one more time for the correct answer; it is there in (E). It must be false that G orders P. You could have reached this same conclusion by focusing on the relationship between B and G. B orders O and M, so in order for G to have one topping in common with B, G's second topping must either be O or M. In other words, G cannot order P. Note that you could have reached this conclusion from

the work you have already done. You noted when walking around the game that there are two basic scenarios, one where B and F order S, which forces C to order M, and another where C orders S, which forces B and F to order M. This question calls for the second of these two, and this is the same scenario you needed for questions two and three (the other you needed for question four). If you saved your work, you could have simply referred to it now. To answer question two you had to determine that if C orders S, then G cannot order P. Again, the correct answer is (E).

6) Question six asks for something that must be false without providing you with any additional conditions, so you will be forced to go through the answer choices. However, this does not mean that you should immediately begin drawing out scenarios. Work the question smartly, using previous work and your knowledge of the rules. (A) is exactly what you worked out in the previous question (G and C ordered S), so it can be true. (B) would have been the case in the previous question if B, F, and G had ordered S, so (B) can be true. (C) would be the case if (B) were true. If B, F, and G have S's, then C and one of D or G must have M's. In fact, the correct answer to question one contains this setup. (D) says that exactly two customers order P. C must order P and neither B nor F can, so the second P would have to come from exactly one of D or G since D and G cannot order the same toppings. Thus, it is possible for two customers to order P. By process of elimination, you now know that the correct answer is (E). It cannot be true that three customers order P because as mentioned, the only customers that can order P are C and one of D or G, but not both.

7) If exactly two customers order M, then it is impossible for B and F to order M, because in addition to B and F, one of D or G would have to order an M. Since B cannot order M, B, and therefore F, must order S. Since B and F order S, C must order M. C's two toppings are therefore P and M. In order for C to have a topping in common with G, G's second topping must be either M or P. In other words, G cannot order O. Since G does not order O, D must order O. The only thing that you cannot determine is which one of D or G orders an M and which one orders P. Now you can go through the answer choices and quickly test each one to determine whether it could be true. This also happens to be the same scenario you would have had to work out for question four, so, once again, time could be saved by using previous work. The correct answer here is (D).

1) The first question is a typical rules question. Go down rule by rule to see whether each answer violates the particular rule you are looking at. Once you have eliminated an answer, do not test it for the other rules. This is also your chance to review the rules to catch any you may have missed or misunderstood. You will know this is the case if you have more than one right answer or no right answer at all. The correct answer here is (D).

2) This question restricts the blue backpack to only two notebooks. Remember, each group must contain one of P or H, so in order to contain exactly two notebooks the blue backpack must contain one of P or H and exactly one other notebook. The first thing to do is determine what the rules say about the blue backpack. One rule says that if G is in the blue backpack then A is in the red backpack. This doesn't tell you anything useful other than the fact that G could be in the blue backpack. Another rule says that if S in the blue backpack, then A is in the blue backpack as well. Since there can only be two notebooks in the blue backpack, you know that S cannot be in the blue backpack, which is to say that S must be in the red backpack. Unfortunately, this is not one of the answer choices. Finally, another rule says that if L is in the blue backpack, then G is in the blue backpack. Having both L and G in the blue backpack in addition to either P or H would mean more than two notebooks. Because placing L in the blue backpack brings about an impossible scenario, L must be in the red backpack. Check whether this is one of the answer choices. It is. The correct answer is (B).

3) This question tells you that Andres carries G in the blue backpack. Look at the chains of causation and find one where G is in the blue backpack. Once you locate this, determine what must be true. If G is in the blue backpack then A must be in the red backpack, S must be in the red backpack, P must be in the blue backpack, and H must be in the red backpack. In other words, if G is in the blue backpack then the red backpack

must have A, S, and H and the blue backpack must have G and P. You are left with M and L and no restrictions on either one. Thus, you know the placement of five of the seven notebooks and know that the remaining two could be in either backpack. With this information in mind, go through the answer choices. The correct answer is (C). L could be in either backpack so L could be in the red backpack. This question is forcing you to prove that you understand that, although the rules say that if L is in the blue backpack then G is in the blue backpack, you can still have G in the blue backpack without having L in the blue backpack.

4) This question asks for something that could be true without giving you any conditions or additional information. This means that you will have to go through the answer choices to find the right answer. That is okay. Each choice will give you enough information to evaluate its validity, so trust the questions and trust yourself. You know what is going on. For each answer choice, look at each of the various chains that you have and see if it is compatible with the information in the choice. (A) is always a good place to start. (A) says that L and H are both in the red backpack. Looking at the different chains of logic, you will see that having L in the red backpack does not tell you anything. It is a consequent of other things, but by itself is not sufficient information to let you know anything. This is the case with placing H in the red backpack as well. Since placing L and H together in the red backpack does not violate any rules, it is possible. The correct answer is (A). If you discovered this, you should not do any more work on this question. (A) works, so that is the answer. If you did not discover this, then at the minimum you should be able to eliminate the other answer choices. You could eliminate both (B) and (C) from the previous two questions. If G is in the blue backpack then both A and S must be in the red backpack. (D) puts L and S together in the blue backpack. However, if L is in the blue backpack then G is in the blue backpack, which again puts S in the red backpack. Finally, (E) places L and H together in the blue backpack. Again, if L is in the blue backpack then G is in the blue backpack. If G is in the blue backpack then P must be in the blue backpack and H must be in the red backpack.

Question Analysis and Answers

5) If Andres takes L on Tuesday and Thursday, then L will be in the blue backpack. Based on the chains of logic extracted from the rules, if L is in the blue backpack then G is in the blue backpack, A is in the red backpack, S is in the red backpack, P is in the blue backpack, and H is in the red backpack. The question asks for what must be true, so find one of these consequences in an answer choice. All the answer choices deal with the days of the week rather than the color of the backpack so remember carefully what each color represents. The correct answer here is (E). If L is in the blue backpack then H must be in the red backpack, which means that H must be a MWF class.

6) If H, G, and A are all in the same backpack, then H, G, and A must be in the red backpack, because if either G or A were in the blue backpack, either G or A would be forced into the red backpack. In other words, it is impossible for G and A to be together in the blue backpack. Now that you know that H, G, and A are in the red backpack, look for any side effects. P and H cannot be together, so P must now be in the blue backpack. Since G is in the red backpack, L must be in the red backpack and since A is in the red backpack, S must also be in the red backpack. These side effects mean that H, G, A, L, and S are all in the red backpack and that P is in the blue backpack. The only notebook left is M, which must be in the blue backpack in order to satisfy the condition that each backpack have at least two notebooks. The correct answer is (C).

7) This question changes the rules such that P and H must be together in the red backpack. The rest of the rules remain the same, so look at the lists of "if...then" statements and see if placing either P or H in the red backpack tells you anything. One of the rules says that whether P is in the red backpack, then G must be in the red backpack. If G is in the red backpack, then L must be in the red backpack as well. At this point you know that P, H, G, and L, four of the seven notebooks, must all be in the red backpack. The remaining three notebooks are A, S, and M. The blue backpack must contain at least two of these three notebooks. The question asks for a notebook that must be in the blue backpack, so the question to ask yourself is which of these three cannot be in the red backpack. A glance at the rules tells you that if A is in the red backpack, then S must be in the red backpack as well. If both A and S are in the red backpack, then only M could be in the blue backpack, which is a violation of the requirement that there be at least two notebooks. Thus, in this setup A cannot be in the red backpack and, therefore, must be in the blue backpack. The correct answer is (B).

1) The first question is a typical rules question. Go down rule by rule to see whether each answer violates the particular rule you are looking at. Once you have eliminated an answer, do not test it for the other rules. This is also your chance to review the rules to catch any you may have missed or misunderstood. You will know this is the case if you have more than one right answer or no right answer at all. The correct answer here is (D).

2) In order to determine who can serve on only one team, all you have to do is compare each answer choice to the diagram. S could be in both C and D or in both C and F, so (A) is not the correct answer. On the other hand, T can only be used once, since it can only be in D or F, but not both. Therefore, (B) is the correct answer. In case you are still wondering, yes, R, V, and L could all be used twice.

3) This question adds the condition that T is on a team with R, in effect creating a TR block. If you look at your diagram, you will notice that F is the only project to which T and R can be assigned together. Thus, what must be true is that R is assigned to project F. The correct answer is (D).

4) The condition for this question is that L cannot be on a team with S. In C, there must be S, one of L or M, and one of R or V. Since there is an S in C and the question says S cannot be with L, M must be in group C, giving you S, M, and R/V in C. Since M is in group C, L must be in group D, giving you V, L, and S/T. Since there is now an L in group D, and L still cannot be with an S, the third person in D must be T. Therefore, it must be true that T is assigned to project D. The correct answer is (C). This question tested the deduction concerning the placement of L and M. Exactly one of L or M must be in C and the other must be in D.

5) Question five places M on exactly two teams. Remember, M cannot be in both C and D, so in order to have two M's, one M must be in F and the other must be in either C or D. Since M can only be in one of C or D, L must be in the other. The key here is to remember that V and L must be together in one of the three groups. As has been determined, L must be in one of C or D, but L could also be in F along with M. However, V cannot be in group F, so the VL block must be in either C or D, in whichever group that M is not in. Thus, any choice that does not contain an M must contain the VL block. With this in mind, check the answer choices for a group of people who cannot compose an entire team. The correct answer is (C). (C) cannot be an accurate list of the people assigned to any of the three projects because if L is the only writer on the team, V must also be on that team. Thus, (C) does not allow for V and L to be together.

6) The only two projects to which R could be assigned are C and F, so if there are two R's then R must be assigned to both C and F. If R is used in C then V cannot be used in C. Since V and L must be together in one of the groups and V can no longer be in C, V and L must be together in D. Since L is assigned to D, M must be assigned to C. The correct answer is therefore (E). It must be true that M is assigned to C. Questions five and six expanded on what you had to determine in question four, testing not only the relationship between L and M, but also how L and M relate to the requirement that V must be assigned to a project with L. This interplay is something that was discussed in the "Walk Around It" section. Knowing what you will be working with before you even start the game makes working the questions much easier because it gives you focus, pointing you to what you need to be looking for.

7) This question is nasty and brutish but it can also be short if you understand the distribution of the writers and graphic artists. If you did not work out the distribution ahead of time, this question would probably be very tough. The question asks for the maximum number of different teams that could be assigned to project F. From the deductions, you know that in F you must have R, S/T, and one or both of L and M. There can be either three or four people assigned to F, depending on whether one or both of the writers are assigned to F. If there are only three people, then you have R, S/T, and L/M. The variations of S, R, L, and M mean that there are four possibilities when there are three people. Written out the long way, these four possibilities are: R, S, M; R, S, L; R, T, L; and R, T, M. If, on the other hand, there are four people assigned to project F, then the team must include R, S/T, L, and M. In this case, there are two possibilities: R, S, L, and M or R, T, L, and M. Thus, there are six possibilities in all. The correct answer is (D).

1) The first question is a typical rules question. Go down rule by rule to see whether each answer violates the particular rule you are looking at. Once you have eliminated an answer, do not test it for the other rules. This is also your chance to review the rules to catch any you may have missed or misunderstood. You will know this is the case if you have more than one right answer or no right answer at all. The correct answer here is (B).

2) This question places H alone in row 4 and M and N together in a row. The fact that H does not sit with anyone means that G cannot sit with H, which, according to a deduction, means that X cannot sit with a lawyer. Keep this in mind. N must always sit in a window seat and can only sit in row 3 or 4. H is already in row 4 so N and M must sit together in row 3 with N in the window seat and M in the aisle seat. Since M is in the aisle, Z must sit in the aisle seat in row 2. Now you are left with G, X, Y, and O to place in the window and aisle seats in rows 1 and 5. O is a lawyer and cannot be in row 5, so O must be in row 1. Since X cannot sit with a lawyer, X must be in row 5. The correct answer here is (E).

3) This question places both H and O in window seats. G and N must sit in window seats as well, and I is already sitting in the window seat in row 2. This gives you all five people sitting in window seats: H, O, G, N, and I. The remaining four (M, Z, X, and Y) must sit in an aisle seat. Thus, M sits in an aisle seat, which forces Z into row 2 with I. Furthermore, since H is sitting in a window seat you know that G and H cannot share a row. If G and H cannot share a row, then X cannot share a row with a lawyer and no lawyers can sit in row 5. There isn't much more to go on, so go through the answer choices and look for any that violate the conditions that you have determined. (C) must be false because in this case, X cannot sit with a lawyer. The correct answer is (C).

4) If Z sits in the window seat of row 3, then because Z must be before N and N must be before H, N sits in row 4 and H sits in row 5. N must sit in a window seat, so that puts him in the window seat in row 4. As of right now, you cannot determine whether H is sitting in the window or the aisle seat of row 5. However, the information that you have does allow you to determine a little bit more. Look at the contrapositive that says if Z and I are not sitting in the same row as each other, then M cannot sit in an aisle seat. In the seating arrangement that you have, Z is not sitting with I, so M must sit in a window seat. According to the rules, G must also sit in a window seat. Thus, both M and G must sit in window seats and, conveniently, there are only two possible window seats left: row 1 and row 5, forcing H to sit in the aisle seat of row 5. Now row 5 is completely occupied, so there is no room for X in row 5. You can make further deductions, but this is sufficient to answer the question. Since row 5 is completely filled, X cannot sit in row 5. The correct answer is (E).

5) This question places G and Y together in row 4. G must sit in a window seat, so G is in the window seat and Y is in the aisle seat. Once you have this basic information, ask yourself what you know about N. From the deductions section, you know that the ordering requirements force N to sit in the window seat of row 3 or 4. For this question, G is in row 4, so N must sit in row 3. This information allows you to eliminate answers (A) and (B) because they place N in some other row. Now consider who N could sit with. Because Z must sit in a lower-numbered row than N, and H must sit in a higher-numbered row than N, it is impossible for N to sit with Z or H. This allows you to eliminate answer choice (C). Now you're down to (D) and (E). The fact that G and Y are sitting in the same row means that G and H cannot sit in the same row, and if G and H cannot sit in the same row, then X cannot sit with a lawyer. N is a lawyer, so it is not possible for N to sit with X, which eliminates answer choice (E). The correct answer here is (D).

6) This question places Z in the row with the empty seat. This makes it impossible for Z to sit in the same row as I, so it is also not possible for M to sit in an aisle seat. Thus, in addition to G, N, and I, who must sit in window seats according to the rules, M must sit in a window seat. The remaining window seat will have either Z or the empty seat. Because of the ordering rule, Z, and therefore the empty space, must be in row 1 or row 3. I is sitting in row 2, and M and N are lawyers and therefore cannot sit in row 5. Thus, only G can sit in the window seat in row 5. Because he is the only one who can, he must. The correct answer is (E).

7) This question adds two conditions. First, M, X, and Y sit in the aisle seats of rows 1, 3, and 5, respectively. Second, Y is the only professional in row 5, which means that Y is sitting next to the empty seat. Because M is in an aisle seat, Z must sit in the aisle seat of row 2. At this point, row 2 and row 5 are filled. The ordering rule now plays an important role. Z must be in a lower-numbered row than N, and N must be in a lower-numbered row than H. Since Z is in row 2 and row 5 is already filled, the order is completely restricted. N must be in row 3 and H must be in row 4. N must sit in the window seat of row 3, which places N next to X. Since X is sitting in the same row as one of the lawyers, G and H must sit together in row 4, with G in the window seat and H in the aisle seat. There is only one person left, O, and only one place left for him, the window seat in row 1. Now you know the entire order so it is rather easy to find one answer choice that cannot be true. The correct answer is (B). G cannot sit in row 3 because G must sit in row 4.

1) The first question is a typical rules question. Go down rule by rule to see whether each answer violates the particular rule you are looking at. Once you have eliminated an answer, do not test it for the other rules. This is also your chance to review the rules to catch any you may have missed or misunderstood. You will know this is the case if you have more than one right answer or no right answer at all. The correct answer here is (E).

2) If F plays immediately after B, then the B..D.. F order is broken, which means that D cannot be played. Also, since this question has I as the sixth song, there are only six songs. You also know that C must be played second. Your diagram at this point looks something like this: _ C _ _ _ I, with the added information that F is immediately after B. The only space for the BF sequence is in the third and fourth or fourth and fifth spaces. Either way, the fourth space is used. This means that E is not fourth, which in turn means that G must be used. If G is used, then A is used also and they are separated by exactly one space. This A_G sequence only fits in the first and third spaces, which means that B is fourth and F is fifth. Now you know the entire order. The correct answer is (D).

3) This question tells you that D is fifth and I is seventh. First of all, the fact that I is seventh means that there are seven songs. Secondly, the fact that D is used means that B and F are used, and their relative order is B..D.. F. Since D is fifth and I is seventh, the only space available for F is sixth, while the precise location of B is unknown. You also know that C must be second. At this point you have a general idea of the location of five of the seven songs. Furthermore, the question asks you for the location of J, so you know J must be used as well. That leaves only one other space. Since this does not leave room for both A and G, neither of them can be used. According to the rules, if G is not used, then E must be fourth. You now know that your diagram looks something like this: _ C _ E

D F I, with a B and J left over. The question wants to know the possible locations for J. J can either be first or third. The correct answer is (A).

4) Since H is played fifth, there are only five songs. You already know that C must be second, so there are only three other spaces to fill. The question wants to know what song cannot be played. The B..D..F sequence would take up all three spaces, but it would also mean that there is no A or G. According to the rules, if there is no G then E must be fourth, but if B, D, and F are used there is no room for that E. This means that the B..D..F sequence does not work. You've already determined that the contrapositive of the B..D.. F rule is that if the B..D..F sequence is not used, then D is not used. Thus, it must be true that D is not used. The correct answer is (B).

5) This question puts D as the fourth song and asks you to use as few songs as possible. This tells you two things right away. If D is fourth, then E is not fourth, which means that A and G must be used. Also, since D is used, B and F must also be used, and their relative order is B..D..F. Finally, you know that C is second. Now consider the condition of this question that says the band plays as few songs as possible. From what you've already determined you know that you must use B, D, F, A, G, and C. That makes six altogether. Try using only those six. B must be before D, which means B could be either first or third. A quick glance tells you that placing B third would not allow you to place A and G and have them separated by exactly one song. If you put B first, the positions that you know for sure are that B is first, C is second, and D is fourth. Your diagram should look something like this: B C _ D_ _. You are left with A, G, and F to place on your diagram. F must be after D, and A and G must be separated by exactly one space. Since A and G must be separated by exactly one space, they only fit into the third and fifth spaces, in any order. This leaves F as the sixth song. You now know the entire order. Only the positions of A and G can change, for they are interchangeable. Since the question states that "each of the following must be false EXCEPT," go through the answer and find one that could be true. The correct answer is (A).

6) This question wants to know the smallest number of songs that can be played. If you did the work in the deductions and "Walk Around It" section, then this is a no-brainer. If, on the other hand, you did not invest the time beforehand, you would have to go through the same thought process now. The smallest number possible is three, since the band could play only A, C, and G, not necessarily in that order. If the band did not play A and G, then they would have to play at least four songs. The correct answer here is (C).

7) The final question gives you information about B and F. Once again, C must be second, so in actuality you know three of the five songs that must be played. C must be second, B must be third, and F must be fifth. Your task is to find the fewest songs that the band could play. You know that F must be the fifth song, so try to limit it to just five. There is no room for A and G to be included and have one space between them, so neither A nor G can be used. Since G is not played, E must be the fourth song. The only song left now is the first song. The first song could not be D because it would break the B..D..F sequence, nor could it be one of H or I since the band must be kicked off after it plays H or I. Therefore, the first song would have to be J. This is an acceptable setup, so the fewest songs the band could play if B is third and F is fifth is five. The correct answer is (A).

1) The first question is a typical rules question. Go down rule by rule to see whether each answer violates the particular rule you are looking at. Once you have eliminated an answer, do not test it for the other rules. This is also your chance to review the rules to catch any you may have missed or misunderstood. You will know this is the case if you have more than one right answer or no right answer at all. The correct answer here is (C).

2) The second question tests your deductions, which in this case means the ability to create the extended list of the relative order of the different cars. This question is very easy to answer by looking at that list. Remember, you are looking for things that MUST be true, not that could be true. The correct answer is (D). S must be after G.

3) The third question asks which cars could arrive first. In the "Walk Around It" section of this game you already determined which cars could be first and last, but if you hadn't, then you would have to do so now. Either way, it is very easy to do. G and T must both be before W, but there is no information that dictates the relative order of G and T, so either of them could be first. B is the wildcard item, so B could be first. Lastly, R must be sometime before S, which means that R could be first as well. That makes four cars that could possibly be first. The correct answer is (D).

4) This question fixes R as the fifth car. From the rules you know that R is before S, which means that S must be sixth. Check whether that is one of the answers. It is indeed. The correct answer is (B).

5) This question wants to know the latest that T could arrive. From the diagram of the relative order you know that T must always be before both W and S, but you do not know how T's order relates to the other three cars, G, R, and B. Placing T as late as possible means that only W and S come after T, which means that S is sixth, W is fifth, and T is fourth. Thus, the latest that T can be is fourth, with only W and S after it. The correct answer is (C).

6) This question fixes the position of B, the wildcard. Since B is third, S must be sixth. What additional information will allow you to determine the entire order? While the diagram of the relative order of the cars gives you a lot of information, it does not reveal the relative order or the absolute positions of G and T. Any statement that fixes the entire order of the cars will have to fix the position of G and T. Go through the answer choices and see whether any choice fixes the placement of G and T. (A) fixes the position of everything except G and T, so it cannot be correct. (B) fixes the placement of both G and T. If T arrived immediately before B, then T is second. If B arrived sometime before G, and G must be before both W and S, then G is fourth, W is fifth, and S is sixth, leaving R for the first position. Thus, (B) is the correct answer.

7) This question asks for the effects of putting B in the second position. Since B is second, S must be sixth. Furthermore, because both G and T must be before W, the earliest W can now be is fourth rather than third. Go to the answer choices and see if you have already determined enough. The correct answer is there in (C). It must be false that W arrived third because this would not leave room for G and T to arrive before W.

1) If A is seventh and A and F must be separated by one space, then F must be fifth. Since F comes before the ABC block, then the ABC block is 6, 7, and 8, but not in that order. B and D must be separated by one space as well, so B will have to be sixth and D will have to be fourth, which means that C must be eighth and G must be first. The only students left are H and E, who are interchangeable in the second and third positions. Go to the answers and find the one that must be true. The correct answer is (C).

2) This question asks for the position in which H must use the bike if C uses the bike as early as possible. The only rule dealing with the order of C is that E and F must both be before C, so the earliest C can be is third. In order to have C after as few people as possible, C must be the first student in the ABC block, which means that A must be the second student in the ABC block. With C third, A must be fourth, and since F and A are separated by one space, F must be second. Since F is second, E must be first, and since A is fourth, B must be fifth. Since B is fifth, D must be seventh. Since the first position is already used, G must be eighth. The only position left for H is sixth. The correct answer is therefore (C).

3) If F is fourth and F...C, then the ABC block must be after F. F must be separated from A by one space, so A must be sixth. If A is the first student in the ABC block, then the ABC block takes up the sixth, seventh, and eighth positions. On the other hand, if A is the second student in the ABC block, then the ABC block takes up the fifth, sixth, and seventh positions. In either case the ABC block must use the sixth and seventh positions. Therefore it cannot be true that D is the seventh student to use the bike. The correct answer is (C). As a reminder, it is often helpful to save your work rather than to erase it, for you can often use work from one question to solve later questions, either by revealing the answer or by revealing possible scenarios.

4) If D is second then B must be fourth. You need A, B, and C to be consecutive, but you also need both E and F to be before the ABC block. There are only two positions remaining before B, so these two positions must be filled by E and F. In order to have A and F separated by exactly one space, F must be third and A must be fifth, leaving E as the first student and C as the sixth student. Since E is first, G must be eighth. The only space left for H is in the seventh position. Thus, fifth, sixth, and seventh must be A, C, and H respectively. The correct answer is (A).

5) This question doesn't give you any firm positions, so just work with the relative order. If B is immediately after F, then you know A is immediately after B, and C is immediately after A. The B_D rule puts D immediately before F. The rules also tell you that E..C so, since D is immediately before C, E must be before D. The only two students who you do not know anything about are H and G. This is everything that you can determine, so go to the answers and find what must be false, based on what you know. The correct answer is (C) because if D were first, there would be no space for E to be before C.

6) This question again does not give you any firm positions, but take what the question says and work it out as far as you can. If A uses the bike sometime after C then C must be the first student in the ABC block and A must be the second student in the ABC block. Thus, the order of the ABC block must be CAB. You need E and F before C, and F must be separated from A by only one space, so F must use the bike immediately before C. B and D must also be separated by one space so the relative order of the students is E..FCAB_D. The only two students left are H and G, and you know G must be either first or eighth, so the space between B and D must be filled with H. What does this mean about the placement of H? If G is first, then H will be seventh and if G is eighth, then H will be sixth. Thus, H can either be sixth or seventh. Find one of these in the answer choices. The correct answer is (D).

7) Occasionally the rules change in the last question of a game. Once you've become familiar with how the game functions, it changes. But that is okay. Accept the changes and do what is required of you. Usually, these become fairly straightforward rules questions. Here, two conditions are changed. B and D are no longer separated by one space, D must come immediately after B. Furthermore, G is no longer first or eighth, G is eighth. Using these two new conditions, build a list of relative order. B must be immediately before D, so B must be the third student in the ABC sequence. A can still be either the first or second student in the ABC block, so you have two possible scenarios: work them out. If A is the first student in the ABC block, then the block looks like this: ACBD. A must still be separated from F by one space and G must be last so the order must look something like this: F_ACBD..G, where G is the last student. The only two students left are H and E, one of whom must fill the space between F and A. If H fills the gap then E must be first. If E fills the gap then H could either be first or seventh. Thus, in this scenario there are three possible orders. If A is the second student in the ABC block then the order must be: E..FCABD..G, leaving only H. H could be immediately before E, immediately after E, or immediately before G. Thus, in this scenario there are also three possible different orders. In total, there are six. The correct answer is therefore (B).

1) The first question is a typical rules question. Go down rule by rule to see whether each answer violates the particular rule you are looking at. Once you have eliminated an answer, do not test it for the other rules. This is also your chance to review the rules to catch any you may have missed or misunderstood. You will know this is the case if you have more than one right answer or no right answer at all. The correct answer here is (D).

2) This question is very easy if you invested the time to understand the game. Even if you did not, this is still a rather easy question to determine. With nine students and two possibly used twice, there can be up to eleven items. There must be a minimum of four in each group, so one group could have the minimum of four and the other could have seven, which as it turns out is the maximum. Another way to think of this: If all nine of the students were used exactly once, then one group would have four and the other would have five. Taking the maximum of two students from the group that has only four and reusing them in the group with five would create one group with four and another with seven. Thus, the greatest number that could be in either group is seven. The correct answer is (C).

3) Question three gives you the complete list of students taking English: K, L, O, M, P, and N. It is your task to determine who could take biology. There are a few rules concerning the setup of biology. You still need K in biology, so K must be one of the students who is in both classes. Furthermore, since M was used in English and M cannot register for both courses, M cannot be included in biology. Finally, if I is in biology then H is not. These facts taken together allow you eliminate (A), which has both I and H in biology, and (B), (D), and (E), which all contain M. The correct answer is (C).

4) This question again gives you the entire setup for English. It says that M, P, N, J, L, and O take English and asks for a group that could not be taking biology. There are only two rules that allow you to say if someone is in English then they are not in biology. First, since M is in English, M cannot take biology, so any group that contains an M would be a group that could not take biology and would therefore be correct. Unfortunately, there are no choices that contain M. Second, the deduction says if J takes English then I cannot take biology. The question placed J in English, so I cannot take biology. Thus, any group that included I would be one that cannot take biology. Any answer that contains I is the correct answer. The correct answer is therefore (A).

5) Question five sets the number of students to nine by saying that each student takes exactly one course. Since each student must be used, the conditional statements become much stricter. Someone not in one group must be in the other. By knowing the people taking English you also know the people taking biology. Treat this as a rules question by going through the rules and determining whether any answer choice breaks a rule. As you look at the answer choices, think of the effects on the group taking biology as well. None of the choices breaks the numerical arrangement rules or the rule about M. Since K must be in biology and can only be used once in this question, (B) cannot be correct because it places K in English. (A) and (E) cannot be correct because they leave both I and H for biology, but if I is in biology then H cannot be in biology. (D) cannot be correct because it does not have P and N together, Thus, the correct answer is (C).

6) For this question you must find a pair of two students who could not both be registered for both classes. The only rules that restrict who can be registered for both classes are the conditional statements and the rule that says M is not in both classes. Unfortunately, none of the answer choices contains M, so the question requires a little more thought. The first conditional statement says that if J is in English, then H is in biology. This does not, however, that if J is in English that H cannot be in English. H could be registered for both classes and this would satisfy the condition that if J is English, H is in biology. Thus, J and H could both be in both classes. This question was testing your understanding of this rule, for if you interpreted the rule to mean that if J is English then H cannot be in English then the incorrect answer (A) would appear correct. The second conditional statement says that if I is in biology, then H is not in biology. This rule means that I and H can never be together in biology and so I and H could not be a pair taking both biology and English. The correct answer is (D).

7) This question is asking for the minimum number of different students who must be used if P and N can each take exactly one course. From the rules you know that both P and N must be used, K must be used, and M must be used. Thus, there are four different students who must register for classes. Suppose that the one course P and N take is the one that M does not take. One possibility here is that M is with K in biology, along with exactly two others: perhaps L and O. If exactly two of K, L, and O also take English with P and N, then the rules can be satisfied with only six students. Since at most two students can register for both classes, it is not possible to go below six, but even with the constraint on P and N in this question, it is possible to have only six, and so the correct answer is (B).

1) The first question is a typical rules question. Go down rule by rule to see whether each answer violates the particular rule you are looking at. Once you have eliminated an answer, do not test it for the other rules. This is also your chance to review the rules to catch any you may have missed or misunderstood. You will know this is the case if you have more than one right answer or no right answer at all. The correct answer here is (C).

2) If B is assigned to lane 1 in the first round, then A's partner in round 2 cannot be B. A's partner must be either B or C, so if it is not B, it must be C. B and E are left as teammates. The correct answer is (D).

3) This question asks for what must be false without giving you any additional conditions in the question or in the answers. The answer, therefore, is based on the rules and the deductions. If you made the deduction that A's partner must be either B or C, this is an easy question to answer. If you didn't make the necessary deduction, you would be forced to do so now. The correct answer is (B).

4) If A and B are assigned to the same team, then obviously B and E cannot be assigned to the same team. Remember, if E is assigned to lane 3 in either round, then he must be on the same team as B. Because E cannot be on the same team as B for this question, E cannot be assigned to lane 3 in either round. If E and his partner, who must be C, cannot play in lane 3, then the other two pairs, AB and DF, must play in lane 3. Since A and B play in lane 1 in round 2, they can only play in lane 3 in round 1. Thus, it must be true that A and B are assigned to lane 3 in the first round. In other words, the correct answer is (A).

Question Analysis and Answers

5) This question again tests your understanding of the possible arrangements of partnerships. E must be with either B or C, with the other of B or C being with A. So E and A cannot be together. Thus, E cannot be in lane 1 in round 2, since A is there by rule; and since E is in lane 2 in round 1, that leaves only lane 3 for E to be in for round 2. Since E must be in lane 3, E must partner with B. So the answer is (D).

6) Question 6 places E in lane 3 in the first round. If E is assigned to lane 3, then his partner must be B. Since E's partner is B, A's partner must be C. Now that you know who goes with whom, look at who goes where. You are looking for the pair of bowlers who must bowl in lane 3 during round 2. A and C are already bowling in lane 1 in round 2, so they cannot bowl in lane 3. Furthermore, E and B already bowl in lane 3 during round 1, so they cannot bowl in lane 3 in round 2. Thus, the remaining partnership, D and F, must bowl in lane 3 in round 2. The correct answer is (E).

7) If E and C are teammates then immediately you know two things: 1) A and B are teammates and 2) E's team cannot be assigned to lane 3. Since E and C cannot be assigned to lane 3, E and C must be assigned to lanes 1 and 2. A and B must be assigned to lane 1 during round 2, so in order for E and C to be assigned to lane 1, E and C must be assigned to lane 1 for round 1. Since E and C must be assigned to lane 1 in round 1, E and C cannot be assigned to any other lanes in round 1. Thus, in order for E and C to be assigned to lane 2, E and C must be assigned to lane 2 in round 2. Since A and B are assigned to lane 1 in round 2 and E and C are assigned to lane 2 in round 2, the team made up of D and F must be assigned to lane 3 in round 2. Therefore, it must be true that D is in lane 3 in round 2. The correct answer is (B).

1) The first question is not a typical rules question, but it is simple once you have the diagram filled in with all the available information. The question wants to know who D's partner could be in round three. If you worked through the deductions section, this would be easy to determine merely by looking at the diagram. You would see that D could not be with Q or T and therefore could only be with P or S. If you did not work through the deductions section, this is still an easy question and will hopefully force you to begin the process of making deductions. D is partners with Q in round 1, and so cannot be partners with Q in round 3. Furthermore, T is partners with F in round 3, so T cannot be partners with anyone else in round 3. Now you've eliminated Q and T as possibilities, leaving only P and S. The correct answer here is (C).

2) This second question tests the deductions. From the deductions you know that C's partner in round 2 must be T and that C's partner in round 3 must be Q. There is only one answer choice that satisfies these requirements. The correct answer is (A). It is important to note that if you did not make deductions before moving to the questions and relied solely on the rules, it would only be possible to eliminate two answer choices, (B) and (C). This question forces you to work out the deductions.

3) Question three tests the deductions again. The question asks what must be false without introducing any new conditions, so the correct answer should be something that you already know, or could have known had you worked out the deductions. Go through the answer choices and compare them to your diagram to see whether or not each answer choice must be false. (A) does not have to be false because you do not know F's partner in round 2; you only know that F's partner must be either P or S. (B) must be true; D and T are partners in round 4. (C) must be false and is, therefore the correct answer. Q cannot be with F in round

2 because Q must be with G in round 2. Here is a recap of how it was determined that Q and F must be together in round 2: Since D is with Q in round 1, D cannot be with Q in any other round, which is to say that D's partner in round 2 cannot be Q. G's partner in round 3 is the same as D's partner in round 2, so G's partner in round 3 cannot be Q. F's partner in round 3 must be T, so neither G, nor F, nor D can be partners with Q. Thus, Q must be partners with C in round 3. C's partner in round 3 (Q) is the same as F's partner in round 4, so F's partner in round 4 is Q. Because Q is partners with D in round 1, C in round 3, and F in round 4, Q's partner in round 2 must be G. Again, (C) is the correct answer. (D) could be false but does not have to be since the placement of P and S is flexible. (E), on the other hand, must be true.

4) This is another question that is easy to solve merely by checking each answer choice against the diagram, but only if you have deduced all that you can. As you go through each answer choice you are looking for an answer that could be true (which is not to say that it must be true). (A) has D with T in an earlier round than D is with S. However, this cannot be true because D must be with T in round 4. (B) puts F with P in an earlier round than F is with S. F must be with either P or S in both round 1 and round 2, so it is possible to place F with P in round 1 and place F with S in round 2. (B) is the correct answer.

5) To answer this question, consult the diagram. You are looking for a player who could partner with P and S in consecutive rounds, although not necessarily in that order. From the diagram (and the previous question) you know that F could be with P or S in rounds 1 and 2, that D could be with P or S in rounds 2 and 3, and that G could be with P or S in rounds 3 and 4. Thus, F, D, and G could all partner with P and S in consecutive rounds. Find the answer choice that has those three players. The correct answer is (C).

6) The previous question just demonstrated that there are three people who must be with one of P or S in consecutive rounds. Thus, if you know which one of P or S any of those players are partners with in any round, you will know which one of P or S that player is with in the other round. You will also be able to place the other of P or S in each round, causing a chain reaction to take place that will enable you to complete the diagram by placing all eight instances of P and S. This question places S with G in round 4. If S is with G in round 4, then C must be with P in round 4 and in round 3 G must be with P. Since G is with P in round 3, D must be with S in round 3. Since D is with S in round 3, D must be with P in round 2, which, in turn, places F with S in round 2. Finally, since F is with S in round 2, in round 1 F must be with P, which means that in round 1 S must be with C. Now you know the entire arrangement. Go through the answer choices and find the answer that must be false. The correct answer is (E). D cannot be partners with S in round 2.

7) Without adding any conditions, this question wants to know which of the answer choices includes a pair of partners that must be in consecutive rounds, regardless of the order in which these partnerships appear. Because there are no new conditions, this question is based on the original diagram where the only information missing is the placement of P and S in each round. Because you do not know any specific placements for P or S, you can eliminate every answer choice that includes P or S. This only leaves one choice. The correct answer is (D).

Question Analysis and Answers

1) The first question is a typical rules question. Go down rule by rule to see whether each answer violates the particular rule you are looking at. Once you have eliminated an answer, do not test it for the other rules. This is also your chance to review the rules to catch any you may have missed or misunderstood. You will know this is the case if you have more than one right answer or no right answer at all. The correct answer here is (A).

2) This question tests a deduction. If you hadn't worked through this deduction beforehand, you would be forced to do so now and it would be harder to do with the answer choices there to distract you. Because anyone who orders T must also order C and B and because no one can order both C and B, no one can order T. The correct answer is (B).

3) If exactly four foods are selected, then there are only two possibilities: either P is selected or P is not selected. Remember, if P is selected, then O, R, and S must also be selected, which would make four foods. This is one scenario. The other possibility is if P is not selected. If P is not selected then you must choose four of the remaining foods. Both C and B and M and R are either/or foods. This means that you have a choice of four of C/B, M/R, S, O, and Y, which means that you are choosing four out of five possible foods. If O is chosen then both R and S must be chosen, leaving only one other food. If O is not chosen, then S, Y, and one of C or B and one of M or R must be chosen. So, in the first scenario Carol chose P, O, R, and S. If P is not chosen and O is chosen, then there must be O, R, S, and one other item. If O is not chosen then S, Y, and one of C or B and one of M or R. The only common item among these three possibilities is S. If only four foods are selected the S must be included. The correct answer is (C).

4) This question is very easy to answer if you took a moment to walk around the game. If you didn't, you would have to go through the same reasoning here. There are nine total foods but

T cannot be chosen, so really Carol can only choose from eight foods. Of these eight foods there are two pairs that are either/or. C and B cannot be together and M and R cannot be together. Thus, there are eight possible choices, but the greatest number of items that Carol can order is six. The correct answer is (C).

5) This question asks if the pairs of foods in the answer choices could both be selected. There are not extra conditions introduced, so you know that the questions are probably going to be based on either the rules or the deductions. The only way to reach the correct answer is to go through the choices one by one and see if they work. The work that you did for question three can also come in handy because you have a few scenarios worked out. (A) cannot be true because the rules say that M and R cannot be selected together. (B) and (D) cannot be true because they include T. (C) can be true. There are no rules that separate M and S. The correct answer is (C). (E) cannot be true because from the deductions you know that if P is included then R must be included and R and M cannot be both be selected. Thus, Carol cannot order P and M at the same time.

6) As opposed to the previous questions, this question asks for a pair that could not both be selected. With the rules and deductions in mind, go to the answer choices. There is nothing wrong with (A). Y is the wildcard, so Y could be with P, which means there is nothing wrong with (B). From the deductions, you know that O and M cannot both be selected. If O is selected then R must be selected and R and M cannot both be selected, so it is impossible for Carol to order both O and M. The correct answer is (C).

7) There are nine total foods but T cannot be chosen, so really there are only eight foods to work with. Of these eight foods there are two pairs that are either/or. C and B cannot be together and M and R cannot be together. Thus, there are eight possible choices, but the greatest number of items that Carol can order is six. From the deductions section you know that if M is chosen then neither O nor P can be chosen. This takes you down to four. The correct answer is (C).

1) The first question is a typical rules question. Go down rule by rule to see whether each answer violates the particular rule you are looking at. Once you have eliminated an answer, do not test it for the other rules. This is also your chance to review the rules to catch any you may have missed or misunderstood. You will know this is the case if you have more than one right answer or no right answer at all. The correct answer here is (B).

2) Question two asks for a deduction. If you did not make this deduction before attempting to answer the questions, this question would force you to make it. V must be always visit site 2. According to the rules V does not visit site 3. Since V does not visit site 3, V must either be on team A in plan 1 and visit sites 1 and 2 or be on team B in plan 2 and visit sites 2 and 4. Either way, V must visit 2, so V must always visit site 2. The correct answer is (D).

3) The third question presents you with a situation, grouping S and Y together, and then asks for what must be false. Begin by asking yourself what you know about S. From the deductions above you know that S always visits 1 and must also visit either 2 or 3. If S and Y were in 1 and 2, then V, who must always visit 2, would also have to be included with S and T. Since 1 and 2 would have V, S, and Y, it would have to be true that T and Y are not together, which, according to the rules, forces T into site 2. This places too many people at site 2. Thus, S and Y must visit 1 and 3 rather than 1 and 2. Since S and Y are in 1 and 3, you must be dealing with plan 2, which means that V and W visit 2 and 4. You are now left with T and R to place. Actually, you already know the placement of R. Remember, if you are following plan 2, then R must visit sites 2 and 4, leaving T to visit sites 1 and 3. Thus, team A, which visits sites 1 and 3, is S, Y, and T, and team B, which visits sites 2 and 4, is V, W, and R. Go through the answer choices and find the one that must be false based upon the setup that you just determined. The correct answer is (D). Y cannot visit site 2 because Y is on team A and visits sites 1 and 3. Alternatively, if you worked out the three possible scenarios, the question is much easier. S

and Y can only be together in one scenario. You must be dealing with plan 2, where S, T, and Y are on team A and visit sites 1 and 3 and V, W, and R are all on team B and visit sites 2 and 4. Since you know the entire setup you can easily go through the answer choices and pick out the one that must be false. The correct answer is (D). Y cannot visit site 2.

4) According to the deductions and the correct answer from question two, V must always visit site 2. This question says V is on team B. Only in plan 2 does team B visit site 2, so you must be dealing with plan 2 and V must visit sites 2 and 4 along with W. Furthermore, since you are dealing with plan 2, R cannot visit site 3, which means that R must be on team B and must also visit sites 2 and 4 along with V and W. The remaining three, S, T, and Y, must visit sites 1 and 3. Alternatively, if you already worked out the scenarios, then you can easily solve this question after knowing that you are dealing with plan 2, because the setup for plan 2 is completely fixed: 1) S, T, Y; 2) V, W, R; 3) S, T, Y; 4) V, W, R. Thus, the only answer choice that does not have to be true is (C). In fact, (C) must be false. T must visit sites 1 and 3.

5) If T visits site 3, and therefore does not visit site 2, then T and Y must be together. You cannot determine whether this TY block visits 3 and 1 or 3 and 4. However, if T and Y visit 1 and 3, then they will be with S, creating a group of S, T, and Y and leaving V, W, and R for the other group. On the other hand, if T and Y visit 3 and 4 they must be with W, creating a group of W, T, and Y and leaving V, S, and R for the other group. Therefore, it is impossible for R and Y to be on the same team. The correct answer is (B). If you already worked out the scenarios, then you could have easily reached this conclusion by using what you know. According to the three scenarios, if T visits site 3 then the team that T is on must include either S, T, and Y, or W, T, and Y. In both cases, the remaining team must include V, R, and one of S or W. Thus, it is impossible for R and Y to be on the same team. The correct answer is (B).

6) This question asks for two surveyors that could be on team A together. You know already that W must be on team B so you can eliminate any answer that contains W, which eliminates (C) and (D). Since you know S must be on team A, the team will include S and exactly two other surveyors. You could arrive at the answer by comparing the three remaining choices to previous work. For instance, in the previous question you determined that S's team could include S, T, and Y or S, V, and R. Look for any of these combinations. V and R are there in choice (B), so (B) is the correct answer. You could also have arrived at the answer by testing each of (A), (B), and (E) individually until you found the right answer. (A) makes team A include S, R, and T. Since there is no room for V, this team would have to visit sites 1 and 3, which means it would have to follow plan 2. However, in plan 2 R cannot visit site 3, so this cannot work. (B) makes team A include S, R, and V, which means team A visits sites 1 and 2 since V must always visit site 2, leaving T, Y, and W to visit sites 3 and 4. This works! (E) does not work because it places S, V, and Y at sites 1 and 2, thereby separating T and Y, which would force T to visit site 2 as well. Either of these approaches would lead you to the correct answer, but there is still a third way that probably works even faster. This third way only works if you took the time to determine all the scenarios. The question asks for two surveyors that could be on team A together. In plan 1 team A visits sites 1 and 2 and, according to the possible scenarios that result from plan 1, must include S, V, and either R or T. In plan 2 team A visits sites 1 and 3 and, according to the possible scenario that results from plan 2, must include S, T, and Y. Look for one of these combinations among the answer choice. (B) contains R and V, which could be the case in plan 1. Thus, (B) is the correct answer.

7) If Y is on the team that visits site 4 then Y must be on team B with W. Now think about the relationship between T and Y. With W and Y at site 4, the third person could be T, which would mean that W, Y, and T visit sites 3 and 4 and S, V, and R visits sites 1 and 2. If, on the other hand, T does not visit site 4 along with Y, then T and Y are separated and T must visit site 2. If this is the case then the teams that visit sites 2 and 4 cannot be the same, so you must be dealing with plan 1

where team A visits sites 1 and 2 and team B visits sites 3 and 4. If T visits sites 1 and 2, and you already know that S visits site 1 and that V visits site 2, then team A would include S, V, and T and team B would have to include W, V, and Y. In one possibility site 2 is visited by S, V, and R and in the other possible setup site 2 is visited by S, V, and T. Thus, if Y is on the team that visits site 4 then both S and V must site 2. Check the answer choices for one of these two people. The correct answer is (B). A more efficient approach to this question is available if you have worked out the three scenarios: If Y is on the team that visits site 4, then Y must be on team B with W. According to the three possible scenarios, this setup places you in plan 1. There are now two possibilities: W and Y could be with either R or T. If W, Y, and R visit sites 3 and 4 then S, V, and T must visit sites 1 and 2. On the other hand, if W, Y, and T visit sites 3 and 4 then S, V, and R must visit sites 1 and 2. In both cases, S and V must visit site 2. Check the answer choices for one of these two people. The correct answer is (B).

8) If R visits site 3, then R must visit site 4 as well, which tells you that he is on team B in plan 1. Since W is already in 4, team B must include R and W. Team A, or the surveyors who visit sites 1 and 2, must include S and V since you already know that S visits site 1 and that V visits site 2. Since you know two of the three people on each team, you also know that there is no room for T and Y to be together. Since T and Y must be split, T must visit site 2, putting him on team A with S and V. Thus, team A includes S, V, and T and team B includes R, W, and Y. The question asks for two surveyors who must visit site 1, so find some combination of two of S, V, and T. The correct answer is (C). Alternatively, if you worked out the three scenarios then you can skip a few of these steps. Using the scenarios, you can reach the answer following these steps: If R visits site 3, then R must visit site 4 as well, which tells you that he is on team B in plan 1. There is only one possible scenario where R visits sites 3 and 4. In this scenario team A, which visits sites 1 and 2 includes S, V, and T. Thus, team A includes S, V, and T and team B includes R, W, and Y. The question asks for two surveyors who must visit site 1, so find some combination of two of S, V, and T. The correct answer is (C).

1) The first question is a typical rules question. Go down rule by rule to see whether each answer violates the particular rule you are looking at. Once you have eliminated an answer, do not test it for the other rules. This is also your chance to review the rules to catch any you may have missed or misunderstood. You will know this is the case if you have more than one right answer or no right answer at all. The correct answer here is (A).

2) The second question is a deduction question. Since it gives you no additional information, it requires you to test each answer choice. But before you do a full scenario for each, it is usually helpful to see if there is one choice that clearly must be false based on the deductions you have already made. Recall that if B and F fill the E _ _ C gap, F cannot be beside C. (B) would place F beside C, so it cannot be true. The correct answer is (B).

3) This question places A immediately before B, which, since B and F are consecutive, means that A, B, and F are consecutive. Having this ABF sequence tells you 1) that B and F are not in the gap between C and E, and 2) that A is not in the gap between C and E. Thus, D and G must be in the gap between C and E, and you know D must be before G. Furthermore, both D and G must be before C, so the setup must be: EDGC, leaving you with only the ABF sequence. The ABF sequence could either be before the other four countries or after the other four countries. With this in mind, go to the answers and look for the choice that cannot be true. The correct answer is (E). G cannot be invaded immediately before E. G must be invaded immediately before C.

4) If E is third, C must come after E because there is not enough room to have C before E while keeping them separated by two spaces. With E third, C must be sixth. D and G must both be before C and B, and F must be adjacent, so there is only one country that

could be seventh: A. This setup leaves two pair of adjacent spaces: 1 and 2 and 4 and 5. One set of adjacent spaces must be filled with B and F, the other with D and G. If B and F are in 4 and 5, remember that F cannot be next to C, so B would have to be fifth. (B) violates this rule, so (B) is the correct answer.

5) Question five places A first and D second. Since A and D are first and second, the gap between C and E must be filled with B and F. Therefore, there is a sequence of CBFE. You do not know whether C or E is at the beginning of this sequence. Interchanging C and E will affect the placement of B and F since F cannot be adjacent to C. Either way, G must be before C, so G must be before the entire CBFE sequence. Therefore, G must be third. You know, then, that E and C, in whichever order they are, must be fourth and seventh, while B and F, in whichever order they are, must be fifth and sixth. Now that you know the setup, go to the answer choices and find the one that could be true. The correct answer is (C).

6) If G is second, then D must be first because D is before G. This allows you to make the same deduction as the previous question: B and F must fill the gap in between C and E. C and E must either be third and sixth or fourth and seventh. Since F cannot be adjacent to C, B must either be before or after C, depending on the order of C and E. Thus, the correct answer is (C).

7) The seventh question tests possible scenarios. If you saved your work then this should be an easy question. In the correct answer to question one and the previous two questions either B or F was in the sixth position. In questions four and six E and C could have been sixth. A is the wildcard and could also be sixth. Furthermore, if C is last then G could be sixth, but because D must be before both G and C, there is no way for D to be sixth. Thus, there are six countries that could be sixth, which means that (E) is the correct answer. It is almost easier here to ask yourself what cannot be sixth. From the initial order of D..G..C, it is clear that D cannot be sixth. Everything else could be sixth.

1) The first question fills one of the slots and tests whether you can determine the consequences of that placement. If T is visited on Thursday morning, then D must be on Thursday afternoon. There must be at least two consecutive empty mornings and with the DT block on Thursday, these two empty consecutive mornings will have to be some combination of Monday and Tuesday, or Tuesday and Wednesday. Either way, Tuesday morning must be empty. The correct answer is (C).

2) If Friday has two empty slots, then, in order to get two consecutive empty mornings, the only other empty slot is Thursday morning. The Thursday afternoon slot will be the last, so it must be either R or T. But T requires D on the same day, which would not be possible because Thursday morning is empty. So R must be the town visited on Thursday. The correct answer is (C).

3) If B, a Wyoming city, is on Friday, then it must be in the morning because a Montana city must be the last city visited. This Montana city must be either R or T, but since D and T go together on the same day, the town visited on Friday afternoon must be R. Now you need a Wyoming city first. You've already used B, so the first town must be D. (Remember your deduction: either B or D must be first city visited.) D would have to be the morning and T would therefore be in the afternoon. That leaves only the S..E.. C sequence. D would be first, T would be second, and S would be third. The correct answer is (D).

4) If there are no visits on Monday morning or on Friday afternoon, then the other empty space must be Tuesday morning in order to have two consecutive empty mornings. Now that you know all three days where there are no cities visited, all the remaining slots must be filled with a city. The only way to have a Wyoming city visited first, which in this case is on Monday afternoon, is if B is visited first, for there is not room for both D and T on Monday. The only way to have a Montana city visited last, which in this case is on Friday morning, is if R is visited last because there is no room for both D and T on Friday. Now you are left with the S..E..C sequence and the DT block. The next slot available in the week is Tuesday afternoon. The only town that could be on Tuesday afternoon is S since there is not room for both D and T on Tuesday and since S must be visited before both E and C. Thus, the first and second towns must be B and S. The correct answer is (B).

5) On any "must" or "could" question, first scan the answers for a rule, a deduction, or scenario that you may already know. If you don't see anything that jumps out at you, then you must go to the list of answers and ask yourself if these could be true. (A) could be true; this was one of the deductions. (B) could be true. Placing S on Thursday morning leaves room for the E and C on Thursday afternoon and Friday morning, and also leaves Friday afternoon for a Montana town. (C) cannot be true. (C) tests your understanding of the relationship between the deductions concerning the cities that must be first and last. (C) says, in effect, that B is not first, which means that D must be first and that T must be visited on that same day. Your other deduction says that R or T must be last. But T is already used, so the last stop must be R. There is therefore no way that R can be before B. The correct answer here is (C). (D) could be true, as it was also one of the deductions. (E) could be true; there are no rules that specify a city must be visited on Monday.

6) This question again tests the deduction about the cities that can be the first and last cities visited. If R is not last then T must be last. T carries D with it and since T must be last, T must be visited in the afternoon of that day while D must be visited in the morning of that day. The correct answer is therefore (D). D must be scheduled for a morning visit.

7) Question seven is looking for some piece of information that will allow you to determine the entire setup. In order to determine the entire setup, you need to fix the placement of the two blocks: the DT block and the block of two empty consecutive mornings. You must also fix which city is first and which city is last. Keep these requirements in mind as you go through the answer choices. Both (A) and (B) deal with the placement of the DT block, but neither allows you to determine where the empty mornings are. (C) does not allow you to determine anything. (D), on the other hand, provides enough information to identify the day and time of each visit. If S and C are on consecutive mornings, beginning on Wednesday, then S must be visited on Wednesday morning, E must be visited on Wednesday afternoon, and C must be visited on Thursday morning. The only slots left for two empty consecutive mornings are Monday morning and Tuesday morning. The answer choice says that no city is visited on Thursday afternoon either, so you now know all three empty slots. The only entire day remaining for the DT block is Friday, and since the last city visited must be a Montana city, T must be the city visited on Friday afternoon while D must be the city visited on Friday morning. This leaves B and R, in that order, for Monday and Tuesday afternoons since B must be the first city visited now that D is not an option. (D) is the correct answer. (E) allows you to determine the placement of the DT block but does not fix the location of the two empty consecutive mornings.

1) The first question is a rules question that is a bit more challenging than some, or at least may appear so. The question deals with the order of treatment, so go through the rules and deductions that deal with the order of treatment. As you do so, see whether any answer choices violate the particular rule you are looking at. The requirement that K is treated either immediately before or after P is violated by (A), (C), and (E). You are only left with (B) and (D). Once you have exhausted the rules themselves, go to your deductions. Remember, you need to test only (B) and (D). It turns out that (D) violates the deduction that G cannot be the fourth animal treated because this does not leave room for four animals to have serious injuries. The correct answer here is (B).

2) Question two is a deduction question. If you did not make the deduction concerning J already, this question makes you do it. As explained in the deductions step, J must have a serious injury because K and H cannot be together and two dogs have to have a serious injury. The correct answer is (B).

3) Question three tests the same deduction as question two. Either K or H must have a serious injury, but not both. The reasoning for this was that K arrives before H but gets treated after H. This is not possible within the same category because within each category the order of treatment is determined by the order of arrival. Since two dogs must have a serious injury but both K and H cannot, one of K and H must have a serious injury and J must have a serious injury. The correct answer is (D).

4) Question four gives you a scenario. It places G as the fifth animal treated and asks for what must be true. Since G is the fifth animal treated and cannot have a serious injury, the first four animals must be the animals with serious injuries. J must have a serious injury according to the deductions, so J must be one of the first four animals treated. If you look at the two scenarios for the possible order of treatment, you will see that the first scenario, where J is in the serious category with K, cannot work here because it would require S, H, P, and K to be ahead of J and would require that at least S and H be in the critical group. However, there is not room for four animals to be ahead of J, nor is there room for a critical group. Thus, J and H must be the two dogs that have serious injuries. This scenario requires K to have a less serious injury than J, which in this case means that K must have a mild injury. In order to keep P adjacent to K, P must have a mild injury as well, because they both must come after G. The four animals with serious injuries are Q, S, J, and H, though not necessarily in that order. The three animals with mild injuries are G, K, and P, though not necessarily in that order since K and P are interchangeable. Go through the answer choices and find that one that must be true. The correct answer is (C). It must be the case that J is injured more seriously than P because J must have a serious injury and P must have a mild injury.

5) This question places P as early as possible in the order of treatment and then asks for what must be true. From comparing the two scenarios it is clear that P can be treated earlier in the first scenario, where J and K are in the serious category, and that in this scenario the earliest that P can be is third. With P third, S and H must be first and second and must make up the critical category since H and K cannot be together in the serious category. In order to have four serious injuries and to have those four seriously injured animals include two cats and two dogs. P, K, J, and Q must have serious injuries and these animals must be treated third, fourth, fifth, and sixth, though not necessarily in that order. G must therefore be treated seventh and must be in the mild category. Go through the answer choices and find what must be true. The correct answer is (C). G must be treated seventh.

6) This question says that there are no animals with mild injuries. This means that there will be four animals with serious injuries and three animals with critical injuries. One of the animals that has a critical injury must be G. Remember, H must have a more serious injury than K, so for this question where there is no mild category, H must have a critical injury. S must be treated ahead of H, so S must have a critical injury as well. You now know the three animals that have critical injuries: G, S, and H. The remaining four, K, P, J, and Q have serious injuries. Since K and J both have serious injuries, J must come after the KP sequence. The question wants to know which animal can be fourth and the only possibilities are K, P, and Q. Find one of these in the answer choices. The correct answer is (D).

7) The seventh question requires you to follow the same logic as in question six except this time it is the critical classification that is done away with. This setup gives you four animals with serious injuries and three with mild injuries, one of which must be G. Since H must have a more serious injury than K, K must also have a mild injury. The question asked for an animal that cannot have a serious injury. You already know of two: K and G. Check if either of these are in the answer choices. Luckily, K is there. The correct answer is (A).

1) The first question is a typical rules question. Go down rule by rule to see whether each answer violates the particular rule you are looking at. Once you have eliminated an answer, do not test it for the other rules. This is also your chance to review the rules to catch any you may have missed or misunderstood. You will know this is the case if you have more than one right answer or no right answer at all. The correct answer here is (D).

2) This question asks for the number of songs that could occupy the position farthest from the middle, or, in other words, the number of songs that could be song 1. If you had thought about this previously, then this would be an easy question to answer quickly. Only L, N, R and S could be first, so the correct answer is four. If you did not arrive at this conclusion in the deductions section, you would be forced to do so now. Regardless, this should be relatively painless. Based on the diagram of relative order, it is clear that out of the five songs that must be used, only L and N could be song 1. Out of the remaining four songs, if Q is used then it must be in position 5 and if P is used then it cannot be song 1 or 7. Thus, neither Q nor P could be song 1. S is the wildcard, so it could be song 1 and R could also be song 1 as long as it is next to N. Once again, there are four songs that could occupy the position farthest from the middle: L, N, R, and P. The correct answer is (D).

3) This question gives you the two songs that must be recorded in addition to the fixed set of five. The CD must include songs P and Q with P closer to the middle than Q. If Q is used then Q must be the fifth song (or third from the middle). P must be closer to the middle than Q, but P cannot be seventh, so P must be sixth. You are now left with the sequence of L..M..H..K, with N sometime before K, to fill the five remaining spaces (1, 2, 3, 4, 7). K must be the last song in this sequence in order to leave room for the other four songs, so K must be seventh. The first four songs must be some combination of L, M, H, and N, but you cannot determine what the order is since you do not know anything about

the order of N relative to the other three. The question wants to know what could be true, so with these limitations in mind, go through the answer choices and find the one that could be true. The correct answer is (D). It could be true that M is third.

4) This question places K as far from the middle as possible. From the list of relative order of the five songs that must be included and as was evident in the previous questions, there must be at least four songs before K. Thus, the earliest, or in other words the farthest from the middle, that K can be is in position 5. L, M, H, and N must come before K, although not necessarily in that order since you cannot determine the exact position of N relative to L, M, and H. This setup leaves positions 6 and 7 for two of P, Q, R, and S. K is already in position 5 so Q cannot be included on the CD and there is no room for R to be adjacent to N, so R cannot be included either. Therefore, P and S must be the two remaining songs and P cannot be seventh, so P must be in position 6 and S must be in position 7. You now have a good idea of the entire order, which makes the question easy to answer. Remember, you are looking for something that must be true, not what merely could be true. The correct answer here is (B).

5) Question five requires more work than the other questions, or at least a little more thought. Even the question itself requires some interpretation. The question asks for a pair of songs that could not both be adjacent to H on the same CD. In other words, you will need to ask yourself whether H can be in between the two songs given to you in each answer choice. If H cannot go between the two songs provided, then you have found the correct answer. As you can see, the only way to determine this is to go through each answer choice. Keep in mind, however, what you know about H. H must come after L and M and before K. (A) places H in between Q and N. Q would have to be fifth, H would have to be fourth, and N would have to be third. This works because it leaves room for L and M to be before H. (B) could also be true because S is the wildcard. (C) places H in between R and Q. Once again, Q would have to be fifth, putting H fourth and R third. Since R is used,

R must be adjacent to N, which forces N into position 2. This does not leave room for L and M to be before H. Thus, the correct answer is (C). H cannot be adjacent to both R and Q.

6) If neither S nor P is included on the CD, then both Q and R must be included. Since Q is included, Q is in position 5. Since R is included, it must be adjacent to N. N, and therefore R, must be before K. Thus, R and N cannot go in positions 6 and 7. They must be in two of the four positions before Q. You still need to place L, M, H, and K. With R and N before Q, there are only two other spaces available before Q. These two positions must be filled with L and M since they are the first two songs in the order of L..M..H..K. Thus, L, M, R, and N must be before Q, while H and K come after Q. The question wants to know every song that could be in position 4. Since L must be before M, L cannot be in position 4. You cannot determine the relative order of M, R, and N, so any one of these three could be in position 4. Thus, the correct answer is (C).

7) This question says that L cannot be first and K cannot be last. If you had determined in the deductions that only K and S can be last, then this question is much easier. By saying that K cannot be last, this question is really saying that S must be last. If S must be used, then only one more of P, Q, and R can be used. Thus, it must be false that both P and Q are used as it says in (B). The correct answer is (B). If you hadn't determined earlier that only K and S can be last, you would be forced to do so now and it would probably take a much longer time because it is not apparent that that is what you are looking for.

1) This is not a typical rules question. You cannot eliminate any of the answers by simply glancing at the rules. Once you accept this the only thing to do is go to the answer choices. The question says, "Each of the following must be false EXCEPT:" so you are actually looking for something that could be true. Try answer choice (A). If F cleans a bedroom on Sunday and Monday, then those bedrooms must be B2 and B3, not necessarily in that order, because the earliest B1 can be is Wednesday. This forces D and G to be consecutive on Tuesday and Wednesday, not necessarily in that order. If D and G are consecutive, then B3 must be immediately before the day off, which is impossible in this setup. Move on to (B). If F cleans bedrooms on Sunday and Wednesday, then once again, these must be B2 and B3, not necessarily in that order, because if B1 were to be on Wednesday, then D would have to be on Sunday. Because F must clean two bedrooms consecutively, B1 would have to be on Thursday. D would, therefore, have to be on Monday, leaving Tuesday for G. Once again D and G are consecutive, requiring B3 to be immediately before the day off and once again this is impossible. Now try (C). If F cleans a bedroom on Sunday, that bedroom must be either B2 or B3. If K is on Monday, then G and D must be consecutive on Tuesday and Wednesday, respectively. Having D on Wednesday forces B1 to Saturday. The only two days left are Thursday and Friday. Since D and G are consecutive, B3 must be immediately before the day off. Thus, B3 must be on Thursday and the day off must be on Friday. However, since Felix cleans a bedroom on Saturday or (in this case and) on Sunday, Felix cannot clean a bedroom on Thursday. (C) must therefore be false because it requires B3 to both be on Thursday and not be on Thursday. Next try (D). G is on Monday and D is on Tuesday. The fact that D is on Tuesday means that B1 is on Friday. Next, D and G are consecutive again so B3 must be immediately before the day off. The only room for this sequence is if B3 is on Wednesday and the day off is on Thursday. In order for there to be two consecutive bedrooms, B2 must be on Saturday, leaving K for Monday. It works! The correct answer is (D).

2) If Tuesday is Felix's day off, then there is no possible way for G and D to be consecutive and at the same time have B3 immediately before the day off. Thus, G and D cannot be consecutive. Because the day off is Tuesday and G must be cleaned sometime before W, the only days on which Felix can clean G are Sunday and Monday. In order for G and D to not be consecutive, D must be on Wednesday. Since you know D is on Wednesday, you also know that B1 must be on Saturday. One rule says if there is a B on Sunday or Saturday then there is not a B on Thursday. Thus, there is no B on Thursday. From the "Walk Around It" section, you know that if no B's can be cleaned on Thursday, then Thursday can only contain K or the day off. The day off has already been used on Tuesday; therefore, K must be on Thursday. The correct answer is therefore (C).

3) If two of the B's are cleaned on Saturday and Sunday, then the two consecutive B's must be on either Sunday and Monday or on Friday and Saturday. If the two B's are on Sunday and Monday, then those two B's would have to be B2 and B3 since B1 must be after D. But this would place D and G on Tuesday and Wednesday, which would require that B3 be before the day off. This is clearly not possible. Thus, the two consecutive B's must be on Friday and Saturday. Thus, either B2 or B3 is on Sunday and the other of B2 or B3 and B1 are on Friday and Saturday. This question asks specifically about the placement of D. What you know about D is that there must be exactly two days between D and B1. At this point you know that B1 must be on either Friday or Saturday, which means that D must be on either Tuesday or Wednesday. If D were on Tuesday, then B1 would be on Friday. G must be before Wednesday, so in this case G would have to be on Monday. This would make D and G consecutive, and if they are consecutive then Felix must clean B3 on the day immediately before his day off. This is impossible with this setup. Thus, D cannot be on Tuesday and must be on Wednesday. The correct answer is therefore (C).

4) Question four places K on Tuesday and then adds the condition that there are no B's before Wednesday. Be clear about what this condition really means. No B's can be before Wednesday, but a B could be on Wednesday. In fact, a B must be on Wednesday. If the three B's were cleaned after Wednesday, which is the same as saying that they are cleaned on Thursday, Friday, and Saturday, then there would be a B on both Saturday and Thursday, in direct violation of the rules. Thus, a B must be cleaned on Wednesday in order to keep this violation of the rules from occurring. With K on Tuesday and a B on Wednesday, D and G must be consecutive on Sunday and Monday, although not necessarily in that order. Since D must be on either Sunday or Monday and there must be exactly two days between D and B1, B1 must be cleaned on either Wednesday or Thursday. Furthermore, since D and G must be consecutive, B3 must be immediately before the day off. Thus, the three bedrooms and the day off must be sometime over the course of Wednesday, Thursday, Friday, and Saturday. Remember, there cannot be a B on both Thursday and Saturday, which means that the day off would have to be on Thursday or Saturday. Since B1 must be on either Wednesday or Thursday, it is impossible for B3 to be on Wednesday and the day off to be on Thursday. Thus, the day off must be Saturday, which means that B3 must be cleaned on Friday. With B3 and the day off on Friday and Saturday, bedrooms 1 and 2 are interchangeable on Wednesday and Thursday. Now it is clear what can and cannot be true. The only answer choice that could be true is (A). Felix can clean bedroom 1 on Thursday.

5) This question introduces the conditions that F cleans D on Sunday and K on Friday. As usual, first go to the rules to see what else you can fill in. If D is on Sunday then B1 will be on Wednesday. At this point you have D on Sunday, B1 on Wednesday, and K on Friday. In all the questions so far it has been apparent that the rule about the placement of D and G has been important. Apply it to this question as well. If D and G are consecutive (which means G is on Monday), then B3 and the day off must be consecutive. If G is on Monday, is there any room for B3 and the day off to be consecutive? No, there is not. Only Tuesday, Thursday, and Saturday would be left. This tells you that there is no way for D and G to be consecutive. The only way that G can fit in the schedule while not being next to D is if G is on Tuesday. You are still left with Monday, Thursday, and Saturday on which to have B2, B3, and the day off. Felix must clean two of the bedrooms on consecutive days. The only way to have two bedrooms consecutive is to have Felix clean a bedroom on Thursday, although you cannot determine whether it is bedroom 2 or 3. Now you have one other bedroom and the day off to place on either Monday or Saturday. One contrapositive says if Felix cleans a bedroom on Thursday, then Felix does not clean a bedroom on Saturday or Sunday. Thus, out of the remaining bedroom and the day off, only the day off can be on Saturday, leaving the remaining bedroom for Monday. Once again, you cannot be sure whether the bedroom on Monday is B2 or B3. Now the question is easy to answer. Which day could be the day on which Felix cleans B2? Felix must clean B2 on either Monday or Thursday. The correct answer is (A).

6) This question places B2 on Sunday. If a bedroom is cleaned on Saturday or Sunday, then Felix cannot clean a bedroom on Thursday. You have already figured out that this means that on Thursday Felix must clean either the kitchen or nothing at all, or rather, Thursday must contain K or the day off. Thus, you already know one day that Felix could take off: Thursday. Based on this information you can eliminate answers (A) and (C). Now look at the only other option, which is if the K is on Thursday. Since K is on Thursday, D cannot be on Monday, leaving Tuesday and Wednesday as possibilities for D. Try Tuesday. If D is on Tuesday then B1 will be on Friday. Also, D will be next to G, which requires that B3 be before the day off. However, there is no room for B3 and the day off to be consecutive. Thus, you know that D cannot be on Tuesday and also that D and G cannot be together, leaving only Wednesday for D and Monday for G. If D is Wednesday then B1 is on Saturday. Felix must clean two bedrooms on consecutive days, so B3 must be on Friday. This leaves Tuesday as the day off. Therefore, the only two days that Felix could take off are Tuesday and Thursday. The correct answer is (D).

7) This question tells you that Felix cleans B3 on Sunday and B1 on Saturday. Felix must clean two bedrooms consecutively, so B2 will have to be either Monday or Friday. If B2 is on Monday, then the only space for G is on Tuesday, which places it next to D. If D and G are consecutive, then B3 must be immediately before the day off. That would make Monday both B2 and the day off, which obviously cannot happen. Since you had the answer narrowed down to Monday and Friday and you just ruled out Monday, the answer must be Friday. Don't do any more work! The answer correct answer is (A). Felix can only clean bedroom 2 on one day.

1) This question tests your deduction about the placement of R, especially as the placement of R relates to S and U. If you did not make this deduction prior to beginning the questions, you would have to make it here. If that is the case, be sure to recognize the answer to this question as a deduction. If R and U vote the same way at the initial meeting and U always votes the same way as S, all three of R, U, and S must vote against the proposal. Since R and U vote the same way, T must also vote the same way, which means T votes against the proposal. The only member left is Q, and Q must always vote with the majority. Thus, this scenario gives you all five members voting against the proposal at the first meeting. The correct answer is (E).

2) If only two vote for the proposal then there are three that vote against it. Q must be with the majority, so Q votes against the proposal with the SU pair. This leaves you with R and T to vote for the proposal. The question also tells you that Q votes against the proposal at the second meeting. Since Q must be with the majority, a majority votes against the proposal at the second meeting, which means that at least three people vote against the proposal at the second meeting. There are only five people, so the highest number that could vote for the proposal in the second meeting is two. The correct answer is (B).

3) This question is a deduction question. If there is a second meeting, then you know from your deductions that R voted for the proposal at the first meeting and, by rule, must vote for it again at the second meeting. The correct answer is (B).

4) If the proposal is adopted at the second meeting, then a majority must vote for it at the second meeting. First of all, this means that Q must vote for the proposal in the second meeting. Secondly, since there is a second meeting, R must have voted for the proposal in the first meeting and must therefore vote for the proposal in the second meeting. So now you know that Q and R must vote for the proposal and that you need one more of S, T, or U to vote for the proposal. S and U must vote together no matter what. If S and U vote for the proposal, then R and U are together, and this means that T must vote for the proposal as well. The other possibility is that S and U vote against the proposal while T votes for it. In either case, T must vote for the proposal. No matter what, both Q and T must vote for the proposal in the second meeting. The correct answer is (B).

5) This question tells you first of all that there is a second meeting, so R must vote for the proposal in the both meetings. Secondly, the question tells you that U votes for the proposal in the second meeting. You deduced from question four that if U votes for the proposal in the second meeting, then everybody must vote for the proposal. Just in case you missed it, if U votes for the proposal then S votes for it as well, giving you R, S, and U voting for the proposal. Since R and U are together, T must be there as well, and Q must vote with the majority. The correct answer is therefore (B). If U votes for the proposal at the second meeting then all five members of the committee must vote for the proposal at the second meeting.

6) This question is also a deduction question. If there is a second meeting, then you not only know that R votes for the proposal at both meetings, but you also know that Q must have voted against the proposal in the first meeting. In other words, it must be false that Q votes for the proposal during both meetings. The correct answer is (B).

1) The first question is a typical rules question. Go down rule by rule to see whether each answer violates the particular rule you are looking at. Once you have eliminated an answer, do not test it for the other rules. This is also your chance to review the rules to catch any you may have missed or misunderstood. You will know this is the case if you have more than one right answer or no right answer at all. The correct answer here is (C).

2) This question tests your deductions, which makes it a very simple question. After working through the deductions you probably know the answer off the top of your head. If you had not worked out the deductions, then you would be forced to do so here. If H does not receive a medal, then B does not receive a medal according to the contrapositive of the rule that says if B wins a medal then H also wins a medal. If B does not win a medal, then according to the deductions you know that G, C, and either I or D win the medals. Thus, this answer is (B).

3) Question three again tests your understanding about the placement of B and the effects that its placement has on the medal winners. If G scores lower than B, then C, G, and I or D cannot be the three countries that win medals. If these three countries do not win medals then it must be true that B wins a medal. If B wins a medal, then C and H must also win medals. You cannot fix the rest of the order, but you do have a good idea. Go through the answer choices and find the correct answer. Keep an eye on questions like this one because the question says EXCEPT. In this case, you are looking for something that does not have to be true, or something that could be false. In this case, everything must be true except (B), which must be false because B wins a medal and D does not. (B) is the correct answer.

4) Question four is a simple question that tests your ability to read your diagram. This was one of the deductions: F and E cannot win medals. Find one of those in the answers. The correct answer is (E).

5) If I finishes in the top three, then you know that B cannot be in the top three because if B were in the top three, then C and H would be the other two countries that receive medals. According to the scenarios already worked out, if B does not win a medal, then G, C, and either I or D must win also. Since G and C must win medals, look for one of them in the answer choices. The correct answer is (B).

6) If F scores lower than exactly four teams, and since H must be before F, and both B and C must be before H, there is only room for one more country before F. Because there is room for only one more country, it is impossible for B to be knocked out of the top three. In other words, B must win a medal. If B wins a medal, then C and H must also win medals. Look through the answer choices for something that must be true; it is there in (D). H and B must win medals. (D) is the correct answer.

7) This is another question based on the deductions. C must always win a medal. The correct answer is therefore (B).

1) The first question is a typical rules question. Go down rule by rule to see whether each answer violates the particular rule you are looking at. Once you have eliminated an answer, do not test it for the other rules. This is also your chance to review the rules to catch any you may have missed or misunderstood. You will know this is the case if you have more than one right answer or no right answer at all. The correct answer here is (D).

2) This question gives you the additional information that K and N are together, and asks for a side effect of that condition. If you had noticed that in both scenarios K and P must be together, then right away you can determine that P must be on the same side as K and N. P is indeed one of the answer choices. The correct answer is (D). Another way to arrive at the same conclusion is to look at the two scenarios. In scenario 1, if K and N are together they would be on side A with P and L. In scenario 2, K and N would be on side B with P, J, and Q. In both scenarios, the KN pair must be with P. The correct answer is still (D).

3) This question does not give you any additional information, so it is testing your deductions. Go through the list of answers and find what must be true according to what you have determined so far. The correct answer is (C). M and R must always be on the same side.

4) Having Q third on side B puts you in the second scenario, so side B must have P, J, N, Q, and K. Look for an answer that has some combination of those. The correct answer is (B).

5) The only scenario where J and M can be together is scenario 1. This would place them on side B as 1 and 2 in either order and would completely determine the group that is on side B. Side B must include J, M, R, and O, with R and O fixed as third and fourth but J and M interchangeable as first and second. Since you know all the songs on side B, you also know the songs that must be on side A: P, L, K, Q, and N. L is third and the K is fourth, leaving P, N, and Q to fill spaces 1, 2, and 5 in some combination. The question is a "must be false except" question, so look for something that could be true. The correct answer is (D). P could be immediately before Q.

6) If O and J are on the same side then you must be dealing with scenario 1 and O and J would have to be on side B, which means that M, J, R, and O are on side B, although not necessarily in that order. Since you know the songs that are on side B, you know that P, L, K, N, and Q must be on side A, although not necessarily in that order. The question asks for three tracks that must be on side A, so go through the answer choices and find any combination of P, L, K, N, and Q. The correct answer is (E).

7) This question undoes the deduction about K because now it is not restricted to being fourth. This might seem to make the question very complicated, but break the question down and see what happens. The question tells you that side A is the side with 5 and that J is fifth. According to the rules, if J is on side A then both M and N must be on side B. Since K cannot be on the same side as M, K must be on side A. L must still be third on side A and P must still be on the side with five, so P is on side A as well. Side A now looks like this: _ _ L _ J. You still need to place K, Q, and P. In order to get K immediately before Q, K must be first and Q must be second, leaving P as song four on side A. The correct answer is therefore (B). Often these questions that eliminate rules are easier than they look. Simply apply the remaining rules.

1) The first question tells you a male dog is in cage three. If you hadn't figured it out already, this question forces you to deduce that the only two possibilities for the male dog in cages 1 through 3 are C and D, as well as what happens when that male must be D. You know you are in scenario 1. Look at what you have in cage 5 and find it in the answers. The correct answer is (D).

2) This question places Y in cage 4. This means that you are in scenario 2 where C is in cage 2. Since Y is in cage 4, B must be in cage 7. Since D is adjacent to B, D is in 6. You are left with any combination of M, S, and T for 1, 3, and 5. Go to the answers and find one of these possibilities. The correct answer is (E).

3) Here you need to find the complete and accurate list for the placement of D. Look at what you've already determined. From scenario 1 you know that D could be in 3, and from scenario 2 you know that D could be in cage 5 or 6. Thus, D could be in 3, 5, and 6. You could have arrived at this question just as easily by realizing that in the first scenario D is in cage 3 and that in question 2 you had to place D in cage 6. There is only one choice that has both 3 and 6. Regardless of how you attempted to arrive at the answer, the correct answer is (D).

4) This question places S and T in adjacent cages. Can you have S and T adjacent in scenario 1? Yes. You could have S and T in cages 1 and 2 in either order. This means that M must be in cage 5. The entire setup looks like this: S T D B M C Y, where S and T are interchangeable. With this setup in mind, look at the answers and find what could be true. The correct answer is (B).

5) This question wants to know what piece of information will allow you to completely determine the order of the dogs in the cages. Scenario 1 tells you the most, but in scenario 1 you still don't know the placement of M, T, and S. Cage 5 must be M or T, while S and the other dog left over are in cages 1 and 2, though not necessarily in that order. You know

the determining factor for each scenario is the placement of C. In order to be in scenario 1, C must be in 6. How would you know if C is in 6? If something else is in cage 2, then you would know that C is in 6. But, as you've determined, you still wouldn't know whether M or T is in cage 5 or the order of S relative to the other of M or T that is in one of the first two cages. So in order to know the whole order, you must know that something other than C is in 2, as well as something about M and T. Look for an answer that tells you both those things. The correct answer is (E). By placing T in cage 2, you know that C is in cage 6, D is in cage 3, B is in cage 4, M is in cage 5, Y is in cage 7, and S is in cage 1.

6) If S is in cage 6, then you know you are dealing with scenario 2, which means that C is in cage 2, and that cages 1 and 3 must be filled by female puppies. Since S in cage 6 and Y must be in either cage 4 or 7, the only two female puppies left are M and T, so they must be in cages 1 and 3, in either order. In other words, M must be placed in cage 1 or 3. The correct answer is (B).

7) Question seven again places you in the second scenario by assigning C to cage 2. The question also assigns M to cage 1. These two pieces of information are the only things set in stone right away: M is in cage 1 and C is in cage 2. You also know that cage 3 must have one of S or T in order for there to be exactly two females in cages 1 through 3. Cages 4 and 7 must be B and Y, although you cannot determine which one is in which. Since you want to find the total number of possibilities, see how many possible scenarios there are when B is in cage 4 and Y is in cage 7. With B in cage 4 and Y in cage 7, D must be in cage 5 while cage 6 must have one of S or T. Thus, when B is in cage 4 and Y is in cage 7, S and T are the only flexible items and interchanging them creates two possibilities. Now test what happens if Y is in cage 4 and B is in cage 7. D would have to be in cage 6 and one of S or T would have to be in cage 5. Once again, S and T are the only flexible items and interchanging them creates another two possibilities. Two plus two equals four so there are four different combinations possible when M is placed in cage 1 and C is placed in cage 2. The correct answer therefore is (C).

1) The first question is a typical rules question. Go down rule by rule to see whether each answer violates the particular rule you are looking at. Once you have eliminated an answer, do not test it for the other rules. This is also your chance to review the rules to catch any you may have missed or misunderstood. You will know this is the case if you have more than one right answer or no right answer at all. The correct answer here is (B).

2) If B is in position 3, then you are dealing with scenario 1, where B is third, A is first, E is second, C is fourth, and D and F are interchangeable in positions 5 and 6. F could therefore host either the fifth or sixth meetings. The correct answer is (E).

3) The question gives you the condition that B is immediately before or after F. This is only possible in the second scenario where B could be fifth and F sixth. If F is sixth then the only meeting that D could host is the first meeting. The correct answer is (A).

4) Question four is perhaps the easiest question provided that you took the time to make deductions and walk around the game. While the question asks for someone who could host the second meeting, you have already had the conscious thought that E must host the second meeting. The correct answer is (D).

5) This question tests your deduction about A and B. If you hadn't figured it out earlier, you would have to do so now. The A_B separation must be either 1 and 3 or 3 and 5. Either way, the third person must be A or B. The correct answer is (A).

6) If F comes sometime before A, you know you are in scenario 2, with F first, E second, A third, C fourth, B fifth, and D sixth. The correct answer is therefore (E).

7) The only condition in question seven is that D hosts his meeting sometime after C hosts his meeting. This situation is possible in both scenarios. In the first scenario where A and B are first and third the setup looks like this: AEBCDF with A and B interchangeable and D and F interchangeable. Thus, in this scenario there are four different possible orders. In the second scenario, if D is after C, then the setup looks like this: FEACBD. Add this one possibility to the other four and you end up with five possible scenarios. The correct answer is (C).

1) The first question is a typical rules question. Go down rule by rule to see whether each answer violates the particular rule you are looking at. Once you have eliminated an answer, do not test it for the other rules. This is also your chance to review the rules to catch any you may have missed or misunderstood. You will know this is the case if you have more than one right answer or no right answer at all. The correct answer here is (C).

2) The button labeled S is the bottom button. Based on the list of relative order, you know that neither S, nor L, nor C can be on the bottom. This leaves you with R, which could be on the bottom and the two wildcards, G and O. Thus, there are three flavors that could possibly be produced by the S button. The correct answer is (C).

3) This question asks for the button that produces the flavor on its label if S is produced from the L button. Both C and L must be above S, so with S in the slot labeled L, the C and L must be in the two slots above L, slots R and O, although you cannot determine which one goes in which. From the deductions it was clear that the buttons that produces the flavor on its labels is O, G, or L. Since the question puts S in the slot with the L button, the L button is out of the question. Likewise, the O button must produce either C or L so O is out of the question. The only remaining button that can produce the flavor on its label is G. The correct answer is therefore (D).

4) This question adds a flavor to the list of relative order that you already have. O must be higher than C. Thus, the order now looks like this: O..CL..S..R. C and L are interchangeable and G is the only wildcard remaining. You have information about five of the six positions. Remember, you must have one button that produces the flavor indicated on the button. The key to this question is placing G such that this condition is satisfied. Go through the answer choices one by one and find that choice that must be false, asking yourself for each answer choice whether or not it could be true. If not, you have found the correct answer. (A) places O with the O button, which means that C, L, S, and R go in the four slots beneath O (L, C, G, and S, respectively) and G goes in the slot labeled R. This setup works since O is with the O button and no others are with their buttons. (B) was the case in answer choice (A) so it works. Now look at (C). It places G in the slot labeled O. In order to keep C and L consecutive and have O above C, the sequence of CL..S..R must go in the four slots beneath the O button, which in turn forces O into the slot labeled with the R button. In this instance, either both C and L will correspond with the C and L buttons or neither of them will. Thus, the requirement that exactly one button produces the flavor indicated on its label cannot be satisfied. For this reason, the correct answer is (C).

5) If G is not the button labeled correctly then either the O button or the L button must be the button labeled correctly. If the O button is labeled correctly then the CL..S..R sequence must be below O in that order, forcing G to the R button. If, on the other hand, the L button is labeled correctly, then C must be produced by the O button, leaving G, O, S, and R. S and R must be somewhere below L, but you cannot determine exactly where. G and O are both wildcards, although neither G nor O can be with their corresponding buttons. With these two scenarios in front of you, you can easily go through the answer choices and find what could be true. The correct answer is (C). In the scenario where L is the button labeled correctly, it is possible for O to be produced by the button labeled G.

6) This question tests the deductions that you have made and used over and over again about which buttons can and cannot be labeled correctly. Even before the questions started you were able to deduce that R, S, and C could not be labeled correctly. R and S cannot be labeled correctly due to their order and C cannot be labeled correctly because that would force L to be labeled correctly as well. Thus, all you need to find is some combination of these three buttons in the answer choices. You could also approach this question by eliminating any answer choice that contains O, L or G, since you know that each of these can be the correctly labeled button. The correct answer is (B).

7) If G is immediately above or below C then there must be a sequence of GCL or LCG. This sequence must be above S and R such that it looks like this: GCL..S..R or LCG.. S..R, leaving only O in either case. The question wants to know which button must be labeled appropriately. According to the deductions, only the O, G, or L button could be labeled correctly. However, in this setup it is impossible for the G button to be labeled correctly because G must be above at least two other drinks. It is likewise impossible for the O button to be labeled correctly because doing so would leave no room to satisfy the requirement that G, C, and L all be consecutive. Thus, L must be the button that is labeled correctly. The correct answer is (C).

1) The first question is a typical rules question. Go down rule by rule to see whether each answer violates the particular rule you are looking at. Once you have eliminated an answer, do not test it for the other rules. This is also your chance to review the rules to catch any you may have missed or misunderstood. You will know this is the case if you have more than one right answer or no right answer at all. If the rules by themselves do not allow you to determine the correct answer, test the answer choices against the deductions. (A), (B), and (C) can all be eliminated because they break rules. (E) can be eliminated because of the deduction that says if S is reviewed on Tuesday then V, and not Y, must also be reviewed on Tuesday. If you didn't make this deduction, you would have to in order to answer this question. Here it is again: S must be reviewed by I. Since (E) has S on Tuesday, I would have to be the manager on Tuesday. However, I cannot review Y, so it is impossible for S and Y to be together on Tuesday. The correct answer here is (D).

2) This question says that K does not review any employees during the week and that W is reviewed on Tuesday. W and T must be reviewed on the same day, so T is on Tuesday as well. Because K does not review any employees, only I and J are available. Between I and J, only J can review both T and W, so J is the reviewer on Tuesday. You have already deduced that Tuesday must contain one of V and Y. Since you know that J is the reviewer on Tuesday and that J cannot review V, you know that Y is reviewed on Tuesday. Due to the R..Y rule, you now also know that R must be reviewed on Monday. You are only left with S and V to place on the diagram. At least one of S and V must be on Wednesday in order to satisfy the condition that at least one employee is reviewed each day. You cannot determine which of S or V is reviewed on Wednesday, but between J and I, only I can review S or V. Therefore, I must conduct the reviews on Wednesday. The correct answer is (D).

3) If Y is reviewed on Tuesday, then according to the R..Y rule, R must be on Monday. In addition, according to the deductions, if Y is reviewed on Tuesday then the TW block must be reviewed on Tuesday as well. In case you missed it, the reasoning behind this deduction is that if Y is on Tuesday, I cannot conduct the reviews on Tuesday, thereby ruling out the possibility that S is reviewed on Tuesday. Tuesday must have one of either S or the TW block, and, since it cannot have S, it must have the TW block. At this point you have used R, T, W, and Y, and have yet to assign any employees to Wednesday. Notice that this list of R, T, W, and Y is, in fact, the list of the employees that J can review. Thus, this scenario uses up all J's employees. This means that J cannot conduct the reviews on Wednesday, for he does not have anybody left to review. In this question you just made another deduction that must be true. Be sure to write it down with the rest of your deductions: if Y is reviewed on Tuesday, then J cannot conduct reviews on Wednesday. The correct answer is (E).

4) This question makes K the reviewer on Monday. K cannot review employee R, so in order for R to be before Y, R must be reviewed on Tuesday and Y must be reviewed on Wednesday. Since Tuesday must contain one of V or Y and Y is used on Wednesday, V must be on Tuesday. This gives you R and V on Tuesday. The only manager that can review both R and V is I, so I is the reviewer on Tuesday. Either S or the TW block must also be on Tuesday but I cannot review T and W, so S must be reviewed on Tuesday. Furthermore, since Y must be reviewed on Wednesday and I cannot review Y, Y must be reviewed by either J or K. At this point you have K conducting reviews of undetermined employees on Monday, I conducting reviews of R, V, and S on Tuesday, and Y being reviewed on Wednesday by either J or K. The only employees remaining are T and W, who must be together. In order to have at least one employee reviewed on each day, the TW block must be reviewed on Monday by K. You now know the reviewer of every employee except one. You cannot determine who conducts a review of Y on Wednesday. The correct answer therefore is (E).

5) This question does not give you any additional information to work with, but it tells you what to focus on: Tuesday. Think about what you know about Tuesday. Tuesday must have one of V and Y and one of S and the TW block. Tuesday cannot contain both of the employees in either of those pairs. First check if one of these is the answer. It is not. What now? After you have exhausted the possibilities that you know of—and only then—you should move to the answer choices and work each one out. Start with (A). If R and S are on Tuesday, then you know I is the reviewer on Tuesday. Because R..Y, Y must be on Wednesday. In order to have at least one person on each day, the TW block would have to be on Monday. This appears to be a valid scenario, so move on to (B). If R and T are on Tuesday, then W must be on Tuesday as well. In order to have R before Y, Y must be on Wednesday, leaving V for Tuesday. This gives you R, T, W, and V on Tuesday. There is no manager who can review all of four of these employees. This scenario does not work. The correct answer is (B). Stop there and move on.

6) This question makes J the reviewer on Tuesday and K the reviewer on Wednesday. I must be included since he is the only manager that can review S, so I must be the reviewer on Monday, which, of course, means that S is on Monday. Since S is on Monday, the TW block must be on Tuesday. Tuesday must also have one of V or Y. Since the question tells you that J conducts reviews on Tuesday, it is easy determine which of V or Y must be there. Between V and Y, J can only review Y. Thus, Y is reviewed on Tuesday. In order to have R before Y, R must be reviewed on Monday. You are only left with V, who must be reviewed on Wednesday in order to have at least one employee reviewed each day. Now you can easily answer the question. V must be reviewed by K on Wednesday. The correct answer is (D).

7) If I conducts reviews on Wednesday, then Y cannot be reviewed on Wednesday. Since Y cannot be reviewed on Monday and now cannot be reviewed on Wednesday, Y must be reviewed on Tuesday. Since R must be reviewed on a day falling sometime before Y and Y is reviewed on Tuesday, R must be reviewed on Monday. Tuesday must also include one of S or the TW block. S must be reviewed by I, but I cannot review Y, who is already on Tuesday, so I cannot review the employees on Tuesday, which means that the TW block must be on Tuesday instead of S. You are left with S and V, at least one of whom must be reviewed by I on Wednesday. At this point you know the placement of exactly four of the employees: R is on Monday, and T, W, and Y are on Tuesday. Wednesday must include at least one of S or V. The managers are a little less restricted. I must be the reviewer on Wednesday. Both J and K can review T, W, and Y, so either J or K is the reviewer on Tuesday. Both I and J can review R, so either I or J is the reviewer on Monday. Now that you know as much as you can, go to the answer choices and find the answer that must be false. The correct answer is (D). K cannot review V on Monday.

1) This question tells you that Johnson meets with a C on Thursday and an L on Friday. The fact that one L is on F means that the other L must be on T. You know that you need one day with 2 A's. The only days available that will allow you to have an A in both the morning and the afternoon are Monday and Wednesday. If the 2 A's are on Monday then an E is on Tuesday in addition to the L that is already there, which fills up Tuesday. The remaining single A could be on Wednesday or Thursday. If A is on Wednesday, then an E is on Thursday, and if A is on Thursday, then E is on Friday. Either way, Thursday would be filled with either an E or an A and the C that was placed there by the question. This leaves Wednesday and Friday as possible days on which Johnson could meet with the S. The only answer choice that contains both Wednesday and Friday is (B). The correct answer, then, is (B). J could also meet with the S on Monday if the 2 A's are on Wednesday. This would force the single A to Monday and would allow S to be on Monday as well.

2) This question tells you that Johnson meets with the E's on two consecutive days. According to the rules, there is an E on the day after any A. In order to satisfy the condition that the E's are on consecutive days, the setup must include two A's on one day, one A and one E on the next day, and one E on the day after that. This setup fills up two entire days and leaves one slot available for the third day. You need to figure out who could fill the one remaining slot on that third day. Notice how this block of three days relates to the condition that the two L's are separated by exactly two days. If the three-day sequence of E's and A's does not include an L, then it would be impossible for the two L's to be separated by two days; they would be separated by three days. Thus, the one empty slot on the third day of the sequence must include an L. In order for the two L's to be two days apart, the second L must be on the day immediately before the two A's. Thus, you know for certain that the setup includes

an L on one day, two A's on the next day, an A and an E on the day after that, and an E and an L on the day after that, although you do not know whose meetings are in the mornings and whose meetings are in the afternoons. Nevertheless, three of the five days are completely filled, and one is partially filled with an L. The remaining people, the S and the two C's, must, in some combination, fill an entire day and the one other slot that is available on the same day as L's meeting. The two C's cannot be on the same day since they must both be in the afternoon. Thus, one C must be with the L and the other must be the S. Therefore, the sequence includes an L and a C one day, two A's on the next, an A and an E on the day after that, and an L and a C on the day after that. The one remaining day must contain an S and a C, but you do not know whether this group has its meeting on Monday or on Friday. If S and C have their meeting on Monday then the L and the C must be on Tuesday. If the S and C are on Friday then the two A's must be on Tuesday. Look for one of these pairs in the answer choices. The correct answer is (C).

3) Since this question introduces the conditions that there is an S on Monday and no A's on Wednesday, the block of two A's must be on either Tuesday or Thursday. If it is on Tuesday, then there must be on E on Wednesday. Because Tuesday is filled, the L _ _ L split must be on Monday and Thursday. At this point Monday and Tuesday are both filled and neither day can contain an E. You can therefore eliminate any answer that has either Monday or Tuesday in it because it is not true that an E must be on either of those days. Eliminating everything that contains a Monday or Tuesday leaves you with only one answer: (E). (E) is the correct answer.

4) If there is an A on Monday, there must be an E on Tuesday. Since the question places a C on Tuesday as well, Tuesday is filled up. This means that the L _ _ L split must be on Monday and Thursday. You still need the block of two A's and the only remaining possibility for its location is Wednesday. Because there are A's on Wednesday, there must be an E on Thursday along with the L that was already there. You now know the entire setup for Monday through Thursday, which means that the two remaining people, the S and the one remaining C, must have their meetings on Friday, with S in the morning and C in the afternoon. The correct answer is (E).

5) Question five places the C's on Tuesday and Friday. This is actually the scenario that you just worked out in question four. Noticing this allows you to answer the question very quickly. However, if you did not notice this, then you would have to work it out again. Placing the C's on Tuesday and Friday makes it impossible for the L _ _ L split to be on Tuesday and Friday because this would leave no way for you to have an E after every day on which there is an A. Therefore, the L _ _ L split must be on Monday and Thursday. The only room left for the 2 A's block is Wednesday, which, in turn, means that there must be an E on Thursday. The only remaining day on which there can be an A while still allowing you to have an E on the following day is Monday, so A is on Monday and an E is on the morning of Tuesday. There is only one space left for S: Friday morning. The correct answer is (E).

6) If J meets with exactly one A on Tuesday then there must be an E on Wednesday. Since there must be an L on either Monday or Tuesday, the block of two A's cannot be on Monday, because placing the two A's on Monday would force an E to be on Tuesday, leaving no room for an L. Since the question told you that there is exactly one A on Tuesday and because there must be an E on Wednesday, the block of two A's cannot be on Tuesday or Wednesday either. The two A's can only be on Thursday, which means that the second E must be on Friday. Since Thursday is filled with two A's, the L _ _ L split must be on Tuesday and Friday, filling both Tuesday and Friday. The only two afternoon slots left are the afternoon slots on Monday and Wednesday. Since the two C's must be in the afternoon, the two C's must fill those two slots. The correct answer is therefore (C). Johnson can meet with the C's on Monday and Wednesday.

1) The first question is a typical rules question. Go down rule by rule to see whether each answer violates the particular rule you are looking at. Once you have eliminated an answer, do not test it for the other rules. This is also your chance to review the rules to catch any you may have missed or misunderstood. You will know this is the case if you have more than one right answer or no right answer at all. The correct answer here is (C).

2) This question tests the deductions and is an easy one to answer quickly if you took the time to make deductions. If you did not, you would have to work through the answer choices, a long and tedious task. Equipped with the deductions, it is easy to determine that the correct answer is (C). J must see a comedy on Saturday. M must see a comedy on Friday and M must see the comedies before J, so J must see a comedy on Saturday. This is a good reminder that it is worth it to take a few seconds to work the game a little bit before you attack the questions. But if you didn't, be sure to note what you have learned in answering this question.

3) Question three does the same thing as question two. It checks to see if you made the proper deductions by asking what must be false. Go through the answer choices and compare each to the diagram. As you do so, it should be easy to spot the correct answer. The correct answer is (D). M cannot view H on Wednesday because M must view W on Wednesday.

4) If W is the first comedy that J views and the earliest that J can view W is Thursday, then in order to view all three comedies, J must view W on Thursday and the remaining two comedies, B and H, on Friday and Saturday, although not necessarily in that order. Since J cannot be the one that sees Q on Thursday, M must view Q on Thursday. Since M views Q on Thursday, M must view F on Saturday. This setup forces M to view L on Tuesday.

Since J cannot view L on Monday, and now cannot view L on Tuesday, J must view L on Wednesday, leaving F and Q for J to see on Monday and Tuesday. Now that you know almost the entire setup, go to the answer choices and find the one that could be false. The correct answer is (E) because B and H are interchangeable on Monday and Friday for M.

5) Question five gives you some additional information to work with: M must view L later in the week than J. L is a drama and M must view dramas on Tuesday, Thursday, and Saturday. Because M must view L after J, M cannot view L on Tuesday. According to the rules, it is also the case that M cannot view L on Saturday. Thus, M must view L on Thursday, leaving F and Q for Tuesday and Saturday, although not necessarily in that order. Since M views L on Thursday, J must be the one who views Q on Thursday. Since J views Q on Thursday, J must view F on Monday. You are trying to find a complete list of the days on which J or M could see F. With the constraints given in the question, J must see F on Monday and M must see F either on Tuesday or Saturday. Thus, the complete and accurate list must be Monday, Tuesday, and Saturday. The correct answer is (C).

6) This question tells you that M views F before viewing H. If you did not make the deduction that M must view one of B or H on Monday and the other on Friday, this would probably be a more difficult question than it really is. If M views F before viewing H, then M cannot view H on Monday. Therefore, M must view B on Monday and H on Friday. Also, since F is before H, F cannot be on Saturday, which means that Q must be on Saturday. Only F and L are left for M to view, and they must be split between Tuesday and Thursday. Since M is not the critic who sees Q on Thursday, J must see Q on Thursday. Since J sees Q on Thursday, he must view F on Monday. Now the rule that says M must view the comedies before H becomes very important. This setup allowed you to determine where M sees each of the comedies: B on Monday, W on Wednesday, and H on Friday. From the deductions you know that J must see W on Thursday or Friday. Now that Q is on Thursday, J must see W on Friday. In order for J to see H after M, J must see H on Saturday. The only two movies left for J to view are B and L, which must be split between Tuesday and Wednesday. You now know almost everything about the setup. There are only two uncertainties: the placement of B and L on Tuesday and Wednesday for J, and the placement of F and L on Tuesday and Thursday for M. Keep in mind that both critics cannot view L on Tuesday. With this setup in mind, go to the question and find the answer choice that could be false. The correct answer is (D). J could see L before M sees L.

7) Question seven requires you to determine what information will allow you to fill in the entire setup. There are two main approaches to this question. You can either jump in and start working out each answer choice to see if it works, or you can invest a little thought and narrow down the possibilities. Consider what the main variables are for the game. What will you have to know in order to know the entire setup? For both critics, you will need to know the placement of one of B and H and of one of F and Q. Any answer choice must include information about both splits. The answer choices that do this are (B), (D), and (E). You must also fix the location of W in Thursday or Friday for J as well as determine which critic sees Q on Thursday. (E) does not allow you to determine this, so you can eliminate (E), leaving only choices (B) and (D). These are the only two that you will have to work out. (B) allows you to fill in all the slots, but violates a rule by forcing both critics see L on Tuesday. Since (B) breaks a rule, the correct answer must be (D). If J sees H and F on Tuesday and Thursday, then J must see Q on Monday, B on Saturday, W on Friday, and L on Wednesday. Since J sees H on Tuesday, M must see H on Monday, and therefore must see B on Friday, Q on Thursday, F on Saturday, and L on Tuesday.

1) The first question is a typical rules question. Go down rule by rule to see whether each answer violates the particular rule you are looking at. Once you have eliminated an answer, do not test it for the other rules. This is also your chance to review the rules to catch any you may have missed or misunderstood. You will know this is the case if you have more than one right answer or no right answer at all. The correct answer here is (E).

2) This question adds the conditions that both H and L are not fired. If H is not fired, then it must be the case that O is not fired, for the rules say that if O is fired then H is fired. You now know that H, L, and O are not fired and that the remaining five must all be fired. Thus, the five employees that are fired are D, E, G, S, and W. W must be fired by B and D must be fired by C. Since both B and C must already fire at least one person, the ES block cannot fit in B or C. Therefore, E and S must be fired by A. You are left only with G, and in order to satisfy the requirement that B fire exactly two people, G must be fired by B. Thus, the correct answer is (A).

3) If O is fired, then the five people who must be fired are G, O, W, H, and one of D or L. Since W is fired, W is fired by B, so if O and W are fired by the same manager, O and W are both fired by B. Whoever is fired between D and L must be fired by C, but you cannot determine anything else. Go to the answer choices and find the one that must be true based on what you know. The correct answer is (E). There is no room for either E or S to be fired.

4) This question adds another block, an HG block, to the already existing ES block. If E and S are fired by B then, according to the deductions, you know that O cannot be fired. Furthermore, since E and S are fired by B, B cannot fire any more employees, which means that W cannot be fired. So far you know that E, S, H, and G must be fired, while neither O nor W can be fired. Thus, the fifth person fired must either be D or L. Regardless of which one is fired, C must do the firing. Since C must fire one of D or L, there is no room for the HG block in C, forcing the HG block into A. The only uncertainty remaining is whether C fires D or L, but you know for sure that A fires H and G and that B fires E and S. Go through the answer choices and find what must be true based on what you have determined. The correct answer is (A). C can only fire one employee.

5) Question five does not give you any conditions to work with so the answer will probably rely on something that you have already determined, especially the deductions. Quickly read through the answer choices and see if anything rings a bell. Do not attempt to work out each choice except as a last resort. Hopefully you will quickly see that (D) must be false and is, therefore, the correct answer. If O is fired, then E and S cannot be fired, and if E and S are fired, then O cannot be. This is something that you either determined in the deductions or had to deduce in order to answer question four correctly.

6) Similar to previous questions, this question creates a new block: G and O. This tells you first of all that O must be used. Since O is used, the five employees who are fired must be G, O, W, H, and one of D or L. W must be fired by B and either D or L must be fired by C, so the only room for the GO block is in A. The remaining employee, H, must be fired by B in order for B to fire two out of the five employees who are fired. Therefore, it must be false that Guillermo is fired by Boris. The correct answer is (B).

7) If D and L are fired then D, L, and G are three out of the five employees who are fired, leaving room for exactly two other employees to be fired. Since exactly two other employees are fired, it is not possible for O to be fired, for if O were fired, both W and H would have to be fired, breaking the rule that five employees are fired. Because O cannot be fired, the employees who might still be fired are E, S, H, and W. E and S constitute a block, such that if one of them is fired the other is also and if one of them is not fired then neither is the other one. Thus, the employees who are fired must be D, L, G, and either both E and S or both H and W. With this in mind, go through the answer choices and find a pair that could not be fired. The correct answer is (C). W and S cannot be fired together because if S is fired, E would have to be fired also, and this would mean that six employees are fired.

1) The first question is a typical rules question. Go down rule by rule to see whether each answer violates the particular rule you are looking at. Once you have eliminated an answer, do not test it for the other rules. This is also your chance to review the rules to catch any you may have missed or misunderstood. You will know this is the case if you have more than one right answer or no right answer at all. If the rules alone are not sufficient to eliminate every answer, don't forget to test the deductions as well, since it is only with your deduction about O and WY that you can eliminate (A). If you have not made that deduction previously, you must make it here. The correct answer here is (B).

2) This question places P in position 8 and asks for which three flags MUST be placed in the front row. If P is in 8, O cannot be in position 8, which means that O must be in the front row. If O is in the front row then G must be placed in the back row. With G, S, and P in the back row, or with position 8 taken, there is no room for the WY sequence. Thus, W and Y must be in the front row as well. O, W, and Y must all be in the front row. The correct answer is (D).

3) The third question begins by testing the deduction about the relationship between G, O, and S. If G is placed in position 2, which is in the front row, then O must be in the back row in position 8 in order to keep it separated from S. The question also tells you that W is facing O. With O in position 8, this means that W is in position 4. W and Y must be consecutive, so with W in position 4, Y must be in position 3. Because Y is in position 3, it is impossible for B to be in position 3. Since B cannot be in position 3, R and Y cannot face each other. Thus, R cannot be in position 7. Now you could get the right answer by looking at the choices and crossing off the ones that must be wrong or by knowing that the only flags left that could possibly be in position 7 are B and P, so one of them must be the correct answer. Either way, the correct answer is (A).

4) This question places P and B in positions 4 and 5, respectively. Because B is not in position 3, R and Y cannot face each other. Unfortunately, this is not the answer, so you must do a little more work. This question really tests your understanding of the relationship between the WY sequence and the rules concerning G and O. The WY sequence must either be in the front row or the back row. If W and Y were in the back row, then the back row would be completely filled, forcing both G and O into the front row. But if G is in the front row, then O is in the back row, which is impossible since the back row is full. Thus, W and Y cannot be in the back row. The correct answer is (D).

5) The fifth question again tests the WY rule. If P and R are in positions 2 and 3, respectively, then the only spaces for W and Y are in positions 7 and 8, though not necessarily in that order. Since there is no room for O in the position 8, O must be in the front row and since O must be in the front row, G must be in the back row in position 5. The correct answer is (C).

6) This question tests the deduction about the placement of R and Y if they are to face each other. Remember, if R and Y face each other, then R and Y could only be in positions 1 and 5 or in positions 4 and 8. If G is in position 1, then O must be in the back row in position 8. Since G is in position 1 and O is in position 8, there is no way for R and Y to face each other. You could also reach this conclusion by recognizing that with O in the back row, there is no room for the WY sequence, so W and Y must be in the front row. One of W or Y must be in position 3, which means that B cannot be in position 3, which in turn means that R and Y cannot face each other. The correct answer is (E).

1) The first question sets up a scenario for you. H and N perform and H is second. Because H is used, then M must be immediately before H, making M first. Now G cannot be first, so he must be fifth. N cannot be next to G, so the only spot available for N is third. The correct answer is (B)

2) If M=6, then you cannot use H, leaving you with only seven singers to fill the remaining time slots. You deduced that if not K then not L. If this were the case, you would only have five singers to fill the seven slots. Therefore, if M=6, then K must be included. The correct answer is (D).

3) This question places L fourth, which means that L..K, making K fifth or sixth. According to the question, both H and I must also give performances. If H, then M is immediately before H. There is only one place for this sequence before L because K is in either 5 or 6. The rule governing I is that I must be second, fourth, or sixth. L is already in 4, so I=2/6. But if I=2 then there is no room for the MH sequence, so I=6. This makes K=5, which in turn makes G=1, M=2, and H=3. Now you know the entire setup. Find what must be false. The correct answer is (C).

4) This question tells you that L=3 and that H is after L. According to the rules, L..K and MH. So K and MH must be 4,5, and 6 (either KMH or MHK). Either way, all three of the spaces are used, so G must be first. The only space that you don't know is 2. The question wants to know who cannot give a performance. Go through the answers: G, M, and K have to give a performance, I could be second, but N cannot give a performance because N cannot be next to G. The correct answer is (E).

Question Analysis and Answers

5) If K does not give a performance, then you know that L does not give a performance either, which means that the other six must give performances. The question places J fourth. The placement of the other performers will be governed by the rules: G=1/5, I=2/6, MH, and N is not next to G. Go to the answers and find the one that could be true. (A) cannot be true because it uses L. (B) cannot be true because J is fourth and M requires H to be immediately after her. (C) could be true. MH could be 5 and 6, with G as 1, I as 2, and N as 3. (C) is the correct answer.

6) This question establishes the conditions that N=2 and I=4. If N=2, then G=5 because N cannot be next to G. You are left with 1, 3, and 6 to fill, which does not leave room for the MH sequence. Therefore, you cannot use H. The correct answer is (A).

7) If L performs fourth, then K must be either fifth or sixth. The question also assigns I as the second performer. According to the rules, G is either going to be first or fifth. In either case there is not room for M and H to be consecutive. Thus, H cannot be used. The correct answer is (E). Since H cannot perform at all, H cannot give the sixth performance.

1) The first question is a typical rules question. Go down rule by rule to see whether each answer violates the particular rule you are looking at. Once you have eliminated an answer, do not test it for the other rules. This is also your chance to review the rules to catch any you may have missed or misunderstood. You will know this is the case if you have more than one right answer or no right answer at all. Don't forget to include any rules contained in the setup paragraph. The correct answer here is (C).

2) Question two places R and T as the only two children assigned O and also assigns N to S. Since R and T are the only children in O, O is filled, leaving D and S to work with. B cannot be in D, so B must be with N in S. Because N is not in D, K cannot be in D either so K must also be in S. Eliminate any answer choice with K or B and you are left with only (B).

3) Question three asks what will allow you to determine all of the assignments. Since there is no additional information, you will have to go through each answer choice. (A) puts B in the same squad as J and M. This does not allow you to determine the entire setup because J, M, and B could be together in either O or S. (B) does make it possible to determine all of the assignments and is therefore the correct answer. If K is assigned to D then both J and N must be assigned to D as well. Because J is not in S, M cannot be in S. The question also places L in O. If L is in O and L and M cannot be together, then M cannot be in O. Thus, M cannot be in O or S. M must be in D. That makes four people in D, which means there must be exactly two people in both O and S. R and T must be together and must be in S since L is already in O. The only person left is B, who must be with L in O. Once you've found this correct answer, you are free to move on. (C) will allow you to fill D but you cannot determine which side the RT block is on. (D) does not allow you to place the RT block, L, or J. Lastly, (E) does not allow you to get anywhere. Once again, the correct answer is (B).

4) Question four is about what cannot be true. Every answer might be true but one. For this particular scenario you will be able to place every single variable into a group, so it makes things a lot easier. The question places M and T in S. In that case, R and J must be in S as well, since R and T must be together and if M is in S then J is in S. S is now filled with four people, leaving two each for the remaining two groups. Since J is not in D, K cannot be in D, leaving K for O. Furthermore, B cannot go in D either, so it goes in O. Finally, L and N are forced into D. You now know the entire setup, so go to the answer choices and find the choice that cannot be true. The correct answer is (E).

5) For question five, you know you are dealing with the 4,2,2 distribution because the question assigns four children to O. This is important to keep in mind as you work through the question. The question assigns J and L as two of the four children assigned to O. Since J is not in S, M is not in S either, and M cannot be in O because of the L/M split. Thus, M must be in D. Also, because J is not in D, K cannot be in D. Therefore, both B and K cannot be in D. At the same time, R and T have to be together. Because M is already in D and there can only be two people in D, the RT block must either be in O or S. If the RT block is in O, then both B and K must be in S. If the RT block is in S, then both B and K must be in O. Notice the side effect: N must always be in D. Thus, it must be false that N is assigned to S. The correct answer is (B).

6) Question 6 adds a rule. The new condition creates a block of M and K. The question also places R and J in D. Since R and T constitute a block, T must go in D also. There is now no room for the MK block in D. Furthermore, since J is not in S you can determine that M is not in S. Therefore, the MK block must be in O. You are left with B, L, and N, but you cannot determine exactly where they are. With that, check your answers. You can immediately scratch out the first three answers because they do not comply with the setup, leaving (D) and (E) as the only possible answers. (D) places the three remaining children into S, which could work. (D) is the correct answer. If you are comfortable with the game, then once you have found the correct answer, you should have the confidence to move on. However, it would be easy to eliminate (E) because if O were to have four children, D could only have two children in it, while according to the setup there are already three children in D.

1) The first question is a typical rules question. Go down rule by rule to see whether each answer violates the particular rule you are looking at. Once you have eliminated an answer, do not test it for the other rules. This is also your chance to review the rules to catch any you may have missed or misunderstood. You will know this is the case if you have more than one right answer or no right answer at all. The correct answer here is (C).

2) This question assigns M to projects D and E and no other projects. This information, added to the deduction that all three of the workers are assigned to either E or F, reveals that in this case the project common to all three workers must be E. Furthermore, because M cannot be assigned to any other projects, only N can be assigned to C, and if N is assigned to C, then he must be assigned to F as well. At this point N has been assigned to the maximum of three projects and M cannot be assigned to any more projects, so L is the only worker who can be assigned to project G. Thus, it must be true that L is assigned to G. The correct answer is (B).

3) If one of M or N is assigned to both E and F and no other projects, then, because L cannot be assigned to C or D, the other one of M or N that is not assigned to E and F must be assigned to both C and D, and, in turn, must be assigned to F as well, since whoever is assigned to C must be assigned to F. Regardless of whether that person is M or N, that worker has reached the maximum number of assignments. Since either M or N will be assigned to C, D, and F, and all three workers must be assigned to either E or F, F must be the project common to all the workers, which means that one of L's two projects must be F. Since one of M or N is assigned to only E and F and the other is assigned to C, D, and F, then just as in the previous question only L can be assigned to G. The question asks for something that must be true, so quickly go through the answer choices and find the one that must be true based on what you know. The correct answer is (A). Since all three workers must be assigned to F, L must be assigned to F.

4) If L and M are the only workers assigned to F, then the project that all three workers have in common must be E, so L, M, and F are all assigned to E. Because N cannot be assigned to project F, N cannot be assigned to project C either, due to the rule that says if C then F. Since neither L nor N can be assigned to C, M must be assigned to C. Now you have used M in projects C, E, and F, which is the maximum number of projects for any worker. L cannot be assigned to D according to the rules, and M cannot be assigned to any more projects, leaving only N to be assigned to D. You are only left with project G, which could be assigned to either L or N. This question is an "EXCEPT" question, so go to the answers and find the answer choice that does not have to be true. The correct answer is (A) because it could be true that N is assigned to G instead of L.

5) This question tells you that M is assigned to G and exactly one other project. Because all three workers must be assigned to exactly one project in common, which, as you have deduced, must be either E or F, the one other project that M is assigned to must be either E or F. Due to the restrictions of this question, you have used M as many times as possible. Because M cannot be assigned to any projects besides G and one of E or F, and because L cannot be assigned to C or D, N must be assigned to both C and D. Because N is assigned to C, N must also be assigned to F. Thus, N must be assigned to C, D, and F. The correct answer is (A).

6) If two workers are assigned to D, these two workers must be M and N, for L cannot be assigned to C or D. For this same reason, at least one of M or N must be assigned to C, which would also make that worker assigned to F. Regardless of which worker is assigned to C, this means that at least one of M or N will be used three times, at projects C, D, and F. Thus, the only project that all three workers could be assigned to together is project F. This is all you can determine from the information given to you, so go to the answer choices and find the answer that must be true. The correct answer is (A). Since all three workers must be assigned to F, L must be assigned to F.

7) This question assigns N to exactly two projects: E and D. Since all three workers must be assigned to either project E or F, and since it is now clear that N cannot be assigned to F, all three workers must be assigned to project E. Since each project must have at least one worker assigned to it and since neither N nor L can now be assigned to project C, M must be assigned to project C. Because M is assigned to C, M must also be assigned to F, which means that M has been assigned to the maximum of three projects. With M assigned to as many projects as possible, and with N assigned to only D and E, L must be the one worker assigned to G. The only uncertainty remaining is whether or not L is assigned to F. With this information, go to the answer choices and find the one answer choice that could be false, the one choice that does not have to be true. The correct answer is (D). L could be assigned to F but does not have to be.

1) The first question is essentially a rules question, though it is slightly more difficult than many typical rules questions because, in order for it to be simple, it requires that you have already worked out the deductions and built your diagram. Furthermore, it is probably easier here to go through the answer choices and see whether each could be true rather than going through the rules and seeing whether any answer choices violate that rule. (A) cannot be true because if Freddie eats S for dinner four times, he would have to eat S on more than two consecutive days, which violates the rule that says Freddie eats the same food for dinner for exactly two days in a row. (B) says Freddie eats P for exactly two meals. This cannot be true because there are fifteen slots and even if Freddie eats four each of C, I, and S, there could only be fourteen meals. (C) says Freddie eats C for breakfast three times. According to the deductions, Freddie must eat C for breakfast on Thursday and Friday, so the third C would have to be on Tuesday. This does not violate any rules and therefore could be true. The correct answer is (C). (D) cannot be true because there is no room for there to be three P's for lunch without violating the rule that Freddie does not eat the same food for lunch on two consecutive days. (E) cannot be true because after making the deductions, you already know where all four of the I's are, and none of these I's are during dinner.

2) The second question tests your deductions concerning the setup on Friday. You know from the deductions that Friday breakfast, lunch, and dinner must be C, I, and P, respectively. The correct answer is (D).

Question Analysis and Answers

3) For this question, you must go through the answer choices and ask yourself whether or not the scenario that each choice gives you must be false. If it does not have to be false, then it is not the correct answer; if it must be false then it is the correct answer. (A) does not have to be false because Freddie must eat I for Friday lunch and can eat either C, S, or P for dinner on Wednesday. (B) must be false and is therefore the correct answer. Freddie eats I for Monday breakfast, so he cannot eat I for dinner on Monday. Besides, you should have already determined all four times that Freddie eats ice cream. Monday dinner is not one of them. Once you've found the correct answer (B), move on!

4) This question says Freddie eats S for dinner only once during the week. Freddie already eats S for dinner on Thursday, so Freddie cannot eat S for dinner on any other day of the week. Freddie still needs to eat the same food for two consecutive dinners. The only possible foods that he could eat consecutively for dinner are C and P since there are no more S's. Remember, both C and P have been used twice already, so whichever one is used for the two consecutive dinners will reach the maximum number of four. Thus, if you know that Freddie eats either C or P somewhere else other than for dinner or somewhere else than he already does, then you know that he could not eat that food for the two consecutive dinners, leaving the other one of the two as the food that is eaten for two consecutive dinners. In other words, if Freddie eats C or P for something other than dinner or where he already eats it, then you know which food he must eat for the two consecutive dinners. With this in mind, go to the answer choices and look for the choice that must be true. The correct answer is (D), because if Freddie eats P for lunch on Monday, then there are three P's, leaving C as the only food that Freddie could eat for two consecutive dinners. The two consecutive C's would have to be on Monday-Tuesday or Tuesday-Wednesday; in both cases C must be on Tuesday.

5) This question introduces two conditions concerning S: Freddie eats S no more than three times and he must eat S for dinner on Tuesday. If Freddie eats S for dinner on Tuesday, then there is an S on Tuesday dinner and an S on Thursday dinner. Since Freddie eats the same food for two consecutive dinners, then the only food that he could eat consecutively is S. Thus, there must be a third S that Freddie eats for dinner, either on Monday or on Wednesday. The rules say that Freddie eats the same dinner for exactly two days in a row, so it cannot be the case that Freddie eats the same dinner three days in a row. Since Freddie cannot eat the same food three days in a row, Freddie cannot eat S on Wednesday. Thus, Freddie must eat S on Monday. Since there are now three S's, there cannot be any additional S's. For lunch on Wednesday, Freddie must eat either C or S, but since there cannot be any more S's, Freddie must eat C for lunch on Wednesday. Since Freddy eats C for lunch on Wednesday, he cannot eat C for dinner on Wednesday. Now that Freddie cannot eat S, C, or I for dinner on Wednesday, it must be true that Freddie must eats P for dinner on Wednesday dinner. This is everything that you can determine right away, so go to the questions and find the choice that must be false. The correct answer is (A). You have determined that under the conditions of this question, Freddie must eat P for Wednesday dinner.

6) This question says that Freddie must eat each of the foods for lunch at least once. There are four foods: C, I, P, and S. On Tuesday and Friday Freddie eats I for lunch. On Thursday Freddie eats P for lunch. Thus, Freddie still needs to eat C and S. There are only two days remaining: Monday and Wednesday. Thus, on Monday Freddie eats either C or S for lunch, and the same is true for Wednesday. Since C is eaten twice for breakfast and once for lunch, C cannot be the food that is eaten for two consecutive dinners, leaving S and P as possibilities. Pay close attention to the rule that Freddie cannot eat the same food twice on the same day. If you know what Freddie eats for any remaining lunch or dinner, you also will know what Freddie cannot eat for that respective lunch or dinner, and eliminating something may very well tell you what Freddie must eat. Now go to the answer choices and look for the answer that must be true. (A) must be false because if Freddie were to eat C for Monday lunch, then Freddie would have to eat S for Wednesday lunch, which would mean that Freddie could not eat S for Wednesday dinner. Since Freddie could not eat S for Wednesday dinner, Freddie's two consecutive dinners of the same food would have to be on Monday-Tuesday or Tuesday-Wednesday. However, the answer choice placed C as Tuesday dinner and C cannot be the food that is eaten twice. (B) is not correct because it could be true but does not have to be true. Freddie could still eat C for lunch on Wednesday. (C) does not have to be correct, and neither does (D) because there could be fewer than four. By process of elimination, (E) is the correct answer. If Freddie has C for Tuesday dinner and C cannot be the food that is eaten consecutively, then the only room for two consecutive foods is Wednesday-Thursday, and the food that must be eaten consecutively is S. If Freddie eats S for Wednesday dinner then he must eat C for Wednesday lunch. Since he has C for Wednesday lunch, he must have S for Monday lunch.

1) Question one is not a typical rules question, but it is not as complicated as it looks. Place S on Saturday in week 2 as the question says. Remember the audition for S is held on the same day in both weeks so S auditions on Saturday in the first week as well. From the deductions you know that R must be on Monday in week 2, so you can eliminate answer choices (B), (C), and (E). If you did not make the deduction that R is on Monday in week 2, working through this question forces you to do it. If you did not determine it until now, be sure to note it as a deduction, as something that must always be true. (A) and (D) are the only two choices to worry about. They differ over the placement of R in week 1. (A) has R on Monday while (D) has R on Friday. T and V must be consecutive, and the only room for them is on Monday and Tuesday or Tuesday and Wednesday. Keep in mind that U must be separated by W by at least one space. If T and V were on Monday and Tuesday, U would be forced next to W, which cannot happen. Thus, T and V cannot be on Monday and Tuesday and must instead be on Tuesday and Wednesday, leaving U for Monday. R, therefore, must be on Friday. The answer here is in (D).

2) Question two places R on Tuesday of the first week. With R on Tuesday and W on Thursday, the only two consecutive days for T and V are Friday and Saturday, though not necessarily in that order. Since Friday, and Saturday are filled, the only day on which S can audition is Wednesday. S auditions on the same day in both weeks, so S is on Wednesday in week 2 as well. The only person left to audition during week 1 is U, who must audition on Monday. In week 2, you have R on Monday, W on Tuesday, and S on Wednesday, leaving T, V, and U for Thursday, Friday, and Saturday. T, V, and U could be in any order as long as T and V remain consecutive. Go to the answer choices and compare them with the setup that you have determined. The only answer that could be true is (E). It could be true that V auditions on Saturday of week 2.

Question Analysis and Answers

3) This question places U as early as possible in both weeks. In week 1, the earliest U could be is Monday, which was the case in question 2. In week 2, the earliest that U could be is Thursday, which was also a possibility in question 2. With U on Thursday in week 2, the only two consecutive days for T and V during week 2 are Friday and Saturday, but not necessarily in that order. Thus, the correct answer must include both Friday and Saturday. With U on Thursday and T and V on Friday and Saturday during week 2, S must audition on Wednesday during week 2. Since S auditions on the same day in both weeks, S must audition on Wednesday during week 1. Since R must come before S and since U is on Monday, R must audition on Tuesday during week 1. The only two consecutive days left for T and V in week 1 are again Friday and Saturday, although not necessarily in that order. Thus, T can only audition on Friday and Saturday. The correct answer is (E).

4) This is a simple question that tests the deduction that R is on Monday during week 2. If R auditions on Friday in one of the weeks, it must be during week 1, while in week 2 he auditions on Monday. The correct answer is (A).

5) Question 5 is a perfect example of why you should remember your work. This question asks you to place R as late possible in both weeks. From the deduction and the previous question, you know that in week 2 R must be on Monday. In week 1, the latest R can be is Friday, because R must come before S. If R is on Friday then S is on Saturday, which means S is on Saturday in both weeks. Before you do too much work, remember question 1, which placed S on Saturday. If S is on Saturday during week 1, then U is on Monday during week 1, T and V are on Tuesday and Wednesday, W is on Thursday, and R is on Friday. In week 2, you are again left with T, V, and U. U cannot be on Wednesday, so either T or V is on Wednesday, the other is on Thursday, and U is on Friday. Thus, in week 1 T and V audition on Tuesday and Wednesday and in week 2 T and V audition on Wednesday and Thursday. Regardless of the specific order of T and V in both weeks, one of them MUST audition on Wednesday. The correct answer is (C).

6) If T auditions on Monday, it must be in week 1 since R must audition on Monday in week 2. T and V are consecutive so V must audition on Tuesday. U cannot audition on Wednesday or Friday, so U must audition on Saturday. The only two slots left are Wednesday and Friday, which must be filled with R and S, respectively, since R must be before S. With S on Friday in week 1, S must audition on Friday in week 2. The only two consecutive days left in week 2 for T and V are Wednesday and Thursday. U must therefore audition on Saturday in week 2 as well. The correct answer is (E).

7) Question seven asks you to find a schedule of auditions that does not conform to the rules, or in other words, one that violates the rules. You can treat this like a basic rules question, but you must also keep in mind the side effects of the given order on the order of the other week that is not mentioned. None of the answer choices break the requirement that R is before S, that T and V are adjacent, or that U and W cannot be adjacent. Answer choice (C), however, does violate the requirement that S auditions on the same day during both weeks. You were able to deduce before even coming to the questions that S can only audition on Wednesday, Friday, or Saturday due to the placement of the W's and the placement of R on Monday during week 2. (C) has S auditioning on Thursday, which clearly violates the rules. The correct answer is (C).

1) The first question is a typical rules question. Go down rule by rule to see whether each answer violates the particular rule you are looking at. Once you have eliminated an answer, do not test it for the other rules. This is also your chance to review the rules to catch any you may have missed or misunderstood. You will know this is the case if you have more than one right answer or no right answer at all. The correct answer here is (D).

2) This question removes Y from the list of possible hires and then assigns T to the afternoon shift. It is your task to find who cannot work part-time. If Y is no longer a possibility, then the people who are left to choose from are R, S, T, W, and one of V or X. T is assigned to the afternoon either part-time or full-time and W must work part-time, so those two must work for sure. Now you are left with R, S, and one of V or X. Neither V nor X can work in the morning, so the only two possibilities for the morning shift are R and S. If R works the morning shift, then V must be hired and must be hired in the afternoon with T. Since W must work part-time and now T and V are working part-time, there are more than three part-time workers, which means that S and W must work together during the night shift. This setup gives you R working full-time in the morning, T and V working part-time in the afternoon, and S and W working part-time during the night. Using this scenario, look at the answer choices and find the applicant that cannot work part-time. S, T, V, and W all work part-time, while R does not. The correct answer is therefore (A). In the scenario you worked out, everyone except R worked part-time so you can conclude that out of the answer choices, only R cannot work part-time.

3) This question tells you that T is the only applicant hired full-time. What does this mean? T must fill one of the groups all by himself. The other two shifts must be filled with part-time workers, which means that there must be four people hired part-time. Since there are more than two applicants hired part-time, both S and W are hired for the night shift. Now you need to determine the possible placement of T. T cannot be hired for the night shift, so T must either be hired for the morning or afternoon shift. If T is hired for the morning shift, then you are left with two of R, V, X, and Y for the afternoon, which works out just fine. On the other hand, if T is hired for the afternoon shift, then the only two employees who can fill the morning shift are R and Y since V and X can only work in the afternoon. However, the rules tell you that if R is hired, then both T and V are hired, which would place V in the afternoon with T. However, since T must work full-time, no one can be hired to work the same shift as T. Thus, T cannot be hired to work the afternoon shift and instead must be hired for the morning shift. Remember, if T works the morning shift then two of R, V, X, and Y work the afternoon shift and S and W work the night shift. The question asks for an answer that must be false, so go through the answer choices and find what must be false, or what cannot be true. The correct answer is (E) because it places another person in the morning with T.

4) If Y works the night shift, then S and W cannot both work the night shift. If S and W do not work the night shift, then there must be exactly two employees hired part-time, W and someone else. W can either work the afternoon or the night shift. If W works part-time with Y during the night shift then the morning shift and the afternoon shift must be each be filled with one full-time worker. You cannot determine exactly who those employees are. On the other hand, if W works part-time in the afternoon then W and whoever W works with are the only part-time workers. This makes Y full-time in the night shift and makes whoever works in the morning a full-time worker as well. From these two scenarios, the only firm information that you can determine is that Y is either with W or alone. Because you cannot determine anything else from the information that the question provides, it is time to move to the answer choices and find the answer that must be false. Look first for something that is obviously false. The correct answer is (B) because Y must work the night shift with W or alone, which means that T cannot work the night shift.

5) This question says that R works in the morning as a part-time employee. W must also work part-time, but, according to the deductions, W cannot work in the morning. Thus, there must be at least two sets of part-time workers. Since there are more than two part-time workers, S and W must be hired for the night shift. Also, since R is hired, both T and V must be hired and X cannot be hired. V can only be hired for the afternoon shift, so V is in the afternoon while you cannot determine which shift T is hired for. At this point you have R working in the morning with one other person, at least V working in the afternoon, and S and W working the night shift. T must be hired and could either be hired for the morning shift with R or for the afternoon shift with V. You do not anything at all about Y, whether Y is hired or not. If Y is hired, Y would have to work part-time in either the morning or the afternoon. Now go to the answers and find the answer choice that could be false (because it is a must be true EXCEPT question). The correct answer is (E) because if Y is hired there would be six applicants hired.

6) If S works full-time, there is no way for S and W to be together. If S and W cannot work together, then there cannot be more than two part-time workers. The question also makes T a part-time worker, so T must be the part-time worker that works a shift with W. W cannot be hired for the morning shift so W and T can only be hired for the afternoon or night shifts. The other two shifts must be filled with full-time workers. That is all you know, so go to the answer choices and look for the answer choice that must be false. The correct answer is (A) because T is with W and W cannot work in the morning.

7) This question tests the deduction about W, which, if you did not deduce at the beginning of the game, you would have had to deduce to solve question six. W cannot work in the morning. The correct answer is therefore (D).

1) The first question is a typical rules question. Go down rule by rule to see whether each answer violates the particular rule you are looking at. Once you have eliminated an answer, do not test it for the other rules. This is also your chance to review the rules to catch any you may have missed or misunderstood. You will know this is the case if you have more than one right answer or no right answer at all. The correct answer here is (C).

2) If you took the time to make the deductions, then you already know the correct answer to this question. The highest possible number of students who could attend the spelling bee is five. (B) is the correct answer.

3) This question says that five students are selected to attend the spelling bee. Look at all three of the possible scenarios. Only in the first scenario, where F and C are both included, and third scenario, where F is not included, can there be five students. Look for a pair of students who must be selected in both of these scenarios. C and H must both be selected in either case. The correct answer is (C).

4) This question says that H and G are among the students who are selected for the spelling bee. According to the rules, if H is selected then C is selected. Thus, H, G, and C must be selected. Compare this to the three scenarios. The only time that H, G, and C can be selected together is if F is not included. Thus, the correct answer is (E).

5) To answer this question, look at the three scenarios. A can be selected in the first scenario, where both F and C are selected, and in the third scenario, where F is not selected. If it is the first scenario then the setup looks like this: A, F, C, and one or both of D/E and H. If it is the third scenario, then you must have at least four of A, D/E, H, C, and G. The question asks for a list of the students who could be selected in addition to A. Compare each answer choice

to the two scenarios. The correct answer is (C). This question also relies heavily on the rules, so many of the answer choices can be eliminated immediately.

6) If C is not selected to attend the spelling bee, then H cannot be selected either. If you take away C and H from the first and third scenarios, you are left with only three people. Therefore, this must be the second scenario, in which there is no C, no H, and no A. The correct answer is therefore (A). A cannot be selected.

7) Question seven asks for a pair of students, at least one of whom must always be selected for the spelling bee. There are two ways to answer this question. First of all, the scenarios were determined by manipulating F. When F is included there are two basic scenarios and when F is not included there is one other scenario. The previous question forced you to determine that C must be included in the scenario in which F is not included, for not including C means not including H either, leaving only three people. Thus, either F or C must always be selected for the spelling bee. The correct answer is therefore (C). The slower approach to this question is to look at each pair of students provided by the answer choices and compare them to the three scenarios. If it is the case that at least one member of the pair must be included in all three scenarios, then you have found the correct answer. (A) says that one of C or D must always be included. This is not correct because neither C nor D must be included in the second scenario, where F, G, B, and D/E are selected. (B) says that one of H or C must always be included. This is also fails in the second scenario, where F, G, B, and D/E are selected. (C) says that one of F or C must always be included. F must be included in the first two scenarios, but F is not in the third scenario. However, in the third scenario, if C is not selected, then H cannot be selected, leaving room for only three people. There must be at least four people, so in the third scenario C must be included. (C) is the correct answer. One of F or C must always be selected. (D) fails in the first and third scenario and (E) fails in the third scenario.

1) The first question is a typical rules question. Go down rule by rule to see whether each answer violates the particular rule you are looking at. Once you have eliminated an answer, do not test it for the other rules. This is also your chance to review the rules to catch any you may have missed or misunderstood. You will know this is the case if you have more than one right answer or no right answer at all. The correct answer here is (A).

2) This question asks for a pair of rooms that cannot be remodeled consecutively. Simply go through each answer choice and compare it to the list of order that you deduced. (A) could be true because S is flexible as long as it is before L. (B) cannot be true. It is impossible for D and L to be consecutive because D must be before G and L must be after G. No matter what, at least G must be between D and L. Thus, the correct answer is (B). The remaining answer choices deal with the placement of S, B, and K, all of which are flexible. Answer choices (C), (D), and (E) could all be true.

3) This question is a simple one to answer if you have the entire list or relative order in front of you, which you should if you approached the game properly. All you need to do is count the number of rooms that could be last. M, D, G, and S all have to be before L and both B and K can be anywhere. Thus, L could be last, and so could B and K. There are exactly three rooms that could be the last room remodeled. The correct answer is (B).

Question Analysis and Answers

4) If S is fourth, then the key to the order of rooms is the relationship between the BK sequence and the M..D..G..L sequence. First of all, L must be after S, leaving two other spaces after S. The BK sequence could either fill those two spaces or come before the S. If the BK sequence is before the S, then there is one remaining space before S, which must be M, and all three of D, G, and L must come after S in that order. On the other hand, if B and K come after S along with L, then M, D, and G must come before S in that order. With these two basic scenarios in mind, go through the answer choices and find the one that must be false. The correct answer is (E). L cannot be sixth. In the scenario where B and K are before S, L must be seventh. In the scenario where B and K come after S, L must be either fifth or seventh in order to allow B and K to remain consecutive.

5) If G is the fourth room remodeled and both M and D must come before G, there is only one other space available before G. Since there is only one space available, there is no room for both B and K. Thus, B and K must come after G, along with L, while S must be before G. You cannot determine the order of S relative to M and D or whether the BK sequence is before or after L. With this knowledge of both what you do know and what you do not, go through the answer choices to find the one that must be true. The correct answer is (D). Remember, you were asked to look for what must be true, not what merely could be true. Answer choices (A), (B), (C), and (E) all *could* be true but only (D) *must* be true.

6) If M is the third room remodeled and D, G, and L must come after M, then there is only room for one other room after M. In other words, there is no room for B and K, so the BK sequence must come before M. With B and K as first and second, though not necessarily in that order, and M third, you know that L must be seventh since D, G, and S must be before L. D, G, and S must be fourth, fifth, and sixth, although not necessarily in that order. The only rule governing their placement is that D must come before G. The question asks for a complete list of the rooms that could be remodeled sixth. You might be tempted to say all three of D, G and S, but since D must come before G, D cannot be sixth. Thus, the only two rooms that could be sixth are S and G. The correct answer, therefore, is (E).

7) This question places K in the third position and places M in the first position while asking for the number of rooms that could be second. If K is third then clearly B could be second, which gives you one possibility. If B comes immediately after K in the fourth position, then the remaining four rooms are D, G, S, and L. D, G, and S must all be before L so L must be seventh. With M first, K third, B fourth, and L seventh, only the second, fifth, and sixth positions remain, and these must be filled with D, G, and S, though not necessarily in that order. You need to find how many of these three could be in the second position; or, put another way, you need to know how many of D, G, and S could be first in a list of those three. Remember, the only rule governing the relationship of these three is that D must be before G. Out of these three then, only G could not be second (or first out of only D, G, and S). Thus, any one of B, D, or S could be second. The correct answer is (C).

1) The first question is a typical rules question. Go down rule by rule to see whether each answer violates the particular rule you are looking at. Once you have eliminated an answer, do not test it for the other rules. This is also your chance to review the rules to catch any you may have missed or misunderstood. You will know this is the case if you have more than one right answer or no right answer at all. The correct answer here is (C).

2) If H participates in B for his individual event, then H cannot play C. Since H must play either C or S, H must play S for his team event. Since the question also adds the condition that H and F participate in the same team event, it must be the case that F participates in S as well. Thus, the correct answer is (B). F participates in S.

3) If F and G both participate in T for their team events, then they must both participate in A for their individual events. The question asks for the possible combinations of events that H participates in. Since H's individual event cannot be the same as F's, H cannot participate in A. H's individual event could either be B or C. Since H's team event cannot be the same as G's, H cannot participate in T. H's team event could either be R or S. Remember, H participates in C, S, or both. If H participates in C for his individual event, then H could play either R or S for the team event. This adds up to two possible combinations. If H participates in S for the team event, then the only new combination is if H participates in B for the individual event. Therefore, there are only three possible combinations. The correct answer is (B).

4) If nobody plays C, then H cannot play C; however, H must play either C or S, so it must be the case that H plays S. Since H and G cannot participate in the same team event, G cannot play S for the team event. According to the question, nobody plays T either, so if G cannot play S or T, G must play R.

The question also states that F participates in B, which is an individual event. Since H and F do not play the same individual event and nobody plays C, H must play A for the individual event. Furthermore, according to the deductions, if F plays something other than A for the individual event, then F and G cannot play the same team event. Here, F and G are playing different individual events, so F and G cannot play the same team event. G is playing R, and nobody can play T, so F must play S. You now know both events for each child and can easily answer the question. It must be true that F and H participate in the same team event. The correct answer is (A).

5) In this question, as with almost every question, simply take the information you are given and work out the chain reaction. If G participates in S, then because G and H cannot participate in the same team event, H cannot participate in S. Since H cannot participate in S, H must participate in C. F and H cannot participate in the same individual event, so F cannot participate in C. Because, according to this question, F cannot participate in B either, F must participate in A. The correct answer is (D). Although, according to the rules, when F and G participate in the same team event they must also participate in same individual event, the reverse is not the case. So even though F and G now participate in the same individual event, this does not mean that F and G must also participate in the same team event.

6) If H participates in A for the individual event, then immediately you know that H must participate in S for the team event. Since G and H cannot participate in the same team event, G cannot participate in S. Furthermore, since F and H cannot participate in the same individual event and H is participating in A, F cannot participate in A. According to the deduction, if F does not participate in A, then F and G cannot participate in the same team event. Thus, it cannot be true that F and G participate in the same team sport. The correct answer is (B).

1) The first question tests the deductions and is simple to answer if you walked around the game. W and T must be on either the east or west side and D and the empty cubicle must be on the opposite side. The correct answer is (B).

2) Question two tests the deductions, which makes this an easy question to answer as long as you worked out the deductions. If you did not, you are forced to do so here. The correct answer is (C). D and V must always be in adjacent cubicles. Again, the reason why D and V must always be adjacent is that all the adjustors except for D (B, C, and E) must have corner cubicles and so does V. This means that D must have a non-corner cubicle. All the non-corner cubicles are adjacent to corner cubicles, so no matter what D must be adjacent to one of B, C, E, or V. But since no adjustor has a cubicle immediately next to the cubicle of another adjustor, D cannot be in a non-corner cubicle adjacent to B, C, or E. Thus, D must always be adjacent to V. If you did not determine this deduction until this question, be sure to realize that it is indeed a deduction, something that must be true throughout the game.

3) This question puts the empty cubicle as far north as possible on the west side. This means that D and the empty cubicle are on the west side. D and the empty cubicle must be in the non-corner cubicles and since the empty cubicle is as forth north as possible, it must be above D. The question wants to know the effects of placing D and the empty cubicle in this setup. Who can occupy the southwest corner? D must be in a non-corner cubicle adjacent to V, who is in a corner cubicle. Thus, V must be in the southwest corner. The correct answer is (E).

4) This question uses the same setup as the previous question. In question two D is as far south as possible. The north wall will have to have two corner offices and one of X or U. With D as far south as possible, you know that V must be in a south corner cubicle adjacent to D. Thus, the only people who could be in the two corner cubicles on the north wall are some combination of B, C, and E. Therefore, the north wall could have two of B, C, and E, and one of X and U. The correct answer is (C) because it contains a combination of the possible people.

5) If V and B are diagonal from each other, then D and the empty cubicle must be on V's side, while W and T are on B's side. Either W or T could be next to B. Since B is in a corner cubicle he must also be next to either X or U. Thus, W, T, X, and U could all be next to B. The correct answer is (A).

6) This question puts B on the south wall and adjacent to the empty cubicle. B must be in the corner, so B is in a corner on the south side, the empty cubicle is adjacent to B in a non-corner cubicle, D is in the non-corner cubicle adjacent to the empty cubicle, and V must be in the corner cubicle adjacent to D, putting V in a corner cubicle on the north wall. The question asks about the south wall, which includes two corner cubicles and one non-corner cubicle. B must be on the south wall because this was a condition of the question. One of X or U must also be on the south wall. The second corner office must be occupied by either C or E since V must be on the north wall. With this information in mind, go to the answer choices and look for a pair that cannot be on the south wall. The correct answer is (C) because V must be on the north wall.

Answers Game 42

1) The first question is a typical rules question. Go down rule by rule to see whether each answer violates the particular rule you are looking at. Once you have eliminated an answer, do not test it for the other rules. This is also your chance to review the rules to catch any you may have missed or misunderstood. You will know this is the case if you have more than one right answer or no right answer at all. The correct answer here is (E).

2) This question asks you what could be true so you are going to have to look at both scenarios and find something that could be true. The best way to do it is go through the answers and see if you have that possibility in one of your scenarios. Look at (A) and see if that combination is in a scenario. You will see it right away in scenario 1. The correct answer is (A).

3) This question adds the condition that four planets must be explored. If you expand both scenarios to include four planets, you will see that in scenario 1 and 2 both W and Y must be explored. Look for one of these as your answer and you will find it in (C).

4) If Spiff does not explore W, then you must be in scenario 2, in which Spiff visits nebula 2, nebula 3, Z, and X for certain. Spiff could also visit one, both, or neither of W and Y. Now go to the answers and find what cannot be true. The correct answer is (B). Spiff cannot visit U.

5) The condition given to you in this question is that Spiff visits as few planets as possible. Look at your scenarios. In scenario 1 Spiff must visit at least three planets, while in scenario 2 he must visit at least two planets, so the smallest number possible is two in scenario 2. This setup would have Spiff visiting Z and X. You will find this answer in (C).

6) If Spiff visits U and only two other planets, then you know you are working with scenario 1 and the two other planets must be V and W. Look for one of those in the answer choices. You will find it in (B).

7) The final question checks to see if you determined the two scenarios and the manner in which they are defined. Imagine how much more difficult this game would have been if you did not make the crucial deduction about the two scenarios until the last question. Luckily, you did the work beforehand. If Spiff visits nebula 1 and nebula 2, then Spiff must also visit V, W, one of U and X, and possibly Y. The only two planets that absolutely must be used are V and W. Thus, the correct answer is (E).

1) If an F and an S are at table 2, then the representative at table 2 must be D. The contrapositive to the rule that says if an S is seated at table 1, then B must be assigned to table 2, states that if B is not assigned to table 2, then there is not an S seated at table 1. This allows you to eliminate answers (D) and (E). Furthermore, since if there is an F at table 1, then C must be at table 2 and in this case C is not at table 2, then there cannot an F at table 1. This allows you to eliminate (A) and (B). Thus, the correct answer is (C).

2) Since this question puts an F at table 1, there must also be at least one F at table 3, B must be assigned to table 1, C must be assigned to table 2, and D must be assigned to table 3. By placing three F's at table 1, the question filled up table 1. There must still be two G's together somewhere. Since only B and C speak G, but B's table is filled with F's, the only place for the two G's is at C's table, table 2. Now you need the three S's. Because there is no room at table 1 and at least one F at table 3, the three S's must be split between tables 2 and 3, with one S at table 2 and two S's at table 3. The correct answer is (C).

3) If there are one F and two J's seated at the same table, then the representative at this table must be B and this table must be filled. That leaves you with two G's and three S's. Out of C and D, only C can speak G, so the two G's are with C, leaving one space available at C's table for either another G or an S. Now you need the three S's. At least two S's would have to be at D's table. The third space at D's table could either be another S or an F. With this information alone you can narrow the answer down to (B) and (E). You are actually looking for a group that could be seated at table 2, so look at (B) and (E) and see whether each could be at table 2. Start with (B). If there are one F and two S's at table 2, then this must be D's table. Since you still need a third S, there must be an S at C's table, along with the two G's that are already there. You've used one of the speakers of F at table

2, so it is impossible to have an F at tables 1 and 3 as well. Therefore, there cannot be an F at table 1. This means that B's table, with the F, J, and F, must be at table 3 and C's table, with a G, G, and an S at table 1. Since there is now an S at table 1, B must be assigned to table 2. This is not the case, so (B) is not the correct answer. The correct answer is (E).

4) If an F and J are together at table 3, then B must be assigned to table 3. The rules tell you that if C is not at table 3, then D is not at table 1. Since B is at table 3, C is not at table 3, so D cannot be at table 1. Thus, D is at table 2 and C is at table 1. The contrapositive of the rule that says if there is an S at table 1, then B is at table 2, tells you that if B is not at table 2, then there are no S's at table 1. In this case, B is at table 3, so there cannot be any S's at table 1. This means that in order to have three S'S, there must be three S's at table 2. You still need to get the two G's together as well, so they must be at table 1. This is everything that you can determine from the condition given to you in the question, so go to the answer choices and find the answer that must be true. The correct answer is (A). There must be three S's at table 2 so there is no room for an F.

5) If two of the guests are F and five are S, then the other two must be G. You know that those two G's must be together. Only two of the representatives speak S, so the five S's must be divided between only two tables, which means one table will have three and the other table will have the other two. This situation leaves no room for the two G's at either of the tables where S is spoken, so the two G's must be with B. So now you have one table with three S's, one with two S's, and one with two G's. B must be assigned to the table with two G's. You still need to place two F's in order to satisfy the requirements of the question. These two F's must be split up, one at each table that only has two. Thus, one table will have three S's, one will have two S's and an F, and one will have two G's and an F. B must be the representative at the table with two G's and an F. Now that you know the make-up of all the tables you need to find the group that

could be at table 3. It appears at first that both (A) and (B) are possibilities. But try (A) out and see what happens. (A) places B at table 3, leaving the other two groups of people for tables 1 and 2, which means that there must be an S at table 1. According to the rules if there is an S at table 1, then B must be at table 2. However, B is already at table 3 so this does not work. The correct answer is (B).

6) If there is a G at tables 2 and 3, then tables 2 and 3 must have one of B or C assigned to them, which means that D is assigned to table 1. The contrapositive of the rule that says if C is not at table 3, then D is not at table 1, says that if D is at table 1, then C is at table 3. Thus, D is at table 1, B is at table 2, and C is at table 3. This does not conform to the setup that results when there is an F at table 1, so there cannot be an F at table 1. D, who is at table 1, can only speak F and S, but now that you know there are not any F's at table 1, you know that there are three S's. You still need one more G at either table 2 or 3, and B at table two can speak G, F, and J, while C at table 3 can only speak G and S. Go to the answers and look for something that could be true. The answer cannot be (A) or (B) because there must be three S's at table 1. (C) could be true because B is at table 2 and he can speak F. Thus, the correct answer is (C). (D) cannot be true because B must be assigned to table 2 and B cannot speak S. (E) cannot be true because only B can speak J and B must be assigned to table 2.

1) This is not your typical rules question, but it is a rules question nonetheless. The question provides information about the advanced courses *only*, so you need to be aware of the side effects as well. Go through the rules one by one and cross off those answers that break the rules. Don't continue to check the answers you have already crossed out. You may also need to go through the deductions. In this case it is easy to eliminate (B) because if K is in F then X must be in F, (D) because Y and Z are not together, and (E) because if M is in S, then Y and Z are also in S. (A) places J and K in advanced classes, leaving L and M as the two boys in beginner's Spanish. If M is in Spanish, the rules say that Y (and Z) must be in advanced Spanish. However, (A) only has K in advanced Spanish, so (A) does not work. The correct answer is (C).

2) Question two asks for something that must be false without providing you with any additional information. This is usually a good sign that the question is testing the deductions, so if you already worked hard on making deductions, simply look through the answer choices for something that you already know. If you did not make deductions, you would have to in order to be able to answer this question. The correct answer here is (D). It is impossible for three students to take beginner's French, for none of the three girls can take beginner's French, and at least two of the four boys must take beginner's Spanish. Since five of the seven students cannot take beginner's French, there can be at most two students who enroll in beginner's French.

3) This question gives you a scenario and asks what must be true. If Y is in French, then Z must be in French as well. Y and Z are both girls and because there are no girls allowed in beginner's French, the YZ block must be in advanced French. Since Y and Z are not in advanced Spanish, it must be the case that M is not in Spanish. Since M cannot be in a Spanish course, it is impossible for K to be in a French course, since if K were in French,

then J and M would have to be the two boys in beginner's Spanish. Thus, K cannot enroll in French, which is the same as saying that K must enroll in Spanish. Therefore it must be true that K enrolls in a Spanish course. The correct answer is (B).

4) Placing L in French does not allow you to determine much else. However, the question also assigns Y to a French course. If Y is in French, then, just as in question two, you know that Y and Z are both in advanced French, that M is in a French course, either beginner's or advanced, and that K is in a Spanish course. With L and M both in French courses, you've used up two of the four boys, so the other two, J and K, must be the two boys who are in beginner's Spanish. The only person left is X, who must be in advanced Spanish in order to satisfy the requirement that there be at least one person in each group. Now look at the answer choices and see which one could be true. (Pay attention to the wording of the question: Each of the following must be false EXCEPT.) The correct answer is (C).

5) This question tests the deduction about K. If you hadn't made the deduction earlier, you would be forced to do so now. What do you know if K is placed in advanced French? If K is in advanced French then X must be in advanced French and L must be in a French course, although at this point it is uncertain whether L enrolls in advanced or beginner's French. J and M must be the two boys in beginner's Spanish, since K and L have already been assigned to French. As of now, you do not have anyone in advanced Spanish and the only candidate remaining who can enroll in a Spanish course is the YZ block, so the YZ block must be in advanced Spanish in order to have at least one student in each course. At this point you know for certain where L must go because L is the only student who can enroll in beginner's French. L must be in beginner's French all by himself. The correct answer is (B).

6) This question places M and J in beginner's Spanish. Remember the rules: if M is in Spanish, then Y, and thus the YZ block, is in advanced Spanish. Four of the seven students are already assigned to Spanish courses. Now you are left with K, L, and X to fill up both beginner's French and advanced French. If you use K in French, then both X and L would have to be in French also, with X definitely in advanced French. In this scenario you still cannot be certain whether K and L are in beginner's or advanced French. If, on the other hand, you put K in Spanish, then L and X must fill up the French groups, with X again in advanced French. Thus, X must take advanced French. Or, in other words, it must be false that X takes a beginner's course. The correct answer here is (C).

7) This question also places an item for you and tests whether you can follow the "if...then" statements to reach a logical conclusion. If M is enrolled in advanced Spanish, then, according to the rules, Y (and thus the YZ block) must be in advanced Spanish as well. With three students enrolled in advanced Spanish, advanced Spanish is filled. You are left with three boys, J, K, and L, to fill up at least two spaces in beginner's Spanish. However, if K were not in beginner's Spanish, which means that K would have to be in French, then L would have to be enrolled in a French course too, leaving you with only J to fill the beginner's Spanish course. There must be at least two boys in beginner's Spanish, so K must be one of them. Thus, K must be with either J or L in beginner's Spanish. The other of J or L must be enrolled in a French course as must X because they are the only two students remaining who can enroll in the two remaining courses. Since no girls are allowed in beginner's French, X must be in advanced French and the other of J or L that is not used in beginner's Spanish must enroll in beginner's French. Now you know the entire setup except for the exact placement of J and L. Find the answer choice that could be false. The correct answer is (A). J could enroll in beginner's French.

1) The first question tests the rules and deductions about the number of stories that must be covered each day: Monday's front page must cover exactly one topic; Tuesday's front page must cover exactly two topics; Wednesday's front page must cover all four topics; Thursday's front page must cover exactly two topics; and Friday's must cover exactly three topics. Thus, the day with the fewest topics included on the front page is Monday. The correct answer here is (A).

2) Question two asks for something that must be true about the setup. Every answer choice deals with the placement of W. The only thing that you know for certain about W is that it must be covered on Wednesday because on Wednesday all four topics must be covered. Thus, the correct answer is (C).

3) Question three introduces two new conditions: W is covered on Friday and E is covered on three consecutive days. If W is covered on Friday, then E must be the one topic covered on Monday. Since E must be covered on three consecutive days and at this point you know there is an E on Monday and an E on Wednesday, there must be an E on Tuesday. Since E is on Tuesday, the second topic covered on Thursday cannot be E, and instead must be W. The correct answer therefore is (B).

4) Question four wants to know if it is possible for any topic to be covered on exactly four of the five days, and, if so, for how many topics that is the case. Take a moment to think about it. Wednesday must have all four topics. Whatever is on Monday cannot be on Friday and vice versa, so no topic can be covered on both Monday and Friday. Tuesday and Thursday have the same relationship as Monday and Friday, so no topic can be covered on both Tuesday and Thursday. If a topic can only be on one of Monday and Friday, one of Tuesday and Thursday, and on Wednesday, then it is impossible for a topic to be covered on four days. The correct answer here is (A).

5) Question five is very similar to question three. Simply plug in the new conditions, follow the chain reactions, and see what happens. If E is covered on Friday then W must be the one topic covered on Monday. With a W on Monday and a W on Friday, in order for it to be the case that the days on which W is covered are not all consecutive, W cannot be covered on Tuesday. Therefore E must be covered on Tuesday and W must be covered on Thursday. Now go through the answer choices and find the one choice that must be false. The correct answer is (D). W, not E, must be covered on Thursday.

6) If E is covered on Monday, then W must be covered on Friday. All that remains is the relationship between Tuesday and Thursday. W must be covered on one of Tuesday or Thursday and E must be covered on the other, but you cannot determine which topic is covered which day. This interchangeability means that there are two different setups possible. The correct answer is (B).

7) If W is covered on Tuesday, then E must be covered on Thursday. The question also requires that as few of the topics as possible are covered on consecutive days, so W cannot be covered on Monday, as this would put the three W's on consecutive days, as well as the three E's on consecutive days. Since W cannot be covered on Monday, E must be covered on Monday, which means that W must be covered on Friday. You now have the entire setup and can easily go through the answer choices and find what must be false. The correct answer is (E). W, not E, is covered on Friday.

1) The first question is a typical rules question. Go down rule by rule to see whether each answer violates the particular rule you are looking at. Once you have eliminated an answer, do not test it for the other rules. This is also your chance to review the rules to catch any you may have missed or misunderstood. You will know this is the case if you have more than one right answer or no right answer at all. The correct answer here is (B).

2) This question tests your deductions. You should've figured out that every student must eat at A so the correct answer is (E). This question really tested your understanding of the rules. Not every student has to eat at D or C, so answer choices (C) and (D) are not correct. Remember, there are five days and no two students can eat at the same place on the same day, so on every day, each of the restaurants must be used. M is the only student who eats at A twice, so two of the five days are used up by M, leaving three days for other people to eat at A. Since none of the remaining three students can eat at A twice and thereby cover the remaining days, each one must eat at A. Again, the correct answer is (E).

3) This question gives you a condition and requires you to determine the side effects of that new information. If M eats at D on Monday, then E must eat at C on Monday. Since E now eats at C on Monday and Tuesday, he cannot eat at C any more, which means he must eat at B on Wednesday. Because E eats at B on Wednesday, M must eat at C on Wednesday. Therefore, the correct answer is (D).

4) If you marked what can and cannot be true in each slot of your diagram, then this question is simple. R cannot eat at B or A on Friday, and therefore can only eat at C or D. The correct answer is (C).

5) This question says that E eats at B two times during the week. E already eats at C on Tuesday and A on Friday and cannot eat at B on Monday, so the two days that E eats at B must be on Wednesday and Thursday. If E eats at B on Wednesday and Thursday then none of the other students can eat at B on Wednesday or Thursday, which means that M must eat at C on Wednesday. Luckily, this is enough work to get the correct answer. It cannot be true that M eats at B on Wednesday. The correct answer is (B).

6) This is a simple question if you took the time to work out the deductions. Simply glance at the diagram and you will see that J must eat at A on Monday. The correct answer is (A).

7) If R eats at C on Thursday, then neither E nor J can eat at C on Thursday. Since J now cannot eat at A, D, or C on Thursday, he must eat at B, which forces E to eat at D on Thursday. If E eats at C on Monday, then M must eat at D on Monday. Since E now eats at C twice (Monday and Tuesday), he cannot eat at C on Wednesday, but instead must eat at B. Since E eats at B on Wednesday, M must eat at C on Wednesday. Now that you have completely filled in Monday through Thursday, go to the answer choices and find the choice the must be true. The correct answer is (C). M must eat at C on Wednesday.

1) The first question is a typical rules question. Go down rule by rule to see whether each answer violates the particular rule you are looking at. Once you have eliminated an answer, do not test it for the other rules. This is also your chance to review the rules to catch any you may have missed or misunderstood. You will know this is the case if you have more than one right answer or no right answer at all. The correct answer here is (D).

2) This question forces you to think about the OM rule and its implications for the placement of the OM block. As you already know, O and M can only be on Monday, Thursday, or Friday. The question puts N on Friday at 8:00. If N is on Friday then there is no room for O and M on Friday, which restricts O and M to Monday or Thursday. The question wants to know the latest day and time that M could be tested. Thursday is the latest day, and since you do not know the relative placement of O and M, M could be at 9:00. Thus, the latest day and time that M could be tested is Thursday at 9:00, or (C).

3) Question three places both T and N sometime before S. P must be tested sometime before N, so T, P, and N must all be before S. S is tested on Tuesday at 9:00, so T, P, and N must fill Monday's two slots and the slot on Tuesday at 8:00, although not necessarily in that order. The OM block can only be on Monday, Thursday, or Friday, but since Monday is filled, the OM block is forced to either Thursday or Friday. Regardless of which day the OM block is tested, there will be only one more 8:00 time slot available (on whichever day the OM block is not tested), which means that it is impossible for both L and R to be tested at 8:00. Since L and R cannot both be tested at 8:00, L cannot be tested at 8:00, for if L is tested at 8:00 then R must also be tested at 8:00. Because L cannot be tested at 8:00, it cannot be true that L is tested on Thursday at 8:00. The correct answer is (C).

4) This question adds the condition that N and O are both before T and wants to know the earliest exam that T could take. If O is before T and O and M constitute a block, then M must be before T as well. Because you want to find the earliest that T can be, it makes sense to put the OM block as early as it can be, which is Monday. According to the question, N must be before T as well, but the rules also say that P must be before N. The earliest that P can be if O and M are on Monday is on Tuesday at 8:00, making the earliest that N can be Wednesday at 9:00. Now that N and O are out of the way, put T in the next available slot, which is Thursday at 8:00. The correct answer is (A).

5) This question eliminates Thursday at 8:00 from the list of available slots. Think about what effects this has. The OM block is now restricted to either Monday or Friday. Also, there are now only three available 8:00 time slots, one of which will contain O or M. This is important in conjunction with the rule that says if L is tested at 8:00 then R is tested at 8:00 on another day. If there are only two free 8:00 slots and L is in one of them, then R will be in the other one, which would not leave any room for any other people to be tested at 8:00. Because you do not have any firm information, you must go to the answer choices and find what could be true. (A) cannot be true for the simple reason that if L is tested at 8:00, then R is tested at 8:00, leaving no 8:00 slot open for N. (B) cannot be true. If N is before S, who is on Tuesday at 9:00, and P is before N, then somebody will be on Monday, which would force the OM block to Friday. Thus, it is impossible for P to be tested sometime after M. (C) must be false. You know that the OM block must be on Monday or Friday, but (C) puts P on Monday and N on Friday, leaving no room for the OM block. (D) could be true, so it is the answer. Once you have found a choice that could be true, move on. You do not need to work through the one remaining answer choice. (E) cannot be true because if L is tested at 8 then R must be tested at 8, and it was already established that one of O or M must also test at 8. With no test-takers on Wednesday or Thursday at 8 and L, R, and one of O or M at 8, there is no room for P to be tested at 8 as well.

6) If R and T are tested in succession on Thursday and Friday at 8:00, then the OM block cannot be on Thursday or Friday. Since the OM block cannot be on Thursday or Friday, the OM block must be on Monday. You must still place P, L, and N somewhere in the setup, keeping in mind that P must be tested sometime before N and that L can still be tested at either 8:00 or 9:00. Now you can go through the answer choices and look for what could be true. The correct answer is (B). L could be tested on Wednesday at 9:00. This question tested the vital ability to interpret conditional statements. The rule that says if L is tested at 8:00 then R must be tested at 8:00 does not mean that if R is tested at 8:00 then L must be tested at 8:00. Knowing that R is tested at 8:00 does not allow you to determine anything about the placement of L.

1) The first question is a typical rules question. Go down rule by rule to see whether each answer violates the particular rule you are looking at. Once you have eliminated an answer, do not test it for the other rules. This is also your chance to review the rules to catch any you may have missed or misunderstood. You will know this is the case if you have more than one right answer or no right answer at all. The correct answer here is (D).

2) Because this question asks for something that cannot be true without first giving you a condition to work with, the answer will depend on what you have already determined, as represented by your diagram. Go through each answer choice and ask yourself if it can be true as you compare it to the diagram. You don't need to write each choice down and work it out fully. All you need to know is whether or not it could be true. How about (A)? In order for F to be fifth, E, G, H, and S would have to go before it. That can work as long as S isn't next to F. (B) could work because G could be preceded by E, F, and S as long as S isn't next to F. (C) could work because although G would have to be first, you can still keep S separated from F and I with either E or J. On the other hand, (D) cannot be true because it does not allow you to keep S isolated from I. If S is fifth, I must be either fourth or sixth. Thus, the correct answer here is (D). S cannot be fifth.

3) If H is visited second, then you know that G must be visited first, because G must be visited before H. Now you are left with the entire E..F..I..J sequence and the S to fill up 3 through 7. Looking at just the E..F.. I..J sequence, the only possible place for S is at the beginning of the sequence (S..E..F.. I..J), which would make S third, or at the end of the sequence (E..F..I..J..S), which would make S seventh. Thus, S can only be third or seventh. Find one of these possibilities in the answer choices. The correct answer is (E).

4) This question identifies E and G as the first and second schools visited. With E and G first and second, the basic order looks like this: EG..F.I.J. H must also be visited sometime after G, but it is not clear how the order of H relates to the other schools. The only school yet to be mentioned is S. S must fit somewhere in the list but cannot be next to F and cannot be next to I. In this setup, only H or J can serve as a buffer between SF and SI. In order to be separated from both F and I, S must either be before the F.I.J sequence or after the F.I.J sequence. S could be placed before F, so as long as H is immediately after S, thereby separating S from F. In this case, S would be third. On the other hand, S could come sometime after J. If S comes after J while H is before J, S would be seventh. It could also be the case that S comes after J and that H is after S. In this case, S would be sixth. These are the only positions in which S could fall in the order of schools visited: third, sixth, or seventh. Thus, S could be in one of three different places in the order. The correct answer is (B).

5) If J is sixth then the only schools that could possibly be visited seventh are H and S. If H were seventh then E, F, G, I, and S would have to occupy positions 1 through 5, though not necessarily in that order. The question also requires that S be visited sometime after E. Because in this instance S must come after E and because J and H are sixth and seventh, neither E, nor H, nor J can serve as a buffer between S and F and S and I. Thus, G would have to separate S from both F and I. The only way to accomplish this in this scenario is if E is first, S is second, G is third, F is fourth, and I is fifth. Therefore, the fourth and fifth schools visited could be F and I. The correct answer is (A).

6) Question six asks for a piece of information that is sufficient to allow you to determine the entire order in which the schools are visited. Before jumping into the answer choices and working out each one, consider what is likely to be the key. At this point, you already know the basic order of E..F.I.J. G must be visited sometime before I, while H must be visited sometime after G. It seems as though S, the one remaining school, is freer to move around in the order than the others. However, as should have been made apparent in the previous questions, the placement of S is severely restricted due to the requirement that S cannot be next to F and that S cannot be next to I. Because the placement of S is severely restricted, the placement of S will also likely restrict the rest of the order. Thus, as you approach the answer choices, work smartly, using what you know about the setup and using previous work. (A) places H second, which was the scenario in question three and which did not allow you to determine the entire setup. (B) places S fourth. Since S is fourth, neither F nor I can be third or fifth. Since F cannot be third and since at least one school must be before F, F must be second. Since I cannot be fifth and since at least one school must come after I, I must be sixth. Thus, the order now looks like this: _ F _ S _ I _. The remaining four positions are easy to fill: E must be before F, so E is first, J must be after I, so J is seventh, and G must be before H, so G is third and H is fifth. Thus, when S is fourth, you can determine the entire order. The correct answer here is (B). Once you have found the correct answer, you do not need to work out the other answer choices. However, (C) is not correct because G can never be sixth, (D) is not correct because it is also an impossible setup, and (E) is not correct because it leaves a very flexible setup.

Answers Game 49

1) There are two ways to approach this first question. You can either treat it as a typical rules question and go down rule by rule to see whether each answer violates the particular rule you are looking at or you can use what you know about team T and eliminate any answer choices that violate what you know. Either way, the correct answer here is (D).

2) Question two asks for the team or teams on which B could serve. According to the deductions, B must serve on team M. Thus, the correct answer is (C).

3) Question three asks for a pair of students who could be together on team H. Team H must include J, S, W, and one of the four M's (Mo, Mi, Ma, Me), so look for some combination of these students in the answer choices. The correct answer is (C). W and Mo could both be on team H.

4) Question four simply asks for a pair of students who could be on the same team as Ma if Ma is on team H. If Ma is on team H then the other three students on team H must be T/C, N, and D. Look for some combination of these students in the answer choices. The correct answer is (E). C and D could be on team H.

5) If T is on the same team as N, then T must be on team T. Since T is on team T, C must be on team M, which means that team M consists of P, B, C, and one of the M's. The question asks for a pair of students who could be on the same team as B. B is on team M, so the students who could be on B's team are P, C, and one of the M's. Look for some combination of these students in the answer choices. The correct answer is (B). Me and C could be on team M with B.

6) Question six asks for a group of three students who could not be on the same team. Go through each answer choice and see if the three students listed in each one could possibly be together on one of the teams. To do this, simply compare each answer choice to the diagram. Remember, you are looking for a group of three who cannot be together. The correct answer is (C). It is impossible for T and W to be on the same team. W must be on team H, while T is either on team M or team T.

1) The first question is a typical rules question. Go down rule by rule to see whether each answer violates the particular rule you are looking at. Once you have eliminated an answer, do not test it for the other rules. This is also your chance to review the rules to catch any you may have missed or misunderstood. You will know this is the case if you have more than one right answer or no right answer at all. The correct answer here is (C).

2) This question places P on Saturday and asks for what must be shown on Friday. This is a simple rules question that tests your ability to understand the contrapositives. The question places P on Saturday. The first rule tells us that if H is on Saturday then P is on Friday. The contrapositive says if P is on Saturday then H is on Friday, so what has to be true is that H is on Friday. The correct answer is (A).

3) Question three is difficult. It places M on Saturday and asks for a movie that must be on Friday. Since M is on Saturday, O has to be on S also. This leaves only two spaces on S. There is a rule that says if L is on Friday then J and K must be on S. Placing L on Friday would thus fill up S, leaving I, L, H, P, and N on Friday. The only other possibility is if L is not on Friday, which is the same as saying that L is on Saturday. If L is on Saturday then there is only one space left on Saturday. Now take a look at the rule governing N and K. If N is on Friday, then K is on Saturday, and if K is on Friday, then N is on Saturday. Since there is not room for both K and N on Saturday, one of K or N must be on Friday, which means that the other of K or N must be on Saturday, thereby filling up Saturday and leaving I, H, P, J, and K/N on Friday. In each of these scenarios, H and P must always be shown on Friday, so look for either H or P in the answer choices. The correct answer is (A). H must always been shown on Friday if M is shown on Saturday.

4) Question 4 places J and M in S and then asks for what must be in the same group. Well, you know from previous work that if M is in S, then O must be there also. But the question makes you work a little further. If Q, J, M, and S are all on Saturday, then there is only room for one more movie on Saturday. Thus, there is no room for the L and N pair. Since L and N cannot be on Saturday, K must be on Saturday, which gives you all five movies on Saturday. The correct answer is (B). K must be shown on Saturday.

5) Question five puts L, M, and P on the same day and asks for a pair that must be together. Ask what group they are in. If L, M, and P were in S, they would drag O with them, filling up the group. But that would place N in F, forcing K to S according to the rules, which would put too many in S. Therefore, L, M, and P must be in F. Since L is on Friday, both J and K must be on Saturday. Go to the answer choices and see if you have the answer. You do. The answer is (B).

6) This question places L on Friday and H on Saturday and asks for a pair that cannot be together. You know that because H is on Saturday that P is on Friday. Also, since L is on Friday, J and K must be on Saturday. So you have three items that you haven't used: M, N, and O. If M is on Saturday, then O is on Saturday; however, there is no room for this, so M must be on Friday and N and O must be split, with one in each group. Thus, it is impossible for N and O to be shown on the same day. The correct answer is (E).

7) Question seven places P in S and K in F. Since P is on S, H must be in F and since K is on F, both N and L must be in S. There is only one spot remaining in S and it must be filled by either O, M, or J. It cannot be M, because M would drag O with it. Therefore it must be O or J. The answer is (C).

Question Analysis and Answers

1) The first question is a typical rules question. Go down rule by rule to see whether each answer violates the particular rule you are looking at. Once you have eliminated an answer, do not test it for the other rules. This is also your chance to review the rules to catch any you may have missed or misunderstood. You will know this is the case if you have more than one right answer or no right answer at all. The correct answer here is (C).

2) This question lets you jump into the chain of logic a little later than in the deductions, where you knew that J was included. This chain starts with L. If L is included, then C is included, and if C is included, then Q is included and K is not. Check to see if K is among the answer choices. It is not, so you need to go further. With C, L, and Q included on the MP3 player, there are already one long song and two short songs. In order to fill the MP3 player, there must be either one more long song or two more short songs, but not a mixture of the two. Because there cannot be a mixture of the two, neither P nor D can be included. Check the answer choices for one of these two. The correct answer is (D). It cannot be true that P is included because P would drag D along with it and there is not room for D.

3) This question says that there are two long songs, which means that there are two long songs and two short songs. If two long songs are included, then some combination of C, D, and F must be included. The rules create an either/or situation for D and F. If F is included, then D is not included, and if D is included, then F is not included. Thus, for two long songs to be included one of them must be C and one of them must be either D or F. Since C must be included, Q must be included. The correct answer is (A).

4) This question is a give-away if you worked out the deductions. If J is included, then the group is J, L, C, Q, and H. Simply go through the answer choices and find the song that is not loaded. The correct answer is (E).

5) If H is not included, then right away you know that J cannot be included because if J is included then H is also. This eliminates (A). The remaining answer choices you will have to eliminate by working them out. (B) cannot be correct because if F is included then D, and therefore P, cannot be included. (C) includes both D and L. If D is included, then P must be included also, and if L is included then C and Q must be included. Thus, this setup gives you two longs songs, C and D, and three short songs, L, Q, and P. This is too many songs, so (C) is not the correct answer. (D) uses C and P. If P is used then D must be used also and if C is used then Q must be used. This gives you two long songs, C and D, and two short songs, P and Q. This works! The correct answer is (D). Once you've found one that works, move on to the next question. In case you must know, (E) cannot work because it leaves no way to fill up the short songs. By including P, answer choice (E) forces D to be used and by using K it forces C to not be used. Thus, there must be one long song and four short songs. With D as the only long song and P and K as the two short songs, there must be two more short songs to fill up the MP3 player. However, neither L nor J can be used since C is not used and the question took away H. Therefore, there are not enough songs available to include four short songs.

6) This question asks for a pair of songs that cannot be included together. Think about how this question relates to the previous question, which asked for a pair that could be loaded together. In question five there were four examples of pairs of songs that could not be included. Take each wrong answer from question five and look for its equivalent in this question. If you find it, then you have found the correct answer for this question. If you're paying attention, then you should notice that in question five you found that D and L could not be loaded together. One of the answer choices for this question is L and P. Since P and D must be included together if one of them is included, these two pairs really mean the same thing. If in question five you found that D and L could not be together, it must also be the case that P and L cannot be together as well. Thus, (E) is the correct answer. If you didn't spot this method for answering the question, you would again have to work through each answer choice. Either way, you will find that (E) is the correct answer. If P is included then D must be included as well and if L is included then C and Q must be included. Thus, this setup gives you two long songs, C and D, and three short songs, L, Q, and P. This is too many songs.

7) If there are exactly four songs that fill up the MP3 player, there must be two long songs and two short songs. As in question 3, when two long songs are loaded, one of those songs must be C and the other must be either D or F. Since C must be included, Q must also be included. Thus, L and Q are the two short songs. There needs to be one more long song, which must be one of D or F. However, since P cannot be used, D cannot be used either. Thus, the fourth song must be F. The correct answer is (B).

1) The first question is a typical rules question. Go down rule by rule to see whether each answer violates the particular rule you are looking at. Once you have eliminated an answer, do not test it for the other rules. This is also your chance to review the rules to catch any you may have missed or misunderstood. You will know this is the case if you have more than one right answer or no right answer at all. The correct answer here is (A).

2) The second question forces you to make a deduction concerning B. If you already have the deduction before going to the questions, this is very easy. Simply look at the diagram: B must learn either 2 or 3 on Monday, 4 on Tuesday, and either 5 or 6 on Wednesday. B cannot learn 1. The correct answer is (A).

3) If B learns 5, he learns it on Wednesday, which forces C to learn 5 on Wednesday. This is because the piece C learns on Wednesday is not more difficult than the piece B learns on Wednesday. Therefore, A must learn piece 6 on W because otherwise there would be no 6. The correct answer is (E).

4) The fourth question is another question that forces you to make a deduction if you haven't done so already. To get the answer, go down the answer choices and compare them to the diagram. Remember, you are looking for the answer that must be false. (C) must be false. Only B can learn 4 on T since A must learn either piece 2 or 3 on Tuesday, and C cannot learn piece 4 at all. Thus, the correct answer is (C).

5) Question five gives you information to apply to the diagram. If A learns the most difficult pieces allowed for her, then A must learn 2 on Monday, 3 on Tuesday, and 6 on Wednesday. Those are the most difficult pieces allowed for A. Since A learns 3 on Tuesday, B must learn 3 on Monday, giving you 3, 4, and 5/6 for B's setup. The only person left is C. One

Question Analysis and Answers

of the three people must learn 5. A is ruled out already, so either B or C must learn 5. If B learns 5 on Wednesday, then C must learn five on Wednesday because C cannot learn a more difficult song than B and if B learns six on Wednesday, C would still have to learn 5 on Wednesday in order to satisfy the requirement that every piece is learned. Thus, C learns 5 on Wednesday. Since 5 is the most difficult piece that C can learn, C's other two pieces must be 1 and 2 or 3. A and B both learned 3, so C cannot learn 3. Thus, C must learn pieces 1, 2, and 5, respectively. Therefore, (E) is the correct answer.

6)   This question says that both A and C learn piece 3. Remember, C can only learn 3 if it is not the piece that A and B both learn. Thus, since both A and C learn 3, A's piece on Tuesday and B's piece on Monday must be piece 2. If A's piece on Tuesday is 2 and, according to the question, he must learn 3, A must learn 3 on Wednesday. Furthermore, since A learns 2 on Tuesday, the only piece he can learn on Monday is piece 1. The slots remaining are B's slot on Wednesday and all of C's slots. C must learn 3 somewhere and can only do so on Monday or Tuesday. If C learned 3 on Monday, then C would have to learn 5 on Tuesday and 6 on Wednesday, forcing B to learn 6 on Wednesday as well. If C learned 3 on Tuesday, then C would have to learn piece 1 on Monday, and, in order to have every piece used, C would have to learn piece 5 on Wednesday and B would have to learn 6 on Wednesday. In both scenarios, 5 must be used only once. This question demonstrates the necessity of working out the question completely. Pieces 6 and 1 *could* be learned only once, but piece 5 *must* be learned only once. The correct answer is (D).

7)   Question seven removes piece 6 from the game. If piece 6 is no longer available then B must learn piece 5 on Wednesday. Likewise, since 6 is no longer available, C would have to learn pieces 1, 2/3, and 5 over the three day period. Thus, both B and C must learn piece 5, which means that 5 is a piece that must be learned by two students. The correct answer is (E).

1)   The first question is a typical rules question. Go down rule by rule to see whether each answer violates the particular rule you are looking at. Once you have eliminated an answer, do not test it for the other rules. This is also your chance to review the rules to catch any you may have missed or misunderstood. You will know this is the case if you have more than one right answer or no right answer at all. The correct answer here is (E).

2)   This question says that M sees Dr. Johnson at 11 and that there is no patient in room B at 10. If M is at 11, then K is also at 11, which fills up the 11 o'clock slots. Since 11 o'clock is filled, P and Q must be in 8 and 10. Nobody is in room B at 10 and P must be in room B, so P must be in room B at 8 and Q must be in room A at 10. With P in room B at 8, nobody in room B at 10, and either K or M in room B at 11, you know that N must be in room B at 9. This is everything that must be true, so go to the answer choices. The correct answer is (D).

3)   This question gives you a scenario and asks for the effects on L, one of the wildcards. The conditions for this scenario are that N immediately follows K, which means that N follows the KM block, and that T is at 10. The important thing to realize is how the placement of the KM block relates to the separation of P and Q. Remember, P and Q must either be in 8 and 10 or 9 and 11. Wherever the KM block is eliminates one of those possibilities. In this case, you also know that N must follow the KM block. Thus, K and M cannot be at 11. K and M cannot be at 10 because T must be at 10. K and M cannot be in 9 either, because placing K and M in 9 puts both N and T in 10, leaving no room for P and Q. Thus, K and M must be at 8, with N immediately after at 9 in room B. Since K and M fill up 8, P and Q must be in 9 and 11. Room B at 9 is filled with N, so Q must be in room A at 9 and P must be in room B at 11. The only person left is L. L could be in either room at 10 or in room A at 11. The correct answer is therefore (B).

4) Room B must have N, P, and either K or M. There is only room for one more person. As long as the answer choices include at least one of the three people that must be in room B, that answer is correct (unless it breaks some other rule, such as having K and M both in room B). If the answer includes two people other than the three who must be in room B, that answer is correct because there is not enough room for two additional people. (A) includes both T and L and is therefore a pair that could not both be in room B. The correct answer is (A).

5) Question 5 says only that there is no patient in room B at 8. Since one of the slots for room B has been eliminated, the remaining three must be filled with N, P, and K/M, though not necessarily in that order. The main issue here is the placement of P and Q. Since this question does not provide enough information to determine fixed positions you will have to go through the answer choices to determine which one could be true. (A) cannot be true because if Q is at 9, then P would have to be at 11, not K and M. (B) cannot be true because it separates P and Q by more than one hour. (C) cannot be true because if P is seen at 11, then Q would have to be seen at 9, and with N in 10 there is no room for the KM block. (D) could be true. If Q is seen at 8, he must be seen in room A and P would have to be seen at 10 in room B. With L in room A at 9, K and M would have to be at 11, leaving T with L at 9 o'clock. (D) is the correct answer. Once you have the answer, move on to the next question. Just so you know, (E) cannot be true because it forces K and M to 9 o'clock and with N at 10, forces P to 11. If P were at 11, then Q would have to be at 9, but there is no room since K and M would have to be there.

6) If K is in room A at 10, then M must be in room B at 10. Since the 10 o'clock time slot is filled, P and Q must be at 9 and 11, though you cannot determine which one is where or even which room Q is in. Thus, P or Q could be in room B at 9, but neither one must be. The only other person who must be in room B is N, so N could be in room B at 9 if Q is in room A and P is in room B at 11. The wildcards are L and T, so either of them could also be seen at 9 in room B. Thus, any one of these five people: P, Q, N, L, and T, could be in room B at 9. The correct answer is (E).

7) Question 7 again forces you to go through each answer choice to find the correct answer, although this time you are looking for something that cannot be true. By this time you should have a good idea of how to work the game and even what is being tested. The key is the relationship between P and Q and the KM block. The correct answer here is (D). If K and M are at 8, then P and Q must be at 9 and 11. (D) puts Q at 10, which is impossible.

1) This question places S in canoe 2 and B in canoe 6. Since there is a paddler in canoe 6, T cannot ride in the same canoe as an experienced paddler, which means T must ride with an inexperienced paddler. Both S and R are inexperienced, so both of them must be sharing their canoes with one other person. The only people remaining are A, Q, and T. Q must be in either canoe 1 or 2, so the only people that R could possibly share with are T and A. But if R shares with A, then you will be left with an inexperienced canoer alone because S would have to share with either Q or T, leaving the other of Q or T alone. This is against the rules, so, R must share with T in canoe 4. The correct answer is (C). T could only ride in canoe 4.

2) If there are no paddlers in canoe 2 and B rides in canoe 3, then you have a CB block in 3. Since Q must be in either 1 or 2 and no paddlers are in 2, Q must be in canoe 1 with another paddler. R must also still share canoe 4 with another paddler. This arrangement gives you three canoes with two people in them, leaving only one paddler. This one remaining paddler cannot be in canoe 2, so there must be one paddler in either canoe 5 or 6. The only ones that can be alone are experienced paddlers, and the only experienced paddler left is A so A must be in canoe 5 or 6. The correct answer is (D).

3) This question places S in canoe 6. S is an inexperienced paddler, so S must share his canoe. Q, an inexperienced paddler, must be in either 1 or 2 and must share his canoe. R must also share her canoe. This means that six of the seven paddlers will be divided among canoe 1 or 2, canoe 4, and canoe 6. C must ride in canoe 3, so C must be alone in canoe 3. The remaining paddlers to divide among the canoes that hold Q, R, and S are A, B, and T. According to the rules, A cannot ride with Q and neither can S, for if S is with an experienced paddler then S is with B. The only place left for A is with R in canoe 4. Therefore, it must be true that A rides in the same canoe as R. The correct answer is (A).

4) You know that Q shares canoe 1 or 2 with someone and that R shares canoe 4 with someone. This question says that C, who is in canoe 3, shares as well and that C shares with an inexperienced paddler. Since Q is in either 1 or 2 and since R is in 4, the only two inexperienced paddlers left are S and T. However, C cannot share with S, for if S shares with an experienced paddler then S must share with B. Thus, C must share with T. Since T is with an experienced paddler, there cannot be any paddlers in canoe 5 or 6. There must be at least four canoes used, so canoes 1 through 4 must all be used. With Q sharing with someone in either 1 or 2, C and T sharing in 3, and R sharing with someone in 4, there must be one canoe with exactly one person in it and this person must be an experienced paddler. The only paddlers left unaccounted for are A, B, and S. The lone experienced paddler must either be A or B, while the other of A or B and S must be split up so that they can share canoes with Q and R. This is everything you can determine, so now you can go to the answers. Look at (A). Can A ride in canoe 1 and S ride in canoe 4? Sure. The correct answer is (A).

5) This question tells you that B shares canoe 4 with R. You know that Q must share as well, but the only available people are now A, S, and T. According to the rules, Q cannot be with A, so Q must share with either S or T. But if you place T with Q, then S must share with either A or C, who are both experienced, and this is against the rules. So now you know that Q is with S and T is with either C or A. Since T must be with an experienced paddler, there cannot be anybody in canoes 5 or 6, which means 1–4 must be used. The correct answer is (A). It cannot be true that there are no paddlers in canoe 4.

6) If A rides in canoe 6, and you know generally where Q, R, and C, are, then you know that you only have S, T, and B to work with. Both T and S have to share with someone because they are inexperienced. You also know that both Q and R must share their canoes with someone else. It turns out that either S or T must share with either one of Q and R, because putting them anywhere else would put S with an experienced paddler other than B, or would put T with an experienced paddler, which is unacceptable because A is in 6. The question asks where B cannot be. Since Q and R both must share with one of S and T, B cannot be in either of those positions. The correct answer is (C).

1) The first question forces you to determine scenario one, if you hadn't figured it out already. Placing F on Saturday is the same as saying that S must be on Wednesday. If you didn't work this scenario out until now, at least realize that it is a scenario, or rather, that this scenario results every time that S is on Wednesday. Once you have worked it out, look at scenario one and determine which answer could be true. The correct answer here is (E).

2) Since you only have two possible scenarios, this "could be" question is rather easy. Go down the list and see if each answer could be true in either of the two scenarios. Here it is actually even easier. You've already deduced that L must be on Monday so it cannot be true that L is on Wednesday. The correct answer is (E).

3) Once again, since you already determined that there are only two scenarios, you also know that there are only two possibilities for F: Friday and Saturday. The correct answer is (E).

4) This question tests your deductions (as all these questions have). You've already done all the necessary work, and the question is even more obvious because in order to answer question two, you had to determine that L must be on Monday. The correct answer is (A).

5) This question asks which prisoner could be scheduled for Thursday. Look at Thursday in both of the scenarios. In both instances, it can only be C or I. The answer is therefore (A).

6) Question five asked about the inmates who could have a hearing on Thursday and now question six asks about the inmates who can have their parole hearing on Friday. All that you need to do to answer this question is look at the two scenarios and determine who can be on Friday. In one scenario either I or C could be on Friday; in the other, F must be on Friday. Thus, the correct answer includes I, C, and F. The correct answer is therefore (C).

**Question Analysis
and Answers**

7) The final question removes the condition that J has his hearing on Tuesday. What this does is take away the precious deduction that there are only two possible scenarios. To answer this one, you have to do a little work. It is given that J is on Thursday and that S is on Wednesday. The four remaining days are Monday, Tuesday, Friday, and Saturday. You must still account for I and C having their hearings on consecutive days and having their hearings before F. The only way to accomplish this is if I and C, though not necessarily in that order, have their hearings on Monday and Tuesday. This leaves F and L to have their hearings on Friday and Saturday, although not necessarily in that order. I and C are interchangeable, as are F and L. Accounting for these uncertainties, there are four possible schedules. The correct answer is (C).

1) The first question is a typical rules question. Go down rule by rule to see whether each answer violates the particular rule you are looking at. Once you have eliminated an answer, do not test it for the other rules. This is also your chance to review the rules to catch any you may have missed or misunderstood. You will know this is the case if you have more than one right answer or no right answer at all. The correct answer here is (A).

2) The second question tests the deduction about A. If A is included, then B must be included, which means that both R and F must also be included. A, B, R, and F make four people total; thus, the minimum number of people who could make up the list of campaigners is four, or (C).

3) This question is much easier if you have the contrapositives of the rules and deductions written down. If S is included in the group, then neither R nor B can be included. If B is not included, then Z must be included, and if Z is included, then A cannot be included. Thus, since in this case neither A nor B can be used, the only liberals that could be included in the group are C, D, and F. This question is testing your understanding of the conditional statements and ultimately whether you understand that F can be included without R. The correct answer is (E).

4) This questions tests your understanding of "if...then" statements in general, or, in other words, your ability to understand that there are only two valid pieces of information contained in an "if...then" statement, the statement itself and the contrapositive. It does so by adding two conditions: that Z is included, and that S is not included. Handle these two conditions one at a time. If Z is included, then the only thing you know is that A cannot be included. If S is not included, then you do not know anything more than the fact that S is not included. Therefore, if Z is included and S is not, the only two things that you know are that A and S are not included. Everyone else could possibly be included, although not at the same time. The question asks for an accurate list of all those who could campaign. Be careful about what the question is asking. It is not asking for a list of people that could campaign at once, but rather for all those who could campaign. In other words, who are the people left to choose from when Z is included and S is not? The correct answer is everyone besides A and S. Find the answer choice that includes B, C, D, F, Q, R, and Z. The correct answer is (C).

5) If S and Z are the only moderates, then immediately you can eliminate the remaining moderates, Q and R. Since Z is included, A cannot be included, and since S is included, neither R nor B can be included. This eliminates A, B, Q, and R. If you look at the answer choices, you are left with only one choice. The correct answer is (A). F could be included, again making you prove that you know that F can be included without R.

6) This question forces A and exactly two out of the four moderates to be included in the group. If A is included, then Z cannot be included and B must be included. If B is included, then both R and F must also be included, while S cannot be part of the group. Thus, A, B, and F, who are all liberals, and R, who is a moderate, must be included in the group, while both Z and S cannot be included. It just so happens that Z and S are both moderates. The four moderates are Q, R, S, and Z. If S and Z cannot be included and at the same time two moderates must be included, then the two moderates that are included are Q and R. Thus you know that A, B, and F are included from the liberal wing and that Q and R are included from the moderate wing. This gives you five people in the group, leaving room for only one more person. Now you are ready to go to the answer choices. You want to find a pair of people that both cannot be included in the group. Since you already know five of the people that must be included, this question is easy. The correct answer is (B). Although C and D are wildcards, they cannot both be included because there is not room for two more people.

7) If Z is the only moderate included in the group of campaigners, then none of the other moderates can be included, which means that neither Q nor R nor S can be included. According to the contrapositive of one of the rules, if R is not included, then B cannot be included. Thus, B cannot be included. Furthermore, since Z is included, A cannot be included. At this point, none of A, B, Q, R, and S can be included. The only three activists remaining are C, D, and F. There are no rules that would restrict any of these three from being included in the group of campaigners. C and D are wildcards, and F can be included without B, as has been shown repeatedly. If these three were all included in addition to Z, there would be four people in the group. The correct answer is (B).

Question Analysis and Answers

1) The first question is a typical rules question. Go down rule by rule to see whether each answer violates the particular rule you are looking at. Once you have eliminated an answer, do not test it for the other rules. This is also your chance to review the rules to catch any you may have missed or misunderstood. You will know this is the case if you have more than one right answer or no right answer at all. The correct answer here is (E).

2) If L is the only person trained in a particular hour, then neither L, nor P, nor M can share their hours, which means that J and N, who both must share, can only share with K and H. Since K must be before H and J must be before N, it must be the case that J shares with K and N shares with H. Thus, the setup for four of the hours looks like this: L..P..KJ..NH, with M as the person in the remaining hour. You cannot determine what hour M is in relative to the other clients. You are looking for what must be true, so go through the answer choices and see which choice corresponds with the setup. The correct answer is (D).

3) This question requires H to train alone. Since H, M, and P must now train alone, J and N must share with L and K, in that order, since L must be before K and J must be before N. Thus, the setup for four of the hours looks like this: LJ..P..KN..H. M must be alone in the remaining hour and you cannot determine which hour that is. The question asks for how many different people could be trained in the first hour. From the setup it is clear that either M or L and J must be in the first hour. Thus, there are three different people that could be trained in the first hour. The correct answer is (C). Be careful with the language in this question. It asks for people rather than scenarios. There are three people that could possibly be in the first hour, but there are only two scenarios.

4) This question asks for something that must be false without giving you any information to work with, so the answer will most likely be something that you have (or should have) already determined. With what you know about the setup, go through each answer choice. Perhaps the easiest way to do it is to read an answer choice and then glance at the diagram to determine whether it could be true or not. (A), (B), (C), and (E) all could be true. The correct answer is (D). It must be false that H and J are together. From the deductions you already knew that J and H cannot train in the same hour, since J must be before N and H's hour is the latest hour that N can go.

5) If the first and last hours are the two hours in which two people train, then you know right away that the basic setup looks like this: LJ..P..K..HN. L and J must be in the first hour and H and N must be in the fifth hour, so the only question is the placement of M in relation to P and K. The question wants to know what must be true, which is now an easy question to answer. The correct answer is (B). It must be true that K trains alone because the first and last hours are the ones in which two people train and there is no way for K to be in either the first or last hour.

6) This question asks for the number of clients who could be alone in the third hour. The basic structure looks like this: L..P..K..H, with M as a wildcard and J and N sharing with two of L, K, or H. The person in the third hour will largely depend on who is first. Essentially, only L or M can be first, although L could share with J. If L is first, then K could be third if P and K follow immediately after L. Since M is the wildcard, M could be also be third when L is first. On the other hand, if M is first, then only P could be third. That is it! The correct answer, therefore, is (B). There are only three people who could be third when the client who trains third does not share that hour with anyone else: K, M, and P.

7) This question asks for the effects of making P the fourth client. Be very careful with the language here. It is impossible for P to be in the fourth hour; this is not what the question says. It says P is the fourth client trained. In the basic structure of L..P..K..H, P is the second person trained. You need to fit two more people in front of P. The only available people are M, J, and N. N must be after P, so the two other people before P must be M and J. M must be alone, so J must share with L. P must now be in the third hour. Thus, the order looks something like this: LJ..M..P..K..H, although M could be in the first hour instead of the second. The only client left is N, who must share with either K or H. The question wants to know what could be true, so go through the answer choices and compare them to the setup for this question. The correct answer is (B). N could train with K.

1) The first question is a typical rules question. Go down rule by rule to see whether each answer violates the particular rule you are looking at. Once you have eliminated an answer, do not test it for the other rules. This is also your chance to review the rules to catch any you may have missed or misunderstood. You will know this is the case if you have more than one right answer or no right answer at all. Don't forget that your deductions count as rules as well. The correct answer here is (B).

2) This question may seem a little confusing but look closely at what it is doing. The phrase that says C works on every day that L works really means that if L works on any day, then C must work on that day also. In other words, *if L then C*. The next phrase says that C does not work on any day on which L does not work. This is simplified as: If not L, then not C. The contrapositive of this statement says *if C then L*. So now you have two statements: If L then C, and if C then L. Thus, this question binds C and L together as a pair. Wherever you have one, you must have the other. One of the rules states that no two technicians can work together on the same day more than two times during the week. This applies directly to the CL pair. The pair cannot work more than two times during the week because wherever one is, the other will be also. H must work on the days on which C and L do not work. Because H needs to have two consecutive days off, C and L have to be together on two days. The remaining four days have only H's. You still have to satisfy the rule that no technician can work three days in a row. The only setup that will prevent you from having three H's consecutive is if H works on Monday, Tuesday, Friday, and Saturday, with the CL pair on Wednesday and Thursday. The only thing you do not know is on which days the meltdowns occur. They could be on any day on which H is alone. Now go to the answer choices and find the one choice that does not have to be false, or, in other words, the one that could be true. The correct answer is (E).

3) If meltdowns occur on Tuesday and Thursday, then H must be alone on Tuesday and Thursday. With H working on Tuesday and Thursday, the only way for H to have two consecutive days off is if H does not work on Friday and Saturday. Because the question added the condition that C does work at all and because H cannot work on Friday or Saturday, L must be the worker who works on Friday and Saturday. Furthermore, since no technician can work three consecutive days, H cannot work on Wednesday, which means that L must also work on Wednesday. Now you know the schedule for Tuesday through Saturday. H still needs one more day of work since H must work at least three days and L must still have his two consecutive days off. The only day left on which H can work is Monday, so H must work on Monday and for L to have two consecutive days off, L cannot work on Monday. Now you know the work schedule for all six days so go to the answer choices and find the one answer choice that could be false, or that does not have to be true. The correct answer is (D). H and L must both work exactly three days so H does not have to work more days than L.

4) This question places L and H together on Tuesday and Friday. You need at least two more days where H works alone in order to allow for the two meltdowns, but you must also ensure that H has two consecutive days off. With H working on Tuesday and Friday, the only way H can have two consecutive days off is if H does not work on either Wednesday or Thursday. Since H cannot work on Wednesday or Thursday, the two days on which H must work alone must be Monday and Saturday. The two meltdowns must, therefore, occur on Monday and Saturday. The correct answer is (A).

5) Question five assigns C to Tuesday and Thursday, L to Saturday, and H to Thursday. H must also work on at least two days all by himself. The only remaining days on which H could work by himself are Monday, Wednesday, and Friday. Since H is already scheduled for Thursday, it is impossible for H to work on both Wednesday and Friday, for this would have H working three days in a row. Since H cannot work on both Wednesday and Friday, H must work on Monday. Therefore, the correct answer is (A).

1) The first question is a typical rules question. Go down rule by rule to see whether each answer violates the particular rule you are looking at. Once you have eliminated an answer, do not test it for the other rules. This is also your chance to review the rules to catch any you may have missed or misunderstood. You will know this is the case if you have more than one right answer or no right answer at all. The correct answer here is (C).

2) Question 2 tests your deductions. This is an easy answer if you took the time to understand how the rules relate to each other. With 1 and 7 together and one of 3, 4, or 5 in each group, 1, 7, and 3/4/5 must always fill up one of the groups. Thus, it is impossible for 1 and 6 to play the same type of music. The correct answer is (B).

3) This is another very easy question if you took the time to work out the scenarios. The key to the scenarios is the placement of 1, 7, and 3/4/5, which must either be in R or O. This question puts 2 in R, which forces 1, 7, and 3/4/5 into O. The correct answer is (E).

4) If buttons 5 and 8 are in R, then you immediately know that 1, 7, and 3/4 must be in O. Since buttons 5 and 6 cannot be assigned to the same type of music, 6 must be assigned to A and since 6 is not assigned to R, 2 must also be assigned to A. Thus, 6, 2, and one of 3 or 4 must be assigned to A. With three buttons assigned to both O and A, only two buttons can play R. The correct answer is (D); only two buttons play rock music, 5 and 8.

5) If 6 and 8 are together then one group must be 6, 8, and 3/4, another must be 1, 7, and 3/4/5, and the remaining group must include 2 and 3/4/5. What is important here is the relationship between 6 and 2. If the newly formed block of 6 and 8 is in R, then the block of 1, 7, and 3/4/5 must be in O, leaving 2 and 3/4/5 for A. If the newly formed block of 6 and 8 is not in R, then according to the rules, button 2 must be assigned to A. Either way, button 2 must be assigned to A. The correct answer is therefore (A). Another way to approach this question is to think of it in terms of the scenarios you deduced. If 6 and 8 are together, then one group must be 6, 8, and 3/4, another must be 1, 7, and 3/4/5, and the remaining group must include 2 and 3/4/5. Buttons 6 and 8 could be together in either the first or the third of the three basic scenarios. In the first scenario 1, 7, and 3/4/5 are assigned to R and 2 must be assigned to A so 6 and 8 would have to be assigned to O. In the third scenario, 6 is already assigned to R, so 6 and 8 would have to be assigned to R, with the block of 1, 7, and 3/4/5 in O, and 2 and 3/4/5 in A. In either case, it must be true that 2 is assigned to alternative.

6) This question asks for a pair of buttons that cannot both play O. This does not mean that the correct answer has to include two buttons neither of which can play oldies; it means only that you have to find two buttons that cannot play O at the same time. An easy way to approach this question is first to think about whether there are any buttons that cannot play O at all. In each of the three scenarios it is evident that button 2 cannot play O. Thus, any answer choice that includes button 2 will be the correct answer. The correct answer is therefore (C). The reason why button 2 can never play O is its relationship to 6 and the block of 1, 7, and 3/4/5. If 1, 7, and 3/4/5 play R then 6 cannot play R, which means that 2 must play A. If the block of 1, 7, and 3/4/5 does not play R, then it must play O, leaving no room for 2. The correct answer is (C).

7) This question assigns 6 to A and also assigns buttons 5 and 8 to the same group. By assigning 6 to A, this question restricts you to either the first scenario or the second scenario. In the first scenario 2 is already in A, so 2 and 6 would be together, putting 5 and 8 in O. Thus, if it were the first scenario it would look this: R: 1, 7, 3/4; O: 8, 5; A: 2, 6, 3/4. In this case there are two possible different combinations because 3 and 4 could be interchanged. If it were the second scenario, 2 and 6 would still be together in A, but now 1, 7, and 3/4/5 would be in O. The second scenario would look like this: R: 8, 5; O: 1, 7, 3/4; A: 2, 6, 3/4. In this case there are also two possible different combinations because 3 and 4 are again interchangeable. Two plus two equals four, so there are four different possible combinations. The correct answer is (C).

1) The first question is a typical rules question. Go down rule by rule to see whether each answer violates the particular rule you are looking at. Once you have eliminated an answer, do not test it for the other rules. This is also your chance to review the rules to catch any you may have missed or misunderstood. You will know this is the case if you have more than one right answer or no right answer at all. The correct answer here is (D).

2) Question two establishes a QW block. According to the deductions, there are only two basic possibilities, one where P is with R and T, and one where Q is with R and T. This question allows you to determine that it is P who is with R and T. In the scenario in which P, R, and T are together, Q, W, and U must be together. Thus, U must be with the QW block. The correct answer is (D).

3) This question assigns V to K. According to the deductions, the RT block must always be with either P or Q. Thus, there is now no room for the RT block in K. Since the RT block cannot be in K or M, the RT block must be in L and the girl assigned to L must be either Q or P. Since L is now filled with R, T, and either Q or P, the fact that V cannot be with W means that W must be assigned to M. With U and W in M, there is no room for the OS block in M, so the OS block must be assigned to K. Thus, K must contain V, O, and S, L must contain R, T, and either Q or P, and M must contain U, W, and the other of Q or P. Now you can go to the answer choices and easily find the one that does not have to be true, or that could be false. The correct answer is (B). P does not have to be assigned to L, for P and Q are interchangeable.

4) If V is assigned to M, then U and V must be together in M. According to the three possible arrangements of teams, the only scenario in which U and V can be together is if Q, R, and T are together in one group, if O, S, and W are together in another group, and if U, V, and P are together in the third group. Thus, U, V, and P must be the three campers assigned to M. All you need to do now is determine which group of three campers is assigned to K. The contrapositive of the rule that says if O is assigned to L, then Q is assigned to M, says that if Q is not assigned to M, then O is not assigned to L. In this case, Q is not assigned to M, so O cannot be assigned to L. If O cannot be in M or L, then O must be in K. Thus, O, S, and W must all be assigned to K. The correct answer is (A).

5) If W is assigned to K, then it is impossible for W and U to be assigned to the same team. In the case where P, R, and T are all together on the same team, W and U must be together, so it cannot be the case that P, R, and T are together. Since P cannot be with the RT block, Q must be with the RT block. Thus, one team must consist of Q, R, and T. When Q, R, and T are together, U must be with P and either V or W. But here, as has already been noted, W and U cannot be together. Therefore, U, P, and V must be the group of campers assigned to M. With Q, R, and T as one group and U, P, and V as another, the one remaining group must include O, S, and W. The question assigned W to K, so O, S, and W must all be assigned to K. With O, S, and W assigned to K and U, P, and V assigned to M, it must be the case that Q, R, and T are assigned to L. Therefore, the correct answer is (C). Q must be assigned to L.

6) Question seven asks for a camper who cannot be assigned to L. From previous work you can clearly see that P, Q, R, and T can all be assigned to L (in fact, you can find Q, R, and T in the correct answer to the first question). Using previous work thereby allows you to eliminate (A), (C), and (E). The correct answer must be either (B) or (D), which means that either W or O cannot be assigned to L. One of the rules says that if O is assigned to L, then Q is assigned to M. Quickly check the three scenarios and see whether it is feasible for O to be assigned to L and Q to be assigned to M. In the first scenario, where P, R, and T are together, O could be assigned to L and Q could be assigned to M. Thus, you can eliminate (D). The correct answer is therefore (B). W cannot be assigned to L. If W were assigned to L, W could have to be with O and S, leaving P, V, and U as the three campers assigned to M. However, according to the rules, if O is assigned to L then Q must be assigned to M. This is clearly not possible.

1) The first question is a typical rules question. Go down rule by rule to see whether each answer violates the particular rule you are looking at. Once you have eliminated an answer, do not test it for the other rules. This is also your chance to review the rules to catch any you may have missed or misunderstood. You will know this is the case if you have more than one right answer or no right answer at all. The correct answer here is (D).

2) The second question assigns B as the manager of project R and D as the manager of project T and wants to know the effects of these assignments on project S. According to the rules, if B is assigned to a project, then E must be assigned to that project as well, so E must be assigned to project R. Next, if D is the manager of T, then, just as you deduced, the only other person that can be with him is E. At this point E has been used twice, so he cannot be used again. You also know that C must the manager of one project, so C is the manager of project S. Since the most experienced researcher is the manager, project S cannot include A or B. The only other researcher left to be the assistant at project S is D. The correct answer is (D).

3) This question assigns D to project S as an assistant and tells you that B is not assigned to any of the projects. It has already been deduced that E cannot be a manager and the question eliminates B, so the managers at each of the three projects must be A, C, and D. Since D is not the manager at project S and, according to a deduction, cannot be the manager of project R, D must be the manager of project T. Wherever D is the manager, E must be the assistant, so D and E must be together in project T. You have used D twice, so D cannot be used again. Thus, neither B nor D can be used in project R, which must have two assistants. If neither B nor D can be used, the only two researchers remaining who could serve as assistants are C and E, leaving A as the manager. Since C must be a manager, he must be the manager

of project S, with D as the only assistant. Now go to the answer choices and find the one that must be false. The correct answer is (C). C cannot be assigned to project T because C must be assigned to projects R and S, and no researcher can be assigned to all three projects.

4) If B is one of exactly two researchers who is assigned to two projects then the other of the two researchers who is assigned to two projects must be E, for if B is assigned to a project, then E must also be assigned to that project. According to the rules, C must be the manager at one of the projects. This means that C must be the researcher with the most experience at one of the projects. B has more experience than C, so C must be the manager at the one project to which B and E are not assigned. Since E cannot be assigned to the project at which C is the manager, the only assistant for C to oversee is D. Since B and E are the only two researchers assigned to two projects, neither C nor D can be assigned to two projects. According to the rules, D must be assigned to project T, so in order for C to oversee D, C and D must be the researchers assigned to project T. Since C and D must be assigned to project T, B and E must be assigned to projects R and S. In order to have at least three researchers in project R, A must be the manager at project R. Thus, this question allows you to determine the entire setup: A, B, and E must be assigned to project R, B and E must be assigned project S, and both C and D must be assigned to project T. Go through the answer choices and find what must be true. The correct answer is (C). C cannot be assigned to project R.

5) This question tells you that E is assigned to project S and no other projects. Look at the rules and deductions concerning E. One rule says that if B is assigned to a project then E must be assigned to that project. The contrapositive says that if E is not assigned to a project, then B cannot be assigned to that project. If there is no E in projects R or T, there cannot be any B's in projects R or T either. In order to have three people in project R without using E or B, A, C, and D must be all be assigned to project R, with A as the manager. One deduction says that if D is the manager, then E must be an assistant. Looking at the contrapositive, this means that since E cannot be used in project T, D cannot be the manager of project T. You also know that B cannot be in projects R or T, so B is not the manager of project T. According to another deduction, A can only be used once, so A cannot be the manager of project T either. Now you know that A, B, D, and E cannot be the manager of project T. Thus, C must be the manager of T. Since E cannot be used, the assistant in project T must be D. By now both C and D have been used twice and A has been used, so B must be the manager of S. Now you are ready to go to the answers and find the choice that could be true (because it is a "must be false EXCEPT" question). The correct answer is (C).

6) If C is only assigned to S, then C must be the manager of S, because according to the rules, C must be a manager. The assistant assigned to project S must be D and/or E. With B as the manager of project R and C unavailable to use as an assistant, the two assistants in project R must be D and E. According to the rules, there must be a D in project T, which means that two D's are already used, so the assistant in project S must be E. Now you have also used two E's, which means that there cannot be an E in project T. Just as in the previous question, this means that there cannot be a B in project T and that D cannot be the manager in project T. If none of C, B, D, and E can be the manager, then A must be the manager. The correct answer is (A).

7) If C and D are the only assistants in project R, then who must be the manager for project R? The manager must be a researcher with more experience than C. The contrapositive that says if E is not assigned to a project, then B cannot be assigned to that project means that B cannot be the manager. This leaves A as the only possible manager of project R. According to the rules you also know that there is a D in project T and that C must be a manager somewhere. Because both C and D have been used once in project R, they both can only be used once more. This question does not allow you to determine the placement of each researcher, but it does limit the possibilities. Now that you have filled in the diagram as much as you can, go to the answer choices and check them one by one on your partially completed diagram. Answer choice (A) must be true based on what you have determined. Move to answer choice (B). If both B and C are assigned to project S, then B will be the manager because he has more experience. However, C must be the manager of one of the projects, so C would have to be the manager of project T. This would give you three C's, one in each project, which is a violation of the rules. Thus, (B) must be false. The correct answer is (B).

1) This is mainly a rules question and requires very little work. Look at the rules one by one, going through the answers with each one. Cross off the ones that don't work and move on. You can easily narrow it down to either (A) or (E). Now remember the rule concerning P, L, and O. There must be room for one in each of 3 groups. In (A) you use up two groups without using any of P, L, or O, leaving you with only two groups to use them in. This does not work. The correct answer is (E). If you didn't make the deduction earlier, then you would have had to make it here. Once you figure out a deduction, regardless of when you make it, remember that it is as true as a rule. Treat it like one.

2) This question tests your understanding of the P, L, and O situation. If Y is not used, then you only have three groups left. You must have one of P, L, or O in each group remaining. Which answer must be false? (A), because that would fill up B and leave P, L, and O for only two groups.

3) This question places K with Q in B, filling up that group. You are again left with only three groups, each having one of P, L, or O. This means that Y, which can only have one person, must have one of P, L, or O. The answer that must be false is (B).

4) If O=G, and K=Y, then what do you know? Look at the contrapositive of the rule *if P=B then K=G*. This tells you that if K is not in G, then P is not in B. So you now know that P cannot be in B or Y. But you also know that P, O, and L need to be separate. This means that P cannot be in G either since O is already in G, so P must be in R. The only place left for L is in B. Now look at the contrapositive of the rule *if N=R then K=R*. This tells you that if K is not in R, then N is not in R, which must be the case here. The only place left for N is in G with O. Now you have NO together, so no one else can be with them. Where does that leave J? J must be in R with P. The correct answer is (E).

5) Once you place L in G and N in R, then you know that K=R as well, according to the rules. You also know, according to your deductions, that O cannot be with N, since there is somebody else with N. Since O also cannot be with L in G, you know that O must be in either B or Y. If Y is filled up or not used, then O must be in B. Look at the answers. The correct answer is (E).

6) This question gives you a few pieces of information: J=Y and NO are together. If N and O are together, they cannot be with anyone else. Remember the deduction that if N=R, then N and O are not together. Here you have the contrapositive: If N and O are together, then N is not in R. The only place NO can be is in G. Now you know two groups, G and Y, are filled up. You have two groups left, B and R, and you know that one of P and L must be in each one. Remember the rules: If P is in B, then K is in G, but you know that N and O are in G together and must be alone, so P is not in B. That puts P in R and L in B. The correct answer is (B).

7) This question asks you to determine what must be true if four people ride in R. It is very easy to do too much work for this question. The only thing that having four people in R tells you immediately is that N and O cannot be together in R. You know that P, L, and O must be in separate boats, but you cannot determine who is in which boat. Knowing this and that Q must be in B, you can easily eliminate (A), (B), (D), and (E). The correct answer, therefore, is (D).

1) The first question is a typical rules question. In this case, however, you cannot determine which group of three is assigned to which group; you only know the people who compose the groups. Thus, you can only use the broad rules about blocks, splits, and numbers to eliminate answer choices. You cannot use the rules that talk about being on a team with a VCR or a computer because you do not know which teams can use VCR's and which can use computers. With that said, go through the applicable rules to see whether any answer choice violates the particular rule you are looking at. Once you have eliminated an answer, do not test it for the other rules. This is also your chance to review the rules to catch any you may have missed or misunderstood. You will know this is the case if you have more than one right answer or no right answer at all. The correct answer here is (E).

2) This question forces you to work out one of the two possible scenarios if you haven't done so already. Since ideally you already have, the answer is easy. All you have to do is look at the finished scenario. The question asks for someone who must be on a team without a VCR, or, in other words, someone who must be on the computer team when M is on a team that can use a VCR. When M and Q are on the VCR team, G must be on the computer team, or else P would have to be with M and Q, leaving no room for a salesperson on that team. The correct answer is (B).

3) This question forces you to work out the second scenario, but in a backwards and confusing way, revealing that it is much easier to do the work before the game. If you didn't, be sure to learn from your mistakes. If you already did the work, then the correct answer is easy to come by. In the second scenario, M, Q, and D/F must be on the computer team, P must be on the VCR only team, and N must be on the mixed team. This question creates a block of F and G and places this block on a team that can use a VCR. Since F now cannot be in the computer group, D must be the salesperson with M and Q in the computer group. In order to place the FG block on a team with a VCR, the FG block must either be with

P or N, leaving O and E to be together with the other of P or N. Thus, the correct answer is (D). If you did not have the second scenario worked out, then this is a much more complicated question. The condition introduced in this question is that F and G are both assigned to a team that has a VCR. F and G are two of four salespeople. Since each team must have at least one salesperson, the remaining two salespeople, D and E, must each be on separate teams. Thus, one team must have D, one must have E, and one must have the block of F and G. Since F is on a team that has a VCR, D cannot be on a team that has a VCR. Therefore, D must be on the computer team. Furthermore, since G is on a team that has a VCR, P cannot be on a team that has a computer. Therefore, P must be on the VCR team. No matter what, P will have to have a salesperson with him. This salesperson could either be E or the FG block. Regardless, there will have to be at least two people other than M and Q on the VCR team, leaving no room for the MQ block on that team. Since, according to the rules, the MQ block cannot be on the mixed team either, the MQ block has to be on the computer team. Thus, the computer team must include M, Q, and D, thereby filling that group. Since P and N cannot be together and P is on the VCR team, N must be on the mixed team. The FG block would have to be with either P or N. Wherever the FG block is, that team will be filled, leaving O and E to be together with the other of P or N. No matter what, O and E must be together. The correct answer, therefore, is (D). Note that the right answer here has to do with the two wildcards, O and E. Although O and E are not restricted outright by any rules, the placement of other items limits the possibilities for their placement.

4) If G does not have access to a VCR, then you must be dealing with the first scenario, in which the MQ block is in the VCR group. In this first scenario, the groups must include the following: VCR: M, Q, salesperson (D, E or F); Mixed: O, P/N, salesperson (D, E, or F); Computer: G, P/N, D/F. The question asks for a list of people that could be on the mixed team. According to the diagram, the mixed team must be some mixture of O, P/N, and D/E/F. The correct answer, then, is (A).

5) If P is in the computer-only group, then you must be in the first scenario. With P in the computer group, N must be in the mixed group. The question does not allow you to fix the position of D, E, or F, so go to the answer choices and find the choice that must be false. The correct answer is (D) since N must be on the team that has access to a computer and a VCR.

6) This question is a little trickier than the others because based on the question itself you cannot determine which of the two scenarios you are dealing with. However, if O and D are together in the first scenario, where M and Q are in the VCR group, then the setup looks like this: VCR: M, Q, E/F; Mixed: O, D, P/N; Computer: G, F, P/N. Before working out the second scenario, check the answer choices against this one. In this setup it is possible for F and P to be together, so the correct answer is (C). It turns out that F and P can also be together in the computer group in the second scenario.

7) Just as in question six, you cannot determine which scenario you are dealing with based solely on the information in the question. N, F, and O could be on the same team in both scenarios. If N, F, and O are together in the first scenario, then they must be together in the mixed group, since M and Q are already in the VCR group and G is already in the computer group. Since F is in the mixed group, D must be in the computer group, which forces E into the VCR group. Thus, the setup looks like this: VCR: M, Q, E; Mixed: N, F, O; Computer: P, D, G. If you stop here and look at the answer choices, you will see that there is seemingly more than one correct answer. Both (C) and (E) must be the case in this first scenario. Since the question asks for what must be true in every case, you must work out the second scenario as well. In the second scenario, you already know that N is in the mixed group, so N, F, and O must again be placed in the mixed group. Since F is in the mixed group, D must be with M and Q in the computer group, forcing P, O, and G into the VCR group. Thus, the setup for this question in the second scenario looks like this: VCR: P, D, G; Mixed: N, F, O; Computer: M, Q, D. In both cases, G is on a team with P. The correct answer is therefore (C).

1) The first question is a typical rules question. Go down rule by rule to see whether each answer violates the particular rule you are looking at. Once you have eliminated an answer, do not test it for the other rules. This is also your chance to review the rules to catch any you may have missed or misunderstood. You will know this is the case if you have more than one right answer or no right answer at all. The correct answer here is (C).

2) This question wants you to put P in the latest position possible for P. You know that P cannot be last and must be sometime before C. C can be last, so if C is sixth, then P could be fifth and satisfy all the conditions governing the placement of P. The correct answer is therefore (D).

3) This question adds another condition: C is before V (C..V). If you add this condition to the initial diagram, you get a list of order that looks like this: T..H..C..V, with P sometime before C, and R as the wildcard. Remember, the last position can only be C or R. Since in this case C must be before V, C can no longer be last. Thus, R must be last. The first position can only be T or R. Since R must be last, T must be first. This is now the order: T..H..C..V..R, with P sometime before C. Since T is first and P must be before C, P could only be in the second or third position. The question wants to know a possible list of the first three orders. T must be the first sandwich ordered, while the second and third sandwiches must be H and P, not necessarily in that order. The correct answer is (B).

4) The question adds two conditions: H is as late as possible and T is not first. The question then asks for a pair of sandwiches, neither of which could be the one that is ordered twice. The rule concerning the sandwich that is ordered twice says only that the sandwich that is ordered twice cannot be the first or last type of sandwich ordered. Thus, in this question you are really looking for the sandwiches that are ordered first and last. Because T is not ordered first and only T or R can be ordered first, R must be ordered first. Since R is ordered first, only C can be ordered last. Thus, the first position must be R and the last must be C. These, then, are two sandwiches neither of which could be the sandwich ordered twice. Find this pair in the answer choices. The correct answer is (D).

5) This last question tests your overall understanding of the game. In the initial diagram you have T before H, H before C, V sometime after H, and P sometime before C. The wildcard is R. The first sandwich must either be R or T, and the last sandwich must either be R or C. In order to determine the exact order of the sandwiches you will need to know the placement of R, which can be determined if R's placement is specified, or if you know that T is not first or that C is not last. You must also fix the placement of V and P to know the entire order. Go through the answer choices looking for information that will allow you to determine what is first and last and also allow you to determine the relationship between V and P. (A) is tempting, but after working it out it is clear that it does not allow you to determine the relative order of P and H. (B) does not fix the placement of P or V. (C) does not allow you to determine the sandwich that is ordered sixth, nor does it allow you to determine the placement of P or V. Answer choice (D) places P after V and tells you that T is the sandwich that is ordered twice. Because T is ordered twice, it cannot be the sandwich ordered first, which means that R must be ordered first. Since R is ordered first and only R or C can be ordered last, C must be ordered last. Thus, the basic order is: R..T..H..C (R is first and C is last). V must be sometime after H, while the answer choice also placed P sometime after V. Thus, (D) creates an order of RTHVPC, which means that (D) provides enough information to determine the exact order in which the sandwiches are ordered. The correct answer is (D).

6) If two C's are ordered, then C cannot be the last sandwich ordered. Since the last sandwich must either be C or R and now cannot be C, the last sandwich must be R. Since R can no longer be the first sandwich ordered, T must be the first sandwich ordered. Thus, this question creates a basic sequence of T..H..C..R, while P must be sometime before C and V must be sometime after H. With this order in mind, go through the answer choices and find the one that must be false, or that cannot be true. The only one answer choice that must be false is (D). H cannot be ordered fourth because there are only six different types of sandwiches and, in this case, all three of C, R, and V must come sometime after H. Thus, the latest that H could be ordered is third. The correct answer is (D). The remaining answer choices could be, and in some cases, must be true.

1) The first question tests the deduction that Luis must watch at least one M. If you made the deduction, then find it in the answer choices. If you did not make the deduction, you are forced to do so here. As noted in the deductions section, Luis must watch six to eight different channels. Three or four of these channels must be some combination of S's and V's. Since S's and V's can account for at most four channels, Luis must watch at least two other channels. These two or more channels must be some combination of M's and G. There is only one G available, so no matter what Luis must watch at least one M. The correct answer is (C).

2) If Luis watches at least two V's then, according to a contrapositive of one of the rules, Luis cannot watch more than two M's. According to the deductions, Luis must watch at least one M, so Luis must watch either one or two M's. Furthermore, because the greatest number of any combination of S's and V's that Luis can watch is four and because Luis must already watch at least two V's, Luis can watch at most two S's. Thus, Luis *must* watch at least two V's and one or two M's, and *can* watch at most two S's. Therefore, if Luis were to watch as many different channels as possible in this scenario without watching the G, he would watch six different channels: two M's and four of some combination of S's and V's. The only way for G to be included is if there are more S's than M's. The greatest number of S's that can be included is two and the fewest number of M's that can be included is one, so if G were included then there would have to be two S's and one M. Including G would produce a setup of one M, two S's, two V's, and the G, for a total of six channels once again. Therefore, if Luis watches at least two V's, Luis cannot watch more than six different channels (though he could watch fewer than six). Hence, the correct answer is (C). Luis cannot watch seven different channels.

3) If Luis watches the G, then Luis must watch more S's than M's. It must be true that Luis watches at least one M, so Luis must watch at least two S's. According to the rules, Luis must watch a total of three or four of some combination of S's and V's. Since in this instance Luis watches at least two S's, it must be the case that Luis watches at most two V's. The correct answer is (E).

4) Question four asks for a possible list of the channels that Luis watches if Luis watches three S's. The rules do not allow you to deduce any additional information, so you will have to go through the answer choices and consider each one. However, work smartly. Before looking at the answer choices, think for a moment about you what do know and what the restrictions are. There must be anywhere between six and eight channels, three of which are S's. Since there are three S's, there can be at most one V. Furthermore, if there are more S's than M's, then G must be included as well. Likewise, if there is a G, then there must be more M's than S's. Only after considering the restrictions should you go through the answer choices. (A) is incorrect because it contains two V's, while there can be at most one V. (B) is incorrect because if there are more S's than M's, G must also be included. (C) could be true and is, therefore, the correct answer. Luis could watch three S's, one V, two M's, and one G. (D) is incorrect because it requires nine channels. (E) is incorrect because including a G requires that there be more S's than M's, which is not the case in (E).

5) Question five requires Luis to watch exactly eight channels. Since Luis watches exactly eight channels and the most S's and V's combined that Luis can watch is four, Luis must watch at least four of some combination of M's and the G. There is only one G, so Luis must watch at least three M's. In other words, it cannot be true that Luis watches exactly two M's. The correct answer is (A).

6) If Luis watches two V's then, in order to reach the required number of three or four of a combination of S's and V's, Luis must watch one or two S's. If Luis watches only one S, then in order to reach the minimum of six channels, Luis would have to watch three more channels from among the M's and the G. However, if there is only one S, then there cannot be more S's than M's, which means that there cannot be a G. Therefore, if Luis only watches one S, Luis must also watch at least three M's. However, according to a contrapositive of one of the rules, if Luis watches two V's then Luis cannot watch more than two M's. Hence, it is impossible for Luis to only watch one S; he must watch two S's. The correct answer is (B). You cannot determine whether or not Luis watches the G, because with Luis watching two V's and two S's, he could either watch two M's or one M and one G.

7) If Luis watches exactly seven channels and exactly three of those channels are M's, then it is impossible for Luis to watch more S's than M's, since doing so would require four S's, the three M's, and the G, for a total of eight channels. Therefore, Luis cannot watch more than three S's. Because Luis cannot watch more S's than M's, Luis cannot watch the G either. Since Luis cannot watch the G, Luis must watch four of some combination of S's and V's in order to reach the required number of seven channels. The rules say that if Luis watches three M's, which is the case here, he cannot watch more than one V. Since Luis cannot watch more than one V and cannot watch more than three S's, in order to have four S's and V's combined Luis must watch exactly one V and exactly three S's. Thus, the four channels that Luis watches in addition to the three M's consist of three S's and one V. Look for one of these in the answer choices. The correct answer is (B).

1) The first question is not a typical rules question; instead, it tests your ability to make deductions. If you took the time to make deductions before moving on to the questions, then this would be a pretty simple answer to get right quickly. Based on your diagram, what schools absolutely cannot receive a 1? O cannot because it must be lower than W, and A cannot since the only category left for A is quality, and W already receives a 1 in quality. Thus, neither O nor A can receive a 1. The correct answer is (D).

2) The second question is another deduction question, although it tries to make you do more work than necessary. The real question is which school cannot be ranked 5, while the condition that the question adds is superfluous. You already know, based on the rule that O must be lower than W in all three criteria, that W cannot receive a 5. Thus, the correct answer is (E). This is another example of the importance of taking the time in the beginning of any game to work out the deductions. Once you work them out, use them. Think about how the deductions relate to every question. It will make your life easier.

3) This is another simple question if you already made the difficult deduction that O cannot be ranked 5 in quality. O must receive a 5 in either cost or location and therefore cannot receive a 5 in quality. Thus, the correct answer is (C). If you did not make this deduction, the best way to approach this problem so that you could solve it quickly is to think that four of the five answer choices could be true. You could go through the answer choices and compare each to the diagram. You can eliminate any choices that the diagram tells you are possible. Any choices that you do not have specific information on you will have to test. Using this method, you can eliminate (A), (B), and (D) because these are explicitly stated as possibilities on the diagram. You are left with (C) and (E). Test (C). If O receives a 5 in quality, then O must receive a 3 in cost and a 4 in location. Since O must receive a lower ranking than W, this setup requires W to receive a 2 in cost and another 2 in location.

This breaks the rule by forcing W to receive a 2 in both cost and location. Thus, (C) is the correct answer. It must be false that O ranks 5 in quality. This is true all the time, so keep it in mind for the rest of the game.

4) Question four places an item in a slot for you. Place this information on your diagram and determine its immediate effects. If W is ranked 4 in location, then O must be ranked 5 in location. Since O is ranked 5 in location, O must be ranked 3 in cost, which also means that W must be ranked 2 in cost. Go through the answer choices and see if any of these results are the correct answer. One of them is there: O is ranked 3 in cost. The correct answer is (C).

5) If S receives a 2 in location, then W cannot receive a 2 in location and must therefore receive a 4, which, just as in the previous questions, forces O to receive a 5 in location, O to receive a 3 in cost, and W to receive a 2 in cost. The only ranking left in location is 1, which must go to the only school left, T. You now have enough information to finish filling in the cost category rankings as well. With A receiving a 4, O receiving a 3, and W receiving a 2 in cost, all that is left for T and S are 1 and 5, although not necessarily in that order. You just determined that T receives a 1 in location, so T cannot receive a 1 in cost. Thus, T receives a 5 in cost and S receives a 1. Now you are left with the rankings in Q, which is precisely what the question is designed to test. The key now becomes the rules that say T has two rankings higher than A and S has two rankings higher than T. As it stands now, T only has one ranking higher than A (in location) and S only has one ranking higher than T (in cost). In the one remaining category, then, S must receive a higher ranking than T and T must receive a higher ranking than A. Since S is going to be the highest, start with S. The highest rank that S can receive in the category of quality is a 3 since it receives a 1 and a 2 in the other categories. Thus, the highest ranking that T can receive for quality is a 4. This forces A to receive a 5 in quality. O is the only school remaining, and the only rank left is the one you are looking for. O must be ranked 2 in quality. The correct answer is (D).

6) Question six again tests your understanding of the relationship between O and W. If W receives a 3 in cost, then O must receive a 5 in cost, which means that O must receive a 4 in location and that W must receive a 2 in location. In the cost category, there are two ranks left, 1 and 2, to assign to one of T or S. In the location category, there are also two ranks left, 1 and 5, to assign to one of T or S. Check the answer choices against the diagram and you will see that the only answer choice that could be true is (A), that S is ranked 5 in location.

7) This question seems rather odd and unlike any of the others, but just do what you have been doing. Given that W is ranked 2 in cost, you are able to fill in the rankings for cost and location for O and W. If W is 2 in cost, W is 4 in location, which means that O is 5 in location and that O is 3 in cost. Since O is 2 in quality, you can also say that A is 5 in quality. You are now missing two rankings in each category. In the cost category you are missing 1 and 5, in the location category you are missing 1 and 2, and in the quality category you are missing 3 and 4. In each category you must assign one of each of the rankings to T and S. In order to rank T and S appropriately, you must remember that T must be ranked higher than A exactly twice and that S must be ranked higher than T exactly twice. The only category where T can receive a lower ranking than A is in the cost category, so since T must receive exactly two rankings higher than S, T must get the lower ranking in cost, which means that T must receive a 5 in cost and S must receive the 1 in cost. Since S is ranked 1 in cost, S cannot be ranked 1 in location, so S receives the 2 in location while T receives the 1. In this case, S's ranking is below T, so S must be higher than T in quality, which means that S receives the 3 and T receives the 4. You now have the entire setup and can easily add the scores for each school. After doing so, it is clear that the school with the lowest sum is S, whose rankings of 1, 2, and 3 add up to 6. The correct answer is (B).

1) The first question is a typical rules question. Go down rule by rule to see whether each answer violates the particular rule you are looking at. Once you have eliminated an answer, do not test it for the other rules. This is also your chance to review the rules to catch any you may have missed or misunderstood. You will know this is the case if you have more than one right answer or no right answer at all. The correct answer here is (D).

2) If C goes to see *Righteous* then, since C and J constitute a block, J must see *Righteous* as well. The only showing of *Righteous* is the evening showing. Therefore, C and J see *Righteous* in the evening. According to the rules if C (and J) goes to an evening show, then F goes to *Ambitious*. Since C and J do see an evening show, F must go to *Ambitious* with D. Four of the seven friends must see either *Righteous* or *Ambitious*. There are two movies left, *Terrified* and *Baffling*, and three friends, E, G, and H. G and H constitute a block; they must see the same movie. Thus, either the GH block or E sees *Terrified* and either the GH block or E sees *Baffling*. In order to answer the question you want to put as many people as possible in matinee showings. Neither *Righteous* nor *Terrified* has matinee showings. Thus, you want to place as many friends as possible in the matinee showings of *Ambitious* and *Baffling*. F and D must see *Ambitious* and could see it as a matinee. Either E or the GH block must see *Baffling* and could see it as a matinee. Since you want to have as many people as possible in matinee showings, you should place the GH block in the *Baffling* matinee showing. You now have F, D, G, and H all seeing matinee showings. Thus, the largest number of friends who could attend matinee showings is four. The correct answer is (B).

3) This question places H and J in evening showings. Since G and H attend the same movie and C and J attend the same movie, both the GH block and the CJ block must be in evening showings, which means that both blocks must be see movies that have evening shows. *Baffling* does not have an evening show, so neither block could attend *Baffling*. Furthermore, D must watch *Ambitious*, so D cannot watch *Baffling* either. Since none of G, G, C, J, or D can watch *Baffling*, the only person who could watch *Baffling* is one of E and F. Therefore, find one of E or F in the answer choices. The correct answer here is (A).

4) The language of this question might seem confusing at first, but relax and try to figure out what it says. The question wants you to find a list of three people, for each of whom it could be impossible to attend a matinee. In order to know which people could not see a matinee, you need to know which people see *Righteous* and *Terrified* because these are the two movies that do not have matinees. So in reality you are looking for a list of three people who could attend *Righteous* or *Terrified* if there are exactly three people in *Baffling*. For each question you must ask yourself, "Can it be possible for these three people to be divided between *Righteous* and *Terrified*? First, you know that D must be in *Ambitious* and therefore it is never impossible for D to attend a matinee, so D cannot be included in the correct answer. Also, because D is in *Ambitious* there are only six friends who could possibly fill the three spots in *Baffling*. Out of these six friends, there are two blocks (CJ and GH) and one split (E and F). In order for there to be exactly three people in *Baffling*, you must use one of the blocks and one person from the split. Thus, the three people that see *Baffling* could either be C, J, and one of E or F, or G, H, and one of E or F. At this point there are three people seeing *Baffling*, one of the blocks and one person from the split, and at least D sees *Ambitious*. You still need at least one person in both *Righteous* and *Terrified*. There are three people left: the other block and the other person from the split. Thus, the correct answer will include one of the blocks and either E or F. Now go to the answer choices. (A) is incorrect because one of E or F can attend a matinee since one of them will be in *Baffling*. (B) is incorrect because one of either the CJ block or the GH block must be in *Baffling*, and therefore one of the blocks will always be able to attend a matinee. (C) is the correct answer. If the CJ block and F are in *Righteous* and *Terrified*, then the GH block and E are left for *Baffling*. Although you should stop once you have the correct answer, (D) is incorrect because it is always possible for D to view a matinee of *Ambitious*, and (E) is incorrect because it includes both blocks (CJ and GH), while one of them must watch *Baffling* and can therefore watch a matinee.

5) Question five asks for something that must be false without providing you with any additional information, so the correct answer will most likely be based on the rules in general or on a specific deduction. In this game, there were not many specific deductions. The main deductions involved the possible numerical distributions and the requirement that one of E or F be alone. With the rules and these deductions is mind, go through the answer choices and find the one that must be false, or cannot be true. Do not spend much time working out each answer choice; simply look at it and see whether it clearly violates any rules and then move on. (A) could be true, and would have to be true if the distribution were 4:1:1:1. (B) could be true and, in fact, was true in the previous question. (C) could be true. There are no rules requiring anyone to see a matinee. (D) could be true. E could see *Terrified* with one of the two blocks as long as F sees a movie alone. (E) cannot be true. If J is one of three friends to see *Righteous*, then C, J, and one of E or F must see *Righteous*. The other of E or F would have to see a movie alone. Since the only showing of *Righteous* is an evening showing, C goes to an evening showing, which means that F must watch *Ambitious*. However, D must also watch *Ambitious*, so in this setup it is impossible for at least one of E or F to be alone. (E) is the correct answer.

6) If exactly six friends attend late shows, then there is only one person left that sees another type of show. *Righteous* does not have a late showing, so that one person who does not see a late show must see *Righteous*. Out of the seven people there are two blocks, one split, and D is assigned to *Ambitious*. Thus, in order for there to be one person who sees *Righteous*, that person must be part of the E and F split. For the remaining three movies, *Terrified*, *Ambitious*, and *Baffling*, you have two blocks (GH and CJ), D in *Ambitious*, and one of E and F. They must all be in late showings. In order to fix the friends their respective movies, you will need to know where one of E or F is, which will tell you where the other one is, and you will need to know the placement of one of the blocks. The correct answer here is (C). If F accompanies D then F is in *Ambitious*, which means that E must see *Righteous*. This leaves you with the two blocks, GH and CJ, and only two movies, *Terrified* and *Baffling*, so there must be one block at each movie. (C) also says that G goes to a movie that has a matinee available. Between *Terrified* and *Baffling*, only *Baffling* has a matinee, which means that G and H must see *Baffling*, leaving C and J for *Terrified*.

1) The first question is a typical rules question. Go down rule by rule to see whether each answer violates the particular rule you are looking at. Once you have eliminated an answer, do not test it for the other rules. This is also your chance to review the rules to catch any you may have missed or misunderstood. You will know this is the case if you have more than one right answer or no right answer at all. The correct answer here is (B).

2) The second question asks for the runner who cannot be fifth in the sequence. From the deductions you already know that O cannot be fifth, so the correct answer is (C). If you hadn't discovered this previously, you would have to do so now. The key to the order for the positions after Q is keeping O and P separated, so you should look first at O and P. If you try and place O in the fifth spot, there is no way you can get P to not be adjacent to O or keep P after L and after M at the same time. The correct answer is (C).

3) This question places R in sixth place and then asks who can finish fourth. You already know that Q is in third place. Since R must be before N and R is sixth, N must be seventh. Now you have just enough information to figure out the relationship between O and P. From the deductions you know that the earliest P can finish is fifth and P can only do so if O is second. In this case, sixth and seventh place are already taken, so P must finish fifth, forcing O into second place and L into first place. The only position left is fourth and the only runner left is M. Thus, M finishes fourth. The correct answer is (B).

4) The fourth question forces you to make the deduction about P's position. If you had made the deduction earlier, you would know that the earliest P could finish the race is fifth. The fact that Q always comes third, coupled with the fact that P comes after both L and M, would seem to prove that the earliest P could finish is fourth, but then P would be next to O and that violates the OP rule. Therefore, the earliest P could be is in the fifth position. The correct answer is (D).

5) Question five further tests the deduction about the placement of O and P. What do you know if O finishes after Q? From the deductions you know that O must finish second or fourth. If O is after Q, then O must be fourth. If you had not made the deduction earlier you would have to do so now. The correct answer is (D).

6) This question again tests your understanding of the placement of P. If you had figured out in the deductions or in question 4 that the earliest P could be is fifth, then it would be easy to see that what must be false is that P is in the fourth position. The correct answer is (D).

7) The seventh question is about how many different possibilities there are for the placement of M. M must be before P, so M could not be last. Also, Q is third, so M cannot finish third. M could finish in any position besides last and third, which means that M could finish in five positions. The correct answer is (D).

8) The last question changes the rules a little bit. The Q rule is changed such that Q comes in fifth place. The question places O in third place instead. P must still finish after both L and M and cannot finish immediately before or after O, so P must finish after Q in either the sixth or seventh position. R and N must both finish after O. With O third, Q fifth, and P in sixth or seventh, R must be fourth, while N must finish either sixth or seventh. Both L and M must either be first or second in no particular order. With this setup in mind, go to the answer choices and find the answer choice that MUST be true. The correct answer is (E).

1) The first question is a typical rules question. Go down rule by rule to see whether each answer violates the particular rule you are looking at. Once you have eliminated an answer, do not test it for the other rules. This is also your chance to review the rules to catch any you may have missed or misunderstood. You will know this is the case if you have more than one right answer or no right answer at all. The correct answer here is (D).

2) This question tests your understanding of how the BWD block relates to the numerical distribution. From the deductions you know that if the BWD block is in bag 2, then it is with J. With four items in bag 2, bag 2 is completely full, leaving the remaining five articles of clothing for bag 1. Therefore, it must be true that there are exactly five items in bag 1. The correct answer is (A).

3) Question three also tests your deductions about the BWD block. If G is in bag 2, then, according to the deduction about C's relationship with J and G, C must be in bag 2 as well. With C and G in bag 2, there is no room for the BWD block, so the BWD block must be in bag 1 with J. Since D and J are the two pairs of pants in bag 1, the pairs of pants in bag 2 must be C and S. Check the answer choices against this information to find what must be false. The correct answer is (A).

4) If S is in bag 1, then the BWD block must be in bag 2, and since the BWD block is in bag 2, it must be with J. B, W, D, and J fill up bag 2, forcing the CG block and the other items, P and R, into bag 1. You now know the entire setup, which makes the question very easy to answer. The correct answer is (C).

5) Question five is a repeat of the first question, except it focuses on bag 2. The most basic information about bag 2 is that it can have only three or four items and must contain exactly two pairs of pants. Keep in mind the relationship between the BWD block and the numerical distribution as you go through the answer choices. You can eliminate (A) and (B) because both are missing pieces of the BWD block and including them would put you over the maximum number. You can eliminate both (D) and (E) because they both contain three pairs of pants. The correct answer is (C).

6) Question six does not give you any additional conditions or information; it simply asks what could be false. Go through each answer choice and ask yourself whether each choice must be true. If it does not have to be true, then it could be false and is the correct answer. (A) must be true because if the BWD block is in bag 1, S must be in bag 2. (B) must be true because C and J must be split. Remember, the BWD block is with exactly one of C or J. C and J can never be together. (C) must be true for the same reason as (A). If S is in bag 1 then the BWD block must be in bag 2. (D) must be true because if P is in bag 2 then there is no room for the BWD block and an additional pair of pants (which would have to be J) in bag 2. Thus, if P is in bag 2 then the BWD block is in bag 1. Since (A), (B), (C), and (D) are not the correct answers, (E) must be the correct answer. It not only could be false, it actually must be false based on what you just reasoned about (D). If P is in bag 2, then the BWD block must be in bag 1, which in turn means that S must be in bag 2.

7) If there are exactly six items in bag 1, then there must be exactly three items in bag 2, one shirt and two pairs of pants. Since the BWD block must be with either J or the CG block, there is no room for the BWD block in bag 2. Thus, the BWD block must be in bag 1. If the BWD block is with J in bag 1, then the CG block and S must be in bag 2. There is one possible combination: CGS. If the BWD block and the CG block are in bag 1, then J and S must be the pants in bag 2. You need one more item in each bag to give you six and three and there are only two items left: P and R. There are no rules about the placement of P and R so either one could be in either bag. This gives you two more possibilities: JSP and JSR. That makes three possible combinations in all. The correct answer is (B).

8) This question asks for a pair of items that could not be together in bag 2. Remember, bag 2 must contain three or four items, and putting the BWD block in bag 2 puts J in bag 2 and completely fills it up. Therefore none of B, W, or D can be in bag 2 with any other article of clothing besides J and the others of B, W, and D. The correct answer is (A) because it puts P and W together in bag 2.

1) The first question is not a typical rules question, but instead tests your understanding of the side effects of the rules. While most of the rules deal with the auditions on Thursday, the question asks for a possible list of actors who audition on Friday. The only things you know for certain about Friday's auditions are that L must audition and that L cannot audition first. Knowing this allows you to eliminate (B) and (E). For the remaining answer choices, you are going to have to determine what side effects they have on Thursday's auditions and then determine if the resulting side effects violate any rules. Start with (A) and place M first, L second, and P third on Friday. This setup forces M to audition sixth, and P to audition second on Thursday. L must be immediately before M, so L would audition fifth. You are left only with positions 1 and 3, and actors R and S. You can place them in either position without violating a rule. Thus, this scenario works. The correct answer here is (A). (C) forces P and S to be non-consecutive on Thursday, which would require that both P and S audition on Friday. (D) does not leave room on Thursday for L and M to audition consecutively.

2) This question makes you get comfortable with the rule concerning P and S. If P and S are not consecutive, then they must both be on Friday. Since R must come after W, the LM sequence must come before W, and since the LM sequence comes before W there is no way that P and S can audition consecutively. Since they are not consecutive, they must both audition on Friday. Thus, the three actors auditioning on Friday are P, S, and L, although not necessarily in that order. You now have enough information to determine the answer since all the answer choices deal with the auditions on Friday. Because the question asks you that "each of the following could be true EXCEPT," you must find the choice that cannot be true. Go to the choices and find it. The correct answer is (D). It cannot be true that R is the first actor to audition on Friday because the three actors that audition on Friday are P, S, and L.

3) This question places P as the third actor to audition on Thursday and then asks about the effects of this placement on the auditions on Friday. Because L must be immediately before M, this setup leaves only positions 1 and 2 or 5 and 6 for L and M, respectively. If L and M were 1 and 2, then M would be second and would audition on Friday. If L and M were 5 and 6, then M would again audition on Friday. Thus, either way M must audition on Friday, giving you both L and M on Friday. Since there are only three auditions on Friday, there is no room for both P and S. According to the contrapositive of the rule dealing with P and S, if P and S are not both on Friday, then P and S are in consecutive positions on Thursday. Since P is third on Thursday and P and S must be consecutive, S must audition second, which forces L and M into positions 5 and 6 and leaves R for the first audition. Now that you know the entire setup on Thursday you can easily determine the sequence on Friday. M will be first, S will be third, and L will be second. The correct answer is (C).

4) This question places W on Friday, which means that both W and L audition on Friday. The first and third positions on Friday are governed by the second and sixth positions on Thursday. Since W cannot be second or sixth on Thursday, W cannot be first or third on Friday. Thus, W is second on Friday. L must then be either first or third on Friday. You already deduced that L must be second or third on Friday, and now, since W is second, you know that L must be third. The actor in the third position on Friday is in the second position on Thursday, so L is second on Thursday, making M third. Because you already have two actors auditioning on Friday, there is no room for both P and S to audition on Friday. According to the contrapositive of the rule concerning P and S, this means that P and S must be consecutive on Thursday. The only room for P and S to be consecutive on Thursday is if they are in positions 5 and 6, although not necessarily in that order. R is the only remaining actor; he must be first. It is now very easy to find the right answer. The correct answer is (B).

5) Question five places S as the second actor to audition on Friday. This question initially takes you through the same reasoning as the previous question did. According to your deductions, L can only be second or third on Friday. Since S is second, L must be third. The actor in the third position on Friday auditions second on Thursday, so L is second, making M third. You are left with R, P, and S to place on Thursday, so you know right away that the fifth position must be occupied by one of R, P, or S. Whoever auditions sixth on Thursday must audition first on Friday and whoever auditions first on Friday must audition sixth on Thursday. If P and S are not consecutive, then P must be the actor who auditions first on Friday, which means that P would have to audition sixth on Thursday and S would have to audition first, leaving R to audition fifth. Unfortunately, R is not one of the answer choices, so look at the remaining possibility. If P and S are consecutive, then P and S would have to audition fifth and sixth on Thursday because these are the only two consecutive positions remaining. Since S is already second on Friday, S cannot also be first, and, therefore, cannot be sixth on Thursday. Thus, if P and S are consecutive, then P must be sixth and must be first on Friday and S must be fifth on Thursday. S is indeed one of the answer choices. The correct answer is (D). This question tests your understanding of the requirement that both P and S must audition on Friday if they have non-consecutive auditions on Thursday. P and S can both still audition on Friday even when they have consecutive auditions on Thursday. If you interpreted this rule incorrectly, you wouldn't have been able to answer this question.

6) If P's and S's auditions on Thursday are not consecutive, then both P and S must audition on Friday. Thus, the three actors who audition on Friday are P, S, and L. Since L cannot be first on Friday, one of P or S must audition first on Friday. This means that either P or S must audition sixth on Thursday. In order to have L and M consecutive, they must be either 1 and 2 or 2 and 3 respectively. If L were first, then M would be second, but because there is no room for M on Friday, M cannot be second on Thursday. Thus, L must be second, making M third. The order on Thursday now looks like this: _ L M W _ P/S. The condition added by the question was that P and S must have non-consecutive auditions on Thursday. In order to satisfy this requirement, the one of P and S that is not sixth must be first, and R must be fifth. The correct answer is therefore (D).

1) The first question is a typical rules question. Go down rule by rule to see whether each answer violates the particular rule you are looking at. Once you have eliminated an answer, do not test it for the other rules. This is also your chance to review the rules to catch any you may have missed or misunderstood. You will know this is the case if you have more than one right answer or no right answer at all. The correct answer here is (B).

2) This question adds the condition that there are two M's: If there are two M's, what is a pair of days on which those two M's could not be eaten? Remember, you need a CB sequence and you need to keep the L and the two M's separated. With these requirements in mind, try each answer choice to see if it is a feasible setup for the placement of the two M's. (A) places the M's on Sunday and Friday. With an M on Sunday, a V on Thursday, and another M on Friday, there is room for the CB sequence and also for the L to be separated from both M's. (B), (C), and (D) also allow room for the CB sequence and for L to be separated from the M's. (E), however, does not. If M is on Tuesday and Friday and V is on Thursday, then the only room for the CB sequence is on Monday and Tuesday, forcing L to either Wednesday or Saturday. Either way, L would be next to an M. The key here is to be aware of the block and the split and to find the situation where you cannot accommodate them. The correct answer is (E).

3) This question places T on Monday and L on Wednesday. Now that Monday, Wednesday, and Thursday are filled, the only two consecutive days for the CB sequence are Friday and Saturday, although you cannot determine the relative order of C and B. The only two remaining days are Sunday and Tuesday and you still need to place an M. M cannot be next to the L on Wednesday, so M must be on Sunday. You are left with an empty space on Tuesday for the one soup that is eaten twice, though you cannot determine which soup that is. Now that you know all that you can, go to the answer choices and find the one answer that cannot be true. The correct answer is (D). It

cannot be true that V is on Sunday because M is eaten on Sunday.

4) From the deductions you know that if Bianca eats C twice, then she must eat a sequence of CBC. With V on Thursday, the only space for the CBC sequence is before B, either on Monday, Tuesday, and Wednesday, or on Tuesday, Wednesday, and Thursday. Either way, you are left with one empty space before the V (either Sunday or Wednesday) and two empty spaces after the V (Friday and Saturday). In order to keep L and M separated, one of them must be before V on either Sunday or Wednesday and one must be after V on either Friday or Saturday. With the CBC sequence and one of L or M before V, Sunday through Thursday are completely filled. L or M must be on Friday or Saturday and the one remaining soup, T, must be on Friday or Saturday as well. Thus, the only days on which Bianca could eat T are Friday and Saturday. The correct answer is (A).

5) Question five places C on Saturday, which means that B must be on Friday. You now have V on Thursday, B on Friday, and C on Saturday. You are looking for the soups that could be eaten twice, or similarly, those that cannot be eaten twice. Since there is no CBC sequence, C is one soup that cannot be eaten twice. With V on Thursday, B on Friday, and C on Saturday, there are four spaces (Monday through Wednesday), to place at least one each of L, M, and T. In order to keep L and M separated and follow the rule that the same soup cannot be eaten on consecutive days, it cannot be true that either one of L or M is used twice. Since you know C, L, and M are the soups that cannot be eaten twice, you know that T, V, and B are the soups that can be. The correct answer is (B).

6) If Bianca eats C on Sunday, then Bianca must eat B on Monday. You now have C on Sunday, B on Monday, and V on Thursday, leaving two pairs of consecutive days: Tuesday and Wednesday, and Friday and Saturday. In order to keep L and M separated, one must be on Tuesday or Wednesday and the other must be on Friday or Saturday. The question wants to know which answer choice is an acceptable list of soups for Friday and Saturday. The correct answer must include exactly one of L or M, but not both. This allows you to eliminate (A), (C), and (E). You also know that Bianca cannot eat V on Friday because she eats V on Thursday and she cannot eat the same soup on consecutive days. Therefore, (D) cannot be the correct answer either. The correct answer is (B).

7) This question tells you that M must be used twice. You need to figure out how you can use M twice and maintain the L and M split. You must then decide which soups can be eaten on Tuesday. First, figure out what days the two M's can go. If both M's are before the V that is on Thursday, then the M's must be on Sunday and Wednesday. If this is the case, the L must go after the V in order to avoid being next to an M. This forces the CB sequence to Monday and Tuesday, although not necessarily in that order. The only other possibility is if there is one M before the V and one M after the V. With an M after the V, not only must the CB sequence be before the V, but the L must be before the V as well. Thus, if there is one M before the V and one after, there must be an M, C, B, and an L in some order on Sunday through Wednesday. Since C and B must be consecutive and L and M cannot be consecutive, the CB sequence must be on Monday and Tuesday, although not necessarily in that order. Thus, in any circumstance, the only soups that Bianca could eat on Tuesday are C and B. The correct answer is therefore (B).

1) The first question is a typical rules question. Go down rule by rule to see whether each answer violates the particular rule you are looking at. Once you have eliminated an answer, do not test it for the other rules. This is also your chance to review the rules to catch any you may have missed or misunderstood. You will know this is the case if you have more than one right answer or no right answer at all. The correct answer here is (A).

2) If the cook uses 1O and 1T in dish X, then the cook cannot use a G or P in dish X, as you may have already determined in the deductions portion of the game. In order to get three spices, the cook must use exactly 2B. Thus, dish X contains 2B, 1O, and 1T. The question asks for the side effects of this setup, the effects on dish Y. This setup for dish X leaves you with 1G, 2O, and 3P to play around with to obtain the four dashes in dish Y. The G/O rule holds true for dish Y, which means that there could be 1G and 3P, or either 1 or 2 O's and 2 or 3 P's, depending on how many O's are included. No matter what, there must be at least two dashes of P. The correct answer is (D).

3) You have already determined the answer to this question, first in the deductions, and if not there, then in question two. The correct answer is (A). The only spice that could be used for two dashes in dish X is B. In fact, there must be exactly 2B's in dish X.

4) This question tells you that the cook uses 2P and 2O in dish Y. You have to determine the consequences of this setup for dish X. First you should notice that this arrangement gives dish Y four dashes, so dish Y is full and cannot have any more dashes. You know that dish X must have either P or T, but if P is in X, then T is in Y. You've already determined that Y is full, so you know that T cannot be in dish Y. Therefore, there cannot be a P in dish X. Since there cannot be a P in dish X, there must be a T in dish X. The correct answer is (E).

5) This question asks you for something that must be false without providing any conditions that further restrict the setup, so the correct answer will most likely rely on something that you have already determined, regardless whether or not you have had the conscious thought of it. Keeping in mind what you know, that dish X must include 2B, 1G/O, and 1P/T, go through the answer choices. Remember, you are looking for something that must be false. If the cook uses a P in dish X, then T must be in dish Y, while if the cook does not use P in dish X, then he must use T. Therefore, T must be used. In other words, it must be false that T is not included. The correct answer is (C).

6) If O is not included in either dish, then the setup for dish X must be 2B, 1G, and 1P/T. The side effects of this setup on the spices included in dish Y are that there cannot be any B's, there can be at most one G, there cannot be any O's, there could be two or three P's (depending on whether P or T is used in dish X), and there could possibly be the one T, (again depending on whether P or T is used in dish X). Go through the answer choices and determine if any of the answer choices break these restrictions. (A) and (B) both include two B's, but both B's must be included in dish X, so (A) and (B) cannot be the correct answer. There can be at most 1G in dish Y, so you can eliminate (D), which includes two G's. Finally, since you must have one of P or T in X, you know that Y cannot have all of P and T as it says in (E). You've narrowed down enough to know that the correct answer is (C).

1) The first question tests your deductions. C must always surface on Thursday and Monday. If you had not figured this out earlier, you would have to figure it out here. Remember that a deduction figured out during the game must be true just as much as one figured out in the beginning, so if you figure it out during the game, note it as a deduction, something that must be true as if it were given to you in the rules. The correct answer here is (D).

2) This question asks for what cannot be true without providing you with any additional conditions or restraints. This is a good hint that the question is testing your deductions, so go through the answer choices and see what cannot be true (or, in other words, what must be false) based on the rules and your deductions. The correct answer is (D). (D) cannot be true, because T must be the only personality that surfaces on any day that he surfaces.

3) This question is another deductions question. It asks you to work out one of the two possible basic scenarios. You would have had to work this scenario out now if you had not done it already. The correct answer here is (D). If T is on Friday, then T must be alone on Friday. Since C must be on two of Monday, Wednesday, and Friday and Friday has been ruled out, C must be on Monday and Wednesday. There cannot be three consecutive days with the same personality, so C cannot be on Tuesday, which means that E cannot be on Tuesday either. The only personality left for Tuesday is T—indeed T is always on Tuesday.

Question Analysis and Answers

4) If E is on Friday, then C is on Friday also, which means you are dealing with the second scenario. If you have already worked the two scenarios, then answering this question correctly is just a matter of comparing the answer choices to what you know. The correct answer here is (E). If C is on Friday, then T must be on Wednesday. If you did not work out the two scenarios while making deductions, question three forces you to work out one of them and now this question forces you have to work out the other. It would be much more difficult to recognize these as the only two basic scenarios if you waited until these two questions forced you to work them out. It is a classic case of losing sight of the forest because of the trees. Regardless, even if you did the work here, the correct answer is still (E). With E on Friday, C must also be on Friday, which means that C is on both Thursday and Friday. C cannot surface three days in a row, so C cannot surface on Wednesday. Since C cannot surface on Wednesday, E cannot surface on Wednesday either, leaving T to surface on Wednesday.

5) Here you are trying to find what cannot be true. Look at the two basic scenarios that you have already worked out and test the answer choices against those two scenarios until you find the one that cannot work. (E) cannot be true and is therefore the correct answer. There is no possible way for T to surface three times and still satisfy the requirements that C surfaces on two of Monday, Wednesday, and Friday and that T cannot surface on Thursday.

6) This question again tests your deductions. You have already deduced that T must surface on Tuesday and that T must be the only personality that surfaces on Tuesday. So where can E *not* be? E cannot surface on Tuesday. The correct answer is (B).

KEY: The key to this game was determining the two basic scenarios that resulted from the interplay between T and C on Friday. Every question asked something you could have known before even looking at the questions.

1) The first question is a typical rules question. Go down rule by rule to see whether each answer violates the particular rule you are looking at. Once you have eliminated an answer, do not test it for the other rules. This is also your chance to review the rules to catch any you may have missed or misunderstood. You will know this is the case if you have more than one right answer or no right answer at all. The correct answer here is (A).

2) If exactly one apple pie is ordered, then G's apple pie is the only apple pie that is ordered. Since whoever orders an R must also order an apple pie, no one other than G can order an R. There needs to be at least as many R's as S's, so if one S is used then G must order an R. In fact, since G can only order either an an S or an R, G must order an R. Otherwise, G would order an S and no one else would be able to order an R. One of the contrapositives says if I orders an S, then H orders an S, which would give you two S's. This cannot be true, so I does not order an S. If I cannot order an S or an R, he must order a T, and if he orders a T then he must also order a cherry pie. At this point you know that it must be true that I orders a T and a cherry pie, so look for one of these in the answer choices. You might be tempted to work out the rest of the scenario to see whether (A) must be true. If you fight the urge and scan the answers for something you already know, then you will be rewarded. The correct answer is (E). I must order a cherry pie. You cannot determine exactly what F and H order. Neither F nor H can order an R, and both of them cannot order an S, so one must order an S and the other a T, or both could order a T.

3) If G does not order an R, then according to your deductions G must order an S. Because H cannot order the same thing as G, and H can only order either an S or a T, H must order a T. Since H orders a T, he must also order a cherry pie. According to one of the contrapositives, if H does not order an S, then I cannot order an S. Here, H must order a T, so I cannot order an S. I can therefore only order either an R or a T. At this point you have G ordering an S, H ordering a T,

and I ordering either an R or a T. Because there must be at least as many R's as S's, it is impossible for F to order an S, or else there would be no way to have at least as many R's. Go to the answers with these things in mind and find the answer that could be true. (A) cannot be true because H must order a cherry pie. (B) cannot be true. I can order either an R or a T. (C) cannot be true because there would be no way to have more R's than S's. (D) could be true. Therefore, the correct answer is (D). H and I could both order T's. (E) must be false because G orders an apple pie and at least one of F or I must order an R, which means that at least one of F or I must also order an apple pie.

4) This question creates the condition that as few pies as possible are ordered. According to the rules, whoever orders an R orders an apple pie and whoever orders a T orders a cherry pie. Therefore, to get as few pies as possible, there must be as many S's as possible, as this is the only steak that does not require a pie to go along with it. Because there must be at least as many R's as S's, the greatest number of S's that can be ordered is two. The other two must be R's, and if one of the friends orders an R then they must also order an apple pie. Thus, it must be true that two apple pies are ordered. The correct answer is therefore (D).

5) This question tests your understanding about the relationship between F and I. If F and I order the same thing, then you know that neither I nor F can order an S, or else there would be no way to have at least as many R's as S's. Since they must order something other than an S, F and I must order either an R or a T. Regardless of whether F and I order R's or T's, they must also order a pie. These two pies plus the apple pie that G must order make a total of three pies. Thus, it must be false that exactly two pies are ordered; the correct answer is therefore (C).

6) Since for this question F is the only person that orders a T and H must either order a T, or an S, H must order an S. Furthermore, from the contrapositive that says if F and G do not both order R's, then I cannot order an S, you can infer that it must be the case that I does not order an S, since you know that F must order a T. Since I cannot order an S or a T, I must order an R, and therefore must also order an apple pie. At this point the only person whose steak order you have not determined is G's, but since there cannot be more S's than R's, G must in fact order an R. The only thing you do not know is whether or not H orders a pie, and, if he does, the type of pie that he orders. Go to the answers and find what could be true. The correct answer is (B). H could order a cherry pie. This is testing your understanding that although if someone orders a T then that person also orders a cherry pie, someone can order a cherry pie without ordering a T.

7) Question seven gives you two conditions: G orders an S and F orders a cherry pie. Since G orders an S, at least one of the friends must order an R. Out of the remaining three friends, only F and I could possibly order an R. However, since F orders a cherry pie, F cannot order an apple pie, which means that F cannot order an R. Thus, I must order an R as well as an apple pie. Since you now know that there is exactly one R, you can easily determine what F and H order, for not only can neither order an R, but also neither can order an S. Thus, both F and H must order T's. Since F and H both order T's, they must also both order a cherry pie. The conditions for this question allow you to determine the entire setup. Go to the answer choices and find the one that must be true. The correct answer is (E). All four friends must order a pie.

Question Analysis and Answers

1) The first question is a typical rules question. Go down rule by rule to see whether each answer violates the particular rule you are looking at. Once you have eliminated an answer, do not test it for the other rules. This is also your chance to review the rules to catch any you may have missed or misunderstood. You will know this is the case if you have more than one right answer or no right answer at all. The correct answer here is (D).

2) In this "could be true" question, compare each answer choice with the diagram. The correct answer is (C). O could be third when C is first.

3) Question three asks for a possible position of H. From the diagram it is clear that H can only be in 3 or 4, depending on whether C is in 1 or 6. Look for 3 or 4 in the answer choices. The correct answer is (C).

4) Once again, simply go through the answer choices and compare each answer with the diagram. Keep in mind that you are looking for what *must* be false, not what could be false. For each answer choice, ask yourself, "Could this be true?" If so, it is not your answer. This question really tests your understanding about the interchangeability of V and D and O and F. The correct answer is (D). It is impossible for H to be adjacent to V because H must be between O and F.

5) This question asks for a pair of stores, either one of which could be third or fourth. The order will change depending on the placement of C. If C is first, then either O or F is third and H is fourth. If C is sixth, H is third and either O or F is fourth. Thus, the answer is H and either O of F. The correct answer is (A).

6) Question six asks for a complete and accurate list of the shops that could occupy storefront 2. If C is first, then either V or D must occupy storefront 2. If C is sixth, then V and D are first and fifth and either O or F must occupy storefront 2. Thus, each of V, D, O, and F could occupy storefront 2. The correct answer is (D). Note that this is the fifth "could be true" question for this game. This type of question seems open ended and might seem to require working out several different scenarios for each question, but having determined and understood that there are only two basic scenarios, and having worked those out, you can do the questions quickly and efficiently. When a game has several "could be true" questions, check to be sure that you aren't doing more work than you have to.

7) Remember, C must be first or sixth, the farthest west or the farthest east. By saying that O is farther east than C, this question is really saying that C must be the farthest west, or in storefront 1. The question asks for something that must be true. The only thing that you know for sure if C is in 1 is that H is in storefront 4. The correct answer is (E).

1) The first question is a typical rules question. Go down rule by rule to see whether each answer violates the particular rule you are looking at. Once you have eliminated an answer, do not test it for the other rules. This is also your chance to review the rules to catch any you may have missed or misunderstood. You will know this is the case if you have more than one right answer or no right answer at all. The correct answer here is (A).

2) Question two places F and G in classes by themselves. If that is the case, F and G are in either S or Z, because P and T already have students. However, if F were in S, then H would have to be with F. Since the question requires that F is alone, F must be in Z and G must be in S. Since G is in S, M cannot teach S. According to the question M teaches twice, but M cannot teach S, because G is there, and M cannot teach T, because K already teaches T. Thus, M must teach both P and Z. H cannot be in a class taught by M, so, because G must be alone in S, H must be in T. Furthermore, because K only teaches one class, C must be in T as well. Thus, K teaches a class with three students: E, C, and H. The correct answer is (A).

3) This question places C and H in Z. Since wherever C is a student, K must be a professor, K must teach Z. This means that K is the professor who teaches twice. K teaches T and Z. Professors L and M must each teach one of the remaining two courses. With D in P, E in T, and both C and H in Z, F and G are the only students left, and at least one of them must be in S. However, F cannot be in S because H is not there. Therefore, G must be in S. Since G is in S and cannot be taught by M, M must teach P, leaving L to teach S. The only person left to place is F and the only restriction on his placement here is that he cannot be in S. Go to the answers and find the choice that could be true. The correct answer is (A). F could take Z.

4) If F takes S, then H is in S. Because H is in S and H cannot take a class taught by M, M cannot teach S. The only students left to place are C and G, at least one of whom must take Z in order to have at least one student in each class. You already know that M cannot be with G and that C must take a class taught by K. Thus, regardless of whether C or G is in Z, M cannot teach Z. Since M cannot teach Z, S, or T, M must teach P. The correct answer is (E).

5) Question five is another "could be true" question and mainly tests your understanding of the distribution of the students. How many students can M teach when he teaches only once? M cannot teach G or H due to the rules. M cannot teach E because E is in a class taught by K. C is also in a class taught by K. That rules out four of the six students. Thus, the greatest number of students M can teach is two, and they must be D and F. The rules assigned D to P, so F must be the other student in P and M must be the teacher. Since M teaches two students, there must be one other class with two students. L cannot teach a class with two students, so the other professor who teaches a class with two students must be K. Also, either K or L must teach two courses. If K teaches one course, then E and C are both in T and L teaches two courses with one student each. (He would have to teach S and Z, with either G or H in each class.) If K teaches two courses, he must teach one course with two students and one course with one student, leaving L to teach one course with one student. With these rules in mind, go to the answer choices. (A) and (B) are easy to eliminate because they violate what you have determined already. (C) could be true and is the correct answer because C and G could take S if K teaches it. Once you have the answer you should move on to the next question; however, for reference, (D) cannot be true because it violates the distribution of students by forcing three into T and (E) cannot be true because if G and H take Z, K would have to teach Z and since C must take a course with K, there would not be any students left to take S.

6) This question again tests your understanding of the possible distribution of the students. If G and H take a class with K, and K also teaches both E and C, then K must teach four students. It is impossible to have four students in the same class, so K must teach two classes with some combination of G, H, E, and C in those two classes. K cannot teach any additional students because each of L and M must teach at least one student. The two classes that K must teach are T and either S or Z. If K teaches S, then the two remaining students, D and F, must be assigned to P and Z, in that order, with either L or M teaching their classes. On the other hand, if K were to teach Z, then D and F would be assigned to P and S, in that order. However, placing F in S requires H to be in S as well, which is impossible here since K must teach H. Thus, K cannot teach Z, which means that nobody that K teaches, G, H, E, and C, can be in Z. With this in mind, go to the answer choices and find the choice that cannot be true. The correct answer is (D).

7) Question seven changes the rules somewhat, but that is okay. Accept the changes and work out the problem just like any other. If K teaches exactly one course, then C must be in T with E. Since there are exactly two people in T and the question also creates another pair of H and G, who must be together in a course taught by M. Since there are two classes with two people in them, the remaining two classes must have one person each. The remaining two students are D and F, so D and F must be alone in their classes. Since D is already in P, the HG pair must either be in S or Z. However, if the HG pair is in Z, then F would be forced into S, which would in turn force H into S. This is impossible. Hence, the HG pair must be in S and F must be in Z. In this setup, either L or M must teach two classes, although you cannot determine which one teaches two. Either L or M must teach P and Z. Go to the answers and find the choice that must be true. The correct answer is (B).

1) The first question is a typical rules question. Go down rule by rule to see whether each answer violates the particular rule you are looking at. Once you have eliminated an answer, do not test it for the other rules. This is also your chance to review the rules to catch any you may have missed or misunderstood. You will know this is the case if you have more than one right answer or no right answer at all. The correct answer here is (D).

2) You can discover how many books Ellen could read during the first week by looking at the list of relative order. The only books that could be read first are B, H, and I. Thus, the answer is (C).

3) Question three asks for something that must be false without giving you any conditions to work with, so the answer will likely be based on what you already know about the order. Go through each answer choice and ask yourself if it can be true. If it cannot, then you have found the correct answer. In this case, (B) is the correct answer. W and B cannot be consecutive because B must be before P and W must come after P.

4) If G is the third book and is immediately after B, then B must be the second book. M, A, and G must all be consecutive, so, since G is third, M and A must be fourth and fifth, although not necessarily in that order. The question asks for the list of books that could be sixth, which is the next book in the sequence. B, G, M, and A have all been used, so the only books remaining are P, I, H, and W. Both P and I must be before W, so it is impossible for W to be sixth. The books that could be sixth, then, are P, I, and H, which means that the correct answer is (D).

5) If Ellen does not read any books during the ninth or tenth week, then both empty spaces are used. W must be adjacent to an empty space, so W must be in the eight week. Based solely on the information provided in the question, you cannot determine anything else. Go through the answer choices and find the one that must be false. (A) could be true because you do not know the order of I relative to any book except W. (B) could be true for the same reason. (C) could be true because you do not know the order of M, A, or G relative to any book except for B. (D) could be true for the same reason. (E) must be false. Since W is eighth, all the other books must be before it. Thus, the correct answer is (E).

6) This question posits that Ellen reads W in the sixth week and I in the fourth week. Since W must be adjacent to an empty space and I cannot be, the empty space cannot be fifth, but instead must come after W in the seventh week. Furthermore, with I in the fourth week and W in the sixth there is no room for the MAG sequence until after W. The MAG sequence cannot be first, second, and third because it must come after B. The only available three consecutive weeks are eight, nine, and ten, so M, A, and G must be eighth, ninth, and tenth, although not necessarily in that order. You are left with B, P, H, and one empty space. This empty space must be either the first or second week since it must be separated from I. With this information, go through the answer choices and find the one that must be false. In other words, ask yourself if each answer choice is a possibility. If it is, then move on. If it is not, then you have found the answer. The correct answer is (B). It cannot be true that Ellen reads no book in the ninth week since one of either M, A, or G must be in the ninth week.

7) This question wants to know the earliest that you can use the two empty weeks. In order to use them both as early as possible, make the first week an empty week. The second empty week must be adjacent to W, coming either before or after it, and B, P, and I must all come before W. Thus, with an empty week, B, P, and I (but not in that order) all ahead of the second empty week, the earliest that the second empty week could be is fifth. The correct answer is (B).

1) The first question is a typical rules question. Go down rule by rule to see whether each answer violates the particular rule you are looking at. Once you have eliminated an answer, do not test it for the other rules. This is also your chance to review the rules to catch any you may have missed or misunderstood. You will know this is the case if you have more than one right answer or no right answer at all. The correct answer here is (D).

2) If G has one C and one P, then you know F must have three flavors made up of one V, one C, and one of B or S, and you also know that G cannot have another flavor. His third part must be another of either C or P. You now know for certain that you must have two C's, which means you must have at least three S's. You know that G cannot have an S, that F could have at most one S, which means that E must have at least two S's. The correct answer is (D).

3) This question places both a P and a B in G's sundae. This gives two flavors to G, which means the third flavor must be another of either P or B and that F must have three flavors (V, C, and one of B or S). The question asks for the greatest number of V's that can be used. Due to the C used by F, you know there must be at least two S's. If F has an S, then the other S must be in E's sundae, leaving at most two parts available for a V in E's sundae. With two V's in E's sundae and one in F's, there could at most be three V's. The answer is (A).

4) This question assigns two B's to F's sundae. Since F already has a V, the two additional B's fill up F's sundae, which means that F cannot have any more flavors. Since F has only two flavors, G must have only one flavor. This setup does not tell you anything about E. At this point you already know that F is filled up, that G must have three parts of the same flavor, and that E's sundae is not restricted. This question tests your ability to keep track

of the number of spaces available and the effect that the inclusion of a C has on the other sundae parts. Here there are only six remaining sundae parts, three for E and three for G. All of G's must be the same flavor. If there is a C, then there must be more total S's than there are C's. What does this mean here? It means that G cannot have any C, because if he did, G would have to have three C's and there would be no way to have more S's than C's. Look for that in the answers. You will find it in (C).

5) This question asks for something that cannot be true, or rather, something that must be false, without providing any additional conditions or restraints. You have to go the answer choices to know what you are looking for, but work smartly, always keeping in mind the rules. Try (A). If E and G both have a C and a P, then you will have two C's, which means there must be three or more S's. G has two flavors, which is his maximum, so you know F must have three flavors. You've already deduced that if F has three flavors he must have a V, a C, and one of B and S, which means you now have three C's and must have at least four S's. There is no room for four S's, so (A) cannot be true. Therefore, the correct answer is (A).

6) This question gives you four P's and two V's to place somewhere on the diagram. You know that F cannot have any P (because it has a V), so the four P's must be split up among E and G. The contrapositive of the rule that says if V then not P says if P then not V. Since you know there are going to be P's in both E and G, there cannot be any V's in either E or G. Thus, the second V must be in F's sundae. F now has two V's, leaving room for only one more flavor. Since F must have more flavors than G, you know that G can only have one flavor. You've already established that he must have at least one P, so he is in fact going to have three P's, leaving the fourth P for E's sundae. Now go to the answers and look for what must be false. The correct answer is (D).

7) If F's sundae does not contain any C's then you know that F cannot have three flavors, for if F had three flavors, F would have to have a C; therefore, F must have exactly two flavors. Since F has only two flavors, G must have exactly one flavor for each of his three parts. The question says that only two C's are used, so you know that the C's cannot be in G because G must have three parts of whatever flavor he has. The two C's must therefore be in E's sundae. Now that you know where the C's are, you need to think about the number of S's and the possible placement of those S's. Since there are exactly two C's, there must be at least three S's. F's sundae cannot contain any S's so the only way to get three S's is for G to have at least two, and if G has any S's at all, then G must have three S's. The correct answer is therefore (D).

KEY: The key here was the interplay between two rules: the relationship between F and G and the relationship between C and S and the effects these two relationships had on one another.

1) The first question is a typical rules question. Go down rule by rule to see whether each answer violates the particular rule you are looking at. Once you have eliminated an answer, do not test it for the other rules. This is also your chance to review the rules to catch any you may have missed or misunderstood. You will know this is the case if you have more than one right answer or no right answer at all. The correct answer here is (A).

2) If each class has 15 students, then each class has exactly two teachers. The question assigns L and K to class 2, filling up class 2. You are left with classes 1 and 3 to fill with two students each. Since you are also left with the JD split, both class 1 and class 3 must contain one of J or D. Any possible pair of teachers for class 3 must therefore contain one of J or D. (B) does not contain one of J or D, so F and H cannot be the teachers assigned to class 3. (B) is therefore the correct answer.

3) Question three tells you that all eight teachers are assigned to a class and also that C, F, and H are the teachers assigned to class 3. Since each classroom may only have two or three teachers assigned to it, class 3 is full. You must divide the remaining five teachers between classes 1 and 2, with one of these classes having three teachers and the other having two. You must still account for the JD split, so both class 1 and class 2 must have one of J or D. Since it is now impossible for G and K to be the only two teachers assigned to a class, G and K cannot be together. Since G and K cannot be together, one of G or K must be assigned to class 1 and the other must be assigned to class 2. The correct answer, therefore, is (C).

4) If C and L are assigned to class 1, then immediately you know that there are three teachers in class 1, so there must be one more teacher in class 1 in addition to C and L. Since H is not assigned to a class, there are only seven available teachers. Since there are three teachers in class 1 and there must be at least two in both class 2 and class 3, it must be the case that there are three teachers in class 1 and exactly two teachers in both class 2 and class 3. The question asks for a list of teachers that could be assigned to class 3. Since there must be two teachers in class 3 you can eliminate (A), (B), and (C). You must choose between (D) and (E). According to the rules, F and K can never be together, which eliminates (E). The correct answer is (D).

5) If G and K are assigned to class 2, then no additional teachers can be assigned to class 2. The question also assigns H and F to class 1. The FK split is no longer a problem, but you still must deal with the JD split. Since no other teachers can be assigned to class 2, one of J and D must be assigned to each of class 1 and 3. Thus, class 1 must have three teachers, H, F, and one of J or D, class 2 must have two teachers, G and K, and you cannot determine how many teachers class 3 has, only that one of J or D must be assigned there. What must be true, therefore, is that there are three students assigned to class 1. The correct answer is (C).

Question Analysis and Answers

6) This question asks for a piece of information that must be false without giving you any conditions to work with, so you must rely on what you have already determined and what each answer choice tells you. Remember, the keys to this game are the class sizes and the two splits. (A) fixes the number of teachers at six while assigning G and F to class 1 and D and L to class 3. In order for class 2 to have two people and in order for each of F, K, J, and D to be used, K and J would have to be assigned to class 2. This works. (B) fixes the number of teachers at seven while assigning C and L to class 2 and F and G to class 3. Since C and L are together there would have to be one more teacher assigned to class 2, giving you three teachers in class 2. Since there are only seven teachers, class 1 would have exactly two teachers. You can accommodate for the FK and the JD splits, so this works as well. (C) forces you to use all eight teachers, which tells you that two classes will have three teachers and one class will have two teachers. Since G and K are in class 1, class 1 must be the class with only two teachers. The question also assigns F, H, and L to class 3. The remaining three teachers, J, D, and C would have to be assigned to class 2, breaking the JD split. Therefore, (C) must be false and is the correct answer.

7) Question seven gives you two conditions to work with. First, classes 1 and 3 must have 20 students each. In other words, classes 1 and 3 have three teachers assigned to them, leaving the remaining two teachers for class 2. Second, the question tells you who those two teachers are in class 2: H and G. With H and G in class 2, class 2 cannot have any more teachers assigned to it. You must still account for the two splits. In order to do so, each of class 1 and 3 must have exactly one of J and D, exactly one of F and K, and exactly one other teacher, whom, by process of elimination, you know must be either C or L. Thus, it is impossible for C and L to be together in class 3. The correct answer is (D).

1) The first question is a typical rules question. Go down rule by rule to see whether each answer violates the particular rule you are looking at. Once you have eliminated an answer, do not test it for the other rules. This is also your chance to review the rules to catch any you may have missed or misunderstood. You will know this is the case if you have more than one right answer or no right answer at all. The correct answer here is (A).

2) This question tests the deductions concerning the players who must be included in the foursomes. According to the deductions, M, C, E, and K must all be included. Look for one of those in the answer choices. The correct answer is (B).

3) This question asks for two golfers that could be the two that are not included in a foursome. There are only two scenarios. In the first, where D is included on a foursome, both G and J must sit out, so this is one pair who could sit out. This, however, is not in any of the answer choices so you must look at the second scenario. In the second scenario D and one other person must sit out. This tells you right away that D must be included in the correct answer, which eliminates all the answer choices except (B) and (D). Next, look at the deductions concerning the players who must be included in the foursomes. M, C, E, and K must always be included, which is to say that they can never sit out. (D) is therefore impossible because it has E sitting out. The correct answer is (B).

4) This question places E in the same foursome as F, which means that F must be used. If F is used then F must be in foursome B, so both F and E are in foursome B. Since E is not in foursome A, you know that N cannot be used at all. This places you in the second scenario because somebody other than G and J is sitting out. In the second scenario D and one other person, in this case N, are sitting out. Thus, it must be true that D is not on a foursome. The correct answer is (B).

5) If M and K play on the same foursome, then both M and K must be in foursome A, since K can never be in foursome B. Furthermore, M and C must always be together, so, actually, K, M, and C must all be in foursome A, leaving space for exactly one more golfer on team A. Since A must include either D or J, there is no room for E to be in A. Since E cannot be in foursome A, N cannot be included in either foursome. Because N is excluded, it is impossible for both G and J to be excluded. Because one of G or J must be included, D cannot be included. Therefore, the two golfers not included on a foursome must be D and N. Since D is not included, J must be the fourth golfer included in foursome A, leaving F, G, E, and H as the four golfers in foursome B. Go through the answer choices and find the one that could be true. The correct answer is (D). F and H could be, and actually must be, on the same foursome.

6) If D is included in a foursome, then you are dealing with the first scenario, about which you practically know everything if you worked out the scenario prior to moving to the questions. Here's a recap: Since D plays and J does not and one of D or J must be in foursome A, D must be in foursome A. Since F plays, F is in foursome B, and K is in foursome A. This setup also forces N to play, which means that E is in foursome A. This gives you D, E, and K in foursome A, which leaves no room for M and C to be together, so M and C must be together in foursome B. Now you have three players in foursome A (D, K, and E), and three players in foursome B (F, M, and C). The two players remaining are N and H, who must be split between the two foursomes. Knowing the entire setup makes this question very easy. Simply check the answer choices against the diagram for the first scenario. Be careful with the language of the question. The question asks for what could be false, so you could ask yourself if the choice has to be true. If the answer choice has to be true then it is incorrect, but if it does not have to be true then you've found the right answer. The correct answer here is (D). N could be in either foursome, so it could be false that N is on foursome A.

7) If H is not included in a foursome, it must be the case that one of G or J is included in a foursome, and since one of G or J must be included, D cannot be included in a foursome. Therefore, the two people who are not assigned to a foursome are D and H. Since D and H are not included, the remaining eight people, M, C, E, K, J, N, F, and G, must all be included in one of the two foursomes. All you need to do is determine which foursome each person must be assigned to. In this scenario, the scenario in which D is not included, both J and K must be assigned to foursome A. F is included and cannot be with K, so F must be in foursome B. Furthermore, because N must be in one of the foursomes, E must be assigned to foursome A. With J, K, and E all in foursome A, there is no room for the MC block in foursome A. The MC block must, therefore, be assigned to foursome B. At this point, J, K, and E are in foursome A and F, M, and C are in foursome B. The only two people remaining are N and G, one of whom will be in foursome A and one of whom will be in foursome B. Now you can easily go through the answer choices and find the pair of golfers who could be included on the same foursome. The correct answer is (C). G could be on either foursome, so G could be with J.

1) The first question is a rules question but it also requires you to use your deductions. Go down rule by rule to see whether each answer violates the particular rule you are looking at. Once you have eliminated an answer, do not test it for the other rules. This is also your chance to review the rules to catch any you may have missed or misunderstood. You will know this is the case if you have more than one right answer or no right answer at all. Don't forget that the deductions you make are as true as the rules they give you. The correct answer here is (C).

2) If N wins match 5, then N will be in the championship game. You deduced already that if N is in the championship game, then he cannot face S or T. Thus, neither S nor T can win match 6. The fact that N wins match 5 also means that M lost match 2. According to the contrapositive that says if M loses match 2, then Z does not win match 6, you know that Z does not win match 6. Now you know that Z, S, and T cannot win match 6. Thus, no combination of those three can play each other. There is also a deduction that says if T and Y meet in a match, then N cannot win match 5. In this case, N does win match 5, so T and Y cannot meet in a match. Out of the four possibilities for match 6, you can eliminate T v. Y, S v. Z and T v. Z, which leaves S v. Y. Now you know every pair of players that must meet in the tournament. The correct answer is (C).

3) If N wins match 2, then N faces F in game 5. If T wins match 3, T will play either Y or Z in match 6. The fact that N wins match 2 means that M lost match 2, which makes the contrapositive true that says if M does not win match 2, then Z cannot win match 6. Thus, if T plays Z, then T must win. Also, the rules say that if T and Y play, then T will win. Therefore, T will win match 6 and make it to the final match regardless of whether he plays Y or Z. Now you know T must play either F or N in match 7. If T plays in the final match, then N cannot play in the final match, so T plays F in match 7. In other words, it must be true that F wins match 5. The correct answer is (A).

4) This question tells you that Y wins match 4 and the winner of match 1 does not win match 5. If Y wins match 4, he will face either S or T in match 6. F must win match 1 and must play either M or N. Since F does not win match 5 as well, the winner of match 2, either M or N, will win match 5 and advance to the championship. The information about M and N leads to a number of conclusions, so try making either M or N win and see what happens. From the rules you know if M wins match 2, then S wins match 3, which would force S to play Y in match 6, the winner of which would play M in the championship. You cannot determine who the winner would be. That scenario works fine. Now see what happens if N wins match 2. From the deductions you know that if N plays in match 7, then Y and T cannot play each other in match 6. That means Y would have to face S in match 6 and Y would be the winner, since S and N cannot play each other in the championship. Regardless of whether M or N wins match 2, S and Y play in match 6. Now that you have as much information as possible, go to the answers and find what must be false. The correct answer is (D).

5) In this question you are looking for a person who must win at least twice, which means you are looking for the people who make it to the final match, match 7. If N wins match 5, then N is definitely going to the championship match. Unfortunately, N is not one of the answers, so you must keep working and find N's opponent. If N is in the championship, he cannot play S or T. Since M lost match 2, Z cannot play in the final. Just as in question 2, the only person left who could make it to the final is Y. The correct answer is (D).

6) If T wins at least one match, he will be in match 6 facing either Y or Z. The fact that T won means that S lost. One contrapositive says if S does not win match 3, then M does not win match 2. Thus, N wins match 2, and faces F in match 5. Another contrapositive says if M does not win match 2, then Z does not win match 6. Thus, if T plays Z in match 6, T will win. But if T plays Y in match 6, T will also win, so either way T will be in the championship. If T is in the championship, N cannot be in the championship, so F wins match 5. Thus, F and T play in the championship match. However, T cannot win the championship, so F must be the winner. The correct answer is (B).

7) If N wins match 2, then N faces F in game 5. Furthermore, since N wins match 2, then Z cannot win match 6. The question wants you to calculate the number of players that could win the tournament. Either one of F or N could advance to the championship from match 5, and any of S, T, Y, or Z could advance to the championship from match 6. However, you can immediately eliminate Z since N wins match 2 and you can also immediately eliminate N, S, and T since they can never be the champions. Thus, out of F, N, S, T, Y, and Z, only F or Y could possibly be the champion. Therefore, the correct answer is (B).

1) This question attempts to make you do much more work than is necessary. Whenever you have a must be true or must be false question, first scan the answers to see if you have already determined what the correct answer is. This question turns out to be an easy rules question. If a tent is navy, then it can hold only one person. (C) must be false!

2) If O and T are in tent 4, then tent 4 must be a green tent (because O is always in a green tent). You still need another green tent for U, but since tent 4 is green, neither tent 3 nor tent 5 can be green. Tent 2 is already full, so it cannot be the green tent that U is in. U's green tent must therefore be tent 1, which means that tent 2 must be brown in order to avoid having two consecutive tents of the same color. In order to place P in a brown tent, there must be a fifth tent. You only have one person left, S, and only one tent, tent 3, so S must be in tent 3. Tent 3 is sandwiched between a brown and a green tent, so tent 3 must be navy. The correct answer is (C).

3) This question places S in tent 3 and makes tent 3 a brown tent. Since tent 3 is brown, tent 2 must be green in order to avoid there being two consecutive tents of the same color. You need to place both O and U in a green tent, but only tents 4 and 5 are available. Since tents 4 and 5 cannot both be green, O and U must be together in the same tent. The correct answer is (B).

4) This question asks for the results of including all five tents in the setup and tells you that tents 1 and 5 are navy. According to the rules, if any tent is navy, then it has only one person in it. Since for this question tents 1 and 5 are navy, tents 1 and 5 must both have only one person in them. Since all five tents are used, there are going to be three tents with one person in them and two tents with two people in them. The question already told you the location of two of the one-person tents and you already know that tent 2 is a two-person

tent, leaving you with tents 3 and 4, one of which must contain one person and one of which must contain two people. Now focus on the assignment of certain campers to certain colored tents. Both O and U must be assigned to a green tent. Tent 2 could be a green tent but it is already filled. There is not room for two more green tents since this would make both tents 3 and 4 green and no two consecutive tents can be the same color. Thus, O and U must be assigned to the same tent, either tent 3 or 4. This tent will be the second two-person tent, forcing the other of tent 3 or 4 to be a one-person tent. P must still be in a brown tent and the only space for a brown tent is in the other of tent 3 or 4 that O and U are not in. Tents 2, 3, and 4 are now filled, leaving S and T to divide between tent 1 and tent 5. Therefore, T could sleep in either tent 1 or tent 5. The correct answer is (C).

5) Question five restricts the setup to only four tents while at the same time placing O and U in separate tents. O and U must both sleep in green tents, so in order to avoid having two consecutive green tents, tent 1 must be a green tent and one of O or U must be sleeping in it. Since tent 1 is green, tent 2 must be brown. You still need P in a brown tent, which, since tent 2 is brown, can only be tent 4. Therefore, it must be false that P is in tent 3. The correct answer is (B).

6) If the conditions are altered such that you must use six tents, then the only way to fill them all is to have five one-person tents and one two-person tent. Q and R are still together in tent 2, so tent 2 is the only two-person tent. All the remaining tents must contain exactly one person each, which means that O and U must sleep in two different green tents. Since P is in tent 1, then tent 1 is brown and tent 2 is green. The only other place for two green tents without placing two green tents consecutively is if the two green tents are tents 4 and 6. The correct answer is therefore (C).

1) The first question is a typical rules question. Go down rule by rule to see whether each answer violates the particular rule you are looking at; don't forget to include the rules that are mentioned in the setup paragraph. Once you have eliminated an answer, do not test it for the other rules. This is also your chance to review the rules to catch any you may have missed or misunderstood. You will know this is the case if you have more than one right answer or no right answer at all. The correct answer here is (B).

2) There are two approaches to this question. If you worked out the deductions completely concerning the toys that J must buy, then this question can be answered quickly. J must buy a Y, a P, and either an S or a V. This question tells you that J buys an S on Monday, so if J buys an S on Monday, then J must buy the P on Wednesday. The other approach, if you did not work out the deductions completely, is to follow the chain reaction through to the end. If J buys an S on Monday, then A buys a V on Monday. If A buys a V on Monday, then A buys an S on Tuesday and E buys a V on Wednesday. With E getting a V on Wednesday, A getting a Y on Wednesday, and J getting an S on Monday, the only toy that J could buy on Wednesday is a P. The correct answer, therefore, is (B).

3) This question again tests your understanding of the possibilities for J. If you learned from the deductions that J must receive a Y, a P, and either an S or a V, or learned the same from the previous question, this is also an easy question to answer. If J buys a V on Wednesday, then J must buy a P on Monday. Or, if you worked it out the longer way, you could easily arrive at the correct answer. If J buys a V on Wednesday, then E must buy an S on Wednesday, which means that A must buy an S on Monday and a V on Tuesday. With A getting an S on Monday, E getting a Y on Monday, and J getting a V on Wednesday, the only toy that J could buy on Monday is a P. Thus, the correct answer is (C). It must be true that J buys a P on Monday. This and the previous question should lead you to deduce that J must receive a P, if you did not already make this deduction.

4) Question four tests another deduction, though this time concerning E. Usually, any question that asks for something that must be true or must be false without giving you any information to work with is going to be based on a deduction that you have, or probably should have, made. Even if you hadn't made the deduction concerning the toy that E must buy on Tuesday, this question would not be too hard because you could pretty easily eliminate all the other answers based on the setup and the previous questions. The correct answer is of course (A). It must always be true that E buys a P on Tuesday due to the relationship between what E buys on Wednesday and what A buys on Monday and Tuesday.

5) If you answered the previous question correctly, this question should not be difficult at all. In the previous question you either reinforced the deduction that E must buy a P on Tuesday or determined it for the first time. Either way, once you know that E must buy a P on Tuesday, you also know that E cannot buy an S on Tuesday. The correct answer is (C).

6) This question asks for information that will allow you to determine the entire setup. You actually have already determined the answer to this question, albeit probably unknowingly, in questions two and three, both of which allowed you to determine everything by telling you that J bought either an S or a V on a certain day. If you did not notice it, that is okay. As discussed in the "Walk Around It" section, in order to determine the entire setup you must know whether J buys an S or a V, on what day J buys her P, and something that tells you the placement of the S's and V's for E and A. Knowing any information about E or A will not allow you to determine enough about the toys that J receives, or rather, will not allow you to determine on which day J buys the P. Therefore, in order to determine the entire setup you need to know something about one of J's slots. This leaves you with (D) and (E) as possible answers. In order for the information about J's toys to allow you to determine everything you must also know whether J buys an S or a V. Only (D) allows you to know for certain whether J buys an S or a V, which also tells you whether E buys an S or a V, where A buys her S and V, and the placement of J's P. The correct answer here is (D).

7) To answer question seven correctly, you must go through the answer choices and ask yourself whether or not each could be true based on what you know from your diagram. All but one of the answer choices must be false; you are looking for that one that could be true. (A) must be false because all three children must buy a Y. (B) must be false because if three S's are chosen, then all three children must buy an S, but since A and E would have S's on Monday and Wednesday, there would be no way for J to buy an S. (C) could be true. In fact, (C) must be true. E must buy a P and J must buy a P. The correct answer here is (C). (D) must be false because A cannot buy a P and in order to have three P's, all three children would have to buy a P. (E) must be false for the same reason as (B). If three V's were chosen, then all three children would have to buy a V, which means that E would buy a V on Wednesday and A would buy a V on Monday, leaving no way for J to buy a V.

1) The first question is a typical rules question. Go down rule by rule to see whether each answer violates the particular rule you are looking at. Once you have eliminated an answer, do not test it for the other rules. This is also your chance to review the rules to catch any you may have missed or misunderstood. You will know this is the case if you have more than one right answer or no right answer at all. The correct answer here is (D).

2) If S is held on day 5, then you immediately know that you are dealing with the first scenario, where the order of events is QVRPSTOU, with R and Q interchangeable in the first and third positions. In this setup, O must be seventh. The correct answer is therefore (E).

3) If T and P are held on days 5 and 7 respectively, then you must be dealing with the third scenario, where the order of events is SVURTQPO. From this it is quite easy to determine that O must be held on day 8. The correct answer is (E).

4) Question four tells you that P is held before U. In other words, you are dealing with the two possible scenarios that contain P_T_U: 1) QVRPSTOU, where Q and R are interchangeable in the first and third positions, and 2) SVRPQTOU, where S and V are interchangeable in the first and second positions. Go through the answer choices and compare each choice to the two possible scenarios. What must be false is that S is third, for either Q or R must be third. Therefore, the correct answer is (C).

5) If Q is held on day 7, then you must be dealing with the fourth scenario, where the order of events is SVOURTQP, with S and V interchangeable in the first and second positions. Thus, O must be held on day 3. The correct answer is (B). Notice that this is the third question that focuses on a wildcard: O. While no rule affects O directly, the placement of other items dictates the placement of O in any workable scenario.

6) If Q is immediately after T, then you must be dealing with the two possible scenarios where U is before T and T is before P (U_T_P). The two choices are: 1) SVURTQPO and 2) SVOURTQP, where S and V are interchangeable. Go through the answer choices and compare each choice to both of these scenarios and ask yourself whether or not each choice could be true. The correct answer is (E). V could be the first event held.

7) This question wants you to find the scenario in which R comes after as many events as possible. In other words, find the scenario that has R as late in the order as R can be. In the first two scenarios the latest that R can be is third. In the third scenario, R must be fourth. In the fourth scenario, R must be fifth. Thus, you must be dealing with the fourth scenario, where the order of events is SVOURTQP, with S and V interchangeable. Go through the answer choices and find the one that must be false. (B) is the correct answer since Q cannot be the third event held. O must be the third event.

1) The first question is a typical rules question. Go down rule by rule to see whether each answer violates the particular rule you are looking at. Once you have eliminated an answer, do not test it for the other rules. This is also your chance to review the rules to catch any you may have missed or misunderstood. You will know this is the case if you have more than one right answer or no right answer at all. The correct answer here is (D).

2) If all four O's are planted and no townhouse can have more than one O, then there is one O at each house. Remember, in every possible scenario at least one of house 1 and house 3 must have two A's and at least one of house 2 and house 4 must have two P's. Adding an O to those townhouses fills up their respective groups, giving you one townhouse with AAO and another with PPO. Since no two townhouses can have the same trees, the remaining two townhouses cannot have two A's and two P's. One will have exactly one A and the other will have exactly one P. Since that is the case, both will also have exactly one each of an E and an O. Thus, the four townhouses must look like this, although not in this order: AAO, PPO, AEO, PEO. Go to the answer choices and find the one that must be true based on this information. The correct answer is (E). There must be two E's.

3) If house 2 has exactly three kinds of trees, then you know house 2 must have P, E, and O. Since house 2 only has one P, house 4 must have two P's and one of either O or E. You cannot determine anything about townhouses 1 or 3. Either one of townhouse 1 or 3 or both could have two A's while exactly one of 1 or 3 could only have one A. With this in mind, go through the answer choices and find what could be true. The correct answer is (E). It could be true that house 3 has exactly three kinds of trees, for house 3 could have an A, an O, and an E.

4) For this question it is helpful to think of how many spaces are available for E's and O's. If there are two houses with two A's and two houses with two P's, then there are exactly four spaces left for E's and O's. This is the minimum number of spaces available for E's and O's. In this setup there would have to be two of each. This cannot be the setup because the question requires there to be more E's than O's. If the houses 1 and 3 are set up with two A's at one house and one A at the other and the house with the P's are set up in the same manner, then there are six spaces left for E's and O's. This is the maximum number of spaces for E's and O's. If the setup is changed such that both houses 1 and 3 have two A's, while only one of houses 2 and 4 has two P's, then there could be five spaces available for E's and O's. Thus, in order for there to be more E's than O's, there must be five or six spaces for the E's and O's to fill. In order to have more E's than O's and fill the five or six spaces, there must either be three E's and two O's or four E's and two O's. Either way, there must be two O's. The correct answer is (D).

5) This question places you squarely in the scenario where there are two houses that have two A's and two houses that have two P's. When this is the case, the setup must look like this: 1: AA and E/O, 2: PP and E/O, 3: AA and E/O, 4: PP and E/O. With this setup in mind, go through the answer choices and find the answer choice that could be false. You can accomplish this by asking yourself for each answer choice if it must be true. If it does not have to be true then it is the correct answer. The correct answer is (C). Two adjacent townhouses could have E's.

6) This question gives you two conditions. First, there are more A's than P's. Second, there are more O's than E's. Remember, there must be three or four of both A and P. If there are going to be more A's than P's then there must be exactly four A's and exactly three P's. This tells you what scenario you are in. Either townhouse 1 or 3 will have AAE while the other will have AAO. Either townhouse 2 or 4 will have PEO while the other will have PP and E/O. In order to have more O's than E's, this last townhouse must actually have PPO, giving you three O's and two E's. Thus, there are four A's, three P's, three O's, and two E's. Now that you know the entire arrangement, the answer should be pretty easy to spot. The correct answer is (E). It could be, and indeed must be, true that there are more P's than E's.

7) For this question you must find what must be true if townhouse 3 has exactly one A. If townhouse 3 has exactly one A, then it must also have an E and an O. With only one A in townhouse 3, there must be exactly two A's in townhouse 1. You cannot determine anything about the arrangement of trees in townhouses 2 or 4. Now that you know everything that you can know, go through the answer choices. The correct answer is (D).

1) The first question is a typical rules question. Go down rule by rule to see whether each answer violates the particular rule you are looking at. Once you have eliminated an answer, do not test it for the other rules. This is also your chance to review the rules to catch any you may have missed or misunderstood. You will know this is the case if you have more than one right answer or no right answer at all. The correct answer here is (D).

2) This question places B on the white bookcase. According to the deductions, both P and B must be on shelf 2. If B is on the white bookcase, then the two P's must be on the black bookcase, with one of the P's on shelf 2. The correct answer is therefore (B). P must be on shelf 2 of the black bookcase.

3) This question asks what must be false without giving you any additional information or conditions. This is a good clue that the answer is something you should already have worked out. Go through each choice and compare it to the diagram and what you know, asking yourself for each whether it must be false. Remember, if it could be true then it is not the correct answer. The correct answer here is (D). P and G cannot be on the same bookcase. Each bookcase must have one of C or N and one of M or S, so the bookcase that also has the two P's does not have room for any other books. (A), (B), (C), and (E) could all be true because you do not know which bookcase M, S, C, or N are on without additional information.

4) If P is on the white bookcase, then B is on the black bookcase on shelf 2. The question asks for the number of different kinds of books that could be on the black bookcase on shelf 1. In the black bookcase B must be on shelf 2, one of M or S must be on the top shelf, one of C or N must be on shelf 1 or shelf 3, and G must be on the other of shelf 1 or shelf 3. Thus, any one of G, C, or N could be on shelf 1, which means that there are three different kinds of books that could be in the black bookcase on shelf 1. The correct answer is (C).

5) This question puts N on a lower numbered shelf than C. In both bookcases, the only available shelves for C and N are shelf 1 and shelf 3. If N is lower than C, then N must be on shelf 1 and C must be on shelf 3. You know this without knowing which bookcase C and N are in and without knowing the placement of B and the two P's. You do not need to work anything else out. The correct answer is (A).

6) If B is on the white bookshelf on a shelf below C, then C must be on shelf 3, B must be on shelf 2, and G must be on shelf 1. Shelf 4 could either be M or S. With B and C on the white bookcase, the black bookshelf will have one of M or S on shelf 4 and P on shelf 2, leaving P and N for shelves 1 and 3, though not necessarily in that order. The question wants to know how many different possible combinations there are for the setup of the black bookcase. Interchanging P and N on shelves 1 and 3 produces two possible scenarios, while interchanging M and S on shelf 4 creates two more. Thus, there are four possible combinations. The correct answer is (C).

1) The first question is a typical rules question. Go down rule by rule to see whether each answer violates the particular rule you are looking at. Once you have eliminated an answer, do not test it for the other rules. This is also your chance to review the rules to catch any you may have missed or misunderstood. You will know this is the case if you have more than one right answer or no right answer at all. The correct answer here is (B).

2) This question designates D's clients, in order from first to last, as C, M, C, W, C. In whichever hour D sees either an M or a W, F must see a C. Thus, F must see C's during the second and fourth hours only. During the remaining three hours, D sees C's, which means that F cannot see C's, but it cannot be determined whether F sees M's or W's in those hours. Go through the answer choices and look for what could be true, comparing each answer choice to what you know. The correct answer is (E). It could be true that F's third client is not an M, for F's third client could be a W.

3) Question three asks for something that must be false without offering any additional restraints or conditions. Thus, in order to answer this question you will have to go through the answer choices, but as you do so, keep in mind what you know about the game. There are only two major conditions: 1) Whenever one hairstylist sees an adult (M or W), then the other sees a C, which also means that whenever one hairstylist sees a C the other must see an adult (M or W). 2) The first and fifth hours must be by appointment. Quickly go through the answer choices and determine which one violates these conditions. Refrain from writing out and working out the scenario that each question provides. Rather, think about it for a moment, and if there doesn't seem to be a problem, move on. Only work them out as a last resort. The correct answer here is (D). D cannot see a W during both the first and fifth hour because the first and fifth hours are by appointment only and only one W has an appointment.

Question Analysis and Answers

4) This question tests the deduction concerning the number of adults and children that can be included in the game. One stylist must see three children and two adults and the other must see two children and three adults. Therefore, of the ten clients, five of them must be C's, which means that the correct answer is (B). As was explained in the deductions section, each hairstylist must see a W, an M, and two C's. The fifth client for both D and F must be one more of an M, a W, or a C. Because whenever one hairstylist sees an adult the other must see a child, the fifth client for one of the hairstylists must be an adult (M or W) and the fifth client for the remaining hairstylist must be a child. Thus, one hairstylist will see an M, a W, two C's, and one more M or W and the other hairstylist will see an M, a W, and three C's. Thus, out of the ten clients served by D and F, there must be five children.

5) Question five largely tests the same understanding of the game as the previous question, which is also to say that it is testing the deductions. One of the hairstylists must have a clientele list that includes a W, an M, a C, a C, and another C, although not necessarily in that order, and the other hairstylist must have a clientele list that includes a W, an M, a C, a C, and another W or M, although not necessarily in that order. Thus, there will be five C's and two or three M's and W's, depending on whether a W or an M is the client without an appointment for one of the hairstylists. Thus, it could be true that of the ten clients there are exactly three W's and exactly five C's. The correct answer is (B).

6) If D's client without an appointment is a W, then D's clientele list must include two W's, two C's and an M. Since D sees three adults and two children, F must see three children and two adults. According to the question, F cannot see any two children in consecutive hours, so in order for F to serve three children, F must see a child in the first hour, the third hour, and the fifth hour. F must still see both an M and a W, so F must see either an M or W in the second hour and the other in the fourth hour. Since F must see adults in the second and fourth hour, D must see a child in both the second and fourth hour, which means that D must see adults in the first, third, and fifth hours. The clients who D sees in the first and fifth hours must have appointments, and one M and one W have appointments, so D must see either an M or a W in the first hour and the other in the fifth hour. You can now determine that D must see the W without an appointment in the third hour. At this point you can go through the answer choices and easily find what could be true. The correct answer is (D). D could serve an M in the fifth hour.

1) The first question is a typical rules question. Go down rule by rule to see whether each answer violates the particular rule you are looking at. Once you have eliminated an answer, do not test it for the other rules. This is also your chance to review the rules to catch any you may have missed or misunderstood. You will know this is the case if you have more than one right answer or no right answer at all. The correct answer here is (B).

2) This question creates a split between C and T. According to the deduction, F and T cannot be together, so if C cannot be with T, C must be with F. Thus, one vehicle contains F and C. Since both F and C are parents, you know that you are in the second scenario. D must be the parent in the other vehicle, and since D is the only parent in that vehicle, S must be in the same vehicle. Thus, one vehicle must have F, C, and two of V, R, and Q, and the other contains D, S, T, and one of V, R, or Q. Therefore, it must be true that S and T are in the same vehicle. The correct answer is (C).

3) Question three creates a CD block. C and D are both parents, so if both are in one vehicle, then the one remaining parent, F, must be in the other vehicle with exactly three children. According to the deductions, if F is the only parent in the vehicle, then that vehicle contains F, V, R, and S. Thus, it must be the case that F and R are in the same vehicle. The correct answer is (D).

4) This question places D in the SUV and Q in the Minivan. Since D is not with Q in the Minivan, either C or F must be the driver of the Minivan. However, according to the rules, F cannot drive the vehicle that Q rides in, which means that F cannot drive the Minivan either. Therefore, in order to have a parent driving the Minivan, C must drive the Minivan. The correct answer is therefore (C). C is in the Minivan. You could have answered this question by working out the possible scenarios, but doing so would require more work than is necessary.

5) Question five asks for something that could be true without giving you any additional conditions to work with so the answer will most likely be something that you have already determined, whether or not you have had the conscious thought. Go through the answer choices and compare each to the two basic scenarios, asking yourself for each whether it must be false. If it does not have to be false, you have found the correct answer. (A) must be false because if V and T are in the Minivan, then R would have to be in the Minivan as well, giving you three children in the Minivan. However, S must be one of the children in the vehicle with three children. (B) must be false also. If R and T are the only children in the Minivan, then Q, S, and V must be in the SUV. F cannot drive Q so F would have to be with R and T, but F cannot be with T either, so this situation creates an impossible outcome. (C) places Q and T in the SUV. This is consistent with the two scenarios, so (C) is the correct answer. Once you find the correct answer, move on. For the sake of thoroughness in the explanation, however, both (D) and (E) must also be false. (D) must be false because if D is in the Minivan, then S must be in the SUV and if S is in the SUV there can only be one parent in the SUV. It cannot be the case that D is the only parent in the Minivan and still be true that there is only one parent in the SUV. (E) must be false because if R is in the SUV then V must be in the SUV as well, which means that C, R, V, and Q are in the SUV, putting S in the vehicle with fewer children as well as placing F and T in the same vehicle.

6) Question six follows the same pattern as question five, except this time you must find something that must be false. Remember, there are only two basic scenarios, but whether or not you are dealing with a specific scenario will depend on the assignments of various people to specific cars. This is where the conditional statements about D and S and R and V become important. While a quick glance at the answer choices compared to the two basic scenarios without considering the effects of the placement of certain people in a certain vehicle seems to tell you that all of the answer choices are possible, go through each answer choice and look for side effects. If you kept your work from question four, you could quickly determine that (A) could be true. S and T could both be in the Minivan without creating any problems. On the other hand, (B) must be false. If R is in the SUV, then V is in the SUV and it is impossible for V, R, and T to be the three children in one vehicle. (B) is therefore the correct answer. Answer choices (C), (D), and (E) all could be true.

7) Question seven removes the rule that restricts F from driving Q while keeping all the other conditions. By changing this rule, the two scenarios are effectively eliminated and the game is much less restricted. There are, however, still many rules, so go through the answer choices and pay close attention to how they relate to the rules. The main rules at work now are the TF split, the requirement that S be in the vehicle that has only one adult, and the two conditional statements. (A) places Q, F, and R in the SUV. If R is in the SUV, then V is also in the SUV. It would be impossible to have Q, F, R, and V because that would force S into the vehicle with two parents. (B) places D, R, and Q in the Minivan. Since D is in the Minivan, S would have to be in the SUV with exactly two other children and one parent. The only two remaining children are T and V. Since F cannot be with T, F would have to be in the Minivan, leaving C for the SUV. This could be true. The correct answer here is (B). (C) places C, R, and D in the SUV. Once again, if R is in the SUV, then V is also in the SUV. This setup will not work because it leaves T and F together in the Minivan. (D) places S, F, and D in the Minivan. This is impossible because F and D are both parents and S must be in the vehicle with only one parent. (E) must be false because it places F and T together.

1) The first question is a typical rules question. Go down rule by rule to see whether each answer violates the particular rule you are looking at. Once you have eliminated an answer, do not test it for the other rules. This is also your chance to review the rules to catch any you may have missed or misunderstood. You will know this is the case if you have more than one right answer or no right answer at all. The correct answer here is (D).

2) Similar to question one, this question asks for a complete and accurate list of sights, but this time it asks you to focus specifically on Saturday. The first thing to do is determine whether or not any answer choice is an obvious violation of a rule. Only (B) can be eliminated right away because it contains an M but no P. It turns out that the focus on Saturday was just a smoke screen. The real focus is on the side effects. Try (A), where L and B are the only sights seen on Saturday. You still need to place the third L. The B has been used already so there cannot be two L's seen on either Thursday or Friday. Thus, since there is already an L on Thursday, there must be an L on Friday. At this point you have an L seen on Thursday, an L seen on Friday, and an L and a B seen on Saturday. You are left with the two M's and the two P's. The M's and P's must be divided among Thursday and Friday. Since there cannot be two M's on Saturday, there must be one M on each of Thursday and Friday, which means that there must be a P on each of Thursday and Friday as well. This does not violate any rules, so the correct answer is (A). (C) must be false because if a P is seen on a day on which an M is not seen, then the two M's would have to be together, which means that the two M's would have to be seen on Saturday. (D) places a B, an M, and a P on Saturday. Since no L is included on Saturday, one of Thursday or Friday would have to have two L's, which means that the B would have to be on either Thursday or Friday instead of Saturday. (E) says that two L's and a B are on Saturday. If there are three sights on Saturday, then the distribution must be, in order, 2–3–3 and

Saturday is filled. Since no M's are seen on Saturday, the two M's must be divided among Thursday and Friday. An L must already be seen on Thursday, and now an M, and therefore a P, must be seen on Thursday as well. This violates the numerical distribution; there can only be two sights on Thursday. Notice what you have learned in answering this question: If there are three sights on Saturday, the three must include at least one M and exactly one P.

3) This question gives you the condition that an M is seen on Thursday. If there is an M, there must also be a P, so Thursday has at least an L, an M, and a P. The remaining sights are two L's, a B, an M, and a P. The M and P will have to be seen on the same day, and it is impossible for the one remaining M to be included on Thursday, so the M and P must be seen on some other day, leaving two L's and a B to deal with. There is, at most, space for only one more sight to be seen on Thursday, which means that the distribution must either be, in order from Thursday to Saturday, 4–2–2 or 3–3–2. Since there is space for only one more sight on Thursday, there cannot be another L, since two L's carry a B along with it. Likewise, if a B is included on Thursday then the two L's would have to be together on either Friday or Saturday, but if two L's are seen on the same day, then a B must be seen as well. Thus, the distribution must be, in order, 3–3–2, with an L, an M, and a P on Thursday. The remaining M, P, two L's, and a B must be divided between Friday and Saturday, with three sights on Friday, two on Saturday, and the M and P on the same day. With this in mind, go to the answer choices and look for the one that could be true. (A) must be false because having a B on Thursday makes the distribution 4–2–2, forcing two L's together without a B. (B) puts an L and a P on Friday. Remember, the M and P must be together, so this really gives you an L, M, and P on Friday, leaving an L and a B for Saturday. This conforms to the rules, so (B) is the correct answer. For the sake of explanation (C) must be false because there are only two P's, one of which must be on Thursday. Thus, there are not enough P's for there to be two P's on Friday. (D) must be

false because the M must be with the P, which means that Saturday would include three sights, an M, a P, and an L; however, there can only be two sights seen on Saturday. (E) again forces three sights to Saturday because two L's carry a B along with it.

4) This question tells you that an L and a B are seen on Friday, which means that there is one L on both Thursday and Friday. Now you need to place the third L. It cannot be on Thursday because if there are 2 L's, there must be a B also, but the B has already been used. The third L cannot be on Saturday either because then there would be no way to place the M's and P's without breaking a rule. Thus, the third L must be on Friday, giving you two L's and a B on Friday. Be sure to make note of this deduction. If an L and a B are on F, then two L's and B must be on Friday. This deduction is just as binding as if it were a rule. This setup leaves you with the M's and P's to put in Thursday and Saturday. The only two possibilities are Thursday: L, P; Friday: L, L, B; Saturday: M, M, P; and Thursday: L, M, P; Friday: L, L, B; Saturday: M, P. Therefore, it could be true that they see an M on T. The correct answer is (B).

5) If there are two M's together, the two M's must be seen on Saturday. Since there is an M on Saturday, there must be at least one P on Saturday as well. The most sights that can be seen on Saturday are three, so Saturday has reached its limit. Remember, there cannot be four sights on Saturday because that would put two sights on Friday, which, in turn, requires that there be only two sights seen on Saturday. If you did not make this deduction in the deductions portion of the game, you would be forced to make it here in order to solve this problem. If you made it now, the trick is to realize that you have made a deduction. If you realize this, then later questions become that much easier. Since Saturday must have three sights, the numerical distribution must be, in order, 2–3–3. You are left with three L's to place on Thursday and Friday, so one of them must have at least two L's. Where there are two L's there must also be a B, so one of Thursday or

Friday must include two L's and a B. This will not fit on Thursday since Thursday can only have two sights, so the LLB group must be on Friday. This leaves an L and a P for Thursday. At this point you have determined the entire setup for this question, so it is very easy to go through the answer choices and pick out the one answer choice that does not have to be false, or, in other words, the one that could be true. The correct answer is (C).

6) If Sarah and Anita do not see a P on Friday, then they cannot see an M on Friday either. At least two sights must be seen on Friday, and the L's and the B are the only sights available to use. Thus, right away you know that Friday must include either two L's and therefore a B or an L and a B. This takes you back to question three where you found that if an L and a B are together on Friday, then there must actually be two L's and a B on Friday. Look for this in the answer choices. If you did not remember your work from question three, you would have to go through the exact same process here and waste valuable time. The correct answer here is (C). Sarah and Anita must see two L's on Friday.

7) If Sarah and Anita see an L and a P on Saturday, then there must be an M there as well, otherwise there would have to be two M's together somewhere other than on Saturday. From either the deductions or a previous question, you know that there cannot be four sights seen on Saturday, so there must be exactly three in this instance, which means that Saturday is full. Since there are three sights on Saturday the distribution must be, in order, 2–3–3. L is on Thursday already, so the one remaining M, and therefore the P, must be seen on Friday. The third L must be seen on Friday as well, or else there would be two L's seen on Thursday, which would require the B to be seen on Thursday as well, again breaking the requirement that there only be two sights seen on Thursday. You now know the whole setup: Thursday: L, B; Friday: L, M, P; Saturday: L, M, P. Go to the answer choices and find the answer that could be true. The correct answer is (B).

1) The first question is a rules question. Go down rule by rule to see whether each answer violates the particular rule you are looking at. In this case you must also pay attention to the side effects of the team assignments that you are given. In other words, pay attention to what is happening on team X as well. Once you have eliminated an answer, do not test it for the other rules. This is also your chance to review the rules to catch any you may have missed or misunderstood. You will know this is the case if you have more than one right answer or no right answer at all. The correct answer here is (D).

2) If F is on the same team as K, then F is on team X. The only certainty about the order on team X is that C is third. According to the question, F is immediately before K. This FK sequence could either be first or second, respectively, or third and fourth, respectively. It cannot be fifth and sixth because K cannot be sixth. With this information in mind, go to the answer choices and find the answer that could be true. (A) cannot be true because F can only be first or third. (B) cannot be true because F must be on team X while D is on team Y. (C) cannot be true either. If F is after G and the earliest G can be is fourth, then the FK sequence would be forced into the fifth and sixth positions; however, K cannot be sixth. (D) could be true. H could be first or second and the FK sequence could be third and fourth, respectively. (D) is the correct answer. (E) cannot be true because F must be immediately before K.

3) If B and F are on team Y with D, M, one of G or H, and one of J or L, then you know something about all six of the positions on team Y. Since all six positions are filled on team Y, you can put the remaining people on team X, which means that I and E must be on team X. Remember, you still don't know exactly which side G or H and J or L are on, only that one of each must be on each team. Go to the answer choices and find the answer that *must* be true. The correct answer is (C).

4) This question makes J, H, and M consecutive on the same team. From this information you know three things right away. First, M must be on team Y, so the JHM sequence must be on team Y. Second, there are two splits: GH and JL. This question gives you the placement of J and H, so you know that L and G must be on team X. Third, according to the rules E, G, and B must be 4, 5, and 6. Since this new JHM sequence only fits in positions four through six on team Y, E, G, and B must be on team X in positions four through six, although their relative order remains unknown. Now look at team X. C is third, and E, G, and B are fourth, fifth, and sixth, although not necessarily in that order. K and L must also be on team X (K based on the deductions, and L because J is on team Y). The only positions left are first and second. K cannot be first, so K must be second, leaving L for the first position. Since you know all six people on team X, you also know all the people on team Y, but you cannot determine the complete order. Now go to the questions and look for the answer choice that *must* be true. The correct answer is (B). L must serve first on team X.

5) This question tests your overall understanding of the game. You know the basic composition of the two teams. C, K, one of J or L, and one of G or H must be on team X while D, M, one of J or L and one of G or H must be on team Y. Each team therefore only has space for two additional players. These two additional players must be chosen from B, E, F, and I. With this in mind, go through the answer choices and find the choice that must be false. The correct answer is (E) because it assigns three of the leftover players to team X while there is only room for two.

6) If J and L are the two players who serve second, then one of J or L is on each team in the second position, although you cannot determine which one is on which team. Because one of J or L must be second on team X, it is now the case that the first, sixth, second, and third positions are all off limits to K. K must, therefore, serve either fourth or fifth on team X. The only room for the IGB sequence is in positions four, five, and six on whichever team they are on. Since K must serve fourth or fifth on team X, the IGB sequence cannot be on team X and must be on team Y, with I serving fourth, G serving fifth, and B serving sixth. With either J or L serving second, D serving third, I serving fourth, G serving fifth, and B serving sixth, it must be the case that M serves first on team Y. Since you now know who something about who serves in all six positions on team Y, you can determine who must be on team X. Team X must include one of J or L (serving second), C (serving third), K (serving fourth or fifth), E, F, and H. According to the rules, E must serve either fourth, fifth, or sixth, as must G and B. G and B are serving fifth, and sixth, respectively, on team Y, so E must serve fourth on team X. Since E must serve fourth on team X and since it was previously determined that K can only serve fourth or fifth, K must serve fifth. The only two people left on team X are F and H, one of whom must serve first and one of whom must serve sixth. Now you can easily go to the answer choices and find the one that could be false, the one that does not have to be true. The correct answer is (D). F could serve first on team X but does not have to, for F could serve sixth without violating any rules.

1) The first question is a typical rules question. Go down rule by rule to see whether each answer violates the particular rule you are looking at. Once you have eliminated an answer, do not test it for the other rules. This is also your chance to review the rules to catch any you may have missed or misunderstood. You will know this is the case if you have more than one right answer or no right answer at all. The correct answer here is (A).

2) This question asks for a person that could form a pair with any of the four people of the opposite sex. There are two ways to approach this. First, you could treat it as a rules question and compare each answer choice to the diagram. Or you could realize that E, H, and A are the wildcards. E and H could conceivably be paired with any of the four groomsmen, while A could conceivably be paired with any of the bridesmaids. Either approach will allow you to quickly decide that the correct answer is (D). H could form a pair with any of the groomsmen.

3) Question three tests your deductions, as is usually the case when a question asks for something that must be true or false without giving you any conditions to work with. As mentioned in the deductions section, G can only be paired with A or C, since G must be before both B and D. Thus, it is impossible for D and G to form a pair. This information is easy to extrapolate from the diagram as long as you are keeping good track of the bridesmaids and groomsmen. The correct answer is (C).

4) If H and A walk second, then position 2 is filled. With position 2 filled, the only way the G..B..D sequence can fit is if G is first, B is third, and D is fourth. The only groomsman left, C, must walk down the aisle with G as the first pair. The two remaining bridesmaids, E and F, must either walk down the aisle third or fourth. B cannot be paired with F, so B and E must be together as the third pair, and D and F must be together as the fourth pair. Thus, it turns out that putting H and A second allows only one scenario. The correct answer is (A).

5) If A walks down the aisle sometime before G, then you have a setup that looks like this: A..G..B..D, where A, B, and D are groomsmen and G is a bridesmaid. Remember, G must be paired with either A or C since she must be before both B and D. For this question A must be before G, so G must be paired with C. Thus, G and C are the couple that walks second. The order now looks like this: A..GC..B..D. You still need to place the remaining three bridesmaids. F must still come sometime after C, but F cannot be paired with B, so F must be paired with D. In other words, the setup must be: A..GC..B..DF. The only two bridesmaids left are E and H, and they must be split between A and B. With this much information it should be easy to find what could be false. The correct answer is (E). B does not have to be paired with E because B could be paired with H.

6) This question assigns D and H as the couple that walks third. If D is third, then according to the basic sequence of G..B..D, G must be in the first pair and B must be in the second pair. Since C must be before D, C must be with G as part of the first pair. Now you have: GC..B..DH..__. The only groomsman left is A, so A must be in the fourth pair. The two bridesmaids left are E and F. B cannot be with F, so B must be with E, leaving F for A. Thus, the entire setup is GC..BE..DH..AF. It is now easy to find what must be true. The correct answer is (B).

7) For this question you must find the information that allows you to determine the entire setup, both the couples and the order in which they walk. You could jump into the answer choices and start working them out and find the correct answer that way, or you could do it the smart way and first take a moment to think about what information you need to deal with. There is a basic order of G..B..D. This order is only restrictive if G is second or if D is third, so look for an answer choice that allows you to determine exactly where G, B and D go. Furthermore, A, H, and E are all wildcards, so the correct answer choice is going to have to allow you to place all three of the wildcards. (A), by placing D fourth, does not allow you to fix the location of B and G. (B), by placing G first, does not allow you to determine the placement of B or D, nor does it include any information about any of the wildcards. (C) includes one of the wildcards, but the placement of D is still flexible. (D) includes two of the wildcards and allows you to determine that G is first, B is second, and D is third. C is the only groomsman left, so C must be part of the first pair with G. All that is left is the placement of E and F and since B and F cannot form a pair, B must be with E and F must be with D. (D) allows you to determine the entire setup and is, therefore, the correct answer. (E) allows you to determine the order of the groomsmen but fails because it does not allow you to determine exactly where E and H go in the order.

1) The first question is not a typical rules question. Instead, it helps to clarify the rules and helps you make one of the deductions if you did not do so previously. You are asked to find the fewest number of times during the week that Ralph can record the wind direction as S. What this does is force you to consider the consequences of not having an S on any given day. According to the rules, if the wind is recorded as N or W on days 1 through 3, then there must be an S on the following day. The contrapositive of this rule is that if there is no S on any given day, then there is neither an N nor a W on the previous day. If there is no N or W on a day, then that day must have an S and an E. Thus, if there is no S on any given day, then the previous day must have an S. Furthermore, if there is no S on any given day, then there must at least be an N on that day, which means that the following day must also have an S. Since any day that does not include an S must be preceded by a day with an S and followed by a day with an S, the fewest number of S's that can be used is two. The correct answer is (C).

2) This question tries to trick you into applying the rules incorrectly. Do not go to the answers and cross off the choices that have north and south together and east and west together. The question asks about two different days, one day in the morning and the other in the afternoon. Therefore, the rules do not seem to apply directly. Here, the easiest (and only) way to determine which answer is correct is to go through the answer choices one by one. (A) places N in the morning of day 3 and E in the afternoon of day 4. Because both N and S and E and W cannot be on the same day together and because there cannot be two consecutive mornings or afternoons that are the same, the afternoon of day 3 cannot be N, nor S, nor E, leaving only W, and the morning of day 3 cannot be E, nor W, nor N, leaving only S. This is an acceptable arrangement according to the rules. Following the same line of reasoning, go to the other answer choices. (B), (C), and (D), all work. Therefore, by the process of elimination you know

that the correct answer here is (E). Placing W in the morning of day 3 means that the morning of day 4 cannot be W. Because S is in the afternoon of day 4, N is not in the afternoon of day 4, and, according to the rules, if there is no N in the afternoon then there cannot be an E in the morning. Since S is in the afternoon and there cannot be an E in the morning, the morning of day 4 would have to be W, which would place two W's in consecutive mornings. Thus, (E) cannot be true. Notice that this question forced you to determine a new deduction that results from the rule that says if the wind direction is E in any morning, then the wind direction is N in that afternoon. If the wind direction is S in any given afternoon, then the morning for that day must be W. This deduction will be true throughout the game, so keep it in mind; it may come in handy.

3) Question three gives you a situation where the wind direction is W in the afternoon of day 3 and E on the afternoon of day 4. Because there is a W on day 3, according to the rules there must be an S on day 4. The afternoon of day 4 is already filled, so the S must be in the morning of day 4. Now you need to determine the wind direction for the morning of day 3. Because E and W cannot be together on the same day, the morning cannot be E, and because the morning of day 4 is S, the morning of day 3 cannot be S. Thus, the morning of day 3 must be N. Now you should notice that there is no S on day 3. According to the deductions, if there is no S on any given day, then the previous day must have an S and an E, with the S in the morning and the E in the afternoon (since if there were an N or W on day 2 there would have to have been an S on day 3). Thus, day 2 must have an S in the morning and an E in the afternoon. Now you have the complete setup for three of the four days. Go to the answer choices and see if you have determined the answer. You have! The correct answer is (B). The wind direction must be S on the morning of day 2.

4) This is the kind of question that tempts you to waste time working out five scenarios when in fact you can work out one using the rules

and deductions, and then use the process of elimination to find the answer. Begin by eliminating (C) and (D) as obvious violations of the rule that says if the wind direction is E in the morning of any day then it must be N in the afternoon of that day. Now take what you know from the deductions and apply it to the answer choices: If the wind direction is S in any given afternoon, then the reading for the morning must be W, so for this question the wind direction on the mornings of days 1 and 4 must be W, which means that day 2 must have S, and since there is already an S in the afternoon on day 1, the S on day 2 must be in the morning. Since the wind direction for the morning of day 2 is S and the wind direction on the afternoon of day 4 is S, day 3 cannot have an S (since that would place two S's in a row in either the morning or the afternoon). Since there is no S on day 3, day 2 must have an E in the afternoon. Now the only possibilities for the morning of day 3 are N or E and the only possibilities for the afternoon of day 3 are N or W. Only (B) meets these constraints so (B) is the correct answer.

5) For question five the wind is N in the afternoon of day 2 and S in the morning of day 4. You need to determine the wind direction for the mornings of days 1, 2, and 3, respectively. Since you have an N on day 2, there must be an S on day 3. You cannot have two consecutive mornings with the same wind direction, so the S on day 3 must be in the afternoon. Using the deduction discovered in question two, which says that if S is in the afternoon of any day, then W must be in the morning of that day, you can determine that the wind direction for the morning of day 3 must be W. Knowing that the wind direction for the morning of day 3 must be W allows you to eliminate all the answer choices except (A) and (B). Now look at day 2. There is an N in the afternoon, so the morning cannot be N or S, and since the morning of day 3 has a W, the morning of day 2 cannot have a W. Thus, the morning of day 2 must have an E. This allows you to eliminate (A), leaving (B) as the correct answer. You can go further and determine exactly what the wind direction is for the morning of day 1, but you do not need to since the process of elimination allowed you to find the correct answer without doing so.

6) This question places W in the afternoon of day 1 and N in the morning of day 3. Take the time to work out the consequences of these placements. Because there is a W in the afternoon of day 1, the morning of day 1 cannot be W or E. In other words, the morning of day 1 must be N or S. Because there is an N in the morning of day 3, the afternoon of day 3 cannot be N or S. In other words, the afternoon of day 3 must be E or W. Now you know that day 3 cannot have an S. According to your deductions, because day 3 does not have an S, day 2 must have an S in the morning and an E in the afternoon. In order to satisfy the requirement that no consecutive mornings or afternoons are the same, the morning of day 1 cannot be S, leaving only N. Also, the afternoon of day 3 cannot be E, leaving only W. Now you know the wind direction for days 1 through 3. Go to the answers and find what could be true based on what you know. The correct answer is (D).

7) This question again tests the deduction that if there is not an S on any day, then on the previous day there must be an S in the morning and an E in the afternoon. The question places an S in the morning of day 1 and a W on the morning of day 3. The morning of day 2 is sandwiched between the S of day 1 and the W of day 3, so the morning of day 2 can only contain an N or an E. If there is an N in the morning of day 2, then the afternoon could be E or W, and if there is an E in the morning of day 2, then the afternoon would have to be N. Either way, it is impossible for day 2 to contain an S. Since there is no S on day 2, day 1 must contain an S in the morning, which it already does, and an E in the afternoon. Furthermore, because day 2 must include an N, day 3 must include an S. Because day 3 has W in the morning, the S on day 3 must be in the afternoon. Finally, on day 4 you know there must also be an S due to the W on the previous day. Since the wind cannot be the same direction for consecutive mornings or afternoons, the S on day 4 must be in the morning. Now you have a good idea of the possibilities in this scenario. Go to the answers and find what must be false according to what you have determined. (A) must be true based on the situation you have worked out. (B) could be true. The wind direction could either be N or E on the morning of day 2. Now take a look at (C). Ralph cannot record the wind direction as E on the afternoon of day 2 because according to what you have determined the wind direction must be E on the afternoon of day 1. Thus, (C) must be false and is therefore the correct answer. Once you've found the correct answer, there is no need to keep testing the other answer choices, but just so you know, (D) and (E) could both be true.

1) The first question is a typical rules question. Go down rule by rule to see whether each answer violates the particular rule you are looking at. Once you have eliminated an answer, do not test it for the other rules. This is also your chance to review the rules to catch any you may have missed or misunderstood. You will know this is the case if you have more than one right answer or no right answer at all. The correct answer here is (C).

2) This question tests your deduction about the scenario that results when E is included. If you hadn't made it earlier, you would have to make it now. According to the rules, if E is included, then both G and L must be included. If L is included, then L must be in cage 2, so in order for E and G to be in adjacent cages, one of them must be in cage 4, leaving no room for K. Therefore, it must be true that H is placed in a new cage. The correct answer is (C). Again, this question forces you to determine the scenario that results when E is relocated: if E is relocated then G, L, and H must also be relocated.

3) This question tests the deduction about L. In both of the possible scenarios L must be one of the animals placed in a new cage. The correct answer is (B).

4) This question tests your ability to relate the rules and your deductions to each other. Based on either your deduction or question 3 you know that L must be in cage 2, which eliminates (E). Since if either E or G is included, E and G must be adjacent and since L must be in cage 2, neither E nor G can be in cage 1. This allows you to eliminate (A) and (B). The rules say that if K is included in a new cage then K is in cage 4, so you can eliminate (D). The correct answer is, therefore, (C). H could be in cage 1.

5) This question adds a new condition that J must be next to an empty cage. First of all, J can only be in scenario 2, so you know you are dealing with scenario 2, which is the scenario where E is not relocated. When E is not relocated, D, H/K, J, and L must be relocated. Thus, you know right away that you cannot have E or G. Since L must be in cage 2, J and the empty cage must be in either cages 3 and 4 or cages 4 and 5. Either way, cage 4 will be used, leaving no room for a K. You are looking for three types of animals that cannot be relocated to new cages and you have determined that neither E nor G nor K can be relocated. Thus, the correct answer is (C).

6) If the rules are changed such that you only need three animals, and J is placed in cage 2, then L cannot be placed in a new cage, for if L is selected for relocation, then L must be placed in cage 2. Since all other conditions remain in effect, you still need one of H or K, which means that the three animal types selected for relocation must be J, H/K, and one other type. Since there is only one more space available, you cannot use E or G, so by the process of elimination you must use D. The rules tell you that if D is included then D is in cage 1. Therefore, it cannot be true that the H is in cage 1. The correct answer is (A).

1) The first question is a typical rules question. Go down rule by rule to see whether each answer violates the particular rule you are looking at. Once you have eliminated an answer, do not test it for the other rules. This is also your chance to review the rules to catch any you may have missed or misunderstood. You will know this is the case if you have more than one right answer or no right answer at all. The correct answer here is (D).

2) If the only I's in the arrangement are white, then there cannot be any yellow I's. The only other type of flower that can include yellow is the R. The rules specify that the number of yellow flowers must be greater than or equal to the number of red flowers and that the number of red flowers must be greater than or equal to the number of pink flowers. There can only be two R's that are yellow, so there must be one or two yellow flowers. If there is only one yellow flower, then there can only be one red flower and at most one pink flower. With this arrangement, it is impossible for there to be nine flowers. Thus, there cannot be only one yellow flower; there must be exactly two yellow flowers. The correct answer is (E).

3) This question specifies that the flower arrangement includes four red flowers. Since the number of yellow flowers must be greater than or equal to the number of red flowers, there must also be at least four yellow flowers. Only nine flowers can be in the arrangement, and, according to the deductions, there must also be at least one white flower. Therefore, in order to satisfy both the condition that there are at least as many yellow flowers as red flowers and the condition that there is at least one white flower, the arrangement must include four red flowers, four yellow flowers, and one white flower. The correct answer is (B).

4) If there are no pink flowers in the arrangement, then the only R's available are two reds and two yellows and the only C's available are two reds and two whites. In other words, there are only four R's available and only four C's available. The I's are not affected by the condition removing pink flowers, so there are still three whites and three yellows to choose from. However, remember the deduction that there can only be one or two I's. If there were only one I, then there would have to be eight more flowers in the arrangement and since both the R's and C's are limited to four flowers each, the arrangement would have to include four R's and four C's, thereby violating the rule that there must be more R's than C's. Thus, there cannot be only one I. There must be two I's. Since there are two I's, there must be seven flowers chosen from among the four available R's and the four available C's. The only way to have seven flowers and satisfy the condition that there are more R's than C's is if there are four R's and three C's. There are only four R's available, so the four R's used must be two red flowers and two yellow flowers. Because there must be two yellow R's and two red R's for a total of four R's, you can eliminate answer choices (A), (B), and (D). Because there must be three C's, you can eliminate (E). The correct answer is (C). It could be false that there is one white C, for there could also be two white C's.

5) Question five asks for something that must be false without introducing any additional conditions or restraints. In order to answer this question, you must go through the answer choices. However, it is not necessary to write down and work out the situation described in each answer choice except as a last resort. First, go through each answer choice quickly, thinking whether or not it will cause side effects. There does not seem to be a problem with (A), for it is conceivable that all six R's are included, which would mean that there are two pink R's. There does not seem to be a problem with (B) because it would allow there to be at least as many yellow flowers as red flowers and at least as many red flowers as pink flowers. (C) was actually the answer to a previous question, so it is possible. (D)

Question Analysis and Answers

is not problematic because the one or more white flowers that must be included could be C's and there could be enough yellow flowers included such that the requirement that there are at least as many yellow flowers as red flowers is satisfied. Now look at (E), which says that the only C's in the arrangement are red. There can never be only one C, since this would not allow there to be nine flowers in the arrangement (remember, the number of C's must be greater than or equal to the number of I's). Since there must be more than one C and since there are only two red C's available, the arrangement must include exactly two red C's. There can be at most two I's, which means that there must be at least five R's. Since there must be at least five R's, there must be at least one pink rose. There must be more white flowers in the arrangement pink flowers, so there must be at least two white flowers. These two white flowers must be I's, which uses as many I's as is possible. With two red C's and two white I's, there is no way to have more yellow flowers than red flowers. The correct answer is (E). It must be false that the only C's in the arrangement are red.

6) Question six tests the deduction concerning the maximum number of pink flowers. The maximum number of pink flowers is two. If there are two pink flowers, then there must be more than two white flowers, and at the same time there must be at least two red flowers and at least two yellow flowers. The only way to satisfy all these conditions is if there are two pink flowers, two red flowers, two yellow flowers, and three white flowers. In order to include three white flowers there must be either two white C's and one white I, or two white I's and one white C. No matter what, there must always be at least one white C. The correct answer is (B).

7) This question says that two pink carnations are included in the arrangement. This is, in effect, saying the same thing as the previous question, except instead of merely saying that the maximum number of pink flowers is included (two), it specifies what type of flowers those pink flower are (C's). Thus, as in the previous question, the arrangement must include two pink flowers, two red flowers, two yellow flowers, and three white flowers. The two pink flowers must be C's and there must also be at least one white C (the answer to the previous question). However, it is impossible for four C's to be included, so there must actually be exactly one white C. Since there must be three white flowers, there must be exactly two white I's. The remaining four flowers (two red flowers and two yellow flowers) would have to R's in order for there to be more R's than C's. Therefore, the R's included in the arrangement must be two reds and two yellows. The correct answer here is (D). It just so happens that this scenario was actually included in the correct answer to the very first question, so you could have arrived at the correct answer to this question by using the correct answer to that question.

1) The first question is a typical rules question. Go down rule by rule to see whether each answer violates the particular rule you are looking at. Once you have eliminated an answer, do not test it for the other rules. This is also your chance to review the rules to catch any you may have missed or misunderstood. You will know this is the case if you have more than one right answer or no right answer at all. The correct answer here is (E).

2) Question two precludes M from being in the starting line-up. Take the time to fill in what you know. If M is not chosen, then L must be in position 5, which then forces K into position 4. If K is included, then I cannot be. So position 1 must have either G or H. Position 2 is also limited because it cannot have J. Including J would force M into position 5, but the question prevents M from being in the line-up. So either G or H must be in position 2. Since either G or H must be in both the first and second positions, you will not be left with either a G for position 3. Thus, having used G and K already and the question having eliminated M, O is the only player remaining who can be assigned to position 3. The correct answer is therefore (E).

3) Question three places I and M in the line-up. Before rushing to the answer choices, take a moment to think. Luckily, from the deductions you already know the entire setup if I is included in the line-up. This makes the question a whole lot easier than it would be if you worked it all out. If I is included, then you know that H must be in position 2 and M must be in position 4. Thus, the correct answer is (B). This is the question that forces you to make the deduction concerning I if you had not made it already. If you were forced to make it now, be sure that you recognize it for what it is, a true deduction about the game.

4) Question four asks for an item that allows you to fill all the positions. You already know that including I allows you to determine everything, so check first for I. Unfortunately, you are not so lucky this time. Now you are forced to go through the answer choices and see what happens for each. Do it quickly. Each answer leaves options in some positions except for (C). Assigning G to position three gives you everything else. If G is in position 3, then, from the deduction about I, you know that I cannot be included. Since I cannot be included and G is already used in position 3, H must be assigned to position 1. Since G and H have now both been used, J must be assigned to position 2. Since J is included, M must be assigned to position 5. Finally, since both G and M are included, K must also be included and must be assigned to position 4. This question was a little more labor-intensive, but it still tested the deduction concerning the placement of I and its consequences. (C) is the correct answer.

5) Question five excludes K from being in the starting line-up. Because there is no K, M and G cannot both be included. Furthermore, since there is no K, both positions 4 and 5 must be one of L or M. Either way, M will be used, which means that there cannot be a G. The correct answer is (A). You can also approach this question by looking at the lineup that results from the deduction about I. When I was included, K was not included, but I, H, M, and O were. I, H, M, and O can therefore be eliminated as answer choices since you are looking for a player that cannot be in the lineup when K is not. Eliminating I, H, M, and O leaves only one answer choice: (A).

6) Question six places I in position 1. Use the deductions. If I is in position 1, then you know the entire order: I is in position 1, H is in position 2, O is in position 3, M is in position 4, and L is in position 5. Now go through the answer choices and see whether or not each pair could be consecutive. The correct answer is (C).

7) Question seven places K in position three. If K is in position three, then L and M must be split between 4 and 5. If L is in position 4, then G must be in position 1. On the other hand, if M is in position 4, then J cannot be in position 2, and G and H must split between positions 1 and 2. Since in either case G must be used, the correct answer is (A).

Question Analysis and Answers

1) The first question is a typical rules question. Go down rule by rule to see whether each answer violates the particular rule you are looking at. Once you have eliminated an answer, do not test it for the other rules. This is also your chance to review the rules to catch any you may have missed or misunderstood. You will know this is the case if you have more than one right answer or no right answer at all. The correct answer here is (A).

2) In this "must be true" question, go through the answer choices and compare each to the diagram. The diagram tells you almost everything that must be true. The order of five of the kites must be G..R..B..R/Y..G. The sixth kite is flexible; it can be an R, a Y, or a B, depending on where it goes. Compare each answer choice to this setup. (A) does not have to be true because there could be two R's. (B) Does not have to be true because there could be a Y in between the B and the G and an additional Y somewhere else. (C) does not have to be true because, as mentioned in (B), there could be two Y's, or even two B's, in which case there would only be one R. (D) must be true and is the correct answer. There must be two G's because the order must look like this: G..R..B..R/Y..G. Obviously, (E) does not have to be true. This question is a good example of why you need to pay attention to what the question is asking. (A), (B), (C), and (E) all could be true, but they do not have to be.

3) This question asks for something that must be true without giving you any additional information or any conditions to work with, so the answer will most likely deal with something that you have already determined, whether or not you have consciously thought of it or not. Have faith in your diagram. Go through the answer choices and compare it to the diagram and determine whether it must be true. You should see it relatively early in (B). Since the setup looks like this: G..R..B..R/Y..G and there is only room for one more kite, a G must be either the highest or the lowest.

4) By stating that the Y's are immediately below the highest kite and immediately above the lowest kite, this question tells you that there are two Y's and gives you their placement. Since there are now two Y's and two G's, and since you know the placement of the two Y's, you can determine the entire setup. It must be: G Y R B Y G. With this as your reference point, go through the answer choices and find the one that must be false. The correct answer is (C). Since there are two G's and two Y's, there must be only one of both B and R.

5) If an R is the highest kite, you know there must be two R's, since there must also be an R lower than G. With the knowledge that an R is the highest kite, the diagram becomes: R..G..R..B..R/Y..G. The kite in between B and G can no longer be an R, since two R's have been used, and it must therefore be a Y in order for Y to be used. Thus, you know the entire order: R G R B Y G. Since you know the entire order, answering the question is simple. Go through the answer choices and find the one that must be false. The correct answer is (D). A Y cannot be the lowest kite; a G must be the lowest.

6) Question six introduces a condition that two kites of the same color must be adjacent in height. First, look at the basic diagram. Five of the kites must follow the order of G..R..B..R/Y..G. The sixth kite must be an R, a Y, or a B. It is clear right away that the two G's can never be adjacent. Two R's could be adjacent as long as Y fills the gap between B and G: G R R B Y G. Two B's could also be adjacent as long as Y fills the gap between B and G: G R B B Y G. Lastly, two Y's could be adjacent if they both fill the gap between B and G: G R B Y Y G. Compare each of the answer choices to these three possibilities and find the one that must be false, or cannot be true. The correct answer is (D). It is not possible in any of these three situations for a Y to be next to an R.

7) If there is exactly one R, then the space in between the B and the G must be filled with a Y, making the setup look like this: G..R..B..Y.. G, with one kite remaining. If the sixth kite is below the R, then R is the second highest kite. If the sixth kite is higher than the R, then R is the third highest kite. Thus, if there is only one R then that kite could either be second or third. The correct answer is (B).

1) The first question is a typical rules question. Go down rule by rule to see whether each answer violates the particular rule you are looking at. Once you have eliminated an answer, do not test it for the other rules. This is also your chance to review the rules to catch any you may have missed or misunderstood. You will know this is the case if you have more than one right answer or no right answer at all. The correct answer here is (B).

2) Determining the total number of graduates who could possibly receive G is quite easy if you took the time to make deductions and work out the two scenarios. If N does not receive S, then K is the only graduate who could receive G. On the other hand, if N does receive S, then either F or D must receive G. Thus, the total number of graduates who could possibly win the award for GPA is three. The correct answer is (C).

3) Question three provides a condition to work with: B receives C. If B receives C, then you must be dealing with the scenario in which N receives S (because when N does not receive S, B must receive L). When N receives S, either F or D receives G, K receives L, B receives either C or R, and the other of F or D also receives either C or R. Since in this case you know that B receives C, the setup requires that N receives S, F or D receives G, K receives L, B receives C, and the other of F or D receives R. With this knowledge, quickly go through the answer choices and find the one that could be true. The correct answer is (D). It could be true that D receives R. You could have eliminated all four of (A), (B), (C), and (E) by noting that K must receive L.

4) Question four tests whether or not you made the deductions about the two scenarios. In order to answer the question correctly, you have to work both of them out. Both scenarios hinge on the award that N receives. In one scenario, N receives S, while in the other, N receives R. Thus, the only two awards that could be presented to N are S and R. The correct answer is (B).

5) Question five provides you with two new conditions. First, K does not receive L. Knowing that K does not receive L allows you to determine that you are dealing with the scenario in which N does not receive S. When N does not receive S, the resulting scenario is that B receives L, K receives G, either D or F receives C, N receives R, and the other of D or F receives S. The only uncertainty is which one of D or F receives C. The second condition introduced in this question, that D does not receive C, removes this uncertainty. F must receive C. Thus, the setup for this question is that B receives L, K receives G, F receives C, N receives R, and D receives S. Now you can easily go through the answer choices and find the one that must be false. The correct answer is (C).

6) This question is very easy to answer if you have already worked out the two possible scenarios, for this is one of the two scenarios. If N receives S then one of B, F, or D might receive the award for citizenship. Thus, the correct answer is (D).

7) Question seven asks for something that must be false without introducing any conditions. To answer this question, you must rely on your overall understanding of the game, especially the two basic scenarios. If you have worked out the scenarios, then this question is rather simple, for all you need to do is compare each answer choice against your work. Otherwise, you'll be busy working out each answer choice completely. The correct answer here is (C). If B receives R, then you would have to be in the scenario in which N receives S, which means that it would be impossible for F to receive S, as is required by (C).

1) The first question is a typical rules question. Go down rule by rule to see whether each answer violates the particular rule you are looking at. Once you have eliminated an answer, do not test it for the other rules. This is also your chance to review the rules to catch any you may have missed or misunderstood. You will know this is the case if you have more than one right answer or no right answer at all. Be careful with this one. While it is asking about the varsity squad, you must also be aware of what is going on in the JV squad. The correct answer here is (B).

2) This question forces you to work out the scenario in which Z is on the JV squad if you did not work it out as part of the deductions process. If you did not work it out until this question, realize that it is one of only two scenarios. When Z is on the JV squad, then Geek 1, J, and one of R or L must also be on the JV squad. Geek 3, Geek 2, S, K, and the other of R or L must be on the varsity squad (see setup section). Since you already know who must be assigned to the varsity squad, simply go through the answer choices and find one that corresponds with the scenario. The correct answer is (C). In this case, K must be on the varsity squad.

3) Question three asks for what could be true without providing any more information. There are two ways to approach this. You can either see if each answer choice violates any rule or you can simply compare each answer choice to your diagram of the two possible scenarios. Either way, the correct answer is (D). Each of the other four answer choices violates one of the conditional rules. This question tests whether or not you understand what conditional statements do and do not mean. (D) says that Geek 3 is on the JV squad and Geek 2 is on the varsity squad. The conditional statement at play here says that if Geek 2 is on the JV squad, then Geek 3 is also on the JV squad. This does not make a block of Geek 3 and Geek 2. It is still possible for Geek 3 to be on the JV squad and for Geek 2 to be on the varsity squad. You had to understand this in order to answer this question correctly (and to correctly work out the two scenarios).

4) For question four you are looking for a piece of information that allows you to determine the placement of each of the nine students. Of the two basic scenarios, the first, where Z is on the JV squad, is much more constrained than the second, where Geek 3 is on the JV squad. Thus, the correct answer is most likely going to work with the first scenario because it will allow you to fill in the remaining assignments easily. The only uncertainty in the first scenario is the exact placement of R and L, so in order to know the entire setup, you will have to know that Z is on the JV squad and which side R or L is on. Look for an answer choice that tells you both of these things. The correct answer is (A). If Geek 3 is on the varsity squad, then Z must be on the JV squad, and if R is with Geek 3 on the varsity squad, then R must be with T on the JV squad.

5) This question asks for something that must be false if Geek 2 is on the varsity squad. A glance at the two scenarios reveals that Geek 2 can be on the varsity squad in either one. In the first scenario Z, Geek 1, J, and one of R or L are on the JV squad, while Geek 3, Geek 2, S, K, and the other of R or L are on the varsity squad. Placing Geek 2 on the varsity squad in the second scenario forces Geek 1 to the JV squad, which means that Geek 3 and Geek 2 are definitely on the JV squad, while Z, Geek 2, and K are definitely on the varsity squad. Armed with the two scenarios, go through the answer choices and find the one that must be false. (A) could be true because you cannot determine the placement of R. (B) could be true in the second scenario. (C) must be false. In both scenarios K must be on the varsity squad. (C) is the correct answer. Once you have found the correct answer, move on. You might have found this much quicker by simply using the deduction that K must be on the varsity squad and scanning the answer choices for something that must be false.

6) Question six asks for a pair of students who could both be assigned to the varsity squad in the first scenario, the scenario in which Z is on the junior varsity squad. Since you've already worked out this scenario, this question is easy to answer. You do not need to spend time reworking it. If Z is on the JV squad, then Geek 1, J, and one of R or L must also be on the JV squad, which means that Geek 3, Geek 2, S, K, and the other of R or L must be on the varsity squad. Look for two of Geek 3, Geek 2, S, K, and one of R or L in the answer choices. The correct answer is (D).

1) The first question is a typical rules question. Go down rule by rule to see whether each answer violates the particular rule you are looking at. Once you have eliminated an answer, do not test it for the other rules. This is also your chance to review the rules to catch any you may have missed or misunderstood. You will know this is the case if you have more than one right answer or no right answer at all. The correct answer here is (C).

2) If Aaron buys a C, then, according to the rules, he cannot buy a B and he cannot buy an R. However, Aaron must buy at least one of a B, an R, or a W. Since in this case he cannot buy a B or an R, he must be a W. Therefore, the correct answer is (D).

3) In question three you are looking for a pair of items that cannot be included together in the group of things that Aaron buys. You must look for the pair that causes a problem. In order to do so, compare each answer choice to the long chain of conditionals that you deduced, if in fact you deduced it. If you did not, you would have to do so in order to answer this question. When you find one that is inconsistent with the chain of conditional statements, you have found the correct answer. There is nothing stopping Aaron from buying a V and a D; doing so would simply mean that he could not buy an L, so (A) is not the correct answer. (B) has Aaron buying a T and a C. Buying a T has no effect on C; there are no rules that link T to C in any way, so (B) is not the correct answer. (C) has Aaron buying an R and a T. This causes a problem. If Aaron buys a T, then he must buy a P and an L, and if he buys a P, then he cannot buy a B and cannot buy an R. Thus, Aaron cannot purchase both an R and a T. The correct answer is (C). In case you must know, both (D) and (E) are consistent with the rules.

4) This question tells you that Aaron buys four products and then proceeds to give you three of those four: a P, a W, and a C. Since he buys a P and a C, he cannot buy a B and cannot buy an R. He can only buy one more item, so he cannot buy any item that would bring another item along with it. T carries P along with it, so Aaron cannot buy a T. Since Aaron does not buy a T, it is not the case that Aaron does not buy a D and does not buy a V. In other words, Aaron must buy either a D or a V for his fourth item. Look for a D or a V in the answer choices. The correct answer is (D).

5) Question five tells you that Aaron buys an R and a B but not a D. Look for the effects of this new information by glancing at the deduced chain of conditional statements. Here is a refresher on that chain: If Aaron does not buy a D and does not buy a V, then he must buy a T. If he buys a T, then he must buy both a P and an L. Purchasing a P has additional effects. If he buys a P, then he does not buy a B and he does not buy an R. Since he must buy at least one of a B, an R, and a W, if he buys a P, then he must also buy a W. Similarly, purchasing an L has additional effects. If Aaron buys an L then he cannot buy both of D and L, though he still might buy one of them. The contrapositive of this entire chain is also the case, such that if Aaron does not buy a W, then he cannot buy a P, and if he cannot buy a P then he cannot buy a T, which in turn means that he cannot *not* buy a D and a V, or, in other words, that he must buy at least one of a D or a V. Now look at what this question told you: Aaron buys a B and an R. This places you in the contrapositive of the chain and allows you to determine that Aaron does not buy a P, which means that Aaron does not buy a T, which in turn means that he must buy at least one of a D or a V. But the question also tells you that Aaron does not buy a D. Since he must buy either a D or a V and cannot buy a D, he must buy a V. Find V in the answer choices. The correct answer is (C).

6) For this question you are told that Aaron buys a V, a C, and a D. Refer to the chain of conditional statements to determine the effects of these purchases. In this case, Aaron buys both a D and V, so he cannot buy an L. Because he does not buy an L, he cannot buy a T. Furthermore, because he buys a C, Aaron cannot purchase a B and cannot purchase an R, and must, therefore, purchase a W. Thus, Aaron must purchase a V, a C, a D, and a W, and cannot purchase an L, a T, a B, or an R. The only item remaining is P, and Aaron could, but does not have to, purchase it. Regardless, Aaron can buy at most five items. The correct answer is (D).

7) Question seven restricts the group of items purchased to exactly four and then tells you what two of those four items are: an L and an R. Using the chain of conditional statements that you deduced from the rules (see question five), determine the side effects of buying an L and buying an R. If Aaron buys an R, then he cannot buy a C or a P. Because he cannot buy a P, he cannot buy a T, and because he cannot buy a T, he cannot *not* buy D and V, which means that he must buy at least one of D or V. However, because Aaron buys an L, it must also be the case that he does not buy both D and V. In other words, Aaron must buy exactly one of D or V; he cannot buy both. Knowing that Aaron must buy exactly one of D or V, and knowing that he cannot buy a C, a P, or a T, allows you to determine the correct answer. (A) includes a C, (B) includes a P, (D) includes a T, and (E) includes both D and V. The correct answer is (C).

1) If B sits in the fourth seat from the front, then B must sit in desk 4. Because M must sit in front of B and because desk 3 is now the only available seat in front of B, M must sit in desk 3. Furthermore, since B must sit immediately before C, C must sit in desk 5. W must now sit in the one remaining seat, desk 6. The student who sits at desk 6 must wear R, so W must wear R. The correct answer is (C).

2) Question two tests your understanding of the relative order of the students. By asking for a list of students who could wear red, this question is really asking for a list of students who could sit in desk 6, since the person at desk 6 must wear R. The relative order of the students is as follows: J..D..M..BC, with W sitting somewhere after D. The only students who could possibly come last in the order of six students are C and W. Thus, the only students who could possibly sit in desk 6 are C and W. The correct answer is (C).

3) Question three asks for the consequences of placing C in desk 5 on the shirts that J can wear. This is, in fact, a trick question because there are no such consequences. J must still wear one of O or S, so look for one or both of these in the answer choices. The correct answer is (E).

4) If B wears T, then B must sit at desk 4, because the student who wears T must sit at desk 4. Because B sits at desk 4, M must sit at desk 3, C must sit at desk 5, and W must sit at desk 6. Go to the answer choices and find the one that could be true based on what you know. The correct answer is (E). W would have to wear R.

5) Question five asks for a complete and accurate list of the shirts that M could wear. M must be after both J and D and before both B and C. Thus, the closest to the front that M could sit is in desk 3 and the farthest away from the front that M could sit is desk 4. If M sits in desk 3 then M must wear P, whereas if M sits in desk 4 M must wear T. Thus, M could wear T or P. The correct answer is (C).

Part V

Summary Answers

Summary Answers

Game 1

1. C
2. D
3. E
4. C
5. D
6. B
7. D

Game 2

1. C
2. A
3. E
4. C
5. A
6. D

Game 3

1. B
2. C
3. C
4. D
5. B
6. D
7. A

Game 4

1. C
2. D
3. A
4. B
5. E
6. E
7. D

Game 5

1. D
2. B
3. C
4. A
5. E
6. C
7. B

Game 6

1. D
2. B
3. D
4. C
5. C
6. E
7. D

Game 7

1. B
2. E
3. C
4. E
5. D
6. E
7. B

Game 8

1. E
2. D
3. A
4. B
5. A
6. C
7. A

Game 9

1. C
2. D
3. D
4. B
5. C
6. B
7. C

Game 10

1. C
2. C
3. C
4. A
5. C
6. D
7. B

Game 11

1. D
2. C
3. C
4. A
5. C
6. D
7. B

Game 12

1. C
2. D
3. B
4. A
5. D
6. E
7. B

Game 13

1. C
2. A
3. C
4. B
5. C
6. E
7. D

Game 14

1. A
2. B
3. C
4. C
5. C
6. C
7. C

Game 15

1. B
2. D
3. D
4. C
5. B
6. B
7. B
8. C

Game 16

1. A
2. B
3. E
4. B
5. C
6. C
7. E

Game 17

1. C
2. C
3. D
4. B
5. C
6. D
7. D

Game 18

1. B
2. B
3. D
4. C
5. C
6. D
7. A

Game 19

1. D
2. D
3. D
4. B
5. C
6. C
7. B

Game 20

1. D
2. C
3. C
4. A
5. A
6. D
7. A

Game 21

1. E
2. B
3. B
4. B
5. B
6. B

Game 22

1. C
2. B
3. B
4. E
5. B
6. D
7. B

Game 23

1. D
2. D
3. C
4. B
5. D
6. E
7. B

Game 24

1. D
2. E
3. D
4. B
5. E
6. B
7. C

Game 25

1. B
2. E
3. A
4. D
5. A
6. E
7. C

Game 26

1. C
2. C
3. D
4. C
5. C
6. B
7. C

Game 27

1. D
2. D
3. E
4. E
5. B
6. D
7. D

Game 28

1. B
2. C
3. E
4. E
5. E
6. C

Game 29

1. C
2. C
3. D
4. E
5. C
6. D
7. D

Game 30

1. E
2. A
3. E
4. A
5. D
6. B
7. C

Game 31

1. B
2. D
3. A
4. D
5. C
6. E

Game 32

1. B
2. D
3. C
4. E
5. C
6. A
7. E

Game 33

1. C
2. B
3. B
4. E
5. B
6. D

Game 34

1. C
2. B
3. A
4. A
5. A
6. A
7. D

Game 35

1. C
2. D
3. B
4. D
5. A
6. E

Game 36

1. D
2. E
3. E
4. A
5. C
6. E
7. C

Game 37

1. D
2. A
3. E
4. B
5. E
6. A
7. D

Game 38

1. C
2. B
3. C
4. E
5. C
6. A
7. C

Game 39

1. A
2. B
3. B
4. E
5. D
6. E
7. C

Game 40

1. C
2. B
3. B
4. A
5. D
6. B

Game 41

1. B
2. C
3. E
4. C
5. A
6. C

Game 42

1. E
2. A
3. C
4. B
5. C
6. B
7. E

Game 43

1. C
2. C
3. E
4. A
5. B
6. C

Game 44

1. C
2. D
3. B
4. C
5. B
6. C
7. A

Game 45

1. A
2. C
3. B
4. A
5. D
6. B
7. E

Game 46

1. B
2. E
3. D
4. C
5. B
6. A
7. C

Game 47

1. D
2. C
3. C
4. A
5. D
6. B

Game 48

1. D
2. D
3. E
4. B
5. A
6. B

Game 49

1. D
2. C
3. C
4. E
5. B
6. C

Game 50

1. C
2. A
3. A
4. B
5. B
6. E
7. C

Game 51

1. C
2. D
3. A
4. E
5. D
6. E
7. B

Game 52

1. A
2. A
3. E
4. C
5. E
6. D
7. E

Game 53

1. E
2. D
3. B
4. A
5. D
6. E
7. D

Game 54

1. C
2. D
3. A
4. A
5. A
6. C

Game 55

1. E
2. E
3. E
4. A
5. A
6. C
7. C

Game 56

1. A
2. C
3. E
4. C
5. A
6. B
7. B

Game 57

1. E
2. D
3. C
4. D
5. B
6. B
7. B

Game 58

1. B
2. E
3. D
4. A
5. A

Game 59

1. C
2. B
3. E
4. D
5. A
6. C
7. C

Game 60

1. D
2. D
3. B
4. A
5. C
6. B

Game 61

1. D
2. D
3. C
4. C
5. C
6. A
7. B

Game 62

1. E
2. A
3. B
4. E
5. E
6. B
7. D

Game 63

1. E
2. B
3. D
4. A
5. D
6. C
7. C

Game 64

1. C
2. D
3. B
4. D
5. D
6. D

Game 65

1. C
2. C
3. E
4. C
5. A
6. B
7. B

Game 66

1. D
2. E
3. C
4. C
5. D
6. A
7. B

Game 67

1. D
2. B
3. A
4. C
5. E
6. C

Game 68

1. B
2. C
3. B
4. D
5. D
6. D
7. D
8. E

Game 69

1. D
2. A
3. A
4. C
5. C
6. E
7. B
8. A

Game 70

1. A
2. D
3. C
4. B
5. D
6. D

Game 71

1. B
2. E
3. D
4. A
5. B
6. B
7. B

Game 72

1. A
2. D
3. A
4. E
5. C
6. C

Game 73

1. D
2. D
3. D
4. E
5. E
6. B

Game 74

1. A
2. E
3. D
4. D
5. C
6. B
7. E

Game 75

1. D
2. C
3. C
4. D
5. A
6. D
7. E

Game 76

1. A
2. A
3. A
4. E
5. C
6. D
7. B

Game 77

1. D
2. C
3. B
4. D
5. E
6. B
7. B

Game 78

1. D
2. D
3. A
4. C
5. A
6. D
7. D

Game 79

1. A
2. B
3. C
4. D
5. C
6. C
7. D

Game 80

1. A
2. B
3. B
4. B
5. D
6. D
7. C

Game 81

1. C
2. C
3. A
4. D
5. D
6. B
7. D

Game 82

1. C
2. C
3. B
4. C
5. B
6. C

Game 83

1. B
2. B
3. C
4. A
5. C
6. D
7. C

Game 84

1. D
2. E
3. E
4. C
5. B
6. E
7. B

Game 85

1. D
2. E
3. E
4. D
5. C
6. E
7. D

Game 86

1. D
2. B
3. D
4. C
5. A
6. C

Game 87

1. B
2. E
3. D
4. B
5. B
6. D

Game 88

1. B
2. C
3. D
4. C
5. C
6. B
7. B

Game 89

1. D
2. A
3. B
4. B
5. C
6. C
7. B

Game 90

1. D
2. D
3. C
4. B
5. E
6. D

Game 91

1. A
2. D
3. C
4. A
5. E
6. B
7. D

Game 92

1. C
2. E
3. B
4. B
5. B
6. D
7. C

Game 93

1. C
2. C
3. B
4. C
5. C
6. A

Game 94

1. D
2. E
3. B
4. C
5. E
6. B
7. D

Game 95

1. E
2. E
3. B
4. C
5. A
6. C
7. A

Game 96

1. A
2. D
3. B
4. C
5. D
6. D
7. B

Game 97

1. B
2. C
3. D
4. B
5. C
6. D
7. C

Game 98

1. B
2. C
3. D
4. A
5. C
6. D

Game 99

1. C
2. D
3. C
4. D
5. C
6. D
7. C

Game 100

1. C
2. C
3. E
4. E
5. C